NETWORK SECURITY ESSENTIALS:

APPLICATIONS AND STANDARDS

SIXTH EDITION

GLOBAL EDITION

William Stallings

Pearson

York • Boston • San Francisco • Toronto • Sydney • Dubai • Singapore • Hong Kong
Cape Town • Sao Paulo • Mexico City • Madrid • Amsterdam • Munich • Paris • Milan

Vice President and Editorial Director, ECS:
Marcia J. Horton
Executive Editor: Tracy Johnson (Dunkelberger)
Editorial Assistant: Kristy Alaura
Program Manager: Carole Snyder
Project Manager: Robert Engelhardt
Media Team Lead: Steve Wright
Acquisitions Editor, Global Edition: Sourabh Maheshwari
Assistant Project Editor, Global Edition: Shaoni Mukherjee
Manager, Media Production, Global Edition: Vikram Kumar

Senior Manufacturing Controller, Production, Global Edition: Trudy Kimber
R&P Manager: Rachel Youdelman
R&P Senior Project Manager: William Opaluch
Senior Operations Specialist: Maura Zaldivar-Garcia
Inventory Manager: Meredith Maresca
Marketing Manager: Demetrius Hall
Product Marketing Manager: Bram Van Kempen
Marketing Assistant: Jon Bryant
Cover Designer: Marta Samsel
Cover Art: Africa Studio
Full-Service Project Management: Chandrasekar Subramanian, SPi Global

Credits and acknowledgments borrowed from other sources and reproduced, with permission, in this textbook appears on page 448.

Pearson Education Limited
Edinburgh Gate
Harlow
Essex CM20 2JE
England

and Associated Companies throughout the world

Visit us on the World Wide Web at:
www.pearsonglobaleditions.com

British Library Cataloguing-in-Publication Data

A catalogue record for this book is available from the British Library

10 9 8 7 6 5 4 3 2 1

ISBN 10: 1-292-15485-3
ISBN 13: 978-1-292-15485-5

Typeset by SPi Global
Printed in Malaysia (CTP-VVP)

For Tricia never
dull never boring
the smartest
and bravest
person I know

CONTENTS

ONLINE CHAPTERS AND APPENDICES[1]

---

[1]Online chapters, appendices, and other documents are at the Companion Website, available via the access code on the inside front cover of this book.

PREFACE

In this age of universal electronic connectivity, of viruses and hackers, of electronic eavesdropping and electronic fraud, there is indeed no time at which security does not matter. Two trends have come together to make the topic of this book of vital interest. First, the explosive growth in computer systems and their interconnections via networks has increased the dependence of both organizations and individuals on the information stored and communicated using these systems. This, in turn, has led to a heightened awareness of the need to protect data and resources from disclosure, to guarantee the authenticity of data and messages, and to protect systems from network-based attacks. Second, the disciplines of cryptography and network security have matured, leading to the development of practical, readily available applications to enforce network security.

WHAT'S NEW IN THE SIXTH EDITION

In the four years since the fifth edition of this book was published, the field has seen continued innovations and improvements. In this new edition, I try to capture these changes while maintaining a broad and comprehensive coverage of the entire field. To begin this process of revision, the fifth edition of this book was extensively reviewed by a number of professors who teach the subject and by professionals working in the field. The result is that, in many places, the narrative has been clarified and tightened, and illustrations have been improved.

Beyond these refinements to improve pedagogy and user-friendliness, there have been substantive changes throughout the book. Roughly the same chapter organization has been retained, but much of the material has been revised and new material has been added. The most noteworthy changes are as follows:

- **Fundamental security design principles:** Chapter 1 includes a new section discussing the security design principles listed as fundamental by the National Centers of Academic Excellence in Information Assurance/Cyber Defense, which is jointly sponsored by the U.S. National Security Agency and the U.S. Department of Homeland Security.

- **Attack surfaces and attack trees:** Chapter 1 includes a new section describing these two concepts, which are useful in evaluating and classifying security threats.

- **Practical use of RSA:** Chapter 3 expands the discussion of RSA encryption and RSA digital signatures to show how padding and other techniques are used to provide practical security using RSA.

- **User authentication model:** Chapter 4 includes a new description of a general model for user authentication, which helps to unify the discussion of the various approaches to user authentication.

- **Cloud security:** The material on cloud security in Chapter 5 has been updated and expanded to reflect its importance and recent developments.

- **Transport Layer Security (TLS):** The treatment of TLS in Chapter 6 has been updated, reorganized to improve clarity, and now includes a discussion of the new TLS version 1.3.

■ **E-mail Security:** Chapter 8 has been completely rewritten to provide a comprehensive and up-to-date discussion of e-mail security. It includes:

— New: discussion of e-mail threats and a comprehensive approach to e-mail security.

— New: discussion of STARTTLS, which provides confidentiality and authentication for SMTP.

— Revised: treatment of S/MIME has been substantially expanded and updated to reflect the latest version 3.2.

— New: discussion of DNSSEC and its role in supporting e-mail security.

— New: discussion of DNS-based Authentication of Named Entities (DANE) and the use of this approach to enhance security for certificate use in SMTP and S/MIME.

— New: discussion of Sender Policy Framework (SPF), which is the standardized way for a sending domain to identify and assert the mail senders for a given domain.

— Revised: discussion of DomainKeys Identified Mail (DKIM) has been revised.

— New: discussion of Domain-based Message Authentication, Reporting, and Conformance (DMARC), allows e-mail senders to specify policy on how their mail should be handled, the types of reports that receivers can send back, and the frequency those reports should be sent.

OBJECTIVES

It is the purpose of this book to provide a practical survey of network security applications and standards. The emphasis is on applications that are widely used on the Internet and for corporate networks, and on standards (especially Internet standards) that have been widely deployed.

SUPPORT OF ACM/IEEE COMPUTER SCIENCE CURRICULA 2013

The book is intended for both academic and professional audiences. As a textbook, it is intended as a one-semester undergraduate course in cryptography and network security for computer science, computer engineering, and electrical engineering majors. The changes to this edition are intended to provide support of the current draft version of the ACM/IEEE Computer Science Curricula 2013 (CS2013). CS2013 adds Information Assurance and Security (IAS) to the curriculum recommendation as one of the Knowledge Areas in the Computer Science Body of Knowledge. The document states that IAS is now part of the curriculum recommendation because of the critical role of IAS in computer science education. CS2013 divides all course work into three categories: Core-Tier 1 (all topics should be included in the curriculum), Core-Tier-2 (all or almost all topics should be included), and elective (desirable to provide breadth and depth). In the IAS area, CS2013 recommends topics in Fundamental Concepts and Network Security in Tier 1 and Tier 2, and Cryptography topics as elective. This text covers virtually all of the topics listed by CS2013 in these three categories.

The book also serves as a basic reference volume and is suitable for self-study.

PLAN OF THE TEXT

The book is organized in three parts:

- **Part One. Cryptography:** A concise survey of the cryptographic algorithms and protocols underlying network security applications, including encryption, hash functions, message authentication, and digital signatures.

- **Part Two. Network Security Applications:** Covers important network security tools and applications, including key distribution, Kerberos, X.509v3 certificates, Extensible Authentication Protocol, S/MIME, IP Security, SSL/TLS, IEEE 802.11i WiFi security, and cloud security.

- **Part Three. System Security:** Looks at system-level security issues, including the threat of and countermeasures for malicious software and intruders, and the use of firewalls.

The book includes a number of pedagogic features, including the use of numerous figures and tables to clarify the discussions. Each chapter includes a list of key words, review questions, homework problems, and suggestions for further reading. The book also includes an extensive glossary, a list of frequently used acronyms, and a list of references. In addition, a test bank is available to instructors.

INSTRUCTOR SUPPORT MATERIALS

The major goal of this text is to make it as effective a teaching tool for this exciting and fast-moving subject as possible. This goal is reflected both in the structure of the book and in the supporting material. The following supplementary materials that will aid the instructor accompany the text:

- **Solutions manual:** Solutions to all end-of-chapter Review Questions and Problems.

- **Projects manual:** Suggested project assignments for all of the project categories listed below.

- **PowerPoint slides:** A set of slides covering all chapters, suitable for use in lecturing.

- **PDF files:** Reproductions of all figures and tables from the book.

- **Test bank:** A chapter-by-chapter set of questions with a separate file of answers.

- **Sample syllabi:** The text contains more material than can be conveniently covered in one semester. Accordingly, instructors are provided with several sample syllabi that guide the use of the text within limited time. These samples are based on real-world experience by professors who used the fourth edition.

All of these support materials are available at the **Instructor Resource Center (IRC)** for this textbook, which can be reached through the Publisher's Website www.pearsonglobaleditions.com/stallings. To gain access to the IRC, please contact your local Pearson sales representative.

PROJECTS AND OTHER STUDENT EXERCISES

For many instructors, an important component of a network security course is a project or set of projects by which the student gets hands-on experience to reinforce concepts from the text. This book provides an unparalleled degree of support, including a projects component in the course. The IRC includes not only guidance on how to assign and structure the projects, but also a set of project assignments that covers a broad range of topics from the text:

- **Hacking project:** This exercise is designed to illuminate the key issues in intrusion detection and prevention.

- **Lab exercises:** A series of projects that involve programming and experimenting with concepts from the book.

- **Research projects:** A series of research assignments that instruct the student to research a particular topic on the Internet and write a report.

- **Programming projects:** A series of programming projects that cover a broad range of topics and that can be implemented in any suitable language on any platform.

- **Practical security assessments:** A set of exercises to examine current infrastructure and practices of an existing organization.

- **Firewall projects:** A portable network firewall visualization simulator is provided, together with exercises for teaching the fundamentals of firewalls.

- **Case studies:** A set of real-world case studies, including learning objectives, case description, and a series of case discussion questions.

- **Writing assignments:** A set of suggested writing assignments, organized by chapter.

- **Reading/report assignments:** A list of papers in the literature—one for each chapter—that can be assigned for the student to read and then write a short report.

This diverse set of projects and other student exercises enables the instructor to use the book as one component in a rich and varied learning experience and to tailor a course plan to meet the specific needs of the instructor and students. See Appendix B in this book for details.

ONLINE CONTENT FOR STUDENTS

For this new edition, a tremendous amount of original supporting material for students has been made available online.

Purchasing this textbook new also grants the reader one year of access to the **Companion Website**, which includes the following materials:

- **Online chapters:** To limit the size and cost of the book, three chapters of the book are provided in PDF format. This includes a chapter on SHA-3, a chapter on SNMP security, and one on legal and ethical issues. The chapters are listed in this book's table of contents.

- **Online appendices:** There are numerous interesting topics that support material found in the text but whose inclusion is not warranted in the printed text. A number of online appendices cover these topics for the interested student. The appendices are listed in this book's table of contents.

- **Homework problems and solutions:** To aid the student in understanding the material, a separate set of homework problems with solutions are available. These enable the students to test their understanding of the text.

- **Key papers:** A number of papers from the professional literature, many hard to find, are provided for further reading.

- **Supporting documents:** A variety of other useful documents are referenced in the text and provided online.

To access the Companion Website, click on the *Premium Content* link at the Companion Website or at pearsonglobaleditions.com/stallings and enter the student access code found on the card in the front of the book.

RELATIONSHIP TO CRYPTOGRAPHY AND NETWORK SECURITY

This book is adapted from *Cryptography and Network Security, Seventh Edition, Global Edition* (CNS7eGE). CNS7eGE provides a substantial treatment of cryptography, key management, and user authentication, including detailed analysis of algorithms and a significant mathematical component, all of which covers nearly 500 pages. *Network Security Essentials: Applications and Standards, Sixth Edition, Global Edition* (NSE6eGE), provides instead a concise overview of these topics in Chapters 2 through 4. NSE6eGE includes all of the remaining material of CNS7eGE. NSE6eGE also covers SNMP security, which is not covered in CNS7eGE. Thus, NSE6eGE is intended for college courses and professional readers whose interest is primarily in the application of network security and who do not need or desire to delve deeply into cryptographic theory and principles.

ACKNOWLEDGMENTS

This new edition has benefited from review by a number of people who gave generously of their time and expertise. The following professors reviewed the manuscript: Jim Helm (Arizona State University, Ira A. Fulton College of Engineering, Information Technology), Ali Saman Tosun (University of Texas at San Antonio, Computer Science Department), Haibo Wang (DIBTS, Texas A&M International University), Xunhua Wang (James Madison University, Department of Computer Science), Robert Kayl (University of Maryland University College), Scott Anderson (Southern Adventist University, School of Computing), and Jonathan Katz (University of Maryland, Department of Computer Science).

Thanks also to the people who provided detailed technical reviews of one or more chapters: Kashif Aftab, Alan Cantrell, Rajiv Dasmohapatra, Edip Demirbilek, Dan Dieterle, Gerardo Iglesias Galvan, Michel Garcia, David Gueguen, Anasuya Threse Innocent, Dennis Kavanagh, Duncan Keir, Robert Knox, Bo Lin, Kousik Nandy, Nickolay Olshevsky, Massimiliano Sembiante, Oscar So, and Varun Tewari.

Nikhil Bhargava (IIT Delhi) developed the set of online homework problems and solutions. Professor Sreekanth Malladi of Dakota State University developed the hacking exercises. Sanjay Rao and Ruben Torres of Purdue developed the laboratory exercises that appear in the IRC.

The following people contributed project assignments that appear in the instructor's supplement: Henning Schulzrinne (Columbia University), Cetin Kaya Koc (Oregon State University), and David Balenson (Trusted Information Systems and George Washington University). Kim McLaughlin developed the test bank.

Finally, I thank the many people responsible for the publication of this text, all of whom did their usual excellent job. This includes the staff at Pearson, particularly my editor Tracy Johnson, program manager Carole Snyder, and production manager Bob Engelhardt. Thanks also to the marketing and sales staffs at Pearson, without whose efforts this text would not be in front of you.

ACKNOWLEDGEMENTS FOR THE GLOBAL EDITION

The publishers would like to thank the following for contributing to and reviewing the Global Edition: A. Kannammal (Coimbatore Institute of Technology), Somitra Sanadhya (IIT Delhi), Atul Kahate (Symbiosis University and Pune University), Anwitaman Datta (NTU Singapore), and Khyat Sharma.

ABOUT THE AUTHOR

Dr. William Stallings has authored 18 titles, and counting revised editions, over 40 books on computer security, computer networking, and computer architecture. His writings have appeared in numerous publications, including the *Proceedings of the IEEE, ACM Computing Reviews*, and *Cryptologia*.

He has 13 times received the award for the best Computer Science textbook of the year from the Text and Academic Authors Association.

In over 30 years in the field, he has been a technical contributor, technical manager, and an executive with several high-technology firms. He has designed and implemented both TCP/IP-based and OSI-based protocol suites on a variety of computers and operating systems, ranging from microcomputers to mainframes. As a consultant, he has advised government agencies, computer and software vendors, and major users on the design, selection, and use of networking software and products.

He created and maintains the *Computer Science Student Resource Site* at Computer-ScienceStudent.com. This site provides documents and links on a variety of subjects of general interest to computer science students (and professionals). He is a member of the editorial board of *Cryptologia*, a scholarly journal devoted to all aspects of cryptology.

Dr. Stallings holds a Ph.D. from MIT in Computer Science and a B.S. from Notre Dame in electrical engineering.

CHAPTER 1

INTRODUCTION

LEARNING OBJECTIVES

After studying this chapter, you should be able to:

◆ Describe the key security requirements of confidentiality, integrity, and availability.

◆ Describe the X.800 security architecture for OSI.

◆ Discuss the types of security threats and attacks that must be dealt with and give examples of the types of threats and attacks that apply to different categories of computer and network assets.

◆ Explain the fundamental security design principles.

◆ Discuss the use of attack surfaces and attack trees.

◆ List and briefly describe key organizations involved in cryptography standards.

The requirements of **information security** within an organization have undergone two major changes in the last several decades. Before the widespread use of data processing equipment, the security of information felt to be valuable to an organization was provided primarily by physical and administrative means. An example of the former is the use of rugged filing cabinets with a combination lock for storing sensitive documents. An example of the latter is personnel screening procedures used during the hiring process.

With the introduction of the computer, the need for automated tools for protecting files and other information stored on the computer became evident. This is especially the case for a shared system, such as a time-sharing system, and the need is even more acute for systems that can be accessed over a public telephone network, data network, or the Internet. The generic name for the collection of tools designed to protect data and to thwart hackers is **computer security**.

The second major change that affected security is the introduction of distributed systems and the use of networks and communications facilities for carrying data between terminal user and computer and between computer and computer. Network security measures are needed to protect data during their transmission. In fact, the term **network security** is somewhat misleading, because virtually all business, government, and academic organizations interconnect their data processing equipment with a collection of interconnected networks. Such a collection is often referred to as an internet,[1] and the term **internet security** is used.

---

[1] We use the term *internet* with a lowercase "i" to refer to any interconnected collection of network. A corporate intranet is an example of an internet. The Internet with a capital "I" may be one of the facilities used by an organization to construct its internet.

There are no clear boundaries between these two forms of security. For example, a computer virus may be introduced into a system physically when it arrives on a flash drive or an optical disk and is subsequently loaded onto a computer. Viruses may also arrive over an internet. In either case, once the virus is resident on a computer system, internal computer security tools are needed to detect and recover from the virus.

This book focuses on internet security, which consists of measures to deter, prevent, detect, and correct security violations that involve the transmission of information. That is a broad statement that covers a host of possibilities. To give you a feel for the areas covered in this book, consider the following examples of security violations:

1. User A transmits a file to user B. The file contains sensitive information (e.g., payroll records) that is to be protected from disclosure. User C, who is not authorized to read the file, is able to monitor the transmission and capture a copy of the file during its transmission.

2. A network manager, D, transmits a message to a computer, E, under its management. The message instructs computer E to update an authorization file to include the identities of a number of new users who are to be given access to that computer. User F intercepts the message, alters its contents to add or delete entries, and then forwards the message to E, which accepts the message as coming from manager D and updates its authorization file accordingly.

3. Rather than intercept a message, user F constructs its own message with the desired entries and transmits that message to E as if it had come from manager D. Computer E accepts the message as coming from manager D and updates its authorization file accordingly.

4. An employee is fired without warning. The personnel manager sends a message to a server system to invalidate the employee's account. When the invalidation is accomplished, the server is to post a notice to the employee's file as confirmation of the action. The employee is able to intercept the message and delay it long enough to make a final access to the server to retrieve sensitive information. The message is then forwarded, the action taken, and the confirmation posted. The employee's action may go unnoticed for some considerable time.

5. A message is sent from a customer to a stockbroker with instructions for various transactions. Subsequently, the investments lose value and the customer denies sending the message.

Although this list by no means exhausts the possible types of security violations, it illustrates the range of concerns of network security.

This chapter provides a general overview of the subject matter that structures the material in the remainder of the book. We begin with a general discussion of network security services and mechanisms and of the types of attacks they are designed for. Then we develop a general overall model within which the security services and mechanisms can be viewed.

1.1 COMPUTER SECURITY CONCEPTS

A Definition of Computer Security

The NIST *Computer Security Handbook* [NIST95] defines the term *computer security* as

> **Computer Security:** The protection afforded to an automated information system in order to attain the applicable objectives of preserving the integrity, availability, and confidentiality of information system resources (includes hardware, software, firmware, information/data, and telecommunications).

This definition introduces three key objectives that are at the heart of computer security.

- **Confidentiality:** This term covers two related concepts:

  Data[2] confidentiality: Assures that private or confidential information is not made available or disclosed to unauthorized individuals.

  Privacy: Assures that individuals control or influence what information related to them may be collected and stored and by whom and to whom that information may be disclosed.

- **Integrity:** This term covers two related concepts:

  Data integrity: Assures that data (both stored and in transmitted packets) and programs are changed only in a specified and authorized manner.

  System integrity: Assures that a system performs its intended function in an unimpaired manner, free from deliberate or inadvertent unauthorized manipulation of the system.

- **Availability:** Assures that systems work promptly and service is not denied to authorized users.

These three concepts form what is often referred to as the **CIA triad**. The three concepts embody the fundamental security objectives for both data and for information and computing services. For example, the NIST *Standards for Security Categorization of Federal Information and Information Systems* (FIPS 199) lists confidentiality, integrity, and availability as the three security objectives for information and for information systems. FIPS 199 provides a useful characterization of these three objectives in terms of requirements and the definition of a loss of security in each category.

- **Confidentiality:** Preserving authorized restrictions on information access and disclosure, including means for protecting personal privacy and proprietary information. A loss of confidentiality is the unauthorized disclosure of information.

---

[2]RFC 4949 defines *information* as "facts and ideas, which can be represented (encoded) as various forms of data," and *data* as "information in a specific physical representation, usually a sequence of symbols that have meaning; especially a representation of information that can be processed or produced by a computer." Security literature typically does not make much of a distinction, nor does this book.

- **Integrity:** Guarding against improper information modification or destruction, including ensuring information nonrepudiation and authenticity. A loss of integrity is the unauthorized modification or destruction of information.
- **Availability:** Ensuring timely and reliable access to and use of information. A loss of availability is the disruption of access to or use of information or an information system.

Although the use of the CIA triad to define security objectives is well established, some in the security field feel that additional concepts are needed to present a complete picture (Figure 1.1). Two of the most commonly mentioned are

- **Authenticity:** The property of being genuine and being able to be verified and trusted; confidence in the validity of a transmission, a message, or message originator. This means verifying that users are who they say they are and that each input arriving at the system came from a trusted source.
- **Accountability:** The security goal that generates the requirement for actions of an entity to be traced uniquely to that entity. This supports nonrepudiation, deterrence, fault isolation, intrusion detection and prevention, and after-action recovery and legal action. Because truly secure systems are not yet an achievable goal, we must be able to trace a security breach to a responsible party. Systems must keep records of their activities to permit later forensic analysis to trace security breaches or to aid in transaction disputes.

Examples

We now provide some examples of applications that illustrate the requirements just enumerated.[3] For these examples, we use three levels of impact on organizations or individuals should there be a breach of security (i.e., a loss of confidentiality, integrity, or availability). These levels are defined in FIPS 199:

- **Low:** The loss could be expected to have a limited adverse effect on organizational operations, organizational assets, or individuals. A limited adverse effect means that, for example, the loss of confidentiality, integrity, or availability might

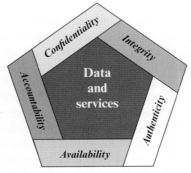

Figure 1.1 Essential Network and Computer Security Requirements

---

[3]These examples are taken from a security policy document published by the Information Technology Security and Privacy Office at Purdue University.

(i) cause a degradation in mission capability to an extent and duration that the organization is able to perform its primary functions, but the effectiveness of the functions is noticeably reduced; (ii) result in minor damage to organizational assets; (iii) result in minor financial loss; or (iv) result in minor harm to individuals.

- ■ **Moderate:** The loss could be expected to have a serious adverse effect on organizational operations, organizational assets, or individuals. A serious adverse effect means that, for example, the loss might (i) cause a significant degradation in mission capability to an extent and duration that the organization is able to perform its primary functions, but the effectiveness of the functions is significantly reduced; (ii) result in significant damage to organizational assets; (iii) result in significant financial loss; or (iv) result in significant harm to individuals that does not involve loss of life or serious, life-threatening injuries.

- ■ **High:** The loss could be expected to have a severe or catastrophic adverse effect on organizational operations, organizational assets, or individuals. A severe or catastrophic adverse effect means that, for example, the loss might (i) cause a severe degradation in or loss of mission capability to an extent and duration that the organization is not able to perform one or more of its primary functions; (ii) result in major damage to organizational assets; (iii) result in major financial loss; or (iv) result in severe or catastrophic harm to individuals involving loss of life or serious, life-threatening injuries.

CONFIDENTIALITY Student grade information is an asset whose confidentiality is considered to be highly important by students. In the United States, the release of such information is regulated by the Family Educational Rights and Privacy Act (FERPA). Grade information should only be available to students, their parents, and employees that require the information to do their job. Student enrollment information may have a moderate confidentiality rating. While still covered by FERPA, this information is seen by more people on a daily basis, is less likely to be targeted than grade information, and results in less damage if disclosed. Directory information (such as lists of students, faculty, or departmental lists) may be assigned a low confidentiality rating or indeed no rating. This information is typically freely available to the public and published on a school's Web site.

INTEGRITY Several aspects of integrity are illustrated by the example of a hospital patient's allergy information stored in a database. The doctor should be able to trust that the information is correct and current. Now suppose that an employee (e.g., a nurse) who is authorized to view and update this information deliberately falsifies the data to cause harm to the hospital. The database needs to be restored to a trusted basis quickly, and it should be possible to trace the error back to the person responsible. Patient allergy information is an example of an asset with a high requirement for integrity. Inaccurate information could result in serious harm or death to a patient and expose the hospital to massive liability.

An example of an asset that may be assigned a moderate level of integrity requirement is a Web site that offers a forum to registered users to discuss some specific topic. Either a registered user or a hacker could falsify some entries or deface the Web site. If the forum exists only for the enjoyment of the users, brings in little or no advertising revenue, and is not used for something important such as research, then potential damage is not severe. The Web master may experience some data, financial, and time loss.

An example of a low-integrity requirement is an anonymous online poll. Many Web sites, such as news organizations, offer these polls to their users with very few safeguards. However, the inaccuracy and unscientific nature of such polls are well understood.

AVAILABILITY The more critical a component or service, the higher is the level of availability required. Consider a system that provides authentication services for critical systems, applications, and devices. An interruption of service results in the inability for customers to access computing resources and for the staff to access the resources they need to perform critical tasks. The loss of the service translates into a large financial loss due to lost employee productivity and potential customer loss.

An example of an asset that typically would be rated as having a moderate availability requirement is a public Web site for a university; the Web site provides information for current and prospective students and donors. Such a site is not a critical component of the university's information system, but its unavailability will cause some embarrassment.

An online telephone directory lookup application would be classified as a low-availability requirement. Although the temporary loss of the application may be an annoyance, there are other ways to access the information, such as a hardcopy directory or the operator.

The Challenges of Computer Security

Computer and network security is both fascinating and complex. Some of the reasons include:

1. Security is not as simple as it might first appear to the novice. The requirements seem to be straightforward; indeed, most of the major requirements for security services can be given self-explanatory, one-word labels: confidentiality, authentication, nonrepudiation, and integrity. But the mechanisms used to meet those requirements can be quite complex, and understanding them may involve rather subtle reasoning.

2. In developing a particular security mechanism or algorithm, one must always consider potential attacks on those security features. In many cases, successful attacks are designed by looking at the problem in a completely different way, therefore exploiting an unexpected weakness in the mechanism.

3. Because of point 2, the procedures used to provide particular services are often counterintuitive. Typically, a security mechanism is complex, and it is not obvious from the statement of a particular requirement that such elaborate measures are needed. It is only when the various aspects of the threat are considered that elaborate security mechanisms make sense.

4. Having designed various security mechanisms, it is necessary to decide where to use them. This is true both in terms of physical placement (e.g., at what points in a network are certain security mechanisms needed) and in a logical sense [e.g., at what layer or layers of an architecture such as TCP/IP (Transmission Control Protocol/Internet Protocol) should mechanisms be placed].

5. Security mechanisms typically involve more than a particular algorithm or protocol. They also require that participants be in possession of some secret information (e.g., an encryption key), which raises questions about the creation, distribution, and protection of that secret information. There also may be a reliance on communications protocols whose behavior may complicate the task of developing the security mechanism. For example, if the proper functioning of the security mechanism requires setting time limits on the transit time of a message from sender to receiver, then any protocol or network that introduces variable, unpredictable delays may render such time limits meaningless.

6. Computer and network security is essentially a battle of wits between a perpetrator who tries to find holes and the designer or administrator who tries to close them. The great advantage that the attacker has is that he or she need only find a single weakness, while the designer must find and eliminate all weaknesses to achieve perfect security.

7. There is a natural tendency on the part of users and system managers to perceive little benefit from security investment until a security failure occurs.

8. Security requires regular, even constant, monitoring, and this is difficult in today's short-term, overloaded environment.

9. Security is still too often an afterthought to be incorporated into a system after the design is complete rather than being an integral part of the design process.

10. Many users (and even security administrators) view strong security as an impediment to efficient and user-friendly operation of an information system or use of information.

The difficulties just enumerated will be encountered in numerous ways as we examine the various security threats and mechanisms throughout this book.

1.2 THE OSI SECURITY ARCHITECTURE

To assess effectively the security needs of an organization and to evaluate and choose various security products and policies, the manager responsible for computer and network security needs some systematic way of defining the requirements for security and characterizing the approaches to satisfying those requirements. This is difficult enough in a centralized data processing environment; with the use of local and wide area networks, the problems are compounded.

ITU-T[4] Recommendation X.800, *Security Architecture for OSI*, defines such a systematic approach.[5] The OSI security architecture is useful to managers as a way of organizing the task of providing security. Furthermore, because this architecture

---

[4]The International Telecommunication Union (ITU) Telecommunication Standardization Sector (ITU-T) is a United Nations-sponsored agency that develops standards, called Recommendations, relating to telecommunications and to open systems interconnection (OSI).

[5]The OSI security architecture was developed in the context of the OSI protocol architecture, which is described in Appendix D. However, for our purposes in this chapter, an understanding of the OSI protocol architecture is not required.

Table 1.1 Threats and Attacks (RFC 4949)

Threat
A potential for violation of security, which exists when there is a circumstance, capability, action, or event that could breach security and cause harm. That is, a threat is a possible danger that might exploit a vulnerability.
Attack
An assault on system security that derives from an intelligent threat. That is, an intelligent act that is a deliberate attempt (especially in the sense of a method or technique) to evade security services and violate the security policy of a system.

was developed as an international standard, computer and communications vendors have developed security features for their products and services that relate to this structured definition of services and mechanisms.

For our purposes, the OSI security architecture provides a useful, if abstract, overview of many of the concepts that this book deals with. The OSI security architecture focuses on security attacks, mechanisms, and services. These can be defined briefly as

- **Security attack:** Any action that compromises the security of information owned by an organization.
- **Security mechanism:** A process (or a device incorporating such a process) that is designed to detect, prevent, or recover from a security attack.
- **Security service:** A processing or communication service that enhances the security of the data processing systems and the information transfers of an organization. The services are intended to counter security attacks, and they make use of one or more security mechanisms to provide the service.

In the literature, the terms *threat* and *attack* are commonly used to mean more or less the same thing. Table 1.1 provides definitions taken from RFC 4949, *Internet Security Glossary*.

1.3 SECURITY ATTACKS

A useful means of classifying security attacks, used both in X.800 and RFC 4949, is in terms of *passive attacks* and *active attacks*. A passive attack attempts to learn or make use of information from the system but does not affect system resources. An active attack attempts to alter system resources or affect their operation.

Passive Attacks

Passive attacks (Figure 1.2a) are in the nature of eavesdropping on, or monitoring of, transmissions. The goal of the opponent is to obtain information that is being transmitted. Two types of passive attacks are the release of message contents and traffic analysis.

The **release of message contents** is easily understood. A telephone conversation, an electronic mail message, and a transferred file may contain sensitive or confidential information. We would like to prevent an opponent from learning the contents of these transmissions.

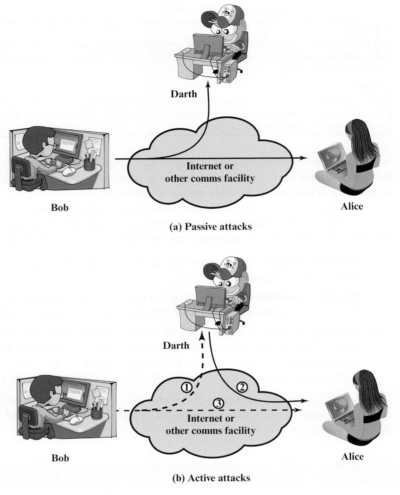

Figure 1.2   Security Attacks

A second type of passive attack, **traffic analysis**, is subtler. Suppose that we had a way of masking the contents of messages or other information traffic so that opponents, even if they captured the message, could not extract the information from the message. The common technique for masking contents is encryption. If we had encryption protection in place, an opponent still might be able to observe the pattern of these messages. The opponent could determine the location and identity of communicating hosts and could observe the frequency and length of messages being exchanged. This information might be useful in guessing the nature of the communication that was taking place.

Passive attacks are very difficult to detect, because they do not involve any alteration of the data. Typically, the message traffic is sent and received in an apparently normal fashion, and neither the sender nor the receiver is aware that a third party has read the messages or observed the traffic pattern. However, it is feasible to prevent the success of these attacks, usually by means of encryption. Thus, the emphasis in dealing with passive attacks is on prevention rather than detection.

Active Attacks

Active attacks (Figure 1.2b) involve some modification of the data stream or the creation of a false stream and can be subdivided into four categories: masquerade, replay, modification of messages, and denial of service.

A **masquerade** takes place when one entity pretends to be a different entity (path 2 of Figure 1.2b is active). A masquerade attack usually includes one of the other forms of active attack. For example, authentication sequences can be captured and replayed after a valid authentication sequence has taken place, thus enabling an authorized entity with few privileges to obtain extra privileges by impersonating an entity that has those privileges.

Replay involves the passive capture of a data unit and its subsequent retransmission to produce an unauthorized effect (paths 1, 2, and 3 active).

Modification of messages simply means that some portion of a legitimate message is altered, or that messages are delayed or reordered, to produce an unauthorized effect (paths 1 and 2 active). For example, a message meaning "Allow John Smith to read confidential file `accounts`" is modified to mean "Allow Fred Brown to read confidential file `accounts`."

The **denial of service** prevents or inhibits the normal use or management of communications facilities (path 3 active). This attack may have a specific target; for example, an entity may suppress all messages directed to a particular destination (e.g., the security audit service). Another form of service denial is the disruption of an entire network—either by disabling the network or by overloading it with messages so as to degrade performance.

Active attacks present the opposite characteristics of passive attacks. Whereas passive attacks are difficult to detect, measures are available to prevent their success. On the other hand, it is quite difficult to prevent active attacks absolutely because of the wide variety of potential physical, software, and network vulnerabilities. Instead, the goal is to detect active attacks and to recover from any disruption or delays caused by them. If the detection has a deterrent effect, it also may contribute to prevention.

1.4 SECURITY SERVICES

X.800 defines a security service as a service that is provided by a protocol layer of communicating open systems and that ensures adequate security of the systems or of data transfers. Perhaps a clearer definition is found in RFC 4949, which provides the following definition: A processing or communication service that is provided by

Table 1.2   Security Services (X.800)

AUTHENTICATION	DATA INTEGRITY
The assurance that the communicating entity is the one that it claims to be.	The assurance that data received are exactly as sent by an authorized entity (i.e., contain no modification, insertion, deletion, or replay).
Peer Entity Authentication Used in association with a logical connection to provide confidence in the identity of the entities connected.	**Connection Integrity with Recovery** Provides for the integrity of all user data on a connection and detects any modification, insertion, deletion, or replay of any data within an entire data sequence, with recovery attempted.
Data-Origin Authentication In a connectionless transfer, provides assurance that the source of received data is as claimed.	**Connection Integrity without Recovery** As above, but provides only detection without recovery.
ACCESS CONTROL The prevention of unauthorized use of a resource (i.e., this service controls who can have access to a resource, under what conditions access can occur, and what those accessing the resource are allowed to do).	**Selective-Field Connection Integrity** Provides for the integrity of selected fields within the user data of a data block transferred over a connection and takes the form of determination of whether the selected fields have been modified, inserted, deleted, or replayed.
DATA CONFIDENTIALITY The protection of data from unauthorized disclosure.	**Connectionless Integrity** Provides for the integrity of a single connectionless data block and may take the form of detection of data modification. Additionally, a limited form of replay detection may be provided.
Connection Confidentiality The protection of all user data on a connection.	**Selective-Field Connectionless Integrity** Provides for the integrity of selected fields within a single connectionless data block; takes the form of determination of whether the selected fields have been modified.
Connectionless Confidentiality The protection of all user data in a single data block.	
Selective-Field Confidentiality The confidentiality of selected fields within the user data on a connection or in a single data block.	**NONREPUDIATION** Provides protection against denial by one of the entities involved in a communication of having participated in all or part of the communication.
Traffic-Flow Confidentiality The protection of the information that might be derived from observation of traffic flows.	**Nonrepudiation, Origin** Proof that the message was sent by the specified party.
	Nonrepudiation, Destination Proof that the message was received by the specified party.

a system to give a specific kind of protection to system resources; security services implement security policies and are implemented by security mechanisms.

X.800 divides these services into five categories and fourteen specific services (Table 1.2). We look at each category in turn.[6]

---

[6]There is no universal agreement about many of the terms used in the security literature. For example, the term *integrity* is sometimes used to refer to all aspects of information security. The term *authentication* is sometimes used to refer both to verification of identity and to the various functions listed under integrity in this chapter. Our usage here agrees with both X.800 and RFC 4949.

Authentication

The **authentication** service is concerned with assuring that a communication is authentic. In the case of a single message, such as a warning or alarm signal, the function of the authentication service is to assure the recipient that the message is from the source that it claims to be from. In the case of an ongoing interaction, such as the connection of a terminal to a host, two aspects are involved. First, at the time of connection initiation, the service assures that the two entities are authentic (i.e., that each is the entity that it claims to be). Second, the service must assure that the connection is not interfered with in such a way that a third party can masquerade as one of the two legitimate parties for the purposes of unauthorized transmission or reception.

Two specific authentication services are defined in X.800:

- **Peer entity authentication:** Provides for the corroboration of the identity of a peer entity in an association. Two entities are considered peers if they implement the same protocol in different systems (e.g., two TCP modules in two communicating systems). Peer entity authentication is provided for use at the establishment of or during the data transfer phase of a connection. It attempts to provide confidence that an entity is not performing either a masquerade or an unauthorized replay of a previous connection.

- **Data origin authentication:** Provides for the corroboration of the source of a data unit. It does not provide protection against the duplication or modification of data units. This type of service supports applications like electronic mail, where there are no prior interactions between the communicating entities.

Access Control

In the context of network security, **access control** is the ability to limit and control the access to host systems and applications via communications links. To achieve this, each entity trying to gain access must first be identified, or authenticated, so that access rights can be tailored to the individual.

Data Confidentiality

Confidentiality is the protection of transmitted data from passive attacks. With respect to the content of a data transmission, several levels of protection can be identified. The broadest service protects all user data transmitted between two users over a period of time. For example, when a TCP connection is set up between two systems, this broad protection prevents the release of any user data transmitted over the TCP connection. Narrower forms of this service can also be defined, including the protection of a single message or even specific fields within a message. These refinements are less useful than the broad approach and may even be more complex and expensive to implement.

The other aspect of confidentiality is the protection of traffic flow from analysis. This requires that an attacker not be able to observe the source and destination, frequency, length, or other characteristics of the traffic on a communications facility.

Data Integrity

As with confidentiality, **integrity** can apply to a stream of messages, a single message, or selected fields within a message. Again, the most useful and straightforward approach is total stream protection.

A connection-oriented integrity service deals with a stream of messages and assures that messages are received as sent with no duplication, insertion, modification, reordering, or replays. The destruction of data is also covered under this service. Thus, the connection-oriented integrity service addresses both message stream modification and denial of service. On the other hand, a connectionless integrity service deals with individual messages without regard to any larger context and generally provides protection against message modification only.

We can make a distinction between service with and without recovery. Because the integrity service relates to active attacks, we are concerned with detection rather than prevention. If a violation of integrity is detected, then the service may simply report this violation, and some other portion of software or human intervention is required to recover from the violation. Alternatively, there are mechanisms available to recover from the loss of integrity of data, as we will review subsequently. The incorporation of automated recovery mechanisms is typically the more attractive alternative.

Nonrepudiation

Nonrepudiation prevents either sender or receiver from denying a transmitted message. Thus, when a message is sent, the receiver can prove that the alleged sender in fact sent the message. Similarly, when a message is received, the sender can prove that the alleged receiver in fact received the message.

Availability Service

Both X.800 and RFC 4949 define **availability** to be the property of a system or a system resource being accessible and usable upon demand by an authorized system entity, according to performance specifications for the system (i.e., a system is available if it provides services according to the system design whenever users request them). A variety of attacks can result in the loss of or reduction in availability. Some of these attacks are amenable to automated countermeasures, such as authentication and encryption, whereas others require some sort of physical action to prevent or recover from loss of availability of elements of a distributed system.

X.800 treats availability as a property to be associated with various security services. However, it makes sense to call out specifically an availability service. An availability service is one that protects a system to ensure its availability. This service addresses the security concerns raised by denial-of-service attacks. It depends on proper management and control of system resources and thus depends on access control service and other security services.

1.5   SECURITY MECHANISMS

Table 1.3 lists the security mechanisms defined in X.800. The mechanisms are divided into those that are implemented in a specific protocol layer, such as TCP or an application-layer protocol, and those that are not specific to any particular protocol layer or security service. These mechanisms will be covered in the appropriate places in the book, so we do not elaborate now except to comment on the

Table 1.3   Security Mechanisms (X.800)

SPECIFIC SECURITY MECHANISMS	PERVASIVE SECURITY MECHANISMS
May be incorporated into the appropriate protocol layer in order to provide some of the OSI security services.	Mechanisms that are not specific to any particular OSI security service or protocol layer.
Encipherment The use of mathematical algorithms to transform data into a form that is not readily intelligible. The transformation and subsequent recovery of the data depend on an algorithm and zero or more encryption keys.	**Trusted Functionality** That which is perceived to be correct with respect to some criteria (e.g., as established by a security policy).
Digital Signature Data appended to, or a cryptographic transformation of, a data unit that allows a recipient of the data unit to prove the source and integrity of the data unit and protect against forgery (e.g., by the recipient).	**Security Label** The marking bound to a resource (which may be a data unit) that names or designates the security attributes of that resource.
Access Control A variety of mechanisms that enforce access rights to resources.	**Event Detection** Detection of security-relevant events.
Data Integrity A variety of mechanisms used to assure the integrity of a data unit or stream of data units.	**Security Audit Trail** Data collected and potentially used to facilitate a security audit, which is an independent review and examination of system records and activities.
Authentication Exchange A mechanism intended to ensure the identity of an entity by means of information exchange.	**Security Recovery** Deals with requests from mechanisms, such as event handling and management functions, and takes recovery actions.
Traffic Padding The insertion of bits into gaps in a data stream to frustrate traffic analysis attempts.	
Routing Control Enables selection of particular physically secure routes for certain data and allows routing changes, especially when a breach of security is suspected.	
Notarization The use of a trusted third party to assure certain properties of a data exchange.	

Table 1.4   Relationship between Security Services and Mechanisms

Service	Encipherment	Digital signature	Access control	Data integrity	Authentication exchange	Traffic padding	Routing control	Notarization
Peer entity authentication	Y	Y			Y			
Data origin authentication	Y	Y						
Access control			Y					
Confidentiality	Y						Y	
Traffic flow confidentiality	Y					Y	Y	
Data integrity	Y	Y		Y				
Nonrepudiation		Y		Y				Y
Availability				Y	Y			

definition of encipherment. X.800 distinguishes between reversible encipherment mechanisms and irreversible encipherment mechanisms. A reversible encipherment mechanism is simply an encryption algorithm that allows data to be encrypted and subsequently decrypted. Irreversible encipherment mechanisms include hash algorithms and message authentication codes, which are used in digital signature and message authentication applications.

Table 1.4, based on one in X.800, indicates the relationship between security services and security mechanisms.

1.6   FUNDAMENTAL SECURITY DESIGN PRINCIPLES

Despite years of research and development, it has not been possible to develop security design and implementation techniques that systematically exclude security flaws and prevent all unauthorized actions. In the absence of such foolproof techniques, it is useful to have a set of widely agreed design principles that can guide the development of protection mechanisms. The National Centers of Academic Excellence in Information Assurance/Cyber Defense, which is jointly sponsored by the U.S. National Security Agency and the U.S. Department of Homeland Security, list the following as fundamental security design principles [NCAE13]:

■ Economy of mechanism
■ Fail-safe defaults
■ Complete mediation

- Open design
- Separation of privilege
- Least privilege
- Least common mechanism
- Psychological acceptability
- Isolation
- Encapsulation
- Modularity
- Layering
- Least astonishment

The first eight listed principles were initially proposed in [SALT75] and have withstood the test of time. In this section, we briefly discuss each principle.

Economy of mechanism means that the design of security measures embodied in both hardware and software should be as simple and small as possible. The motivation for this principle is that relatively simple, small design is easier to test and verify thoroughly. With a complex design, there are many more opportunities for an adversary to discover subtle weaknesses to exploit that may be difficult to spot ahead of time. The more complex the mechanism, the more likely it is to possess exploitable flaws. Simple mechanisms tend to have fewer exploitable flaws and require less maintenance. Further, because configuration management issues are simplified, updating or replacing a simple mechanism becomes a less intensive process. In practice, this is perhaps the most difficult principle to honor. There is a constant demand for new features in both hardware and software, complicating the security design task. The best that can be done is to keep this principle in mind during system design to try to eliminate unnecessary complexity.

Fail-safe default means that access decisions should be based on permission rather than exclusion. That is, the default situation is lack of access, and the protection scheme identifies conditions under which access is permitted. This approach exhibits a better failure mode than the alternative approach, where the default is to permit access. A design or implementation mistake in a mechanism that gives explicit permission tends to fail by refusing permission, a safe situation that can be quickly detected. On the other hand, a design or implementation mistake in a mechanism that explicitly excludes access tends to fail by allowing access, a failure that may long go unnoticed in normal use. For example, most file access systems work on this principle and virtually all protected services on client/server systems work this way.

Complete mediation means that every access must be checked against the access control mechanism. Systems should not rely on access decisions retrieved from a cache. In a system designed to operate continuously, this principle requires that, if access decisions are remembered for future use, careful consideration should be given to how changes in authority are propagated into such local memories. File access systems appear to provide an example of a system that complies with this principle. However, typically, once a user has opened a file, no check is made to see if permissions change. To fully implement complete mediation, every time a user reads a field or record in a file, or a data item in a database, the system must exercise access control. This resource-intensive approach is rarely used.

Open design means that the design of a security mechanism should be open rather than secret. For example, although encryption keys must be secret, encryption algorithms should be open to public scrutiny. The algorithms can then be reviewed by many experts, and users can therefore have high confidence in them. This is the philosophy behind the National Institute of Standards and Technology (NIST) program of standardizing encryption and hash algorithms and has led to the widespread adoption of NIST-approved algorithms.

Separation of privilege is defined in [SALT75] as a practice in which multiple privilege attributes are required to achieve access to a restricted resource. A good example of this is multifactor user authentication, which requires the use of multiple techniques, such as a password and a smart card, to authorize a user. The term is also now applied to any technique in which a program is divided into parts that are limited to the specific privileges they require in order to perform a specific task. This is used to mitigate the potential damage of a computer security attack. One example of this latter interpretation of the principle is removing high privilege operations to another process and running that process with the higher privileges required to perform its tasks. Day-to-day interfaces are executed in a lower privileged process.

Least privilege means that every process and every user of the system should operate using the least set of privileges necessary to perform the task. A good example of the use of this principle is role-based access control, described in Chapter 4. The system security policy can identify and define the various roles of users or processes. Each role is assigned only those permissions needed to perform its functions. Each permission specifies a permitted access to a particular resource (such as read and write access to a specified file or directory, connect access to a given host and port, etc.). Unless a permission is granted explicitly, the user or process should not be able to access the protected resource. More generally, any access control system should allow each user only the privileges that are authorized for that user. There is also a temporal aspect to the least privilege principle. For example, system programs or administrators who have special privileges should have those privileges only when necessary; when they are doing ordinary activities, the privileges should be withdrawn. Leaving them in place just opens the door to accidents.

Least common mechanism means that the design should minimize the functions shared by different users, providing mutual security. This principle helps reduce the number of unintended communication paths and reduces the amount of hardware and software on which all users depend, thus making it easier to verify if there are any undesirable security implications.

Psychological acceptability implies that the security mechanisms should not interfere unduly with the work of users, while at the same time meeting the needs of those who authorize access. If security mechanisms hinder the usability or accessibility of resources, then users may opt to turn off those mechanisms. Where possible, security mechanisms should be transparent to the users of the system or at most introduce minimal obstruction. In addition to not being intrusive or burdensome, security procedures must reflect the user's mental model of protection. If the protection procedures do not make sense to the user or if the user must translate his image of protection into a substantially different protocol, the user is likely to make errors.

Isolation is a principle that applies in three contexts. First, public access systems should be isolated from critical resources (data, processes, etc.) to prevent disclosure or tampering. In cases where the sensitivity or criticality of the information is high, organizations may want to limit the number of systems on which that data is stored and isolate them, either physically or logically. Physical isolation may include ensuring that no physical connection exists between an organization's public access information resources and an organization's critical information. When implementing logical isolation solutions, layers of security services and mechanisms should be established between public systems and secure systems responsible for protecting critical resources. Second, the processes and files of individual users should be isolated from one another except where it is explicitly desired. All modern operating systems provide facilities for such isolation, so that individual users have separate, isolated process space, memory space, and file space, with protections for preventing unauthorized access. Finally, security mechanisms should be isolated in the sense of preventing access to those mechanisms. For example, logical access control may provide a means of isolating cryptographic software from other parts of the host system, and for protecting cryptographic software from tampering and the keys from replacement or disclosure.

Encapsulation can be viewed as a specific form of isolation based on object-oriented functionality. Protection is provided by encapsulating a collection of procedures and data objects in a domain of its own so that the internal structure of a data object is accessible only to the procedures of the protected subsystem, and the procedures may be called only at designated domain entry points.

Modularity in the context of security refers both to the development of security functions as separate, protected modules and to the use of a modular architecture for mechanism design and implementation. With respect to the use of separate security modules, the design goal here is to provide common security functions and services, such as cryptographic functions, as common modules. For example, numerous protocols and applications make use of cryptographic functions. Rather than implementing such functions in each protocol or application, a more secure design is provided by developing a common cryptographic module that can be invoked by numerous protocols and applications. The design and implementation effort can then focus on the secure design and implementation of a single cryptographic module and including mechanisms to protect the module from tampering. With respect to the use of a modular architecture, each security mechanism should be able to support migration to new technology or upgrade of new features without requiring an entire system redesign. The security design should be modular so that individual parts of the security design can be upgraded without the requirement to modify the entire system.

Layering refers to the use of multiple, overlapping protection approaches addressing the people, technology, and operational aspects of information systems. By using multiple, overlapping protection approaches, the failure or circumvention of any individual protection approach will not leave the system unprotected. We will see throughout this text that a layering approach is often used to provide multiple barriers between an adversary and protected information or services. This technique is often referred to as *defense in depth*.

Least astonishment means that a program or user interface should always respond in the way that is least likely to astonish the user. For example, the mechanism for authorization should be transparent enough to a user that the user has a good intuitive understanding of how the security goals map to the provided security mechanism.

1.7 ATTACK SURFACES AND ATTACK TREES

In Section 1.3, we provided an overview of the spectrum of security threats and attacks facing computer and network systems. Section 11.1 goes into more detail about the nature of attacks and the types of adversaries that present security threats. This section elaborates on two concepts that are useful in evaluating and classifying threats: attack surfaces and attack trees.

Attack Surfaces

An attack surface consists of the reachable and exploitable vulnerabilities in a system [MANA11, HOWA03]. Examples of attack surfaces are the following:

- Open ports on outward facing Web and other servers, and code listening on those ports
- Services available on the inside of a firewall
- Code that processes incoming data, e-mail, XML, office documents, and industry-specific custom data exchange formats
- Interfaces, SQL, and Web forms
- An employee with access to sensitive information vulnerable to a social engineering attack

Attack surfaces can be categorized in the following way:

- **Network attack surface:** This category refers to vulnerabilities over an enterprise network, wide-area network, or the Internet. Included in this category are network protocol vulnerabilities, such as those used for a denial-of-service attack, disruption of communications links, and various forms of intruder attacks.
- **Software attack surface:** This refers to vulnerabilities in application, utility, or operating system code. A particular focus in this category is Web server software.
- **Human attack surface:** This category refers to vulnerabilities created by personnel or outsiders, such as social engineering, human error, and trusted insiders.

An attack surface analysis is useful for assessing the scale and severity of threats to a system. A systematic analysis of points of vulnerability makes developers and security analysts aware of where security mechanisms are required. Once an attack surface is defined, designers may be able to find ways to make the surface smaller, thus making the task of the adversary more difficult. The attack surface also provides guidance on setting priorities for testing, strengthening security measures, or modifying the service or application.

As illustrated in Figure 1.3, the use of layering, or defense in depth, and attack surface reduction complement each other in mitigating security risk.

Attack Trees

An attack tree is a branching, hierarchical data structure that represents a set of potential techniques for exploiting security vulnerabilities [MAUW05, MOOR01, SCHN99]. The security incident that is the goal of the attack is represented as the root node of the tree, and the ways that an attacker could reach that goal are iteratively and incrementally represented as branches and subnodes of the tree. Each subnode defines a subgoal, and each subgoal may have its own set of further subgoals, etc. The final nodes on the paths outward from the root, that is, the leaf nodes, represent different ways to initiate an attack. Each node other than a leaf is either an AND-node or an OR-node. To achieve the goal represented by an AND-node, the subgoals represented by all of that node's subnodes must be achieved; and for an OR-node, at least one of the subgoals must be achieved. Branches can be labeled with values representing difficulty, cost, or other attack attributes, so that alternative attacks can be compared.

The motivation for the use of attack trees is to effectively exploit the information available on attack patterns. Organizations such as CERT publish security advisories that have enabled the development of a body of knowledge about both general attack strategies and specific attack patterns. Security analysts can use the attack tree to document security attacks in a structured form that reveals key vulnerabilities. The attack tree can guide both the design of systems and applications, and the choice and strength of countermeasures.

Figure 1.4, based on a figure in [DIMI07], is an example of an attack tree analysis for an Internet banking authentication application. The root of the tree is

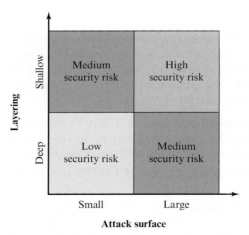

Figure 1.3   Defense in Depth and Attack Surface

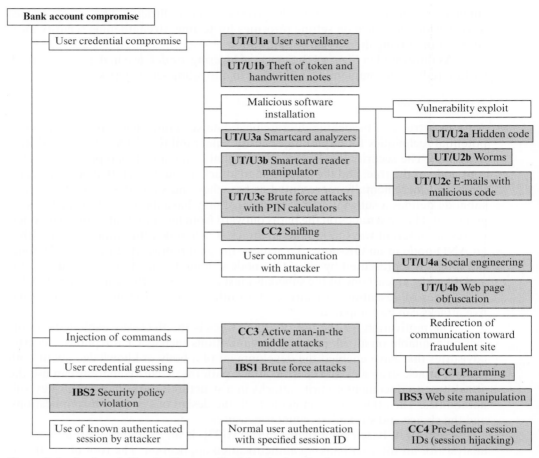

Figure 1.4 An Attack Tree for Internet Banking Authentication

the objective of the attacker, which is to compromise a user's account. The shaded boxes on the tree are the leaf nodes, which represent events the comprise the attacks. Note that in this tree in this example, all the nodes other than leaf nodes are OR-nodes. The analysis to generate this tree considered the three components involved in authentication:

- **User terminal and user (UT/U):** These attacks target the user equipment, including the tokens that may be involved, such as smartcards or other password generators, as well as the actions of the user.
- **Communications channel (CC):** This type of attack focuses on communication links.
- **Internet banking server (IBS):** These types of attacks are offline attacks against the servers that host the Internet banking application.

Five overall attack strategies can be identified, each of which exploits one or more of the three components. The five strategies are as follows:

- **User credential compromise:** This strategy can be used against many elements of the attack surface. There are procedural attacks, such as monitoring a user's action to observe a PIN or other credential, or theft of the user's token or handwritten notes. An adversary may also compromise token information using a variety of token attack tools, such as hacking the smartcard or using a brute force approach to guess the PIN. Another possible strategy is to embed malicious software to compromise the user's login and password. An adversary may also attempt to obtain credential information via the communication channel (sniffing). Finally, an adversary may use various means to engage in communication with the target user, as shown in Figure 1.4.

- **Injection of commands:** In this type of attack, the attacker is able to intercept communication between the UT and the IBS. Various schemes can be used to be able to impersonate the valid user and so gain access to the banking system.

- **User credential guessing:** It is reported in [HILT06] that brute force attacks against some banking authentication schemes are feasible by sending random usernames and passwords. The attack mechanism is based on distributed zombie personal computers, hosting automated programs for username- or password-based calculation.

- **Security policy violation:** For example, violating the bank's security policy in combination with weak access control and logging mechanisms, an employee may cause an internal security incident and expose a customer's account.

- **Use of known authenticated session:** This type of attack persuades or forces the user to connect to the IBS with a preset session ID. Once the user authenticates to the server, the attacker may utilize the known session ID to send packets to the IBS, spoofing the user's identity.

Figure 1.4 provides a thorough view of the different types of attacks on an Internet banking authentication application. Using this tree as a starting point, security analysts can assess the risk of each attack and, using the design principles outlined in the preceding section, design a comprehensive security facility. [DIMI07] provides a good account of the results of this design effort.

1.8 A MODEL FOR NETWORK SECURITY

A model for much of what we will be discussing is captured, in very general terms, in Figure 1.5. A message is to be transferred from one party to another across some sort of Internet service. The two parties, who are the *principals* in this transaction, must cooperate for the exchange to take place. A logical information channel is established by defining a route through the Internet from source to destination and by the cooperative use of communication protocols (e.g., TCP/IP) by the two principals.

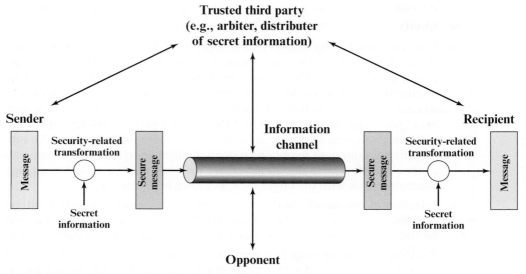

Figure 1.5   Model for Network Security

Security aspects come into play when it is necessary or desirable to protect the information transmission from an opponent who may present a threat to confidentiality, authenticity, and so on. All of the techniques for providing security have two components:

1. A security-related transformation on the information to be sent. Examples include the encryption of the message, which scrambles the message so that it is unreadable by the opponent, and the addition of a code based on the contents of the message, which can be used to verify the identity of the sender.

2. Some secret information shared by the two principals and, it is hoped, unknown to the opponent. An example is an encryption key used in conjunction with the transformation to scramble the message before transmission and unscramble it on reception.[7]

A trusted third party may be needed to achieve secure transmission. For example, a third party may be responsible for distributing the secret information to the two principals while keeping it from any opponent. Or a third party may be needed to arbitrate disputes between the two principals concerning the authenticity of a message transmission.

This general model shows that there are four basic tasks in designing a particular security service:

1. Design an algorithm for performing the security-related transformation. The algorithm should be such that an opponent cannot defeat its purpose.

2. Generate the secret information to be used with the algorithm.

---

[7]Chapter 3 discusses a form of encryption, known as asymmetric encryption, in which only one of the two principals needs to have the secret information.

3. Develop methods for the distribution and sharing of the secret information.

4. Specify a protocol to be used by the two principals that make use of the security algorithm and the secret information to achieve a particular security service.

Parts One and Two of this book concentrate on the types of security mechanisms and services that fit into the model shown in Figure 1.5. However, there are other security-related situations of interest that do not neatly fit this model but are considered in this book. A general model of these other situations is illustrated by Figure 1.6, which reflects a concern for protecting an information system from unwanted access. Most readers are familiar with the concerns caused by the existence of hackers who attempt to penetrate systems that can be accessed over a network. The hacker can be someone who, with no malign intent, simply gets satisfaction from breaking and entering a computer system. The intruder can be a disgruntled employee who wishes to do damage or a criminal who seeks to exploit computer assets for financial gain (e.g., obtaining credit card numbers or performing illegal money transfers).

Another type of unwanted access is the placement in a computer system of logic that exploits vulnerabilities in the system and that can affect application programs as well as utility programs, such as editors and compilers. Programs can present two kinds of threats:

1. **Information access threats:** Intercept or modify data on behalf of users who should not have access to that data.

2. **Service threats:** Exploit service flaws in computers to inhibit use by legitimate users.

Viruses and worms are two examples of software attacks. Such attacks can be introduced into a system by means of a disk that contains the unwanted logic concealed in otherwise useful software. They also can be inserted into a system across a network; this latter mechanism is of more concern in network security.

The **security mechanisms** needed to cope with unwanted access fall into two broad categories (see Figure 1.6). The first category might be termed a gatekeeper function. It includes password-based login procedures that are designed to deny access to all but authorized users and screening logic that is designed to detect and reject worms, viruses, and other similar attacks. Once either an unwanted user

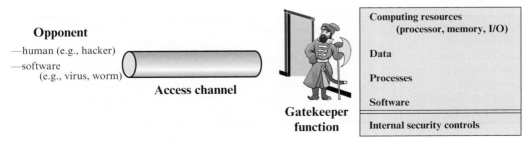

Figure 1.6 Network Access Security Model

or unwanted software gains access, the second line of defense consists of a variety of internal controls that monitor activity and analyze stored information in an attempt to detect the presence of unwanted intruders. These issues are explored in Part Three.

1.9 STANDARDS

Many of the security techniques and applications described in this book have been specified as standards. Additionally, standards have been developed to cover management practices and the overall architecture of security mechanisms and services. Throughout this book, we describe the most important standards in use or being developed for various aspects of cryptography and network security. Various organizations have been involved in the development or promotion of these standards. The most important (in the current context) of these organizations are as follows.

- **National Institute of Standards and Technology:** NIST is a U.S. federal agency that deals with measurement science, standards, and technology related to U.S. government use and to the promotion of U.S. private-sector innovation. Despite its national scope, NIST **Federal Information Processing Standards (FIPS)** and **Special Publications (SP)** have a worldwide impact.
- **Internet Society:** ISOC is a professional membership society with worldwide organizational and individual membership. It provides leadership in addressing issues that confront the future of the Internet and is the organization home for the groups responsible for Internet infrastructure standards, including the Internet Engineering Task Force (IETF) and the Internet Architecture Board (IAB). These organizations develop Internet standards and related specifications, all of which are published as **Requests for Comments (RFCs)**.

A more detailed discussion of these organizations is contained in Appendix C.

1.10 KEY TERMS, REVIEW QUESTIONS, AND PROBLEMS

Key Terms

access control	denial of service	passive attack
active attack	encryption	replay
authentication	integrity	security attacks
authenticity	intruder	security mechanisms
availability	masquerade	security services
data confidentiality	nonrepudiation	traffic analysis
data integrity	OSI security architecture	

Review Questions

1.1 What is the OSI security architecture?

1.2 Briefly explain masquerade attack with an example.

1.3 What is the difference between security threats and attacks?

1.4 Why are passive attacks difficult to detect and active attacks difficult to prevent?

1.5 Identify the different security attacks prevented by the security mechanisms defined in X.800.

1.6 List and briefly define the fundamental security design principles.

1.7 Explain the difference between an attack surface and an attack tree.

Problems

1.1 Consider an automated teller machine (ATM) in which users provide a personal identification number (PIN) and a card for account access. Give examples of confidentiality, integrity, and availability requirements associated with the system. In each case, indicate the degree of importance of the requirement.

1.2 Repeat Problem 1.1 for a telephone switching system that routes calls through a switching network based on the telephone number requested by the caller.

1.3 Consider a desktop publishing system used to produce documents for various organizations.
   a. Give an example of a type of publication for which confidentiality of the stored data is the most important requirement.
   b. Give an example of a type of publication in which data integrity is the most important requirement.
   c. Give an example in which system availability is the most important requirement.

1.4 For each of the following assets, assign a low, moderate, or high impact level for the loss of confidentiality, availability, and integrity, respectively. Justify your answers.
   a. A portal maintained by the Government to provide information regarding its departments and services.
   b. A hospital managing the medical records of its patients.
   c. A financial organization managing routine administrative information (not privacy-related information).
   d. An information system used for large acquisitions in a contracting organization that contains both sensitive, pre-solicitation phase contract information and routine administrative information. Assess the impact for the two data sets separately and the information system as a whole.
   e. The Examinations department of a University maintains examination particulars, such as question papers of forthcoming examinations, grades obtained, and examiner details. The University's administrative department maintains the students' attendance particulars and internal assessment results. Assess the impact for the two data sets separately and the information system as a whole.

1.5 Draw a matrix similar to Table 1.4 that shows the relationship between security attacks and mechanisms.

1.6 Draw a matrix similar to Table 1.4 that shows the relationship between security mechanisms and services.

1.7 Develop an attack tree for gaining access to customer account details from the database of a bank.

1.8 Consider a company whose operations are housed in two buildings on the same property; one building is headquarters, the other building contains network and computer services. The property is physically protected by a fence around the perimeter. The only entrance to the property is through the fenced perimeter. In addition to the perimeter fence, physical security consists of a guarded front gate. The local networks are split between the Headquarters' LAN and the Network Services' LAN. Internet users connect to the Web server through a firewall. Dial-up users get access to a particular server on the Network Services' LAN. Develop an attack tree in which the root node represents disclosure of proprietary secrets. Include physical, social engineering, and technical attacks. The tree may contain both AND and OR nodes. Develop a tree that has at least 15 leaf nodes.

1.9 Read all of the classic papers cited in the Recommended Reading section for this chapter, available at the Author Web site at WilliamStallings.com/NetworkSecurity. The papers are available at box.com/NetSec6e. Compose a 500–1000 word paper (or 8 to 12 slide PowerPoint presentation) that summarizes the key concepts that emerge from these papers, emphasizing concepts that are common to most or all of the papers.

PART ONE: CRYPTOGRAPHY

CHAPTER 2

SYMMETRIC ENCRYPTION AND MESSAGE CONFIDENTIALITY

LEARNING OBJECTIVES

After studying this chapter, you should be able to:

◆ Present an overview of the main concepts of symmetric cryptography.

◆ Explain the difference between cryptanalysis and brute-force attack.

◆ Summarize the functionality of DES.

◆ Present an overview of AES.

◆ Explain the concepts of randomness and unpredictability with respect to random numbers.

◆ Understand the differences among true random number generators, pseudorandom number generators, and pseudorandom functions.

◆ Present an overview of stream ciphers and RC4.

◆ Compare and contrast ECB, CBC, CFB, and counter modes of operation.

Symmetric encryption, also referred to as conventional encryption, secret-key, or single-key encryption, was the only type of encryption in use prior to the development of public-key encryption in the late 1970s.[1] It remains by far the most widely used of the two types of encryption.

This chapter begins with a look at a general model for the symmetric encryption process; this will enable us to understand the context within which the algorithms are used. Then we look at three important block encryption algorithms: DES, triple DES, and AES. This is followed by a discussion of random and pseudorandom number generation. Next, the chapter introduces symmetric stream encryption and describes the widely used stream cipher RC4. Finally, we look at the important topic of block cipher modes of operation.

2.1 SYMMETRIC ENCRYPTION PRINCIPLES

A **symmetric encryption** scheme has five ingredients (Figure 2.1):

■ **Plaintext:** This is the original message or data that is fed into the algorithm as input.

■ **Encryption algorithm:** The **encryption** algorithm performs various substitutions and transformations on the plaintext.

■ **Secret key:** The secret key is also input to the algorithm. The exact substitutions and transformations performed by the algorithm depend on the key.

---

[1]Public-key encryption was first described in the open literature in 1976; the National Security Agency (NSA) claims to have discovered it some years earlier.

- **Ciphertext:** This is the scrambled message produced as output. It depends on the plaintext and the secret key. For a given message, two different keys will produce two different ciphertexts.

- **Decryption algorithm:** This is essentially the encryption algorithm run in reverse. It takes the ciphertext and the same secret key and produces the original plaintext.

There are two requirements for secure use of symmetric encryption:

1. We need a strong encryption algorithm. At a minimum, we would like the algorithm to be such that an opponent who knows the algorithm and has access to one or more ciphertexts would be unable to decipher the ciphertext or figure out the key. This requirement is usually stated in a stronger form: The opponent should be unable to decrypt ciphertext or discover the key even if he or she is in possession of a number of ciphertexts together with the plaintext that produced each ciphertext.

2. Sender and receiver must have obtained copies of the secret key in a secure fashion and must keep the key secure. If someone can discover the key and knows the algorithm, all communication using this key is readable.

It is important to note that the security of symmetric encryption depends on the secrecy of the key, not the secrecy of the algorithm. That is, it is assumed that it is impractical to decrypt a message on the basis of the ciphertext *plus* knowledge of the encryption/decryption algorithm. In other words, we do not need to keep the algorithm secret; we need to keep only the key secret.

This feature of symmetric encryption is what makes it feasible for widespread use. The fact that the algorithm need not be kept secret means that manufacturers can and have developed low-cost chip implementations of data encryption algorithms. These chips are widely available and incorporated into a number of products. With the use of symmetric encryption, the principal security problem is maintaining the secrecy of the key.

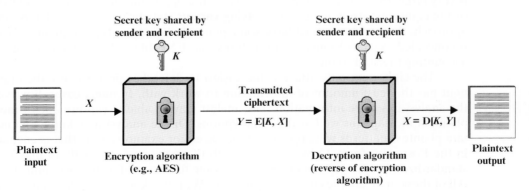

Figure 2.1   Simplified Model of Symmetric Encryption

Cryptography

Cryptographic systems are generically classified along three independent dimensions:

1. **The type of operations used for transforming plaintext to ciphertext.** All encryption algorithms are based on two general principles: substitution, in which each element in the plaintext (bit, letter, group of bits or letters) is mapped into another element; and transposition, in which elements in the plaintext are rearranged. The fundamental requirement is that no information be lost (i.e., that all operations be reversible). Most systems, referred to as product systems, involve multiple stages of substitutions and transpositions.

2. **The number of keys used.** If both sender and receiver use the same key, the system is referred to as symmetric, single-key, secret-key, or conventional encryption. If the sender and receiver each use a different key, the system is referred to as asymmetric, two-key, or public-key encryption.

3. **The way in which the plaintext is processed.** A **block cipher** processes the input one block of elements at a time, producing an output block for each input block. A **stream cipher** processes the input elements continuously, producing output one element at a time, as it goes along.

Cryptanalysis

The process of attempting to discover the plaintext or key is known as **cryptanalysis**. The strategy used by the cryptanalyst depends on the nature of the encryption scheme and the information available to the cryptanalyst.

Table 2.1 summarizes the various types of cryptanalytic attacks based on the amount of information known to the cryptanalyst. The most difficult problem is presented when all that is available is the *ciphertext only*. In some cases, not even the encryption algorithm is known, but in general, we can assume that the opponent does know the algorithm used for encryption. One possible attack under these circumstances is the brute-force approach of trying all possible keys. If the key space is very large, this becomes impractical. Thus, the opponent must rely on an analysis of the ciphertext itself, generally applying various statistical tests to it. To use this approach, the opponent must have some general idea of the type of plaintext that is concealed, such as English or French text, an EXE file, a Java source listing, an accounting file, and so on.

The ciphertext-only attack is the easiest to defend against because the opponent has the least amount of information to work with. In many cases, however, the analyst has more information. The analyst may be able to capture one or more plaintext messages as well as their encryptions. Or the analyst may know that certain plaintext patterns will appear in a message. For example, a file that is encoded in the Postscript format always begins with the same pattern, or there may be a standardized header or banner to an electronic funds transfer message, and so on. All of these are examples of *known plaintext*. With this knowledge, the analyst may be able to deduce the key on the basis of the way in which the known plaintext is transformed.

Table 2.1 Types of Attacks on Encrypted Messages

Type of Attack	Known to Cryptanalyst
Ciphertext only	■ Encryption algorithm ■ Ciphertext to be decoded
Known plaintext	■ Encryption algorithm ■ Ciphertext to be decoded ■ One or more plaintext–ciphertext pairs formed with the secret key
Chosen plaintext	■ Encryption algorithm ■ Ciphertext to be decoded ■ Plaintext message chosen by cryptanalyst, together with its corresponding ciphertext generated with the secret key
Chosen ciphertext	■ Encryption algorithm ■ Ciphertext to be decoded ■ Purported ciphertext chosen by cryptanalyst, together with its corresponding decrypted plaintext generated with the secret key
Chosen text	■ Encryption algorithm ■ Ciphertext to be decoded ■ Plaintext message chosen by cryptanalyst, together with its corresponding ciphertext generated with the secret key ■ Purported ciphertext chosen by cryptanalyst, together with its corresponding decrypted plaintext generated with the secret key

Closely related to the known-plaintext attack is what might be referred to as a probable-word attack. If the opponent is working with the encryption of some general prose message, he or she may have little knowledge of what is in the message. However, if the opponent is after some very specific information, then parts of the message may be known. For example, if an entire accounting file is being transmitted, the opponent may know the placement of certain key words in the header of the file. As another example, the source code for a program developed by a corporation might include a copyright statement in some standardized position.

If the analyst is able somehow to get the source system to insert into the system a message chosen by the analyst, then a *chosen-plaintext* attack is possible. In general, if the analyst is able to choose the messages to encrypt, the analyst may deliberately pick patterns that can be expected to reveal the structure of the key.

Table 2.1 lists two other types of attack: chosen ciphertext and chosen text. These are less commonly employed as cryptanalytic techniques but are nevertheless possible avenues of attack.

Only relatively weak algorithms fail to withstand a ciphertext-only attack. Generally, an encryption algorithm is designed to withstand a known-plaintext attack.

An encryption scheme is **computationally secure** if the ciphertext generated by the scheme meets one or both of the following criteria:

■ The cost of breaking the cipher exceeds the value of the encrypted information.

■ The time required to break the cipher exceeds the useful lifetime of the information.

Unfortunately, it is very difficult to estimate the amount of effort required to cryptanalyze ciphertext successfully. However, assuming there are no inherent mathematical weaknesses in the algorithm, then a brute-force approach is indicated. A **brute-force attack** involves trying every possible key until an intelligible translation of the ciphertext into plaintext is obtained. On average, half of all possible keys must be tried to achieve success. That is, if there are x different keys, on average an attacker would discover the actual key after $x/2$ tries. It is important to note that there is more to a brute-force attack than simply running through all possible keys. Unless known plaintext is provided, the analyst must be able to recognize plaintext as plaintext. If the message is just plaintext in English, then the result pops out easily, although the task of recognizing English would have to be automated. If the text message has been compressed before encryption, then recognition is more difficult. And if the message is some more general type of data, such as a numerical file, and this has been compressed, the problem becomes even more difficult to automate. Thus, to supplement the brute-force approach, some degree of knowledge about the expected plaintext is needed, and some means of automatically distinguishing plaintext from garble is also needed.

Feistel Cipher Structure

Many symmetric block encryption algorithms, including DES, have a structure first described by Horst Feistel of IBM in 1973 [FEIS73] and shown in Figure 2.2. The inputs to the encryption algorithm are a plaintext block of length $2w$ bits and a key K. The plaintext block is divided into two halves, LE_0 and RE_0. The two halves of the data pass through n rounds of processing and then combine to produce the ciphertext block. Each round i has as inputs LE_{i-1} and RE_{i-1} derived from the previous round, as well as a subkey K_i derived from the overall K. In general, the subkeys K_i are different from K and from each other and are generated from the key by a subkey generation algorithm. In Figure 2.2, 16 rounds are used, although any number of rounds could be implemented. The right-hand side of Figure 2.2 shows the decryption process.

All rounds have the same structure. A substitution is performed on the left half of the data. This is done by applying a *round function* F to the right half of the data and then taking the exclusive-OR (XOR) of the output of that function and the left half of the data. The round function has the same general structure for each round but is parameterized by the round subkey K_i. Following this substitution, a permutation is performed that consists of the interchange of the two halves of the data.

The **Feistel structure** is a particular example of the more general structure used by all symmetric block ciphers. In general, a symmetric block cipher consists of a sequence of rounds, with each round performing substitutions and permutations conditioned by a secret key value. The exact realization of a symmetric block cipher depends on the choice of the following parameters and design features.

- **Block size:** Larger block sizes mean greater security (all other things being equal) but reduced encryption/decryption speed. A block size of 128 bits is a reasonable trade-off and is nearly universal among recent block cipher designs.

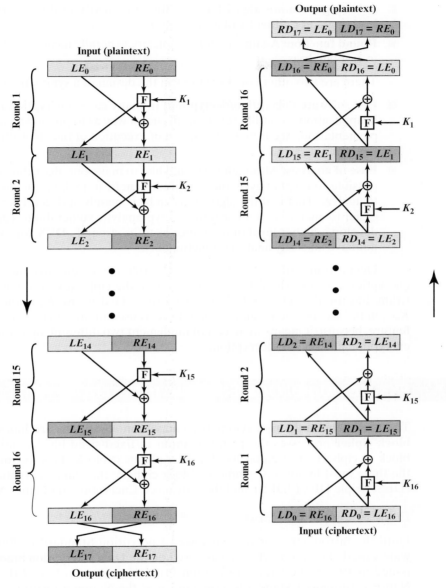

Figure 2.2   Feistel Encryption and Decryption (16 rounds)

- **Key size:** Larger key size means greater security but may decrease encryption/decryption speed. The most common key length in modern algorithms is 128 bits.

- **Number of rounds:** The essence of a symmetric block cipher is that a single round offers inadequate security but that multiple rounds offer increasing security. A typical size is from 10 to 16 rounds.

- **Subkey generation algorithm:** Greater complexity in this algorithm should lead to greater difficulty of cryptanalysis.

- **Round function:** Again, greater complexity generally means greater resistance to cryptanalysis.

There are two other considerations in the design of a symmetric block cipher:

- **Fast software encryption/decryption:** In many cases, encryption is embedded in applications or utility functions in such a way as to preclude a hardware implementation. Accordingly, the speed of execution of the algorithm becomes a concern.

- **Ease of analysis:** Although we would like to make our algorithm as difficult as possible to cryptanalyze, there is great benefit in making the algorithm easy to analyze. That is, if the algorithm can be concisely and clearly explained, it is easier to analyze that algorithm for cryptanalytic vulnerabilities and therefore develop a higher level of assurance as to its strength. DES, for example, does not have an easily analyzed functionality.

Decryption with a symmetric block cipher is essentially the same as the encryption process. The rule is as follows: Use the ciphertext as input to the algorithm, but use the subkeys K_i in reverse order. That is, use K_n in the first round, K_{n-1} in the second round, and so on until K_1 is used in the last round. This is a nice feature, because it means we need not implement two different algorithms—one for encryption and one for decryption.

2.2 SYMMETRIC BLOCK ENCRYPTION ALGORITHMS

The most commonly used symmetric encryption algorithms are block ciphers. A **block cipher** processes the plaintext input in fixed-sized blocks and produces a block of ciphertext of equal size for each plaintext block. This section focuses on the three most important symmetric block ciphers: the Data Encryption Standard (DES), triple DES (3DES), and the Advanced Encryption Standard (AES).

Data Encryption Standard

Until the introduction of the Advanced Encryption Standard in 2001, the most widely used encryption scheme was based on the **Data Encryption Standard (DES)** issued in 1977 as Federal Information Processing Standard 46 (FIPS 46) by the National Bureau of Standards, now known as the National Institute of Standards and Technology (NIST). The algorithm itself is referred to as the Data Encryption Algorithm (DEA).[2]

---

[2]The terminology is a bit confusing. Until recently, the terms *DES* and *DEA* could be used interchangeably. However, the most recent edition of the DES document includes a specification of the DEA described here plus the triple DEA (3DES) described subsequently. Both DEA and 3DES are part of the Data Encryption Standard. Furthermore, until the recent adoption of the official term *3DES*, the triple DEA algorithm was typically referred to as *triple DES* and written as 3DES. For the sake of convenience, we will use 3DES.

DESCRIPTION OF THE ALGORITHM The plaintext is 64 bits in length and the key is 56 bits in length; longer plaintext amounts are processed in 64-bit blocks. The DES structure is a minor variation of the Feistel network shown in Figure 2.2. There are 16 rounds of processing. From the original 56-bit key, 16 subkeys are generated, one of which is used for each round.

The process of decryption with DES is essentially the same as the encryption process. The rule is as follows: Use the ciphertext as input to the DES algorithm, but use the subkeys K_i in reverse order. That is, use K_{16} on the first iteration, K_{15} on the second iteration, and so on until K_1 is used on the 16th and last iteration.

THE STRENGTH OF DES Concerns about the strength of DES fall into two categories: concerns about the algorithm itself and concerns about the use of a 56-bit key. The first concern refers to the possibility that cryptanalysis is possible by exploiting the characteristics of the DES algorithm. Over the years, there have been numerous attempts to find and exploit weaknesses in the algorithm, making DES the most-studied encryption algorithm in existence. Despite numerous approaches, no one has so far succeeded in discovering a fatal weakness in DES.[3]

A more serious concern is key length. With a key length of 56 bits, there are 2^{56} possible keys, which is approximately 7.2×10^{16} keys. Thus, on the face of it, a brute-force attack appears impractical. Assuming that on average half the key space has to be searched, a single machine performing one DES encryption per microsecond would take more than a thousand years to break the cipher.

However, the assumption of one encryption per microsecond is overly conservative. DES finally and definitively proved insecure in July 1998, when the Electronic Frontier Foundation (EFF) announced that it had broken a DES encryption using a special-purpose "DES cracker" machine that was built for less than $250,000. The attack took less than three days. The EFF has published a detailed description of the machine, enabling others to build their own cracker [EFF98]. And, of course, hardware prices will continue to drop as speeds increase, making DES virtually worthless.

With current technology, it is not even necessary to use special, purpose-built hardware. Rather, the speed of commercial, off-the-shelf processors threaten the security of DES. A paper from Seagate Technology [SEAG08] suggests that a rate of one billion (10^9) key combinations per second is reasonable for today's multicore computers. Recent offerings confirm this. Both Intel and AMD now offer hardware-based instructions to accelerate the use of AES. Tests run on a contemporary multi-core Intel machine resulted in an encryption rate of about half a billion [BASU12]. Another recent analysis suggests that with contemporary supercomputer technology, a rate of 10^{13} encryptions/s is reasonable [AROR12].

Considering these results, Table 2.2 shows how much time is required for a brute-force attack for various key sizes. As can be seen, a single PC can break DES in about a year; if multiple PCs work in parallel, the time is drastically shortened. And today's supercomputers should be able to find a key in about an hour. Key sizes of 128 bits or greater are effectively unbreakable using simply a brute-force approach. Even if we managed to speed up the attacking system by a factor of 1 trillion (10^{12}), it would still take over 100,000 years to break a code using a 128-bit key.

---

[3]At least, no one has publicly acknowledged such a discovery.

54 CHAPTER 2 / SYMMETRIC ENCRYPTION AND MESSAGE CONFIDENTIALITY

Table 2.2 Average Time Required for Exhaustive Key Search

Key Size (bits)	Cipher	Number of Alternative Keys	Time Required at 10^9 Decryptions/s	Time Required at 10^{13} Decryptions/s
56	DES	$2^{56} \approx 7.2 \times 10^{16}$	2^{55} ns = 1.125 years	1 hour
128	AES	$2^{128} \approx 3.4 \times 10^{38}$	2^{127} ns = 5.3×10^{21} years	5.3×10^{17} years
168	Triple DES	$2^{168} \approx 3.7 \times 10^{50}$	2^{167} ns = 5.8×10^{33} years	5.8×10^{29} years
192	AES	$2^{192} \approx 6.3 \times 10^{57}$	2^{191} ns = 9.8×10^{40} years	9.8×10^{36} years
256	AES	$2^{256} \approx 1.2 \times 10^{77}$	2^{255} ns = 1.8×10^{60} years	1.8×10^{56} years

Fortunately, there are a number of alternatives to DES, the most important of which are triple DES and AES, discussed in the remainder of this section.

Triple DES

Triple DES (3DES) was first standardized for use in financial applications in ANSI standard X9.17 in 1985. 3DES was incorporated as part of the Data Encryption Standard in 1999 with the publication of FIPS 46-3.

3DES uses three keys and three executions of the DES algorithm. The function follows an encrypt-decrypt-encrypt (EDE) sequence (Figure 2.3a):

$$C = E(K_3, D(K_2, E(K_1, P)))$$

where

$$C = \text{ciphertext}$$
$$P = \text{plaintext}$$
$$E[K, X] = \text{encryption of } X \text{ using key } K$$
$$D[K, Y] = \text{decryption of } Y \text{ using key } K$$

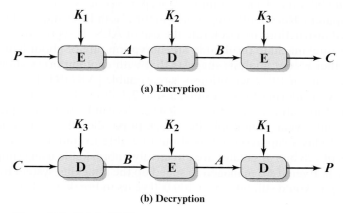

(a) Encryption

(b) Decryption

Figure 2.3 Triple DES

Decryption is simply the same operation with the keys reversed (Figure 2.3b):

$$P = D(K_1, E(K_2, D(K_3, C)))$$

There is no cryptographic significance to the use of decryption for the second stage of 3DES encryption. Its only advantage is that it allows users of 3DES to decrypt data encrypted by users of the older single DES:

$$C = E(K_1, D(K_1, E(K_1, P))) = E[K, P]$$

With three distinct keys, 3DES has an effective key length of 168 bits. FIPS 46-3 also allows for the use of two keys, with $K_1 = K_3$; this provides for a key length of 112 bits. FIPS 46-3 includes the following guidelines for 3DES.

- 3DES is the FIPS-approved symmetric encryption algorithm of choice.
- The original DES, which uses a single 56-bit key, is permitted under the standard for legacy systems only. New procurements should support 3DES.
- Government organizations with legacy DES systems are encouraged to transition to 3DES.
- It is anticipated that 3DES and the Advanced Encryption Standard (AES) will coexist as FIPS-approved algorithms, allowing for a gradual transition to AES.

It is easy to see that 3DES is a formidable algorithm. Because the underlying cryptographic algorithm is DEA, 3DES can claim the same resistance to cryptanalysis based on the algorithm as is claimed for DEA. Furthermore, with a 168-bit key length, brute-force attacks are effectively impossible.

Ultimately, AES is intended to replace 3DES, but this process will take a number of years. NIST anticipates that 3DES will remain an approved algorithm (for U.S. government use) for the foreseeable future.

Advanced Encryption Standard

3DES has two attractions that assure its widespread use over the next few years. First, with its 168-bit key length, it overcomes the vulnerability to brute-force attack of DEA. Second, the underlying encryption algorithm in 3DES is the same as in DEA. This algorithm has been subjected to more scrutiny than any other encryption algorithm over a longer period of time, and no effective cryptanalytic attack based on the algorithm rather than brute force has been found. Accordingly, there is a high level of confidence that 3DES is very resistant to cryptanalysis. If security were the only consideration, then 3DES would be an appropriate choice for a standardized encryption algorithm for decades to come.

The principal drawback of 3DES is that the algorithm is relatively sluggish in software. The original DEA was designed for mid-1970s hardware implementation and does not produce efficient software code. 3DES, which has three times as many rounds as DEA, is correspondingly slower. A secondary drawback is that both DEA and 3DES use a 64-bit block size. For reasons of both efficiency and security, a larger block size is desirable.

Because of these drawbacks, 3DES is not a reasonable candidate for long-term use. As a replacement, NIST in 1997 issued a call for proposals for a new

Advanced Encryption Standard (AES), which should have a security strength equal to or better than 3DES and significantly improved efficiency. In addition to these general requirements, NIST specified that AES must be a symmetric block cipher with a block length of 128 bits and support for key lengths of 128, 192, and 256 bits. Evaluation criteria included security, computational efficiency, memory requirements, hardware and software suitability, and flexibility.

In a first round of evaluation, 15 proposed algorithms were accepted. A second round narrowed the field to five algorithms. NIST completed its evaluation process and published a final standard (FIPS PUB 197) in November of 2001. NIST selected Rijndael as the proposed AES algorithm. The two researchers who developed and submitted Rijndael for the AES are both cryptographers from Belgium: Dr. Joan Daemen and Dr. Vincent Rijmen.

OVERVIEW OF THE ALGORITHM   AES uses a block length of 128 bits and a key length that can be 128, 192, or 256 bits. In the description of this section, we assume a key length of 128 bits, which is likely to be the one most commonly implemented.

The input to the encryption and decryption algorithms is a single 128-bit block. In FIPS PUB 197, this block is depicted as a square matrix of bytes. This block is copied into the **State** array, which is modified at each stage of encryption or decryption. After the final stage, **State** is copied to an output matrix. Similarly, the 128-bit key is depicted as a square matrix of bytes. This key is then expanded into an array of key schedule words: Each word is four bytes and the total key schedule is 44 words for the 128-bit key. The ordering of bytes within a matrix is by column. So, for example, the first four bytes of a 128-bit plaintext input to the encryption cipher occupy the first column of the **in** matrix, the second four bytes occupy the second column, and so on. Similarly, the first four bytes of the expanded key, which form a word, occupy the first column of the **w** matrix.

The following comments give some insight into AES.

1. One noteworthy feature of this structure is that it is not a Feistel structure. Recall that in the classic Feistel structure, half of the data block is used to modify the other half of the data block, and then the halves are swapped. AES does not use a Feistel structure but processes the entire data block in parallel during each round using substitutions and permutation.

2. The key that is provided as input is expanded into an array of forty-four 32-bit words, $w[i]$. Four distinct words (128 bits) serve as a round key for each round.

3. Four different stages are used, one of permutation and three of substitution (Figure 2.4):
   - **Substitute bytes:** Uses a table, referred to as an S-box,[4] to perform a byte-by-byte substitution of the block.
   - **Shift rows:** A simple permutation that is performed row by row.

---

[4]The term *S-box*, or substitution box, is commonly used in the description of symmetric ciphers to refer to a table used for a table-lookup type of substitution mechanism.

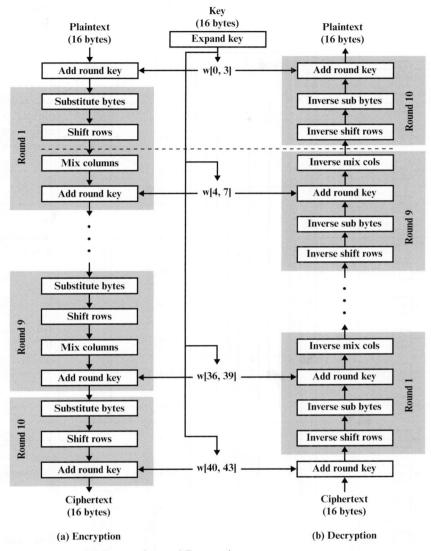

Figure 2.4   AES Encryption and Decryption

■ **Mix columns:** A substitution that alters each byte in a column as a function of all of the bytes in the column.

■ **Add round key:** A simple bitwise XOR of the current block with a portion of the expanded key.

4. The structure is quite simple. For both encryption and decryption, the cipher begins with an Add Round Key stage, followed by nine rounds that each includes all four stages, followed by a tenth round of three stages. Figure 2.5 depicts the structure of a full encryption round.

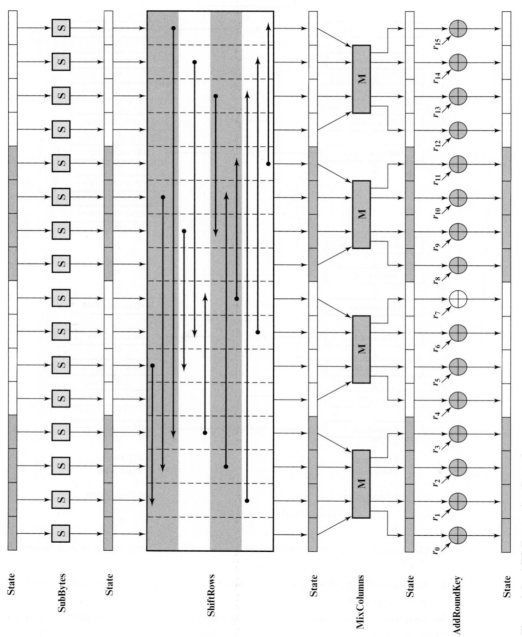

Figure 2.5 AES Encryption Round

5. Only the Add Round Key stage makes use of the key. For this reason, the cipher begins and ends with an Add Round Key stage. Any other stage, applied at the beginning or end, is reversible without knowledge of the key and so would add no security.

6. The Add Round Key stage by itself would not be formidable. The other three stages together scramble the bits, but by themselves, they would provide no security because they do not use the key. We can view the cipher as alternating operations of XOR encryption (Add Round Key) of a block, followed by scrambling of the block (the other three stages), followed by XOR encryption, and so on. This scheme is both efficient and highly secure.

7. Each stage is easily reversible. For the Substitute Byte, Shift Row, and Mix Columns stages, an inverse function is used in the decryption algorithm. For the Add Round Key stage, the inverse is achieved by XORing the same round key to the block, using the result that $A \oplus B \oplus B = A$.

8. As with most block ciphers, the decryption algorithm makes use of the expanded key in reverse order. However, the decryption algorithm is not identical to the encryption algorithm. This is a consequence of the particular structure of AES.

9. Once it is established that all four stages are reversible, it is easy to verify that decryption does recover the plaintext. Figure 2.4 lays out encryption and decryption going in opposite vertical directions. At each horizontal point (e.g., the dashed line in the figure), **State** is the same for both encryption and decryption.

10. The final round of both encryption and decryption consists of only three stages. Again, this is a consequence of the particular structure of AES and is required to make the cipher reversible.

2.3 RANDOM AND PSEUDORANDOM NUMBERS

Random numbers play an important role in the use of encryption for various network security applications. We provide an overview in this section. The topic is examined in more detail in Appendix E.

The Use of Random Numbers

A number of network security algorithms based on cryptography make use of random numbers. For example,

- Generation of keys for the RSA public-key encryption algorithm (described in Chapter 3) and other public-key algorithms.
- Generation of a stream key for symmetric stream cipher (discussed in the following section).

- Generation of a symmetric key for use as a temporary **session key**. This function is used in a number of networking applications, such as Transport Layer Security (Chapter 5), Wi-Fi (Chapter 6), e-mail security (Chapter 7), and IP security (Chapter 8).

- In a number of key distribution scenarios, such as Kerberos (Chapter 4), random numbers are used for handshaking to prevent replay attacks.

These applications give rise to two distinct and not necessarily compatible requirements for a sequence of random numbers: randomness and unpredictability.

RANDOMNESS Traditionally, the concern in the generation of a sequence of allegedly random numbers has been that the sequence of numbers be random in some well-defined statistical sense. The following criteria are used to validate that a sequence of numbers is random.

- **Uniform distribution:** The distribution of bits in the sequence should be uniform; that is, the frequency of occurrence of ones and zeros should be approximately the same.

- **Independence:** No one subsequence in the sequence can be inferred from the others.

Although there are well-defined tests for determining that a sequence of numbers matches a particular distribution, such as the uniform distribution, there is no such test to "prove" independence. Rather, a number of tests can be applied to demonstrate if a sequence does not exhibit independence. The general strategy is to apply a number of such tests until the confidence that independence exists is sufficiently strong.

In the context of our discussion, the use of a sequence of numbers that appear statistically random often occurs in the design of algorithms related to cryptography. For example, a fundamental requirement of the RSA public-key encryption scheme discussed in Chapter 3 is the ability to generate prime numbers. In general, it is difficult to determine if a given large number N is prime. A brute-force approach would be to divide N by every odd integer less than $\sqrt{N}$. If N is on the order, say, of 10^{150} (a not uncommon occurrence in public-key cryptography), such a brute-force approach is beyond the reach of human analysts and their computers. However, a number of effective algorithms exist that test the primality of a number by using a sequence of randomly chosen integers as input to relatively simple computations. If the sequence is sufficiently long (but far, far less than $\sqrt{10^{150}}$), the primality of a number can be determined with near certainty. This type of approach, known as randomization, crops up frequently in the design of algorithms. In essence, if a problem is too hard or time-consuming to solve exactly, a simpler, shorter approach based on randomization is used to provide an answer with any desired level of confidence.

UNPREDICTABILITY In applications such as reciprocal authentication and session key generation, the requirement is not so much that the sequence of numbers be statistically random but that the successive members of the sequence are unpredictable. With "true" random sequences, each number is statistically independent of other numbers in the sequence and therefore unpredictable. However, as is discussed shortly, true random numbers are not always used; rather, sequences of numbers that appear to be random are generated by some algorithm. In this latter case, care must be taken that an opponent not be able to predict future elements of the sequence on the basis of earlier elements.

TRNGs, PRNGs, and PRFs

Cryptographic applications typically make use of algorithmic techniques for random number generation. These algorithms are deterministic and therefore produce sequences of numbers that are not statistically random. However, if the algorithm is good, the resulting sequences will pass many reasonable tests of randomness. Such numbers are referred to as **pseudorandom numbers**.

You may be somewhat uneasy about the concept of using numbers generated by a deterministic algorithm as if they were random numbers. Despite what might be called philosophical objections to such a practice, it generally works. That is, under most circumstances, pseudorandom numbers will perform as well as if they were random for a given use. The phrase "as well as" is unfortunately subjective, but the use of pseudorandom numbers is widely accepted. The same principle applies in statistical application, in which a statistician takes a sample of a population and assumes that the results will be approximately the same as if the whole population were measured.

Figure 2.6 contrasts a **true random number generator (TRNG)** with two forms of pseudorandom number generators. A TRNG takes as input a source that is effectively random; the source is often referred to as an **entropy source**. In essence, the entropy source is drawn from the physical environment of the computer

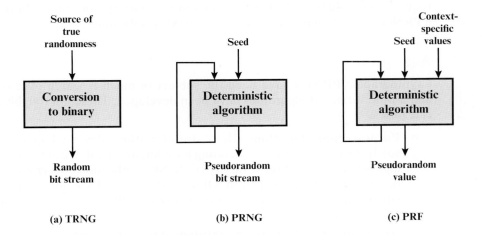

TRNG = true random number generator
PRNG = pseudorandom number generator
PRF = pseudorandom function

Figure 2.6   Random and Pseudorandom Number Generators

and could include things such as keystroke timing patterns, disk electrical activity, mouse movements, and instantaneous values of the system clock. The source, or combination of sources, serves as input to an algorithm that produces random binary output. The TRNG may simply involve conversion of an analog source to a binary output. The TRNG may involve additional processing to overcome any bias in the source.

In contrast, a PRNG takes as input a fixed value, called the **seed**, and produces a sequence of output bits using a deterministic algorithm. Typically, as shown in Figure 2.6, there is some feedback path by which some of the results of the algorithm are fed back as input as additional output bits are produced. The important thing to note is that the output bit stream is determined solely by the input value or values, so that an adversary who knows the algorithm and the seed can reproduce the entire bit stream.

Figure 2.6 shows two different forms of PRNGs, based on application.

- **Pseudorandom number generator:** An algorithm that is used to produce an open-ended sequence of bits is referred to as a PRNG. A common application for an open-ended sequence of bits is as input to a symmetric stream cipher, as discussed in the following section.

- **Pseudorandom function (PRF):** A PRF is used to produce a pseudorandom string of bits of some fixed length. Examples are symmetric encryption keys and nonces. Typically, the PRF takes as input a seed plus some context specific values, such as a user ID or an application ID. A number of examples of PRFs will be seen throughout this book.

Other than the number of bits produced, there is no difference between a PRNG and a PRF. The same algorithms can be used in both applications. Both require a seed and both must exhibit randomness and unpredictability. Furthermore, a PRNG application may also employ context-specific input.

Algorithm Design

Cryptographic PRNGs have been the subject of much research over the years, and a wide variety of algorithms have been developed. These fall roughly into two categories:

- **Purpose-built algorithms:** These are algorithms designed specifically and solely for the purpose of generating pseudorandom bit streams. Some of these algorithms are used for a variety of PRNG applications; several of these are described in the next section. Others are designed specifically for use in a stream cipher. The most important example of the latter is RC4, described in the next section.

- **Algorithms based on existing cryptographic algorithms:** Cryptographic algorithms have the effect of randomizing input. Indeed, this is a requirement of such algorithms. For example, if a symmetric block cipher produced ciphertext that had certain regular patterns in it, it would aid in the process of cryptanalysis. Thus, cryptographic algorithms can serve as the core of PRNGs. Three broad categories of cryptographic algorithms are commonly used to create PRNGs:

— **Symmetric block ciphers**

— **Asymmetric ciphers**

— **Hash functions and message authentication codes**

Any of these approaches can yield a cryptographically strong PRNG. A purpose-built algorithm may be provided by an operating system for general use. For applications that already use certain cryptographic algorithms for encryption or authentication, it makes sense to re-use the same code for the PRNG. Thus, all of these approaches are in common use.

2.4 STREAM CIPHERS AND RC4

A *block cipher* processes the input one block of elements at a time, producing an output block for each input block. A *stream cipher* processes the input elements continuously, producing output one element at a time as it goes along. Although block ciphers are far more common, there are certain applications in which a stream cipher is more appropriate. Examples are given subsequently in this book. In this section, we look at perhaps the most popular symmetric stream cipher, RC4. We begin with an overview of stream cipher structure, and then examine RC4.

Stream Cipher Structure

A typical stream cipher encrypts plaintext one byte at a time, although a stream cipher may be designed to operate on one bit at a time or on units larger than a byte at a time. Figure 2.7 is a representative diagram of stream cipher structure. In this structure, a key is input to a pseudorandom bit generator that produces a

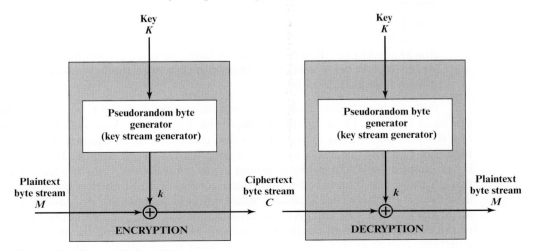

Figure 2.7 Stream Cipher Diagram

stream of 8-bit numbers that are apparently random. The pseudorandom stream is unpredictable without knowledge of the input key and has an apparently random character. The output of the generator, called a **keystream**, is combined one byte at a time with the plaintext stream using the bitwise exclusive-OR (XOR) operation. For example, if the next byte generated by the generator is 01101100 and the next plaintext byte is 11001100, then the resulting ciphertext byte is

$$
\begin{array}{rl}
11001100 & \text{plaintext} \\
\oplus\ \underline{01101100} & \text{key stream} \\
10100000 & \text{ciphertext}
\end{array}
$$

Decryption requires the use of the same pseudorandom sequence:

$$
\begin{array}{rl}
10100000 & \text{ciphertext} \\
\oplus\ \underline{01101100} & \text{key stream} \\
11001100 & \text{plaintext}
\end{array}
$$

[KUMA97] lists the following important design considerations for a stream cipher.

1. The encryption sequence should have a large period. A pseudorandom number generator uses a function that produces a deterministic stream of bits that eventually repeats. The longer the period of repeat, the more difficult it will be to do cryptanalysis.

2. The keystream should approximate the properties of a true random number stream as close as possible. For example, there should be an approximately equal number of 1s and 0s. If the keystream is treated as a stream of bytes, then all of the 256 possible byte values should appear approximately equally often. The more random-appearing the keystream is, the more randomized the ciphertext is, making cryptanalysis more difficult.

3. Note from Figure 2.7 that the output of the pseudorandom number generator is conditioned on the value of the input key. To guard against brute-force attacks, the key needs to be sufficiently long. The same considerations as apply for block ciphers are valid here. Thus, with current technology, a key length of at least 128 bits is desirable.

With a properly designed pseudorandom number generator, a stream cipher can be as secure as block cipher of comparable key length. A potential advantage of a stream cipher is that stream ciphers that do not use block ciphers as a building block are typically faster and use far less code than do block ciphers. The example in this chapter, RC4, can be implemented in just a few lines of code. In recent years, this advantage has diminished with the introduction of AES, which is quite efficient in software. Furthermore, hardware acceleration techniques are now available for AES. For example, the Intel AES Instruction Set has machine instructions for one round of encryption and decryption and key generation. Using the hardware instructions results in speedups of about an order of magnitude compared to pure software implementations [XU10].

One advantage of a block cipher is that you can reuse keys. In contrast, if two plaintexts are encrypted with the same key using a stream cipher, then cryptanalysis is often quite simple [DAWS96]. If the two ciphertext streams are XORed together, the result is the XOR of the original plaintexts. If the plaintexts are text strings, credit card numbers, or other byte streams with known properties, then cryptanalysis may be successful.

For applications that require encryption/decryption of a stream of data (such as over a data-communications channel or a browser/Web link), a stream cipher might be the better alternative. For applications that deal with blocks of data (such as file transfer, e-mail, and database), block ciphers may be more appropriate. However, either type of cipher can be used in virtually any application.

The RC4 Algorithm

RC4 is a stream cipher designed in 1987 by Ron Rivest for RSA Security. It is a variable key-size stream cipher with byte-oriented operations. The algorithm is based on the use of a random permutation. Analysis shows that the period of the cipher is overwhelmingly likely to be greater than 10100 [ROBS95a]. Eight to sixteen machine operations are required per output byte, and the cipher can be expected to run very quickly in software. RC4 is used in the Secure Sockets Layer/Transport Layer Security (SSL/TLS) standards that have been defined for communication between Web browsers and servers. It is also used in the Wired Equivalent Privacy (WEP) protocol and the newer WiFi Protected Access (WPA) protocol that are part of the IEEE 802.11 wireless LAN standard. RC4 was kept as a trade secret by RSA Security. In September 1994, the RC4 algorithm was anonymously posted on the Internet on the Cypherpunks anonymous remailers list.

The RC4 algorithm is remarkably simple and quite easy to explain. A variable-length key of from 1 to 256 bytes (8 to 2048 bits) is used to initialize a 256-byte state vector S, with elements S[0], S[1], . . . , S[255]. At all times, S contains a permutation of all 8-bit numbers from 0 through 255. For encryption and decryption, a byte k (see Figure 2.7) is generated from S by selecting one of the 255 entries in a systematic fashion. As each value of k is generated, the entries in S are once again permuted.

INITIALIZATION OF S To begin, the entries of S are set equal to the values from 0 through 255 in ascending order; that is, S[0] = 0, S[1] = 1, . . . , S[255] = 255. A temporary vector, T, is also created. If the length of the key K is 256 bytes, then K is transferred to T. Otherwise, for a key of length *keylen* bytes, the first *keylen* elements of T are copied from K, and then K is repeated as many times as necessary to fill out T. These preliminary operations can be summarized as:

```
/* Initialization */
for i = 0 to 255 do
S[i] = i;
T[i] = K[i mod keylen];
```

Next we use T to produce the initial permutation of S. This involves starting with S[0] and going through to S[255] and, for each S[i], swapping S[i] with another byte in S according to a scheme dictated by T[i]:

```
/* Initial Permutation of S */
j = 0;
for i = 0 to 255 do
  j = (j + S[i] + T[i]) mod 256;
  Swap (S[i], S[j]);
```

Because the only operation on S is a swap, the only effect is a permutation. S still contains all the numbers from 0 through 255.

STREAM GENERATION Once the S vector is initialized, the input key is no longer used. Stream generation involves cycling through all the elements of S[i] and, for each S[i], swapping S[i] with another byte in S according to a scheme dictated by the current configuration of S. After S[255] is reached, the process continues, starting over again at S[0]:

```
/* Stream Generation */
i, j = 0;
while (true)
  i = (i + 1) mod 256;
  j = (j + S[i]) mod 256;
  Swap (S[i], S[j]);
  t = (S[i] + S[j]) mod 256;
  k = S[t];
```

To encrypt, XOR the value *k* with the next byte of plaintext. To decrypt, XOR the value *k* with the next byte of ciphertext.

Figure 2.8 illustrates the RC4 logic.

STRENGTH OF RC4 A number of papers have been published analyzing methods of attacking RC4 (e.g., [KNUD98], [FLUH00], [MANT01]). None of these approaches is practical against RC4 with a reasonable key length, such as 128 bits. A more serious problem is reported in [FLUH01]. The authors demonstrate that the WEP protocol, intended to provide confidentiality on 802.11 wireless LAN networks, is vulnerable to a particular attack approach. In essence, the problem is not with RC4 itself but the way in which keys are generated for use as input to RC4. This particular problem does not appear to be relevant to other applications using RC4 and can be remedied in WEP by changing the way in which keys are generated. This problem points out the difficulty in designing a secure system that involves both cryptographic functions and protocols that make use of them.

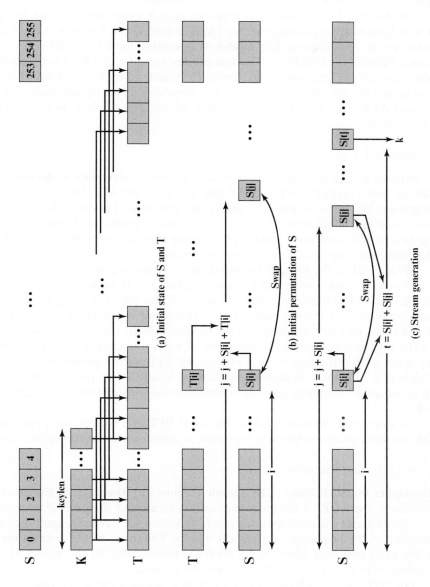

Figure 2.8   RC4

2.5   CIPHER BLOCK MODES OF OPERATION

A symmetric block cipher processes one block of data at a time. In the case of DES and 3DES, the block length is $b = 64$ bits; for AES, the block length is $b = 128$ bits. For longer amounts of plaintext, it is necessary to break the plaintext into b-bit blocks (padding the last block if necessary). To apply a block cipher in a variety of applications, five **modes of operation** have been defined by NIST (Special Publication 800-38A). The five modes are intended to cover virtually all of the possible applications of encryption for which a block cipher could be used. These modes are intended for use with any symmetric block cipher, including triple DES and AES. The most important modes are described briefly in the remainder of this section.

Electronic Codebook Mode

The simplest way to proceed is using what is known as **electronic codebook (ECB) mode**, in which plaintext is handled b bits at a time and each block of plaintext is encrypted using the same key. The term *codebook* is used because, for a given key, there is a unique ciphertext for every b-bit block of plaintext. Therefore, one can imagine a gigantic codebook in which there is an entry for every possible b-bit plaintext pattern showing its corresponding ciphertext.

With ECB, if the same b-bit block of plaintext appears more than once in the message, it always produces the same ciphertext. Because of this, for lengthy messages, the ECB mode may not be secure. If the message is highly structured, it may be possible for a cryptanalyst to exploit these regularities. For example, if it is known that the message always starts out with certain predefined fields, then the cryptanalyst may have a number of known plaintext–ciphertext pairs to work with. If the message has repetitive elements with a period of repetition a multiple of b bits, then these elements can be identified by the analyst. This may help in the analysis or may provide an opportunity for substituting or rearranging blocks.

To overcome the security deficiencies of ECB, we would like a technique in which the same plaintext block, if repeated, produces different ciphertext blocks.

Cipher Block Chaining Mode

In the **cipher block chaining (CBC) mode** (Figure 2.9), the input to the encryption algorithm is the XOR of the current plaintext block and the preceding ciphertext block; the same key is used for each block. In effect, we have chained together the processing of the sequence of plaintext blocks. The input to the encryption function for each plaintext block bears no fixed relationship to the plaintext block. Therefore, repeating patterns of b bits are not exposed.

For decryption, each cipher block is passed through the decryption algorithm. The result is XORed with the preceding ciphertext block to produce the plaintext block. To see that this works, we can write

$$C_j = \mathrm{E}(K, [C_{j-1} \oplus P_j])$$

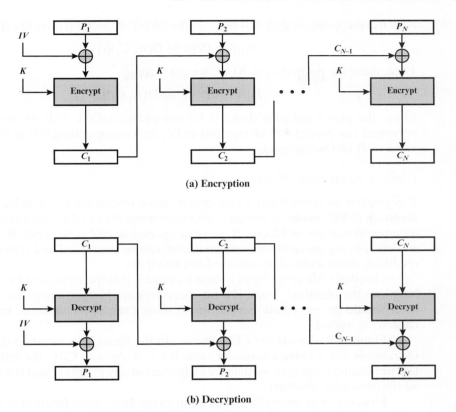

(a) Encryption

(b) Decryption

Figure 2.9   Cipher Block Chaining (CBC) Mode

where $E[K, X]$ is the encryption of plaintext X using key K, and $\oplus$ is the exclusive-OR operation. Then

$$D(K, C_j) = D(K, E(K, [C_{j-1} \oplus P_j]))$$
$$D(K, C_j) = C_{j-1} \oplus P_j$$
$$C_{j-1} \oplus D(K, C_j) = C_{j-1} \oplus C_{j-1} \oplus P_j = P_j$$

which verifies Figure 2.9b.

To produce the first block of ciphertext, an initialization vector (IV) is XORed with the first block of plaintext. On decryption, the IV is XORed with the output of the decryption algorithm to recover the first block of plaintext.

The IV must be known to both the sender and receiver. For maximum security, the IV should be protected as well as the key. This could be done by sending the IV using ECB encryption. One reason for protecting the IV is as follows: If an opponent is able to fool the receiver into using a different value for IV, then the opponent is able to invert selected bits in the first block of plaintext. To see this, consider the following:

$$C_1 = E(K, [IV \oplus P_1])$$
$$P_1 = IV \oplus D(K, C_1)$$

Now use the notation that $X[j]$ denotes the jth bit of the b-bit quantity X. Then

$$P_1[i] = IV[i] \oplus D(K, C_1)[i]$$

Then, using the properties of XOR, we can state

$$P_1[i]' = IV[i]' \oplus D(K, C_1)[i]$$

where the prime notation denotes bit complementation. This means that if an opponent can predictably change bits in IV, the corresponding bits of the received value of P_1 can be changed.

Cipher Feedback Mode

It is possible to convert any block cipher into a stream cipher by using the **cipher feedback (CFB) mode**. A stream cipher eliminates the need to pad a message to be an integral number of blocks. It also can operate in real time. Thus, if a character stream is being transmitted, each character can be encrypted and transmitted immediately using a character-oriented stream cipher.

One desirable property of a stream cipher is that the ciphertext be of the same length as the plaintext. Thus, if 8-bit characters are being transmitted, each character should be encrypted using 8 bits. If more than 8 bits are used, transmission capacity is wasted.

Figure 2.10 depicts the CFB scheme. In the figure, it is assumed that the unit of transmission is s bits; a common value is $s = 8$. As with CBC, the units of plaintext are chained together, so that the ciphertext of any plaintext unit is a function of all the preceding plaintext.

First, consider encryption. The input to the encryption function is a b-bit shift register that is initially set to some initialization vector (IV). The leftmost (most significant) s bits of the output of the encryption function are XORed with the first unit of plaintext P_1 to produce the first unit of ciphertext C_1, which is then transmitted. In addition, the contents of the shift register are shifted left by s bits, and C_1 is placed in the rightmost (least significant) s bits of the shift register. This process continues until all plaintext units have been encrypted.

For decryption, the same scheme is used, except that the received ciphertext unit is XORed with the output of the encryption function to produce the plaintext unit. Note that it is the *encryption* function that is used, not the decryption function. This is easily explained. Let $S_s(X)$ be defined as the most significant s bits of X. Then

$$C_1 = P_1 \oplus S_s[E(K, IV)]$$

Therefore,

$$P_1 = C_1 \oplus S_s[E(K, IV)]$$

The same reasoning holds for subsequent steps in the process.

Counter Mode

Although interest in the **counter mode (CTR)** has increased recently, with applications to ATM (asynchronous transfer mode) network security and IPSec (IP security), this mode was proposed early on (e.g., [DIFF79]).

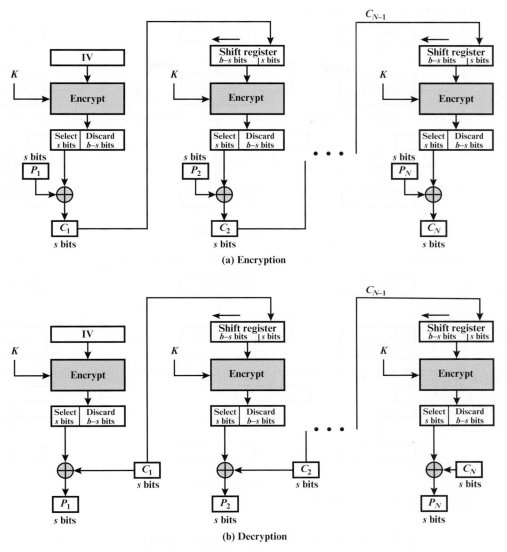

Figure 2.10   *s*-bit Cipher Feedback (CFB) Mode

Figure 2.11 depicts the CTR mode. A counter equal to the plaintext block size is used. The only requirement stated in NIST Special Publication 800-38A is that the counter value must be different for each plaintext block that is encrypted. Typically, the counter is initialized to some value and then incremented by 1 for each subsequent block (modulo 2^b, where b is the block size). For encryption, the counter is encrypted and then XORed with the plaintext block to produce the ciphertext block; there is no chaining. For decryption, the same sequence of counter values is used, with each encrypted counter XORed with a ciphertext block to recover the corresponding plaintext block.

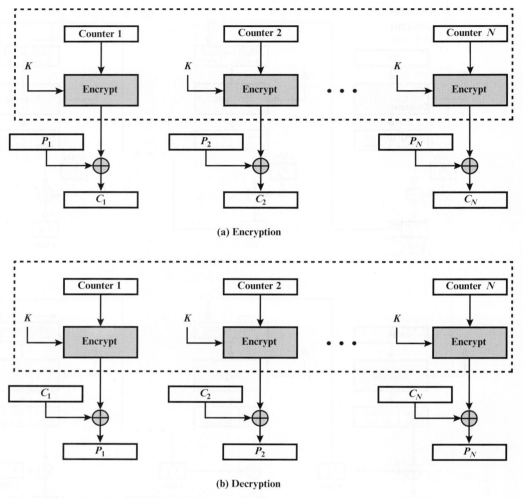

Figure 2.11 Counter (CTR) Mode

[LIPM00] lists the following advantages of CTR mode.

■ **Hardware efficiency:** Unlike the chaining modes, encryption (or decryption) in CTR mode can be done in parallel on multiple blocks of plaintext or ciphertext. For the chaining modes, the algorithm must complete the computation on one block before beginning on the next block. This limits the maximum throughput of the algorithm to the reciprocal of the time for one execution of block encryption or decryption. In CTR mode, the throughput is only limited by the amount of parallelism that is achieved.

■ **Software efficiency:** Similarly, because of the opportunities for parallel execution in CTR mode, processors that support parallel features (such as aggressive pipelining, multiple instruction dispatch per clock cycle, a large number of registers, and SIMD instructions) can be effectively utilized.

- **Preprocessing:** The execution of the underlying encryption algorithm does not depend on input of the plaintext or ciphertext. Therefore, if sufficient memory is available and security is maintained, preprocessing can be used to prepare the output of the encryption boxes that feed into the XOR functions in Figure 2.11. When the plaintext or ciphertext input is presented, then the only computation is a series of XORs. Such a strategy greatly enhances throughput.

- **Random access:** The ith block of plaintext or ciphertext can be processed in random-access fashion. With the chaining modes, block C_i cannot be computed until the $i - 1$ prior block are computed. There may be applications in which a ciphertext is stored, and it is desired to decrypt just one block; for such applications, the random access feature is attractive.

- **Provable security:** It can be shown that CTR is at least as secure as the other modes discussed in this section.

- **Simplicity:** Unlike ECB and CBC modes, CTR mode requires only the implementation of the encryption algorithm and not the decryption algorithm. This matters most when the decryption algorithm differs substantially from the encryption algorithm, as it does for AES. In addition, the decryption key scheduling need not be implemented.

2.6 KEY TERMS, REVIEW QUESTIONS, AND PROBLEMS

Key Terms

Advanced Encryption Standard (AES)	cryptography	keystream
block cipher	Data Encryption Standard (DES)	link encryption
brute-force attack	decryption	plaintext
cipher block chaining (CBC) mode	electronic codebook (ECB) mode	session key
cipher feedback (CFB) mode	encryption	stream cipher
ciphertext	end-to-end encryption	subkey
counter mode (CTR)	Feistel cipher	symmetric encryption
cryptanalysis	key distribution	triple DES (3DES)

Review Questions

2.1 What is symmetric encryption? What are the two requirements for secure use of symmetric encryption?

2.2 What is cryptanalysis? Summarize the various types of cryptanalytic attacks on encrypted messages.

2.3 List the parameters of a symmetric block cipher for greater security.

2.4 What is a block cipher? Name the important symmetric block ciphers.

2.5 Describe the data encryption algorithm for 64-bit length plaintext and 56-bit length key.

2.6 Describe the encryption and decryption of triple DES.

2.7 What are the advantages and disadvantages of triple DES?

2.8 List the important design criteria for a stream cipher.

Problems

2.1 This problem uses a real-world example of a symmetric cipher, from an old U.S. Special Forces manual (public domain). The document, filename *SpecialForces.pdf*, is available at box.com/NetSec6e.

    a. Using the two keys (memory words) *cryptographic* and *network security*, encrypt the following message:

> Be at the third pillar from the left outside the lyceum theatre tonight at seven. If you are distrustful bring two friends.

Make reasonable assumptions about how to treat redundant letters and excess letters in the memory words and how to treat spaces and punctuation. Indicate what your assumptions are. *Note:* The message is from the Sherlock Holmes novel *The Sign of Four*.

    b. Decrypt the ciphertext. Show your work.

    c. Comment on when it would be appropriate to use this technique and what its advantages are.

2.2 Consider a very simple symmetric block encryption algorithm in which 64-bit blocks of plaintext are encrypted using a 128-bit key. Encryption is defined as

$$C = (P \oplus K_1) \boxplus K_0$$

where C = ciphertext, K = secret key, K_0 = leftmost 64 bits of K, K_1 = rightmost 64 bits of K, $\oplus$ = bitwise exclusive OR, and $\boxplus$ is addition mod 2^{64}.

    a. Show the decryption equation. That is, show the equation for P as a function of C, K_0, and K_1.

    b. Suppose an adversary has access to two sets of plaintexts and their corresponding ciphertexts and wishes to determine K. We have the two equations:

$$C = (P \oplus K_1) \boxplus K_0; C' = (P' \oplus K_1) \boxplus K_0$$

First, derive an equation in one unknown (e.g., K_0). Is it possible to proceed further to solve for K_0?

2.3 Perhaps the simplest "serious" symmetric block encryption algorithm is the Tiny Encryption Algorithm (TEA). TEA operates on 64-bit blocks of plaintext using a 128-bit key. The plaintext is divided into two 32-bit blocks (L_0, R_0), and the key is divided into four 32-bit blocks (K_0, K_1, K_2, K_3). Encryption involves repeated application of a pair of rounds, defined as follows for rounds i and $i + 1$:

$$L_i = R_{i-1}$$
$$R_i = L_{i-1} \boxplus F(R_{i-1}, K_0, K_1, \delta_i)$$
$$L_{i+1} = R_i$$
$$R_{i+1} = L_i \boxplus F(R_i, K_2, K_3, \delta_{i+1})$$

where F is defined as

$$F(M, K_j, K_k, \delta_i) = ((M << 4) \boxplus K_j) \oplus ((M >> 5) \boxplus K_k) \oplus (M \boxplus \delta_i)$$

and where the logical shift of x by y bits is denoted by $x << y$, the logical right shift of x by y bits is denoted by $x >> y$, and δ_i is a sequence of predetermined constants.

    a. Comment on the significance and benefit of using the sequence of constants.

    b. Illustrate the operation of TEA using a block diagram or flow chart type of depiction.

    c. If only one pair of rounds is used, then the ciphertext consists of the 64-bit block (L_2, R_2). For this case, express the decryption algorithm in terms of equations.

    d. Repeat part (c) using an illustration similar to that used for part (b).

2.4 Is the DES decryption the inverse of DES encryption? Justify your answer.

2.5 Consider a Feistel cipher composed of 14 rounds with block length 128 bits and key length 128 bits. Suppose that, for a given k, the key scheduling algorithm determines values for the first seven round keys, $k_1, k_2, \ldots, k_8$, and then sets

$$k_8 = k_7, k_9 = k_6, k_{10} = k_5, \ldots, k_{14} = k_1$$

Suppose you have a ciphertext c. Explain how, with access to an encryption oracle, you can decrypt c and determine m using just a single oracle query. This shows that such a cipher is vulnerable to a chosen plaintext attack. (An encryption oracle can be thought of as a device that, when given a plaintext, returns the corresponding ciphertext. The internal details of the device are not known to you, and you cannot break open the device. You can only gain information from the oracle by making queries to it and observing its responses.)

2.6 For any block cipher, the fact that it is a nonlinear function is crucial to its security. To see this, suppose that we have a linear block cipher EL that encrypts 256-bit blocks of plaintext into 256-bit blocks of ciphertext. Let $EL(k, m)$ denote the encryption of a 256-bit message m under a key k (the actual bit length of k is irrelevant). Thus,

$$EL(k, [m_1 \oplus m_2]) = EL(k, m_1) \oplus EL(k, m_2) \text{ for all 256-bit patterns } m_1, m_2$$

Describe how, with 256 chosen ciphertexts, an adversary can decrypt any ciphertext without knowledge of the secret key k. (A "chosen ciphertext" means that an adversary has the ability to choose a ciphertext and then obtain its decryption. Here, you have 256 plaintext–ciphertext pairs to work with, and you have the ability to choose the value of the ciphertexts.)

2.7 Suppose you have a true random bit generator where each bit in the generated stream has the same probability of being a 0 or 1 as any other bit in the stream and that the bits are not correlated; that is, the bits are generated from identical independent distribution. However, the bit stream is biased. The probability of a 1 is $0.5 - \delta$ and the probability of a 0 is $0.5 + \delta$ where $0 < \delta < 0.5$. A simple deskewing algorithm is as follows: Examine the bit stream as a sequence of nonoverlapping pairs. Discard all 00 and 11 pairs. Replace each 01 pair with 0 and each 10 pair with 1.

    a. What is the probability of occurrence of each pair in the original sequence?

    b. What is the probability of occurrence of 0 and 1 in the modified sequence?

    c. What is the expected number of input bits to produce x output bits?

    d. Suppose that the algorithm uses overlapping successive bit pairs instead of non-overlapping successive bit pairs. That is, the first output bit is based on input bits 1 and 2, the second output bit is based on input bits 2 and 3, and so on. What can you say about the output bit stream?

2.8 Another approach to deskewing is to consider the bit stream as a sequence of non-overlapping groups of n bits each and output the parity of each group. That is, if a group contains an odd number of ones, the output is 1; otherwise the output is 0.

    a. Express this operation in terms of a basic Boolean function.

    b. Assume, as in the Problem 2.7, that the probability of a 1 is $0.5 - \delta$. If each group consists of 2 bits, what is the probability of an output of 1?

    c. If each group consists of 3 bits, what is the probability of an output of 1?

    d. Generalize the result to find the probability of an output of 1 for input groups of n bits.

2.9   Is it appropriate to reuse keys in RC4? Why or why not?

2.10   RC4 has a secret internal state which is a permutation of all the possible values of the vector **S** and the two indices i and j.
  a. Using a straightforward scheme to store the internal state, how many bits are used?
  b. Suppose we think of it from the point of view of how much information is represented by the state. In that case, we need to determine how many different states there are, then take the log to the base 2 to find out how many bits of information this represents. Using this approach, how many bits would be needed to represent the state?

2.11   Alice and Bob agree to communicate privately via e-mail using a scheme based on RC4, but they want to avoid using a new secret key for each transmission. Alice and Bob privately agree on a 128-bit key k. To encrypt a message m consisting of a string of bits, the following procedure is used.
  1. Choose a random 80-bit value v
  2. Generate the ciphertext $c = RC4(v \| k) \oplus m$
  3. Send the bit string $(v \| c)$
     a. Suppose Alice uses this procedure to send a message m to Bob. Describe how Bob can recover the message m from $(v \| c)$ using k.
     b. If an adversary observes several values $(v_1 \| c_1), (v_2 \| c_2), \ldots$ transmitted between Alice and Bob, how can he or she determine when the same key stream has been used to encrypt two messages?

2.12   With the ECB mode, if there is an error in a block of the transmitted ciphertext, only the corresponding plaintext block is affected. However, in the CBC mode, this error propagates. For example, an error in the transmitted C_1 (Figure 2.9) obviously corrupts P_1 and P_2.
  a. Are any blocks beyond P_2 affected?
  b. Suppose that there is a bit error in the source version of P_1. Through how many ciphertext blocks is this error propagated? What is the effect at the receiver?

2.13   Is it possible to perform decryption operations in parallel on multiple blocks of ciphertext in CBC mode? How about encryption?

2.14   Why should the IV in CBC be protected?

2.15   CBC-Pad is a block cipher mode of operation used in the RC5 block cipher, but it could be used in any block cipher. CBC-Pad handles plaintext of any length. The ciphertext is longer than the plaintext by at most the size of a single block. Padding is used to assure that the plaintext input is a multiple of the block length. It is assumed that the original plaintext is an integer number of bytes. This plaintext is padded at the end by from 1 to bb bytes, where bb equals the block size in bytes. The pad bytes are all the same and set to a byte that represents the number of bytes of padding. For example, if there are 8 bytes of padding, each byte has the bit pattern 00001000. Why not allow zero bytes of padding? That is, if the original plaintext is an integer multiple of the block size, why not refrain from padding?

2.16   Padding may not always be appropriate. For example, one might wish to store the encrypted data in the same memory buffer that originally contained the plaintext. In that case, the ciphertext must be the same length as the original plaintext. A mode for that purpose is the ciphertext stealing (CTS) mode. Figure 2.12a shows an implementation of this mode.
  a. Explain how it works.
  b. Describe how to decrypt C_{n-1} and C_n.

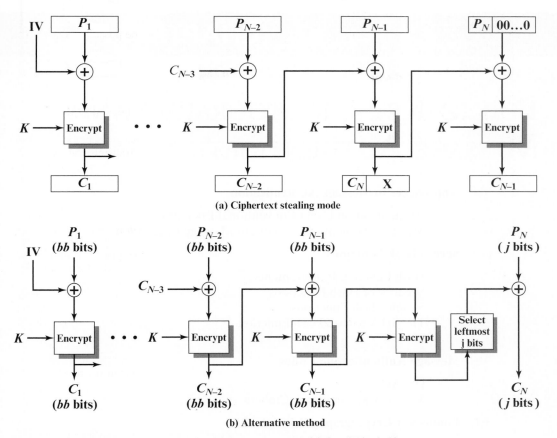

Figure 2.12   Block Cipher Modes for Plaintext not a Multiple of Block Size

2.17   Figure 2.12b shows an alternative to CTS for producing ciphertext of equal length to
the plaintext when the plaintext is not an integer multiple of the block size.
a.   Explain the algorithm.
b.   Explain why CTS is preferable to this approach illustrated in Figure 2.12b.

2.18   If a bit error occurs in the transmission of a ciphertext character in 8-bit CFB mode,
how far does the error propagate?

CHAPTER 3

PUBLIC-KEY CRYPTOGRAPHY AND MESSAGE AUTHENTICATION

LEARNING OBJECTIVES

After studying this chapter, you should be able to:

◆ Define the term *message authentication code.*

◆ List and explain the requirements for a message authentication code.

◆ Explain why a hash function used for message authentication needs to be secured.

◆ Understand the differences among preimage resistant, second preimage resistant, and collision resistant properties.

◆ Understand the operation of SHA-512.

◆ Present an overview of HMAC.

◆ Present an overview of the basic principles of public-key cryptosystems.

◆ Explain the two distinct uses of public-key cryptosystems.

◆ Present an overview of the RSA algorithm.

◆ Define Diffie–Hellman key exchange.

◆ Understand the man-in-the-middle attack.

In addition to message confidentiality, message authentication is an important network security function. This chapter examines three aspects of message authentication. First, we look at the use of message authentication codes and hash functions to provide message authentication. Then we look at public-key encryption principles and two specific public-key algorithms. These algorithms are useful in the exchange of conventional encryption keys. Then we look at the use of public-key encryption to produce digital signatures, which provides an enhanced form of message authentication.

3.1 APPROACHES TO MESSAGE AUTHENTICATION

Encryption protects against passive attack (eavesdropping). A different requirement is to protect against active attack (falsification of data and transactions). Protection against such attacks is known as message authentication.

A message, file, document, or other collection of data is said to be authentic when it is genuine and comes from its alleged source. Message authentication is a procedure that allows communicating parties to verify that received messages are authentic.[1] The two important aspects are to verify that the contents of the message have not been altered and that the source is authentic. We may also wish to verify a message's timeliness (it has not been artificially delayed and replayed) and sequence relative to other messages flowing between two parties. All of these concerns come under the category of data integrity as described in Chapter 1.

---

[1]For simplicity, for the remainder of this chapter, we refer to *message authentication.* By this we mean both authentication of transmitted messages and of stored data (*data authentication*).

Authentication Using Conventional Encryption

It would seem possible to perform authentication simply by the use of symmetric encryption. If we assume that only the sender and receiver share a key (which is as it should be), then only the genuine sender would be able to encrypt a message successfully for the other participant, provided the receiver can recognize a valid message. Furthermore, if the message includes an error-detection code and a sequence number, the receiver is assured that no alterations have been made and that sequencing is proper. If the message also includes a timestamp, the receiver is assured that the message has not been delayed beyond that normally expected for network transit.

In fact, symmetric encryption alone is not a suitable tool for data authentication. To give one simple example, in the ECB mode of encryption, if an attacker reorders the blocks of ciphertext, then each block will still decrypt successfully. However, the reordering may alter the meaning of the overall data sequence. Although sequence numbers may be used at some level (e.g., each IP packet), it is typically not the case that a separate sequence number will be associated with each b-bit block of plaintext. Thus, block reordering is a threat.

Message Authentication without Message Encryption

In this section, we examine several approaches to message authentication that do not rely on encryption. In all of these approaches, an authentication tag is generated and appended to each message for transmission. The message itself is not encrypted and can be read at the destination independent of the authentication function at the destination.

Because the approaches discussed in this section do not encrypt the message, message confidentiality is not provided. As was mentioned, message encryption by itself does not provide a secure form of authentication. However, it is possible to combine authentication and confidentiality in a single algorithm by encrypting a message plus its authentication tag. Typically, however, message authentication is provided as a separate function from message encryption. [DAVI89] suggests three situations in which message authentication without confidentiality is preferable:

1. There are a number of applications in which the same message is broadcast to a number of destinations. Two examples are notification to users that the network is now unavailable and an alarm signal in a control center. It is cheaper and more reliable to have only one destination responsible for monitoring authenticity. Thus, the message must be broadcast in plaintext with an associated message authentication tag. The responsible system performs authentication. If a violation occurs, the other destination systems are alerted by a general alarm.

2. Another possible scenario is an exchange in which one side has a heavy load and cannot afford the time to decrypt all incoming messages. Authentication is carried out on a selective basis with messages being chosen at random for checking.

3. Authentication of a computer program in plaintext is an attractive service. The computer program can be executed without having to decrypt it every time, which would be wasteful of processor resources. However, if a message authentication tag were attached to the program, it could be checked whenever assurance is required of the integrity of the program.

Thus, there is a place for both authentication and encryption in meeting security requirements.

MESSAGE AUTHENTICATION CODE One authentication technique involves the use of a secret key to generate a small block of data, known as a **message authentication code (MAC)**, that is appended to the message. This technique assumes that two communicating parties, say A and B, share a common secret key K_{AB}. When A has a message to send to B, it calculates the message authentication code as a function of the message and the key: $MAC_M = F(K_{AB}, M)$. The message plus code are transmitted to the intended recipient. The recipient performs the same calculation on the received message, using the same secret key, to generate a new message authentication code. The received code is compared to the calculated code (Figure 3.1). If we assume that only the receiver and the sender know the identity of the secret key, and if the received code matches the calculated code, then the following statements apply:

1. The receiver is assured that the message has not been altered. If an attacker alters the message but does not alter the code, then the receiver's calculation of the code will differ from the received code. Because the attacker is assumed not to know the secret key, the attacker cannot alter the code to correspond to the alterations in the message.

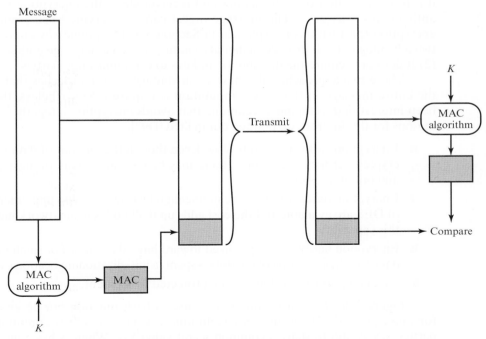

Figure 3.1   Message Authentication Using a Message Authentication Code

2. The receiver is assured that the message is from the alleged sender. Because no one else knows the secret key, no one else could prepare a message with a proper code.

3. If the message includes a sequence number (such as is used with HDLC and TCP), then the receiver can be assured of the proper sequence, because an attacker cannot successfully alter the sequence number.

A number of algorithms could be used to generate the code. The NIST specification, FIPS PUB 113, recommends the use of DES. DES is used to generate an encrypted version of the message, and the last number of bits of ciphertext are used as the code. A 16- or 32-bit code is typical.

The process just described is similar to encryption. One difference is that the authentication algorithm need not be reversible, as it must for decryption. Because of the mathematical properties of the authentication function, it is less vulnerable to being broken than encryption.

ONE-WAY HASH FUNCTION An alternative to the message authentication code is the **one-way hash function**. As with the message authentication code, a hash function accepts a variable-size message M as input and produces a fixed-size message digest $H(M)$ as output. Unlike the MAC, a hash function does not take a secret key as input. To authenticate a message, the message digest is sent with the message in such a way that the message digest is authentic.

Figure 3.2 illustrates three ways in which the message can be authenticated. The message digest can be encrypted using conventional encryption (part a); if it is assumed that only the sender and receiver share the encryption key, then authenticity is assured. The message digest can be encrypted using public-key encryption (part b); this is explained in Section 3.5. The public-key approach has two advantages: (1) It provides a digital signature as well as message authentication. (2) It does not require the distribution of keys to communicating parties.

These two approaches also have an advantage over approaches that encrypt the entire message in that less computation is required. Nevertheless, there has been interest in developing a technique that avoids encryption altogether. Several reasons for this interest are pointed out in [TSUD92]:

- Encryption software is quite slow. Even though the amount of data to be encrypted per message is small, there may be a steady stream of messages into and out of a system.

- Encryption hardware costs are nonnegligible. Low-cost chip implementations of DES are available, but the cost adds up if all nodes in a network must have this capability.

- Encryption hardware is optimized toward large data sizes. For small blocks of data, a high proportion of the time is spent in initialization/invocation overhead.

- An encryption algorithm may be protected by a patent.

Figure 3.2c shows a technique that uses a hash function but no encryption for message authentication. This technique assumes that two communicating parties, say A and B, share a common secret value S_{AB}. When A has a message to send to B, it calculates the hash function over the concatenation of the secret value

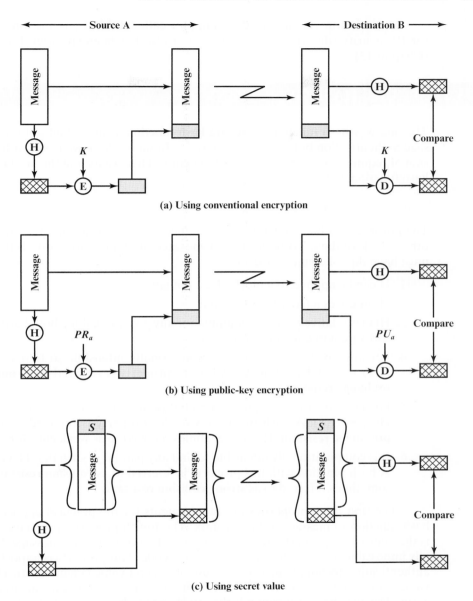

(a) Using conventional encryption

(b) Using public-key encryption

(c) Using secret value

Figure 3.2 Message Authentication Using a One-Way Hash Function

and the message: $MD_M = H(S_{AB} \| M)$.[2] It then sends $[M \| MD_M]$ to B. Because B possesses S_{AB}, it can recompute $H(S_{AB} \| M)$ and verify MD_M. Because the secret value itself is not sent, it is not possible for an attacker to modify an intercepted message. As long as the secret value remains secret, it is also not possible for an attacker to generate a false message.

---

[2] $\|$ denotes concatenation

A variation on the third technique, called HMAC, is the one adopted for IP security (described in Chapter 9); it also has been specified for SNMPv3 (Chapter 13).

3.2 SECURE HASH FUNCTIONS

The one-way hash function, or **secure hash function**, is important not only in message authentication but in digital signatures. In this section, we begin with a discussion of requirements for a secure hash function. Then we look at the most important hash function, SHA.

Hash Function Requirements

The purpose of a hash function is to produce a "fingerprint" of a file, message, or other block of data. To be useful for message authentication, a hash function H must have the following properties:

1. H can be applied to a block of data of any size.
2. H produces a fixed-length output.
3. $H(x)$ is relatively easy to compute for any given x, making both hardware and software implementations practical.
4. For any given code h, it is computationally infeasible to find x such that $H(x) = h$. A hash function with this property is referred to as **one-way** or **preimage resistant**.[3]
5. For any given block x, it is computationally infeasible to find $y \neq x$ with $H(y) = H(x)$. A hash function with this property is referred to as **second pre-image resistant**. This is sometimes referred to as **weak collision resistant**.
6. It is computationally infeasible to find any pair (x, y) such that $H(x) = H(y)$. A hash function with this property is referred to as **collision resistant**. This is sometimes referred to as **strong collision resistant**.

The first three properties are requirements for the practical application of a hash function to message authentication. The fourth property, preimage resistant, is the "one-way" property: It is easy to generate a code given a message, but virtually impossible to generate a message given a code. This property is important if the authentication technique involves the use of a secret value (Figure 3.2c). The secret value itself is not sent; however, if the hash function is not one way, an attacker can easily discover the secret value: If the attacker can observe or intercept a transmission, the attacker obtains the message M and the hash code $C = H(S_{AB} \| M)$. The attacker then inverts the hash function to obtain $S_{AB} \| M = H^{-1}(C)$. Because the attacker now has both M and $S_{AB} \| M$, it is a trivial matter to recover S_{AB}.

The second preimage resistant property guarantees that it is impossible to find an alternative message with the same hash value as a given message. This prevents

---

[3]For $f(x) = y$, x is said to be a preimage of y. Unless f is one-to-one, there may be multiple preimage values for a given y.

forgery when an encrypted hash code is used (Figures 3.2a and b). If this property were not true, an attacker would be capable of the following sequence: First, observe or intercept a message plus its encrypted hash code; second, generate an unencrypted hash code from the message; third, generate an alternate message with the same hash code.

A hash function that satisfies the first five properties in the preceding list is referred to as a weak hash function. If the sixth property is also satisfied, then it is referred to as a strong hash function. The sixth property, collision resistant, protects against a sophisticated class of attack known as the birthday attack. Details of this attack are beyond the scope of this book. The attack reduces the strength of an m-bit hash function from 2^m to $2^{m/2}$. See [STAL13] for details.

In addition to providing authentication, a message digest also provides data integrity. It performs the same function as a frame check sequence: If any bits in the message are accidentally altered in transit, the message digest will be in error.

Security of Hash Functions

As with symmetric encryption, there are two approaches to attacking a secure hash function: cryptanalysis and brute-force attack. As with symmetric encryption algorithms, cryptanalysis of a hash function involves exploiting logical weaknesses in the algorithm.

The strength of a hash function against brute-force attacks depends solely on the length of the hash code produced by the algorithm. For a hash code of length n, the level of effort required is proportional to the following:

Preimage resistant	2^n
Second preimage resistant	2^n
Collision resistant	$2^{n/2}$

If collision resistance is required (and this is desirable for a general-purpose secure hash code), then the value $2^{n/2}$ determines the strength of the hash code against brute-force attacks. Van Oorschot and Wiener [VANO94] presented a design for a $10 million collision search machine for MD5, which has a 128-bit hash length, that could find a collision in 24 days. Thus, a 128-bit code may be viewed as inadequate. The next step up, if a hash code is treated as a sequence of 32 bits, is a 160-bit hash length. With a hash length of 160 bits, the same search machine would require over four thousand years to find a collision. With today's technology, the time would be much shorter, so that 160 bits now appears suspect.

Simple Hash Functions

All hash functions operate using the following general principles. The input (message, file, etc.) is viewed as a sequence of n-bit blocks. The input is processed one block at a time in an iterative fashion to produce an n-bit hash function.

One of the simplest hash functions is the bit-by-bit exclusive-OR (XOR) of every block. This can be expressed as

$$C_i = b_{i1} \oplus b_{i2} \oplus \cdots \oplus b_{im}$$

where

C_i = ith bit of the hash code, $1 \leq i \leq n$

m = number of n-bit blocks in the input

b_{ij} = ith bit in jth block

$\oplus$ = XOR operation

Figure 3.3 illustrates this operation; it produces a simple parity for each bit position and is known as a longitudinal redundancy check. It is reasonably effective for random data as a data integrity check. Each n-bit hash value is equally likely. Thus, the probability that a data error will result in an unchanged hash value is 2^{-n}. With more predictably formatted data, the function is less effective. For example, in most normal text files, the high-order bit of each octet is always zero. So if a 128-bit hash value is used, instead of an effectiveness of 2^{-128}, the hash function on this type of data has an effectiveness of 2^{-112}.

A simple way to improve matters is to perform a 1-bit circular shift, or rotation, on the hash value after each block is processed. The procedure can be summarized as

1. Initially set the n-bit hash value to zero.
2. Process each successive n-bit block of data:
    a. Rotate the current hash value to the left by one bit.
    b. XOR the block into the hash value.

This has the effect of "randomizing" the input more completely and overcoming any regularities that appear in the input.

Although the second procedure provides a good measure of data integrity, it is virtually useless for data security when an encrypted hash code is used with a plaintext message, as in Figures 3.2a and b. Given a message, it is an easy matter to produce a new message that yields that hash code: Simply prepare the desired alternate message and then append an n-bit block that forces the combined new message plus block to yield the desired hash code.

Although a simple XOR or rotated XOR (RXOR) is insufficient if only the hash code is encrypted, you may still feel that such a simple function could be useful when the message as well as the hash code are encrypted. But one must be careful. A technique originally proposed by the National Bureau of Standards used

	bit 1	bit 2	• • •	bit n
Block 1	b_{11}	b_{21}		b_{n1}
Block 2	b_{12}	b_{22}		b_{n2}
	• • •	• • •	• • •	• • •
Block m	b_{1m}	b_{2m}		b_{nm}
Hash code	C_1	C_2		C_n

Figure 3.3   Simple Hash Function Using Bitwise XOR

the simple XOR applied to 64-bit blocks of the message and then an encryption of the entire message using the cipher block chaining (CBC) mode. We can define the scheme as follows: Given a message consisting of a sequence of 64-bit blocks $X_1, X_2, \ldots, X_N$, define the hash code C as the block-by-block XOR or all blocks and append the hash code as the final block:

$$C = X_{N+1} = X_1 \oplus X_2 \oplus \cdots \oplus X_N$$

Next, encrypt the entire message plus hash code using CBC mode to produce the encrypted message $Y_1, Y_2, \ldots, Y_{N+1}$. [JUEN85] points out several ways in which the ciphertext of this message can be manipulated in such a way that it is not detectable by the hash code. For example, by the definition of CBC (Figure 2.9), we have

$$X_1 = IV \oplus \mathrm{D}(K, Y_1)$$
$$X_i = Y_{i-1} \oplus \mathrm{D}(K, Y_i)$$
$$X_{N+1} = Y_N \oplus \mathrm{D}(K, Y_{N+1})$$

But X_{N+1} is the hash code:

$$X_{N+1} = X_1 \oplus X_2 \oplus \cdots \oplus X_N$$
$$= [IV \oplus \mathrm{D}(K, Y_1)] \oplus [Y_1 \oplus \mathrm{D}(K, Y_2)] \oplus \cdots \oplus [Y_{N-1} \oplus \mathrm{D}(K, Y_N)]$$

Because the terms in the preceding equation can be XORed in any order, it follows that the hash code would not change if the ciphertext blocks were permuted.

The SHA Secure Hash Function

In recent years, the most widely used hash function has been the Secure Hash Algorithm (SHA). Indeed, because virtually every other widely used hash function had been found to have substantial cryptanalytic weaknesses, SHA was more or less the last remaining standardized hash algorithm by 2005. SHA was developed by the National Institute of Standards and Technology (NIST) and published as a federal information processing standard (FIPS 180) in 1993. When weaknesses were discovered in SHA (now known as SHA-0), a revised version was issued as FIPS 180-1 in 1995 and is referred to as **SHA-1**. The actual standards document is entitled "Secure Hash Standard." SHA is based on the hash function MD4, and its design closely models MD4.

SHA-1 produces a hash value of 160 bits. In 2002, NIST produced a revised version of the standard, FIPS 180-2, that defined three new versions of SHA with hash value lengths of 256, 384, and 512 bits known as SHA-256, SHA-384, and SHA-512, respectively. Collectively, these hash algorithms are known as **SHA-2**. These new versions have the same underlying structure and use the same types of modular arithmetic and logical binary operations as SHA-1. A revised document was issued as FIP PUB 180-3 in 2008, which added a 224-bit version (Table 3.1). SHA-1 and SHA-2 are also specified in RFC 6234, which essentially duplicates the material in FIPS 180-3 but adds a C code implementation.

In 2005, NIST announced the intention to phase out approval of SHA-1 and move to a reliance on SHA-2 by 2010. Shortly thereafter, a research team described an attack in which two separate messages could be found that deliver the same SHA-1 hash using 2^{69} operations, far fewer than the 2^{80} operations previously

Table 3.1 Comparison of SHA Parameters

	SHA-1	SHA-224	SHA-256	SHA-384	SHA-512
Message Digest Size	160	224	256	384	512
Message Size	$<2^{64}$	$<2^{64}$	$<2^{64}$	$<2^{128}$	$<2^{128}$
Block Size	512	512	512	1024	1024
Word Size	32	32	32	64	64
Number of Steps	80	64	64	80	80

Note: All sizes are measured in bits.

thought needed to find a collision with an SHA-1 hash [WANG05]. This result should hasten the transition to SHA-2.

In this section, we provide a description of SHA-512. The other versions are quite similar.

The algorithm takes as input a message with a maximum length of less than 2^{128} bits and produces as output a 512-bit message digest. The input is processed in 1024-bit blocks. Figure 3.4 depicts the overall processing of a message to produce a digest. The processing consists of the following steps.

Step 1 **Append padding bits:** The message is padded so that its length is congruent to 896 modulo 1024 [length $\equiv$ 896 (mod 1024)]. Padding is always added, even if the message is already of the desired length. Thus, the number of padding bits is in the range of 1 to 1024. The padding consists of a single 1 bit followed by the necessary number of 0 bits.

Step 2 **Append length:** A block of 128 bits is appended to the message. This block is treated as an unsigned 128-bit integer (most significant byte first) and contains the length of the original message (before the padding).

The outcome of the first two steps yields a message that is an integer multiple of 1024 bits in length. In Figure 3.4, the expanded message is represented as the sequence of 1024-bit blocks $M_1, M_2, \ldots, M_N$, so that the total length of the expanded message is $N \times 1024$ bits.

Step 3 **Initialize hash buffer:** A 512-bit buffer is used to hold intermediate and final results of the hash function. The buffer can be represented as eight 64-bit registers (a, b, c, d, e, f, g, h). These registers are initialized to the following 64-bit integers (hexadecimal values):

a = 6A09E667F3BCC908 e = 510E527FADE682D1

b = BB67AE8584CAA73B f = 9B05688C2B3E6C1F

c = 3C6EF372FE94F82B g = 1F83D9ABFB41BD6B

d = A54FF53A5F1D36F1 h = 5BE0CD19137E2179

These values are stored in big-endian format, which is the most significant byte of a word in the low-address (leftmost) byte position. These words were obtained by taking the first sixty-four bits of the fractional parts of the square roots of the first eight prime numbers.

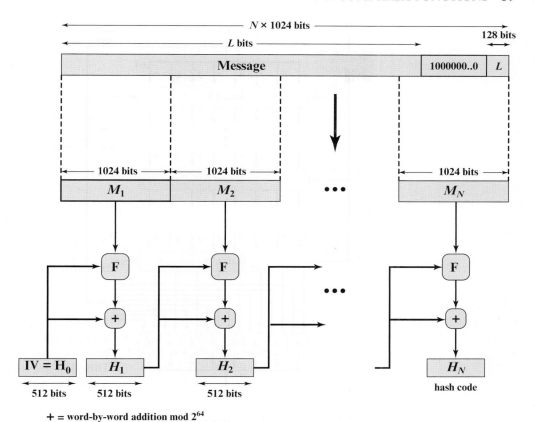

Figure 3.4   Message Digest Generation Using SHA-512

Step 4   **Process message in 1024-bit (128-word) blocks:** The heart of the algorithm is a module that consists of 80 rounds; this module is labeled F in Figure 3.4. The logic is illustrated in Figure 3.5.

Each round takes as input the 512-bit buffer value **abcdefgh** and updates the contents of the buffer. At input to the first round, the buffer has the value of the intermediate hash value, H_{i-1}. Each round t makes use of a 64-bit value W_t derived from the current 1024-bit block being processed (M_i). Each round also makes use of an additive constant K_t, where $0 \leq t \leq 79$ indicates one of the 80 rounds. These words represent the first 64 bits of the fractional parts of the cube roots of the first 80 prime numbers. The constants provide a "randomized" set of 64-bit patterns, which should eliminate any regularities in the input data.

The output of the 80th round is added to the input to the first round (H_{i-1}) to produce H_i. The addition is done independently for each of the eight words in the buffer with each of the corresponding words in H_{i-1}, using addition modulo 2^{64}.

Step 5   **Output:** After all N 1024-bit blocks have been processed, the output from the Nth stage is the 512-bit message digest.

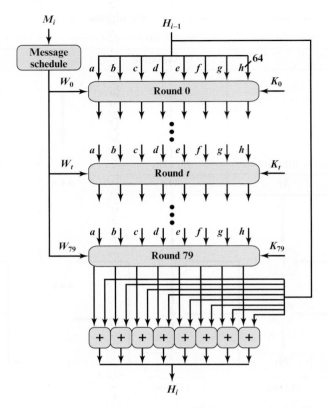

Figure 3.5 SHA-512 Processing of a Single 1024-Bit Block

The SHA-512 algorithm has the property that every bit of the hash code is a function of every bit of the input. The complex repetition of the basic function F produces results that are well mixed; that is, it is unlikely that two messages chosen at random, even if they exhibit similar regularities, will have the same hash code. Unless there is some hidden weakness in SHA-512, which has not so far been published, the difficulty of coming up with two messages having the same message digest is on the order of 2^{256} operations, while the difficulty of finding a message with a given digest is on the order of 2^{512} operations.

SHA-3

SHA-2, particularly the 512-bit version, would appear to provide unassailable security. However, SHA-2 shares the same structure and mathematical operations as its predecessors, and this is a cause for concern. Because it would take years to find a suitable replacement for SHA-2, should it become vulnerable, NIST announced in 2007 a competition to produce the next-generation NIST hash function, which is to be called SHA-3. Following are the basic requirements that must be satisfied by any candidate for SHA-3:

1. It must be possible to replace SHA-2 with SHA-3 in any application by a simple drop-in substitution. Therefore, SHA-3 must support hash value lengths of 224, 256, 384, and 512 bits.

2. SHA-3 must preserve the online nature of SHA-2. That is, the algorithm must process comparatively small blocks (512 or 1024 bits) at a time instead of requiring that the entire message be buffered in memory before processing it.

In 2012, NIST selected a winning submission and formally published SHA-3. A detailed presentation of SHA-3 is provided in Chapter 15.

3.3 MESSAGE AUTHENTICATION CODES

HMAC

In recent years, there has been increased interest in developing a MAC derived from a cryptographic hash code, such as SHA-1. The motivations for this interest are as follows:

- Cryptographic hash functions generally execute faster in software than conventional encryption algorithms such as DES.
- Library code for cryptographic hash functions is widely available.

A hash function such as SHA-1 was not designed for use as a MAC and cannot be used directly for that purpose because it does not rely on a secret key. There have been a number of proposals for the incorporation of a secret key into an existing hash algorithm. The approach that has received the most support is HMAC [BELL96a, BELL96b]. HMAC has been issued as RFC 2104, has been chosen as the mandatory-to-implement MAC for IP Security, and is used in other Internet protocols, such as Transport Layer Security (TLS) and Secure Electronic Transaction (SET).

HMAC DESIGN OBJECTIVES RFC 2104 lists the following design objectives for HMAC.

- To use, without modifications, available hash functions. In particular, hash functions that perform well in software, and for which code is freely and widely available
- To allow for easy replaceability of the embedded hash function in case faster or more secure hash functions are found or required
- To preserve the original performance of the hash function without incurring a significant degradation
- To use and handle keys in a simple way
- To have a well-understood cryptographic analysis of the strength of the authentication mechanism based on reasonable assumptions on the embedded hash function

The first two objectives are important to the acceptability of HMAC. HMAC treats the hash function as a "black box." This has two benefits. First, an existing implementation of a hash function can be used as a module in implementing HMAC.

In this way, the bulk of the HMAC code is prepackaged and ready to use without modification. Second, if it is ever desired to replace a given hash function in an HMAC implementation, all that is required is to remove the existing hash function module and drop in the new module. This could be done if a faster hash function were desired. More important, if the security of the embedded hash function were compromised, the security of HMAC could be retained simply by replacing the embedded hash function with a more secure one.

The last design objective in the preceding list is, in fact, the main advantage of HMAC over other proposed hash-based schemes. HMAC can be proven secure provided that the embedded hash function has some reasonable cryptographic strengths. We return to this point later in this section, but first we examine the structure of HMAC.

HMAC Algorithm Figure 3.6 illustrates the overall operation of HMAC. The following terms are defined:

H = embedded hash function (e.g., SHA-1)

M = message input to HMAC (including the padding specified in the embedded hash function)

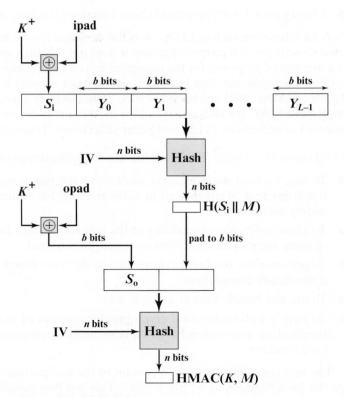

Figure 3.6   HMAC Structure

$Y_i = i$th block of $M, 0 \le i \le (L - 1)$

$L =$ number of blocks in M

$b =$ number of bits in a block

$n =$ length of hash code produced by embedded hash function

$K =$ secret key; if key length is greater than b, the key is input to the hash function to produce an n-bit key; recommended length is $> n$

$K^+ = K$ padded with zeros on the left so that the result is b bits in length

ipad $= 00110110$ (36 in hexadecimal) repeated $b/8$ times

opad $= 01011100$ (5C in hexadecimal) repeated $b/8$ times

Then HMAC can be expressed as

$$\text{HMAC}(K, M) = \text{H}[(K^+ \oplus \text{opad}) \| \text{H}[(K^+ \oplus \text{ipad}) \| M]]$$

In words, HMAC is defined as follows:

1. Append zeros to the left end of K to create a b-bit string K^+ (e.g., if K is of length 160 bits and $b = 512$, then K will be appended with 44 zero bytes).
2. XOR (bitwise exclusive-OR) K^+ with ipad to produce the b-bit block S_i.
3. Append M to S_i.
4. Apply H to the stream generated in step 3.
5. XOR K^+ with opad to produce the b-bit block S_o.
6. Append the hash result from step 4 to S_o.
7. Apply H to the stream generated in step 6 and output the result.

Note that the XOR with ipad results in flipping one-half of the bits of K. Similarly, the XOR with opad results in flipping one-half of the bits of K, but a different set of bits. In effect, by passing S_i and S_o through the hash algorithm, we have pseudorandomly generated two keys from K.

HMAC should execute in approximately the same time as the embedded hash function for long messages. HMAC adds three executions of the basic hash function (for S_i, S_o, and the block produced from the inner hash).

MACs Based on Block Ciphers

In this section, we look at several MACs based on the use of a block cipher.

CIPHER-BASED MESSAGE AUTHENTICATION CODE (CMAC) The Cipher-based Message Authentication Code mode of operation is for use with AES and triple DES. It is specified in SP 800-38B.

First, let us consider the operation of CMAC when the message is an integer multiple n of the cipher block length b. For AES, $b = 128$, and for triple DES, $b = 64$. The message is divided into n blocks ($M_1, M_2, \ldots, M_n$). The algorithm makes use of a k-bit encryption key K and an n-bit key, K_1. For AES, the key size k is 128, 192, or 256 bits; for triple DES, the key size is 112 or 168 bits. CMAC is calculated as follows (Figure 3.7).

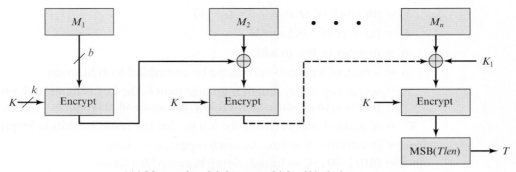

(a) Message length is integer multiple of block size

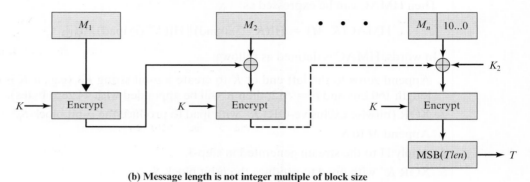

(b) Message length is not integer multiple of block size

Figure 3.7   Cipher-Based Message Authentication Code (CMAC)

$$C_1 = \mathrm{E}(K, M_1)$$
$$C_2 = \mathrm{E}(K, [M_2 \oplus C_1])$$
$$C_3 = \mathrm{E}(K, [M_3 \oplus C_2])$$
$$\cdot$$
$$\cdot$$
$$\cdot$$
$$C_n = \mathrm{E}(K, [M_N \oplus C_{n-1} \oplus K_1])$$
$$T = \mathrm{MSB}_{Tlen}(C_n)$$

where

T = message authentication code, also referred to as the tag

$Tlen$ = bit length of T

$\mathrm{MSB}_s(X)$ = the s leftmost bits of the bit string X

If the message is not an integer multiple of the cipher block length, then the final block is padded to the right (least significant bits) with a 1 and as many

0s as necessary so that the final block is also of length b. The CMAC operation then proceeds as before, except that a different n-bit key K_2 is used instead of K_1.

To generate the two n-bit keys, the block cipher is applied to the block that consists entirely of 0 bits. The first subkey is derived from the resulting ciphertext by a left shift of one bit and, conditionally, by XORing a constant that depends on the block size. The second subkey is derived in the same manner from the first subkey.

COUNTER WITH CIPHER BLOCK CHAINING-MESSAGE AUTHENTICATION CODE The Counter with Cipher Block Chaining-Message Authentication Code (CCM) mode of operation, defined in SP 800-38C, is referred to as an **authenticated encryption** mode. "Authenticated encryption" is a term used to describe encryption systems that simultaneously protect confidentiality and authenticity (integrity) of communications. Many applications and protocols require both forms of security, but until recently the two services have been designed separately.

The key algorithmic ingredients of CCM are the AES encryption algorithm (Section 2.2), the CTR mode of operation (Section 2.5), and the CMAC authentication algorithm. A single key K is used for both encryption and MAC algorithms. The input to the CCM encryption process consists of three elements.

1. Data that will be both authenticated and encrypted. This is the plaintext message P of data block.
2. Associated data A that will be authenticated but not encrypted. An example is a protocol header that must be transmitted in the clear for proper protocol operation but which needs to be authenticated.
3. A nonce N that is assigned to the payload and the associated data. This is a unique value that is different for every instance during the lifetime of a protocol association and is intended to prevent replay attacks and certain other types of attacks.

Figure 3.8 illustrates the operation of CCM. For authentication, the input includes the nonce, the associated data, and the plaintext. This input is formatted as a sequence of blocks B_0 through B_r. The first block contains the nonce plus some formatting bits that indicate the lengths of the N, A, and P elements. This is followed by zero or more blocks that contain A, followed by zero or more blocks that contain P. The resulting sequence of blocks serves as input to the CMAC algorithm, which produces a MAC value with length $Tlen$, which is less than or equal to the block length (Figure 3.8a).

For encryption, a sequence of counters is generated that must be independent of the nonce. The authentication tag is encrypted in CTR mode using the single counter Ctr_0. The $Tlen$ most significant bits of the output are XORed with the tag to produce an encrypted tag. The remaining counters are used for the CTR mode encryption of the plaintext (Figure 2.11). The encrypted plaintext is concatenated with the encrypted tag to form the ciphertext output (Figure 3.8b).

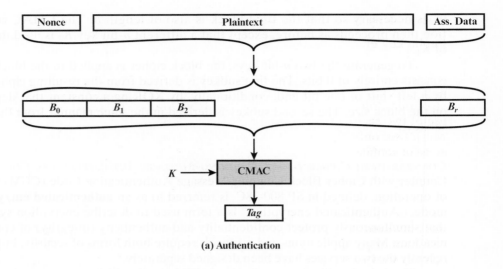

(a) Authentication

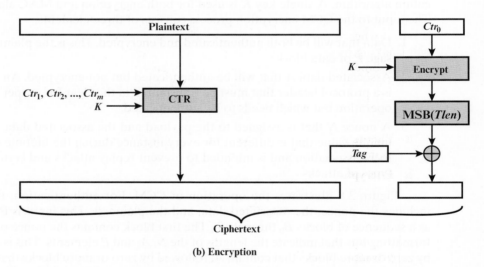

(b) Encryption

Figure 3.8   Counter with Cipher Block Chaining-Message Authentication Code

3.4 PUBLIC-KEY CRYPTOGRAPHY PRINCIPLES

Of equal importance to conventional encryption is **public-key encryption**, which finds use in message authentication and key distribution. This section looks first at the basic concept of public-key encryption and takes a preliminary look at key distribution issues. Section 3.5 examines the two most important public-key algorithms: RSA and Diffie–Hellman. Section 3.6 introduces digital signatures.

Public–Key Encryption Structure

Public-key encryption, first publicly proposed by Diffie and Hellman in 1976 [DIFF76], is the first truly revolutionary advance in encryption in literally thousands of years. Public-key algorithms are based on mathematical functions rather than on simple operations on bit patterns, such as are used in symmetric encryption algorithms. More important, public-key cryptography is asymmetric, involving the use of two separate keys—in contrast to the symmetric conventional encryption, which uses only one key. The use of two keys has profound consequences in the areas of confidentiality, key distribution, and authentication.

Before proceeding, we should first mention several common misconceptions concerning public-key encryption. One is that public-key encryption is more secure from cryptanalysis than conventional encryption. In fact, the security of any encryption scheme depends on (1) the length of the key and (2) the computational work involved in breaking a cipher. There is nothing in principle about either conventional or public-key encryption that makes one superior to another from the point of view of resisting cryptanalysis. A second misconception is that public-key encryption is a general-purpose technique that has made conventional encryption obsolete. On the contrary, because of the computational overhead of current public-key encryption schemes, there seems no foreseeable likelihood that conventional encryption will be abandoned. Finally, there is a feeling that key distribution is trivial when using public-key encryption, compared to the rather cumbersome handshaking involved with key distribution centers for conventional encryption. In fact, some form of protocol is needed, often involving a central agent, and the procedures involved are no simpler or any more efficient than those required for conventional encryption.

A public-key encryption scheme has six ingredients (Figure 3.9a).

- **Plaintext:** This is the readable message or data that is fed into the algorithm as input.

- **Encryption algorithm:** The encryption algorithm performs various transformations on the plaintext.

- **Public and private key:** This is a pair of keys that have been selected so that if one is used for encryption, the other is used for decryption. The exact transformations performed by the encryption algorithm depend on the public or private key that is provided as input.

- **Ciphertext:** This is the scrambled message produced as output. It depends on the plaintext and the key. For a given message, two different keys will produce two different ciphertexts.

- **Decryption algorithm:** This algorithm accepts the ciphertext and the matching key and produces the original plaintext.

As the names suggest, the public key of the pair is made public for others to use, while the private key is known only to its owner. A general-purpose public-key cryptographic algorithm relies on one key for encryption and a different but related key for decryption.

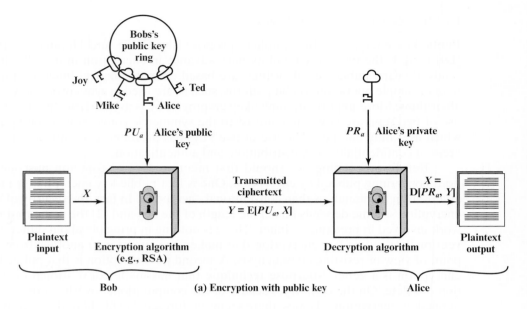

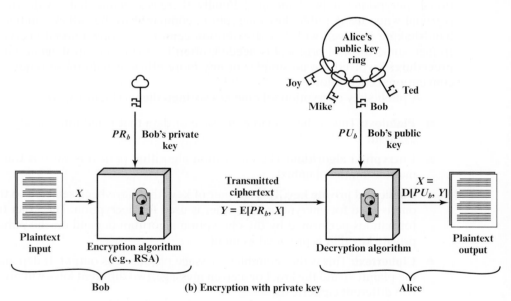

Figure 3.9 Public-Key Cryptography

The essential steps are the following:

1. Each user generates a pair of keys to be used for the encryption and decryption of messages.

2. Each user places one of the two keys in a public register or other accessible file. This is the public key. The companion key is kept private. As Figure 3.9a

suggests, each user maintains a collection of public keys obtained from others.

3. If Bob wishes to send a private message to Alice, Bob encrypts the message using Alice's public key.

4. When Alice receives the message, she decrypts it using her private key. No other recipient can decrypt the message because only Alice knows Alice's private key.

With this approach, all participants have access to public keys, and private keys are generated locally by each participant and therefore need never be distributed. As long as a user protects his or her private key, incoming communication is secure. At any time, a user can change the private key and publish the companion public key to replace the old public key.

The key used in conventional encryption is typically referred to as a **secret key**. The two keys used for public-key encryption are referred to as the **public key** and the **private key**. Invariably, the private key is kept secret, but it is referred to as a private key rather than a secret key to avoid confusion with conventional encryption.

Applications for Public-Key Cryptosystems

Before proceeding, we need to clarify one aspect of public-key cryptosystems that is otherwise likely to lead to confusion. Public-key systems are characterized by the use of a cryptographic type of algorithm with two keys, one held private and one available publicly. Depending on the application, the sender uses either the sender's private key, the receiver's public key, or both to perform some type of cryptographic function. In broad terms, we can classify the use of public-key cryptosystems into three categories:

■ **Encryption/decryption:** The sender encrypts a message with the recipient's public key.

■ **Digital signature:** The sender "signs" a message with its private key. Signing is achieved by a cryptographic algorithm applied to the message or to a small block of data that is a function of the message.

■ **Key exchange:** Two sides cooperate to exchange a session key. Several different approaches are possible, involving the private key(s) of one or both parties.

Some algorithms are suitable for all three applications, whereas others can be used only for one or two of these applications. Table 3.2 indicates the applications supported by the algorithms discussed in this chapter: RSA and Diffie–Hellman. This table also includes the Digital Signature Standard (DSS) and elliptic-curve cryptography, also mentioned later in this chapter.

One general observation can be made at this point. Public-key algorithms require considerably more computation than symmetric algorithms for comparable security and a comparable plaintext length. Accordingly, public-key algorithms are used only for short messages or data blocks, such as to encrypt a secret key or PIN.

Table 3.2   Applications for Public-Key Cryptosystems

Algorithm	Encryption/Decryption	Digital Signature	Key Exchange
RSA	Yes	Yes	Yes
Diffie–Hellman	No	No	Yes
DSS	No	Yes	No
Elliptic curve	Yes	Yes	Yes

Requirements for Public-Key Cryptography

The cryptosystem illustrated in Figure 3.9 depends on a cryptographic algorithm based on two related keys. Diffie and Hellman postulated this system without demonstrating that such algorithms exist. However, they did lay out the conditions that such algorithms must fulfill [DIFF76]:

1. It is computationally easy for a party B to generate a pair (public key PU_b, private key PR_b).

2. It is computationally easy for a sender A, knowing the public key and the message to be encrypted, M, to generate the corresponding ciphertext:

$$C = E(PU_b, M)$$

3. It is computationally easy for the receiver B to decrypt the resulting ciphertext using the private key to recover the original message:

$$M = D(PR_b, C) = D[PR_b, E(PU_b, M)]$$

4. It is computationally infeasible for an opponent, knowing the public key, PU_b, to determine the private key, PR_b.

5. It is computationally infeasible for an opponent, knowing the public key, PU_b, and a ciphertext, C, to recover the original message, M.

We can add a sixth requirement that, although useful, is not necessary for all public-key applications.

1. Either of the two related keys can be used for encryption, with the other used for decryption.

$$M = D[PU_b, E(PR_b, M)] = D[PR_b, E(PU_b, M)]$$

3.5 PUBLIC-KEY CRYPTOGRAPHY ALGORITHMS

Two widely used public-key algorithms are RSA and Diffie–Hellman. We look at both of these in this section and then briefly introduce two other algorithms.[4]

---

[4]This section uses some elementary concepts from number theory. For a review, see Appendix A.

The RSA Public-Key Encryption Algorithm

One of the first public-key schemes was developed in 1977 by Ron Rivest, Adi Shamir, and Len Adleman at MIT and first published in 1978 [RIVE78]. The RSA scheme has until recently reigned supreme as the most widely accepted and implemented approach to public-key encryption. Currently, both RSA and elliptic-curve cryptography are widely used. **RSA** is a block cipher in which the plaintext and ciphertext are integers between 0 and $n - 1$ for some n.

BASIC RSA ENCRYPTION AND DECRYPTION Encryption and decryption are of the following form period for some plaintext block M and ciphertext block C:

$$C = M^e \bmod n$$
$$M = C^d \bmod n = (M^e)^d \bmod n = M^{ed} \bmod n$$

Both sender and receiver must know the values of n and e, and only the receiver knows the value of d. This is a public-key encryption algorithm with a public key of $KU = \{e, n\}$ and a private key of $KR = \{d, n\}$. For this algorithm to be satisfactory for public-key encryption, the following requirements must be met.

1. It is possible to find values of e, d, n such that $M^{ed} \bmod n = M$ for all $M < n$.
2. It is relatively easy to calculate M^e and C^d for all values of $M < n$.
3. It is infeasible to determine d given e and n.

The first two requirements are easily met. The third requirement can be met for large values of e and n.

Figure 3.10 summarizes the RSA algorithm. Begin by selecting two prime numbers p and q and calculating their product n, which is the modulus for encryption and decryption. Next, we need the quantity $\phi(n)$, referred to as the Euler totient of n, which is the number of positive integers less than n and relatively prime to n. Then select an integer e that is relatively prime to $\phi(n)$ [i.e., the greatest common divisor of e and $\phi(n)$ is 1]. Finally, calculate d as the multiplicative inverse of e, modulo $\phi(n)$. It can be shown that d and e have the desired properties.

Suppose that user A has published its public key and that user B wishes to send the message M to A. Then B calculates $C = M^e \pmod{n}$ and transmits C. On receipt of this ciphertext, user A decrypts by calculating $M = C^d \pmod{n}$.

An example, from [SING99], is shown in Figure 3.11. For this example, the keys were generated as follows:

1. Select two prime numbers, $p = 17$ and $q = 11$.
2. Calculate $n = pq = 17 \times 11 = 187$.
3. Calculate $\phi(n) = (p - 1)(q - 1) = 16 \times 10 = 160$.
4. Select e such that e is relatively prime to $\phi(n) = 160$ and less than $\phi(n)$; we choose $e = 7$.
5. Determine d such that $de \bmod 160 = 1$ and $d < 160$. The correct value is $d = 23$, because $23 \times 7 = 161 = (1 \times 160) + 1$.

The resulting keys are public key $PU = \{7, 187\}$ and private key $PR = \{23, 187\}$. The example shows the use of these keys for a plaintext input of $M = 88$.

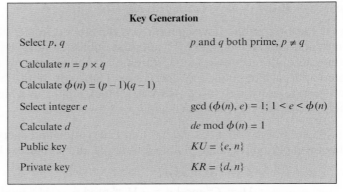

Figure 3.10   The RSA Algorithm

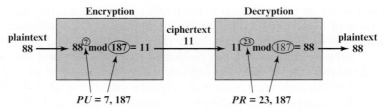

Figure 3.11   Example of RSA Algorithm

For encryption, we need to calculate $C = 88^7 \bmod 187$. Exploiting the properties of modular arithmetic, we can do this as follows:

$$88^7 \bmod 187 = [(88^4 \bmod 187) \times (88^2 \bmod 187) \times (88^1 \bmod 187)] \bmod 187$$

$$88^1 \bmod 187 = 88 \; 88^2 \bmod 187 = 7744 \bmod 187 = 77$$

$$88^4 \bmod 187 = 59{,}969{,}536 \bmod 187 = 132$$

$$88^7 \bmod 187 = (88 \times 77 \times 132) \bmod 187 = 894{,}432 \bmod 187 = 11$$

For decryption, we calculate $M = 11^{23} \bmod 187$:

$$11^{23} \bmod 187 = [(11^1 \bmod 187) \times (11^2 \bmod 187) \times (11^4 \bmod 187) \times$$
$$(11^8 \bmod 187) \times (11^8 \bmod 187)] \bmod 187$$

$$11^1 \bmod 187 = 11$$
$$11^2 \bmod 187 = 121$$
$$11^4 \bmod 187 = 14{,}641 \bmod 187 = 55$$
$$11^8 \bmod 187 = 214{,}358{,}881 \bmod 187 = 33$$
$$11^{23} \bmod 187 = (11 \times 121 \times 55 \times 33 \times 33) \bmod 187$$
$$= 79{,}720{,}245 \bmod 187 = 88$$

SECURITY CONSIDERATIONS The security of RSA depends on it being used in such a way as to counter potential attacks. Four possible attack approaches are as follows:

- **Mathematical attacks:** There are several approaches, all equivalent in effort to factoring the product of two primes. The defense against mathematical attacks is to use a large key size. Thus, the larger the number of bits in d, the better. However, because the calculations involved, both in key generation and in encryption/decryption, are complex, the larger the size of the key, the slower the system will run. SP 800-131A (*Transitions: Recommendation for Transitioning the Use of Cryptographic Algorithms and Key Lengths*, November 2015) recommends the use of a 2048-bit key size. A recent report from the European Union Agency for Network and Information Security (*Algorithms, key size and parameters report—2014*, November 2014) recommends a 3072-bit key length. Either of these lengths should provide adequate security for a considerable time into the future.

- **Timing attacks:** These depend on the running time of the decryption algorithm. Various approaches to mask the time required so as to thwart attempts to deduce key size have been suggested, such as introducing a random delay.

- **Chosen ciphertext attacks:** This type of attack exploits properties of the RSA algorithm by selecting blocks of data that, when processed using the target's private key, yield information needed for cryptanalysis. These attacks can be thwarted by suitable padding of the plaintext.

To counter sophisticated chosen ciphertext attacks, RSA Security Inc., a leading RSA vendor and former holder of the RSA patent, recommends modifying the plaintext using a procedure known as optimal asymmetric encryption padding (OAEP). A full discussion of the threats and OAEP are beyond our scope; see [POIN02] for an introduction and [BELL94a] for a thorough analysis. Here, we simply summarize the OAEP procedure.

Figure 3.12 depicts OAEP encryption. As a first step, the message M to be encrypted is padded. A set of optional parameters, P, is passed through a hash function, H. The output is then padded with zeros to get the desired length in the overall data block (DB). Next, a random seed is generated and passed through another hash function, called the mask generating function (MGF). The resulting hash value is bit-by-bit XORed with DB to produce a maskedDB. The maskedDB is in turn passed

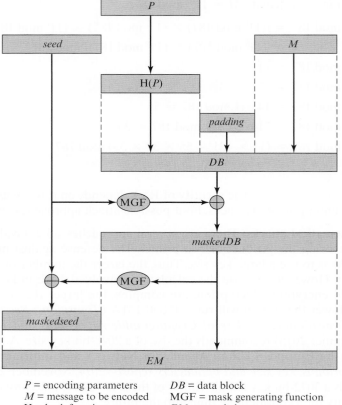

P = encoding parameters   *DB* = data block
M = message to be encoded   MGF = mask generating function
H = hash function   *EM* = encoded message

Figure 3.12   Encryption Using Optimal Asymmetric Encryption Padding (OAEP)

through the MGF to form a hash that is XORed with the seed to produce the masked seed. The concatenation of the maskedseed and the maskedDB forms the encoded message *EM*. Note that the EM includes the padded message masked by the seed, and the seed masked by the maskedDB. The EM is then encrypted using RSA.

Diffie–Hellman Key Exchange

The first published public-key algorithm appeared in the seminal paper by Diffie and Hellman that defined public-key cryptography [DIFF76] and is generally referred to as the **Diffie–Hellman key exchange**. A number of commercial products employ this key exchange technique.

The purpose of the algorithm is to enable two users to securely exchange a secret key that then can be used for subsequent encryption of messages. The algorithm itself is limited to the exchange of the keys.

The Diffie–Hellman algorithm depends for its effectiveness on the difficulty of computing discrete logarithms. Briefly, we can define the discrete logarithm in the following way. First, we define a primitive root of a prime number p as one whose powers generate all the integers from 1 to $p - 1$. That is, if a is a primitive root of the prime number p, then the numbers

$$a \bmod p, a^2 \bmod p, \ldots, ap^{-1} \bmod p$$

are distinct and consist of the integers from 1 through $p - 1$ in some permutation.

For any integer b less than p and a primitive root a of prime number p, one can find a unique exponent i such that

$$b = a^i \bmod p \quad 0 \le i \le (p - 1)$$

The exponent i is referred to as the discrete logarithm, or index, of b for the base a, mod p. We denote this value as $\mathrm{dlog}_{a,p}(b)$.[5]

THE ALGORITHM   With this background, we can define the Diffie–Hellman key exchange, which is summarized in Figure 3.13. For this scheme, there are two publicly known numbers: a prime number q and an integer α that is a primitive root of q. Suppose the users A and B wish to exchange a key. User A selects a random integer $X_A < q$ and computes $Y_A = \alpha^{X_A} \bmod q$. Similarly, user B independently selects a random integer $X_B < q$ and computes $Y_B = \alpha^{X_B} \bmod q$. Each side keeps the X value private and makes the Y value available publicly to the other side. User A computes the key as $K = (Y_B)^{X_A} \bmod q$ and user B computes the key as $K = (Y_A)^{X_B} \bmod q$. These two calculations produce identical results:

$$
\begin{aligned}
K &= (Y_B)^{X_A} \bmod q \\
  &= (\alpha^{X_B} \bmod q)^{X_A} \bmod q \\
  &= (\alpha^{X_B})^{X_A} \bmod q \\
  &= \alpha^{X_B X_A} \bmod q \\
  &= (\alpha^{X_A})^{X_B} \bmod q \\
  &= (\alpha^{X_A} \bmod q)^{X_B} \bmod q \\
  &= (Y_A)^{X_B} \bmod q
\end{aligned}
$$

The result is that the two sides have exchanged a secret value. Furthermore, because X_A and X_B are private, an adversary only has the following ingredients to work with: $q, \alpha, Y_A,$ and Y_B. Thus, the adversary is forced to take a discrete logarithm to determine the key. For example, to determine the private key of user B, an adversary must compute

$$X_B = \mathrm{dlog}_{\alpha,q}(Y_B)$$

The adversary can then calculate the key K in the same manner as user B does.

The security of the Diffie–Hellman key exchange lies in the fact that, while it is relatively easy to calculate exponentials modulo a prime, it is very difficult to calculate discrete logarithms. For large primes, the latter task is considered infeasible.

---

[5]Many texts refer to the discrete logarithm as the *index*. There is no generally agreed notation for this concept, much less an agreed name.

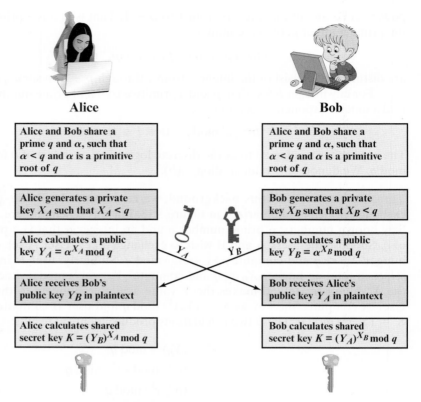

Figure 3.13 The Diffie–Hellman Key Exchange

Here is an example. Key exchange is based on the use of the prime number $q = 353$ and a primitive root of 353, in this case $\alpha = 3$. A and B select secret keys $X_A = 97$ and $X_B = 233$, respectively. Each computes its public key:

A computes $Y_A = 3^{97} \bmod 353 = 40$. B computes $Y_B = 3^{233} \bmod 353 = 248$.

After they exchange public keys, each can compute the common secret key:

A computes $K = (Y_B)^{X_A} \bmod 353 = 248^{97} \bmod 353 = 160$.
B computes $K = (Y_A)^{X_B} \bmod 353 = 40^{233} \bmod 353 = 160$.

We assume an attacker would have available the following information:

$$q = 353; \quad a = 3; \quad Y_A = 40; \quad Y_B = 248$$

In this simple example, it would be possible to determine the secret key 160 by brute force. In particular, an attacker E can determine the common key by discovering a solution to the equation $3^a \bmod 353 = 40$ or the equation $3^b \bmod 353 = 248$. The brute-force approach is to calculate powers of 3 modulo 353, stopping when the result equals either 40 or 248. The desired answer is reached with the exponent value of 97, which provides $3^{97} \bmod 353 = 40$.

With larger numbers, the problem becomes impractical.

KEY EXCHANGE PROTOCOLS Figure 3.13 shows a simple protocol that makes use of the Diffie–Hellman calculation. Suppose that user A wishes to set up a connection with user B and use a secret key to encrypt messages on that connection. User A can generate a one-time private key X_A, calculate Y_A, and send that to user B. User B responds by generating a private value X_B, calculating Y_B, and sending Y_B to user A. Both users can now calculate the key. The necessary public values q and α would need to be known ahead of time. Alternatively, user A could pick values for q and include those in the first message.

As an example of another use of the Diffie–Hellman algorithm, suppose that a group of users (e.g., all users on a LAN) each generate a long-lasting private value X_A and calculate a public value Y_A. These public values, together with global public values for q and α, are stored in some central directory. At any time, user B can access user A's public value, calculate a secret key, and use that to send an encrypted message to user A. If the central directory is trusted, then this form of communication provides both confidentiality and a degree of authentication. Because only A and B can determine the key, no other user can read the message (confidentiality). Recipient A knows that only user B could have created a message using this key (authentication). However, the technique does not protect against replay attacks.

MAN-IN-THE-MIDDLE ATTACK The protocol depicted in Figure 3.13 is insecure against a man-in-the-middle attack. Suppose Alice and Bob wish to exchange keys, and Darth is the adversary. The attack proceeds as follows (Figure 3.14):

1. Darth prepares for the attack by generating two random private keys X_{D1} and X_{D2}, and then computing the corresponding public keys Y_{D1} and Y_{D2}.
2. Alice transmits Y_A to Bob.
3. Darth intercepts Y_A and transmits Y_{D1} to Bob. Darth also calculates $K2 = (Y_A)^{X_{D2}} \bmod q$.
4. Bob receives Y_{D1} and calculates $K1 = (Y_{D1})^{X_B} \bmod q$.
5. Bob transmits Y_B to Alice.
6. Darth intercepts Y_B and transmits Y_{D2} to Alice. Darth calculates $K1 = (Y_B)^{X_{D1}} \bmod q$.
7. Alice receives Y_{D2} and calculates $K2 = (Y_{D2})^{X_A} \bmod q$.

At this point, Bob and Alice think that they share a secret key. Instead Bob and Darth share secret key $K1$, and Alice and Darth share secret key $K2$. All future communication between Bob and Alice is compromised in the following way:

1. Alice sends an encrypted message M: $E(K2, M)$.
2. Darth intercepts the encrypted message and decrypts it to recover M.
3. Darth sends Bob $E(K1, M)$ or $E(K1, M')$, where M' is any message. In the first case, Darth simply wants to eavesdrop on the communication without altering it. In the second case, Darth wants to modify the message going to Bob.

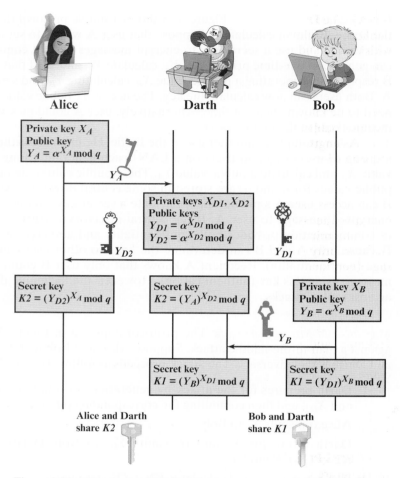

Figure 3.14 Man-in-the-Middle Attack

The key exchange protocol is vulnerable to such an attack because it does not authenticate the participants. This vulnerability can be overcome with the use of digital signatures and public-key certificates; these topics are explored later in this chapter and in Chapter 4.

Other Public-Key Cryptography Algorithms

Two other public-key algorithms have found commercial acceptance: DSS and elliptic-curve cryptography.

DIGITAL SIGNATURE STANDARD The National Institute of Standards and Technology (NIST) has published Federal Information Processing Standard FIPS PUB 186, known as the **Digital Signature Standard (DSS)**. The DSS makes use of the SHA-1 and presents a new digital signature technique, the Digital Signature Algorithm

(DSA). The DSS was originally proposed in 1991 and revised in 1993 in response to public feedback concerning the security of the scheme. There was a further minor revision in 1996. The DSS uses an algorithm that is designed to provide only the digital signature function. Unlike RSA, it cannot be used for encryption or key exchange.

ELLIPTIC-CURVE CRYPTOGRAPHY The vast majority of the products and standards that use public-key cryptography for encryption and digital signatures use RSA. The bit length for secure RSA use has increased over recent years, and this has put a heavier processing load on applications using RSA. This burden has ramifications, especially for electronic commerce sites that conduct large numbers of secure transactions. Recently, a competing system has begun to challenge RSA: **elliptic curve cryptography (ECC)**. Already, ECC is showing up in standardization efforts, including the IEEE P1363 Standard for Public-Key Cryptography.

The principal attraction of ECC compared to RSA is that it appears to offer equal security for a far smaller bit size, thereby reducing processing overhead. On the other hand, although the theory of ECC has been around for some time, it is only recently that products have begun to appear and that there has been sustained cryptanalytic interest in probing for weaknesses. Thus, the confidence level in ECC is not yet as high as that in RSA.

ECC is fundamentally more difficult to explain than either RSA or Diffie–Hellman, and a full mathematical description is beyond the scope of this book. The technique is based on the use of a mathematical construct known as the elliptic curve.

3.6 DIGITAL SIGNATURES

NIST FIPS PUB 186-4 [*Digital Signature Standard (DSS)*, July 2013] defines a digital signature as follows: The result of a cryptographic transformation of data that, when properly implemented, provides a mechanism for verifying origin authentication, data integrity, and signatory non-repudiation.

Thus, a digital signature is a data-dependent bit pattern, generated by an agent as a function of a file, message, or other form of data block. Another agent can access the data block and its associated signature and verify that (1) the data block has been signed by the alleged signer and that (2) the data block has not been altered since the signing. Further, the signer cannot repudiate the signature.

FIPS 186-4 specifies the use of one of three digital signature algorithms:

- **Digital Signature Algorithm (DSA):** The original NIST-approved algorithm, which is based on the difficulty of computing discrete logarithms.
- **RSA Digital Signature Algorithm:** Based on the RSA public-key algorithm.
- **Elliptic Curve Digital Signature Algorithm (ECDSA):** Based on elliptic-curve cryptography.

In this section, we provide a brief overview of the digital signature process, then describe the RSA digital signature algorithm.

Digital Signature Generation and Verification

Figure 3.15 is a generic model of the process of making and using digital signatures. All of the digital signature schemes in FIPS 186-4 have this structure. Suppose that Bob wants to send a message to Alice. Although it is not important that the message be kept as a secret, he wants Alice to be certain that the message is indeed from him. For this purpose, Bob uses a secure hash function, such as SHA-512, to generate a hash value for the message. That hash value, together with Bob's private key, serve as input to a digital signature generation algorithm that produces a short block that functions as a digital signature. Bob sends the message with the signature attached. When Alice receives the message plus signature, she (1) calculates

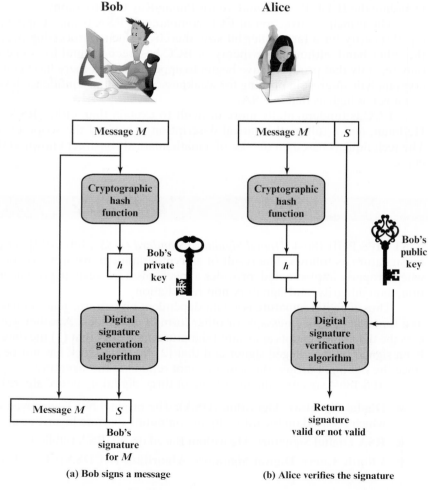

Figure 3.15   Simplified Depiction of Essential Elements of Digital Signature Process

a hash value for the message and (2) provides the hash value and Bob's public key as inputs to a digital signature verification algorithm. If the algorithm returns the result that the signature is valid, Alice is assured that the message must have been signed by Bob. No one else has Bob's private key and therefore no one else could have created a signature that could be verified for this message with Bob's public key. In addition, it is impossible to alter the message without access to Bob's private key, so the message is authenticated both in terms of source and in terms of data integrity.

It is important to emphasize that the encryption process just described does not provide confidentiality. That is, the message being sent is safe from alteration, but not safe from eavesdropping. This is obvious in the case of a signature based on a portion of the message, because the rest of the message is transmitted in the clear. Even in the case of complete encryption, there is no protection of confidentiality because any observer can decrypt the message by using the sender's public key.

RSA Digital Signature Algorithm

The essence of the RSA digital signature algorithm is to encrypt the hash of the message to be signed using RSA. However, as with the use of RSA for encryption of keys or short messages, the RSA digital signature algorithm first modifies the hash value to enhance security. There are several approaches to this, one of which is the RSA Probabilistic Signature Scheme (RSA-PSS). RSA-PSS is the latest of the RSA schemes and the one that RSA Laboratories recommends as the most secure of the RSA digital signature schemes. We provide a brief overview here; for more detail see [STAL16].

Figure 3.16 illustrates the RSS-PSS signature generation process. The steps are as follows:

1. Generate a hash value, or message digest, mHash from the message M to be signed.
2. Pad mHash with a constant value padding1 and pseudorandom value salt to form M'
3. Generate hash value H from M'.
4. Generate a block DB consisting of a constant value padding 2 and salt.
5. Use the mask generating function MGF, which produces a randomized output from input H of the same length as DB.
6. Create the encoded message (EM) block by padding H with the hexadecimal constant BC and the XOR of H and DB.
7. Encrypt EM with RSA using the signer's private key.

The objective with this algorithm is to make it more difficult for an adversary to find another message that maps to the same message digest as a given message or to find two messages that map to the same message digest. Because the salt changes with every use, signing the same message twice using the same private key will yield two different signatures. This is an added measure of security.

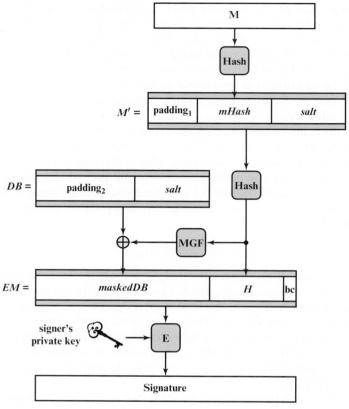

Figure 3.16   RSA-PSS Encoding and Signature Generation

3.7 KEY TERMS, REVIEW QUESTIONS, AND PROBLEMS

Key Terms

authenticated encryption	key exchange	public-key certificate
Diffie–Hellman key exchange	MD5	public-key encryption
digital signature	message authentication	RSA
Digital Signature Standard (DSS)	message authentication code (MAC)	secret key
elliptic-curve cryptography (ECC)	message digest	secure hash function
HMAC	one-way hash function	SHA-1
	private key	strong collision resistant
	public key	weak collision resistant

Review Questions

3.1   List three approaches to message authentication.

3.2   What is a message authentication code?

3.3   What is a one-way hash function? How is it different from message authentication code?
3.4   List the properties of a strong hash function.
3.5   Compare SHA-1 and SHA-2 with respect to SHA parameters.
3.6   List the design objectives for HMAC.
3.7   Differentiate between public-key cryptosystem and symmetric encryption algorithm.
3.8   List the public-key cryptography algorithm used in digital signatures, encryption/decryption, and key exchange.
3.9   In what way is the Diffie–Hellman key exchange algorithm insecure against a man-in-the-middle attack?

Problems

3.1   Consider a 32-bit hash function defined as the concatenation of two 16-bit functions: XOR and RXOR, which are defined in Section 3.2 as "two simple hash functions."
   a.   Will this checksum detect all errors caused by an odd number of error bits? Explain.
   b.   Will this checksum detect all errors caused by an even number of error bits? If not, characterize the error patterns that will cause the checksum to fail.
   c.   Comment on the effectiveness of this function for use as a hash function for authentication.
3.2   Suppose H(m) is a collision-resistant hash function that maps a message of arbitrary bit length into an n-bit hash value. Is it true that, for all messages x, x' with $x \neq x'$, we have H(x) $\neq$ H(x')? Explain your answer.
3.3   State the value of the padding field in SHA-512 if the length of the message is
   a.   4987 bits
   b.   4199 bits
   c.   1227 bits
3.4   State the value of the length field in SHA-512 if the length of the message is
   a.   3967 bits
   b.   3968 bits
   c.   3969 bits
3.5   a.   Consider the following hash function. Messages are in the form of a sequence of decimal numbers, $M = (a_1, a_2, \ldots, a_t)$. The hash value h is calculated as $\left(\sum_{i=1}^{t} a_i \right) \bmod n$, for some predefined value n. Does this hash function satisfy any of the requirements for a hash function listed in Section 3.2? Explain your answer.
   b.   Repeat part (a) for the hash function $h = \left(\sum_{i=1}^{t} (a_i)^2 \right) \bmod n$.
   c.   Calculate the hash function of part (b) for $M = (237, 632, 913, 423, 349)$ and $n = 757$.

3.6   This problem introduces a hash function similar in spirit to SHA that operates on letters instead of binary data. It is called the *toy tetragraph hash* (tth).[6] Given a message consisting of a sequence of letters, tth produces a hash value consisting of four letters. First, tth divides the message into blocks of 16 letters, ignoring spaces, punctuation, and capitalization. If the message length is not divisible by 16, it is padded out with nulls. A four-number running total is maintained that starts out with the value (0, 0, 0, 0); this is input to the compression function for processing the first block. The compression function consists of two rounds. **Round 1:** Get the next block of text and arrange it as a row-wise 4 block of text and covert it to numbers (A = 0, B = 1, etc.). For example, for the block ABCDEFGHIJKLMNOP, we have

---

[6] I thank William K. Mason of the magazine staff of *The Cryptogram* for providing this example.

A	B	C	D
E	F	G	H
I	J	K	L
M	N	O	P

0	1	2	3
4	5	6	7
8	9	10	11
12	13	14	15

Then, add each column mod 26 and add the result to the running total, mod 26. In this example, the running total is (24, 2, 6, 10). **Round 2:** Using the matrix from round 1, rotate the first row left by 1, second row left by 2, third row left by 3, and reverse the order of the fourth row. In our example:

B	C	D	A
G	H	E	F
L	I	J	K
P	O	N	M

1	2	3	0
6	7	4	5
11	8	9	10
15	14	13	12

Now, add each column mod 26 and add the result to the running total. The new running total is (5, 7, 9, 11). This running total is now the input into the first round of the compression function for the next block of text. After the final block is processed, convert the final running total to letters. For example, if the message is ABCDE FGHIJKLMNOP, then the hash is FHJL.

    a. Draw figures comparable to Figures 3.4 and 3.5 to depict the overall tth logic and the compression function logic.

    b. Calculate the hash function for the 48-letter message "I leave twenty million dollars to my friendly cousin Bill."

    c. To demonstrate the weakness of tth, find a 48-letter block that produces the same hash as that just derived. *Hint:* Use lots of A's.

3.7 It is possible to use a hash function to construct a block cipher with a structure similar to DES. Because a hash function is one way and a block cipher must be reversible (to decrypt), how is it possible?

3.8 Now consider the opposite problem: Use an encryption algorithm to construct a one-way hash function. Consider using RSA with a known key. Then process a message consisting of a sequence of blocks as follows: Encrypt the first block, XOR the result with the second block and encrypt again, and so on. Show that this scheme is not secure by solving the following problem. Given a two-block message B1, B2, and its hash, we have

$$\text{RSAH}(B1, B2) = \text{RSA}(\text{RSA}(B1) \oplus B2)$$

Given an arbitrary block C1, choose C2 so that $\text{RSAH}(C1, C2) = \text{RSAH}(B1, B2)$. Thus, the hash function does not satisfy weak collision resistance.

3.9 One of the most widely used MACs, referred to as the Data Authentication Algorithm, is based on DES. The algorithm is both a FIPS publication (FIPS PUB 113) and an ANSI standard (X9.17). The algorithm can be defined as using the cipher block chaining (CBC) mode of operation of DES with an initialization vector of zero (Figure 2.9). The data (e.g., message, record, file, or program) to be authenticated is grouped into contiguous 64-bit blocks: $P_1, P_2, \ldots, P_N$. If necessary, the final block is padded on the right with 0s to form a full 64-bit block. The MAC consists of either the entire ciphertext block C_N or the leftmost M bits of the block with $16 \leq M \leq 64$. Show that the same result can be produced using the cipher feedback mode.

3.10 In this problem, we will compare the security services that are provided by digital signatures (DS) and message authentication codes (MAC). We assume that Oscar is able to observe all messages sent from Alice to Bob and vice versa. Oscar has no knowledge of any keys but the public one in case of DS. State whether and how (i) DS and (ii) MAC protect against each attack. The value `auth(x)` is computed with a DS or a MAC algorithm, respectively.

    a. (Message integrity) Alice sends a message `x = "Transfer $1000 to Mark"` in the clear and also sends `auth(x)` to Bob. Oscar intercepts the message and replaces "Mark" with "Oscar." Will Bob detect this?

    b. (Replay) Alice sends a message `x = "Transfer $1000 to Oscar"` in the clear and also sends `auth(x)` to Bob. Oscar observes the message and signature and sends them 100 times to Bob. Will Bob detect this?

    c. (Sender Authentication with cheating third party) Oscar claims that he sent some message x with a valid `auth(x)` to Bob, but Alice claims the same. Can Bob clear the question in either case?

    d. (Authentication with Bob cheating) Bob claims that he received a message x with a valid signature `auth(x)` from Alice (e.g., "Transfer $1000 from Alice to Bob") but Alice claims she has never sent it. Can Alice clear this question in either case?

3.11 Figure 3.17 shows an alternative means of implementing HMAC.

    a. Describe the operation of this implementation.

    b. What potential benefit does this implementation have over that shown in Figure 3.6?

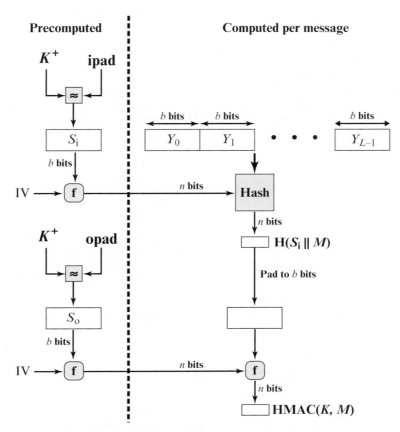

Figure 3.17 Efficient Implementation of HMAC

3.12 In this problem, we demonstrate that for CMAC, a variant that XORs the second key after applying the final encryption doesn't work. Let us consider this for the case of the message being an integer multiple of the block size. Then the variant can be expressed as $VMAC(K, M) = CBC(K, M) \oplus K_1$. Now suppose an adversary is able to ask for the MACs of three messages: the message $\mathbf{0} = 0^n$, where n is the cipher block size; the message $\mathbf{1} = 1^n$; and the message $\mathbf{1} \| \mathbf{0}$. As a result of these three queries, the adversary gets $T_0 = CBC(K, \mathbf{0}) \oplus K_1$; $T_1 = CBC(K, \mathbf{1}) \oplus K_1$ and $T_2 = CBC(K, [CBC(K, \mathbf{1})]) \oplus K_1$. Show that the adversary can compute the correct MAC for the (unqueried) message $\mathbf{0} \| (T_0 \oplus T_1)$.

3.13 Prior to the discovery of any specific public-key schemes, such as RSA, an existence proof was developed whose purpose was to demonstrate that public-key encryption is possible in theory. Consider the functions $f_1(x_1) = z_1$; $f_2(x_2, y_2) = z_2$; $f_3(x_3, y_3) = z_3$, where all values are integers with $1 \le x_i, y_i, z_i \le N$. Function f_1 can be represented by a vector M1 of length N in which the kth entry is the value of $f_1(k)$. Similarly, f_2 and f_3 can be represented by $N \times N$ matrices M2 and M3. The intent is to represent the encryption/decryption process by table lookups for tables with very large values of N. Such tables would be impractically huge but in principle could be constructed. The scheme works as follows: Construct M1 with a random permutation of all integers between 1 and N; that is, each integer appears exactly once in M1. Construct M2 so that each row contains a random permutation of the first N integers. Finally, fill in M3 to satisfy the condition:

$$f_3(f_2(f_1(k), p), k) = p \quad \text{for all } k, p \text{ with } 1 \le k, p \le N$$

In words,
1. M1 takes an input k and produces an output x.
2. M2 takes inputs x and p giving output z.
3. M3 takes inputs z and k and produces p.

The three tables, once constructed, are made public.

a. It should be clear that it is possible to construct M3 to satisfy the preceding condition. As an example, fill in M3 for the following simple case:

$$\text{M1} = \begin{array}{|c|} \hline 5 \\ \hline 4 \\ \hline 2 \\ \hline 3 \\ \hline 1 \\ \hline \end{array} \quad \text{M2} = \begin{array}{|c|c|c|c|c|} \hline 5 & 2 & 3 & 4 & 1 \\ \hline 4 & 2 & 5 & 1 & 3 \\ \hline 1 & 3 & 2 & 4 & 5 \\ \hline 3 & 1 & 4 & 2 & 5 \\ \hline 2 & 5 & 3 & 4 & 1 \\ \hline \end{array} \quad \text{M3} = \begin{array}{|c|c|c|c|c|} \hline & & & & \\ \hline & & & & \\ \hline & & & & \\ \hline & & & & \\ \hline & & & & \\ \hline \end{array}$$

Convention: The ith element of M1 corresponds to $k = i$. The ith row of M2 corresponds to $x = i$; the jth column of M2 corresponds to $p = j$. The ith row of M3 corresponds to $z = i$; the jth column of M3 corresponds to $k = j$.

b. Describe the use of this set of tables to perform encryption and decryption between two users.

c. Argue that this is a secure scheme.

3.14 Perform encryption and decryption using the RSA algorithm (Figure 3.10) for the following:
a. $p = 3$; $q = 11$, $e = 7$; $M = 2$
b. $p = 5$; $q = 11$, $e = 3$; $M = 5$
c. $p = 7$; $q = 11$, $e = 17$; $M = 2$
d. $p = 11$; $q = 13$, $e = 11$; $M = 3$
e. $p = 17$; $q = 11$, $e = 7$; $M = 88$

Hint: Decryption is not as hard as you think; use some finesse.

3.15 In a public-key system using RSA, you intercept the ciphertext $C = 16$ sent to a user whose public key is $e = 6$, $n = 40$. What is the plaintext M?

3.16   In an RSA system, the public key of a given user is $e = 7, n = 137$. What is the private key of this user?

3.17   Suppose we have a set of blocks encoded with the RSA algorithm and we don't have the private key. Assume $n = pq$, e is the public key. Suppose also someone tells us they know one of the plaintext blocks has a common factor with n. Does this help us in any way?

3.18   Show how RSA can be represented by matrices M1, M2, and M3 of Problem 3.4.

3.19   Consider the following scheme.
1.   Pick an odd number, E.
2.   Pick two prime numbers, P and Q, where $(P - 1)(Q - 1)$ is relatively prime to E.
3.   Multiply P and Q to get N.
5.   Calculate $D = \dfrac{(P - 1)(Q - 1)(E + 1) + 1}{E}$

Is this scheme equivalent to RSA? Show why or why not.

3.20   Suppose Bob uses the RSA cryptosystem with a very large modulus n for which the factorization cannot be found in a reasonable amount of time. Suppose Alice sends a message to Bob by representing each alphabetic character as an integer between 0 and 25 (A $\rightarrow$ 0, ... , Z $\rightarrow$ 25), and then encrypting each number separately using RSA with large e and large n. Is this method secure? If not, describe the most efficient attack against this encryption method.

3.21   Consider a Diffie–Hellman scheme with a common prime $q = 353$ and a primitive root $\alpha = 3$.
a.   If user A has public key $Y_A = 40$, what is A's private key X_A?
b.   If user B has public key $Y_B = 248$, what is the shared secret key K?

PART TWO: NETWORK SECURITY APPLICATIONS

CHAPTER 4

KEY DISTRIBUTION AND USER AUTHENTICATION

LEARNING OBJECTIVES

After studying this chapter, you should be able to:

◆ Understand the issues involved in the use of symmetric encryption to distribute symmetric keys.

◆ Give a presentation on Kerberos.

◆ Explain the differences between versions 4 and 5 of Kerberos.

◆ Understand the issues involved in the use of asymmetric encryption to distribute symmetric keys.

◆ List and explain the elements in an X.509 certificate.

◆ Present an overview of public-key infrastructure concepts.

◆ Understand the need for a federated identity management system.

This chapter covers two important related concepts. First is the complex topic of cryptographic key distribution, involving cryptographic, protocol, and management considerations. This chapter gives the reader a feel for the issues involved and provides a broad survey of the various aspects of key management and distribution.

This chapter also examines some of the authentication functions that have been developed to support network-based user authentication. The chapter includes a detail discussion of one of the earliest and also one of the most widely used key distribution and user authentication services: Kerberos. Next, the chapter looks at key distribution schemes that rely on asymmetric encryption. This is followed by a discussion of X.509 certificates and public-key infrastructure. Finally, the concept of federated identity management is introduced.

4.1 REMOTE USER AUTHENTICATION PRINCIPLES

In most computer security contexts, user authentication is the fundamental building block and the primary line of defense. User authentication is the basis for most types of access control and for user accountability. RFC 4949 (Internet Security Glossary) defines user authentication as the process of verifying an identity claimed by or for a system entity. This process consists of two steps:

■ Identification step: Presenting an identifier to the security system. (Identifiers should be assigned carefully, because authenticated identities are the basis for other security services, such as access control service.)

■ Verification step: Presenting or generating authentication information that corroborates the binding between the entity and the identifier.

For example, user Alice Toklas could have the user identifier ABTOKLAS. This information needs to be stored on any server or computer system that Alice wishes to use and could be known to system administrators and other users. A typical item of authentication information associated with this user ID is a password, which is kept secret (known only to Alice and to the system). If no one is able to obtain or guess Alice's password, then the combination of Alice's user ID and password enables administrators to set up Alice's access permissions and audit her activity. Because Alice's ID is not secret, system users can send her e-mail, but because her password is secret, no one can pretend to be Alice.

In essence, identification is the means by which a user provides a claimed identity to the system; user authentication is the means of establishing the validity of the claim. Note that user authentication is distinct from message authentication. As defined in Chapter 3, message authentication is a procedure that allows communicating parties to verify that the contents of a received message have not been altered and that the source is authentic. This chapter is concerned solely with user authentication.

The NIST Model for Electronic User Authentication

NIST SP 800-63-2 (*Electronic Authentication Guideline*, August 2013) defines electronic user authentication as the process of establishing confidence in user identities that are presented electronically to an information system. Systems can use the authenticated identity to determine if the authenticated individual is authorized to perform particular functions, such as database transactions or access to system resources. In many cases, the authentication and transaction or other authorized function take place across an open network such as the Internet. Equally, authentication and subsequent authorization can take place locally, such as across a local area network.

SP 800-63-2 defines a general model for user authentication that involves a number of entities and procedures. We discuss this model with reference to Figure 4.1.

The initial requirement for performing user authentication is that the user must be registered with the system. The following is a typical sequence for registration. An applicant applies to a registration authority (RA) to become a subscriber of a credential service provider (CSP). In this model, the RA is a trusted entity that establishes and vouches for the identity of an applicant to a CSP. The CSP then engages

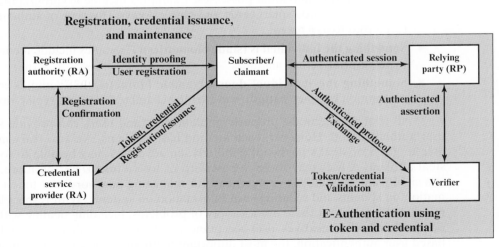

Figure 4.1 The NIST SP 800-63-2 E-Authentication Architectural Model

in an exchange with the subscriber. Depending on the details of the overall authentication system, the CSP issues some sort of electronic credential to the subscriber. The credential is a data structure that authoritatively binds an identity and additional attributes to a token possessed by a subscriber, and can be verified when presented to the verifier in an authentication transaction. The token could be an encryption key or an encrypted password that identifies the subscriber. The token may be issued by the CSP, generated directly by the subscriber, or provided by a third party. The token and credential may be used in subsequent authentication events.

Once a user is registered as a subscriber, the actual authentication process can take place between the subscriber and one or more systems that perform authentication and, subsequently, authorization. The party to be authenticated is called a claimant and the party verifying that identity is called a verifier. When a claimant successfully demonstrates possession and control of a token to a verifier through an authentication protocol, the verifier can verify that the claimant is the subscriber named in the corresponding credential. The verifier passes on an assertion about the identity of the subscriber to the relying party (RP). That assertion includes identity information about a subscriber, such as the subscriber name, an identifier assigned at registration, or other subscriber attributes that were verified in the registration process. The RP can use the authenticated information provided by the verifier to make access control or authorization decisions.

An implemented system for authentication will differ from or be more complex than this simplified model, but the model illustrates the key roles and functions needed for a secure authentication system.

Means of Authentication

There are four general means of authenticating a user's identity, which can be used alone or in combination:

- **Something the individual knows:** Examples include a password, a personal identification number (PIN), or answers to a prearranged set of questions.
- **Something the individual possesses:** Examples include cryptographic keys, electronic keycards, smart cards, and physical keys. This type of authenticator is referred to as a *token*.
- **Something the individual is (static biometrics):** Examples include recognition by fingerprint, retina, and face.
- **Something the individual does (dynamic biometrics):** Examples include recognition by voice pattern, handwriting characteristics, and typing rhythm.

All of these methods, properly implemented and used, can provide secure user authentication. However, each method has problems. An adversary may be able to guess or steal a password. Similarly, an adversary may be able to forge or steal a token. A user may forget a password or lose a token. Furthermore, there is a significant administrative overhead for managing password and token information on systems and securing such information on systems. With respect to biometric authenticators, there are a variety of problems, including dealing with false positives and false negatives, user acceptance, cost, and convenience. For network-based user authentication, the most important methods involve cryptographic keys and something the individual knows, such as a password.

4.2 SYMMETRIC KEY DISTRIBUTION USING SYMMETRIC ENCRYPTION

For symmetric encryption to work, the two parties to an exchange must share the same key, and that key must be protected from access by others. Furthermore, frequent key changes are usually desirable to limit the amount of data compromised if an attacker learns the key. Therefore, the strength of any cryptographic system rests with the "key distribution technique," a term that refers to the means of delivering a key to two parties that wish to exchange data, without allowing others to see the key. Key distribution can be achieved in a number of ways. For two parties A and B, there are the following options:

1. A key could be selected by A and physically delivered to B.
2. A third party could select the key and physically deliver it to A and B.
3. If A and B have previously and recently used a key, one party could transmit the new key to the other, using the old key to encrypt the new key.
4. If A and B each have an encrypted connection to a third party C, C could deliver a key on the encrypted links to A and B.

Options 1 and 2 call for manual delivery of a key. For link encryption, this is a reasonable requirement, because each link encryption device is only going to be exchanging data with its partner on the other end of the link. However, for end-to-end encryption over a network, manual delivery is awkward. In a distributed system, any given host or terminal may need to engage in exchanges with many other hosts and terminals over time. Thus, each device needs a number of keys supplied dynamically. The problem is especially difficult in a wide-area distributed system.

Option 3 is a possibility for either link encryption or end-to-end encryption, but if an attacker ever succeeds in gaining access to one key, then all subsequent keys are revealed. Even if frequent changes are made to the link encryption keys, these should be done manually. To provide keys for end-to-end encryption, option 4 is preferable.

For **option 4**, two kinds of keys are used:

- **Session key:** When two end systems (hosts, terminals, etc.) wish to communicate, they establish a logical connection (e.g., virtual circuit). For the duration of that logical connection, called a session, all user data are encrypted with a one-time session key. At the conclusion of the session the session key is destroyed.
- **Permanent key:** A permanent key is a key used between entities for the purpose of distributing session keys.

A necessary element of option 4 is a **key distribution center (KDC)**. The KDC determines which systems are allowed to communicate with each other. When permission is granted for two systems to establish a connection, the key distribution center provides a one-time session key for that connection.

In general terms, the operation of a KDC proceeds as follows:

1. When host A wishes to set up a connection to host B, it transmits a connection-request packet to the KDC. The communication between A and the KDC is encrypted using a master key shared only by A and the KDC.

2. If the KDC approves the connection request, it generates a unique one-time session key. It encrypts the session key using the permanent key it shares with A and delivers the encrypted session key to A. Similarly, it encrypts the session key using the permanent key it shares with B and delivers the encrypted session key to B.

3. A and B can now set up a logical connection and exchange messages and data, all encrypted using the temporary session key.

The automated key distribution approach provides the flexibility and dynamic characteristics needed to allow a number of users to access a number of servers and for the servers to exchange data with each other. The most widely used application that implements this approach is Kerberos, described in the next section.

4.3 KERBEROS

Kerberos is a key distribution and user authentication service developed at MIT. The problem that Kerberos addresses is this: Assume an open distributed environment in which users at workstations wish to access services on servers distributed throughout the network. We would like for servers to be able to restrict access to authorized users and to be able to authenticate requests for service. In this environment, a workstation cannot be trusted to identify its users correctly to network services. In particular, the following three threats exist:

1. A user may gain access to a particular workstation and pretend to be another user operating from that workstation.

2. A user may alter the network address of a workstation so that the requests sent from the altered workstation appear to come from the impersonated workstation.

3. A user may eavesdrop on exchanges and use a replay attack to gain entrance to a server or to disrupt operations.

In any of these cases, an unauthorized user may be able to gain access to services and data that he or she is not authorized to access. Rather than building elaborate authentication protocols at each server, Kerberos provides a centralized authentication server whose function is to authenticate users to servers and servers to users. Kerberos relies exclusively on symmetric encryption, making no use of public-key encryption.

Two versions of Kerberos are in use. Version 4 [MILL88, STEI88] implementations still exist, although this version is being phased out. Version 5 [KOHL94] corrects some of the security deficiencies of version 4 and has been issued as a proposed Internet Standard (RFC 4120).

Because of the complexity of Kerberos, it is best to start with a description of version 4. This enables us to see the essence of the Kerberos strategy without considering some of the details required to handle subtle security threats. Then, we examine version 5.

Kerberos Version 4

Version 4 of Kerberos makes use of DES, in a rather elaborate protocol, to provide the authentication service. Viewing the protocol as a whole, it is difficult to see the need for the many elements contained therein. Therefore, we adopt a strategy used by Bill Bryant [BRYA88] and build up to the full protocol by looking first at several hypothetical dialogues. Each successive dialogue adds additional complexity to counter security vulnerabilities revealed in the preceding dialogue.

After examining the protocol, we look at some other aspects of version 4.

A SIMPLE AUTHENTICATION DIALOGUE In an unprotected network environment, any client can apply to any server for service. The obvious security risk is that of impersonation. An opponent can pretend to be another client and obtain unauthorized privileges on server machines. To counter this threat, servers must be able to confirm the identities of clients who request service. Each server can be required to undertake this task for each client/server interaction, but in an open environment, this places a substantial burden on each server.

An alternative is to use an **authentication server (AS)** that knows the passwords of all users and stores these in a centralized database. In addition, the AS shares a unique secret key with each server. These keys have been distributed physically or in some other secure manner. Consider the following hypothetical dialogue:[1]

(1) $C \rightarrow AS$: $ID_C \| P_C \| ID_V$

(2) $AS \rightarrow C$:   *Ticket*

(3) $C \rightarrow V$: $ID_C \| Ticket$

$$Ticket = E(K_v, [ID_C \| AD_C \| ID_V])$$

where

$$\begin{aligned}
C &= \text{client} \\
AS &= \text{authentication server} \\
V &= \text{server} \\
ID_C &= \text{identifier of user on C} \\
ID_V &= \text{identifier of V} \\
P_C &= \text{password of user on C} \\
AD_C &= \text{network address of C} \\
K_v &= \text{secret encryption key shared by AS and V}
\end{aligned}$$

In this scenario, the user logs on to a workstation and requests access to server V. The client module C in the user's workstation requests the user's password and

---

[1] The portion to the left of the colon indicates the sender and receiver, the portion to the right indicates the contents of the message, and the symbol $\|$ indicates concatenation.

then sends a message to the AS that includes the user's ID, the server's ID, and the user's password. The AS checks its database to see if the user has supplied the proper password for this user ID and whether this user is permitted access to server V. If both tests are passed, the AS accepts the user as authentic and must now convince the server that this user is authentic. To do so, the AS creates a **ticket** that contains the user's ID and network address and the server's ID. This ticket is encrypted using the secret key shared by the AS and this server. This ticket is then sent back to C. Because the ticket is encrypted, it cannot be altered by C or by an opponent.

With this ticket, C can now apply to V for service. C sends a message to V containing C's ID and the ticket. V decrypts the ticket and verifies that the user ID in the ticket is the same as the unencrypted user ID in the message. If these two match, the server considers the user authenticated and grants the requested service.

Each of the ingredients of message (3) is significant. The ticket is encrypted to prevent alteration or forgery. The server's ID (ID_V) is included in the ticket so that the server can verify that it has decrypted the ticket properly. ID_C is included in the ticket to indicate that this ticket has been issued on behalf of C. Finally, AD_C serves to counter the following threat. An opponent could capture the ticket transmitted in message (2), then use the name ID_C, and transmit a message of form (3) from another workstation. The server would receive a valid ticket that matches the user ID and grant access to the user on that other workstation. To prevent this attack, the AS includes in the ticket the network address from which the original request came. Now the ticket is valid only if it is transmitted from the same workstation that initially requested the ticket.

A MORE SECURE AUTHENTICATION DIALOGUE   Although the foregoing scenario solves some of the problems of authentication in an open network environment, problems remain. Two in particular stand out. First, we would like to minimize the number of times that a user has to enter a password. Suppose each ticket can be used only once. If user C logs on to a workstation in the morning and wishes to check his or her mail at a mail server, C must supply a password to get a ticket for the mail server. If C wishes to check the mail several times during the day, each attempt requires reentering the password. We can improve matters by saying that tickets are reusable. For a single logon session, the workstation can store the mail-server ticket after it is received and use it on behalf of the user for multiple accesses to the mail server.

However, under this scheme, it remains the case that a user would need a new ticket for every different service. If a user wished to access a print server, a mail server, a file server, and so on, the first instance of each access would require a new ticket and hence require the user to enter the password.

The second problem is that the earlier scenario involved a plaintext transmission of the password [message (1)]. An eavesdropper could capture the password and use any service accessible to the victim.

To solve these additional problems, we introduce a scheme for avoiding plaintext passwords and a new server, known as the **ticket-granting server (TGS)**. The new (but still hypothetical) scenario is as follows.

Once per user logon session:

> **(1)** C → AS: $ID_C \| ID_{tgs}$
> **(2)** AS → C: $E(K_c, Ticket_{tgs})$

Once per type of service:

> **(3)** C → TGS: $ID_C \| ID_V \| Ticket_{tgs}$
> **(4)** TGS → C: $Ticket_v$

Once per service session:

> **(5)** C → V: $ID_C \| Ticket_v$

$$Ticket_{tgs} = E(K_{tgs}, [ID_C \| AD_C \| ID_{tgs} \| TS_1 \| Lifetime_1])$$

$$Ticket_v = E(K_v, [ID_C \| AD_C \| ID_v \| TS_2 \| Lifetime_2])$$

The new service, TGS, issues **tickets** to users who have been authenticated to AS. Thus, the user first requests a ticket-granting ticket ($Ticket_{tgs}$) from the AS. The client module in the user workstation saves this ticket. Each time the user requires access to a new service, the client applies to the TGS, using the ticket to authenticate itself. The TGS then grants a ticket for the particular service. The client saves each service-granting ticket and uses it to authenticate its user to a server each time a particular service is requested. Let us look at the details of this scheme:

1. The client requests a ticket-granting ticket on behalf of the user by sending its user's ID to the AS, together with the TGS ID, indicating a request to use the TGS service.

2. The AS responds with a ticket that is encrypted with a key that is derived from the user's password (K_C), which is already stored at the AS. When this response arrives at the client, the client prompts the user for his or her password, generates the key, and attempts to decrypt the incoming message. If the correct password is supplied, the ticket is successfully recovered.

Because only the correct user should know the password, only the correct user can recover the ticket. Thus, we have used the password to obtain credentials from Kerberos without having to transmit the password in plaintext. The ticket itself consists of the ID and network address of the user and the ID of the TGS. This corresponds to the first scenario. The idea is that the client can use this ticket to request multiple service-granting tickets. So the ticket-granting ticket is to be reusable. However, we do not wish an opponent to be able to capture the ticket and use it. Consider the following scenario: An opponent captures the login ticket and waits until the user has logged off his or her workstation. Then the opponent either gains access to that workstation or configures his workstation with the same network address as that of the victim. The opponent would be able to reuse the ticket to spoof the TGS. To counter this, the ticket includes a **timestamp**, indicating the date and time at which the ticket was issued, and a **lifetime**, indicating the length of time for which the ticket is valid (e.g., eight hours). Thus, the client now has a reusable ticket and need not bother the user for a password for each new service request. Finally, note that the ticket-granting ticket is encrypted with a secret key known only to the AS and the TGS. This prevents alteration of the ticket. The ticket is reencrypted with a key based on the user's password. This assures that the ticket can be recovered only by the correct user, providing the authentication.

Now that the client has a ticket-granting ticket, access to any server can be obtained with steps 3 and 4.

3. The client requests a service-granting ticket on behalf of the user. For this purpose, the client transmits a message to the TGS containing the user's ID, the ID of the desired service, and the ticket-granting ticket.

4. The TGS decrypts the incoming ticket using a key shared only by the AS and the TGS (K_{tgs}) and verifies the success of the decryption by the presence of its ID. It checks to make sure that the lifetime has not expired. Then it compares the user ID and network address with the incoming information to authenticate the user. If the user is permitted access to the server V, the TGS issues a ticket to grant access to the requested service.

The service-granting ticket has the same structure as the ticket-granting ticket. Indeed, because the TGS is a server, we would expect that the same elements are needed to authenticate a client to the TGS and to authenticate a client to an application server. Again, the ticket contains a timestamp and lifetime. If the user wants access to the same service at a later time, the client can simply use the previously acquired service-granting ticket and need not bother the user for a password. Note that the ticket is encrypted with a secret key (K_v) known only to the TGS and the server, preventing alteration.

Finally, with a particular service-granting ticket, the client can gain access to the corresponding service with step 5.

5. The client requests access to a service on behalf of the user. For this purpose, the client transmits a message to the server containing the user's ID and the service-granting ticket. The server authenticates by using the contents of the ticket.

This new scenario satisfies the two requirements of only one password query per user session and protection of the user password.

THE VERSION 4 AUTHENTICATION DIALOGUE Although the foregoing scenario enhances security compared to the first attempt, two additional problems remain. The heart of the first problem is the lifetime associated with the ticket-granting ticket. If this lifetime is very short (e.g., minutes), then the user will be repeatedly asked for a password. If the lifetime is long (e.g., hours), then an opponent has a greater opportunity for replay. An opponent could eavesdrop on the network and capture a copy of the ticket-granting ticket and then wait for the legitimate user to log out. Then the opponent could forge the legitimate user's network address and send the message of step (3) to the TGS. This would give the opponent unlimited access to the resources and files available to the legitimate user.

Similarly, if an opponent captures a service-granting ticket and uses it before it expires, the opponent has access to the corresponding service.

Thus, we arrive at an additional requirement. A network service (the TGS or an application service) must be able to prove that the person using a ticket is the same person to whom that ticket was issued.

The second problem is that there may be a requirement for servers to authenticate themselves to users. Without such authentication, an opponent could sabotage the configuration so that messages to a server were directed to another location. The false server then would be in a position to act as a real server, capture any information from the user, and deny the true service to the user.

We examine these problems in turn and refer to Table 4.1, which shows the actual Kerberos protocol. Figure 4.2 provides simplified overview.

First, consider the problem of captured ticket-granting tickets and the need to determine that the ticket presenter is the same as the client for whom the ticket was issued. The threat is that an opponent will steal the ticket and use it before it expires. To get around this problem, let us have the AS provide both the client and the TGS with a secret piece of information in a secure manner. Then the client can prove its identity to the TGS by revealing the secret information, again in a secure manner. An efficient way of accomplishing this is to use an encryption key as the secure information; this is referred to as a session key in Kerberos.

Table 4.1a shows the technique for distributing the session key. As before, the client sends a message to the AS requesting access to the TGS. The AS responds with a message, encrypted with a key derived from the user's password (K_C), that contains the ticket. The encrypted message also contains a copy of the session key, $K_{C,tgs}$, where the subscripts indicate that this is a session key for C and TGS. Because this session key is inside the message encrypted with K_C, only the user's client can read it. The same session key is included in the ticket, which can be read only by the TGS. Thus, the session key has been securely delivered to both C and the TGS.

Note that several additional pieces of information have been added to this first phase of the dialogue. Message (1) includes a timestamp, so that the AS knows that the message is timely. Message (2) includes several elements of the ticket in a

Table 4.1   Summary of Kerberos Version 4 Message Exchanges

(1) C $\rightarrow$ AS $ID_c \| ID_{tgs} \| TS_1$

(2) AS $\rightarrow$ C $E(K_c, [K_{c,tgs} \| ID_{tgs} \| TS_2 \| Lifetime_2 \| Ticket_{tgs}])$

$Ticket_{tgs} = E(K_{tgs}, [K_{c,tgs} \| ID_C \| AD_C \| ID_{tgs} \| TS_2 \| Lifetime_2])$

(a) Authentication Service Exchange to obtain ticket-granting ticket

(3) C $\rightarrow$ TGS $ID_v \| Ticket_{tgs} \| Authenticator_c$

(4) TGS $\rightarrow$ C $E(K_{c,tgs}, [K_{c,v} \| ID_v \| TS_4 \| Ticket_v])$

$Ticket_{tgs} = E(K_{tgs}, [K_{c,tgs} \| ID_C \| AD_C \| ID_{tgs} \| TS_2 \| Lifetime_2])$

$Ticket_v = E(K_v, [K_{c,v} \| ID_C \| AD_C \| ID_v \| TS_4 \| Lifetime_4])$

$Authenticator_c = E(K_{c,tgs}, [ID_C \| AD_C \| TS_3])$

(b) Ticket-Granting Service Exchange to obtain service-granting ticket

(5) C $\rightarrow$ V $Ticket_v \| Authenticator_c$

(6) V $\rightarrow$ C $E(K_{c,v}, [TS_5 + 1])$(for mutual authentication)

$Ticket_v = E(K_v, [K_{c,v} \| ID_C \| AD_C \| ID_v \| TS_4 \| Lifetime_4])$

$Authenticator_c = E(K_{c,v}, [ID_C \| AD_C \| TS_5])$

(c) Client/Server Authentication Exchange to obtain service

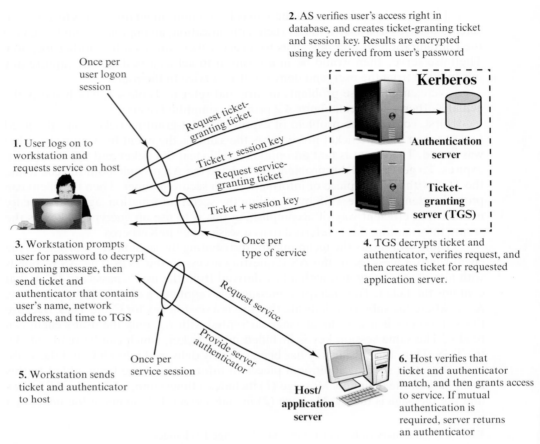

2. AS verifies user's access right in database, and creates ticket-granting ticket and session key. Results are encrypted using key derived from user's password

Once per user logon session

Request ticket-granting ticket

Ticket + session key

Request service-granting ticket

Ticket + session key

1. User logs on to workstation and requests service on host

Kerberos

Authentication server

Ticket-granting server (TGS)

Once per type of service

3. Workstation prompts user for password to decrypt incoming message, then send ticket and authenticator that contains user's name, network address, and time to TGS

4. TGS decrypts ticket and authenticator, verifies request, and then creates ticket for requested application server.

Request service

Provide server authenticator

Once per service session

5. Workstation sends ticket and authenticator to host

Host/ application server

6. Host verifies that ticket and authenticator match, and then grants access to service. If mutual authentication is required, server returns an authenticator

Figure 4.2 Overview of Kerberos

form accessible to C. This enables C to confirm that this ticket is for the TGS and to learn its expiration time.

Armed with the ticket and the session key, C is ready to approach the TGS. As before, C sends the TGS a message that includes the ticket plus the ID of the requested service [message (3) in Table 4.1b]. In addition, C transmits an authenticator, which includes the ID and address of C's user and a timestamp. Unlike the ticket, which is reusable, the authenticator is intended for use only once and has a very short lifetime. The TGS can decrypt the ticket with the key that it shares with the AS. This ticket indicates that user C has been provided with the session key $K_{C,tgs}$. In effect, the ticket says, "Anyone who uses $K_{C,tgs}$ must be C." The TGS uses the session key to decrypt the authenticator. The TGS can then check the name and address from the authenticator with that of the ticket and with the network address of the incoming message. If all match, then the TGS is assured that the sender of the ticket is indeed the ticket's real owner. In effect, the authenticator says, "At time TS_3, I hereby use $K_{C,tgs}$." Note that the ticket does not prove anyone's identity but is a way to distribute keys securely. It is the authenticator that proves the client's identity. Because the

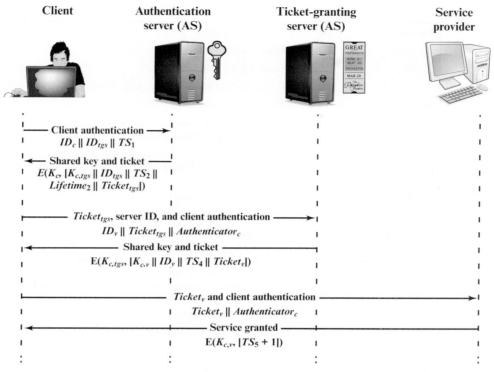

Figure 4.3 Kerberos Exchanges

authenticator can be used only once and has a short lifetime, the threat of an opponent stealing both the ticket and the authenticator for presentation later is countered.

The reply from the TGS in message (4) follows the form of message (2). The message is encrypted with the session key shared by the TGS and C and includes a session key to be shared between C and the server V, the ID of V, and the timestamp of the ticket. The ticket itself includes the same session key.

C now has a reusable service-granting ticket for V. When C presents this ticket, as shown in message (5), it also sends an authenticator. The server can decrypt the ticket, recover the session key, and decrypt the authenticator.

If mutual authentication is required, the server can reply as shown in message (6) of Table 4.1. The server returns the value of the timestamp from the authenticator, incremented by 1, and encrypted in the session key. C can decrypt this message to recover the incremented timestamp. Because the message was encrypted by the session key, C is assured that it could have been created only by V. The contents of the message assure C that this is not a replay of an old reply.

Finally, at the conclusion of this process, the client and server share a secret key. This key can be used to encrypt future messages between the two or to exchange a new random session key for that purpose.

Figure 4.3 illustrates the Kerberos exchanges among the parties. Table 4.2 summarizes the justification for each of the elements in the Kerberos protocol.

Table 4.2 Rationale for the Elements of the Kerberos Version 4 Protocol

Message (1)	Client requests ticket-granting ticket.
ID_C	Tells AS identity of user from this client.
ID_{tgs}	Tells AS that user requests access to TGS.
TS_1	Allows AS to verify that client's clock is synchronized with that of AS.
Message (2)	AS returns ticket-granting ticket.
K_c	Encryption is based on user's password, enabling AS and client to verify password, and protecting contents of message (2).
$K_{c,tgs}$	Copy of session key accessible to client created by AS to permit secure exchange between client and TGS without requiring them to share a permanent key.
ID_{tgs}	Confirms that this ticket is for the TGS.
TS_2	Informs client of time this ticket was issued.
$Lifetime_2$	Informs client of the lifetime of this ticket.
$Ticket_{tgs}$	Ticket to be used by client to access TGS.

(a) Authentication Service Exchange

Message (3)	Client requests service-granting ticket.
ID_V	Tells TGS that user requests access to server V.
$Ticket_{tgs}$	Assures TGS that this user has been authenticated by AS.
$Authenticator_c$	Generated by client to validate ticket.
Message (4)	TGS returns service-granting ticket.
$K_{c,tgs}$	Key shared only by C and TGS protects contents of message (4).
$K_{c,v}$	Copy of session key accessible to client created by TGS to permit secure exchange between client and server without requiring them to share a permanent key.
ID_V	Confirms that this ticket is for server V.
TS_4	Informs client of time this ticket was issued.
$Ticket_V$	Ticket to be used by client to access server V.
$Ticket_{tgs}$	Reusable so that user does not have to reenter password.
K_{tgs}	Ticket is encrypted with key known only to AS and TGS, to prevent tampering.
$K_{c,tgs}$	Copy of session key accessible to TGS used to decrypt authenticator, thereby authenticating ticket.
ID_C	Indicates the rightful owner of this ticket.
AD_C	Prevents use of ticket from workstation other than one that initially requested the ticket.
ID_{tgs}	Assures server that it has decrypted ticket properly.
TS_2	Informs TGS of time this ticket was issued.
$Lifetime_2$	Prevents replay after ticket has expired.
$Authenticator_c$	Assures TGS that the ticket presenter is the same as the client for whom the ticket was issued has very short lifetime to prevent replay.

$K_{c,tgs}$	Authenticator is encrypted with key known only to client and TGS, to prevent tampering.
ID_C	Must match ID in ticket to authenticate ticket.
AD_C	Must match address in ticket to authenticate ticket.
TS_3	Informs TGS of time this authenticator was generated.

(b) Ticket-Granting Service Exchange

Message (5)	Client requests service.
$Ticket_V$	Assures server that this user has been authenticated by AS.
$Authenticator_c$	Generated by client to validate ticket.
Message (6)	Optional authentication of server to client.
$K_{c,v}$	Assures C that this message is from V.
$TS_5 + 1$	Assures C that this is not a replay of an old reply.
$Ticket_v$	Reusable so that client does not need to request a new ticket from TGS for each access to the same server.
K_v	Ticket is encrypted with key known only to TGS and server, to prevent tampering.
$K_{c,v}$	Copy of session key accessible to client; used to decrypt authenticator, thereby authenticating ticket.
ID_C	Indicates the rightful owner of this ticket.
AD_C	Prevents use of ticket from workstation other than one that initially requested the ticket.
ID_V	Assures server that it has decrypted ticket properly.
TS_4	Informs server of time this ticket was issued.
$Lifetime_4$	Prevents replay after ticket has expired.
$Authenticator_c$	Assures server that the ticket presenter is the same as the client for whom the ticket was issued; has very short lifetime to prevent replay.
$K_{c,v}$	Authenticator is encrypted with key known only to client and server, to prevent tampering.
ID_C	Must match ID in ticket to authenticate ticket.
AD_c	Must match address in ticket to authenticate ticket.
TS_5	Informs server of time this authenticator was generated.

(c) Client/Server Authentication Exchange

KERBEROS REALMS AND MULTIPLE KERBERI A full-service Kerberos environment consisting of a Kerberos server, a number of clients, and a number of application servers requires the following:

1. The Kerberos server must have the user ID and hashed passwords of all participating users in its database. All users are registered with the Kerberos server.

2. The Kerberos server must share a secret key with each server. All servers are registered with the Kerberos server.

Such an environment is referred to as a **Kerberos realm**. The concept of **realm** can be explained as follows. A Kerberos realm is a set of managed nodes that share the same Kerberos database. The Kerberos database resides on the Kerberos master computer system, which should be kept in a physically secure room. A read-only copy of the Kerberos database might also reside on other Kerberos computer systems. However, all changes to the database must be made on the master computer system. Changing or accessing the contents of a Kerberos database requires the Kerberos master password. A related concept is that of a **Kerberos principal**, which is a service or user that is known to the Kerberos system. Each Kerberos principal is identified by its principal name. Principal names consist of three parts: a service or user name, an instance name, and a realm name.

Networks of clients and servers under different administrative organizations typically constitute different realms. That is, it generally is not practical or does not conform to administrative policy to have users and servers in one administrative domain registered with a Kerberos server elsewhere. However, users in one realm may need access to servers in other realms, and some servers may be willing to provide service to users from other realms, provided that those users are authenticated.

Kerberos Version 5

Kerberos version 5 is specified in RFC 4120 and provides a number of improvements over version 4 [KOHL94]. To begin, we provide an overview of the changes from version 4 to version 5 and then look at the version 5 protocol.

DIFFERENCES BETWEEN VERSIONS 4 AND 5 Version 5 is intended to address the limitations of version 4 in two areas: environmental shortcomings and technical deficiencies. We briefly summarize the improvements in each area. Kerberos version 4 did not fully address the need to be of general purpose. This led to the following **environmental shortcomings**.

1. **Encryption system dependence:** Version 4 requires the use of DES. Export restriction on DES as well as doubts about the strength of DES were thus of concern. In version 5, ciphertext is tagged with an encryption-type identifier so that any encryption technique may be used. Encryption keys are tagged with a type and a length, allowing the same key to be used in different algorithms and allowing the specification of different variations on a given algorithm.

2. **Internet protocol dependence:** Version 4 requires the use of Internet Protocol (IP) addresses. Other address types, such as the ISO network address, are not accommodated. Version 5 network addresses are tagged with type and length, allowing any network address type to be used.

3. **Message byte ordering:** In version 4, the sender of a message employs a byte ordering of its own choosing and tags the message to indicate least significant byte in lowest address or most significant byte in lowest address. This technique works but does not follow established conventions. In version 5, all message structures are defined using Abstract Syntax Notation One (ASN.1) and Basic Encoding Rules (BER), which provide an unambiguous byte ordering.

4. **Ticket lifetime:** Lifetime values in version 4 are encoded in an 8-bit quantity in units of five minutes. Thus, the maximum lifetime that can be expressed

is $2^8 \times 5 = 1280$ minutes (a little over 21 hours). This may be inadequate for some applications (e.g., a long-running simulation that requires valid Kerberos credentials throughout execution). In version 5, tickets include an explicit start time and end time, allowing tickets with arbitrary lifetimes.

5. **Authentication forwarding:** Version 4 does not allow credentials issued to one client to be forwarded to some other host and used by some other client. This capability would enable a client to access a server and have that server access another server on behalf of the client. For example, a client issues a request to a print server that then accesses the client's file from a file server, using the client's credentials for access. Version 5 provides this capability.

6. **Interrealm authentication:** In version 4, interoperability among N realms requires on the order of N^2 Kerberos-to-Kerberos relationships, as described earlier. Version 5 supports a method that requires fewer relationships, as described shortly.

Apart from these environmental limitations, there are **technical deficiencies** in the version 4 protocol itself. Most of these deficiencies were documented in [BELL90], and version 5 attempts to address these. The deficiencies are the following.

1. **Double encryption:** Note in Table 4.1 [messages (2) and (4)] that tickets provided to clients are encrypted twice—once with the secret key of the target server and then again with a secret key known to the client. The second encryption is not necessary and is computationally wasteful.

2. **PCBC encryption:** Encryption in version 4 makes use of a nonstandard mode of DES known as **propagating cipher block chaining (PCBC)**.[2] It has been demonstrated that this mode is vulnerable to an attack involving the interchange of ciphertext blocks [KOHL89]. PCBC was intended to provide an integrity check as part of the encryption operation. Version 5 provides explicit integrity mechanisms, allowing the standard CBC mode to be used for encryption. In particular, a checksum or hash code is attached to the message prior to encryption using CBC.

3. **Session keys:** Each ticket includes a session key that is used by the client to encrypt the authenticator sent to the service associated with that ticket. In addition, the session key subsequently may be used by the client and the server to protect messages passed during that session. However, because the same ticket may be used repeatedly to gain service from a particular server, there is the risk that an opponent will replay messages from an old session to the client or the server. In version 5, it is possible for a client and server to negotiate a subsession key, which is to be used only for that one connection. A new access by the client would result in the use of a new subsession key.

4. **Password attacks:** Both versions are vulnerable to a password attack. The message from the AS to the client includes material encrypted with a key based on the client's password.[3] An opponent can capture this message and attempt

---

[2]This is described in Appendix F.

[3]Appendix F describes the mapping of passwords to encryption keys.

to decrypt it by trying various passwords. If the result of a test decryption is of the proper form, then the opponent has discovered the client's password and may subsequently use it to gain authentication credentials from Kerberos. This is the same type of password attack described in Chapter 10, with the same kinds of countermeasures being applicable. Version 5 does provide a mechanism known as preauthentication, which should make password attacks more difficult, but it does not prevent them.

THE VERSION 5 AUTHENTICATION DIALOGUE Table 4.3 summarizes the basic version 5 dialogue. This is best explained by comparison with version 4 (Table 4.1).

First, consider the **authentication service exchange**. Message (1) is a client request for a ticket-granting ticket. As before, it includes the ID of the user and the TGS. The following new elements are added:

- **Realm:** Indicates realm of user.
- **Options:** Used to request that certain flags be set in the returned ticket.
- **Times:** Used by the client to request the following time settings in the ticket:

    from: the desired start time for the requested ticket

    till: the requested expiration time for the requested ticket

    rtime: requested renew-till time

- **Nonce:** A random value to be repeated in message (2) to assure that the response is fresh and has not been replayed by an opponent.

Table 4.3 Summary of Kerberos Version 5 Message Exchanges

(1) C → AS	$Options \| ID_c \| Realm_c \| ID_{tgs} \| Times \| Nonce_1$
(2) AS → C	$Realm_c \| ID_C \| Ticket_{tgs} \| E(K_c, [K_{c, tgs} \| Times \| Nonce_1 \| Realm_{tgs} \| ID_{tgs}])$
	$Ticket_{tgs} = E(K_{tgs}, [Flags \| K_{c,tgs} \| Realm_c \| ID_C \| AD_C \| Times])$

(a) Authentication Service Exchange to obtain ticket-granting ticket

(3) C → TGS	$Options \| ID_v \| Times \| \| Nonce_2 \| Ticket_{tgs} \| Authenticator_c$
(4) TGS → C	$Realm_c \| ID_C \| Ticket_v \| E(K_{c,tgs}, [K_{c,v} \| Times \| Nonce_2 \| Realm_v \| ID_v])$
	$Ticket_{tgs} = E(K_{tgs}, [Flags \| K_{c,tgs} \| Realm_c \| ID_C \| AD_C \| Times])$
	$Ticket_v = E(K_v, [Flags \| K_{c,v} \| Realm_c \| ID_C \| AD_C \| Times])$
	$Authenticator_c = E(K_{c, tgs}, [ID_C \| Realm_c \| TS_1])$

(b) Ticket-Granting Service Exchange to obtain service-granting ticket

(5) C → V	$Options \| Ticket_v \| Authenticator_c$
(6) V → C	$E_{K_{c,v}}[TS_2 \| Subkey \| Seq\#]$
	$Ticket_v = E(K_v, [Flags \| K_{c, v} \| Realm_c \| ID_C \| AD_C \| Times])$
	$Authenticator_c = E(K_{c,v}, [ID_C \| Realm_c \| TS_2 \| Subkey \| Seq\#])$

(c) Client/Server Authentication Exchange to obtain service

Message (2) returns a ticket-granting ticket, identifying information for the client, and a block encrypted using the encryption key based on the user's password. This block includes the session key to be used between the client and the TGS, times specified in message (1), the nonce from message (1), and TGS identifying information. The ticket itself includes the session key, identifying information for the client, the requested time values, and flags that reflect the status of this ticket and the requested options. These flags introduce significant new functionality to version 5. For now, we defer a discussion of these flags and concentrate on the overall structure of the version 5 protocol.

Let us now compare the **ticket-granting service exchange** for versions 4 and 5. We see that message (3) for both versions includes an authenticator, a ticket, and the name of the requested service. In addition, version 5 includes requested times and options for the ticket and a nonce—all with functions similar to those of message (1). The authenticator itself is essentially the same as the one used in version 4.

Message (4) has the same structure as message (2). It returns a ticket plus information needed by the client, with the information encrypted using the session key now shared by the client and the TGS.

Finally, for the **client/server authentication exchange**, several new features appear in version 5. In message (5), the client may request as an option that mutual authentication is required. The authenticator includes several new fields:

- **Subkey:** The client's choice for an encryption key to be used to protect this specific application session. If this field is omitted, the session key from the ticket ($K_{C,V}$) is used.
- **Sequence number:** An optional field that specifies the starting sequence number to be used by the server for messages sent to the client during this session. Messages may be sequence numbered to detect replays.

If mutual authentication is required, the server responds with message (6). This message includes the timestamp from the authenticator. Note that in version 4, the timestamp was incremented by one. This is not necessary in version 5, because the nature of the format of messages is such that it is not possible for an opponent to create message (6) without knowledge of the appropriate encryption keys. The subkey field, if present, overrides the subkey field, if present, in message (5). The optional sequence number field specifies the starting sequence number to be used by the client.

4.4 KEY DISTRIBUTION USING ASYMMETRIC ENCRYPTION

One of the major roles of public-key encryption is to address the problem of key distribution. There are actually two distinct aspects to the use of public-key encryption in this regard.

- The distribution of public keys.
- The use of public-key encryption to distribute secret keys.

We examine each of these areas in turn.

Public-Key Certificates

On the face of it, the point of public-key encryption is that the public key is public. Thus, if there is some broadly accepted public-key algorithm, such as RSA, any participant can send his or her public key to any other participant or broadcast the key to the community at large. Although this approach is convenient, it has a major weakness. Anyone can forge such a public announcement. That is, some user could pretend to be user A and send a public key to another participant or broadcast such a public key. Until such time as user A discovers the forgery and alerts other participants, the forger is able to read all encrypted messages intended for A and can use the forged keys for authentication.

The solution to this problem is the **public-key certificate**. In essence, a certificate consists of a public key plus a user ID of the key owner, with the whole block signed by a trusted third party. Typically, the third party is a certificate authority (CA) that is trusted by the user community, such as a government agency or a financial institution. A user can present his or her public key to the authority in a secure manner and obtain a certificate. The user can then publish the certificate. Anyone needing this user's public key can obtain the certificate and verify that it is valid by way of the attached trusted signature. Figure 4.4 illustrates the process.

One scheme has become universally accepted for formatting public-key certificates: the X.509 standard. X.509 certificates are used in most network security applications, including IP security, secure sockets layer (SSL), and S/MIME—all of which are discussed in subsequent chapters. X.509 is examined in detail in the next section.

Public-Key Distribution of Secret Keys

With conventional encryption, a fundamental requirement for two parties to communicate securely is that they share a secret key. Suppose Bob wants to create a messaging application that will enable him to exchange e-mail securely with anyone

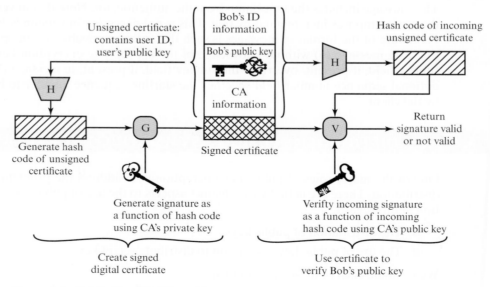

Figure 4.4 Public-Key Certificate Use

who has access to the Internet or to some other network that the two of them share. Suppose Bob wants to do this using conventional encryption. With conventional encryption, Bob and his correspondent, say, Alice, must come up with a way to share a unique secret key that no one else knows. How are they going to do that? If Alice is in the next room from Bob, Bob could generate a key and write it down on a piece of paper or store it on a diskette and hand it to Alice. But if Alice is on the other side of the continent or the world, what can Bob do? He could encrypt this key using conventional encryption and e-mail it to Alice, but this means that Bob and Alice must share a secret key to encrypt this new secret key. Furthermore, Bob and everyone else who uses this new e-mail package faces the same problem with every potential correspondent: Each pair of correspondents must share a unique secret key.

One approach is the use of Diffie–Hellman key exchange. This approach is indeed widely used. However, it suffers the drawback that, in its simplest form, Diffie–Hellman provides no authentication of the two communicating partners.

A powerful alternative is the use of public-key certificates. When Bob wishes to communicate with Alice, Bob can do the following:

1. Prepare a message.
2. Encrypt that message using conventional encryption with a one-time conventional session key.
3. Encrypt the session key using public-key encryption with Alice's public key.
4. Attach the encrypted session key to the message and send it to Alice.

Only Alice is capable of decrypting the session key and therefore of recovering the original message. If Bob obtained Alice's public key by means of Alice's public-key certificate, then Bob is assured that it is a valid key.

4.5 X.509 CERTIFICATES

ITU-T recommendation X.509 is part of the X.500 series of recommendations that define a directory service. The directory is, in effect, a server or distributed set of servers that maintains a database of information about users. The information includes a mapping from user name to network address, as well as other attributes and information about the users.

X.509 defines a framework for the provision of authentication services by the X.500 directory to its users. The directory may serve as a repository of public-key certificates. Each certificate contains the public key of a user and is signed with the private key of a trusted certification authority. In addition, X.509 defines alternative authentication protocols based on the use of public-key certificates.

X.509 is an important standard because the certificate structure and authentication protocols defined in X.509 are used in a variety of contexts. For example, the X.509 certificate format is used in S/MIME (Chapter 8), IP Security (Chapter 9), and SSL/TLS (Chapter 6).

X.509 was initially issued in 1988. The standard was subsequently revised in 1993 to address some of the security concerns documented in [IANS90] and [MITC90]. The standard is currently at version 7, issued in 2012.

X.509 is based on the use of public-key cryptography and digital signatures. The standard does not dictate the use of a specific digital signature algorithm nor a specific hash function. Figure 4.5 illustrates the overall X.509 scheme for generation of a public-key certificate. The certificate for Bob's public key includes unique identifying information for Bob, Bob's public key, and identifying information about the CA, plus other information as explained subsequently. This information is then signed by computing a hash value of the information and generating a digital signature using the hash value and the CA's private key.

Certificates

The heart of the X.509 scheme is the public-key certificate associated with each user. These user certificates are assumed to be created by some trusted certification authority (CA) and placed in the directory by the CA or by the user. The directory server itself is not responsible for the creation of public keys or for the certification function; it merely provides an easily accessible location for users to obtain certificates.

Figure 4.5a shows the general format of a certificate, which includes the following elements.

- **Version:** Differentiates among successive versions of the certificate format; the default is version 1. If the Issuer Unique Identifier or Subject Unique Identifier are present, the value must be version 2. If one or more extensions

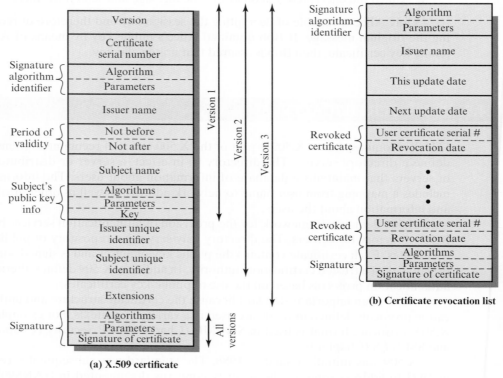

(a) **X.509 certificate**

(b) **Certificate revocation list**

Figure 4.5   X.509 Formats

are present, the version must be version 3. Although the X.509 specification is currently at version 7, no changes have been made to the fields that make up the certificate since version 3.

■ **Serial number:** An integer value, unique within the issuing CA, that is unambiguously associated with this certificate.

■ **Signature algorithm identifier:** The algorithm used to sign the certificate, together with any associated parameters. Because this information is repeated in the Signature field at the end of the certificate, this field has little, if any, utility.

■ **Issuer name:** X.500 name of the CA that created and signed this certificate.

■ **Period of validity:** Consists of two dates: the first and last on which the certificate is valid.

■ **Subject name:** The name of the user to whom this certificate refers. That is, this certificate certifies the public key of the subject who holds the corresponding private key.

■ **Subject's public-key information:** The public key of the subject, plus an identifier of the algorithm for which this key is to be used, together with any associated parameters.

■ **Issuer unique identifier:** An optional bit string field used to identify uniquely the issuing CA in the event the X.500 name has been reused for different entities.

■ **Subject unique identifier:** An optional bit string field used to identify uniquely the subject in the event the X.500 name has been reused for different entities.

■ **Extensions:** A set of one or more extension fields. Extensions were added in version 3 and are discussed later in this section.

■ **Signature:** Covers all of the other fields of the certificate. One component of this field is the digital signature applied to the other fields of the certificate. This field includes the signature algorithm identifier.

The unique identifier fields were added in version 2 to handle the possible reuse of subject and/or issuer names over time. These fields are rarely used.

The standard uses the following notation to define a certificate:

$$CA \ll A \gg \ = CA\{V, SN, AI, CA, UCA, A, UA, Ap, T^A\}$$

where

$Y \ll X \gg =$ the certificate of user X issued by certification authority Y

$Y\{I\} =$ the signing of I by Y; consists of I with an encrypted hash code appended

$V =$ version of the certificate

$SN =$ serial number of the certificate

$AI =$ identifier of the algorithm used to sign the certificate

$CA =$ name of certificate authority

$UCA =$ optional unique identifier of the CA

A = name of user A

UA = optional unique identifier of the user A

Ap = public key of user A

T^A = period of validity of the certificate

The CA signs the certificate with its private key. If the corresponding public key is known to a user, then that user can verify that a certificate signed by the CA is valid. This is the typical digital signature approach, as illustrated in Figure 3.15.

OBTAINING A USER'S CERTIFICATE   User certificates generated by a CA have the following characteristics:

- Any user with access to the public key of the CA can verify the user public key that was certified.

- No party other than the certification authority can modify the certificate without this being detected.

Because certificates are unforgeable, they can be placed in a directory without the need for the directory to make special efforts to protect them.

If all users subscribe to the same CA, then there is a common trust of that CA. All user certificates can be placed in the directory for access by all users. In addition, a user can transmit his or her certificate directly to other users. In either case, once B is in possession of A's certificate, B has confidence that messages it encrypts with A's public key will be secure from eavesdropping and that messages signed with A's private key are unforgeable.

If there is a large community of users, it may not be practical for all users to subscribe to the same CA. Because it is the CA that signs certificates, each participating user must have a copy of the CA's own public key to verify signatures. This public key must be provided to each user in an absolutely secure way (with respect to integrity and authenticity) so that the user has confidence in the associated certificates. Thus, with many users, it may be more practical for there to be a number of CAs, each of which securely provides its public key to some fraction of the users.

Now suppose that A has obtained a certificate from certification authority X_1 and B has obtained a certificate from CA X_2. If A does not securely know the public key of X_2, then B's certificate, issued by X_2, is useless to A. A can read B's certificate, but A cannot verify the signature. However, if the two CAs have securely exchanged their own public keys, the following procedure will enable A to obtain B's public key.

1. A obtains (from the directory) the certificate of X_2 signed by X_1. Because A securely knows X_1's public key, A can obtain X_2's public key from its certificate and verify it by means of X_1's signature on the certificate.

2. A then goes back to the directory and obtains the certificate of B signed by X_2. Because A now has a trusted copy of X_2's public key, A can verify the signature and securely obtain B's public key.

A has used a chain of certificates to obtain B's public key. In the notation of X.509, this chain is expressed as

$$X_1 \ll X_2 \gg X_2 \ll B \gg$$

In the same fashion, B can obtain A's public key with the reverse chain:

$$X_2 \ll X_1 \gg X_1 \ll A \gg$$

This scheme need not be limited to a chain of two certificates. An arbitrarily long path of CAs can be followed to produce a chain. A chain with N elements would be expressed as

$$X_1 \ll X_2 \gg X_2 \ll X_3 \gg \ldots X_N \ll B \gg$$

In this case, each pair of CAs in the chain (X_i, X_{i+1}) must have created certificates for each other.

All of these certificates of CAs by CAs need to appear in the directory, and the user needs to know how they are linked to follow a path to another user's public-key certificate. X.509 suggests that CAs be arranged in a hierarchy so that navigation is straightforward.

Figure 4.6, taken from X.509, is an example of such a hierarchy. The connected circles indicate the hierarchical relationship among the CAs; the associated boxes indicate certificates maintained in the directory for each CA entry. The directory entry for each CA includes two types of certificates:

- **Forward certificates:** Certificates of X generated by other CAs.
- **Reverse certificates:** Certificates generated by X that are the certificates of other CAs.

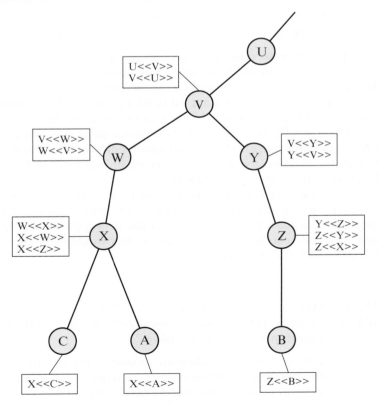

Figure 4.6   X.509 Hierarchy: A Hypothetical Example

In this example, user A can acquire the following certificates from the directory to establish a certification path to B:

$$X \ll W \gg W \ll V \gg V \ll Y \gg Y \ll Z \gg Z \ll B \gg$$

When A has obtained these certificates, it can unwrap the certification path in sequence to recover a trusted copy of B's public key. Using this public key, A can send encrypted messages to B. If A wishes to receive encrypted messages back from B or to sign messages sent to B, then B will require A's public key, which can be obtained from the certification path:

$$Z \ll Y \gg Y \ll V \gg V \ll W \gg W \ll X \gg X \ll A \gg$$

B can obtain this set of certificates from the directory or A can provide them as part of its initial message to B.

REVOCATION OF CERTIFICATES Recall from Figure 4.5 that each certificate includes a period of validity, much like a credit card. Typically, a new certificate is issued just before the expiration of the old one. In addition, it may be desirable on occasion to revoke a certificate before it expires for one of the following reasons.

1. The user's private key is assumed to be compromised.
2. The user is no longer certified by this CA. Reasons for this include subject's name has changed, the certificate is superseded, or the certificate was not issued in conformance with the CA's policies.
3. The CA's certificate is assumed to be compromised.

Each CA must maintain a list consisting of all revoked but not expired certificates issued by that CA, including both those issued to users and to other CAs. These lists also should be posted on the directory.

Each certificate revocation list (CRL) posted to the directory is signed by the issuer and includes (Figure 4.5b) the issuer's name, the date the list was created, the date the next CRL is scheduled to be issued, and an entry for each revoked certificate. Each entry consists of the serial number of a certificate and revocation date for that certificate. Because serial numbers are unique within a CA, the serial number is sufficient to identify the certificate.

When a user receives a certificate in a message, the user must determine whether the certificate has been revoked. The user could check the directory each time a certificate is received. To avoid the delays (and possible costs) associated with directory searches, it is likely that the user would maintain a local cache of certificates and lists of revoked certificates.

X.509 Version 3

The X.509 version 2 format does not convey all of the information that recent design and implementation experience has shown to be needed. [FORD95] lists the following requirements not satisfied by version 2:

1. The Subject field is inadequate to convey the identity of a-key owner to a public-key user. X.509 names may be relatively short and lacking in obvious identification details that may be needed by the user.

2. The Subject field is also inadequate for many applications, which typically recognize entities by an Internet e-mail address, a URL, or some other Internet-related identification.

3. There is a need to indicate security policy information. This enables a security application or function, such as IPSec, to relate an X.509 certificate to a given policy.

4. There is a need to limit the damage that can result from a faulty or malicious CA by setting constraints on the applicability of a particular certificate.

5. It is important to be able to identify different keys used by the same owner at different times. This feature supports key life cycle management, in particular the ability to update key pairs for users and CAs on a regular basis or under exceptional circumstances.

Rather than continue to add fields to a fixed format, standards developers felt that a more flexible approach was needed. Thus, version 3 includes a number of optional extensions that may be added to the version 2 format. Each extension consists of an extension identifier, a criticality indicator, and an extension value. The criticality indicator indicates whether an extension can be safely ignored. If the indicator has a value of TRUE and an implementation does not recognize the extension, it must treat the certificate as invalid.

The certificate extensions fall into three main categories: key and policy information, subject and issuer attributes, and certification path constraints.

KEY AND POLICY INFORMATION These extensions convey additional information about the subject and issuer keys, plus indicators of certificate policy. A certificate policy is a named set of rules that indicates the applicability of a certificate to a particular community and/or class of application with common security requirements. For example, a policy might be applicable to the authentication of electronic data interchange (EDI) transactions for the trading of goods within a given price range.

This area includes the following:

■ **Authority key identifier:** Identifies the public key to be used to verify the signature on this certificate or CRL. Enables distinct keys of the same CA to be differentiated. One use of this field is to handle CA key pair updating.

■ **Subject key identifier:** Identifies the public key being certified. Useful for subject key pair updating. Also, a subject may have multiple key pairs and, correspondingly, different certificates for different purposes (e.g., digital signature and encryption key agreement).

■ **Key usage:** Indicates a restriction imposed as to the purposes for which, and the policies under which, the certified public key may be used. May indicate one or more of the following: digital signature, nonrepudiation, key encryption, data encryption, key agreement, CA signature verification on certificates, and CA signature verification on CRLs.

■ **Private-key usage period:** Indicates the period of use of the private key corresponding to the public key. Typically, the private key is used over a different period from the validity of the public key. For example, with digital signature keys, the usage period for the signing private key is typically shorter than that for the verifying public key.

- **Certificate policies:** Certificates may be used in environments where multiple policies apply. This extension lists policies that the certificate is recognized as supporting, together with optional qualifier information.
- **Policy mappings:** Used only in certificates for CAs issued by other CAs. Policy mappings allow an issuing CA to indicate that one or more of that issuer's policies can be considered equivalent to another policy used in the subject CA's domain.

CERTIFICATE SUBJECT AND ISSUER ATTRIBUTES These extensions support alternative names, in alternative formats, for a certificate subject or certificate issuer and can convey additional information about the certificate subject to increase a certificate user's confidence that the certificate subject is a particular person or entity. For example, information such as postal address, position within a corporation, or picture image may be required.

The extension fields in this area include the following:

- **Subject alternative name:** Contains one or more alternative names, using any of a variety of forms. This field is important for supporting certain applications, such as electronic mail, EDI, and IPSec, which may employ their own name forms.
- **Issuer alternative name:** Contains one or more alternative names, using any of a variety of forms.
- **Subject directory attributes:** Conveys any desired X.500 directory attribute values for the subject of this certificate.

CERTIFICATION PATH CONSTRAINTS These extensions allow constraint specifications to be included in certificates issued for CAs by other CAs. The constraints may restrict the types of certificates that can be issued by the subject CA or that may occur subsequently in a certification chain.

The extension fields in this area include the following:

- **Basic constraints:** Indicates if the subject may act as a CA. If so, a certification path length constraint may be specified.
- **Name constraints:** Indicates a name space within which all subject names in subsequent certificates in a certification path must be located.
- **Policy constraints:** Specifies constraints that may require explicit certificate policy identification or inhibit policy mapping for the remainder of the certification path.

4.6 PUBLIC-KEY INFRASTRUCTURE

RFC 4949 (*Internet Security Glossary*) defines public-key infrastructure (PKI) as the set of hardware, software, people, policies, and procedures needed to create, manage, store, distribute, and revoke digital certificates based on asymmetric cryptography. The principal objective for developing a PKI is to enable secure, convenient, and efficient acquisition of public keys. The Internet Engineering Task Force (IETF) Public Key Infrastructure X.509 (PKIX) working group has been the driving force behind setting up a formal (and generic) model based on X.509 that is suitable for deploying a certificate-based architecture on the Internet. This section describes the PKIX model.

Figure 4.7 shows the interrelationship among the key elements of the PKIX model. These elements are

- **End entity:** A generic term used to denote end users, devices (e.g., servers, routers), or any other entity that can be identified in the subject field of a public key certificate. End entities typically consume and/or support PKI-related services.

- **Certification authority (CA):** The issuer of certificates and (usually) certificate revocation lists (CRLs). It may also support a variety of administrative functions, although these are often delegated to one or more registration authorities.

- **Registration authority (RA):** An optional component that can assume a number of administrative functions from the CA. The RA is often associated

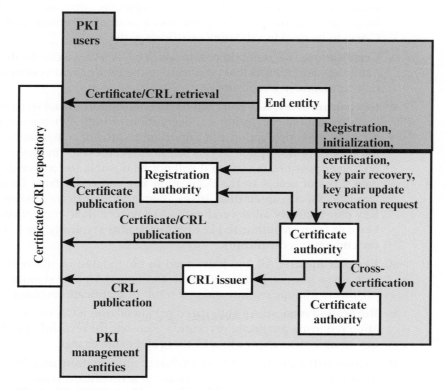

Figure 4.7 PKIX Architectural Model

with the end entity registration process, but can assist in a number of other areas as well.

- **CRL issuer:** An optional component that a CA can delegate to publish CRLs.
- **Repository:** A generic term used to denote any method for storing certificates and CRLs so that they can be retrieved by end entities.

PKIX Management Functions

PKIX identifies a number of management functions that potentially need to be supported by management protocols. These are indicated in Figure 4.7 and include the following:

- **Registration:** This is the process whereby a user first makes itself known to a CA (directly, or through an RA), prior to that CA issuing a certificate or certificates for that user. Registration begins the process of enrolling in a PKI. Registration usually involves some off-line or online procedure for mutual authentication. Typically, the end entity is issued one or more shared secret keys used for subsequent authentication.
- **Initialization:** Before a client system can operate securely, it is necessary to install key materials that have the appropriate relationship with keys stored elsewhere in the infrastructure. For example, the client needs to be securely initialized with the public key and other assured information of the trusted CA(s) to be used in validating certificate paths.
- **Certification:** This is the process in which a CA issues a certificate for a user's public key and returns that certificate to the user's client system and/or posts that certificate in a repository.
- **Key pair recovery:** Key pairs can be used to support digital signature creation and verification, encryption and decryption, or both. When a key pair is used for encryption/decryption, it is important to provide a mechanism to recover the necessary decryption keys when normal access to the keying material is no longer possible, otherwise it will not be possible to recover the encrypted data. Loss of access to the decryption key can result from forgotten passwords/PINs, corrupted disk drives, damage to hardware tokens, and so on. Key pair recovery allows end entities to restore their encryption/decryption key pair from an authorized key backup facility (typically, the CA that issued the end entity's certificate).
- **Key pair update:** All key pairs need to be updated regularly (i.e., replaced with a new key pair) and new certificates issued. Update is required when the certificate lifetime expires and as a result of certificate revocation.
- **Revocation request:** An authorized person advises a CA of an abnormal situation requiring certificate revocation. Reasons for revocation include private key compromise, change in affiliation, and name change.
- **Cross-certification:** Two CAs exchange information used in establishing a cross-certificate. A cross-certificate is a certificate issued by one CA to another CA that contains a CA signature key used for issuing certificates.

PKIX Management Protocols

The PKIX working group has defined two alternative management protocols between PKIX entities that support the management functions listed in the preceding subsection. RFC 2510 defines the certificate management protocols (CMP). Within CMP, each of the management functions is explicitly identified by specific protocol exchanges. CMP is designed to be a flexible protocol able to accommodate a variety of technical, operational, and business models.

RFC 2797 defines certificate management messages over CMS (CMC), where CMS refers to RFC 2630, cryptographic message syntax. CMC is built on earlier work and is intended to leverage existing implementations. Although all of the PKIX functions are supported, the functions do not all map into specific protocol exchanges.

4.7 FEDERATED IDENTITY MANAGEMENT

Federated identity management is a relatively new concept dealing with the use of a common identity management scheme across multiple enterprises and numerous applications and supporting many thousands, even millions, of users. We begin our overview with a discussion of the concept of identity management and then examine federated identity management.

Identity Management

Identity management is a centralized, automated approach to provide enterprise-wide access to resources by employees and other authorized individuals. The focus of identity management is defining an identity for each user (human or process), associating attributes with the identity, and enforcing a means by which a user can verify identity. The central concept of an identity management system is the use of single sign-on (SSO). SSO enables a user to access all network resources after a single authentication.

Typical services provided by a federated identity management system include the following:

- **Point of contact:** Includes authentication that a user corresponds to the user name provided, and management of user/server sessions.
- **SSO protocol services:** Provides a vendor-neutral security token service for supporting a single sign on to federated services.
- **Trust services:** Federation relationships require a trust relationship-based federation between business partners. A trust relationship is represented by the combination of the security tokens used to exchange information about a user, the cryptographic information used to protect these security tokens, and optionally the identity mapping rules applied to the information contained within this token.
- **Key services:** Management of keys and certificates.
- **Identity services:** Services that provide the interface to local data stores, including user registries and databases, for identity-related information management.

■ **Authorization:** Granting access to specific services and/or resources based on the authentication.

■ **Provisioning:** Includes creating an account in each target system for the user, enrollment or registration of user in accounts, establishment of access rights or credentials to ensure the privacy and integrity of account data.

■ **Management:** Services related to runtime configuration and deployment.

Note that Kerberos contains a number of elements of an identity management system.

Figure 4.8 [LINN06] illustrates entities and data flows in a generic identity management architecture. A **principal** is an identity holder. Typically, this is a human user that seeks access to resources and services on the network. User devices, agent processes, and server systems may also function as principals. Principals authenticate themselves to an **identity provider**. The identity provider associates authentication information with a principal, as well as attributes and one or more identifiers.

Increasingly, digital identities incorporate attributes other than simply an identifier and authentication information (such as passwords and biometric information). An **attribute service** manages the creation and maintenance of such attributes. For example, a user needs to provide a shipping address each time an order is placed at a new Web merchant, and this information needs to be revised when the user moves. Identity management enables the user to provide this information once, so that it is maintained in a single place and released to data consumers in accordance with authorization and privacy policies. Users may create some of the attributes to be associated with their digital identity, such as address. **Administrators** may also assign attributes to users, such as roles, access permissions, and employee information.

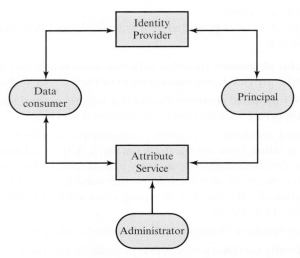

Figure 4.8   Generic Identity Management Architecture

Data consumers are entities that obtain and employ data maintained and provided by identity and attribute providers, which are often used to support authorization decisions and to collect audit information. For example, a database server or file server is a data consumer that needs a client's credentials so as to know what access to provide to that client.

Identity Federation

Identity federation is, in essence, an extension of identity management to multiple security domains. Such domains include autonomous internal business units, external business partners, and other third-party applications and services. The goal is to provide the sharing of digital identities so that a user can be authenticated a single time and then access applications and resources across multiple domains. Because these domains are relatively autonomous or independent, no centralized control is possible. Rather, the cooperating organizations must form a federation based on agreed standards and mutual levels of trust to securely share digital identities.

Federated identity management refers to the agreements, standards, and technologies that enable the portability of identities, identity attributes, and entitlements across multiple enterprises and numerous applications and supports many thousands, even millions, of users. When multiple organizations implement interoperable federated identity schemes, an employee in one organization can use a single sign-on to access services across the federation with trust relationships associated with the identity. For example, an employee may log onto her corporate intranet and be authenticated to perform authorized functions and access authorized services on that intranet. The employee could then access her health benefits from an outside health-care provider without having to reauthenticate.

Beyond SSO, federated identity management provides other capabilities. One is a standardized means of representing attributes. Increasingly, digital identities incorporate attributes other than simply an identifier and authentication information (such as passwords and biometric information). Examples of attributes include account numbers, organizational roles, physical location, and file ownership. A user may have multiple identifiers; for example, each identifier may be associated with a unique role with its own access permissions.

Another key function of federated identity management is identity mapping. Different security domains may represent identities and attributes differently. Furthermore, the amount of information associated with an individual in one domain may be more than is necessary in another domain. The federated identity management protocols map identities and attributes of a user in one domain to the requirements of another domain.

Figure 4.9 illustrates entities and data flows in a generic federated identity management architecture.

The identity provider acquires attribute information through dialogue and protocol exchanges with users and administrators. For example, a user needs to provide a shipping address each time an order is placed at a new Web merchant, and this information needs to be revised when the user moves. Identity management enables the user to provide this information once, so that it is maintained in a

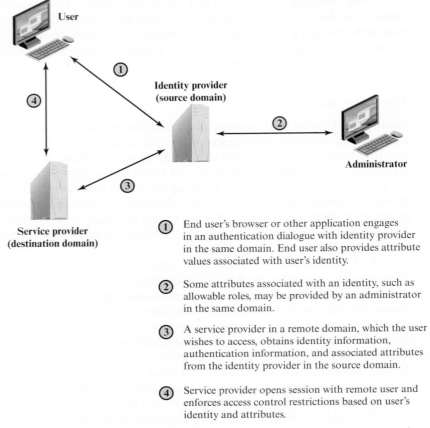

Figure 4.9 Federated Identity Operation

single place and released to data consumers in accordance with authorization and privacy policies.

Service providers are entities that obtain and employ data maintained and provided by identity providers, often to support authorization decisions and to collect audit information. For example, a database server or file server is a data consumer that needs a client's credentials so as to know what access to provide to that client. A service provider can be in the same domain as the user and the identity provider. The power of this approach is for federated identity management, in which the service provider is in a different domain (e.g., a vendor or supplier network).

STANDARDS Federated identity management uses a number of standards as the building blocks for secure identity exchange across different domains or heterogeneous systems. In essence, organizations issue some form of security tickets for their users that can be processed by cooperating partners. Identity federation standards are thus concerned with defining these tickets in terms of content and format, providing protocols for exchanging tickets, and performing a number of management tasks. These tasks include configuring systems to perform attribute transfers and identity mapping, and performing logging and auditing functions. The key standards are as follows:

- **The Extensible Markup Language (XML):** A markup language uses sets of embedded tags or labels to characterize text elements within a document so as to indicate their appearance, function, meaning, or context. XML documents appear similar to HTML (Hypertext Markup Language) documents that are visible as Web pages, but provide greater functionality. XML includes strict definitions of the data type of each field, thus supporting database formats and semantics. XML provides encoding rules for commands that are used to transfer and update data objects.

- **The Simple Object Access Protocol (SOAP):** A minimal set of conventions for invoking code using XML over HTTP. It enables applications to request services from one another with XML-based requests and receive responses as data formatted with XML. Thus, XML defines data objects and structures, and SOAP provides a means of exchanging such data objects and performing remote procedure calls related to these objects. See [ROS06] for an informative discussion.

- **WS-Security:** A set of SOAP extensions for implementing message integrity and confidentiality in Web services. To provide for secure exchange of SOAP messages among applications, WS-Security assigns security tokens to each message for use in authentication.

- **Security Assertion Markup Language (SAML):** An XML-based language for the exchange of security information between online business partners. SAML conveys authentication information in the form of assertions about subjects. Assertions are statements about the subject issued by an authoritative entity.

The challenge with federated identity management is to integrate multiple technologies, standards, and services to provide a secure, user-friendly utility. The key, as in most areas of security and networking, is the reliance on a few mature standards widely accepted by industry. Federated identity management seems to have reached this level of maturity.

EXAMPLES To get some feel for the functionality of identity federation, we look at three scenarios, taken from [COMP06]. In the first scenario (Figure 4.10a), Workplace.com contracts with Health.com to provide employee health benefits. An employee uses a Web interface to sign on to Workplace.com and goes through an authentication procedure there. This enables the employee to access authorized services and resources at Workplace.com. When the employee clicks on a link to access health benefits, her browser is redirected to Health.com. At the same time, the Workplace.com software passes the user's identifier to Health.com in a secure manner. The two organizations are part of a federation that cooperatively exchanges user identifiers. Health.com maintains user identities for every employee at Workplace.com and associates with each identity health-benefits information

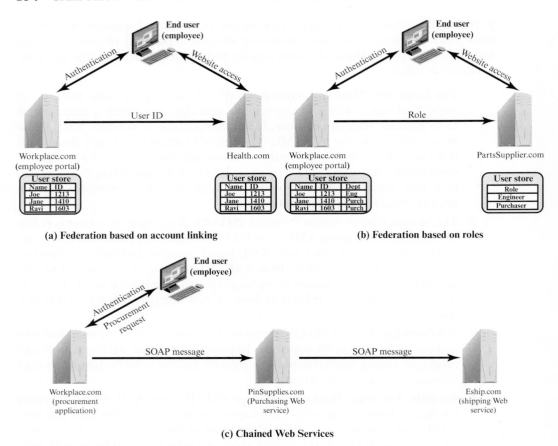

Figure 4.10   Federated Identity Scenarios

and access rights. In this example, the linkage between the two companies is based on account information and user participation is browser based.

Figure 4.10b shows a second type of browser-based scheme. PartsSupplier.com is a regular supplier of parts to Workplace.com. In this case, a role-based access control (RBAC) scheme is used for access to information. An engineer of Workplace.com authenticates at the employee portal at Workplace.com and clicks on a link to access information at PartsSupplier.com. Because the user is authenticated in the role of an engineer, he is taken to the technical documentation and troubleshooting portion of PartsSupplier.com's Web site without having to sign on. Similarly, an employee in a purchasing role signs on at Workplace.com and is authorized, in that role, to place purchases at PartsSupplier.com without having to authenticate to PartsSupplier.com. For this scenario, PartsSupplier.com does not have identity information for individual employees at Workplace.com. Rather, the linkage between the two federated partners is in terms of roles.

The scenario illustrated in Figure 4.10c can be referred to as document based rather than browser based. In this third example, Workplace.com has a purchasing agreement with PinSupplies.com, and PinSupplies.com has a business relationship with E-Ship.com. An employee of Workplace.com signs on and is authenticated to make purchases. The employee goes to a procurement application that provides a list of Workplace.com's suppliers and the parts that can be ordered. The user clicks on the PinSupplies button and is presented with a purchase order Web page (HTML page). The employee fills out the form and clicks the submit button. The procurement application generates an XML/SOAP document that it inserts into the envelope body of an XML-based message. The procurement application then inserts the user's credentials in the envelope header of the message, together with Workplace.com's organizational identity. The procurement application posts the message to the PinSupplies.com's purchasing Web service. This service authenticates the incoming message and processes the request. The purchasing Web service then sends a SOAP message its shipping partner to fulfill the order. The message includes a PinSupplies.com security token in the envelope header and the list of items to be shipped as well as the end user's shipping information in the envelope body. The shipping Web service authenticates the request and processes the shipment order.

4.8 KEY TERMS, REVIEW QUESTIONS, AND PROBLEMS

Key Terms

authentication	key distribution center (KDC)	public-key certificate
authentication server (AS)	key management	public-key directory
federated identity management	master key	realm
identity management	mutual authentication	replay attack
Kerberos	nonce	ticket
Kerberos realm	one-way authentication	ticket-granting server (TGS)
key distribution	propagating cipher block chaining (PCBC) mode	timestamp
		X.509 certificate

Review Questions

4.1 Explain the operation of a key distribution center.

4.2 What are the advantages of the automated key distribution approach?

4.3 What is Kerberos?

4.4 Identify the security threats that exist in an open distributed network.

4.5 In the context of Kerberos, what is a realm?

4.6 What are the ingredients of a authentication server's ticket? Explain the significance of each.

4.7 List the environmental shortcomings and technical deficiencies of Kerberos version 4.

4.8 Identify the weakness of a public key distribution with a public key algorithm. How can it be fixed?

4.9 What is a X.509 certificate?

4.10 Explain the different fields of the public-key certificate of the X.509 scheme.

    4.11   What is public-key infrastructure?

    4.12   What are the key elements of the PKIX model?

    4.13   Name the PKIX certificate management protocols.

    4.14   What is federated identity management?

Problems

4.1   "We are under great pressure, Holmes." Detective Lestrade looked nervous. "We have learned that copies of sensitive government documents are stored in computers of one foreign embassy here in London. Normally these documents exist in electronic form only on a selected few government computers that satisfy the most stringent security requirements. However, sometimes they must be sent through the network connecting all government computers. But all messages in this network are encrypted using a top secret encryption algorithm certified by our best crypto experts. Even the NSA and the KGB are unable to break it. And now these documents have appeared in hands of diplomats of a small, otherwise insignificant, country. And we have no idea how it could happen."

"But you do have some suspicion who did it, do you?" asked Holmes.

"Yes, we did some routine investigation. There is a man who has legal access to one of the government computers and has frequent contacts with diplomats from the embassy. But the computer he has access to is not one of the trusted ones where these documents are normally stored. He is the suspect, but we have no idea how he could obtain copies of the documents. Even if he could obtain a copy of an encrypted document, he couldn't decrypt it."

"Hmm, please describe the communication protocol used on the network." Holmes opened his eyes, thus proving that he had followed Lestrade's talk with an attention that contrasted with his sleepy look.

"Well, the protocol is as follows. Each node N of the network has been assigned a unique secret key K_n. This key is used to secure communication between the node and a trusted server. That is, all the keys are stored also on the server. User A, wishing to send a secret message M to user B, initiates the following protocol:

1. A generates a random number R and sends to the server his name A, destination B, and $E(K_a, R)$.
2. Server responds by sending $E(K_b, R)$ to A.
3. A sends $E(R, M)$ together with $E(K_b, R)$ to B.
4. B knows K_b, thus decrypts $E(K_b, R)$ to get R and will subsequently use R to decrypt $E(R, M)$ to get M.

You see that a random key is generated every time a message has to be sent. I admit the man could intercept messages sent between the top secret trusted nodes, but I see no way he could decrypt them."

"Well, I think you have your man, Lestrade. The protocol isn't secure because the server doesn't authenticate users who send him a request. Apparently designers of the protocol have believed that sending $E(K_x, R)$ implicitly authenticates user X as the sender, as only X (and the server) knows K_x. But you know that $E(K_x, R)$ can be intercepted and later replayed. Once you understand where the hole is, you will be able to obtain enough evidence by monitoring the man's use of the computer he has access to. Most likely he works as follows: After intercepting $E(K_a, R)$ and $E(R, M)$ (see steps 1 and 3 of the protocol), the man, let's denote him as Z, will continue by pretending to be A and . . .

Finish the sentence for Holmes.

4.2   There are three typical ways to use nonces as challenges. Suppose N_a is a nonce generated by A, A and B share key K, and f() is a function (such as increment). The three usages are

Usage 1	Usage 2	Usage 3
(1) A → B: N_a	(1) A → B: $E(K, N_a)$	(1) A → B: $E(K, N_a)$
(2) B → A: $E(K, N_a)$	(2) B → A: N_a	(2) B → A: $E(K, f(N_a))$

Describe situations for which each usage is appropriate.

4.3   Show that a random error in one block of ciphertext is propagated to all subsequent blocks of plaintext in PCBC mode (see Figure F.2 in Appendix F).

4.4   Suppose that, in PCBC mode, blocks C_i and C_{i+1} are interchanged during transmission. Show that this affects only the decrypted blocks P_i and P_{i+1} but not subsequent blocks.

4.5   In addition to providing a standard for public-key certificate formats, X.509 specifies an authentication protocol. The original version of X.509 contains a security flaw. The essence of the protocol is

$$A \rightarrow B: \quad A\,\{t_A, r_A, ID_B\}$$
$$B \rightarrow A: \quad B\,\{t_B, r_B, ID_A, r_A\}$$
$$A \rightarrow B: \quad A\,\{r_B\}$$

where t_A and t_B are timestamps, r_A and r_B are nonces, and the notation X {Y} indicates that the message Y is transmitted, encrypted, and signed by X.

The text of X.509 states that checking timestamps t_A and t_B is optional for three-way authentication. But consider the following example: Suppose A and B have used the preceding protocol on some previous occasion, and that opponent C has intercepted the preceding three messages. In addition, suppose that timestamps are not used and are all set to 0. Finally, suppose C wishes to impersonate A to B. C initially sends the first captured message to B:

$$C \rightarrow B: \quad A\,\{0, r_A, ID_B\}$$

B responds, thinking it is talking to A but is actually talking to C:

$$B \rightarrow C: \quad B\,\{0, r'_B, ID_A, r_A\}$$

C meanwhile causes A to initiate authentication with C by some means. As a result, A sends C the following:

$$A \rightarrow C: \quad A\,\{0, r'_A, ID_C\}$$

C responds to A using the same nonce provided to C by B.

$$C \rightarrow A: \quad C\,\{0, r'_B, ID_A, r'_A\}$$

A responds with

$$A \rightarrow C: \quad A\,\{r'_B\}$$

This is exactly what C needs to convince B that it is talking to A, so C now repeats the incoming message back out to B.

$$C \rightarrow B: \quad A\,\{r'_B\}$$

So B will believe it is talking to A, whereas it is actually talking to C. Suggest a simple solution to this problem that does not involve the use of timestamps.

4.6   Consider a one-way authentication technique based on asymmetric encryption:

$$A \rightarrow B: \quad ID_A$$
$$B \rightarrow A: \quad R_1$$
$$A \rightarrow B: \quad E(PR_a, R_1)$$

   a. Explain the protocol.
   b. What type of attack is this protocol susceptible to?

4.7   Consider a one-way authentication technique based on asymmetric encryption:

$$A \rightarrow B: \quad ID_A$$
$$B \rightarrow A: \quad E(PU_a, R_2)$$
$$A \rightarrow B: \quad R_2$$

   a. Explain the protocol.
   b. What type of attack is this protocol susceptible to?

4.8   In Kerberos, how do servers verify the authenticity of the client using the ticket?

4.9   In Kerberos, how does an authentication server protect a ticket from being altered by the client or opponent?

4.10   How is ticket reuse by an opponent prevented in Kerberos?

4.11   What is the purpose of a session key in Kerberos? How is it distributed by the AS?

4.12   The 1988 version of X.509 lists properties that RSA keys must satisfy to be secure, given current knowledge about the difficulty of factoring large numbers. The discussion concludes with a constraint on the public exponent and the modulus n:

   It must be ensured that $e > \log_2(n)$ to prevent attack by taking the eth root mod n to disclose the plaintext.

   Although the constraint is correct, the reason given for requiring it is incorrect. What is wrong with the reason given and what is the correct reason?

4.13   Find at least one intermediate certification authority's certificate and one trusted root certification authority's certificate on your computer (e.g., in the browser). Print screenshots of both the general and details tab for each certificate.

4.14   NIST defines the term "cryptoperiod" as the time span during which a specific key is authorized for use or in which the keys for a given system or application may remain in effect. One document on key management uses the following time diagram for a shared secret key.

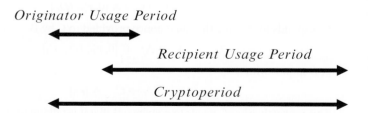

Explain the overlap by giving an example application in which the originator's usage period for the shared secret key begins before the recipient's usage period and also ends before the recipient's usage period.

4.15 Consider the following protocol, designed to let A and B decide on a fresh, shared session key K'_{AB}. We assume that they already share a long-term key K_{AB}.
1. $A \rightarrow B$: A, N_A
2. $B \rightarrow A$: $E(K_{AB}, [N_A, K'_{AB}])$
3. $A \rightarrow B$: $E(K'_{AB}, N_A)$
   a. We first try to understand the protocol designer's reasoning:
      ■ Why would A and B believe after the protocol ran that they share K'_{AB} with the other party?
      ■ Why would they believe that this shared key is fresh?
   In both cases, you should explain both the reasons of both A and B, so your answer should complete the following sentences.
      A believes that she shares K'_{AB} with B since . . .
      B believes that he shares K'_{AB} with A since . . .
      A believes that K'_{AB} is fresh since . . .
      B believes that K'_{AB} is fresh since . . .
   b. Assume now that A starts a run of this protocol with B. However, the connection is intercepted by the adversary C. Show how C can start a new run of the protocol using reflection, causing A to believe that she has agreed on a fresh key with B (in spite of the fact that she has only been communicating with C). Thus, in particular, the belief in (a) is false.
   c. Propose a modification of the protocol that prevents this attack.

4.16 List the different management functions of the PKIX model.

4.17 Explain the entities and data flows of generic identity management architecture.

4.18 Consider the following protocol:

$$A \rightarrow KDC: \quad ID_A \| ID_B \| N_1$$
$$KDC \rightarrow A: \quad E(K_a, [K_S \| ID_B \| N_1 \| E(K_b, [K_S \| ID_A])])$$
$$A \rightarrow B: \quad E(K_b, [K_S \| ID_A])$$
$$B \rightarrow A: \quad E(K_S, N_2) \quad A \rightarrow B: \quad E(K_S, f(N_2))$$

a. Explain the protocol.
b. Can you think of a possible attack on this protocol? Explain how it can be done.
c. Mention a possible technique to get around the attack — not a detailed mechanism, just the basics of the idea.

Note: The remaining problems deal with a cryptographic product developed by IBM, which is briefly described in a document at this book's Web site in IBMCrypto.pdf. *Try these problems after reviewing the document.*

4.19 What is the effect of adding the instruction EMK_i?

$$EMK_i: X \rightarrow E(KMH_i, X) \quad i = 0, 1$$

4.20 Suppose N different systems use the IBM Cryptographic Subsystem with host master keys $KMH[i](i = 1, 2, \ldots, N)$. Devise a method for communicating between systems without requiring the system to either share a common host master key or to divulge their individual host master keys. *Hint*: Each system needs three variants of its host master key.

4.21 The principal objective of the IBM Cryptographic Subsystem is to protect transmissions between a terminal and the processing system. Devise a procedure, perhaps adding instructions, which will allow the processor to generate a session key KS and distribute it to Terminal i and Terminal j without having to store a key-equivalent variable in the host.

CHAPTER 5

NETWORK ACCESS CONTROL AND CLOUD SECURITY

LEARNING OBJECTIVES

After studying this chapter, you should be able to:

◆ Discuss the principal elements of a network access control system.

◆ Discuss the principal network access enforcement methods.

◆ Present an overview of the Extensible Authentication Protocol.

◆ Understand the operation and role of the IEEE 802.1X Port-Based Network Access Control mechanism.

◆ Present an overview of cloud computing concepts.

◆ Understand the unique security issues related to cloud computing.

This chapter begins our discussion of network security, focusing on two key topics: network access control and cloud security. We begin with an overview of network access control systems, summarizing the principal elements and techniques involved in such a system. Next, we discuss the Extensible Authentication Protocol and IEEE 802.1X, two widely implemented standards that are the foundation of many network access control systems.

The remainder of the chapter deals with cloud security. We begin with an overview of cloud computing, and follow this with a discussion of cloud security issues.

5.1 NETWORK ACCESS CONTROL

Network access control (NAC) is an umbrella term for managing access to a network. NAC authenticates users logging into the network and determines what data they can access and actions they can perform. NAC also examines the health of the user's computer or mobile device (the endpoints).

Elements of a Network Access Control System

NAC systems deal with three categories of components:

■ **Access requestor (AR):** The AR is the node that is attempting to access the network and may be any device that is managed by the NAC system, including workstations, servers, printers, cameras, and other IP-enabled devices. ARs are also referred to as **supplicants**, or simply, clients.

■ **Policy server:** Based on the AR's posture and an enterprise's defined policy, the policy server determines what access should be granted. The policy server often relies on backend systems, including antivirus, patch management, or a user directory, to help determine the host's condition.

■ **Network access server (NAS):** The NAS functions as an access control point for users in remote locations connecting to an enterprise's internal network. Also called a **media gateway**, a **remote access server (RAS)**, or a **policy server**, an NAS may include its own authentication services or rely on a separate authentication service from the policy server.

Figure 5.1 is a generic network access diagram. A variety of different ARs seek access to an enterprise network by applying to some type of NAS. The first step is generally to authenticate the AR. Authentication typically involves some sort of secure protocol and the use of cryptographic keys. Authentication may be performed by the NAS, or the NAS may mediate the authentication process. In the latter case, authentication takes place between the supplicant and an authentication server that is part of the policy server or that is accessed by the policy server.

The authentication process serves a number of purposes. It verifies a supplicant's claimed identity, which enables the policy server to determine what access privileges, if any, the AR may have. The authentication exchange may result in the

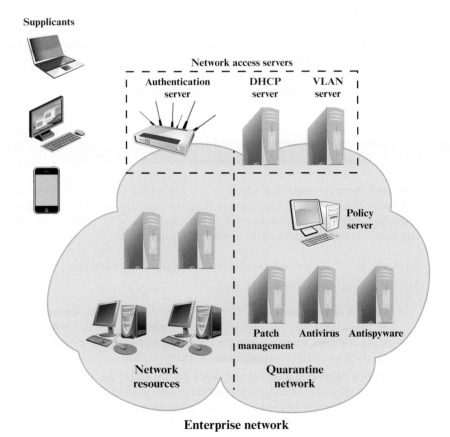

Figure 5.1   Network Access Control Context

establishment of session keys to enable future secure communication between the supplicant and resources on the enterprise network.

Typically, the policy server or a supporting server will perform checks on the AR to determine if it should be permitted interactive remote access connectivity. These checks—sometimes called health, suitability, screening, or assessment checks—require software on the user's system to verify compliance with certain requirements from the organization's secure configuration baseline. For example, the user's antimalware software must be up-to-date, the operating system must be fully patched, and the remote computer must be owned and controlled by the organization. These checks should be performed before granting the AR access to the enterprise network. Based on the results of these checks, the organization can determine whether the remote computer should be permitted to use interactive remote access. If the user has acceptable authorization credentials but the remote computer does not pass the health check, the user and remote computer should be denied network access or have limited access to a quarantine network so that authorized personnel can fix the security deficiencies. Figure 5.1 indicates that the quarantine portion of the enterprise network consists of the policy server and related AR suitability servers. There may also be application servers that do not require the normal security threshold be met.

Once an AR has been authenticated and cleared for a certain level of access to the enterprise network, the NAS can enable the AR to interact with resources in the enterprise network. The NAS may mediate every exchange to enforce a security policy for this AR, or may use other methods to limit the privileges of the AR.

Network Access Enforcement Methods

Enforcement methods are the actions that are applied to ARs to regulate access to the enterprise network. Many vendors support multiple enforcement methods simultaneously, allowing the customer to tailor the configuration by using one or a combination of methods. The following are common NAC enforcement methods.

- **IEEE 802.1X:** This is a link layer protocol that enforces authorization before a port is assigned an IP address. IEEE 802.1X makes use of the Extensible Authentication Protocol for the authentication process. Sections 5.2 and 5.3 cover the Extensible Authentication Protocol and IEEE 802.1X, respectively.

- **Virtual local area networks (VLANs):** In this approach, the enterprise network, consisting of an interconnected set of LANs, is segmented logically into a number of virtual LANs.[1] The NAC system decides to which of the network's VLANs it will direct an AR, based on whether the device needs security remediation, Internet access only, or some level of network access to enterprise resources. VLANs can be created dynamically and VLAN membership, of both enterprise servers and ARs, may overlap. That is, an enterprise server or an AR may belong to more than one VLAN.

---

[1] A VLAN is a logical subgroup within a LAN that is created via software rather than manually moving cables in the wiring closet. It combines user stations and network devices into a single unit regardless of the physical LAN segment they are attached to and allows traffic to flow more efficiently within populations of mutual interest. VLANs are implemented in port-switching hubs and LAN switches.

■ **Firewall:** A firewall provides a form of NAC by allowing or denying network traffic between an enterprise host and an external user. Firewalls are discussed in Chapter 12.

■ **DHCP management:** The Dynamic Host Configuration Protocol (DHCP) is an Internet protocol that enables dynamic allocation of IP addresses to hosts. A DHCP server intercepts DHCP requests and assigns IP addresses instead. Thus, NAC enforcement occurs at the IP layer based on subnet and IP assignment. A DCHP server is easy to install and configure, but is subject to various forms of IP spoofing, providing limited security.

There are a number of other enforcement methods available from vendors. The ones in the preceding list are perhaps the most common, and IEEE 802.1X is by far the most commonly implemented solution.

5.2 EXTENSIBLE AUTHENTICATION PROTOCOL

The Extensible Authentication Protocol (EAP), defined in RFC 3748, acts as a framework for network access and authentication protocols. EAP provides a set of protocol messages that can encapsulate various authentication methods to be used between a client and an authentication server. EAP can operate over a variety of network and link level facilities, including point-to-point links, LANs, and other networks, and can accommodate the authentication needs of the various links and networks. Figure 5.2 illustrates the protocol layers that form the context for EAP.

Authentication Methods

EAP supports multiple authentication methods. This is what is meant by referring to EAP as *extensible*. EAP provides a generic transport service for the exchange of authentication information between a client system and an authentication server. The basic EAP transport service is extended by using a specific authentication protocol, or method, that is installed in both the EAP client and the authentication server.

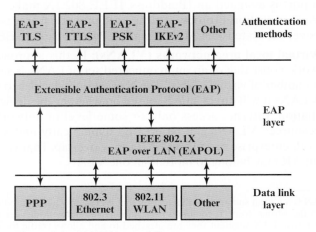

Figure 5.2   EAP Layered Context

Numerous methods have been defined to work over EAP. The following are commonly supported EAP methods:

- **EAP-TLS (EAP Transport Layer Security):** EAP-TLS (RFC 5216) defines how the TLS protocol (described in Chapter 6) can be encapsulated in EAP messages. EAP-TLS uses the handshake protocol in TLS, not its encryption method. Client and server authenticate each other using digital certificates. Client generates a pre-master secret key by encrypting a random number with the server's public key and sends it to the server. Both client and server use the pre-master to generate the same secret key.

- **EAP-TTLS (EAP Tunneled TLS):** EAP-TTLS is like EAP-TLS, except only the server has a certificate to authenticate itself to the client first. As in EAP-TLS, a secure connection (the "tunnel") is established with secret keys, but that connection is used to continue the authentication process by authenticating the client and possibly the server again using any EAP method or legacy method such as PAP (Password Authentication Protocol) and CHAP (Challenge-Handshake Authentication Protocol). EAP-TTLS is defined in RFC 5281.

- **EAP-GPSK (EAP Generalized Pre-Shared Key):** EAP-GPSK, defined in RFC 5433, is an EAP method for mutual authentication and session key derivation using a Pre-Shared Key (PSK). EAP-GPSK specifies an EAP method based on pre-shared keys and employs secret key-based cryptographic algorithms. Hence, this method is efficient in terms of message flows and computational costs, but requires the existence of pre-shared keys between each peer and EAP server. The set up of these pairwise secret keys is part of the peer registration, and thus, must satisfy the system preconditions. It provides a protected communication channel when mutual authentication is successful for both parties to communicate over and is designed for authentication over insecure networks such as IEEE 802.11. EAP-GPSK does not require any public-key cryptography. The EAP method protocol exchange is done in a minimum of four messages.

- **EAP-IKEv2:** It is based on the Internet Key Exchange protocol version 2 (IKEv2), which is described in Chapter 9. It supports mutual authentication and session key establishment using a variety of methods. EAP-TLS is defined in RFC 5106.

EAP Exchanges

Whatever method is used for authentication, the authentication information and authentication protocol information are carried in EAP messages.

RFC 3748 defines the goal of the exchange of EAP messages to be successful authentication. In the context of RFC 3748, *successful authentication* is an exchange of EAP messages, as a result of which the authenticator decides to allow access by the peer, and the peer decides to use this access. The authenticator's decision typically involves both authentication and authorization aspects; the peer may successfully authenticate to the authenticator, but access may be denied by the authenticator due to policy reasons.

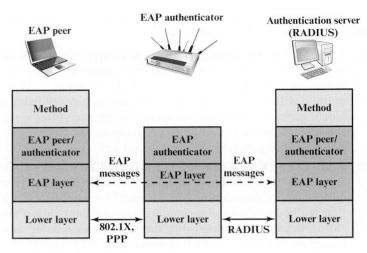

Figure 5.3   EAP Protocol Exchanges

Figure 5.3 indicates a typical arrangement in which EAP is used. The following components are involved:

- **EAP peer:** Client computer that is attempting to access a network.
- **EAP authenticator:** An access point or NAS that requires EAP authentication prior to granting access to a network.
- **Authentication server:** A server computer that negotiates the use of a specific EAP method with an EAP peer, validates the EAP peer's credentials, and authorizes access to the network. Typically, the authentication server is a Remote Authentication Dial-In User Service (RADIUS) server.

The authentication server functions as a backend server that can authenticate peers as a service to a number of EAP authenticators. The EAP authenticator then makes the decision of whether to grant access. This is referred to as the **EAP pass-through mode**. Less commonly, the authenticator takes over the role of the EAP server; that is, only two parties are involved in the EAP execution.

As a first step, a lower-level protocol, such as PPP (point-to-point protocol) or IEEE 802.1X, is used to connect to the EAP authenticator. The software entity in the EAP peer that operates at this level is referred to as the **supplicant**. EAP messages containing the appropriate information for a chosen EAP method are then exchanged between the EAP peer and the authentication server.

EAP messages may include the following fields:

- **Code:** Identifies the Type of EAP message. The codes are Request (1), Response (2), Success (3), and Failure (4).
- **Identifier:** Used to match Responses with Requests.
- **Length:** Indicates the length, in octets, of the EAP message, including the Code, Identifier, Length, and Data fields.

- **Data:** Contains information related to authentication. Typically, the Data field consists of a Type subfield, indicating the type of data carried, and a Type-Data field.

The Success and Failure messages do not include a Data field.

The EAP authentication exchange proceeds as follows. After a lower-level exchange that established the need for an EAP exchange, the authenticator sends a Request to the peer to request an identity, and the peer sends a Response with the identity information. This is followed by a sequence of Requests by the authenticator and Responses by the peer for the exchange of authentication information. The information exchanged and the number of Request–Response exchanges needed depend on the authentication method. The conversation continues until either (1) the authenticator determines that it cannot authenticate the peer and transmits an EAP Failure or (2) the authenticator determines that successful authentication has occurred and transmits an EAP Success.

Figure 5.4 gives an example of an EAP exchange. Not shown in the figure is a message or signal sent from the EAP peer to the authenticator using some protocol other than EAP and requesting an EAP exchange to grant network access. One protocol used for this purpose is IEEE 802.1X, discussed in the next section. The first pair of EAP Request and Response messages is of Type identity, in which the authenticator requests the peer's identity, and the peer returns its claimed identity in the Response message. This Response is passed through the authenticator to the authentication server. Subsequent EAP messages are exchanged between the peer and the authentication server.

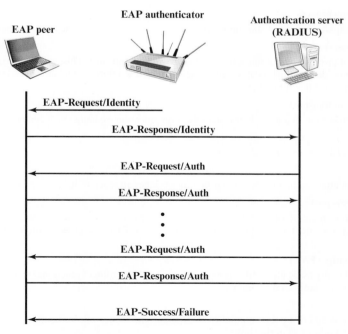

Figure 5.4   EAP Message Flow in Pass-Through Mode

Upon receiving the identity Response message from the peer, the server selects an EAP method and sends the first EAP message with a Type field related to an authentication method. If the peer supports and accepts the selected EAP method, it replies with the corresponding Response message of the same type. Otherwise, the peer sends a NAK, and the EAP server either selects another EAP method or aborts the EAP execution with a failure message. The selected EAP method determines the number of Request/Response pairs. During the exchange the appropriate authentication information, including key material, is exchanged. The exchange ends when the server determines that authentication has succeeded or that no further attempt can be made and authentication has failed.

5.3 IEEE 802.1X PORT-BASED NETWORK ACCESS CONTROL

IEEE 802.1X Port-Based Network Access Control was designed to provide access control functions for LANs. Table 5.1 briefly defines key terms used in the IEEE 802.11 standard. The terms *supplicant*, *network access point*, and *authentication*

Table 5.1 Terminology Related to IEEE 802.1X

Authenticator

An entity at one end of a point-to-point LAN segment that facilities authentication of the entity to the other end of the link.

Authentication exchange

The two-party conversation between systems performing an authentication process.

Authentication process

The cryptographic operations and supporting data frames that perform the actual authentication.

Authentication server (AS)

An entity that provides an authentication service to an authenticator. This service determines, from the credentials provided by supplicant, whether the supplicant is authorized to access the services provided by the system in which the authenticator resides.

Authentication transport

The datagram session that actively transfers the authentication exchange between two systems.

Bridge port

A port of an IEEE 802.1D or 802.1Q bridge.

Edge port

A bridge port attached to a LAN that has no other bridges attached to it.

Network access port

A point of attachment of a system to a LAN. It can be a physical port, such as a single LAN MAC attached to a physical LAN segment, or a logical port, for example, an IEEE 802.11 association between a station and an access point.

Port access entity (PAE)

The protocol entity associated with a port. It can support the protocol functionality associated with the authenticator, the supplicant, or both.

Supplicant

An entity at one end of a point-to-point LAN segment that seeks to be authenticated by an authenticator attached to the other end of that link.

server correspond to the EAP terms *peer*, *authenticator*, and *authentication server*, respectively.

Until the AS authenticates a supplicant (using an authentication protocol), the authenticator only passes control and authentication messages between the supplicant and the AS; the 802.1X control channel is unblocked, but the 802.11 data channel is blocked. Once a supplicant is authenticated and keys are provided, the authenticator can forward data from the supplicant, subject to predefined access control limitations for the supplicant to the network. Under these circumstances, the data channel is unblocked.

As indicated in Figure 5.5, 802.1X uses the concepts of controlled and uncontrolled ports. Ports are logical entities defined within the authenticator and refer to physical network connections. Each logical port is mapped to one of these two types of physical ports. An uncontrolled port allows the exchange of protocol data units (PDUs) between the supplicant and the AS, regardless of the authentication state of the supplicant. A controlled port allows the exchange of PDUs between a supplicant and other systems on the network only if the current state of the supplicant authorizes such an exchange.

The essential element defined in 802.1X is a protocol known as EAPOL (EAP over LAN). EAPOL operates at the network layers and makes use of an IEEE 802 LAN, such as Ethernet or Wi-Fi, at the link level. EAPOL enables a supplicant to communicate with an authenticator and supports the exchange of EAP packets for authentication.

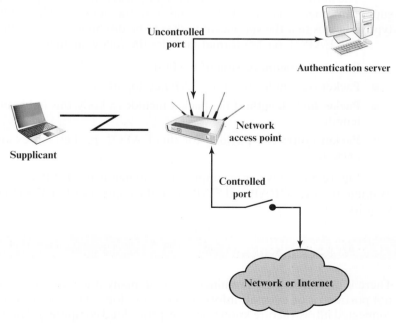

Figure 5.5 802.1X Access Control

Table 5.2   Common EAPOL Frame Types

Frame Type	Definition
EAPOL-EAP	Contains an encapsulated EAP packet.
EAPOL-Start	A supplicant can issue this packet instead of waiting for a challenge from the authenticator.
EAPOL-Logoff	Used to return the state of the port to unauthorized when the supplicant is finished using the network.
EAPOL-Key	Used to exchange cryptographic keying information.

The most common EAPOL packets are listed in Table 5.2. When the supplicant first connects to the LAN, it does not know the MAC address of the authenticator. Actually it doesn't know whether there is an authenticator present at all. By sending an **EAPOL-Start** packet to a special group-multicast address reserved for IEEE 802.1X authenticators, a supplicant can determine whether an authenticator is present and let it know that the supplicant is ready. In many cases, the authenticator will already be notified that a new device has connected from some hardware notification. For example, a hub knows that a cable is plugged in before the device sends any data. In this case the authenticator may preempt the Start message with its own message. In either case the authenticator sends an EAP-Request Identity message encapsulated in an **EAPOL-EAP** packet. The EAPOL-EAP is the EAPOL frame type used for transporting EAP packets.

The authenticator uses the **EAP-Key** packet to send cryptographic keys to the supplicant once it has decided to admit it to the network. The **EAP-Logoff** packet type indicates that the supplicant wishes to be disconnected from the network.

The EAPOL packet format includes the following fields:

- **Protocol version:** version of EAPOL.
- **Packet type:** indicates start, EAP, key, logoff, etc.
- **Packet body length:** If the packet includes a body, this field indicates the body length.
- **Packet body:** The payload for this EAPOL packet. An example is an EAP packet.

Figure 5.6 shows an example of exchange using EAPOL. In Chapter 7, we examine the use of EAP and EAPOL in the context of IEEE 802.11 wireless LAN security.

5.4   CLOUD COMPUTING

There is an increasingly prominent trend in many organizations to move a substantial portion of or even all information technology (IT) operations to an Internet-connected infrastructure known as enterprise cloud computing. This section provides an overview of cloud computing. For a more detailed treatment, see [STAL16b].

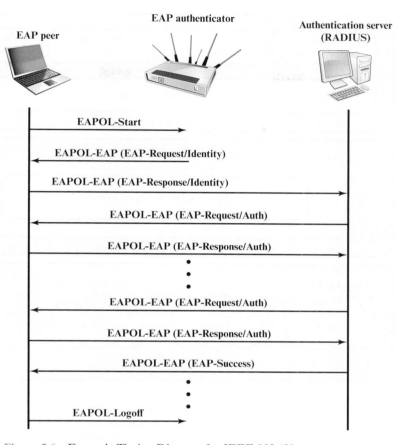

EAP peer

EAP authenticator

Authentication server
(RADIUS)

EAPOL-Start

EAPOL-EAP (EAP-Request/Identity)

EAPOL-EAP (EAP-Response/Identity)

EAPOL-EAP (EAP-Request/Auth)

EAPOL-EAP (EAP-Response/Auth)

EAPOL-EAP (EAP-Request/Auth)

EAPOL-EAP (EAP-Response/Auth)

EAPOL-EAP (EAP-Success)

EAPOL-Logoff

Figure 5.6 Example Timing Diagram for IEEE 802.1X

Cloud Computing Elements

NIST defines cloud computing, in NIST SP 800-145 (*The NIST Definition of Cloud Computing*), as follows:

Cloud computing: A model for enabling ubiquitous, convenient, on-demand network access to a shared pool of configurable computing resources (e.g., networks, servers, storage, applications, and services) that can be rapidly provisioned and released with minimal management effort or service provider interaction. This cloud model promotes availability and is composed of five essential characteristics, three service models, and four deployment models.

The definition refers to various models and characteristics, whose relationship is illustrated in Figure 5.7. The essential characteristics of cloud computing include the following:

- **Broad network access:** Capabilities are available over the network and accessed through standard mechanisms that promote use by heterogeneous

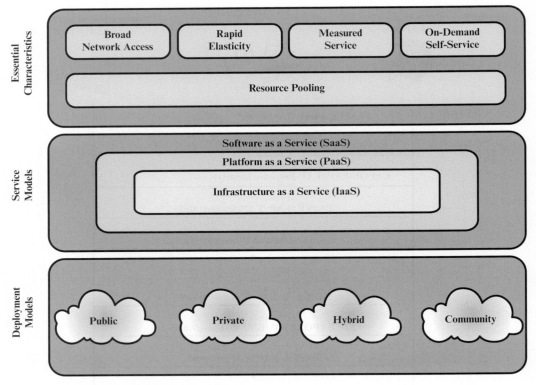

Figure 5.7   Cloud Computing Elements

thin or thick client platforms (e.g., mobile phones, laptops, and PDAs) as well as other traditional or cloud-based software services.

- **Rapid elasticity:** Cloud computing gives you the ability to expand and reduce resources according to your specific service requirement. For example, you may need a large number of server resources for the duration of a specific task. You can then release these resources upon completion of the task.

- **Measured service:** Cloud systems automatically control and optimize resource use by leveraging a metering capability at some level of abstraction appropriate to the type of service (e.g., storage, processing, bandwidth, and active user accounts). Resource usage can be monitored, controlled, and reported, providing transparency for both the provider and consumer of the utilized service.

- **On-demand self-service:** A consumer can unilaterally provision computing capabilities, such as server time and network storage, as needed automatically without requiring human interaction with each service provider. Because the service is on demand, the resources are not permanent parts of your IT infrastructure.

- **Resource pooling:** The provider's computing resources are pooled to serve multiple consumers using a multi-tenant model, with different physical and virtual resources dynamically assigned and reassigned according to consumer demand. There is a degree of location independence in that the customer generally has no control or knowledge of the exact location of the provided resources, but may be able to specify location at a higher level of abstraction (e.g., country, state, or data center). Examples of resources include storage, processing, memory, network bandwidth, and virtual machines. Even private clouds tend to pool resources between different parts of the same organization.

NIST defines three **service models**, which can be viewed as nested service alternatives:

- **Software as a service (SaaS):** The capability provided to the consumer is to use the provider's applications running on a cloud infrastructure. The applications are accessible from various client devices through a thin client interface such as a Web browser. Instead of obtaining desktop and server licenses for software products it uses, an enterprise obtains the same functions from the cloud service. SaaS saves the complexity of software installation, maintenance, upgrades, and patches. Examples of services at this level are Gmail, Google's e-mail service, and Salesforce.com, which helps firms keep track of their customers.

- **Platform as a service (PaaS):** The capability provided to the consumer is to deploy onto the cloud infrastructure consumer-created or acquired applications created using programming languages and tools supported by the provider. PaaS often provides middleware-style services such as database and component services for use by applications. In effect, PaaS is an operating system in the cloud.

- **Infrastructure as a service (IaaS):** The capability provided to the consumer is to provision processing, storage, networks, and other fundamental computing resources where the consumer is able to deploy and run arbitrary software, which can include operating systems and applications. IaaS enables customers to combine basic computing services, such as number crunching and data storage, to build highly adaptable computer systems.

NIST defines four **deployment models**:

- **Public cloud:** The cloud infrastructure is made available to the general public or a large industry group and is owned by an organization selling cloud services. The cloud provider is responsible both for the cloud infrastructure and for the control of data and operations within the cloud.

- **Private cloud:** The cloud infrastructure is operated solely for an organization. It may be managed by the organization or a third party and may exist on premise or off premise. The cloud provider (CP) is responsible only for the infrastructure and not for the control.

- **Community cloud:** The cloud infrastructure is shared by several organizations and supports a specific community that has shared concerns (e.g., mission, security requirements, policy, and compliance considerations). It may be managed by the organizations or a third party and may exist on premise or off premise.

- **Hybrid cloud:** The cloud infrastructure is a composition of two or more clouds (private, community, or public) that remain unique entities but are bound together by standardized or proprietary technology that enables data and application portability (e.g., cloud bursting for load balancing between clouds).

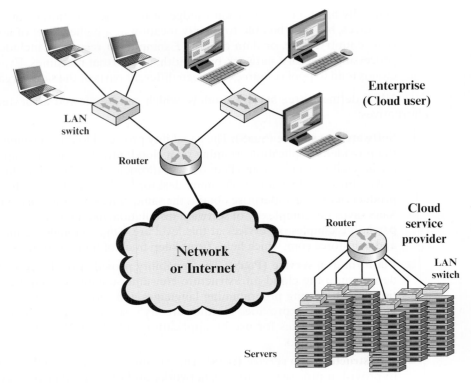

Figure 5.8 Cloud Computing Context

Figure 5.8 illustrates the typical cloud service context. An enterprise maintains workstations within an enterprise LAN or set of LANs, which are connected by a router through a network or the Internet to the cloud service provider. The cloud service provider maintains a massive collection of servers, which it manages with a variety of network management, redundancy, and security tools. In the figure, the cloud infrastructure is shown as a collection of blade servers, which is a common architecture.

Cloud Computing Reference Architecture

NIST SP 500-292 (*NIST Cloud Computing Reference Architecture*) establishes a reference architecture, described as follows:

> The NIST cloud computing reference architecture focuses on the requirements of "what" cloud services provide, not a "how to" design solution and implementation. The reference architecture is intended to facilitate the understanding of the operational intricacies in cloud computing. It does not represent the system architecture of a specific cloud computing system; instead it is a tool for describing, discussing, and developing a system-specific architecture using a common framework of reference.

NIST developed the reference architecture with the following objectives in mind:

- to illustrate and understand the various cloud services in the context of an overall cloud computing conceptual model
- to provide a technical reference for consumers to understand, discuss, categorize, and compare cloud services
- to facilitate the analysis of candidate standards for security, interoperability, and portability and reference implementations

The reference architecture, depicted in Figure 5.9, defines five major actors in terms of the roles and responsibilities:

- **Cloud consumer:** A person or organization that maintains a business relationship with, and uses service from, cloud providers.
- **Cloud provider:** A person, organization, or entity responsible for making a service available to interested parties.
- **Cloud auditor:** A party that can conduct independent assessment of cloud services, information system operations, performance, and security of the cloud implementation.
- **Cloud broker:** An entity that manages the use, performance, and delivery of cloud services, and negotiates relationships between CPs and cloud consumers.
- **Cloud carrier:** An intermediary that provides connectivity and transport of cloud services from CPs to cloud consumers.

The roles of the cloud consumer and provider have already been discussed. To summarize, a **cloud provider** can provide one or more of the cloud services to meet IT and business requirements of **cloud consumers**. For each of the three service

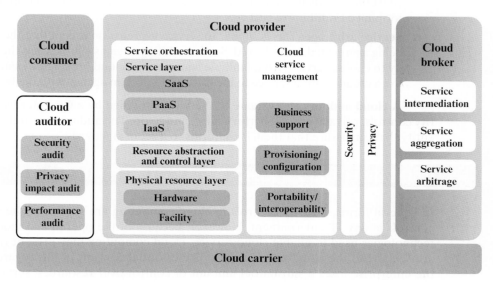

Figure 5.9   NIST Cloud Computing Reference Architecture

models (SaaS, PaaS, IaaS), the CP provides the storage and processing facilities needed to support that service model, together with a cloud interface for cloud service consumers. For SaaS, the CP deploys, configures, maintains, and updates the operation of the software applications on a cloud infrastructure so that the services are provisioned at the expected service levels to cloud consumers. The consumers of SaaS can be organizations that provide their members with access to software applications, end users who directly use software applications, or software application administrators who configure applications for end users.

For PaaS, the CP manages the computing infrastructure for the platform and runs the cloud software that provides the components of the platform, such as run-time software execution stack, databases, and other middleware components. Cloud consumers of PaaS can employ the tools and execution resources provided by CPs to develop, test, deploy, and manage the applications hosted in a cloud environment.

For IaaS, the CP acquires the physical computing resources underlying the service, including the servers, networks, storage, and hosting infrastructure. The IaaS cloud consumer in turn uses these computing resources, such as a virtual computer, for their fundamental computing needs.

The **cloud carrier** is a networking facility that provides connectivity and transport of cloud services between cloud consumers and CPs. Typically, a CP will set up service level agreements (SLAs) with a cloud carrier to provide services consistent with the level of SLAs offered to cloud consumers, and may require the cloud carrier to provide dedicated and secure connections between cloud consumers and CPs.

A **cloud broker** is useful when cloud services are too complex for a cloud consumer to easily manage. Three areas of support can be offered by a cloud broker:

- **Service intermediation:** These are value-added services, such as identity management, performance reporting, and enhanced security.
- **Service aggregation:** The broker combines multiple cloud services to meet consumer needs not specifically addressed by a single CP, or to optimize performance or minimize cost.
- **Service arbitrage:** This is similar to service aggregation except that the services being aggregated are not fixed. Service arbitrage means a broker has the flexibility to choose services from multiple agencies. The cloud broker, for example, can use a credit-scoring service to measure and select an agency with the best score.

A **cloud auditor** can evaluate the services provided by a CP in terms of security controls, privacy impact, performance, and so on. The auditor is an independent entity that can assure that the CP conforms to a set of standards.

5.5 CLOUD SECURITY RISKS AND COUNTERMEASURES

In general terms, security controls in cloud computing are similar to the security controls in any IT environment. However, because of the operational models and technologies used to enable cloud service, cloud computing may present risks that are specific to the cloud environment. The essential concept in this regard is that the enterprise loses a substantial amount of control over resources, services, and applications but must maintain accountability for security and privacy policies.

The Cloud Security Alliance [CSA10] lists the following as the top cloud-specific security threats, together with suggested countermeasures:

- **Abuse and nefarious use of cloud computing:** For many CPs, it is relatively easy to register and begin using cloud services, some even offering free limited trial periods. This enables attackers to get inside the cloud to conduct various attacks, such as spamming, malicious code attacks, and denial of service. PaaS providers have traditionally suffered most from this kind of attacks; however, recent evidence shows that hackers have begun to target IaaS vendors as well. The burden is on the CP to protect against such attacks, but cloud service clients must monitor activity with respect to their data and resources to detect any malicious behavior.

  Countermeasures include (1) stricter initial registration and validation processes; (2) enhanced credit card fraud monitoring and coordination; (3) comprehensive introspection of customer network traffic; and (4) monitoring public blacklists for one's own network blocks.

- **Insecure interfaces and APIs:** CPs expose a set of software interfaces or APIs that customers use to manage and interact with cloud services. The security and availability of general cloud services are dependent upon the security of these basic APIs. From authentication and access control to encryption and activity monitoring, these interfaces must be designed to protect against both accidental and malicious attempts to circumvent policy.

  Countermeasures include (1) analyzing the security model of CP interfaces; (2) ensuring that strong authentication and access controls are implemented in concert with encrypted transmission; and (3) understanding the dependency chain associated with the API.

- **Malicious insiders:** Under the cloud computing paradigm, an organization relinquishes direct control over many aspects of security and, in doing so, confers an unprecedented level of trust onto the CP. One grave concern is the risk of malicious insider activity. Cloud architectures necessitate certain roles that are extremely high risk. Examples include CP system administrators and managed security service providers.

  Countermeasures include the following: (1) enforce strict supply chain management and conduct a comprehensive supplier assessment; (2) specify human resource requirements as part of legal contract; (3) require transparency into overall information security and management practices, as well as compliance reporting; and (4) determine security breach notification processes.

- **Shared technology issues:** IaaS vendors deliver their services in a scalable way by sharing infrastructure. Often, the underlying components that make up this infrastructure (CPU caches, GPUs, etc.) were not designed to offer strong isolation properties for a multi-tenant architecture. CPs typically approach this risk by the use of isolated virtual machines for individual clients. This approach is still vulnerable to attack, by both insiders and outsiders, and so can only be a part of an overall security strategy.

  Countermeasures include the following: (1) implement security best practices for installation/configuration; (2) monitor environment for unauthorized changes/activity; (3) promote strong authentication and access control for administrative access and operations; (4) enforce SLAs for patching and vulnerability remediation; and (5) conduct vulnerability scanning and configuration audits.

■ **Data loss or leakage:** For many clients, the most devastating impact from a security breach is the loss or leakage of data. We address this issue in the next subsection.

Countermeasures include the following: (1) implement strong API access control; (2) encrypt and protect integrity of data in transit; (3) analyze data protection at both design and run time; and (4) implement strong key generation, storage and management, and destruction practices.

■ **Account or service hijacking:** Account or service hijacking, usually with stolen credentials, remains a top threat. With stolen credentials, attackers can often access critical areas of deployed cloud computing services, allowing them to compromise the confidentiality, integrity, and availability of those services.

Countermeasures include the following: (1) prohibit the sharing of account credentials between users and services; (2) leverage strong two-factor authentication techniques where possible; (3) employ proactive monitoring to detect unauthorized activity; and (4) understand CP security policies and SLAs.

■ **Unknown risk profile:** In using cloud infrastructures, the client necessarily cedes control to the CP on a number of issues that may affect security. Thus the client must pay attention to and clearly define the roles and responsibilities involved for managing risks. For example, employees may deploy applications and data resources at the CP without observing the normal policies and procedures for privacy, security, and oversight.

Countermeasures include (1) disclosure of applicable logs and data; (2) partial/full disclosure of infrastructure details (e.g., patch levels and firewalls); and (3) monitoring and alerting on necessary information.

Similar lists have been developed by the European Network and Information Security Agency [ENIS09] and NIST [JANS11].

5.6 DATA PROTECTION IN THE CLOUD

As can be seen from the previous section, there are numerous aspects to cloud security and numerous approaches to providing cloud security measures. A further example is seen in the NIST guidelines for cloud security, specified in SP-800-14 and listed in Table 5.3. Thus, the topic of cloud security is well beyond the scope of this chapter. In this section, we focus on one specific element of cloud security.

There are many ways to compromise data. Deletion or alteration of records without a backup of the original content is an obvious example. Unlinking a record from a larger context may render it unrecoverable, as can storage on unreliable media. Loss of an encoding key may result in effective destruction. Finally, unauthorized parties must be prevented from gaining access to sensitive data.

Table 5.3   NIST Guidelines on Security and Privacy Issues and Recommendations

Governance

Extend organizational practices pertaining to the policies, procedures, and standards used for application development and service provisioning in the cloud, as well as the design, implementation, testing, use, and monitoring of deployed or engaged services.

Put in place audit mechanisms and tools to ensure organizational practices are followed throughout the system life cycle.

Compliance

Understand the various types of laws and regulations that impose security and privacy obligations on the organization and potentially impact cloud computing initiatives, particularly those involving data location, privacy and security controls, records management, and electronic discovery requirements.

Review and assess the cloud provider's offerings with respect to the organizational requirements to be met and ensure that the contract terms adequately meet the requirements.

Ensure that the cloud provider's electronic discovery capabilities and processes do not compromise the privacy or security of data and applications.

Trust

Ensure that service arrangements have sufficient means to allow visibility into the security and privacy controls and processes employed by the cloud provider, and their performance over time.

Establish clear, exclusive ownership rights over data.

Institute a risk management program that is flexible enough to adapt to the constantly evolving and shifting risk landscape for the life cycle of the system.

Continuously monitor the security state of the information system to support ongoing risk management decisions.

Architecture

Understand the underlying technologies that the cloud provider uses to provision services, including the implications that the technical controls involved have on the security and privacy of the system, over the full system life cycle and across all system components.

Identity and access management

Ensure that adequate safeguards are in place to secure authentication, authorization, and other identity and access management functions, and are suitable for the organization.

Software isolation

Understand virtualization and other logical isolation techniques that the cloud provider employs in its multi-tenant software architecture, and assess the risks involved for the organization.

Data protection

Evaluate the suitability of the cloud provider's data management solutions for the organizational data concerned and the ability to control access to data, to secure data while at rest, in transit, and in use, and to sanitize data.

Take into consideration the risk of collating organizational data with those of other organizations whose threat profiles are high or whose data collectively represent significant concentrated value.

Fully understand and weigh the risks involved in cryptographic key management with the facilities available in the cloud environment and the processes established by the cloud provider.

Availability

Understand the contract provisions and procedures for availability, data backup and recovery, and disaster recovery, and ensure that they meet the organization's continuity and contingency planning requirements.

Ensure that during an intermediate or prolonged disruption or a serious disaster, critical operations can be immediately resumed, and that all operations can be eventually reinstituted in a timely and organized manner.

Incident response

Understand the contract provisions and procedures for incident response and ensure that they meet the requirements of the organization.

Table 5.3   Continued

> Ensure that the cloud provider has a transparent response process in place and sufficient mechanisms to share information during and after an incident.
> Ensure that the organization can respond to incidents in a coordinated fashion with the cloud provider in accordance with their respective roles and responsibilities for the computing environment.

The threat of data compromise increases in the cloud, due to the number of and interactions between risks and challenges that are either unique to the cloud or more dangerous because of the architectural or operational characteristics of the cloud environment.

Database environments used in cloud computing can vary significantly. Some providers support a **multi-instance model**, which provides a unique DBMS running on a virtual machine instance for each cloud subscriber. This gives the subscriber complete control over role definition, user authorization, and other administrative tasks related to security. Other providers support a **multi-tenant model**, which provides a predefined environment for the cloud subscriber that is shared with other tenants, typically through tagging data with a subscriber identifier. Tagging gives the appearance of exclusive use of the instance, but relies on the CP to establish and maintain a sound secure database environment.

Data must be secured while at rest, in transit, and in use, and access to the data must be controlled. The client can employ encryption to protect data in transit, though this involves key management responsibilities for the CP. The client can enforce access control techniques but, again, the CP is involved to some extent depending on the service model used.

For data at rest, the ideal security measure is for the client to encrypt the database and only store encrypted data in the cloud, with the CP having no access to the encryption key. So long as the key remains secure, the CP has no ability to read the data, although corruption and other denial-of-service attacks remain a risk.

A straightforward solution to the security problem in this context is to encrypt the entire database and not provide the encryption/decryption keys to the service provider. This solution by itself is inflexible. The user has little ability to access individual data items based on searches or indexing on key parameters, but rather would have to download entire tables from the database, decrypt the tables, and work with the results. To provide more flexibility, it must be possible to work with the database in its encrypted form.

An example of such an approach, depicted in Figure 5.10, is reported in [DAMI05] and [DAMI03]. A similar approach is described in [HACI02]. Four entities are involved:

- **Data owner:** An organization that produces data to be made available for controlled release, either within the organization or to external users.
- **User:** Human entity that presents requests (queries) to the system. The user could be an employee of the organization who is granted access to the database via the server, or a user external to the organization who, after authentication, is granted access.
- **Client:** Frontend that transforms user queries into queries on the encrypted data stored on the server.

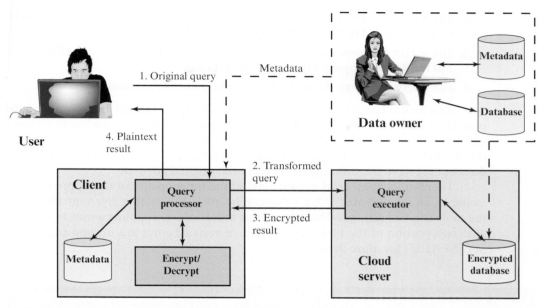

Figure 5.10   An Encryption Scheme for a Cloud-Based Database

■ **Server:** An organization that receives the encrypted data from a data owner and makes them available for distribution to clients. The server could in fact be owned by the data owner but, more typically, is a facility owned and maintained by an external provider. For our discussion, the server is a cloud server.

Before continuing this discussion, we need to define some database terms. In relational database parlance, the basic building block is a **relation**, which is a flat table. Rows are referred to as **tuples**, and columns are referred to as **attributes**. A **primary key** is defined to be a portion of a row used to uniquely identify a row in a table; the primary key consists of one or more column names.[2] For example, in an employee table, the employee ID is sufficient to uniquely identify a row in a particular table.

Let us first examine the simplest possible arrangement based on this scenario. Suppose that each individual item in the database is encrypted separately, all using the same encryption key. The encrypted database is stored at the server, but the server does not have the encryption key. Thus, the data are secure at the server. Even if someone were able to hack into the server's system, all he or she would have access to is encrypted data. The client system does have a copy of the encryption key. A user at the client can retrieve a record from the database with the following sequence:

1. The user issues a query for fields from one or more records with a specific value of the primary key.

---

[2]Note that a primary key has nothing to do with cryptographic keys. A primary key in a database is a means of indexing into the database.

2. The query processor at the client encrypts the primary key, modifies the query accordingly, and transmits the query to the server.

3. The server processes the query using the encrypted value of the primary key and returns the appropriate record or records.

4. The query processor decrypts the data and returns the results.

This method is certainly straightforward but is quite limited. For example, suppose the Employee table contains a salary attribute and the user wishes to retrieve all records for salaries less than $70K. There is no obvious way to do this, because the attribute value for salary in each record is encrypted. The set of encrypted values does not preserve the ordering of values in the original attribute.

There are a number of ways to extend the functionality of this approach. For example, an unencrypted index value can be associated with a given attribute and the table can be partitioned based on these index values, enabling a user to retrieve a certain portion of the table. The details of such schemes are beyond our scope. See [STAL15] for more detail.

5.7 CLOUD SECURITY AS A SERVICE

The term **Security as a Service (SecaaS)** has generally meant a package of security services offered by a service provider that offloads much of the security responsibility from an enterprise to the security service provider. Among the services typically provided are authentication, antivirus, antimalware/-spyware, intrusion detection, and security event management. In the context of cloud computing, cloud security as a service, designated SecaaS, is a segment of the SaaS offering of a CP.

The Cloud Security Alliance defines SecaaS as the provision of security applications and services via the cloud either to cloud-based infrastructure and software or from the cloud to the customers' on-premise systems [CSA11b]. The Cloud Security Alliance has identified the following SecaaS categories of service:

- Identity and access management
- Data loss prevention
- Web security
- E-mail security
- Security assessments
- Intrusion management
- Security information and event management
- Encryption
- Business continuity and disaster recovery
- Network security

In this section, we examine these categories with a focus on security of the cloud-based infrastructure and services (Figure 5.11).

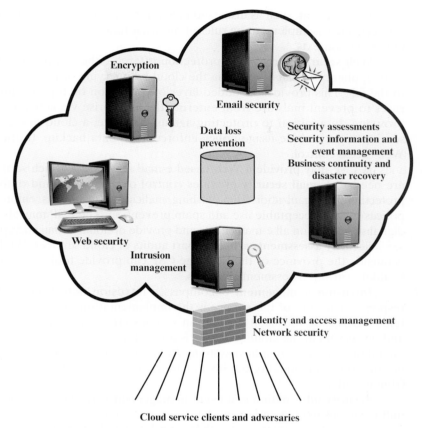

Figure 5.11 Elements of Cloud Security as a Service

Identity and access management (IAM) includes people, processes, and systems that are used to manage access to enterprise resources by assuring that the identity of an entity is verified, and then granting the correct level of access based on this assured identity. One aspect of identity management is identity provisioning, which has to do with providing access to identified users and subsequently deprovisioning, or deny access, to users when the client enterprise designates such users as no longer having access to enterprise resources in the cloud. Another aspect of identity management is for the cloud to participate in the federated identity management scheme (see Chapter 4) used by the client enterprise. Among other requirements, the cloud service provider (CSP) must be able to exchange identity attributes with the enterprise's chosen identity provider.

The access management portion of IAM involves authentication and access control services. For example, the CSP must be able to authenticate users in a trustworthy manner. The access control requirements in SPI environments include establishing trusted user profile and policy information, using it to control access within the cloud service, and doing this in an auditable way.

Data loss prevention (DLP) is the monitoring, protecting, and verifying the security of data at rest, in motion, and in use. Much of DLP can be implemented by the cloud client, such as discussed in Section 5.6. The CSP can also provide DLP services, such as implementing rules about what functions can be performed on data in various contexts.

Web security is real-time protection offered either on premise through software/appliance installation or via the cloud by proxying or redirecting Web traffic to the CP. This provides an added layer of protection on top of things like antiviruses to prevent malware from entering the enterprise via activities such as Web browsing. In addition to protecting against malware, a cloud-based Web security service might include usage policy enforcement, data backup, traffic control, and Web access control.

A CSP may provide a Web-based e-mail service, for which security measures are needed. **E-mail security** provides control over inbound and outbound e-mail, protecting the organization from phishing, malicious attachments, enforcing corporate polices such as acceptable use and spam prevention. The CSP may also incorporate digital signatures on all e-mail clients and provide optional e-mail encryption.

Security assessments are third-part audits of cloud services. While this service is outside the province of the CSP, the CSP can provide tools and access points to facilitate various assessment activities.

Intrusion management encompasses intrusion detection, prevention, and response. The core of this service is the implementation of intrusion detection systems (IDSs) and intrusion prevention systems (IPSs) at entry points to the cloud and on servers in the cloud. An IDS is a set of automated tools designed to detect unauthorized access to a host system. We discuss this in Chapter 11. An IPS incorporates IDS functionality but also includes mechanisms designed to block traffic from intruders.

Security information and event management (SIEM) aggregates (via push or pull mechanisms) log and event data from virtual and real networks, applications, and systems. This information is then correlated and analyzed to provide real-time reporting and alerting on information/events that may require intervention or other type of response. The CSP typically provides an integrated service that can put together information from a variety of sources both within the cloud and within the client enterprise network.

Encryption is a pervasive service that can be provided for data at rest in the cloud, e-mail traffic, client-specific network management information, and identity information. Encryption services provided by the CSP involve a range of complex issues, including key management, how to implement virtual private network (VPN) services in the cloud, application encryption, and data content access.

Business continuity and disaster recovery comprise measures and mechanisms to ensure operational resiliency in the event of any service interruptions. This is an area where the CSP, because of economies of scale, can offer obvious benefits to a cloud service client [WOOD10]. The CSP can provide backup at multiple locations, with reliable failover and disaster recovery facilities. This service must include a flexible infrastructure, redundancy of functions and hardware, monitored operations, geographically distributed data centers, and network survivability.

Network security consists of security services that allocate access, distribute, monitor, and protect the underlying resource services. Services include perimeter and server firewalls and denial-of-service protection. Many of the other services listed in this section, including intrusion management, identity and access management, data loss protection, and Web security, also contribute to the network security service.

5.8 ADDRESSING CLOUD COMPUTING SECURITY CONCERNS

Numerous documents have been developed to guide businesses thinking about the security issues associated with cloud computing. In addition to SP 800-144, which provides overall guidance, NIST has issued SP 800-146 (*Cloud Computing Synopsis and Recommendations,* May 2012). NIST's recommendations systematically consider each of the major types of cloud services consumed by businesses including Software as a Service (SaaS), Infrastructure as a Service (IaaS), and Platform as a Service (PaaS). While security issues vary somewhat depending on the type of cloud service, there are multiple NIST recommendations that are independent of service type. Not surprisingly, NIST recommends selecting cloud providers that support strong encryption, have appropriate redundancy mechanisms in place, employ authentication mechanisms, and offer subscribers sufficient visibility about mechanisms used to protect subscribers from other subscribers and the provider. SP 800-146 also lists the overall security controls that are relevant in a cloud computing environment and that must be assigned to the different cloud actors. These are shown in Table 5.4.

As more businesses incorporate cloud services into their enterprise network infrastructures, cloud computing security will persist as an important issue. Examples of cloud computing security failures have the potential to have a chilling effect on business interest in cloud services and this is inspiring service providers to be serious about incorporating security mechanisms that will allay concerns of potential subscribers. Some service providers have moved their operations to Tier 4 data centers to address user concerns about availability and redundancy. Because so many businesses remain reluctant to embrace cloud computing in a big way, cloud service providers will have to continue to work hard to convince potential customers that computing support for core business processes and mission critical applications can be moved safely and securely to the cloud.

Table 5.4   Control Functions and Classes

Technical	Operational	Management
Access Control	Awareness and Training	Certification, Accreditation, and Security Assessment
Audit and Accountability	Configuration and Management	
Identification and Authentication	Contingency Planning	Planning Risk Assessment
System and Communication Protection	Incident Response	System and Services Acquisition
	Maintenance	
	Media Protection	
	Physical and Environmental Protection	
	Personnel Security System and Information Integrity	

5.9 KEY TERMS, REVIEW QUESTIONS, AND PROBLEMS

Key Terms

access requestor (AR)	EAP-IKEv2	Network Access Server
authentication server	EAP over LAN (EAPOL)	(NAS)
cloud	EAP method	Platform as a Service (PaaS)
cloud auditor	EAP pass-through mode	policy server
cloud broker	EAP peer	private cloud
cloud carrier	EAP-TLS	public cloud
cloud computing	EAP-TTLS	Remote Access Server (RAS)
cloud consumer	Extensible Authentication	Security as a Service (SecaaS)
cloud provider	Protocol (EAP)	Software as a Service (SaaS)
community cloud	firewall	supplicant
Dynamic Host Configuration	IEEE 802.1X	Virtual Local Area Network
Protocol (DHCP)	media gateway	(VLAN)
EAP authenticator	Network Access Control	
EAP-GPSK	(NAC)	

Review Questions

5.1 Provide a brief definition of network access control.

5.2 What is an EAP?

5.3 List and briefly define four EAP authentication methods.

5.4 What is DHCP? How useful is it to help achieve security of IP addresses?

5.5 Why is EAPOL an essential element of IEEE 802.1X?

5.6 What are the essential characteristics of cloud computing?

5.7 List and briefly define the deployment models of cloud computing.

5.8 What is the cloud computing reference architecture?

5.9 Describe some of the main cloud-specific security threats.

Problems

5.1 Investigate the network access control scheme used at your school or place of employment. Draw a diagram and describe the principal components.

5.2 Figure 5.3 suggests that EAP can be described in the context of a four-layer model. Indicate the functions and formats of each of the four layers. You may need to refer to RFC 3748.

5.3 List some commonly used cloud-based data services. Explore and compare these services based on their use of encryption, flexibility, efficiency, speed, and ease of use. Study security breaches on these services in recent past. What changes were made by the services after these attacks?

CHAPTER 6

TRANSPORT-LEVEL SECURITY

LEARNING OBJECTIVES

After studying this chapter, you should be able to:

◆ Summarize Web security threats and Web traffic security approaches.

◆ Present an overview of Transport Layer Security (TLS).

◆ Understand the differences between Secure Sockets Layer and Transport Layer Security.

◆ Compare the pseudorandom function used in Transport Layer Security with those discussed earlier in the book.

◆ Present an overview of HTTPS (HTTP over SSL).

◆ Present an overview of Secure Shell (SSH).

Virtually all businesses, most government agencies, and many individuals now have Web sites. The number of individuals and companies with Internet access is expanding rapidly and all of these have graphical Web browsers. As a result, businesses are enthusiastic about setting up facilities on the Web for electronic commerce. But the reality is that the Internet and the Web are extremely vulnerable to compromises of various sorts. As businesses wake up to this reality, the demand for secure Web services grows.

The topic of Web security is a broad one and can easily fill a book. In this chapter, we begin with a discussion of the general requirements for Web security and then focus on three standardized schemes that are becoming increasingly important as part of Web commerce and that focus on security at the transport layer: SSL/TLS, HTTPS, and SSH.

6.1 WEB SECURITY CONSIDERATIONS

The World Wide Web is fundamentally a client/server application running over the Internet and TCP/IP intranets. As such, the security tools and approaches discussed so far in this book are relevant to the issue of Web security. However, the following characteristics of Web usage suggest the need for tailored security tools:

■ Although Web browsers are very easy to use, Web servers are relatively easy to configure and manage, and Web content is increasingly easy to develop, the underlying software is extraordinarily complex. This complex software may hide many potential security flaws. The short history of the Web is filled with examples of new and upgraded systems, properly installed, that are vulnerable to a variety of security attacks.

■ A Web server can be exploited as a launching pad into the corporation's or agency's entire computer complex. Once the Web server is subverted, an attacker may be able to gain access to data and systems not part of the Web itself but connected to the server at the local site.

■ Casual and untrained (in security matters) users are common clients for Web-based services. Such users are not necessarily aware of the security risks that exist and do not have the tools or knowledge to take effective countermeasures.

Web Security Threats

Table 6.1 provides a summary of the types of security threats faced when using the Web. One way to group these threats is in terms of passive and active attacks. Passive attacks include eavesdropping on network traffic between browser and server and gaining access to information on a Web site that is supposed to be restricted. Active attacks include impersonating another user, altering messages in transit between client and server, and altering information on a Web site.

Another way to classify Web security threats is in terms of the location of the threat: Web server, Web browser, and network traffic between browser and server. Issues of server and browser security fall into the category of computer system security; Part Six of this book addresses the issue of system security in general but is also applicable to Web system security. Issues of traffic security fall into the category of network security and are addressed in this chapter.

Web Traffic Security Approaches

A number of approaches to providing Web security are possible. The various approaches that have been considered are similar in the services they provide and, to some extent, in the mechanisms that they use, but they differ with respect to their scope of applicability and their relative location within the TCP/IP protocol stack.

Table 6.1   A Comparison of Threats on the Web

	Threats	**Consequences**	**Countermeasures**
Integrity	• Modification of user data • Trojan horse browser • Modification of memory • Modification of message traffic in transit	• Loss of information • Compromise of machine • Vulnerability to all other threats	Cryptographic checksums
Confidentiality	• Eavesdropping on the net • Theft of info from server • Theft of data from client • Info about network configuration • Info about which client talks to server	• Loss of information • Loss of privacy	Encryption, Web proxies
Denial of Service	• Killing of user threads • Flooding machine with bogus requests • Filling up disk or memory • Isolating machine by DNS attacks	• Disruptive • Annoying • Prevent user from getting work done	Difficult to prevent
Authentication	• Impersonation of legitimate users • Data forgery	• Misrepresentation of user • Belief that false information is valid	Cryptographic techniques

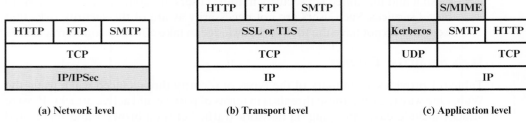

(a) Network level   (b) Transport level   (c) Application level

Figure 6.1 Relative Location of Security Facilities in the TCP/IP Protocol Stack

Figure 6.1 illustrates this difference. One way to provide Web security is to use IP security (IPsec) (Figure 6.1a). The advantage of using IPsec is that it is transparent to end users and applications and provides a general-purpose solution. Furthermore, IPsec includes a filtering capability so that only selected traffic need incur the overhead of IPsec processing.

Another relatively general-purpose solution is to implement security just above TCP (Figure 6.1b). The foremost example of this approach is the Secure Sockets Layer (SSL) and the follow-on Internet standard known as Transport Layer Security (TLS). At this level, there are two implementation choices. For full generality, SSL (or TLS) could be provided as part of the underlying protocol suite and therefore be transparent to applications. Alternatively, TLS can be embedded in specific packages. For example, virtually all browsers come equipped with TLS, and most Web servers have implemented the protocol.

Application-specific security services are embedded within the particular application. Figure 6.1c shows examples of this architecture. The advantage of this approach is that the service can be tailored to the specific needs of a given application.

6.2 TRANSPORT LAYER SECURITY

One of the most widely used security services is **Transport Layer Security (TSL)**; the current version is Version 1.2, defined in RFC 5246. TLS is an Internet standard that evolved from a commercial protocol known as **Secure Sockets Layer (SSL)**. Although SSL implementations are still around, it has been deprecated by IETF and is disabled by most corporations offering TLS software. TLS is a general-purpose service implemented as a set of protocols that rely on TCP. At this level, there are two implementation choices. For full generality, TLS could be provided as part of the underlying protocol suite and therefore be transparent to applications. Alternatively, TLS can be embedded in specific packages. For example, most browsers come equipped with TLS, and most Web servers have implemented the protocol.

TLS Architecture

TLS is designed to make use of TCP to provide a reliable end-to-end secure service. TLS is not a single protocol but rather two layers of protocols, as illustrated in Figure 6.2.

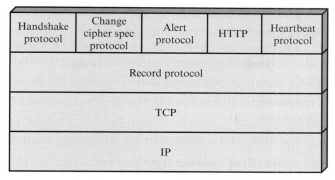

Handshake protocol	Change cipher spec protocol	Alert protocol	HTTP	Heartbeat protocol
Record protocol				
TCP				
IP				

Figure 6.2 TLS Protocol Stack

The TLS Record Protocol provides basic security services to various higher-layer protocols. In particular, the **Hypertext Transfer Protocol (HTTP)**, which provides the transfer service for Web client/server interaction, can operate on top of TLS. Three higher-layer protocols are defined as part of TLS: the Handshake Protocol; the Change Cipher Spec Protocol; and the Alert Protocol. These TLS-specific protocols are used in the management of TLS exchanges and are examined later in this section. A fourth protocol, the Heartbeat Protocol, is defined in a separate RFC and is also discussed subsequently in this section.

Two important TLS concepts are the TLS session and the TLS connection, which are defined in the specification as follows:

- **Connection:** A connection is a transport (in the OSI layering model definition) that provides a suitable type of service. For TLS, such connections are peer-to-peer relationships. The connections are transient. Every connection is associated with one session.

- **Session:** A TLS session is an association between a client and a server. Sessions are created by the Handshake Protocol. Sessions define a set of cryptographic security parameters, which can be shared among multiple connections. Sessions are used to avoid the expensive negotiation of new security parameters for each connection.

Between any pair of parties (applications such as HTTP on client and server), there may be multiple secure connections. In theory, there may also be multiple simultaneous sessions between parties, but this feature is not used in practice.

There are a number of states associated with each session. Once a session is established, there is a current operating state for both read and write (i.e., receive and send). In addition, during the Handshake Protocol, pending read and write states are created. Upon successful conclusion of the Handshake Protocol, the pending states become the current states.

A session state is defined by the following parameters:

- **Session identifier:** An arbitrary byte sequence chosen by the server to identify an active or resumable session state.

- **Peer certificate:** An X509.v3 certificate of the peer. This element of the state may be null.

- **Compression method:** The algorithm used to compress data prior to encryption.
- **Cipher spec:** Specifies the bulk data encryption algorithm (such as null, AES, etc.) and a hash algorithm (such as MD5 or SHA-1) used for MAC calculation. It also defines cryptographic attributes such as the hash_size.
- **Master secret:** 48-byte secret shared between the client and server.
- **Is resumable:** A flag indicating whether the session can be used to initiate new connections.

A connection state is defined by the following parameters:

- **Server and client random:** Byte sequences that are chosen by the server and client for each connection.
- **Server write MAC secret:** The secret key used in MAC operations on data sent by the server.
- **Client write MAC secret:** The symmetric key used in MAC operations on data sent by the client.
- **Server write key:** The symmetric encryption key for data encrypted by the server and decrypted by the client.
- **Client write key:** The symmetric encryption key for data encrypted by the client and decrypted by the server.
- **Initialization vectors:** When a block cipher in CBC mode is used, an initialization vector (IV) is maintained for each key. This field is first initialized by the TLS Handshake Protocol. Thereafter, the final ciphertext block from each record is preserved for use as the IV with the following record.
- **Sequence numbers:** Each party maintains separate sequence numbers for transmitted and received messages for each connection. When a party sends or receives a "change cipher spec message," the appropriate sequence number is set to zero. Sequence numbers may not exceed $2^{64} - 1$.

TLS Record Protocol

The TLS Record Protocol provides two services for TLS connections:

- **Confidentiality:** The Handshake Protocol defines a shared secret key that is used for conventional encryption of TLS payloads.
- **Message Integrity:** The Handshake Protocol also defines a shared secret key that is used to form a message authentication code (MAC).

Figure 6.3 indicates the overall operation of the TLS Record Protocol. The Record Protocol takes an application message to be transmitted, fragments the data into manageable blocks, optionally compresses the data, applies a MAC, encrypts, adds a header, and transmits the resulting unit in a TCP segment. Received data are decrypted, verified, decompressed, and reassembled before being delivered to higher-level users.

The first step is **fragmentation**. Each upper-layer message is fragmented into blocks of 2^{14} bytes (16,384 bytes) or less. Next, **compression** is optionally applied. Compression must be lossless and may not increase the content length by more than

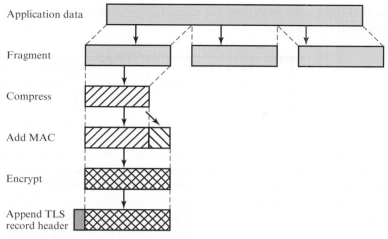

Figure 6.3 TLS Record Protocol Operation

1024 bytes.[1] In TLSv2, no compression algorithm is specified, so the default compression algorithm is null.

The next step in processing is to compute a **message authentication code** over the compressed data. TLS makes use of the HMAC algorithm defined in RFC 2104. Recall from Chapter 3 that HMAC is defined as

$$\text{HMAC}_K(M) = \text{H}[(K^+ \oplus \text{opad}) \| \text{H}[(K^+ \oplus \text{ipad}) \| M]]$$

where

H = embedded hash function (for TLS, either MD5 or SHA-1)

M = message input to HMAC

K^+ = secret key padded with zeros on the left so that the result is equal to the block length of the hash code (for MD5 and SHA-1, block length = 512 bits)

ipad = 00110110 (36 in hexadecimal) repeated 64 times (512 bits)

opad = 01011100 (5C in hexadecimal) repeated 64 times (512 bits)

For TLS, the MAC calculation encompasses the fields indicated in the following expression:

HMAC_hash(MAC_write_secret, seq_num ‖ TLSCompressed.type ‖ TLSCompressed.version ‖ TLSCompressed.length ‖ TLSCompressed.fragment)

The MAC calculation covers all of the fields XXX, plus the field `TLSCompressed.version`, which is the version of the protocol being employed.

Next, the compressed message plus the MAC are **encrypted** using symmetric encryption. Encryption may not increase the content length by more than 1024 bytes,

---

[1]Of course, one hopes that compression shrinks rather than expands the data. However, for very short blocks, it is possible, because of formatting conventions, that the compression algorithm will actually provide output that is longer than the input.

so that the total length may not exceed $2^{14} + 2048$. The following encryption algorithms are permitted:

Block Cipher		Stream Cipher	
Algorithm	**Key Size**	**Algorithm**	**Key Size**
AES	128, 256	RC4-128	128
3DES	168		

For stream encryption, the compressed message plus the MAC are encrypted. Note that the MAC is computed before encryption takes place and that the MAC is then encrypted along with the plaintext or compressed plaintext.

For block encryption, padding may be added after the MAC prior to encryption. The padding is in the form of a number of padding bytes followed by a one-byte indication of the length of the padding. The padding can be any amount that results in a total that is a multiple of the cipher's block length, up to a maximum of 255 bytes. For example, if the cipher block length is 16 bytes (e.g., AES) and if the plaintext (or compressed text if compression is used) plus MAC plus padding length byte is 79 bytes long, then the padding length (in bytes) can be 1, 17, 33, and so on, up to 161. At a padding length of 161, the total length is $79 + 161 = 240$. A variable padding length may be used to frustrate attacks based on an analysis of the lengths of exchanged messages.

The final step of TLS Record Protocol processing is to prepend a header consisting of the following fields:

- **Content Type (8 bits):** The higher-layer protocol used to process the enclosed fragment.
- **Major Version (8 bits):** Indicates major version of TLS in use. For TLSv2, the value is 3.
- **Minor Version (8 bits):** Indicates minor version in use. For TLSv2, the value is 1.
- **Compressed Length (16 bits):** The length in bytes of the plaintext fragment (or compressed fragment if compression is used). The maximum value is $2^{14} + 2048$.

The content types that have been defined are `change_cipher_spec`, `alert`, `handshake`, and `application_data`. The first three are the TLS-specific protocols, discussed next. Note that no distinction is made among the various applications (e.g., HTTP) that might use TLS; the content of the data created by such applications is opaque to TLS.

Figure 6.4 illustrates the TLS record format.

Change Cipher Spec Protocol

The Change Cipher Spec Protocol is one of the four TLS-specific protocols that use the TLS Record Protocol, and it is the simplest. This protocol consists of a single message (Figure 6.5a), which consists of a single byte with the value 1. The sole purpose of this message is to cause the pending state to be copied into the current state, which updates the cipher suite to be used on this connection.

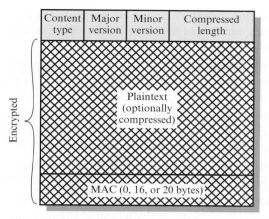

Figure 6.4   TLS Record Format

Alert Protocol

The Alert Protocol is used to convey TLS-related alerts to the peer entity. As with other applications that use TLS, alert messages are compressed and encrypted, as specified by the current state.

Each message in this protocol consists of two bytes (Figure 6.5b). The first byte takes the value warning (1) or fatal (2) to convey the severity of the message. If the level is fatal, TLS immediately terminates the connection. Other connections on the same session may continue, but no new connections on this session may be established. The second byte contains a code that indicates the specific alert. The following alerts are always fatal:

- **unexpected_message:** An inappropriate message was received.
- **bad_record_mac:** An incorrect MAC was received.
- **decompression_failure:** The decompression function received improper input (e.g., unable to decompress or decompress to greater than maximum allowable length).
- **handshake_failure:** Sender was unable to negotiate an acceptable set of security parameters given the options available.
- **illegal_parameter:** A field in a handshake message was out of range or inconsistent with other fields.

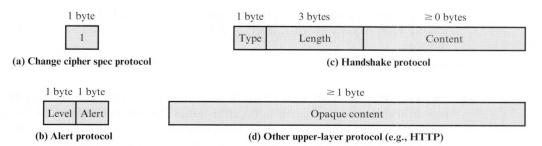

Figure 6.5   TLS Record Protocol Payload

- **decryption_failed:** A ciphertext decrypted in an invalid way; either it was not an even multiple of the block length or its padding values, when checked, were incorrect.

- **record_overflow:** A TLS record was received with a payload (ciphertext) whose length exceeds $2^{14} + 2048$ bytes, or the ciphertext decrypted to a length of greater than $2^{14} + 1024$ bytes.

- **unknown_ca:** A valid certificate chain or partial chain was received, but the certificate was not accepted because the CA certificate could not be located or could not be matched with a known, trusted CA.

- **access_denied:** A valid certificate was received, but when access control was applied, the sender decided not to proceed with the negotiation.

- **decode_error:** A message could not be decoded, because either a field was out of its specified range or the length of the message was incorrect.

- **export_restriction:** A negotiation not in compliance with export restrictions on key length was detected.

- **protocol_version:** The protocol version the client attempted to negotiate is recognized but not supported.

- **insufficient_security:** Returned instead of handshake_failure when a negotiation has failed specifically because the server requires ciphers more secure than those supported by the client.

- **internal_error:** An internal error unrelated to the peer or the correctness of the protocol makes it impossible to continue.

The remaining alerts are the following.

- **close_notify:** Notifies the recipient that the sender will not send any more messages on this connection. Each party is required to send a close_notify alert before closing the write side of a connection.

- **bad_certificate:** A received certificate was corrupt (e.g., contained a signature that did not verify).

- **unsupported_certificate:** The type of the received certificate is not supported.

- **certificate_revoked:** A certificate has been revoked by its signer.

- **certificate_expired:** A certificate has expired.

- **certificate_unknown:** Some other unspecified issue arose in processing the certificate, rendering it unacceptable.

- **decrypt_error:** A handshake cryptographic operation failed, including being unable to verify a signature, decrypt a key exchange, or validate a finished message.

- **user_canceled:** This handshake is being canceled for some reason unrelated to a protocol failure.

- **no_renegotiation:** Sent by a client in response to a hello request or by the server in response to a client hello after initial handshaking. Either of these messages would normally result in renegotiation, but this alert indicates that the sender is not able to renegotiate. This message is always a warning.

Handshake Protocol

The most complex part of TLS is the **Handshake Protocol**. This protocol allows the server and client to authenticate each other and to negotiate an encryption and MAC algorithm and cryptographic keys to be used to protect data sent in a TLS record. The Handshake Protocol is used before any application data is transmitted.

The Handshake Protocol consists of a series of messages exchanged by client and server. All of these have the format shown in Figure 6.5c. Each message has three fields:

- **Type (1 byte):** Indicates one of 10 messages. Table 6.2 lists the defined message types.
- **Length (3 bytes):** The length of the message in bytes.
- **Content (≥ 0 bytes):** The parameters associated with this message; these are listed in Table 6.2.

Figure 6.6 shows the initial exchange needed to establish a logical connection between client and server. The exchange can be viewed as having four phases.

PHASE 1. ESTABLISH SECURITY CAPABILITIES Phase 1 initiates a logical connection and establishes the security capabilities that will be associated with it. The exchange is initiated by the client, which sends a **client_hello message** with the following parameters:

- **Version:** The highest TLS version understood by the client.
- **Random:** A client-generated random structure consisting of a 32-bit timestamp and 28 bytes generated by a secure random number generator. These values serve as nonces and are used during key exchange to prevent replay attacks.
- **Session ID:** A variable-length session identifier. A nonzero value indicates that the client wishes to update the parameters of an existing connection or to create a new connection on this session. A zero value indicates that the client wishes to establish a new connection on a new session.

Table 6.2   TLS Handshake Protocol Message Types

Message Type	Parameters
hello_request	null
client_hello	version, random, session id, cipher suite, compression method
server_hello	version, random, session id, cipher suite, compression method
certificate	chain of X.509v3 certificates
server_key_exchange	parameters, signature
certificate_request	type, authorities
server_done	null
certificate_verify	signature
client_key_exchange	parameters, signature
finished	hash value

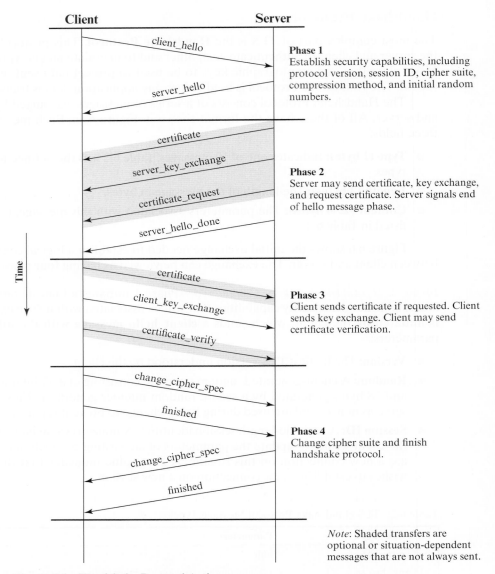

Figure 6.6   Handshake Protocol Action

■ **CipherSuite:** This is a list that contains the combinations of cryptographic algorithms supported by the client, in decreasing order of preference. Each element of the list (each cipher suite) defines both a key exchange algorithm and a CipherSpec; these are discussed subsequently.

■ **Compression Method:** This is a list of the compression methods the client supports.

After sending the client_hello message, the client waits for the **server_ hello message**, which contains the same parameters as the client_hello message. For the `server_hello` message, the following conventions apply. The Version field contains the lowest of the version suggested by the client and the highest supported by the server. The Random field is generated by the server and is independent of the client's Random field. If the SessionID field of the client was nonzero, the same value is used by the server; otherwise the server's SessionID field contains the value for a new session. The CipherSuite field contains the single cipher suite selected by the server from those proposed by the client. The Compression field contains the compression method selected by the server from those proposed by the client.

The first element of the Ciphersuite parameter is the key exchange method (i.e., the means by which the cryptographic keys for conventional encryption and MAC are exchanged). The following key exchange methods are supported.

- **RSA:** The secret key is encrypted with the receiver's RSA public key. A public-key certificate for the receiver's key must be made available.

- **Fixed Diffie–Hellman:** This is a Diffie–Hellman key exchange in which the server's certificate contains the Diffie–Hellman public parameters signed by the certificate authority (CA). That is, the public-key certificate contains the Diffie–Hellman public-key parameters. The client provides its Diffie–Hellman public-key parameters either in a certificate, if client authentication is required, or in a key exchange message. This method results in a fixed secret key between two peers based on the Diffie–Hellman calculation using the fixed public keys.

- **Ephemeral Diffie–Hellman:** This technique is used to create ephemeral (temporary, one-time) secret keys. In this case, the Diffie–Hellman public keys are exchanged and signed using the sender's private RSA or DSS key. The receiver can use the corresponding public key to verify the signature. Certificates are used to authenticate the public keys. This would appear to be the most secure of the three Diffie–Hellman options because it results in a temporary, authenticated key.

- **Anonymous Diffie–Hellman:** The base Diffie–Hellman algorithm is used with no authentication. That is, each side sends its public Diffie–Hellman parameters to the other with no authentication. This approach is vulnerable to man-in-the-middle attacks, in which the attacker conducts anonymous Diffie–Hellman with both parties.

Following the definition of a key exchange method is the CipherSpec, which includes the following fields:

- **CipherAlgorithm:** Any of the algorithms mentioned earlier: RC4, RC2, DES, 3DES, DES40, or IDEA
- **MACAlgorithm:** MD5 or SHA-1
- **CipherType:** Stream or Block
- **IsExportable:** True or False
- **HashSize:** 0, 16 (for MD5), or 20 (for SHA-1) bytes
- **Key Material:** A sequence of bytes that contain data used in generating the write keys
- **IV Size:** The size of the Initialization Value for Cipher Block Chaining (CBC) encryption

PHASE 2. SERVER AUTHENTICATION AND KEY EXCHANGE The server begins this phase by sending its certificate if it needs to be authenticated; the message contains one or a chain of X.509 certificates. The **certificate message** is required for any agreed-on key exchange method except anonymous Diffie–Hellman. Note that if fixed Diffie–Hellman is used, this certificate message functions as the server's key exchange message because it contains the server's public Diffie–Hellman parameters.

Next, a **server_key_exchange message** may be sent if it is required. It is not required in two instances: (1) The server has sent a certificate with fixed Diffie–Hellman parameters; or (2) RSA key exchange is to be used. The server_key_ exchange message is needed for the following:

- **Anonymous Diffie–Hellman:** The message content consists of the two global Diffie–Hellman values (a prime number and a primitive root of that number) plus the server's public Diffie–Hellman key (see Figure 10.1).

- **Ephemeral Diffie–Hellman:** The message content includes the three Diffie–Hellman parameters provided for anonymous Diffie–Hellman plus a signature of those parameters.

- **RSA key exchange (in which the server is using RSA but has a signature-only RSA key):** Accordingly, the client cannot simply send a secret key encrypted with the server's public key. Instead, the server must create a temporary RSA public/private key pair and use the server_key_exchange message to send the public key. The message content includes the two parameters of the temporary RSA public key (exponent and modulus; see Figure 9.5) plus a signature of those parameters.

Some further details about the signatures are warranted. As usual, a signature is created by taking the hash of a message and encrypting it with the sender's private key. In this case, the hash is defined as

$$hash(\text{ClientHello.random} \parallel \text{ServerHello.random} \parallel \text{ServerParams})$$

So the hash covers not only the Diffie–Hellman or RSA parameters but also the two nonces from the initial hello messages. This ensures against replay attacks and misrepresentation. In the case of a DSS signature, the hash is performed using the SHA-1 algorithm. In the case of an RSA signature, both an MD5 and an SHA-1 hash are calculated, and the concatenation of the two hashes (36 bytes) is encrypted with the server's private key.

Next, a nonanonymous server (server not using anonymous Diffie–Hellman) can request a certificate from the client. The **certificate_request message** includes two parameters: certificate_type and certificate_authorities. The certificate type indicates the public-key algorithm and its use:

- RSA, signature only
- DSS, signature only
- RSA for fixed Diffie–Hellman; in this case the signature is used only for authentication, by sending a certificate signed with RSA
- DSS for fixed Diffie–Hellman; again, used only for authentication

The second parameter in the certificate_request message is a list of the distinguished names of acceptable certificate authorities.

The final message in phase 2, and one that is always required, is the **server_ done message**, which is sent by the server to indicate the end of the server hello and associated messages. After sending this message, the server will wait for a client response. This message has no parameters.

PHASE 3. CLIENT AUTHENTICATION AND KEY EXCHANGE Upon receipt of the server_done message, the client should verify that the server provided a valid certificate (if required) and check that the server_hello parameters are acceptable. If all is satisfactory, the client sends one or more messages back to the server.

If the server has requested a certificate, the client begins this phase by sending a **certificate message**. If no suitable certificate is available, the client sends a no_certificate alert instead.

Next is the **client_key_exchange message**, which must be sent in this phase. The content of the message depends on the type of key exchange, as follows:

- **RSA:** The client generates a 48-byte *pre-master secret* and encrypts with the public key from the server's certificate or temporary RSA key from a server_ key_exchange message. Its use to compute a *master secret* is explained later.
- **Ephemeral or Anonymous Diffie–Hellman:** The client's public Diffie–Hellman parameters are sent.
- **Fixed Diffie–Hellman:** The client's public Diffie–Hellman parameters were sent in a certificate message, so the content of this message is null.

Finally, in this phase, the client may send a **certificate_verify message** to provide explicit verification of a client certificate. This message is only sent following any client certificate that has signing capability (i.e., all certificates except those containing fixed Diffie–Hellman parameters). This message signs a hash code based on the preceding messages, defined as

CertificateVerify.signature.md5_hash

   MD5(handshake_messages);

Certificate.signature.sha_hash

   SHA(handshake_messages);

where handshake_messages refers to all Handshake Protocol messages sent or received starting at client_hello but not including this message. If the user's private key is DSS, then it is used to encrypt the SHA-1 hash. If the user's private key is RSA, it is used to encrypt the concatenation of the MD5 and SHA-1 hashes. In either case, the purpose is to verify the client's ownership of the private key for the client certificate. Even if someone is misusing the client's certificate, he or she would be unable to send this message.

PHASE 4. FINISH Phase 4 completes the setting up of a secure connection. The client sends a **change_cipher_spec message** and copies the pending CipherSpec into the current CipherSpec. Note that this message is not considered part of the Handshake Protocol but is sent using the Change Cipher Spec Protocol. The client then immediately sends the **finished message** under the new algorithms, keys, and secrets.

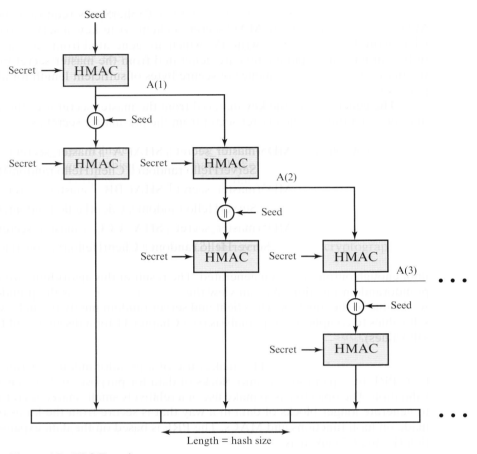

Figure 6.7 TLS Function `P_hash(secret, seed)`

To make PRF as secure as possible, it uses two hash algorithms in a way that should guarantee its security if either algorithm remains secure. PRF is defined as

$$\text{PRF(secret, label, seed)} = \text{P\_<hash>(secret, label || seed)}$$

PRF takes as input a secret value, an identifying label, and a seed value and produces an output of arbitrary length.

Heartbeat Protocol

In the context of computer networks, a heartbeat is a periodic signal generated by hardware or software to indicate normal operation or to synchronize other parts of a system. A heartbeat protocol is typically used to monitor the availability of a protocol entity. In the specific case of TLS, a Heartbeat protocol was defined in 2012 in RFC 6250 (*Transport Layer Security (TLS) and Datagram Transport Layer Security (DTLS) Heartbeat Extension*).

The Heartbeat protocol runs on top of the TLS Record Protocol and consists of two message types: `heartbeat_request` and `heartbeat_response`. The use of the Heartbeat protocol is established during Phase 1 of the Handshake protocol (Figure 6.6). Each peer indicates whether it supports heartbeats. If heartbeats are supported, the peer indicates whether it is willing to receive `heartbeat_request` messages and respond with `heartbeat_response` messages or only willing to send `heartbeat_request` messages.

A `heartbeat_request` message can be sent at any time. Whenever a request message is received, it should be answered promptly with a corresponding `heartbeat_response` message. The `heartbeat_request` message includes payload length, payload, and padding fields. The payload is a random content between 16 bytes and 64 Kbytes in length. The corresponding `heartbeat_response` message must include an exact copy of the received payload. The padding is also random content. The padding enables the sender to perform a path MTU (maximum transfer unit) discovery operation, by sending requests with increasing padding until there is no answer anymore, because one of the hosts on the path cannot handle the message.

The heartbeat serves two purposes. First, it assures the sender that the recipient is still alive, even though there may not have been any activity over the underlying TCP connection for a while. Second, the heartbeat generates activity across the connection during idle periods, which avoids closure by a firewall that does not tolerate idle connections.

The requirement for the exchange of a payload was designed into the Heartbeat protocol to support its use in a connectionless version of TLS known as Datagram Transport Layer Security (DTLS). Because a connectionless service is subject to packet loss, the payload enables the requestor to match response messages to request messages. For simplicity, the same version of the Heartbeat protocol is used with both TLS and DTLS. Thus, the payload is required for both TLS and DTLS.

SSL/TLS ATTACKS

Since the first introduction of SSL in 1994, and the subsequent standardization of TLS, numerous attacks have been devised against these protocols. The appearance of each attack has necessitated changes in the protocol, the encryption tools used, or some aspect of the implementation of SSL and TLS to counter these threats.

ATTACK CATEGORIES We can group the attacks into four general categories:

- **Attacks on the handshake protocol:** As early as 1998, an approach to compromising the handshake protocol based on exploiting the formatting and implementation of the RSA encryption scheme was presented [BLEI98]. As countermeasures were implemented the attack was refined and adjusted to not only thwart the countermeasures but also speed up the attack [e.g., BARD12].

- **Attacks on the record and application data protocols:** A number of vulnerabilities have been discovered in these protocols, leading to patches to counter the new threats. As a recent example, in 2011, researchers Thai Duong and Juliano Rizzo demonstrated a proof of concept called BEAST (Browser Exploit Against SSL/TLS) that turned what had been considered only a theoretical vulnerability

finished, the client may then initiate the first HTTP request. All HTTP data is to be sent as TLS application data. Normal HTTP behavior, including retained connections, should be followed.

There are three levels of awareness of a connection in HTTPS. At the HTTP level, an HTTP client requests a connection to an HTTP server by sending a connection request to the next lowest layer. Typically, the next lowest layer is TCP, but it also may be TLS/SSL. At the level of TLS, a session is established between a TLS client and a TLS server. This session can support one or more connections at any time. As we have seen, a TLS request to establish a connection begins with the establishment of a TCP connection between the TCP entity on the client side and the TCP entity on the server side.

Connection Closure

An HTTP client or server can indicate the closing of a connection by including the following line in an HTTP record: `Connection: close`. This indicates that the connection will be closed after this record is delivered.

The closure of an HTTPS connection requires that TLS close the connection with the peer TLS entity on the remote side, which will involve closing the underlying TCP connection. At the TLS level, the proper way to close a connection is for each side to use the TLS alert protocol to send a `close_notify` alert. TLS implementations must initiate an exchange of closure alerts before closing a connection. A TLS implementation may, after sending a closure alert, close the connection without waiting for the peer to send its closure alert, generating an "incomplete close". Note that an implementation that does this may choose to reuse the session. This should only be done when the application knows (typically through detecting HTTP message boundaries) that it has received all the message data that it cares about.

HTTP clients also must be able to cope with a situation in which the underlying TCP connection is terminated without a prior `close_notify` alert and without a `Connection: close` indicator. Such a situation could be due to a programming error on the server or a communication error that causes the TCP connection to drop. However, the unannounced TCP closure could be evidence of some sort of attack. So the HTTPS client should issue some sort of security warning when this occurs.

6.4 SECURE SHELL (SSH)

Secure Shell (SSH) is a protocol for secure network communications designed to be relatively simple and inexpensive to implement. The initial version, SSH1 was focused on providing a secure remote logon facility to replace TELNET and other remote logon schemes that provided no security. SSH also provides a more general client/server capability and can be used for such network functions as file transfer and e-mail. A new version, SSH2, fixes a number of security flaws in the original scheme. SSH2 is documented as a proposed standard in IETF RFCs 4250 through 4256.

SSH client and server applications are widely available for most operating systems. It has become the method of choice for remote login and X tunneling and

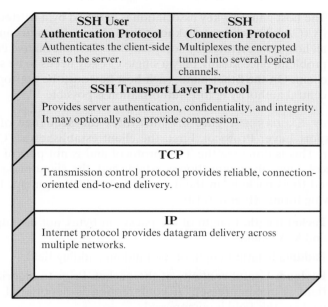

Figure 6.8   SSH Protocol Stack

is rapidly becoming one of the most pervasive applications for encryption technology outside of embedded systems.

SSH is organized as three protocols that typically run on top of TCP (Figure 6.8):

- **Transport Layer Protocol:** Provides server authentication, data confidentiality, and data integrity with forward secrecy (i.e., if a key is compromised during one session, the knowledge does not affect the security of earlier sessions). The transport layer may optionally provide compression.

- **User Authentication Protocol:** Authenticates the user to the server.

- **Connection Protocol:** Multiplexes multiple logical communications channels over a single, underlying SSH connection.

Transport Layer Protocol

HOST KEYS Server authentication occurs at the transport layer, based on the server possessing a public/private key pair. A server may have multiple host keys using multiple different asymmetric encryption algorithms. Multiple hosts may share the same host key. In any case, the server host key is used during key exchange to authenticate the identity of the host. For this to be possible, the client must have a priori knowledge of the server's public host key. RFC 4251 dictates two alternative trust models that can be used:

1. The client has a local database that associates each host name (as typed by the user) with the corresponding public host key. This method requires no centrally administered infrastructure and no third-party coordination. The downside is that the database of name-to-key associations may become burdensome to maintain.

2. The host name-to-key association is certified by a trusted certification authority (CA). The client only knows the CA root key and can verify the validity of all host keys certified by accepted CAs. This alternative eases the maintenance problem, since ideally, only a single CA key needs to be securely stored on the client. On the other hand, each host key must be appropriately certified by a central authority before authorization is possible.

PACKET EXCHANGE Figure 6.9 illustrates the sequence of events in the SSH Transport Layer Protocol. First, the client establishes a TCP connection to the server. This is done via the TCP protocol and is not part of the Transport Layer Protocol. Once the connection is established, the client and server exchange data, referred to as packets, in the data field of a TCP segment. Each packet is in the following format (Figure 6.10).

- **Packet length:** Length of the packet in bytes, not including the packet length and MAC fields.
- **Padding length:** Length of the random padding field.
- **Payload:** Useful contents of the packet. Prior to algorithm negotiation, this field is uncompressed. If compression is negotiated, then in subsequent packets, this field is compressed.

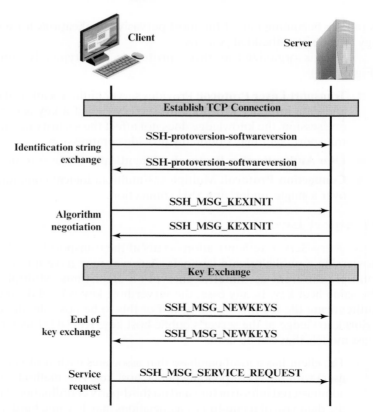

Figure 6.9   SSH Transport Layer Protocol Packet Exchanges

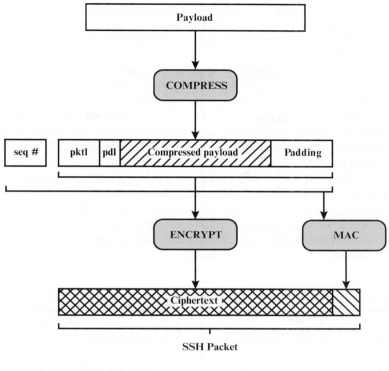

pktl = packet length
pdl = padding length

Figure 6.10   SSH Transport Layer Protocol Packet Formation

- **Random padding:** Once an encryption algorithm has been negotiated, this field is added. It contains random bytes of padding so that the total length of the packet (excluding the MAC field) is a multiple of the cipher block size, or 8 bytes for a stream cipher.

- **Message authentication code (MAC):** If message authentication has been negotiated, this field contains the MAC value. The MAC value is computed over the entire packet plus a sequence number, excluding the MAC field. The sequence number is an implicit 32-bit packet sequence that is initialized to zero for the first packet and incremented for every packet. The sequence number is not included in the packet sent over the TCP connection.

Once an encryption algorithm has been negotiated, the entire packet (excluding the MAC field) is encrypted after the MAC value is calculated.

The SSH Transport Layer packet exchange consists of a sequence of steps (Figure 6.9). The first step, the **identification string exchange**, begins with the client sending a packet with an identification string of the form:

```
SSH-protoversion-softwareversion SP comments CR LF
```

where SP, CR, and LF are space character, carriage return, and line feed, respectively. An example of a valid string is SSH-2.0-billsSSH_3.6.3q3<CR><LF>. The server responds with its own identification string. These strings are used in the Diffie–Hellman key exchange.

Next comes **algorithm negotiation**. Each side sends an SSH_MSG_KEXINIT containing lists of supported algorithms in the order of preference to the sender. There is one list for each type of cryptographic algorithm. The algorithms include key exchange, encryption, MAC algorithm, and compression algorithm. Table 6.3 shows the allowable options for encryption, MAC, and compression. For each category, the algorithm chosen is the first algorithm on the client's list that is also supported by the server.

The next step is **key exchange**. The specification allows for alternative methods of key exchange, but at present, only two versions of Diffie–Hellman key exchange are specified. Both versions are defined in RFC 2409 and require only one packet in each direction. The following steps are involved in the exchange. In this, C is the client; S is the server; p is a large safe prime; g is a generator for a subgroup of $GF(p)$; q is the order of the subgroup; V_S is S's identification string; V_C is

Table 6.3   SSH Transport Layer Cryptographic Algorithms

Cipher		MAC algorithm	
3des-cbc*	Three-key 3DES in CBC mode	hmac-sha1*	HMAC-SHA1; digest length = key length = 20
blowfish-cbc	Blowfish in CBC mode	hmac-sha1-96**	First 96 bits of HMAC-SHA1; digest length = 12; key length = 20
twofish256-cbc	Twofish in CBC mode with a 256-bit key	hmac-md5	HMAC-MD5; digest length = key length = 16
twofish192-cbc	Twofish with a 192-bit key	hmac-md5-96	First 96 bits of HMAC-MD5; digest length = 12; key length = 16
twofish128-cbc	Twofish with a 128-bit key		

Cipher (cont.)		Compression algorithm	
aes256-cbc	AES in CBC mode with a 256-bit key	none*	No compression
aes192-cbc	AES with a 192-bit key	zlib	Defined in RFC 1950 and RFC 1951
aes128-cbc**	AES with a 128-bit key		
Serpent256-cbc	Serpent in CBC mode with a 256-bit key		
Serpent192-cbc	Serpent with a 192-bit key		
Serpent128-cbc	Serpent with a 128-bit key		
arcfour	RC4 with a 128-bit key		
cast128-cbc	CAST-128 in CBC mode		

* = Required
** = Recommended

C's identification string; K_S is S's public host key; I_C is C's SSH_MSG_KEXINIT message and I_S is S's SSH_MSG_KEXINIT message that have been exchanged before this part begins. The values of p, g, and q are known to both client and server as a result of the algorithm selection negotiation. The hash function hash() is also decided during algorithm negotiation.

1. C generates a random number $x(1 < x < q)$ and computes $e = g^x \bmod p$. C sends e to S.

2. S generates a random number $y(0 < y < q)$ and computes $f = g^y \bmod p$. S receives e. It computes $K = e^y \bmod p, H = \text{hash}(\text{V\_C} \| \text{V\_S} \| \text{I\_C} \| \text{I\_S} \| \text{K\_S} \| e \| f \| K)$, and signature s on H with its private host key. S sends $(\text{K\_S} \| f \| s)$ to C. The signing operation may involve a second hashing operation.

3. C verifies that K_S really is the host key for S (e.g., using certificates or a local database). C is also allowed to accept the key without verification; however, doing so will render the protocol insecure against active attacks (but may be desirable for practical reasons in the short term in many environments). C then computes $K = f^x \bmod p, H = \text{hash}(\text{V\_C} \| \text{V\_S} \| \text{I\_C} \| \text{I\_S} \| \text{K\_S} \| e \| f \| K)$, and verifies the signature s on H.

As a result of these steps, the two sides now share a master key K. In addition, the server has been authenticated to the client, because the server has used its private key to sign its half of the Diffie–Hellman exchange. Finally, the hash value H serves as a session identifier for this connection. Once computed, the session identifier is not changed, even if the key exchange is performed again for this connection to obtain fresh keys.

The **end of key exchange** is signaled by the exchange of SSH_MSG_NEWKEYS packets. At this point, both sides may start using the keys generated from K, as discussed subsequently.

The final step is **service request**. The client sends an SSH_MSG_SERVICE_REQUEST packet to request either the User Authentication or the Connection Protocol. Subsequent to this, all data is exchanged as the payload of an SSH Transport Layer packet, protected by encryption and MAC.

KEY GENERATION The keys used for encryption and MAC (and any needed IVs) are generated from the shared secret key K, the hash value from the key exchange H, and the session identifier, which is equal to H unless there has been a subsequent key exchange after the initial key exchange. The values are computed as follows.

- Initial IV client to server: $\text{HASH}(K \| H \| \text{"A"} \| \text{session\_id})$
- Initial IV server to client: $\text{HASH}(K \| H \| \text{"B"} \| \text{session\_id})$
- Encryption key client to server: $\text{HASH}(K \| H \| \text{"C"} \| \text{session\_id})$
- Encryption key server to client: $\text{HASH}(K \| H \| \text{"D"} \| \text{session\_id})$
- Integrity key client to server: $\text{HASH}(K \| H \| \text{"E"} \| \text{session\_id})$
- Integrity key server to client: $\text{HASH}(K \| H \| \text{"F"} \| \text{session\_id})$

where HASH() is the hash function determined during algorithm negotiation.

User Authentication Protocol

The User Authentication Protocol provides the means by which the client is authenticated to the server.

MESSAGE TYPES AND FORMATS Three types of messages are always used in the User Authentication Protocol. Authentication requests from the client have the format:

byte	SSH_MSG_USERAUTH_REQUEST (50)
string	user name
string	service name
string	method name
. . .	method specific fields

where user name is the authorization identity the client is claiming, service name is the facility to which the client is requesting access (typically the SSH Connection Protocol), and method name is the authentication method being used in this request. The first byte has decimal value 50, which is interpreted as SSH_MSG_USERAUTH_REQUEST.

If the server either (1) rejects the authentication request or (2) accepts the request but requires one or more additional authentication methods, the server sends a message with the format:

byte	SSH_MSG_USERAUTH_FAILURE (51)
name-list	authentications that can continue
boolean	partial success

where the name-list is a list of methods that may productively continue the dialog. If the server accepts authentication, it sends a single byte message: SSH_MSG_USERAUTH_SUCCESS (52).

MESSAGE EXCHANGE The message exchange involves the following steps.

1. The client sends a SSH_MSG_USERAUTH_REQUEST with a requested method of none.
2. The server checks to determine if the user name is valid. If not, the server returns SSH_MSG_USERAUTH_FAILURE with the partial success value of false. If the user name is valid, the server proceeds to step 3.
3. The server returns SSH_MSG_USERAUTH_FAILURE with a list of one or more authentication methods to be used.
4. The client selects one of the acceptable authentication methods and sends a SSH_MSG_USERAUTH_REQUEST with that method name and the required method-specific fields. At this point, there may be a sequence of exchanges to perform the method.

5. If the authentication succeeds and more authentication methods are required, the server proceeds to step 3, using a partial success value of true. If the authentication fails, the server proceeds to step 3, using a partial success value of false.

6. When all required authentication methods succeed, the server sends a `SSH_MSG_USERAUTH_SUCCESS` message, and the Authentication Protocol is over.

AUTHENTICATION METHODS   The server may require one or more of the following authentication methods.

■ **publickey:** The details of this method depend on the public-key algorithm chosen. In essence, the client sends a message to the server that contains the client's public key, with the message signed by the client's private key. When the server receives this message, it checks whether the supplied key is acceptable for authentication and, if so, it checks whether the signature is correct.

■ **password:** The client sends a message containing a plaintext password, which is protected by encryption by the Transport Layer Protocol.

■ **hostbased:** Authentication is performed on the client's host rather than the client itself. Thus, a host that supports multiple clients would provide authentication for all its clients. This method works by having the client send a signature created with the private key of the client host. Thus, rather than directly verifying the user's identity, the SSH server verifies the identity of the client host—and then believes the host when it says the user has already authenticated on the client side.

Connection Protocol

The SSH Connection Protocol runs on top of the SSH Transport Layer Protocol and assumes that a secure authentication connection is in use.[2] That secure authentication connection, referred to as a **tunnel**, is used by the Connection Protocol to multiplex a number of logical channels.

CHANNEL MECHANISM   All types of communication using SSH, such as a terminal session, are supported using separate channels. Either side may open a channel. For each channel, each side associates a unique channel number, which need not be the same on both ends. Channels are flow controlled using a window mechanism. No data may be sent to a channel until a message is received to indicate that window space is available.

---

[2]RFC 4254, *The Secure Shell (SSH) Connection Protocol*, states that the Connection Protocol runs on top of the Transport Layer Protocol and the User Authentication Protocol. RFC 4251, *SSH Protocol Architecture*, states that the Connection Protocol runs over the User Authentication Protocol. In fact, the Connection Protocol runs over the Transport Layer Protocol, but assumes that the User Authentication Protocol has been previously invoked.

6.5 KEY TERMS, REVIEW QUESTIONS, AND PROBLEMS

Key Terms

Alert protocol	HTTPS (HTTP over SSL)	Secure Socket Layer (SSL)
Change Cipher Spec protocol	Master Secret	Transport Layer Security
Handshake protocol	Secure Shell (SSH)	(TLS)

Review Questions

6.1 What are the advantages of each of the three approaches shown in Figure 6.1?

6.2 What protocols comprise TLS?

6.3 What is the difference between a TLS connection and a TLS session?

6.4 List and briefly define the parameters that define a TLS session state.

6.5 List and briefly define the parameters that define a TLS session connection.

6.6 What services are provided by the TLS Record Protocol?

6.7 What steps are involved in the TLS Record Protocol transmission?

6.8 Give brief details about different levels of awareness of a connection in HTTPS.

6.9 Which protocol was replaced by SSH and why? Which version is currently in the process of being standardized?

6.10 List and briefly define the SSH protocols.

Problems

6.1 In SSL and TLS, why is there a separate Change Cipher Spec Protocol rather than including a `change_cipher_spec` message in the Handshake Protocol?

6.2 What purpose does the MAC serve during the change cipher spec TLS exchange?

6.3 Consider the following threats to Web security and describe how each is countered by a particular feature of TLS.

    a. Brute-Force Cryptanalytic Attack: An exhaustive search of the key space for a conventional encryption algorithm.

    b. Known Plaintext Dictionary Attack: Many messages will contain predictable plaintext, such as the HTTP GET command. An attacker constructs a dictionary containing every possible encryption of the known-plaintext message. When an encrypted message is intercepted, the attacker takes the portion containing the encrypted known plaintext and looks up the ciphertext in the dictionary. The ciphertext should match against an entry that was encrypted with the same secret key. If there are several matches, each of these can be tried against the full ciphertext to determine the right one. This attack is especially effective against small key sizes (e.g., 40-bit keys).

    c. Replay Attack: Earlier TLS handshake messages are replayed.

    d. Man-in-the-Middle Attack: An attacker interposes during key exchange, acting as the client to the server and as the server to the client.

    e. Password Sniffing: Passwords in HTTP or other application traffic are eavesdropped.

    f. IP Spoofing: Uses forged IP addresses to fool a host into accepting bogus data.

g. IP Hijacking: An active, authenticated connection between two hosts is disrupted and the attacker takes the place of one of the hosts.

h. SYN Flooding: An attacker sends TCP SYN messages to request a connection but does not respond to the final message to establish the connection fully. The attacked TCP module typically leaves the "half-open connection" around for a few minutes. Repeated SYN messages can clog the TCP module.

6.4 Based on what you have learned in this chapter, is it possible in TLS for the receiver to reorder TLS record blocks that arrive out of order? If so, explain how it can be done. If not, why not?

6.5 For SSH packets, what is the advantage, if any, of not including the MAC in the scope of the packet encryption?

CHAPTER

7

WIRELESS NETWORK SECURITY

LEARNING OBJECTIVES

After studying this chapter, you should be able to:

◆ Present an overview of security threats and countermeasures for wireless networks.

◆ Understand the unique security threats posed by the use of mobile devices with enterprise networks.

◆ Describe the principal elements in a mobile device security strategy.

◆ Understand the essential elements of the IEEE 802.11 wireless LAN standard.

◆ Summarize the various components of the IEEE 802.11i wireless LAN security architecture.

This chapter begins with a general overview of wireless security issues. We then focus on the relatively new area of mobile device security, examining threats and counter-measures for mobile devices used in the enterprise. Then, we look at the IEEE 802.11i standard for wireless LAN security. This standard is part of IEEE 802.11, also referred to as Wi-Fi. We begin the discussion with an overview of IEEE 802.11, and then we look in some detail at IEEE 802.11i.

7.1 WIRELESS SECURITY

Wireless networks, and the wireless devices that use them, introduce a host of security problems over and above those found in wired networks. Some of the key factors contributing to the higher security risk of wireless networks compared to wired networks include the following [MA10]:

■ **Channel:** Wireless networking typically involves broadcast communications, which is far more susceptible to eavesdropping and jamming than wired networks. Wireless networks are also more vulnerable to active attacks that exploit vulnerabilities in communications protocols.

■ **Mobility:** Wireless devices are, in principal and usually in practice, far more portable and mobile than wired devices. This mobility results in a number of risks, described subsequently.

■ **Resources:** Some wireless devices, such as smartphones and tablets, have sophisticated operating systems but limited memory and processing resources with which to counter threats, including denial of service and malware.

■ **Accessibility:** Some wireless devices, such as sensors and robots, may be left unattended in remote and/or hostile locations. This greatly increases their vulnerability to physical attacks.

SECURING WIRELESS ACCESS POINTS The main threat involving wireless access points is unauthorized access to the network. The principal approach for preventing such access is the IEEE 802.1X standard for port-based network access control. The standard provides an authentication mechanism for devices wishing to attach to a LAN or wireless network. The use of 802.1X can prevent rogue access points and other unauthorized devices from becoming insecure backdoors.

Section 5.3 provides an introduction to 802.1X.

USE OF UNTRUSTED NETWORKS If a mobile device is used on premises, it can connect to organization resources over the organization's own in-house wireless networks. However, for off-premises use, the user will typically access organizational resources via Wi-Fi or cellular access to the Internet and from the Internet to the organization. Thus, traffic that includes an off-premises segment is potentially susceptible to eavesdropping or man-in-the-middle types of attacks. Thus, the security policy must be based on the assumption that the networks between the mobile device and the organization are not trustworthy.

USE OF APPLICATIONS CREATED BY UNKNOWN PARTIES By design, it is easy to find and install third-party applications on mobile devices. This poses the obvious risk of installing malicious software. An organization has several options for dealing with this threat, as described subsequently.

INTERACTION WITH OTHER SYSTEMS A common feature found on smartphones and tablets is the ability to automatically synchronize data, apps, contacts, photos, and so on with other computing devices and with cloud-based storage. Unless an organization has control of all the devices involved in synchronization, there is considerable risk of the organization's data being stored in an unsecured location, plus the risk of the introduction of malware.

USE OF UNTRUSTED CONTENT Mobile devices may access and use content that other computing devices do not encounter. An example is the Quick Response (QR) code, which is a two-dimensional barcode. QR codes are designed to be captured by a mobile device camera and used by the mobile device. The QR code translates to a URL, so that a malicious QR code could direct the mobile device to malicious Web sites.

USE OF LOCATION SERVICES The GPS capability on mobile devices can be used to maintain a knowledge of the physical location of the device. While this feature might be useful to an organization as part of a presence service, it creates security risks. An attacker can use the location information to determine where the device and user are located, which may be of use to the attacker.

Mobile Device Security Strategy

With the threats listed in the preceding discussion in mind, we outline the principal elements of a mobile device security strategy. They fall into three categories: device security, client/server traffic security, and barrier security (Figure 7.2).

DEVICE SECURITY A number of organizations will supply mobile devices for employee use and preconfigure those devices to conform to the enterprise security policy. However, many organizations will find it convenient or even necessary to adopt a bring-your-own-device (BYOD) policy that allows the personal mobile devices of employees to have access to corporate resources. IT managers should be able to inspect each device before allowing network access. IT will want to establish configuration guidelines for operating systems and applications. For example, "rooted" or "jail-broken" devices are not permitted on the network, and mobile

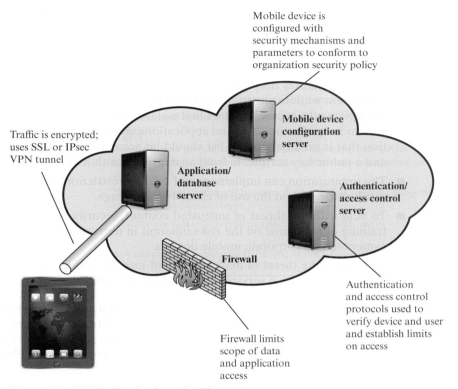

Mobile device is configured with security mechanisms and parameters to conform to organization security policy

Mobile device configuration server

Traffic is encrypted; uses SSL or IPsec VPN tunnel

Application/ database server

Authentication/ access control server

Firewall

Authentication and access control protocols used to verify device and user and establish limits on access

Firewall limits scope of data and application access

Figure 7.2   Mobile Device Security Elements

devices cannot store corporate contacts on local storage. Whether a device is owned by the organization or BYOD, the organization should configure the device with security controls, including the following:

- Enable auto-lock, which causes the device to lock if it has not been used for a given amount of time, requiring the user to re-enter a four-digit PIN or a password to re-activate the device.

- Enable password or PIN protection. The PIN or password is needed to unlock the device. In addition, it can be configured so that e-mail and other data on the device are encrypted using the PIN or password and can only be retrieved with the PIN or password.

- Avoid using auto-complete features that remember user names or passwords.

- Enable remote wipe.

- Ensure that SSL protection is enabled, if available.

- Make sure that software, including operating systems and applications, is up to date.

- Install antivirus software as it becomes available.

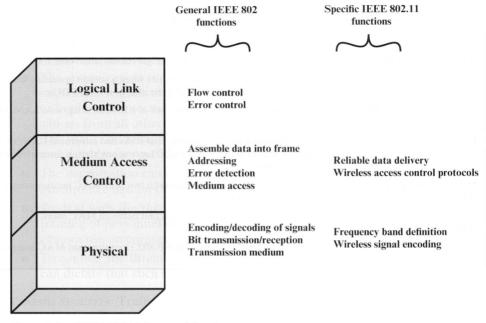

Figure 7.3 IEEE 802.11 Protocol Stack

MEDIA ACCESS CONTROL All LANs consist of collections of devices that share the network's transmission capacity. Some means of controlling access to the transmission medium is needed to provide an orderly and efficient use of that capacity. This is the function of a **media access control (MAC)** layer. The MAC layer receives data from a higher-layer protocol, typically the Logical Link Control (LLC) layer, in the form of a block of data known as the **MAC service data unit (MSDU)**. In general, the MAC layer performs the following functions:

■ On transmission, assemble data into a frame, known as a **MAC protocol data unit (MPDU)** with address and error-detection fields.

■ On reception, disassemble frame, and perform address recognition and error detection.

■ Govern access to the LAN transmission medium.

The exact format of the MPDU differs somewhat for the various MAC protocols in use. In general, all of the MPDUs have a format similar to that of Figure 7.4. The fields of this frame are as follows.

■ **MAC Control:** This field contains any protocol control information needed for the functioning of the MAC protocol. For example, a priority level could be indicated here.

■ **Destination MAC Address:** The destination physical address on the LAN for this MPDU.

■ **Source MAC Address:** The source physical address on the LAN for this MPDU.

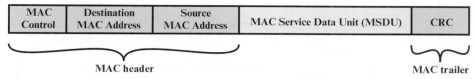

MAC Control	Destination MAC Address	Source MAC Address	MAC Service Data Unit (MSDU)	CRC

MAC header   MAC trailer

Figure 7.4   General IEEE 802 MPDU Format

- **MAC Service Data Unit:** The data from the next higher layer.
- **CRC:** The cyclic redundancy check field; also known as the Frame Check Sequence (FCS) field. This is an error-detecting code, such as that which is used in other data-link control protocols. The CRC is calculated based on the bits in the entire MPDU. The sender calculates the CRC and adds it to the frame. The receiver performs the same calculation on the incoming MPDU and compares that calculation to the CRC field in that incoming MPDU. If the two values don't match, then one or more bits have been altered in transit.

The fields preceding the MSDU field are referred to as the **MAC header**, and the field following the MSDU field is referred to as the **MAC trailer**. The header and trailer contain control information that accompany the data field and that are used by the MAC protocol.

LOGICAL LINK CONTROL In most data-link control protocols, the data-link protocol entity is responsible not only for detecting errors using the CRC, but for recovering from those errors by retransmitting damaged frames. In the LAN protocol architecture, these two functions are split between the MAC and LLC layers. The MAC layer is responsible for detecting errors and discarding any frames that contain errors. The LLC layer optionally keeps track of which frames have been successfully received and retransmits unsuccessful frames.

IEEE 802.11 Network Components and Architectural Model

Figure 7.5 illustrates the model developed by the 802.11 working group. The smallest building block of a wireless LAN is a **basic service set (BSS)**, which consists of wireless stations executing the same MAC protocol and competing for access to the same shared wireless medium. A BSS may be isolated, or it may connect to a backbone **distribution system (DS)** through an **access point (AP)**. The AP functions as a bridge and a relay point. In a BSS, client stations do not communicate directly with one another. Rather, if one station in the BSS wants to communicate with another station in the same BSS, the MAC frame is first sent from the originating station to the AP and then from the AP to the destination station. Similarly, a MAC frame from a station in the BSS to a remote station is sent from the local station to the AP and then relayed by the AP over the DS on its way to the destination station. The BSS generally corresponds to what is referred to as a cell in the literature. The DS can be a switch, a wired network, or a wireless network.

When all the stations in the BSS are mobile stations that communicate directly with one another (not using an AP), the BSS is called an **independent BSS (IBSS)**. An IBSS is typically an ad hoc network. In an IBSS, the stations all communicate directly, and no AP is involved.

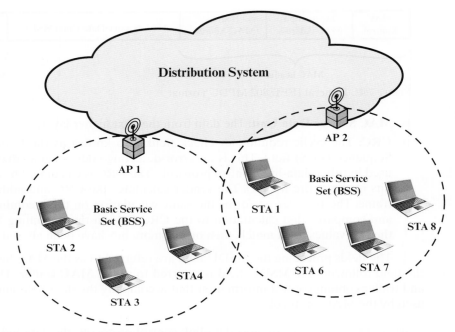

Figure 7.5   IEEE 802.11 Extended Service Set

A simple configuration is shown in Figure 7.5, in which each station belongs to a single BSS; that is, each station is within wireless range only of other stations within the same BSS. It is also possible for two BSSs to overlap geographically, so that a single station could participate in more than one BSS. Furthermore, the association between a station and a BSS is dynamic. Stations may turn off, come within range, and go out of range.

An **extended service set (ESS)** consists of two or more basic service sets interconnected by a distribution system. The extended service set appears as a single logical LAN to the logical link control (LLC) level.

IEEE 802.11 Services

IEEE 802.11 defines nine services that need to be provided by the wireless LAN to achieve functionality equivalent to that which is inherent to wired LANs. Table 7.2 lists the services and indicates two ways of categorizing them.

1. The service provider can be either the station or the DS. Station services are implemented in every 802.11 station, including AP stations. Distribution services are provided between BSSs; these services may be implemented in an AP or in another special-purpose device attached to the distribution system.

2. Three of the services are used to control IEEE 802.11 LAN access and confidentiality. Six of the services are used to support delivery of MSDUs between stations. If the MSDU is too large to be transmitted in a single MPDU, it may be fragmented and transmitted in a series of MPDUs.

Table 7.2   IEEE 802.11 Services

Service	Provider	Used to support
Association	Distribution system	MSDU delivery
Authentication	Station	LAN access and security
Deauthentication	Station	LAN access and security
Disassociation	Distribution system	MSDU delivery
Distribution	Distribution system	MSDU delivery
Integration	Distribution system	MSDU delivery
MSDU delivery	Station	MSDU delivery
Privacy	Station	LAN access and security
Reassociation	Distribution system	MSDU delivery

Following the IEEE 802.11 document, we next discuss the services in an order designed to clarify the operation of an IEEE 802.11 ESS network. **MSDU delivery**, which is the basic service, already has been mentioned. Services related to security are introduced in Section 7.4.

DISTRIBUTION OF MESSAGES WITHIN A DS The two services involved with the distribution of messages within a DS are distribution and integration. **Distribution** is the primary service used by stations to exchange MPDUs when the MPDUs must traverse the DS to get from a station in one BSS to a station in another BSS. For example, suppose a frame is to be sent from station 2 (STA 2) to station 7 (STA 7) in Figure 7.5. The frame is sent from STA 2 to AP 1, which is the AP for this BSS. The AP gives the frame to the DS, which has the job of directing the frame to the AP associated with STA 7 in the target BSS. AP 2 receives the frame and forwards it to STA 7. How the message is transported through the DS is beyond the scope of the IEEE 802.11 standard.

If the two stations that are communicating are within the same BSS, then the distribution service logically goes through the single AP of that BSS.

The **integration** service enables transfer of data between a station on an IEEE 802.11 LAN and a station on an integrated IEEE 802.x LAN. The term *integrated* refers to a wired LAN that is physically connected to the DS and whose stations may be logically connected to an IEEE 802.11 LAN via the integration service. The integration service takes care of any address translation and media conversion logic required for the exchange of data.

ASSOCIATION-RELATED SERVICES The primary purpose of the MAC layer is to transfer MSDUs between MAC entities; this purpose is fulfilled by the distribution service. For that service to function, it requires information about stations within the ESS that is provided by the association-related services. Before the distribution service can deliver data to or accept data from a station, that station must be *associated*. Before looking at the concept of association, we need to describe the concept of mobility. The standard defines three transition types, based on mobility:

- **No transition:** A station of this type is either stationary or moves only within the direct communication range of the communicating stations of a single BSS.

- **BSS transition:** This is defined as a station movement from one BSS to another BSS within the same ESS. In this case, delivery of data to the station requires that the addressing capability be able to recognize the new location of the station.

- **ESS transition:** This is defined as a station movement from a BSS in one ESS to a BSS within another ESS. This case is supported only in the sense that the station can move. Maintenance of upper-layer connections supported by 802.11 cannot be guaranteed. In fact, disruption of service is likely to occur.

To deliver a message within a DS, the distribution service needs to know where the destination station is located. Specifically, the DS needs to know the identity of the AP to which the message should be delivered in order for that message to reach the destination station. To meet this requirement, a station must maintain an association with the AP within its current BSS. Three services relate to this requirement:

- **Association:** Establishes an initial association between a station and an AP. Before a station can transmit or receive frames on a wireless LAN, its identity and address must be known. For this purpose, a station must establish an association with an AP within a particular BSS. The AP can then communicate this information to other APs within the ESS to facilitate routing and delivery of addressed frames.

- **Reassociation:** Enables an established association to be transferred from one AP to another, allowing a mobile station to move from one BSS to another.

- **Disassociation:** A notification from either a station or an AP that an existing association is terminated. A station should give this notification before leaving an ESS or shutting down. However, the MAC management facility protects itself against stations that disappear without notification.

7.4 IEEE 802.11i WIRELESS LAN SECURITY

There are two characteristics of a wired LAN that are not inherent in a wireless LAN.

1. In order to transmit over a wired LAN, a station must be physically connected to the LAN. On the other hand, with a wireless LAN, any station within radio range of the other devices on the LAN can transmit. In a sense, there is a form of authentication with a wired LAN in that it requires some positive and presumably observable action to connect a station to a wired LAN.

2. Similarly, in order to receive a transmission from a station that is part of a wired LAN, the receiving station also must be attached to the wired LAN. On the other hand, with a wireless LAN, any station within radio range can receive. Thus, a wired LAN provides a degree of privacy, limiting reception of data to stations connected to the LAN.

These differences between wired and wireless LANs suggest the increased need for robust security services and mechanisms for wireless LANs. The original 802.11 specification included a set of security features for privacy and authentication that were quite weak. For privacy, 802.11 defined the **Wired Equivalent Privacy (WEP)** algorithm. The privacy portion of the 802.11 standard contained major weaknesses. Subsequent to the development of WEP, the 802.11i task group has developed a set of capabilities to address the WLAN security issues. In order to accelerate the introduction of strong security into WLANs, the Wi-Fi Alliance promulgated **Wi-Fi Protected Access (WPA)** as a Wi-Fi standard. WPA is a set of security mechanisms that eliminates most 802.11 security issues and was based on the current state of the 802.11i standard. The final form of the 802.11i standard is referred to as **Robust Security Network (RSN)**. The Wi-Fi Alliance certifies vendors in compliance with the full 802.11i specification under the WPA2 program.

The RSN specification is quite complex, and occupies 145 pages of the 2012 IEEE 802.11 standard. In this section, we provide an overview.

IEEE 802.11i Services

The 802.11i RSN security specification defines the following services.

- **Authentication:** A protocol is used to define an exchange between a user and an AS that provides mutual authentication and generates temporary keys to be used between the client and the AP over the wireless link.

- **Access control:**[1] This function enforces the use of the authentication function, routes the messages properly, and facilitates key exchange. It can work with a variety of authentication protocols.

- **Privacy with message integrity:** MAC-level data (e.g., an LLC PDU) are encrypted along with a message integrity code that ensures that the data have not been altered.

Figure 7.6a indicates the security protocols used to support these services, while Figure 7.6b lists the cryptographic algorithms used for these services.

IEEE 802.11i Phases of Operation

The operation of an IEEE 802.11i RSN can be broken down into five distinct phases of operation. The exact nature of the phases will depend on the configuration and the end points of the communication. Possibilities include (see Figure 7.5):

1. Two wireless stations in the same BSS communicating via the access point (AP) for that BSS.

2. Two wireless stations (STAs) in the same ad hoc IBSS communicating directly with each other.

---

[1]In this context, we are discussing access control as a security function. This is a different function than media access control (MAC) as described in Section 7.3. Unfortunately, the literature and the standards use the term *access control* in both contexts.

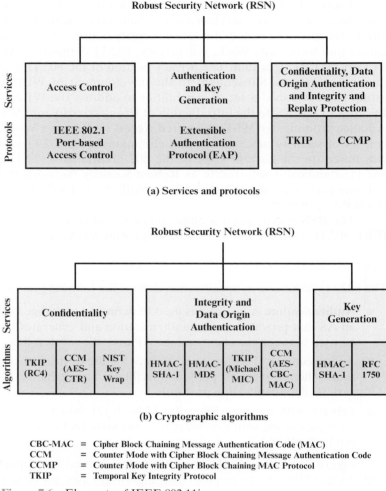

(a) Services and protocols

(b) Cryptographic algorithms

CBC-MAC	=	Cipher Block Chaining Message Authentication Code (MAC)
CCM	=	Counter Mode with Cipher Block Chaining Message Authentication Code
CCMP	=	Counter Mode with Cipher Block Chaining MAC Protocol
TKIP	=	Temporal Key Integrity Protocol

Figure 7.6   Elements of IEEE 802.11i

3. Two wireless stations in different BSSs communicating via their respective APs across a distribution system.

4. A wireless station communicating with an end station on a wired network via its AP and the distribution system.

IEEE 802.11i security is concerned only with secure communication between the STA and its AP. In case 1 in the preceding list, secure communication is assured if each STA establishes secure communications with the AP. Case 2 is similar, with the AP functionality residing in the STA. For case 3, security is not provided across the distribution system at the level of IEEE 802.11, but only within each BSS. End-to-end security (if required) must be provided at a higher layer. Similarly, in case 4, security is only provided between the STA and its AP.

With these considerations in mind, Figure 7.7 depicts the five phases of operation for an RSN and maps them to the network components involved. One new component is the authentication server (AS). The rectangles indicate the exchange of sequences of MPDUs. The five phases are defined as follows.

- **Discovery:** An AP uses messages called Beacons and Probe Responses to advertise its IEEE 802.11i security policy. The STA uses these to identify an AP for a WLAN with which it wishes to communicate. The STA associates with the AP, which it uses to select the cipher suite and authentication mechanism when the Beacons and Probe Responses present a choice.

- **Authentication:** During this phase, the STA and AS prove their identities to each other. The AP blocks non-authentication traffic between the STA and AS until the authentication transaction is successful. The AP does not participate in the authentication transaction other than forwarding traffic between the STA and AS.

- **Key generation and distribution:** The AP and the STA perform several operations that cause cryptographic keys to be generated and placed on the AP and the STA. Frames are exchanged between the AP and STA only.

- **Protected data transfer:** Frames are exchanged between the STA and the end station through the AP. As denoted by the shading and the encryption module icon, secure data transfer occurs between the STA and the AP only; security is not provided end-to-end.

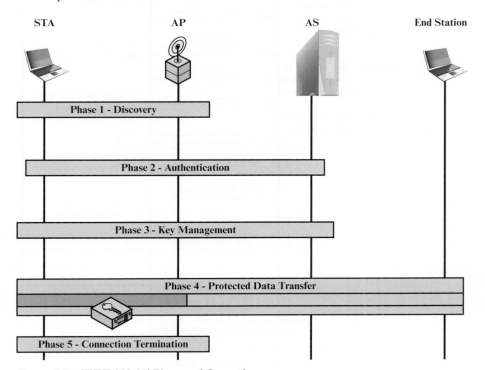

Figure 7.7   IEEE 802.11i Phases of Operation

- **Connection termination:** The AP and STA exchange frames. During this phase, the secure connection is torn down and the connection is restored to the original state.

Discovery Phase

We now look in more detail at the RSN phases of operation, beginning with the discovery phase, which is illustrated in the upper portion of Figure 7.8. The purpose of this phase is for an STA and an AP to recognize each other, agree on a set of security capabilities, and establish an association for future communication using those security capabilities.

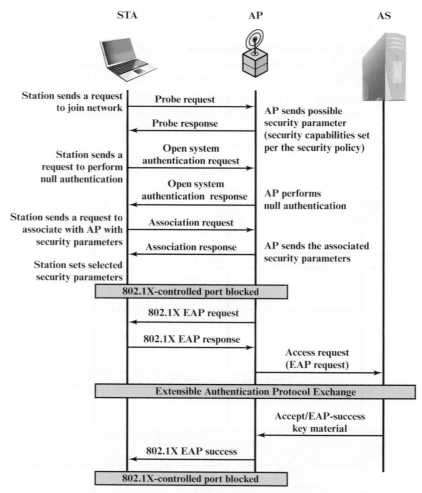

Figure 7.8 IEEE 802.11i Phases of Operation: Capability Discovery, Authentication, and Association

SECURITY CAPABILITIES During this phase, the STA and AP decide on specific techniques in the following areas:

- Confidentiality and MPDU integrity protocols for protecting unicast traffic (traffic only between this STA and AP)
- Authentication method
- Cryptography key management approach

Confidentiality and integrity protocols for protecting multicast/broadcast traffic are dictated by the AP, since all STAs in a multicast group must use the same protocols and ciphers. The specification of a protocol, along with the chosen key length (if variable) is known as a *cipher suite*. The options for the confidentiality and integrity cipher suite are

- WEP, with either a 40-bit or 104-bit key, which allows backward compatibility with older IEEE 802.11 implementations
- TKIP
- CCMP
- Vendor-specific methods

The other negotiable suite is the authentication and key management (AKM) suite, which defines (1) the means by which the AP and STA perform mutual authentication and (2) the means for deriving a root key from which other keys may be generated. The possible AKM suites are

- IEEE 802.1X
- Pre-shared key (no explicit authentication takes place and mutual authentication is implied if the STA and AP share a unique secret key)
- Vendor-specific methods

MPDU EXCHANGE The discovery phase consists of three exchanges.

- **Network and security capability discovery:** During this exchange, STAs discover the existence of a network with which to communicate. The AP either periodically broadcasts its security capabilities (not shown in figure), indicated by RSN IE (Robust Security Network Information Element), in a specific channel through the Beacon frame; or responds to a station's Probe Request through a Probe Response frame. A wireless station may discover available access points and corresponding security capabilities by either passively monitoring the Beacon frames or actively probing every channel.
- **Open system authentication:** The purpose of this frame sequence, which provides no security, is simply to maintain backward compatibility with the IEEE 802.11 state machine, as implemented in existing IEEE 802.11 hardware. In essence, the two devices (STA and AP) simply exchange identifiers.
- **Association:** The purpose of this stage is to agree on a set of security capabilities to be used. The STA then sends an Association Request frame to the AP. In this frame, the STA specifies one set of matching capabilities

(one authentication and key management suite, one pairwise cipher suite, and one group-key cipher suite) from among those advertised by the AP. If there is no match in capabilities between the AP and the STA, the AP refuses the Association Request. The STA blocks it too, in case it has associated with a rogue AP or someone is inserting frames illicitly on its channel. As shown in Figure 7.8, the IEEE 802.1X controlled ports are blocked, and no user traffic goes beyond the AP. The concept of blocked ports is explained subsequently.

Authentication Phase

As was mentioned, the authentication phase enables mutual authentication between an STA and an authentication server (AS) located in the DS. Authentication is designed to allow only authorized stations to use the network and to provide the STA with assurance that it is communicating with a legitimate network.

IEEE 802.1X ACCESS CONTROL APPROACH   IEEE 802.11i makes use of another standard that was designed to provide access control functions for LANs. The standard is IEEE 802.1X, Port-Based Network Access Control. The authentication protocol that is used, the Extensible Authentication Protocol (EAP), is defined in the IEEE 802.1X standard. IEEE 802.1X uses the terms *supplicant*, *authenticator*, and *authentication server* (AS). In the context of an 802.11 WLAN, the first two terms correspond to the wireless station and the AP. The AS is typically a separate device on the wired side of the network (i.e., accessible over the DS) but could also reside directly on the authenticator.

Before a supplicant is authenticated by the AS using an authentication protocol, the authenticator only passes control or authentication messages between the supplicant and the AS; the 802.1X control channel is unblocked, but the 802.11 data channel is blocked. Once a supplicant is authenticated and keys are provided, the authenticator can forward data from the supplicant, subject to predefined access control limitations for the supplicant to the network. Under these circumstances, the data channel is unblocked.

As indicated in Figure 5.5, 802.1X uses the concepts of controlled and uncontrolled ports. Ports are logical entities defined within the authenticator and refer to physical network connections. For a WLAN, the authenticator (the AP) may have only two physical ports: one connecting to the DS and one for wireless communication within its BSS. Each logical port is mapped to one of these two physical ports. An uncontrolled port allows the exchange of PDUs between the supplicant and the other AS, regardless of the authentication state of the supplicant. A controlled port allows the exchange of PDUs between a supplicant and other systems on the LAN only if the current state of the supplicant authorizes such an exchange. IEEE 802.1X is covered in more detail in Chapter 5.

The 802.1X framework, with an upper-layer authentication protocol, fits nicely with a BSS architecture that includes a number of wireless stations and an AP. However, for an IBSS, there is no AP. For an IBSS, 802.11i provides a more complex solution that, in essence, involves pairwise authentication between stations on the IBSS.

MPDU Exchange The lower part of Figure 7.8 shows the MPDU exchange dictated by IEEE 802.11 for the authentication phase. We can think of authentication phase as consisting of the following three phases.

- **Connect to AS:** The STA sends a request to its AP (the one with which it has an association) for connection to the AS. The AP acknowledges this request and sends an access request to the AS.

- **EAP exchange:** This exchange authenticates the STA and AS to each other. A number of alternative exchanges are possible, as explained subsequently.

- **Secure key delivery:** Once authentication is established, the AS generates a master session key (MSK), also known as the Authentication, Authorization, and Accounting (AAA) key and sends it to the STA. As explained subsequently, all the cryptographic keys needed by the STA for secure communication with its AP are generated from this MSK. IEEE 802.11i does not prescribe a method for secure delivery of the MSK but relies on EAP for this. Whatever method is used, it involves the transmission of an MPDU containing an encrypted MSK from the AS, via the AP, to the AS.

EAP Exchange As mentioned, there are a number of possible EAP exchanges that can be used during the authentication phase. Typically, the message flow between STA and AP employs the EAP over LAN (EAPOL) protocol, and the message flow between the AP and AS uses the Remote Authentication Dial In User Service (RADIUS) protocol, although other options are available for both STA-to-AP and AP-to-AS exchanges. [FRAN07] provides the following summary of the authentication exchange using EAPOL and RADIUS.

1. The EAP exchange begins with the AP issuing an EAP-Request/Identity frame to the STA.

2. The STA replies with an EAP-Response/Identity frame, which the AP receives over the uncontrolled port. The packet is then encapsulated in RADIUS over EAP and passed on to the RADIUS server as a RADIUS-Access-Request packet.

3. The AAA server replies with a RADIUS-Access-Challenge packet, which is passed on to the STA as an EAP-Request. This request is of the appropriate authentication type and contains relevant challenge information.

4. The STA formulates an EAP-Response message and sends it to the AS. The response is translated by the AP into a Radius-Access-Request with the response to the challenge as a data field. Steps 3 and 4 may be repeated multiple times, depending on the EAP method in use. For TLS tunneling methods, it is common for authentication to require 10 to 20 round trips.

5. The AAA server grants access with a Radius-Access-Accept packet. The AP issues an EAP-Success frame. (Some protocols require confirmation of the EAP success inside the TLS tunnel for authenticity validation.) The controlled port is authorized, and the user may begin to access the network.

Note from Figure 7.8 that the AP controlled port is still blocked to general user traffic. Although the authentication is successful, the ports remain blocked until the temporal keys are installed in the STA and AP, which occurs during the 4-Way Handshake.

Key Management Phase

During the key management phase, a variety of cryptographic keys are generated and distributed to STAs. There are two types of keys: pairwise keys used for communication between an STA and an AP and group keys used for multicast communication. Figure 7.9, based on [FRAN07], shows the two key hierarchies, and Table 7.3 defines the individual keys.

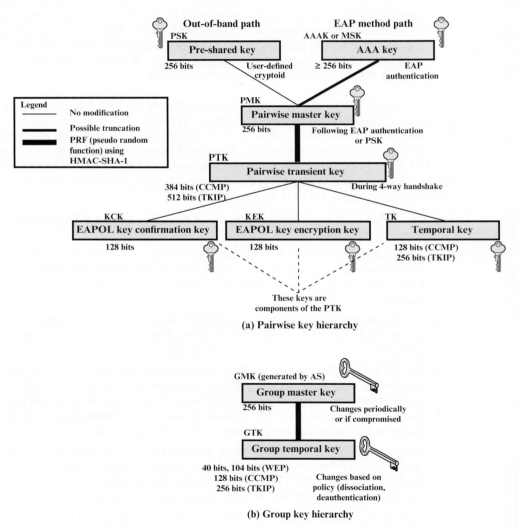

Figure 7.9 IEEE 802.11i Key Hierarchies

Table 7.3   IEEE 802.11i Keys for Data Confidentiality and Integrity Protocols

Abbreviation	Name	Description / Purpose	Size (bits)	Type
AAA Key	Authentication, Accounting, and Authorization Key	Used to derive the PMK. Used with the IEEE 802.1X authentication and key management approach. Same as MMSK.	≥ 256	Key generation key, root key
PSK	Pre-shared Key	Becomes the PMK in pre-shared key environments.	256	Key generation key, root key
PMK	Pairwise Master Key	Used with other inputs to derive the PTK.	256	Key generation key
GMK	Group Master Key	Used with other inputs to derive the GTK.	128	Key generation key
PTK	Pair-wise Transient Key	Derived from the PMK. Comprises the EAPOL-KCK, EAPOL-KEK, and TK and (for TKIP) the MIC key.	512 (TKIP) 384 (CCMP)	Composite key
TK	Temporal Key	Used with TKIP or CCMP to provide confidentiality and integrity protection for unicast user traffic.	256 (TKIP) 128 (CCMP)	Traffic key
GTK	Group Temporal Key	Derived from the GMK. Used to provide confidentiality and integrity protection for multicast/broadcast user traffic.	256 (TKIP) 128 (CCMP) 40,104 (WEP)	Traffic key
MIC Key	Message Integrity Code Key	Used by TKIP's Michael MIC to provide integrity protection of messages.	64	Message integrity key
EAPOL-KCK	EAPOL-Key Confirmation Key	Used to provide integrity protection for key material distributed during the 4-Way Handshake.	128	Message integrity key
EAPOL-KEK	EAPOL-Key Encryption Key	Used to ensure the confidentiality of the GTK and other key material in the 4-Way Handshake.	128	Traffic key / key encryption key
WEP Key	Wired Equivalent Privacy Key	Used with WEP.	40,104	Traffic key

PAIRWISE KEYS Pairwise keys are used for communication between a pair of devices, typically between an STA and an AP. These keys form a hierarchy beginning with a master key from which other keys are derived dynamically and used for a limited period of time.

At the top level of the hierarchy are two possibilities. A **pre-shared key (PSK)** is a secret key shared by the AP and a STA and installed in some fashion outside the scope of IEEE 802.11i. The other alternative is the **master session key (MSK)**, also known as the AAAK, which is generated using the IEEE 802.1X protocol during the authentication phase, as described previously. The actual method of key generation depends on the details of the authentication protocol used. In either case (PSK or MSK), there is a unique key shared by the AP with each STA with which it communicates. All the other keys derived from this master key are also unique between an AP and an STA. Thus, each STA, at any time, has one set of keys, as depicted in the hierarchy of Figure 7.9a, while the AP has one set of such keys for each of its STAs.

The **pairwise master key (PMK)** is derived from the master key. If a PSK is used, then the PSK is used as the PMK; if a MSK is used, then the PMK is derived from the MSK by truncation (if necessary). By the end of the authentication phase, marked by the 802.1X EAP Success message (Figure 7.8), both the AP and the STA have a copy of their shared PMK.

The PMK is used to generate the **pairwise transient key (PTK)**, which in fact consists of three keys to be used for communication between an STA and AP after they have been mutually authenticated. To derive the PTK, the HMAC-SHA-1 function is applied to the PMK, the MAC addresses of the STA and AP, and nonces generated when needed. Using the STA and AP addresses in the generation of the PTK provides protection against session hijacking and impersonation; using nonces provides additional random keying material.

The three parts of the PTK are as follows.

- **EAP Over LAN (EAPOL) Key Confirmation Key (EAPOL-KCK):** Supports the integrity and data origin authenticity of STA-to-AP control frames during operational setup of an RSN. It also performs an access control function: proof-of-possession of the PMK. An entity that possesses the PMK is authorized to use the link.

- **EAPOL Key Encryption Key (EAPOL-KEK):** Protects the confidentiality of keys and other data during some RSN association procedures.

- **Temporal Key (TK):** Provides the actual protection for user traffic.

GROUP KEYS Group keys are used for multicast communication in which one STA sends MPDU's to multiple STAs. At the top level of the group key hierarchy is the **group master key (GMK)**. The GMK is a key-generating key used with other inputs to derive the **group temporal key (GTK)**. Unlike the PTK, which is generated using material from both AP and STA, the GTK is generated by the AP and transmitted to its associated STAs. Exactly how this GTK is generated is undefined. IEEE 802.11i, however, requires that its value is computationally indistinguishable from random. The GTK is distributed securely using the pairwise keys that are already established. The GTK is changed every time a device leaves the network.

Pairwise Key Distribution The upper part of Figure 7.10 shows the MPDU exchange for distributing pairwise keys. This exchange is known as the **4-way handshake**. The STA and AP use this handshake to confirm the existence of the

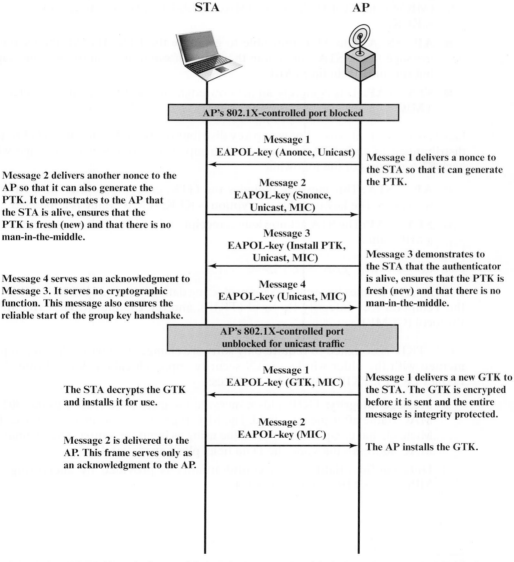

Figure 7.10   IEEE 802.11i Phases of Operation: 4-Way Handshake and Group Key Handshake

PMK, verify the selection of the cipher suite, and derive a fresh PTK for the following data session. The four parts of the exchange are as follows.

- **AP → STA:** Message includes the MAC address of the AP and a nonce (Anonce).

- **STA → AP:** The STA generates its own nonce (Snonce) and uses both nonces and both MAC addresses, plus the PMK, to generate a PTK. The STA then sends a message containing its MAC address and Snonce, enabling the AP to generate the same PTK. This message includes a message integrity code (MIC)[2] using HMAC-MD5 or HMAC-SHA-1-128. The key used with the MIC is KCK.

- **AP → STA:** The AP is now able to generate the PTK. The AP then sends a message to the STA, containing the same information as in the first message, but this time including a MIC.

- **STA → AP:** This is merely an acknowledgment message, again protected by a MIC.

GROUP KEY DISTRIBUTION For group key distribution, the AP generates a GTK and distributes it to each STA in a multicast group. The two-message exchange with each STA consists of the following:

- **AP → STA:** This message includes the GTK, encrypted either with RC4 or with AES. The key used for encryption is KEK. A MIC value is appended.

- **STA → AP:** The STA acknowledges receipt of the GTK. This message includes a MIC value.

Protected Data Transfer Phase

IEEE 802.11i defines two schemes for protecting data transmitted in 802.11 MPDUs: the Temporal Key Integrity Protocol (TKIP), and the Counter Mode-CBC MAC Protocol (CCMP).

TKIP TKIP is designed to require only software changes to devices that are implemented with the older wireless LAN security approach called Wired Equivalent Privacy (WEP). TKIP provides two services:

- **Message integrity:** TKIP adds a message integrity code (MIC) to the 802.11 MAC frame after the data field. The MIC is generated by an algorithm, called Michael, that computes a 64-bit value using as input the source and destination MAC address values and the Data field, plus key material.

- **Data confidentiality:** Data confidentiality is provided by encrypting the MPDU plus MIC value using RC4.

---

[2] While *MAC* is commonly used in cryptography to refer to a Message Authentication Code, the term *MIC* is used instead in connection with 802.11i because *MAC* has another standard meaning, Media Access Control, in networking.

The 256-bit TK (Figure 7.9) is employed as follows. Two 64-bit keys are used with the Michael message digest algorithm to produce a message integrity code. One key is used to protect STA-to-AP messages, and the other key is used to protect AP-to-STA messages. The remaining 128 bits are truncated to generate the RC4 key used to encrypt the transmitted data.

For additional protection, a monotonically increasing TKIP sequence counter (TSC) is assigned to each frame. The TSC serves two purposes. First, the TSC is included with each MPDU and is protected by the MIC to protect against replay attacks. Second, the TSC is combined with the session TK to produce a dynamic encryption key that changes with each transmitted MPDU, thus making cryptanalysis more difficult.

CCMP CCMP is intended for newer IEEE 802.11 devices that are equipped with the hardware to support this scheme. As with TKIP, CCMP provides two services:

- **Message integrity:** CCMP uses the cipher block chaining message authentication code (CBC-MAC), described in Chapter 3.
- **Data confidentiality:** CCMP uses the CTR block cipher mode of operation with AES for encryption. CTR is described in Chapter 2.

The same 128-bit AES key is used for both integrity and confidentiality. The scheme uses a 48-bit packet number to construct a nonce to prevent replay attacks.

The IEEE 802.11i Pseudorandom Function

At a number of places in the IEEE 802.11i scheme, a pseudorandom function (PRF) is used. For example, it is used to generate nonces, to expand pairwise keys, and to generate the GTK. Best security practice dictates that different pseudorandom number streams be used for these different purposes. However, for implementation efficiency, we would like to rely on a single pseudorandom number generator function.

The PRF is built on the use of HMAC-SHA-1 to generate a pseudorandom bit stream. Recall that HMAC-SHA-1 takes a message (block of data) and a key of length at least 160 bits and produces a 160-bit hash value. SHA-1 has the property that the change of a single bit of the input produces a new hash value with no apparent connection to the preceding hash value. This property is the basis for pseudorandom number generation.

The IEEE 802.11i PRF takes four parameters as input and produces the desired number of random bits. The function is of the form PRF(K, A, B, Len), where

K = a secret key

A = a text string specific to the application (e.g., nonce generation or pairwise key expansion)

B = some data specific to each case

Len = desired number of pseudorandom bits

For example, for the pairwise transient key for CCMP:

```
PTK = PRF (PMK, "Pairwise key expansion", min (AP-
      Addr, STA-Addr) || max (AP-Addr, STA-Addr) || min
      (Anonce, Snonce) || max (Anonce, Snonce), 384)
```

So, in this case, the parameters are

K = PMK

A = the text string "Pairwise key expansion"

B = a sequence of bytes formed by concatenating the two MAC addresses and the two nonces

Len = 384 bits

Similarly, a nonce is generated by

```
Nonce = PRF (Random Number, "InitCounter", MAC || Time, 256)
```

where **Time** is a measure of the network time known to the nonce generator.
The group temporal key is generated by

```
GTK = PRF (GMK, "Group key expansion", MAC || Gnonce, 256)
```

Figure 7.11 illustrates the function PRF(K, A, B, *Len*). The parameter K serves as the key input to HMAC. The message input consists of four items concatenated together: the parameter A, a byte with value 0, the parameter B, and a counter i. The counter is initialized to 0. The HMAC algorithm is run once, producing a 160-bit hash value. If more bits are required, HMAC is run again with the same inputs, except that i is incremented each time until the necessary number of bits is generated. We can express the logic as

```
PRF (K, A, B, Len)
    R ← null string
    for i ← 0 to ((Len + 159)/160 - 1) do
    R ← R || HMAC-SHA-1 (K, A || 0 || B || i)
    Return Truncate-to-Len (R, Len)
```

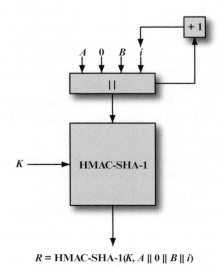

R = HMAC-SHA-1(K, A || 0 || B || i)

Figure 7.11 IEEE 802.11i Pseudorandom Function

7.5 KEY TERMS, REVIEW QUESTIONS, AND PROBLEMS

Key Terms

4-way handshake	independent BSS (IBSS)	pseudorandom function
access point (AP)	logical link control (LLC)	Robust Security Network
basic service set (BSS)	media access control (MAC)	(RSN)
Counter Mode-CBC MAC	MAC protocol data unit	Temporal Key Integrity
Protocol (CCMP)	(MPDU)	Protocol (TKIP)
distribution system (DS)	MAC service data unit	Wi-Fi
extended service set (ESS)	(MSDU)	Wi-Fi Protected Access
group keys	message integrity code	(WPA)
IEEE 802.1X	(MIC)	Wired Equivalent Privacy
IEEE 802.11	Michael	(WEP)
IEEE 802.11i	pairwise keys	Wireless LAN (WLAN)

Review Questions

7.1 What is the basic building block of an 802.11 WLAN?

7.2 List and briefly define threats to a wireless network.

7.3 List and briefly define IEEE 802.11 services.

7.4 List some security threats related to mobile devices.

7.5 How is the concept of an association related to that of mobility?

7.6 What security areas are addressed by IEEE 802.11i?

7.7 Briefly describe the five IEEE 802.11i phases of operation.

7.8 What is the difference between TKIP and CCMP?

Problems

7.1 In IEEE 802.11, open system authentication simply consists of two communications. An authentication is requested by the client, which contains the station ID (typically the MAC address). This is followed by an authentication response from the AP/router containing a success or failure message. An example of when a failure may occur is if the client's MAC address is explicitly excluded in the AP/router configuration.

   a. What are the benefits of this authentication scheme?

   b. What are the security vulnerabilities of this authentication scheme?

7.2 Prior to the introduction of IEEE 802.11i, the security scheme for IEEE 802.11 was Wired Equivalent Privacy (WEP). WEP assumed all devices in the network share a secret key. The purpose of the authentication scenario is for the STA to prove that it possesses the secret key. Authentication proceeds as shown in Figure 7.12. The STA sends a message to the AP requesting authentication. The AP issues a challenge, which is a sequence of 128 random bytes sent as plaintext. The STA encrypts the challenge with the shared key and returns it to the AP. The AP decrypts the incoming value and compares it to the challenge that it sent. If there is a match, the AP confirms that authentication has succeeded.

   a. What are the benefits of this authentication scheme?

   b. This authentication scheme is incomplete. What is missing and why is this important? *Hint:* The addition of one or two messages would fix the problem.

   c. What is a cryptographic weakness of this scheme?

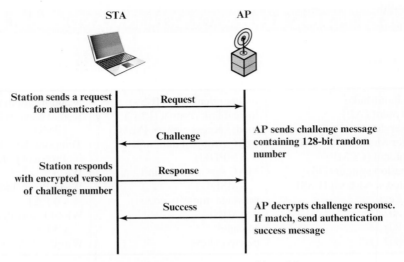

Figure 7.12   WEP Authentication; refer to Problem 7.2

7.3   For WEP, data integrity and data confidentiality are achieved using the RC4 stream encryption algorithm. The transmitter of an MPDU performs the following steps, referred to as encapsulation:

1. The transmitter selects an initial vector (IV) value.
2. The IV value is concatenated with the WEP key shared by transmitter and receiver to form the seed, or key input, to RC4.
3. A 32-bit cyclic redundancy check (CRC) is computed over all the bits of the MAC data field and appended to the data field. The CRC is a common error-detection code used in data link control protocols. In this case, the CRC serves as a integrity check value (ICV).
4. The result of step 3 is encrypted using RC4 to form the ciphertext block.
5. The plaintext IV is prepended to the ciphertext block to form the encapsulated MPDU for transmission.
   a. Draw a block diagram that illustrates the encapsulation process.
   b. Describe the steps at the receiver end to recover the plaintext and perform the integrity check.
   c. Draw a block diagram that illustrates part b.

7.4   A potential weakness of the CRC as an integrity check is that it is a linear function. This means that you can predict which bits of the CRC are changed if a single bit of the message is changed. Furthermore, it is possible to determine which combination of bits could be flipped in the message so that the net result is no change in the CRC. Thus, there are a number of combinations of bit flippings of the plaintext message that leave the CRC unchanged, so message integrity is defeated. However, in WEP, if an attacker does not know the encryption key, the attacker does not have access to the plaintext, only to the ciphertext block. Does this mean that the ICV is protected from the bit flipping attack? Explain.

CHAPTER 8

ELECTRONIC MAIL SECURITY

LEARNING OBJECTIVES

After studying this chapter, you should be able to:

◆ Summarize the key functional components of the Internet mail architecture.

◆ Explain the basic functionality of SMTP, POP3, and IMAP.

◆ Explain the need for MIME as an enhancement to ordinary e-mail.

◆ Describe the key elements of MIME.

◆ Understand the functionality of S/MIME and the security threats it addresses.

◆ Understand the basic mechanisms of STARTTLS and its role in e-mail security.

◆ Understand the basic mechanisms of DANE and its role in e-mail security.

◆ Understand the basic mechanisms of SPF and its role in e-mail security.

◆ Understand the basic mechanisms of DKIM and its role in e-mail security.

◆ Understand the basic mechanisms of DMARC and its role in e-mail security.

In virtually all distributed environments, electronic mail is the most heavily used network-based application. Users expect to be able to, and do, send e-mail to others who are connected directly or indirectly to the Internet, regardless of host operating system or communications suite. With the explosively growing reliance on e-mail, there grows a demand for authentication and confidentiality services. Two schemes stand out as approaches that enjoy widespread use: Pretty Good Privacy (PGP) and S/MIME. Both are examined in this chapter. This chapter concludes with a discussion of DomainKeys Identified Mail.

8.1 INTERNET MAIL ARCHITECTURE

For an understanding of the topics in this chapter, it is useful to have a basic grasp of the Internet mail architecture, which is currently defined in RFC 5598 (*Internet Mail Architecture*, July 2009). This section provides an overview of the basic concepts.

E-mail Components

At its most fundamental level, the Internet mail architecture consists of a user world in the form of Message User Agents (MUA), and the transfer world, in the form of the **Message Handling Service (MHS)**, which is composed of Message Transfer Agents (MTA). The MHS accepts a message from one user and delivers it to one or more other users, creating a virtual MUA-to-MUA exchange environment. This architecture involves three types of interoperability. One is directly between users: messages must be formatted by the MUA on behalf of the message author so that the message can be displayed to the message recipient by the destination MUA. There are also interoperability requirements between the MUA and the MHS—first when a message is posted from an MUA to the MHS and later when it is delivered from the MHS to the destination MUA. Interoperability is required among the MTA components along the transfer path through the MHS.

Figure 8.1 illustrates the key components of the Internet mail architecture, which include the following.

- **Message User Agent (MUA):** Operates on behalf of user actors and user applications. It is their representative within the e-mail service. Typically, this function is housed in the user's computer and is referred to as a client e-mail program or a local network e-mail server. The author MUA formats a message and performs initial submission into the MHS via a MSA. The recipient MUA processes received mail for storage and/or display to the recipient user.

- **Mail Submission Agent (MSA):** Accepts the message submitted by an MUA and enforces the policies of the hosting domain and the requirements of Internet standards. This function may be located together with the MUA or

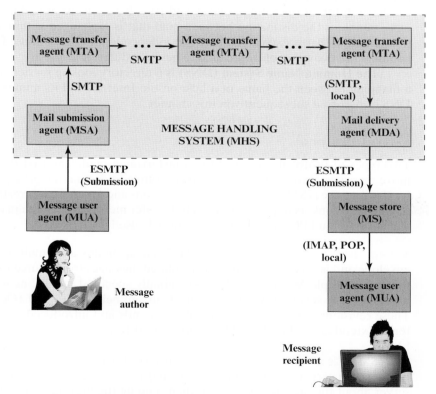

Figure 8.1 Function Modules and Standardized Protocols Used between them in the Internet Mail Architecture

as a separate functional model. In the latter case, the Simple Mail Transfer Protocol (SMTP) is used between the MUA and the MSA.

- **Message Transfer Agent (MTA):** Relays mail for one application-level hop. It is like a packet switch or IP router in that its job is to make routing assessments and to move the message closer to the recipients. Relaying is performed by a sequence of MTAs until the message reaches a destination MDA. An MTA also adds trace information to the message header. SMTP is used between MTAs and between an MTA and an MSA or MDA.

- **Mail Delivery Agent (MDA):** Responsible for transferring the message from the MHS to the MS.

- **Message Store (MS):** An MUA can employ a long-term MS. An MS can be located on a remote server or on the same machine as the MUA. Typically, an MUA retrieves messages from a remote server using POP (Post Office Protocol) or IMAP (Internet Message Access Protocol).

Two other concepts need to be defined. An **administrative management domain (ADMD)** is an Internet e-mail provider. Examples include a department that operates a local mail relay (MTA), an IT department that operates an enterprise mail relay, and an ISP that operates a public shared e-mail service. Each ADMD can have different operating policies and trust-based decision making. One obvious example is the distinction between mail that is exchanged within an organization and mail that is exchanged between independent organizations. The rules for handling the two types of traffic tend to be quite different.

The **Domain Name System (DNS)** is a directory lookup service that provides a mapping between the name of a host on the Internet and its numerical address. DNS is discussed subsequently in this chapter.

E-mail Protocols

Two types of protocols are used for transferring e-mail. The first type is used to move messages through the Internet from source to destination. The protocol used for this purpose is SMTP, with various extensions and in some cases restrictions. The second type consists of protocols used to transfer messages between mail servers, of which IMAP and POP are the most commonly used.

SIMPLE MAIL TRANSFER PROTOCOL   SMTP encapsulates an e-mail message in an envelope and is used to relay the encapsulated messages from source to destination through multiple MTAs. SMTP was originally specified in 1982 as RFC 821 and has undergone several revisions, the most current being RFC 5321 (October 2008). These revisions have added additional commands and introduced extensions. The term Extended SMTP (ESMTP) is often used to refer to these later versions of SMTP.

SMTP is a text-based client-server protocol where the client (e-mail sender) contacts the server (next-hop recipient) and issues a set of commands to tell the server about the message to be sent, then sending the message itself. The majority of these commands are ASCII text messages sent by the client and a resulting return code (and additional ASCII text) returned by the server.

The transfer of a message from a source to its ultimate destination can occur over a single SMTP client/server conversation over a single TCP connection. Alternatively, an SMTP server may be an intermediate relay that assumes the role of an SMTP client after receiving a message and then forwards that message to an SMTP server along a route to the ultimate destination.

The operation of SMTP consists of a series of commands and responses exchanged between the SMTP sender and receiver. The initiative is with the SMTP sender, who establishes the TCP connection. Once the connection is established, the SMTP sender sends commands over the connection to the receiver. Each command consists of a single line of text, beginning with a four-letter command code followed in some cases by an argument field. Each command generates exactly one reply from the SMTP receiver. Most replies are a single-line, although multiple-line replies are possible. Each reply begins with a three-digit code and may be followed by additional information.

Figure 8.2 illustrates the SMTP exchange between a client (C) and server (S). The interchange begins with the client establishing a TCP connection to TCP port 25 on the server (not shown in figure). This causes the server to activate SMTP and send a 220 reply to the client. The HELO command identifies the sending domain, which the server acknowledges and accepts with a 250 reply. The SMTP sender is transmitting mail that originates with the user Smith@bar.com. The MAIL command identifies the originator of the message. The message is addressed to three users on machine foo.com, namely, Jones, Green, and Brown. The client

```
S: 220 foo.com Simple Mail Transfer Service Ready
C: HELO bar.com
S: 250 OK
C: MAIL FROM:<Smith@bar.com>
S: 250 OK
C: RCPT TO:<Jones@foo.com>
S: 250 OK
C: RCPT TO:<Green@foo.com>
S: 550 No such user here
C: RCPT TO:<Brown@foo.com>
S: 250 OK
C: DATA
S: 354 Start mail input; end with <crlf>.<crlf>
C: Blah blah blah . . .
C: . . . etc. etc. etc.
C: <crlf><crlf>
S: 250 OK
C: QUIT
S: 221 foo.com Service closing transmission channel
```

Figure 8.2   Example SMTP Transaction Scenario

identifies each of these in a separate RCPT command. The SMTP receiver indicates that it has mailboxes for Jones and Brown but does not have information on Green. Because at least one of the intended recipients has been verified, the client proceeds to send the text message, by first sending a DATA command to ensure the server is ready for the data. After the server acknowledges receipt of all the data, it issues a 250 OK message. Then the client issues a QUIT command and the server closes the connection.

A significant security-related extension for SMTP, called STARTTLS, is defined in RFC 3207 (*SMTP Service Extension for Secure SMTP over Transport Layer Security*, February 2002). STARTTLS enables the addition of confidentiality and authentication in the exchange between SMTP agents. This gives SMTP agents the ability to protect some or all of their communications from eavesdroppers and attackers. If the client does initiate the connection over a TLS-enabled port (e.g., port 465 was previously used for SMTP over SSL), the server may prompt with a message indicating that the STARTTLS option is available. The client can then issue the STARTTLS command in the SMTP command stream, and the two parties proceed to establish a secure TLS connection. An advantage of using STARTTLS is that the server can offer SMTP service on a single port, rather than requiring separate port numbers for secure and cleartext operations. Similar mechanisms are available for running TLS over IMAP and POP protocols.

Historically, MUA/MSA message transfers have used SMTP. The standard currently preferred is SUBMISSION, defined in RFC 6409 (*Message Submission for Mail*, November 2011). Although SUBMISSION derives from SMTP, it uses a separate TCP port and imposes distinct requirements, such as access authorization.

MAIL ACCESS PROTOCOLS (POP3, IMAP) Post Office Protocol (POP3) allows an e-mail client (user agent) to download an e-mail from an e-mail server (MTA). POP3 user agents connect via TCP to the server (typically port 110). The user agent enters a username and password (either stored internally for convenience or entered each time by the user for stronger security). After authorization, the UA can issue POP3 commands to retrieve and delete mail.

As with POP3, Internet Mail Access Protocol (IMAP) also enables an e-mail client to access mail on an e-mail server. IMAP also uses TCP, with server TCP port 143. IMAP is more complex than POP3. IMAP provides stronger authentication than POP3 and provides other functions not supported by POP3.

8.2 E-MAIL FORMATS

To understand S/MIME, we need first to have a general understanding of the underlying e-mail format that it uses, namely, MIME. But to understand the significance of MIME, we need to go back to the traditional e-mail format standard, RFC 822, which is still in common use. The most recent version of this format specification is RFC 5322 (*Internet Message Format*, October 2008). Accordingly, this section first provides an introduction to these two earlier standards and then moves on to a discussion of S/MIME.

RFC 5322

RFC 5322 defines a format for text messages that are sent using electronic mail. It has been the standard for Internet-based text mail messages and remains in common use. In the RFC 5322 context, messages are viewed as having an envelope and contents. The envelope contains whatever information is needed to accomplish transmission and delivery. The contents compose the object to be delivered to the recipient. The RFC 5322 standard applies only to the contents. However, the content standard includes a set of header fields that may be used by the mail system to create the envelope, and the standard is intended to facilitate the acquisition of such information by programs.

The overall structure of a message that conforms to RFC 5322 is very simple. A message consists of some number of header lines (*the header*) followed by unrestricted text (*the body*). The header is separated from the body by a blank line. Put differently, a message is ASCII text, and all lines up to the first blank line are assumed to be header lines used by the user agent part of the mail system.

A header line usually consists of a keyword, followed by a colon, followed by the keyword's arguments; the format allows a long line to be broken up into several lines. The most frequently used keywords are *From*, *To*, *Subject*, and *Date*. Here is an example message:

```
Date: October 8, 2009 2:15:49 PM EDT
From: "William Stallings" <ws@shore.net>
Subject: The Syntax in RFC 5322
To: Smith@Other-host.com
Cc: Jones@Yet-Another-Host.com

Hello. This section begins the actual
message body, which is delimited from the
message heading by a blank line.
```

Another field that is commonly found in RFC 5322 headers is *Message-ID*. This field contains a unique identifier associated with this message.

Multipurpose Internet Mail Extensions

Multipurpose Internet Mail Extension (MIME) is an extension to the RFC 5322 framework that is intended to address some of the problems and limitations of the use of Simple Mail Transfer Protocol (SMTP) or some other mail transfer protocol and RFC 5322 for electronic mail. RFCs 2045 through 2049 define MIME, and there have been a number of updating documents since then.

As justification for the use of MIME, [PARZ06] lists the following limitations of the SMTP/5322 scheme.

1. SMTP cannot transmit executable files or other binary objects. A number of schemes are in use for converting binary files into a text form that can be used by SMTP mail systems, including the popular UNIX UUencode/UUdecode scheme. However, none of these is a standard or even a *de facto* standard.

2. SMTP cannot transmit text data that includes national language characters, because these are represented by 8-bit codes with values of 128 decimal or higher, and SMTP is limited to 7-bit ASCII.

3. SMTP servers may reject mail message over a certain size.

4. SMTP gateways that translate between ASCII and the character code EBCDIC do not use a consistent set of mappings, resulting in translation problems.

5. SMTP gateways to X.400 electronic mail networks cannot handle nontextual data included in X.400 messages.

6. Some SMTP implementations do not adhere completely to the SMTP standards defined in RFC 821. Common problems include:
   —Deletion, addition, or reordering of carriage return and linefeed
   —Truncating or wrapping lines longer than 76 characters
   —Removal of trailing white space (tab and space characters)
   —Padding of lines in a message to the same length
   —Conversion of tab characters into multiple space characters

MIME is intended to resolve these problems in a manner that is compatible with existing RFC 5322 implementations.

OVERVIEW The MIME specification includes the following elements.

1. Five new message header fields are defined, which may be included in an RFC 5322 header. These fields provide information about the body of the message.

2. A number of content formats are defined, thus standardizing representations that support multimedia electronic mail.

3. Transfer encodings are defined that enable the conversion of any content format into a form that is protected from alteration by the mail system.

In this subsection, we introduce the five message header fields. The next two subsections deal with content formats and transfer encodings.

The five header fields defined in MIME are as follows:

■ **MIME-Version:** Must have the parameter value 1.0. This field indicates that the message conforms to RFCs 2045 and 2046.

■ **Content-Type:** Describes the data contained in the body with sufficient detail that the receiving user agent can pick an appropriate agent or mechanism to represent the data to the user or otherwise deal with the data in an appropriate manner.

- **Content-Transfer-Encoding:** Indicates the type of transformation that has been used to represent the body of the message in a way that is acceptable for mail transport.
- **Content-ID:** Used to identify MIME entities uniquely in multiple contexts.
- **Content-Description:** A text description of the object with the body; this is useful when the object is not readable (e.g., audio data).

Any or all of these fields may appear in a normal RFC 5322 header. A compliant implementation must support the MIME-Version, Content-Type, and Content-Transfer-Encoding fields; the Content-ID and Content-Description fields are optional and may be ignored by the recipient implementation.

MIME CONTENT TYPES The bulk of the MIME specification is concerned with the definition of a variety of content types. This reflects the need to provide standardized ways of dealing with a wide variety of information representations in a multimedia environment.

Table 8.1 lists the content types specified in RFC 2046. There are seven different major types of content and a total of 15 subtypes. In general, a content type declares the general type of data, and the subtype specifies a particular format for that type of data.

Table 8.1   MIME Content Types

Type	Subtype	Description
Text	Plain	Unformatted text; may be ASCII or ISO 8859.
	Enriched	Provides greater format flexibility.
Multipart	Mixed	The different parts are independent but are to be transmitted together. They should be presented to the receiver in the order that they appear in the mail message.
	Parallel	Differs from Mixed only in that no order is defined for delivering the parts to the receiver.
	Alternative	The different parts are alternative versions of the same information. They are ordered in increasing faithfulness to the original, and the recipient's mail system should display the "best" version to the user.
	Digest	Similar to Mixed, but the default type/subtype of each part is message/rfc822.
Message	rfc822	The body is itself an encapsulated message that conforms to RFC 822.
	Partial	Used to allow fragmentation of large mail items, in a way that is transparent to the recipient.
	External-body	Contains a pointer to an object that exists elsewhere.
Image	jpeg	The image is in JPEG format, JFIF encoding.
	gif	The image is in GIF format.
Video	mpeg	MPEG format.
Audio	Basic	Single-channel 8-bit ISDN μ-law encoding at a sample rate of 8 kHz.
Application	PostScript	Adobe Postscript format.
	octet-stream	General binary data consisting of 8-bit bytes.

For the **text type** of body, no special software is required to get the full meaning of the text aside from support of the indicated character set. The primary subtype is *plain text*, which is simply a string of ASCII characters or ISO 8859 characters. The *enriched* subtype allows greater formatting flexibility.

The **multipart type** indicates that the body contains multiple, independent parts. The Content-Type header field includes a parameter (called boundary) that defines the delimiter between body parts. This boundary should not appear in any parts of the message. Each boundary starts on a new line and consists of two hyphens followed by the boundary value. The final boundary, which indicates the end of the last part, also has a suffix of two hyphens. Within each part, there may be an optional ordinary MIME header.

Here is a simple example of a multipart message containing two parts—both consisting of simple text (taken from RFC 2046):

```
From: Nathaniel Borenstein <nsb@bellcore.com>
To: Ned Freed <ned@innosoft.com>
Subject: Sample message
MIME-Version: 1.0
Content-type: multipart/mixed; boundary="simple boundary"

This is the preamble. It is to be ignored, though it is a
handy place for mail composers to include an explanatory
note to non-MIME conformant readers.
—simple boundary

This is implicitly typed plain ASCII text. It does NOT end
with a linebreak.
—simple boundary
Content-type: text/plain; charset=us-ascii

This is explicitly typed plain ASCII text. It DOES end
with a linebreak.

—simple boundary—
This is the epilogue. It is also to be ignored.
```

There are four subtypes of the multipart type, all of which have the same overall syntax. The **multipart/mixed subtype** is used when there are multiple independent body parts that need to be bundled in a particular order. For the **multipart/parallel subtype**, the order of the parts is not significant. If the recipient's system is appropriate, the multiple parts can be presented in parallel. For example, a picture or text part could be accompanied by a voice commentary that is played while the picture or text is displayed.

For the **multipart/alternative subtype**, the various parts are different representations of the same information. The following is an example:

```
From: Nathaniel Borenstein <nsb@bellcore.com>
To: Ned Freed <ned@innosoft.com>
Subject: Formatted text mail
```

```
MIME-Version: 1.0
Content-Type: multipart/alternative;
boundary=boundary42

—boundary42

Content-Type: text/plain; charset=us-ascii

    . . . plain text version of message goes here. . . .

—boundary42
Content-Type: text/enriched

    . . . RFC 1896 text/enriched version of same message
goes here . . .

—boundary42—
```

In this subtype, the body parts are ordered in terms of increasing preference. For this example, if the recipient system is capable of displaying the message in the text/enriched format, this is done; otherwise, the plain text format is used.

The **multipart/digest subtype** is used when each of the body parts is interpreted as an RFC 5322 message with headers. This subtype enables the construction of a message whose parts are individual messages. For example, the moderator of a group might collect e-mail messages from participants, bundle these messages, and send them out in one encapsulating MIME message.

The **message type** provides a number of important capabilities in MIME. The **message/rfc822 subtype** indicates that the body is an entire message, including header and body. Despite the name of this subtype, the encapsulated message may be not only a simple RFC 5322 message, but also any MIME message.

The **message/partial subtype** enables fragmentation of a large message into a number of parts, which must be reassembled at the destination. For this subtype, three parameters are specified in the Content-Type: Message/Partial field: an *id* common to all fragments of the same message, a *sequence number* unique to each fragment, and the *total* number of fragments.

The **message/external-body subtype** indicates that the actual data to be conveyed in this message are not contained in the body. Instead, the body contains the information needed to access the data. As with the other message types, the message/external-body subtype has an outer header and an encapsulated message with its own header. The only necessary field in the outer header is the Content-Type field, which identifies this as a message/external-body subtype. The inner header is the message header for the encapsulated message. The Content-Type field in the outer header must include an access-type parameter, which indicates the method of access, such as FTP (file transfer protocol).

The **application type** refers to other kinds of data, typically either uninterpreted binary data or information to be processed by a mail-based application.

MIME TRANSFER ENCODINGS   The other major component of the MIME specification, in addition to content type specification, is a definition of transfer encodings for message bodies. The objective is to provide reliable delivery across the largest range of environments.

The MIME standard defines two methods of encoding data. The Content-Transfer-Encoding field can actually take on six values, as listed in Table 8.2. However, three of these values (7-bit, 8-bit, and binary) indicate that no encoding has been done but provide some information about the nature of the data. For SMTP transfer, it is safe to use the 7-bit form. The 8-bit and binary forms may be usable in other mail transport contexts. Another Content-Transfer-Encoding value is x-token, which indicates that some other encoding scheme is used for which a name is to be supplied. This could be a vendor-specific or application-specific scheme. The two actual encoding schemes defined are quoted-printable and base64. Two schemes are defined to provide a choice between a transfer technique that is essentially human readable and one that is safe for all types of data in a way that is reasonably compact.

The **quoted-printable** transfer encoding is useful when the data consists largely of octets that correspond to printable ASCII characters. In essence, it represents nonsafe characters by the hexadecimal representation of their code and introduces reversible (soft) line breaks to limit message lines to 76 characters.

The **base64 transfer encoding**, also known as radix-64 encoding, is a common one for encoding arbitrary binary data in such a way as to be invulnerable to the processing by mail-transport programs. It is also used in PGP and is described in Appendix H.

A MULTIPART EXAMPLE Figure 8.3, taken from RFC 2045, is the outline of a complex multipart message. The message has five parts to be displayed serially: two introductory plain text parts, an embedded multipart message, a richtext part, and a closing encapsulated text message in a non-ASCII character set. The embedded multipart message has two parts to be displayed in parallel: a picture and an audio fragment.

CANONICAL FORM An important concept in MIME and S/MIME is that of canonical form. Canonical form is a format, appropriate to the content type, that is standardized for use between systems. This is in contrast to native form, which is a format that may be peculiar to a particular system. RFC 2049 defines these two forms as follows:

- **Native form:** The body to be transmitted is created in the system's native format. The native character set is used and, where appropriate, local end-of-line conventions are used as well. The body may be any format that corresponds to

Table 8.2   MIME Transfer Encodings

7 bit	The data are all represented by short lines of ASCII characters.
8 bit	The lines are short, but there may be non-ASCII characters (octets with the high-order bit set).
binary	Not only may non-ASCII characters be present but the lines are not necessarily short enough for SMTP transport.
quoted-printable	Encodes the data in such a way that if the data being encoded are mostly ASCII text, the encoded form of the data remains largely recognizable by humans.
base64	Encodes data by mapping 6-bit blocks of input to 8-bit blocks of output, all of which are printable ASCII characters.
x-token	A named nonstandard encoding.

```
MIME-Version: 1.0
    From: Nathaniel Borenstein <nsb@bellcore.com>
    To: Ned Freed <ned@innosoft.com>
    Subject: A multipart example
    Content-Type: multipart/mixed;
       boundary=unique-boundary-1
This is the preamble area of a multipart message. Mail readers that
understand multipart format should ignore this preamble. If you are reading
this text, you might want to consider changing to a mail reader that
understands how to properly display multipart messages.

    —unique-boundary-1
    . . . Some text appears here . . .
[Note that the preceding blank line means no header fields were given and
this is text, with charset US ASCII. It could have been done with explicit
typing as in the next part.]

    —unique-boundary-1
    Content-type: text/plain; charset=US-ASCII
This could have been part of the previous part, but illustrates explicit
versus implicit typing of body parts.

    —unique-boundary-1
    Content-Type: multipart/parallel; boundary=unique-boundary-2

    —unique-boundary-2
    Content-Type: audio/basic
    Content-Transfer-Encoding: base64
    . . . base64-encoded 8000 Hz single-channel mu-law-format audio data goes
here . . . .

    —unique-boundary-2
    Content-Type: image/jpeg
    Content-Transfer-Encoding: base64
    . . . base64-encoded image data goes here . . . .

    —unique-boundary-2—
    —unique-boundary-1
    Content-type: text/enriched

This is richtext. as defined in RFC 1896

    Isn't it cool?

    —unique-boundary-1
    Content-Type: message/rfc822

From: (mailbox in US-ASCII)
To: (address in US-ASCII)
Subject: (subject in US-ASCII)
Content-Type: Text/plain; charset=ISO-8859-1
Content-Transfer-Encoding: Quoted-printable

    . . . Additional text in ISO-8859-1 goes here . . .

    —unique-boundary-1—
```

Figure 8.3   Example MIME Message Structure

the local model for the representation of some form of information. Examples include a UNIX-style text file, or a Sun raster image, or a VMS indexed file, and audio data in a system-dependent format stored only in memory. In essence, the data are created in the native form that corresponds to the type specified by the media type.

■ **Canonical form:** The entire body, including out-of-band information such as record lengths and possibly file attribute information, is converted to a universal canonical form. The specific media type of the body as well as its associated attributes dictates the nature of the canonical form that is used. Conversion to the proper canonical form may involve character set conversion, transformation of audio data, compression, or various other operations specific to the various media types.

8.3 E-MAIL THREATS AND COMPREHENSIVE E-MAIL SECURITY

For both organizations and individuals, e-mail is both pervasive and especially vulnerable to a wide range of security threats. In general terms, e-mail security threats can be classified as follows:

■ **Authenticity-related threats:** Could result in unauthorized access to an enterprise's e-mail system.

■ **Integrity-related threats:** Could result in unauthorized modification of e-mail content.

■ **Confidentiality-related threats:** Could result in unauthorized disclosure of sensitive information.

■ **Availability-related threats:** Could prevent end users from being able to send or receive e-mail.

A useful list of specific e-mail threats, together with approaches to mitigation, is provided in SP 800-177 (*Trustworthy E-mail*, September 2015) and is shown in Table 8.3.

SP 800-177 recommends use of a variety of standardized protocols as a means for countering these threats. These include:

■ **STARTTLS:** An SMTP security extension that provides authentication, integrity, non-repudiation (via digital signatures) and confidentiality (via encryption) for the entire SMTP message by running SMTP over TLS.

■ **S/MIME:** Provides authentication, integrity, non-repudiation (via digital signatures) and confidentiality (via encryption) of the message body carried in SMTP messages.

■ **DNS Security Extensions (DNSSEC):** Provides authentication and integrity protection of DNS data, and is an underlying tool used by various e-mail security protocols.

■ **DNS-based Authentication of Named Entities (DANE):** Is designed to overcome problems in the certificate authority (CA) system by providing an alternative channel for authenticating public keys based on DNSSEC, with the

Table 8.3   E-mail Threats and Mitigations

Threat	Impact on Purported Sender	Impact on Receiver	Mitigation
E-mail sent by unauthorized MTA in enterprise (e.g., malware botnet)	Loss of reputation, valid e-mail from enterprise may be blocked as possible spam/phishing attack.	UBE and/or e-mail containing malicious links may be delivered into user inboxes.	Deployment of domain-based authentication techniques. Use of digital signatures over e-mail.
E-mail message sent using spoofed or unregistered sending domain	Loss of reputation, valid e-mail from enterprise may be blocked as possible spam/phishing attack.	UBE and/or e-mail containing malicious links may be delivered into user inboxes.	Deployment of domain-based authentication techniques. Use of digital signatures over e-mail.
E-mail message sent using forged sending address or e-mail address (i.e., phishing, spear phishing)	Loss of reputation, valid e-mail from enterprise may be blocked as possible spam/phishing attack.	UBE and/or e-mail containing malicious links may be delivered. Users may inadvertently divulge sensitive information or PII.	Deployment of domain-based authentication techniques. Use of digital signatures over e-mail.
E-mail modified in transit	Leak of sensitive information or PII.	Leak of sensitive information, altered message may contain malicious information.	Use of TLS to encrypt e-mail transfer between servers. Use of end-to-end e-mail encryption.
Disclosure of sensitive information (e.g., PII) via monitoring and capturing of e-mail traffic	Leak of sensitive information or PII.	Leak of sensitive information, altered message may contain malicious information.	Use of TLS to encrypt e-mail transfer between servers. Use of end-to-end e-mail encryption.
Unsolicited Bulk E-mail (UBE) (i.e., spam)	None, unless purported sender is spoofed.	UBE and/or e-mail containing malicious links may be delivered into user inboxes.	Techniques to address UBE.
DoS/DDoS attack against an enterprises' e-mail servers	Inability to send e-mail.	Inability to receive e-mail.	Multiple mail servers, use of cloud-based e-mail providers.

result that the same trust relationships used to certify IP addresses are used to certify servers operating on those addresses.

- **Sender Policy Framework (SPF):** Uses the Domain Name System (DNS) to allow domain owners to create records that associate the domain name with a specific IP address range of authorized message senders. It is a simple matter for receivers to check the SPF TXT record in the DNS to confirm that the purported sender of a message is permitted to use that source address and reject mail that does not come from an authorized IP address.

- **DomainKeys Identified Mail (DKIM):** Enables an MTA to sign selected headers and the body of a message. This validates the source domain of the mail and provides message body integrity.

- **Domain-based Message Authentication, Reporting, and Conformance (DMARC):** Lets senders know the proportionate effectiveness of their SPF and DKIM policies, and signals to receivers what action should be taken in various individual and bulk attack scenarios.

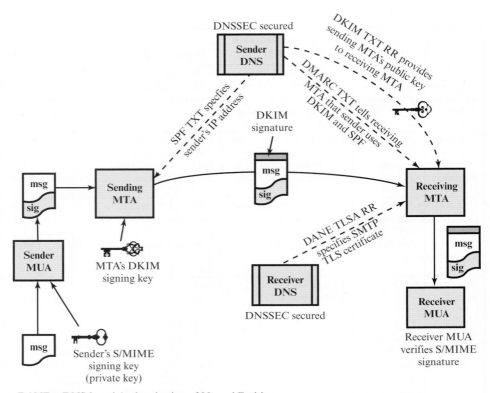

DANE = DNS-based Authentication of Named Entities
DKIM = DomainKeys Identified Mail
DMARC = Domain-based Message Authentication, Reporting, and Conformance
DNSSEC = Domain Name System Security Extensions
SPF = Sender Policy Framework
S/MIME = Secure Multi-Purpose Internet Mail Extensions
TLSA RR = Transport Layer Security Authentication Resource Record

Figure 8.4   The Interrelationship of DNSSEC, SPF, DKIM, DMARC, DANE, and S/MIME for Assuring Message Authenticity and Integrity

Figure 8.4 shows how these components interact to provide message authenticity and integrity. Not shown, for simplicity, is that S/MIME also provides message confidentiality by encrypting messages.

8.4   S/MIME

Secure/Multipurpose Internet Mail Extension (S/MIME) is a security enhancement to the MIME Internet e-mail format standard based on technology from RSA Data Security. S/MIME is a complex capability that is defined in a number of documents. The most important documents relevant to S/MIME include the following:

■ **RFC 5750, S/MIME Version 3.2 Certificate Handling:** Specifies conventions for X.509 certificate usage by (S/MIME) v3.2.

- **RFC 5751, S/MIME) Version 3.2 Message Specification:** The principal defining document for S/MIME message creation and processing.
- **RFC 4134, Examples of S/MIME Messages:** Gives examples of message bodies formatted using S/MIME.
- **RFC 2634, Enhanced Security Services for S/MIME:** Describes four optional security service extensions for S/MIME.
- **RFC 5652, Cryptographic Message Syntax (CMS):** Describes the Cryptographic Message Syntax (CMS). This syntax is used to digitally sign, digest, authenticate, or encrypt arbitrary message content.
- **RFC 3370, CMS Algorithms:** Describes the conventions for using several cryptographic algorithms with the CMS.
- **RFC 5752, Multiple Signatures in CMS:** Describes the use of multiple, parallel signatures for a message.
- **RFC 1847, Security Multiparts for MIME — Multipart/Signed and Multipart/ Encrypted:** Defines a framework within which security services may be applied to MIME body parts. The use of a digital signature is relevant to S/MIME, as explained subsequently.

Operational Description

S/MIME provides for four message-related services: authentication, confidentiality, compression, and e-mail compatibility (Table 8.4). This subsection provides an overview. We then look in more detail at this capability by examining message formats and message preparation.

AUTHENTICATION Authentication is provided by means of a digital signature, using the general scheme discussed in Chapter 3 and illustrated in Figure 3.15. Most commonly RSA with SHA-256 is used. The sequence is as follows:

1. The sender creates a message.
2. SHA-256 is used to generate a 256-bit message digest of the message.

Table 8.4 Summary of S/MIME Services

Function	Typical Algorithm	Typical Action
Digital signature	RSA/SHA-256	A hash code of a message is created using SHA-256. This message digest is encrypted using SHA-256 with the sender's private key and included with the message.
Message encryption	AES-128 with CBC	A message is encrypted using AES-128 with CBC with a one-time session key generated by the sender. The session key is encrypted using RSA with the recipient's public key and included with the message.
Compression	unspecified	A message may be compressed for storage or transmission.
E-mail compatibility	Radix-64 conversion	To provide transparency for e-mail applications, an encrypted message may be converted to an ASCII string using radix-64 conversion.

3. The message digest is encrypted with RSA using the sender's private key, and the result is appended to the message. Also appended is identifying information for the signer, which will enable the receiver to retrieve the signer's public key.

4. The receiver uses RSA with the sender's public key to decrypt and recover the message digest.

5. The receiver generates a new message digest for the message and compares it with the decrypted hash code. If the two match, the message is accepted as authentic.

The combination of SHA-256 and RSA provides an effective digital signature scheme. Because of the strength of RSA, the recipient is assured that only the possessor of the matching private key can generate the signature. Because of the strength of SHA-256, the recipient is assured that no one else could generate a new message that matches the hash code and, hence, the signature of the original message.

Although signatures normally are found attached to the message or file that they sign, this is not always the case: Detached signatures are supported. A detached signature may be stored and transmitted separately from the message it signs. This is useful in several contexts. A user may wish to maintain a separate signature log of all messages sent or received. A detached signature of an executable program can detect subsequent virus infection. Finally, detached signatures can be used when more than one party must sign a document, such as a legal contract. Each person's signature is independent and therefore is applied only to the document. Otherwise, signatures would have to be nested, with the second signer signing both the document and the first signature, and so on.

CONFIDENTIALITY S/MIME provides confidentiality by encrypting messages. Most commonly AES with a 128-bit key is used, with the cipher block chaining (CBC) mode. The key itself is also encrypted, typically with RSA, as explained below.

As always, one must address the problem of key distribution. In S/MIME, each symmetric key, referred to as a content-encryption key, is used only once. That is, a new key is generated as a random number for each message. Because it is to be used only once, the content-encryption key is bound to the message and transmitted with it. To protect the key, it is encrypted with the receiver's public key. The sequence can be described as follows:

1. The sender generates a message and a random 128-bit number to be used as a content-encryption key for this message only.

2. The message is encrypted using the content-encryption key.

3. The content-encryption key is encrypted with RSA using the recipient's public key and is attached to the message.

4. The receiver uses RSA with its private key to decrypt and recover the content-encryption key.

5. The content-encryption key is used to decrypt the message.

Several observations may be made. First, to reduce encryption time, the combination of symmetric and public-key encryption is used in preference to simply using public-key encryption to encrypt the message directly: Symmetric algorithms are substantially faster than asymmetric ones for a large block of content. Second, the use of the public-key algorithm solves the session-key distribution problem, because only the recipient is able to recover the session key that is bound to the message. Note that we do not need a session-key exchange protocol of the type discussed in Chapter 4, because we are not beginning an ongoing session. Rather, each message is a one-time independent event with its own key. Furthermore, given the store-and-forward nature of electronic mail, the use of handshaking to assure that both sides have the same session key is not practical. Finally, the use of one-time symmetric keys strengthens what is already a strong symmetric encryption approach. Only a small amount of plaintext is encrypted with each key, and there is no relationship among the keys. Thus, to the extent that the public-key algorithm is secure, the entire scheme is secure.

CONFIDENTIALITY AND AUTHENTICATION As Figure 8.5 illustrates, both confidentiality and encryption may be used for the same message. The figure shows a sequence in which a signature is generated for the plaintext message and appended to the message. Then the plaintext message and signature are encrypted as a single block using symmetric encryption and the symmetric encryption key is encrypted using public-key encryption.

S/MIME allows the signing and message encryption operations to be performed in either order. If signing is done first, the identity of the signer is hidden by the encryption. Plus, it is generally more convenient to store a signature with a plaintext version of a message. Furthermore, for purposes of third-party verification, if the signature is performed first, a third party need not be concerned with the symmetric key when verifying the signature.

If encryption is done first, it is possible to verify a signature without exposing the message content. This can be useful in a context in which automatic signature verification is desired, as no private key material is required to verify a signature. However, in this case the recipient cannot determine any relationship between the signer and the unencrypted content of the message.

E-MAIL COMPATIBILITY When S/MIME is used, at least part of the block to be transmitted is encrypted. If only the signature service is used, then the message digest is encrypted (with the sender's private key). If the confidentiality service is used, the message plus signature (if present) are encrypted (with a one-time symmetric key). Thus, part or all of the resulting block consists of a stream of arbitrary 8-bit octets. However, many electronic mail systems only permit the use of blocks consisting of ASCII text. To accommodate this restriction, S/MIME provides the service of converting the raw 8-bit binary stream to a stream of printable ASCII characters, a process referred to as 7-bit encoding.

The scheme typically used for this purpose is Base64 conversion. Each group of three octets of binary data is mapped into four ASCII characters. See Appendix K for a description.

One noteworthy aspect of the Base64 algorithm is that it blindly converts the input stream to Base64 format regardless of content, even if the input happens to be ASCII text. Thus, if a message is signed but not encrypted and the conversion is applied to the entire block, the output will be unreadable to the casual observer, which provides a certain level of confidentiality.

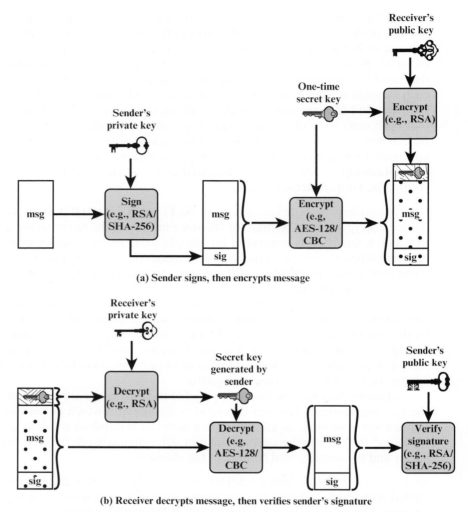

(a) Sender signs, then encrypts message

(b) Receiver decrypts message, then verifies sender's signature

Figure 8.5   Simplified S/MIME Functional Flow

RFC 5751 also recommends that even if outer 7-bit encoding is not used, the original MIME content should be 7-bit encoded. The reason for this is that it allows the MIME entity to be handled in any environment without changing it. For example, a trusted gateway might remove the encryption, but not the signature, of a message, and then forward the signed message on to the end recipient so that they can verify the signatures directly. If the transport internal to the site is not 8-bit clean, such as on a wide area network with a single mail gateway, verifying the signature will not be possible unless the original MIME entity was only 7-bit data.

COMPRESSION S/MIME also offers the ability to compress a message. This has the benefit of saving space both for e-mail transmission and for file storage.

Compression can be applied in any order with respect to the signing and message encryption operations. RFC 5751 provides the following guidelines:

- Compression of binary encoded encrypted data is discouraged, since it will not yield significant compression. Base64 encrypted data could very well benefit, however.

- If a lossy compression algorithm is used with signing, you will need to compress first, then sign.

S/MIME Message Content Types

S/MIME uses the following message content types, which are defined in RFC 5652, Cryptographic Message Syntax:

- **Data:** Refers to the inner MIME-encoded message content, which may then be encapsulated in a SignedData, EnvelopedData, or CompressedData content type.

- **SignedData:** Used to apply a digital signature to a message.

- **EnvelopedData:** This consists of encrypted content of any type and encrypted-content encryption keys for one or more recipients.

- **CompressedData:** Used to apply data compression to a message.

The Data content type is also used for a procedure known as clear signing. For clear signing, a digital signature is calculated for a MIME-encoded message and the two parts, the message and signature, form a multipart MIME message. Unlike SignedData, which involves encapsulating the message and signature in a special format, clear-signed messages can be read and their signatures verified by e-mail entities that do not implement S/MIME.

Approved Cryptographic Algorithms

Table 8.5 summarizes the cryptographic algorithms used in S/MIME. S/MIME uses the following terminology taken from RFC 2119 (*Key Words for use in RFCs to Indicate Requirement Levels*, March 1997) to specify the requirement level:

- **MUST:** The definition is an absolute requirement of the specification. An implementation must include this feature or function to be in conformance with the specification.

- **SHOULD:** There may exist valid reasons in particular circumstances to ignore this feature or function, but it is recommended that an implementation include the feature or function.

The S/MIME specification includes a discussion of the procedure for deciding which content encryption algorithm to use. In essence, a sending agent has two decisions to make. First, the sending agent must determine if the receiving agent is capable of decrypting using a given encryption algorithm. Second, if the receiving agent is only capable of accepting weakly encrypted content, the sending agent must decide if it is acceptable to send using weak encryption. To support this decision process, a sending agent may announce its decrypting capabilities in order of preference for any message that it sends out. A receiving agent may store that information for future use.

Table 8.5 Cryptographic Algorithms Used in S/MIME

Function	Requirement
Create a message digest to be used in forming a digital signature.	MUST support SHA-256 SHOULD support SHA-1 Receiver SHOULD support MD5 for backward compatibility
Use message digest to form a digital signature.	MUST support RSA with SHA-256 SHOULD support —DSA with SHA-256 —RSASSA-PSS with SHA-256 —RSA with SHA-1 —DSA with SHA-1 —RSA with MD5
Encrypt session key for transmission with a message.	MUST support RSA encryption SHOULD support —RSAES-OAEP —Diffie–Hellman ephemeral-static mode
Encrypt message for transmission with a one-time session key.	MUST support AES-128 with CBC SHOULD support —AES-192 CBC and AES-256 CBC —Triple DES CBC

The following rules, in the following order, should be followed by a sending agent.

1. If the sending agent has a list of preferred decrypting capabilities from an intended recipient, it SHOULD choose the first (highest preference) capability on the list that it is capable of using.

2. If the sending agent has no such list of capabilities from an intended recipient but has received one or more messages from the recipient, then the outgoing message SHOULD use the same encryption algorithm as was used on the last signed and encrypted message received from that intended recipient.

3. If the sending agent has no knowledge about the decryption capabilities of the intended recipient and is willing to risk that the recipient may not be able to decrypt the message, then the sending agent SHOULD use triple DES.

4. If the sending agent has no knowledge about the decryption capabilities of the intended recipient and is not willing to risk that the recipient may not be able to decrypt the message, then the sending agent MUST use RC2/40.

If a message is to be sent to multiple recipients and a common encryption algorithm cannot be selected for all, then the sending agent will need to send two messages. However, in that case, it is important to note that the security of the message is made vulnerable by the transmission of one copy with lower security.

S/MIME Messages

S/MIME makes use of a number of new MIME content types. All of the new application types use the designation PKCS. This refers to a set of public-key cryptography specifications issued by RSA Laboratories and made available for the S/MIME effort.

We examine each of these in turn after first looking at the general procedures for S/MIME message preparation.

SECURING A MIME ENTITY S/MIME secures a MIME entity with a signature, encryption, or both. A MIME entity may be an entire message (except for the RFC 5322 headers), or if the MIME content type is multipart, then a MIME entity is one or more of the subparts of the message. The MIME entity is prepared according to the normal rules for MIME message preparation. Then the MIME entity plus some security-related data, such as algorithm identifiers and certificates, are processed by S/MIME to produce what is known as a PKCS object. A PKCS object is then treated as message content and wrapped in MIME (provided with appropriate MIME headers). This process should become clear as we look at specific objects and provide examples.

In all cases, the message to be sent is converted to canonical form. In particular, for a given type and subtype, the appropriate canonical form is used for the message content. For a multipart message, the appropriate canonical form is used for each subpart.

The use of transfer encoding requires special attention. For most cases, the result of applying the security algorithm will be to produce an object that is partially or totally represented in arbitrary binary data. This will then be wrapped in an outer MIME message and transfer encoding can be applied at that point, typically base64. However, in the case of a multipart signed message (described in more detail later), the message content in one of the subparts is unchanged by the security process. Unless that content is 7 bit, it should be transfer encoded using base64 or quoted-printable so that there is no danger of altering the content to which the signature was applied.

We now look at each of the S/MIME content types.

ENVELOPEDDATA An application/pkcs7-mime subtype is used for one of four categories of S/MIME processing, each with a unique smime-type parameter. In all cases, the resulting entity, (referred to as an *object*) is represented in a form known as Basic Encoding Rules (BER), which is defined in ITU-T Recommendation X.209. The BER format consists of arbitrary octet strings and is therefore binary data. Such an object should be transfer encoded with base64 in the outer MIME message. We first look at envelopedData.

The steps for preparing an envelopedData MIME entity are:

1. Generate a pseudorandom session key for a particular symmetric encryption algorithm (RC2/40 or triple DES).

2. For each recipient, encrypt the session key with the recipient's public RSA key.

3. For each recipient, prepare a block known as `RecipientInfo` that contains an identifier of the recipient's public-key certificate,[1] an identifier of the algorithm used to encrypt the session key, and the encrypted session key.

4. Encrypt the message content with the session key.

---

[1]This is an X.509 certificate, discussed later in this section.

The RecipientInfo blocks followed by the encrypted content constitute the `envelopedData`. This information is then encoded into base64. A sample message (excluding the RFC 5322 headers) is given below.

```
Content-Type: application/pkcs7-mime; smime-type=enveloped-
      data; name=smime.p7m
Content-Transfer-Encoding: base64
Content-Disposition: attachment; filename=smime.p7m
```

```
rfvbnj756tbBghyHhHUujhJhjH77n8HHGT9HG4VQpfyF467GhIGfHfYT6
7n8HHGghyHhHUujhJh4VQpfyF467GhIGfHfYGTrfvbnjT6jH7756tbB9H
f8HHGTrfvhJhjH776tbB9HG4VQbnj7567GhIGfHfYT6ghyHhHUujpfyF4
0GhIGfHfQbnj756YT64V
```

To recover the encrypted message, the recipient first strips off the base64 encoding. Then the recipient's private key is used to recover the session key. Finally, the message content is decrypted with the session key.

SIGNEDDATA The `signedData` smime-type can be used with one or more signers. For clarity, we confine our description to the case of a single digital signature. The steps for preparing a signedData MIME entity are as follows.

1. Select a message digest algorithm (SHA or MD5).
2. Compute the message digest (hash function) of the content to be signed.
3. Encrypt the message digest with the signer's private key.
4. Prepare a block known as `SignerInfo` that contains the signer's public-key certificate, an identifier of the message digest algorithm, an identifier of the algorithm used to encrypt the message digest, and the encrypted message digest.

The `signedData` entity consists of a series of blocks, including a message digest algorithm identifier, the message being signed, and `SignerInfo`. The `signedData` entity may also include a set of public-key certificates sufficient to constitute a chain from a recognized root or top-level certification authority to the signer. This information is then encoded into base64. A sample message (excluding the RFC 5322 headers) is the following.

```
Content-Type: application/pkcs7-mime; smime-type=signed-
      data; name=smime.p7m
Content-Transfer-Encoding: base64
Content-Disposition: attachment; filename=smime.p7m
```

```
567GhIGfHfYT6ghyHhHUujpfyF4f8HHGTrfvhJhjH776tbB9HG4VQbnj7
77n8HHGT9HG4VQpfyF467GhIGfHfYT6rfvbnj756tbBghyHhHUujhJhjH
HUujhJh4VQpfyF467GhIGfHfYGTrfvbnjT6jH7756tbB9H7n8HHGghyHh
6YT64V0GhIGfHfQbnj75
```

To recover the signed message and verify the signature, the recipient first strips off the base64 encoding. Then the signer's public key is used to decrypt the message digest. The recipient independently computes the message digest and compares it to the decrypted message digest to verify the signature.

CLEAR SIGNING   Clear signing is achieved using the multipart content type with a signed subtype. As was mentioned, this signing process does not involve transforming the message to be signed, so that the message is sent "in the clear." Thus, recipients with MIME capability but not S/MIME capability are able to read the incoming message.

A multipart/signed message has two parts. The first part can be any MIME type but must be prepared so that it will not be altered during transfer from source to destination. This means that if the first part is not 7 bit, then it needs to be encoded using base64 or quoted-printable. Then this part is processed in the same manner as `signedData`, but in this case an object with `signedData` format is created that has an empty message content field. This object is a detached signature. It is then transfer encoded using base64 to become the second part of the multipart/signed message. This second part has a MIME content type of application and a subtype of pkcs7-signature. Here is a sample message:

```
Content-Type: multipart/signed;
    protocol="application/pkcs7-signature";
    micalg=sha1; boundary=boundary42

—boundary42
Content-Type: text/plain

This is a clear-signed message.

—boundary42
Content-Type: application/pkcs7-signature; name=smime.p7s
Content-Transfer-Encoding: base64
Content-Disposition: attachment; filename=smime.p7s

ghyHhHUujhJhjH77n8HHGTrfvbnj756tbB9HG4VQpfyF467GhIGfHfYT6
4VQpfyF467GhIGfHfYT6jH77n8HHGghyHhHUujhJh756tbB9HGTrfvbnj
n8HHGTrfvhJhjH776tbB9HG4VQbnj7567GhIGfHfYT6ghyHhHUujpfyF4
7GhIGfHfYT64VQbnj756
—boundary42—
```

The protocol parameter indicates that this is a two-part clear-signed entity. The `micalg` parameter indicates the type of message digest used. The receiver can verify the signature by taking the message digest of the first part and comparing this to the message digest recovered from the signature in the second part.

REGISTRATION REQUEST   Typically, an application or user will apply to a certification authority for a public-key certificate. The application/pkcs10 S/MIME entity is used to transfer a certification request. The certification request includes `certificationRequestInfo` block, followed by an identifier of the public-key encryption algorithm, followed by the signature of the `certificationRequestInfo` block, made using the sender's private key. The `certificationRequestInfo` block includes a name of the certificate subject (the entity whose public key is to be certified) and a bit-string representation of the user's public key.

CERTIFICATES-ONLY MESSAGE   A message containing only certificates or a certificate revocation list (CRL) can be sent in response to a registration request. The message is an application/pkcs7-mime type/subtype with an smime-type parameter of degenerate. The steps involved are the same as those for creating a `signedData` message, except that there is no message content and the `signerInfo` field is empty.

S/MIME Certificate Processing

S/MIME uses public-key certificates that conform to version 3 of X.509 (see Chapter 4). S/MIME managers and/or users must configure each client with a list of trusted keys and with certificate revocation lists. That is, the responsibility is local for maintaining the certificates needed to verify incoming signatures and to encrypt outgoing messages. On the other hand, the certificates are signed by certification authorities.

USER AGENT ROLE   An S/MIME user has several key management functions to perform.

- **Key generation:** The user of some related administrative utility (e.g., one associated with LAN management) MUST be capable of generating separate Diffie–Hellman and DSS key pairs and SHOULD be capable of generating RSA key pairs. Each key pair MUST be generated from a good source of nondeterministic random input and be protected in a secure fashion. A user agent SHOULD generate RSA key pairs with a length in the range of 768 to 1024 bits and MUST NOT generate a length of less than 512 bits.
- **Registration:** A user's public key must be registered with a certification authority in order to receive an X.509 public-key certificate.
- **Certificate storage and retrieval:** A user requires access to a local list of certificates in order to verify incoming signatures and to encrypt outgoing messages. Such a list could be maintained by the user or by some local administrative entity on behalf of a number of users.

Enhanced Security Services

RFC 2634 defines four enhanced security services for S/MIME:

- **Signed receipts:** A signed receipt may be requested in a `SignedData` object. Returning a signed receipt provides proof of delivery to the originator of a message and allows the originator to demonstrate to a third party that the recipient received the message. In essence, the recipient signs the entire original message plus the original (sender's) signature and appends the new signature to form a new S/MIME message.

- **Security labels:** A security label may be included in the authenticated attributes of a `SignedData` object. A security label is a set of security information regarding the sensitivity of the content that is protected by S/MIME encapsulation. The labels may be used for access control, by indicating which users are permitted access to an object. Other uses include priority (secret, confidential, restricted, and so on) or role based, describing which kind of people can see the information (e.g., patient's health-care team, medical billing agents).

- **Secure mailing lists:** When a user sends a message to multiple recipients, a certain amount of per-recipient processing is required, including the use of each recipient's public key. The user can be relieved of this work by employing the services of an S/MIME Mail List Agent (MLA). An MLA can take a single incoming message, perform the recipient-specific encryption for each recipient, and forward the message. The originator of a message need only send the message to the MLA with encryption performed using the MLA's public key.

- **Signing certificates:** This service is used to securely bind a sender's certificate to their signature through a signing certificate attribute.

8.5 PRETTY GOOD PRIVACY

An alternative e-mail security protocol is Pretty Good Privacy (PGP), which has essentially the same functionality as S/MIME. PGP was created by Phil Zimmerman and implemented as a product first released in 1991. It was made available free of charge and became quite popular for personal use. The initial PGP protocol was proprietary and used some encryption algorithms with intellectual property restrictions. In 1996, version 5.x of PGP was defined in IETF RFC 1991, *PGP Message Exchange Formats*. Subsequently, OpenPGP was developed as a new standard protocol based on PGP version 5.x. OpenPGP is defined in RFC 4880 (*OpenPGP Message Format*, November 2007) and RFC 3156 (*MIME Security with OpenPGP*, August 2001).

There are two significant differences between S/MIME and OpenPGP:

- **Key Certification:** S/MIME uses X.509 certificates that are issued by Certificate Authorities (or local agencies that have been delegated authority by a CA to issue certificates). In OpenPGP, users generate their own OpenPGP public and private keys and then solicit signatures for their public keys from individuals or organizations to which they are known. Whereas X.509 certificates are trusted if there is a valid PKIX chain to a trusted root, an OpenPGP public key is trusted if it is signed by another OpenPGP public key that is trusted by the recipient. This is called the *Web-of-Trust*.

- **Key Distribution:** OpenPGP does not include the sender's public key with each message, so it is necessary for recipients of OpenPGP messages to separately obtain the sender's public key in order to verify the message. Many organizations post OpenPGP keys on TLS-protected websites: People who wish to verify digital signatures or send these organizations encrypted mail need to manually download these keys and add them to their OpenPGP clients. Keys may also be registered with the OpenPGP public key servers, which are servers that maintain a database of PGP public keys organized by e-mail address. Anyone may post a public key to the OpenPGP key servers, and that public key may contain any e-mail address. There is no vetting of OpenPGP keys, so users must use the Web-of-Trust to decide whether to trust a given public key.

SP 800-177 recommends the use of S/MIME rather than PGP because of the greater confidence in the CA system of verifying public keys.

Appendix H provides an overview of PGP.

8.6 DNSSEC

DNS Security Extensions (DNSSEC) are used by several protocols that provide e-mail security. This section provides a brief overview of the Domain Name System (DNS) and then looks at DNSSEC.

Domain Name System

DNS is a directory lookup service that provides a mapping between the name of a host on the Internet and its numeric IP address. DNS is essential to the functioning of the Internet. The DNS is used by MUAs and MTAs to find the address of the next hop server for mail delivery. Sending MTAs query DNS for the Mail Exchange Resource Record (MX RR) of the recipient's domain (the right hand side of the "@" symbol) in order to find the receiving MTA to contact.

Four elements comprise the DNS:

- **Domain name space:** DNS uses a tree-structured name space to identify resources on the Internet.

- **DNS database:** Conceptually, each node and leaf in the name space tree structure names a set of information (e.g., IP address, name server for this domain name) that is contained in resource record. The collection of all RRs is organized into a distributed database.

- **Name servers:** These are server programs that hold information about a portion of the domain name tree structure and the associated RRs.

- **Resolvers:** These are programs that extract information from name servers in response to client requests. A typical client request is for an IP address corresponding to a given domain name.

THE DNS DATABASE DNS is based on a hierarchical database containing **resource records (RRs)** that include the name, IP address, and other information about hosts. The key features of the database are as follows:

- **Variable-depth hierarchy for names:** DNS allows essentially unlimited levels and uses the period (.) as the level delimiter in printed names, as described earlier.

Table 8.6   Resource Record Types

Type	Description
A	A host address. This RR type maps the name of a system to its IPv4 address. Some systems (e.g., routers) have multiple addresses, and there is a separate RR for each.
AAAA	Similar to A type, but for IPv6 addresses.
CNAME	Canonical name. Specifies an alias name for a host and maps this to the canonical (true) name.
HINFO	Host information. Designates the processor and operating system used by the host.
MINFO	Mailbox or mail list information. Maps a mailbox or mail list name to a host name.
MX	Mail exchange. Identifies the system(s) via which mail to the queried domain name should be relayed.
NS	Authoritative name server for this domain.
PTR	Domain name pointer. Points to another part of the domain name space.
SOA	Start of a zone of authority (which part of naming hierarchy is implemented). Includes parameters related to this zone.
SRV	For a given service provides name of server or servers in domain that provide that service.
TXT	Arbitrary text. Provides a way to add text comments to the database.
WKS	Well-known services. May list the application services available at this host.

- **Distributed database:** The database resides in DNS servers scattered throughout the Internet.
- **Distribution controlled by the database:** The DNS database is divided into thousands of separately managed zones, which are managed by separate administrators. Distribution and update of records is controlled by the database software.

Using this database, DNS servers provide a name-to-address directory service for network applications that need to locate specific servers. For example, every time an e-mail message is sent or a Web page is accessed, there must be a DNS name lookup to determine the IP address of the e-mail server or Web server.

Table 8.6 lists the various types of resource records.

DNS OPERATION DNS operation typically includes the following steps (Figure 8.6):

1. A user program requests an IP address for a domain name.
2. A resolver module in the local host or local ISP queries a local name server in the same domain as the resolver.
3. The local name server checks to see if the name is in its local database or cache, and, if so, returns the IP address to the requestor. Otherwise, the name server queries other available name servers, if necessary going to the root server, as explained subsequently.
4. When a response is received at the local name server, it stores the name/address mapping in its local cache and may maintain this entry for the amount of time specified in the time-to-live field of the retrieved RR.
5. The user program is given the IP address or an error message.

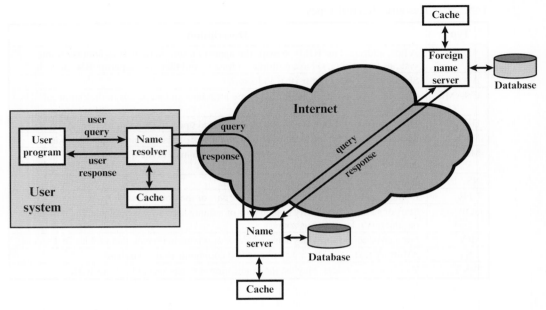

Figure 8.6 DNS Name Resolution

The distributed DNS database that supports the DNS functionality must be updated frequently because of the rapid and continued growth of the Internet. Further, the DNS must cope with dynamic assignment of IP addresses, such as is done for home DSL users by their ISP. Accordingly, dynamic updating functions for DNS have been defined. In essence, DNS name servers automatically send out updates to other relevant name servers as conditions warrant.

DNS Security Extensions

DNSSEC provides end-to-end protection through the use of digital signatures that are created by responding zone administrators and verified by a recipient's resolver software. In particular, DNSSEC avoids the need to trust intermediate name servers and resolvers that cache or route the DNS records originating from the responding zone administrator before they reach the source of the query. DNSSEC consists of a set of new resource record types and modifications to the existing DNS protocol, and is defined in the following documents:

- **RFC 4033, DNS Security Introduction and Requirements:** Introduces the DNS security extensions and describes their capabilities and limitations. The document also discusses the services that the DNS security extensions do and do not provide.

- **RFC 4034, Resource Records for the DNS Security Extensions:** Defines four new resource records that provide security for DNS.

■ **RFC 4035, Protocol Modifications for the DNS Security Extensions:** Defines the concept of a signed zone, along with the requirements for serving and resolving by using DNSSEC. These techniques allow a security-aware resolver to authenticate both DNS resource records and authoritative DNS error indications.

DNSSEC OPERATION In essence, DNSSEC is designed to protect DNS clients from accepting forged or altered DNS resource records. It does this by using digital signatures to provide:

■ **Data origin authentication:** Ensures that data has originated from the correct source.

■ **Data integrity verification:** Ensures that the content of a RR has not been modified.

The DNS zone administrator digitally signs every Resource Record set (RRset) in the zone, and publishes this collection of digital signatures, along with the zone administrator's public key, in the DNS itself. In DNSSEC, trust in the public key (for signature verification) of the source is established not by going to a third party or a chain of third parties (as in public key infrastructure [PKI] chaining), but by starting from a trusted zone (such as the root zone) and establishing the chain of trust down to the current source of response through successive verifications of signature of the public key of a child by its parent. The public key of the trusted zone is called the *trust anchor*.

RESOURCE RECORDS FOR DNSSEC RFC 4034 defines four new DNS resource records:

■ **DNSKEY:** Contains a public key.

■ **RRSIG:** A resource record digital signature.

■ **NSEC:** Authenticated denial of existence record.

■ **DS:** Delegation signer.

An RRSIG is associated with each RRset, where an RRset is the set of resource records that have the same label, class, and type. When a client requests data, an RRset is returned, together with the associated digital signature in an RRSIG record. The client obtains the relevant DNSKEY public key and verifies the signature for this RRset.

DNSSEC depends on establishing the authenticity of the DNS hierarchy leading to the domain name in question, and thus its operation depends on beginning the use of cryptographic digital signatures in the root zone. The DS resource record facilitates key signing and authentication between DNS zones to create an authentication chain, or trusted sequence of signed data, from the root of the DNS tree down to a specific domain name. To secure all DNS lookups, including those for non-existent domain names and record types, DNSSEC uses the NSEC resource record to authenticate negative responses to queries. NSEC is used to identify the range of DNS names or resource record types that do not exist among the sequence of domain names in a zone.

8.7 DNS-BASED AUTHENTICATION OF NAMED ENTITIES

DANE is a protocol to allow X.509 certificates, commonly used for Transport Layer Security (TLS), to be bound to DNS names using DNSSEC. It is proposed in RFC 6698 as a way to authenticate TLS client and server entities without a certificate authority (CA).

The rationale for DANE is the vulnerability of the use of CAs in a global PKI system. Every browser developer and operating system supplier maintains a list of CA root certificates as trust anchors. These are called the software's root certificates and are stored in its root certificate store. The PKIX procedure allows a certificate recipient to trace a certificate back to the root. So long as the root certificate remains trustworthy, and the authentication concludes successfully, the client can proceed with the connection.

However, if any of the hundreds of CAs operating on the Internet is compromised, the effects can be widespread. The attacker can obtain the CA's private key, get issued certificates under a false name, or introduce new bogus root certificates into a root certificate store. There is no limitation of scope for the global PKI and a compromise of a single CA damages the integrity of the entire PKI system. In addition, some CAs have engaged in poor security practices. For example, some CAs have issued wildcard certificates that allow the holder to issue sub-certificates for any domain or entity, anywhere in the world.

The purpose of DANE is to replace reliance on the security of the CA system with reliance on the security provided by DNSSEC. Given that the DNS administrator for a domain name is authorized to give identifying information about the zone, it makes sense to allow that administrator to also make an authoritative binding between the domain name and a certificate that might be used by a host at that domain name.

TLSA Record

DANE defines a new DNS record type, TLSA, that can be used for a secure method of authenticating SSL/TLS certificates. The TLSA provides for:

- Specifying constraints on which CA can vouch for a certificate, or which specific PKIX end-entity certificate is valid.
- Specifying that a service certificate or a CA can be directly authenticated in the DNS itself.

The TLSA RR enables certificate issue and delivery to be tied to a given domain. A server domain owner creates a TLSA resource record that identifies the certificate and its public key. When a client receives an X.509 certificate in the TLS negotiation, it looks up the TLSA RR for that domain and matches the TLSA data against the certificate as part of the client's certificate validation procedure.

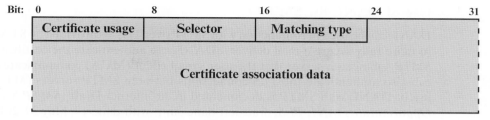

Figure 8.7   TLSA RR Transmission Format

Figure 8.7 shows the format of a TLSA RR as it is transmitted to a requesting entity. It contains four fields. The **Certificate Usage** field defines four different usage models, to accommodate users who require different forms of authentication. The usage models are:

- **PKIX-TA (CA constraint):** Specifies which CA should be trusted to authenticate the certificate for the service. This usage model limits which CA can be used to issue certificates for a given service on a host. The server certificate chain must pass PKIX validation that terminates with a trusted root certificate stored in the client.

- **PKIX-EE (service certificate constraint):** Defines which specific end entity service certificate should be trusted for the service. This usage model limits which end entity certificate can be used by a given service on a host. The server certificate chain must pass PKIX validation that terminates with a trusted root certificate stored in the client.

- **DANE-TA (trust anchor assertion):** Specifies a domain-operated CA to be used as a trust anchor. This usage model allows a domain name administrator to specify a new trust anchor—for example, if the domain issues its own certificates under its own CA that is not expected to be in the end users' collection of trust anchors. The server certificate chain is self-issued and does not need to verify against a trusted root stored in the client.

- **DANE-EE (domain-issued certificate):** Specifies a domain-operated CA to be used as a trust anchor. This certificate usage allows a domain name administrator to issue certificates for a domain without involving a third-party CA. The server certificate chain is self-issued and does not need to verify against a trusted root stored in the client.

The first two usage models are designed to co-exist with and strengthen the public CA system. The final two usage models operate without the use of public CAs.

The **Selector** field indicates whether the full certificate will be matched or just the value of the public key. The match is made between the certificate presented in TLS negotiation and the certificate in the TLSA RR. The **Matching Type** field indicates how the match of the certificate is made. The options are exact match, SHA-256 hash match, or SHA-512 hash match. The **Certificate Association Data** is the raw certificate data in hex format.

Use of DANE for SMTP

DANE can be used in conjunction with SMTP over TLS, as provided by STARTTLS, to more fully secure e-mail delivery. DANE can authenticate the certificate of the SMTP submission server that the user's mail client (MUA) communicates with. It can also authenticate the TLS connections between SMTP servers (MTAs). The use of DANE with SMTP is documented in an Internet Draft (*SMTP Security via Opportunistic DANE TLS*, draft-ietf-dane-smtp-with-dane-19, May 29, 2015).

As discussed in Section 8.1, SMTP can use the STARTTLS extension to run SMTP over TLS, so that the entire e-mail message plus SMTP envelope are encrypted. This is done opportunistically, that is, if both sides support STARTTLS. Even when TLS is used to provide confidentiality, it is vulnerable to attack in the following ways:

■ Attackers can strip away the TLS capability advertisement and downgrade the connection to not use TLS.

■ TLS connections are often unauthenticated (e.g., the use of self-signed certificates as well as mismatched certificates is common).

DANE can address both these vulnerabilities. A domain can use the presence of the TLSA RR as an indicator that encryption must be performed, thus preventing malicious downgrade. A domain can authenticate the certificate used in the TLS connection setup using a DNSSEC-signed TLSA RR.

Use of DNSSEC for S/MIME

DNSSEC can be used in conjunction with S/MIME to more fully secure e-mail delivery, in a manner similar to the DANE functionality. This use is documented in an Internet Draft (*Using Secure DNS to Associate Certificates with Domain Names for S/MIME*, draft-ietf-dane-smime-09, August 27, 2015), which proposes a new SMIMEA DNS RR. The purpose of the SMIMEA RR is to associate certificates with DNS domain names.

As discussed in Section 8.4, S/MIME messages often contain certificates that can assist in authenticating the message sender and can be used in encrypting messages sent in reply. This feature requires that the receiving MUA validate the certificate associated with the purported sender. SMIMEA RRs can provide a secure means of doing this validation.

In essence, the SMIMEA RR will have the same format and content as the TLSA RR, with the same functionality. The difference is that it is geared to the needs of MUAs in dealing with domain names as specified in e-mail addresses in the message body, rather than domain names specified in the outer SMTP envelope.

8.8 SENDER POLICY FRAMEWORK

SPF is the standardized way for a sending domain to identify and assert the mail senders for a given domain. The problem that SPF addresses is the following: With the current e-mail infrastructure, any host can use any domain name for each of the various identifiers in the mail header, not just the domain name where the host is located. Two major drawbacks of this freedom are:

- It is a major obstacle to reducing unsolicited bulk e-mail (UBE), also known as spam. It makes it difficult for mail handlers to filter out e-mails on the basis of known UBE sources.

- ADMDs (see Section 8.1) are understandably concerned about the ease with which other entities can make use of their domain names, often with malicious intent.

RFC 7208 defines the SPF. It provides a protocol by which ADMDs can authorize hosts to use their domain names in the "MAIL FROM" or "HELO" identities. Compliant ADMDs publish Sender Policy Framework (SPF) records in the DNS specifying which hosts are permitted to use their names, and compliant mail receivers use the published SPF records to test the authorization of sending Mail Transfer Agents (MTAs) using a given "HELO" or "MAIL FROM" identity during a mail transaction.

SPF works by checking a sender's IP address against the policy encoded in any SPF record found at the sending domain. The sending domain is the domain used in the SMTP connection, not the domain indicated in the message header as displayed in the MUA. This means that SPF checks can be applied before the message content is received from the sender.

Figure 8.8 is an example in which SPF would come into play. Assume that the sender's IP address is 192.168.0.1. The message arrives from the MTA with domain mta.example.net. The sender uses the MAIL FROM tag of alice@example.org, indicating that the message originates in the example.org domain. But the message header specifies alice.sender@example.net. The receiver uses SPF to query for the SPF RR that corresponds to example.com to check if the IP address 192.168.0.1 is

```
S: 220 foo.com Simple Mail Transfer Service Ready
C: HELO mta.example.net
S: 250 OK
C: MAIL FROM:<alice@example.org>
S: 250 OK
C: RCPT TO:<Jones@foo.com>
S: 250 OK
C: DATA
S: 354 Start mail input; end with <crlf>.<crlf>
C: To: bob@foo.com
C: From: alice.sender@example.net
C: Date: Today
C: Subject: Meeting Today
   . . .
```

Figure 8.8   Example in which SMTP Envelope Header Does Not Match Message Header

listed as a valid sender, and then takes appropriate action based on the results of checking the RR.

SPF on the Sender Side

A sending domain needs to identify all the senders for a given domain and add that information into the DNS as a separate resource record. Next, the sending domain encodes the appropriate policy for each sender using the SPF syntax. The encoding is done in a TXT DNS resource record as a list of mechanisms and modifiers. Mechanisms are used to define an IP address or range of addresses to be matched, and modifiers indicate the policy for a given match. Table 8.7 lists the most important mechanisms and modifiers used in SPF.

The SPF syntax is fairly complex and can express complex relationships between senders. For more detail, see RFC 7208.

SPF on the Receiver Side

If SPF is implemented at a receiver, the SPF entity uses the SMTP envelope MAIL FROM: address domain and the IP address of the sender to query an SPF TXT RR. The SPF checks can be started before the body of the e-mail message is received,

Table 8.7   Common SPF Mechanisms and Modifiers

Tag	Description
ip4	Specifies an IPv4 address or range of addresses that are authorized senders for a domain.
ip6	Specifies an IPv6 address or range of addresses that are authorized senders for a domain.
mx	Asserts that the listed hosts for the Mail Exchange RRs are also valid senders for the domain.
include	Lists another domain where the receiver should look for an SPF RR for further senders. This can be useful for large organizations with many domains or sub-domains that have a single set of shared senders. The include mechanism is recursive, in that the SPF check in the record found is tested in its entirety before proceeding. It is not simply a concatenation of the checks.
all	Matches every IP address that has not otherwise been matched.

(a) SPF Mechanisms

Modifier	Description
+	The given mechanism check must pass. This is the default mechanism and does not need to be explicitly listed.
−	The given mechanism is not allowed to send e-mail on behalf of the domain.
~	The given mechanism is in transition and if an e-mail is seen from the listed host/IP address, then it should be accepted but marked for closer inspection.
?	The SPF RR explicitly states nothing about the mechanism. In this case, the default behavior is to accept the e-mail. (This makes it equivalent to '+' unless some sort of discrete or aggregate message review is conducted.)

(b) SPF Mechanism Modifiers

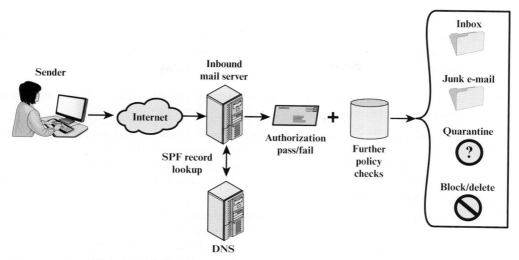

Figure 8.9   Sender Policy Framework Operation

which may result in blocking the transmission of the e-mail content. Alternatively, the entire message can be absorbed and buffered until all the checks are finished. In either case, checks must be completed before the mail message is sent to the end user's inbox.

The checking involves the following rules:

1. If no SPF TXT RR is returned, the default behavior is to accept the message.
2. If the SPF TXT RR has formatting errors, the default behavior is to accept the message.
3. Otherwise the mechanisms and modifiers in the RR are used to determine disposition of the e-mail message.

Figure 8.9 illustrates SPF operation.

8.9 DOMAINKEYS IDENTIFIED MAIL

DomainKeys Identified Mail (DKIM) is a specification for cryptographically signing e-mail messages, permitting a signing domain to claim responsibility for a message in the mail stream. Message recipients (or agents acting in their behalf) can verify the signature by querying the signer's domain directly to retrieve the appropriate public key and thereby can confirm that the message was attested to by a party in possession of the private key for the signing domain. DKIM is an Internet Standard (RFC 6376: *DomainKeys Identified Mail (DKIM) Signatures*). DKIM has been widely adopted by a range of e-mail providers, including corporations, government agencies, gmail, Yahoo!, and many Internet Service Providers (ISPs).

E-mail Threats

RFC 4686 (*Analysis of Threats Motivating DomainKeys Identified Mail*) describes the threats being addressed by DKIM in terms of the characteristics, capabilities, and location of potential attackers.

CHARACTERISTICS   RFC 4686 characterizes the range of attackers on a spectrum of three levels of threat.

1. At the low end are attackers who simply want to send e-mail that a recipient does not want to receive. The attacker can use one of a number of commercially available tools that allow the sender to falsify the origin address of messages. This makes it difficult for the receiver to filter spam on the basis of originating address or domain.

2. At the next level are professional senders of bulk spam mail. These attackers often operate as commercial enterprises and send messages on behalf of third parties. They employ more comprehensive tools for attack, including Mail Transfer Agents (MTAs) and registered domains and networks of compromised computers (zombies), to send messages and (in some cases) to harvest addresses to which to send.

3. The most sophisticated and financially motivated senders of messages are those who stand to receive substantial financial benefit, such as from an e-mail-based fraud scheme. These attackers can be expected to employ all of the above mechanisms and additionally may attack the Internet infrastructure itself, including DNS cache-poisoning attacks and IP routing attacks.

CAPABILITIES   RFC 4686 lists the following as capabilities that an attacker might have.

1. Submit messages to MTAs and Message Submission Agents (MSAs) at multiple locations in the Internet.

2. Construct arbitrary Message Header fields, including those claiming to be mailing lists, resenders, and other mail agents.

3. Sign messages on behalf of domains under their control.

4. Generate substantial numbers of either unsigned or apparently signed messages that might be used to attempt a denial-of-service attack.

5. Resend messages that may have been previously signed by the domain.

6. Transmit messages using any envelope information desired.

7. Act as an authorized submitter for messages from a compromised computer.

8. Manipulation of IP routing. This could be used to submit messages from specific IP addresses or difficult-to-trace addresses, or to cause diversion of messages to a specific domain.

9. Limited influence over portions of DNS using mechanisms such as cache poisoning. This might be used to influence message routing or to falsify advertisements of DNS-based keys or signing practices.

10. Access to significant computing resources, for example, through the conscription of worm-infected "zombie" computers. This could allow the "bad actor" to perform various types of brute-force attacks.

11. Ability to eavesdrop on existing traffic, perhaps from a wireless network.

LOCATION DKIM focuses primarily on attackers located outside of the administrative units of the claimed originator and the recipient. These administrative units frequently correspond to the protected portions of the network adjacent to the originator and recipient. It is in this area that the trust relationships required for authenticated message submission do not exist and do not scale adequately to be practical. Conversely, within these administrative units, there are other mechanisms (such as authenticated message submission) that are easier to deploy and more likely to be used than DKIM. External bad actors are usually attempting to exploit the "any-to-any" nature of e-mail that motivates most recipient MTAs to accept messages from anywhere for delivery to their local domain. They may generate messages without signatures, with incorrect signatures, or with correct signatures from domains with little traceability. They may also pose as mailing lists, greeting cards, or other agents that legitimately send or resend messages on behalf of others.

DKIM Strategy

DKIM is designed to provide an e-mail authentication technique that is transparent to the end user. In essence, a user's e-mail message is signed by a private key of the administrative domain from which the e-mail originates. The signature covers all of the content of the message and some of the RFC 5322 message headers. At the receiving end, the MDA can access the corresponding public key via a DNS and verify the signature, thus authenticating that the message comes from the claimed administrative domain. Thus, mail that originates from somewhere else but claims to come from a given domain will not pass the authentication test and can be rejected. This approach differs from that of S/MIME and PGP, which use the originator's private key to sign the content of the message. The motivation for DKIM is based on the following reasoning:[2]

1. S/MIME depends on both the sending and receiving users employing S/MIME. For almost all users, the bulk of incoming mail does not use S/MIME, and the bulk of the mail the user wants to send is to recipients not using S/MIME.

2. S/MIME signs only the message content. Thus, RFC 5322 header information concerning origin can be compromised.

3. DKIM is not implemented in client programs (MUAs) and is therefore transparent to the user; the user need not take any action.

4. DKIM applies to all mail from cooperating domains.

5. DKIM allows good senders to prove that they did send a particular message and to prevent forgers from masquerading as good senders.

---

[2] The reasoning is expressed in terms of the use of S/MIME. The same argument applies to PGP.

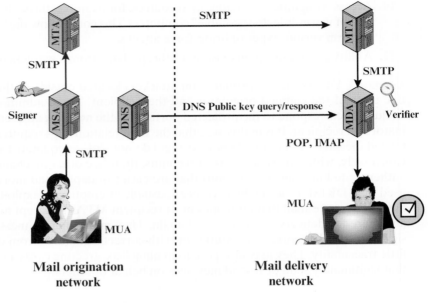

DNS = Domain Name System
MDA = Mail Delivery Agent
MSA = Mail Submission Agent
MTA = Message Transfer Agent
MUA = Message User Agent

Figure 8.10   Simple Example of DKIM Deployment

Figure 8.10 is a simple example of the operation of DKIM. We begin with a message generated by a user and transmitted into the MHS to an MSA that is within the user's administrative domain. An e-mail message is generated by an e-mail client program. The content of the message, plus selected RFC 5322 headers, is signed by the e-mail provider using the provider's private key. The signer is associated with a domain, which could be a corporate local network, an ISP, or a public e-mail facility such as gmail. The signed message then passes through the Internet via a sequence of MTAs. At the destination, the MDA retrieves the public key for the incoming signature and verifies the signature before passing the message on to the destination e-mail client. The default signing algorithm is RSA with SHA-256. RSA with SHA-1 also may be used.

DKIM Functional Flow

Figure 8.11 provides a more detailed look at the elements of DKIM operation. Basic message processing is divided between a signing Administrative Management Domain (ADMD) and a verifying ADMD. At its simplest, this is between the originating ADMD and the delivering ADMD, but it can involve other ADMDs in the handling path.

Signing is performed by an authorized module within the signing ADMD and uses private information from a Key Store. Within the originating ADMD,

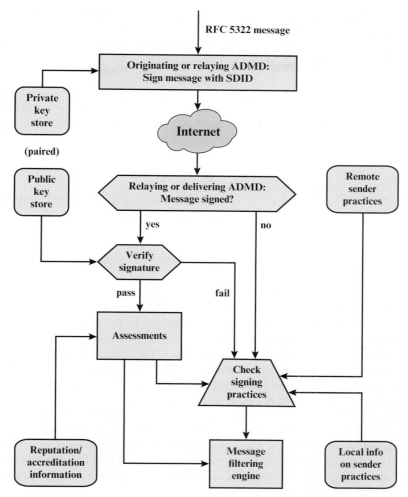

Figure 8.11 DKIM Functional Flow

this might be performed by the MUA, MSA, or an MTA. Verifying is performed by an authorized module within the verifying ADMD. Within a delivering ADMD, verifying might be performed by an MTA, MDA or MUA. The module verifies the signature or determines whether a particular signature was required. Verifying the signature uses public information from the Key Store. If the signature passes, reputation information is used to assess the signer and that information is passed to the message filtering system. If the signature fails or there is no signature using the author's domain, information about signing practices related to the author can be retrieved remotely and/or locally, and that information is passed to the message filtering system. For example, if the sender (e.g., gmail) uses DKIM but no DKIM signature is present, then the message may be considered fraudulent.

The signature is inserted into the RFC 5322 message as an additional header entry, starting with the keyword Dkim-Signature. You can view examples from your own incoming mail by using the View Long Headers (or similar wording) option for an incoming message. Here is an example:

```
Dkim-Signature:     v=1; a=rsa-sha256; c=relaxed/relaxed;
                    d=gmail.com; s=gamma; h=domainkey-
                    signature:mime-version:received:date:
                    message-id:subject :from:to:content-type:
                    content-transfer-encoding;
                    bh=5mZvQDyCRuyLb1Y28K4zgS2MPOemFToDBgvbJ
                    7GO90s=;
                    b=PcUvPSDygb4ya5Dyj1rbZGp/VyRiScuaz7TTG
                    J5qW5slM+klzv6kcfYdGDHzEVJW+Z
                    FetuPfF1ETOVhELtwH0zjSccOyPkEiblOf6gILO
                    bm3DDRm3Ys1/FVrbhVOlA+/jH9Aei
                    uIIw/5iFnRbSH6qPDVv/beDQqAWQfA/wF7O5k=
```

Before a message is signed, a process known as canonicalization is performed on both the header and body of the RFC 5322 message. Canonicalization is necessary to deal with the possibility of minor changes in the message made en route, including character encoding, treatment of trailing white space in message lines, and the "folding" and "unfolding" of header lines. The intent of canonicalization is to make a minimal transformation of the message (for the purpose of signing; the message itself is not changed, so the canonicalization must be performed again by the verifier) that will give it its best chance of producing the same canonical value at the receiving end. DKIM defines two header canonicalization algorithms ("simple" and "relaxed") and two for the body (with the same names). The simple algorithm tolerates almost no modification, while the relaxed algorithm tolerates common modifications.

The signature includes a number of fields. Each field begins with a tag consisting of a tag code followed by an equals sign and ends with a semicolon. The fields include the following:

- **v=** DKIM version/
- **a=** Algorithm used to generate the signature; must be either rsa-sha1 or rsa-sha256
- **c=** Canonicalization method used on the header and the body.
- **d=** A domain name used as an identifier to refer to the identity of a responsible person or organization. In DKIM, this identifier is called the Signing Domain IDentifier (SDID). In our example, this field indicates that the sender is using a gmail address.
- **s=** In order that different keys may be used in different circumstances for the same signing domain (allowing expiration of old keys, separate departmental signing, or the like), DKIM defines a selector (a name associated with a key) that is used by the verifier to retrieve the proper key during signature verification.

- **h=** Signed Header fields. A colon-separated list of header field names that identify the header fields presented to the signing algorithm. Note that in our example above, the signature covers the domainkey-signature field. This refers to an older algorithm (since replaced by DKIM) that is still in use.

- **bh=** The hash of the canonicalized body part of the message. This provides additional information for diagnosing signature verification failures.

- **b=** The signature data in base64 format; this is the encrypted hash code.

8.10 DOMAIN-BASED MESSAGE AUTHENTICATION, REPORTING, AND CONFORMANCE

Domain-Based Message Authentication, Reporting, and Conformance (DMARC) allows e-mail senders to specify policy on how their mail should be handled, the types of reports that receivers can send back, and the frequency those reports should be sent. It is defined in RFC 7489 (*Domain-based Message Authentication, Reporting, and Conformance*, March 2015).

DMARC works with SPF and DKIM. SPF and DKM enable senders to advise receivers, via DNS, whether mail purporting to come from the sender is valid, and whether it should be delivered, flagged, or discarded. However, neither SPF nor DKIM include a mechanism to tell receivers if SPF or DKIM are in use, nor do they have feedback mechanism to inform senders of the effectiveness of the anti-spam techniques. For example, if a message arrives at a receiver without a DKIM signature, DKIM provides no mechanism to allow the receiver to learn if the message is authentic but was sent from a sender that did not implement DKIM, or if the message is a spoof. DMARC addresses these issues essentially by standardizing how e-mail receivers perform e-mail authentication using SPF and DKIM mechanisms.

Identifier Alignment

DKIM, SPF, and DMARC authenticate various aspects of an individual message. DKIM authenticates the domain that affixed a signature to the message. SPF focuses on the SMTP envelope, defined in RFC 5321. It can authenticate either the domain that appears in the MAIL FROM portion of the SMTP envelope or the HELO domain, or both. These may be different domains, and they are typically not visible to the end user.

DMARC authentication deals with the From domain in the message header, as defined in RFC 5322. This field is used as the central identity of the DMARC mechanism because it is a required message header field and therefore guaranteed to be present in compliant messages, and most MUAs represent the RFC 5322 From field as the originator of the message and render some or all of this header field's content to end users. The e-mail address in this field is the one used by end users to identify the source of the message and therefore is a prime target for abuse.

DMARC requires that From address match (be aligned with) an Authenticated Identifier from DKIM or SPF. In the case of DKIM, the match is made between the DKIM signing domain and the From domain. In the case of SPF, the match is between the SPF-authenticated domain and the From domain.

DMARC on the Sender Side

A mail sender that uses DMARC must also use SPF or DKIM, or both. The sender posts a DMARC policy in the DNS that advises receivers on how to treat messages that purport to originate from the sender's domain. The policy is in the form of a DNS TXT resource record. The sender also needs to establish e-mail addresses to receive aggregate and forensic reports. As these e-mail addresses are published unencrypted in the DNS TXT RR, they are easily discovered, leaving the poster subject to unsolicited bulk e-mail. Thus, the poster of the DNS TXT RR needs to employ some kind of abuse countermeasures.

Similar to SPF and DKIM, the DMARC policy in the TXT RR is encoded in a series of `tag=value` pairs separated by semicolons. Table 8.8 describes the common tags.

Once the DMARC RR is posted, messages from the sender are typically processed as follows:

1. The domain owner constructs an SPF policy and publishes it in its DNS database. The domain owner also configures its system for DKIM signing. Finally, the domain owner publishes via the DNS a DMARC message-handling policy.

2. The author generates a message and hands the message to the domain owner's designated mail submission service.

3. The submission service passes relevant details to the DKIM signing module in order to generate a DKIM signature to be applied to the message.

4. The submission service relays the now-signed message to its designated transport service for routing to its intended recipient(s).

DMARC on the Receiver Side

A message generated on the sender side may pass through other relays but eventually arrives at a receiver's transport service. The typical processing order for DMARC on the receiving side is the following:

1. The receiver performs standard validation tests, such as checking against IP blocklists and domain reputation lists, as well as enforcing rate limits from a particular source.

2. The receiver extracts the RFC 5322 From address from the message. This must contain a single, valid address or else the mail is refused as an error.

3. The receiver queries for the DMARC DNS record based on the sending domain. If none exists, terminate DMARC processing.

4. The receiver performs DKIM signature checks. If more than one DKIM signature exists in the message, one must verify.

5. The receiver queries for the sending domain's SPF record and performs SPF validation checks.

6. The receiver conducts Identifier Alignment checks between the RFC 5321 From and the results of the SPF and DKIM records (if present).

Table 8.8   DMARC Tag and Value Descriptions

Tag (Name)	Description
v= (Version)	Version field that must be present as the first element. By default the value is always **DMARC1**.
p= (Policy)	Mandatory policy field. May take values **none** or **quarantine** or **reject**. This allows for a gradually tightening policy where the sender domain recommends no specific action on mail that fails DMARC checks **(p= none)**, through treating failed mail as suspicious **(p= quarantine),** to rejecting all failed mail **(p= reject),** preferably at the SMTP transaction stage.
aspf= (SPF Policy)	Values are **r** (default) for relaxed and **s** for strict SPF domain enforcement. Strict alignment requires an exact match between the From address domain and the (passing) SPF check must exactly match the MailFrom address (HELO address). Relaxed requires that only the From and MailFrom address domains be in alignment. For example, the MailFrom address domain **smtp.example.org** and the From address **announce@example.org** are in alignment, but not a strict match.
adkim= (DKIM Policy)	Optional. Values are **r** (default) for relaxed and **s** for strict DKIM domain enforcement. Strict alignment requires an exact match between the From domain in the message header and the DKIM domain presented in the **(d=** DKIM), tag. Relaxed requires only that the domain part is in alignment (as in **aspf**).
fo= (Failure reporting options)	Optional. Ignore if a **ruf** argument is not also present. Value **0** indicates the receiver should generate a DMARC failure report if all underlying mechanisms fail to produce an aligned pass result. Value **1** means generate a DMARC failure report if any underlying mechanism produces something other than an aligned pass result. Other possible values are **d** (generate a DKIM failure report if a signature failed evaluation), and **s** (generate an SPF failure report if the message failed SPF evaluation). These values are not exclusive and may be combined.
ruf=	Optional, but requires the **fo** argument to be present. Lists a series of URIs (currently just **mailto:**<emailaddress>) that list where to send forensic feedback reports. This is for reports on message-specific failures.
rua=	Optional list of URIs (like in **ruf=**, using the **mailto:** URI) listing where to send aggregate feedback back to the sender. These reports are sent based on the interval requested using the **ri=** option with a default of 86400 seconds if not listed.
ri= (Reporting interval)	Optional with the default value of 86400 seconds. The value listed is the reporting interval desired by the sender.
pct= (Percent)	Optional with the default value of **100**. Expresses the percentage of a sender's mail that should be subject to the given DMARC policy. This allows senders to ramp up their policy enforcement gradually and prevent having to commit to a rigorous policy before getting feedback on their existing policy.
sp= (Receiver Policy)	Optional with a default value of **none**. Other values include the same range of values as the **p=** argument. This is the policy to be applied to mail from all identified subdomains of the given DMARC RR.

7. The results of these steps are passed to the DMARC module along with the Author's domain. The DMARC module attempts to retrieve a policy from the DNS for that domain. If none is found, the DMARC module determines the organizational domain and repeats the attempt to retrieve a policy from the DNS.

8. If a policy is found, it is combined with the Author's domain and the SPF and DKIM results to produce a DMARC policy result (a "pass" or "fail") and can optionally cause one of two kinds of reports to be generated.

9. Recipient transport service either delivers the message to the recipient inbox or takes other local policy action based on the DMARC result.

10. When requested, Recipient transport service collects data from the message delivery session to be used in providing feedback.

Figure 8.12, based on one at DMARC.org, summarizes the sending and receiving functional flow.

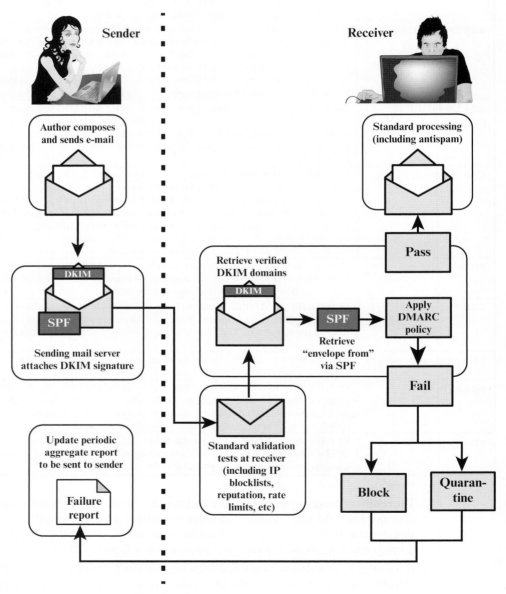

Figure 8.12 DMARC Functional Flow

DMARC Reports

DMARC reporting provides the sender's feedback on their SPF, DKIM, Identifier Alignment, and message disposition policies, which enable the sender to make these policies more effective. Two types of reports are sent: aggregate reports and forensic reports.

Aggregate reports are sent by receivers periodically and include aggregate figures for successful and unsuccessful message authentications, including:

- The sender's DMARC policy for that interval.
- The message disposition by the receiver (i.e., delivered, quarantined, rejected).
- SPF result for a given SPF identifier.
- DKIM result for a given DKIM identifier.
- Whether identifiers are in alignment or not.
- Results classified by sender subdomain.
- The sending and receiving domain pair.
- The policy applied, and whether this is different from the policy requested.
- The number of successful authentications.
- Totals for all messages received.

This information enables the sender to identify gaps in e-mail infrastructure and policy. SP 800-177 recommends that a sending domain begin by setting a DMARC policy of **p= none**, so that the ultimate disposition of a message that fails some check is determined by the receiver's local policy. As DMARC aggregate reports are collected, the sender will have a quantitatively better assessment of the extent to which the sender's e-mail is authenticated by outside receivers, and will be able to set a policy of **p = reject**, indicating that any message that fails the SPF, DKIM, and alignment checks really should be rejected. From their own traffic analysis, receivers can develop a determination of whether a sender's **p = reject** policy is sufficiently trustworthy to act on.

A forensic report helps the sender refine the component SPF and DKIM mechanisms as well as alerting the sender that their domain is being used as part of a phishing/spam campaign. Forensic reports are similar in format to aggregation reports, with these changes:

- Receivers include as much of the message and message header as is reasonable to allow the domain to investigate the failure. Add an Identity-Alignment field, with DKIM and SPF DMARC-method fields as appropriate.
- Optionally add a Delivery-Result field.
- Add DKIM Domain, DKIM Identity, and DKIM selector fields, if the message was DKIM signed. Optionally also add DKIM Canonical header and body fields.
- Add an additional DMARC authentication failure type, for use when some authentication mechanisms fail to produce aligned identifiers.

8.11 KEY TERMS, REVIEW QUESTIONS, AND PROBLEMS

Key Terms

administrative management domain (ADMD)	Domain Name System (DNS)	Message User Agent (MUA)
base64	DomainKeys Identified Mail (DKIM)	Multipurpose Internet Mail Extensions (MIME)
Cryptographic Message Syntax (CMS)	electronic mail	Post Office Protocol (POP3)
detached signature	Internet Mail Access Protocol (IMAP)	Pretty Good Privacy (PGP)
DNS-based Authentication of Named Entities (DANE)	Mail Delivery Agent (MDA)	Sender Policy Framework (SPF)
DNS Security Extensions (DNSSEC)	Mail Submission Agent (MSA)	session key
Domain-based Message Authentication, Reporting, and Conformance (DMARC)	Message Handling Service (MHS)	Simple Mail Transfer Protocol (SMTP)
	Message Store	STARTTLS
	Message Transfer Agents (MTA)	SUBMISSION
		S/MIME
		trust

Review Questions

8.1 What types of interoperability issues are involved in internet mail architecture and how are they handled?

8.2 What are the SMTP and MIME standards?

8.3 What is the difference between a MIME content type and a MIME transfer encoding?

8.4 Briefly explain base64 encoding.

8.5 Why is base64 conversion useful for an e-mail application?

8.6 What is S/MIME?

8.7 What are the four principal services provided by S/MIME?

8.8 What is the utility of a detached signature?

8.9 What is DKIM?

Problems

8.1 The character sequence "<CR><LF>.<CR><LF>" indicates the end of mail data to a SMTP-server. What happens if the mail data itself contains that character sequence?

8.2 What are POP3 and IMAP?

8.3 If a lossless compression algorithm, such as ZIP, is used with S/MIME, why is it preferable to generate a signature before applying compression?

8.4 Before the deployment of the Domain Name System, a simple text file (HOSTS.TXT) centrally maintained at the SRI Network Information Center was used to enable mapping between host names and addresses. Each host connected to the Internet had to have an updated local copy of it to be able to use host names instead of having to cope directly with their IP addresses. Discuss the main advantages of the DNS over the old centralized HOSTS.TXT system.

8.5 For this problem and the next few, consult Appendix H. In Figure H.2, each entry in the public-key ring contains an Owner Trust field that indicates the degree of trust associated with this public-key owner. Why is that not enough? That is, if this owner is trusted and this is supposed to be the owner's public key, why is that trust not enough to permit PGP to use this public key?

8.6   What is the basic difference between X.509 and PGP in terms of key hierarchies and key trust?

8.7   In PGP, what is the expected number of session keys generated before a previously created key is produced?

8.8   A PGP user may have multiple public keys. So that a recipient knows which public key is being used by a sender, a key ID, consisting of the least significant 64 bits of the public key, is sent with the message. What is the probability that a user with N public keys will have at least one duplicate key ID?

8.9   The first 16 bits of the message digest in a PGP signature are translated in the clear. This enables the recipient to determine if the correct public key was used to decrypt the message digest by comparing this plaintext copy of the first two octets with the first two octets of the decrypted digest.
   a. To what extent does this compromise the security of the hash algorithm?
   b. To what extent does it in fact perform its intended function, namely, to help determine if the correct RSA key was used to decrypt the digest?

8.10 Consider base64 conversion as a form of encryption. In this case, there is no key. But suppose that an opponent knew only that some form of substitution algorithm was being used to encrypt English text and did not guess that it was base64. How effective would this algorithm be against cryptanalysis?

8.11 Encode the text "ciphertext" using the following techniques. Assume characters are stored in 8-bit ASCII with zero parity.
   a. base64
   b. Quoted-printable

8.12 Use a 2 × 2 matrix to categorize the properties of the four certificate usage models in DANE.

IP SECURITY

LEARNING OBJECTIVES

After studying this chapter, you should be able to:

◆ Present an overview of IP security (IPsec).

◆ Explain the difference between transport mode and tunnel mode.

◆ Understand the concept of security association.

◆ Explain the difference between the security association database and the security policy database.

◆ Summarize the traffic processing functions performed by IPsec for outbound packets and for inbound packets.

◆ Present an overview of Encapsulating Security Payload.

◆ Discuss the alternatives for combining security associations.

◆ Present an overview of Internet Key Exchange.

◆ Summarize the alternative cryptographic suites approved for use with IPsec.

There are application-specific security mechanisms for a number of application areas, including electronic mail (S/MIME, PGP), client/server (Kerberos), Web access (Secure Sockets Layer), and others. However, users have security concerns that cut across protocol layers. For example, an enterprise can run a secure, private IP network by disallowing links to untrusted sites, encrypting packets that leave the premises, and authenticating packets that enter the premises. By implementing security at the IP level, an organization can ensure secure networking not only for applications that have security mechanisms but also for the many security-ignorant applications.

IP-level security encompasses three functional areas: authentication, confidentiality, and key management. The authentication mechanism assures that a received packet was, in fact, transmitted by the party identified as the source in the packet header. In addition, this mechanism assures that the packet has not been altered in transit. The confidentiality facility enables communicating nodes to encrypt messages to prevent eavesdropping by third parties. The key management facility is concerned with the secure exchange of keys.

We begin this chapter with an overview of IP security (IPsec) and an introduction to the IPsec architecture. We then look at each of the three functional areas in detail. Appendix D reviews Internet protocols.

9.1 IP SECURITY OVERVIEW

In 1994, the Internet Architecture Board (IAB) issued a report titled "Security in the Internet Architecture" (RFC 1636). The report identified key areas for security mechanisms. Among these were the need to secure the network infrastructure from unauthorized monitoring and control of network traffic and the need to secure end-user-to-end-user traffic using authentication and encryption mechanisms.

To provide security, the IAB included authentication and encryption as necessary security features in the next-generation IP, which has been issued as IPv6. Fortunately, these security capabilities were designed to be usable both with the current IPv4 and the future IPv6. This means that vendors can begin offering these features now, and many vendors now do have some IPsec capability in their products. The IPsec specification now exists as a set of Internet standards.

Applications of IPsec

IPsec provides the capability to secure communications across a LAN, across private and public WANs, and across the Internet. Examples of its use include:

- **Secure branch office connectivity over the Internet:** A company can build a secure virtual private network over the Internet or over a public WAN. This enables a business to rely heavily on the Internet and reduce its need for private networks, saving costs and network management overhead.

- **Secure remote access over the Internet:** An end user whose system is equipped with IP security protocols can make a local call to an Internet Service Provider (ISP) and gain secure access to a company network. This reduces the cost of toll charges for traveling employees and telecommuters.

- **Establishing extranet and intranet connectivity with partners:** IPsec can be used to secure communication with other organizations, ensuring authentication and confidentiality and providing a key exchange mechanism.

- **Enhancing electronic commerce security:** Even though some Web and electronic commerce applications have built-in security protocols, the use of IPsec enhances that security. IPsec guarantees that all traffic designated by the network administrator is both encrypted and authenticated, adding an additional layer of security to whatever is provided at the application layer.

The principal feature of IPsec that enables it to support these varied applications is that it can encrypt and/or authenticate *all* traffic at the IP level. Thus, all distributed applications (including remote logon, client/server, e-mail, file transfer, Web access, and so on) can be secured. Figure 9.1a shows a simplified packet format for an IPsec option known as tunnel mode, described subsequently. Tunnel mode makes use of an IPsec function, a combined authentication/encryption function called Encapsulating Security Payload (ESP), and a key exchange function. For VPNs, both authentication and encryption are generally desired, because it is important both to (1) assure that unauthorized users do not penetrate the VPN, and (2) assure that eavesdroppers on the Internet cannot read messages sent over the VPN.

Figure 9.1b is a typical scenario of IPsec usage. An organization maintains LANs at dispersed locations. Nonsecure IP traffic is conducted on each LAN. For traffic offsite, through some sort of private or public WAN, IPsec protocols are used. These protocols operate in networking devices, such as a router or firewall, that connect each LAN to the outside world. The IPsec networking device will typically encrypt all traffic going into the WAN and decrypt traffic coming from the WAN; these operations are transparent to workstations and servers on the LAN. Secure

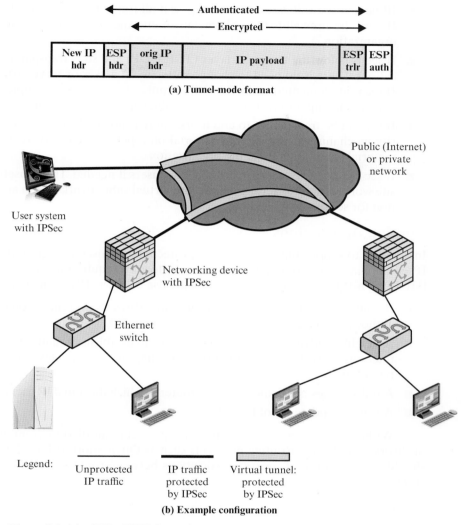

◀───────── **Authenticated** ──────────▶

◀───────── **Encrypted** ──────────▶

New IP hdr	ESP hdr	orig IP hdr	IP payload	ESP trlr	ESP auth

(a) Tunnel-mode format

Public (Internet) or private network

User system with IPSec

Networking device with IPSec

Ethernet switch

Legend:

─────	─────	▭
Unprotected IP traffic	IP traffic protected by IPSec	Virtual tunnel: protected by IPSec

(b) Example configuration

Figure 9.1   An IPSec VPN Scenario

transmission is also possible with individual users who dial into the WAN. Such user workstations must implement the IPsec protocols to provide security.

Benefits of IPsec

Some of the benefits of IPsec:

■ When IPsec is implemented in a firewall or router, it provides strong security that can be applied to all traffic crossing the perimeter. Traffic within a company or workgroup does not incur the overhead of security-related processing.

■ IPsec in a firewall is resistant to bypass if all traffic from the outside must use IP and the firewall is the only means of entrance from the Internet into the organization.

■ IPsec is below the transport layer (TCP, UDP) and so is transparent to applications. There is no need to change software on a user or server system when IPsec is implemented in the firewall or router. Even if IPsec is implemented in end systems, upper-layer software, including applications, is not affected.

■ IPsec can be transparent to end users. There is no need to train users on security mechanisms, issue keying material on a per-user basis, or revoke keying material when users leave the organization.

■ IPsec can provide security for individual users if needed. This is useful for off-site workers and for setting up a secure virtual subnetwork within an organization for sensitive applications.

Routing Applications

In addition to supporting end users and protecting premises systems and networks, IPsec can play a vital role in the routing architecture required for internetworking. [HUIT98] lists the following examples of the use of IPsec. IPsec can assure that

■ A router advertisement (a new router advertises its presence) comes from an authorized router.

■ A neighbor advertisement (a router seeks to establish or maintain a neighbor relationship with a router in another routing domain) comes from an authorized router.

■ A redirect message comes from the router to which the initial IP packet was sent.

■ A routing update is not forged.

Without such security measures, an opponent can disrupt communications or divert some traffic. Routing protocols such as Open Shortest Path First (OSPF) should be run on top of security associations between routers that are defined by IPsec.

IPsec Documents

IPsec encompasses three functional areas: authentication, confidentiality, and key management. The totality of the IPsec specification is scattered across dozens of RFCs and draft IETF documents, making this the most complex and difficult to grasp of all IETF specifications. The best way to grasp the scope of IPsec is to consult the latest version of the IPsec document roadmap, which as of this writing is RFC 6071 (*IP Security (IPsec) and Internet Key Exchange (IKE) Document Roadmap*, February 2011). The documents can be categorized into the following groups.

■ **Architecture:** Covers the general concepts, security requirements, definitions, and mechanisms defining IPsec technology. The current specification is RFC 4301, *Security Architecture for the Internet Protocol.*

- **Authentication Header (AH):** AH is an extension header to provide message authentication. The current specification is RFC 4302, *IP Authentication Header*. Because message authentication is provided by ESP, the use of AH is deprecated. It is included in IPsecv3 for backward compatibility but should not be used in new applications. We do not discuss AH in this chapter.

- **Encapsulating Security Payload (ESP):** ESP consists of an encapsulating header and trailer used to provide encryption or combined encryption/authentication. The current specification is RFC 4303, *IP Encapsulating Security Payload (ESP)*.

- **Internet Key Exchange (IKE):** This is a collection of documents describing the key management schemes for use with IPsec. The main specification is RFC 7296, *Internet Key Exchange (IKEv2) Protocol*, but there are a number of related RFCs.

- **Cryptographic algorithms:** This category encompasses a large set of documents that define and describe cryptographic algorithms for encryption, message authentication, pseudorandom functions (PRFs), and cryptographic key exchange.

- **Other:** There are a variety of other IPsec-related RFCs, including those dealing with security policy and management information base (MIB) content.

IPsec Services

IPsec provides security services at the IP layer by enabling a system to select required security protocols, determine the algorithm(s) to use for the service(s), and put in place any cryptographic keys required to provide the requested services. Two protocols are used to provide security: an authentication protocol designated by the header of the protocol, Authentication Header (AH); and a combined encryption/authentication protocol designated by the format of the packet for that protocol, Encapsulating Security Payload (ESP). RFC 4301 lists the following services:

- Access control
- Connectionless integrity
- Data origin authentication
- Rejection of replayed packets (a form of partial sequence integrity)
- Confidentiality (encryption)
- Limited traffic flow confidentiality

Transport and Tunnel Modes

Both AH and ESP support two modes of use: transport and tunnel mode. The operation of these two modes is best understood in the context of a description of ESP, which is covered in Section 9.3. Here we provide a brief overview.

TRANSPORT MODE   Transport mode provides protection primarily for upper-layer protocols. That is, transport mode protection extends to the payload of an IP packet.[1] Examples include a TCP or UDP segment or an ICMP packet, all of which operate directly above IP in a host protocol stack. Typically, transport mode is used for end-to-end communication between two hosts (e.g., a client and a server, or two workstations). When a host runs AH or ESP over IPv4, the payload is the data that normally follow the IP header. For IPv6, the payload is the data that normally follow both the IP header and any IPv6 extensions headers that are present, with the possible exception of the destination options header, which may be included in the protection.

ESP in transport mode encrypts and optionally authenticates the IP payload but not the IP header. AH in transport mode authenticates the IP payload and selected portions of the IP header.

TUNNEL MODE   Tunnel mode provides protection to the entire IP packet. To achieve this, after the AH or ESP fields are added to the IP packet, the entire packet plus security fields is treated as the payload of new outer IP packet with a new outer IP header. The entire original, inner, packet travels through a tunnel from one point of an IP network to another; no routers along the way are able to examine the inner IP header. Because the original packet is encapsulated, the new, larger packet may have totally different source and destination addresses, adding to the security. Tunnel mode is used when one or both ends of a security association (SA) are a security gateway, such as a firewall or router that implements IPsec. With tunnel mode, a number of hosts on networks behind firewalls may engage in secure communications without implementing IPsec. The unprotected packets generated by such hosts are tunneled through external networks by tunnel mode SAs set up by the IPsec software in the firewall or secure router at the boundary of the local network.

Here is an example of how tunnel mode IPsec operates. Host A on a network generates an IP packet with the destination address of host B on another network. This packet is routed from the originating host to a firewall or secure router at the boundary of A's network. The firewall filters all outgoing packets to determine the need for IPsec processing. If this packet from A to B requires IPsec, the firewall performs IPsec processing and encapsulates the packet with an outer IP header. The source IP address of this outer IP packet is this firewall, and the destination address may be a firewall that forms the boundary to B's local network. This packet is now routed to B's firewall, with intermediate routers examining only the outer IP header. At B's firewall, the outer IP header is stripped off, and the inner packet is delivered to B.

ESP in tunnel mode encrypts and optionally authenticates the entire inner IP packet, including the inner IP header. AH in tunnel mode authenticates the entire inner IP packet and selected portions of the outer IP header.

Table 9.1 summarizes transport and tunnel mode functionality.

---

[1]In this chapter, the term *IP packet* refers to either an IPv4 datagram or an IPv6 packet.

Table 9.1   Tunnel Mode and Transport Mode Functionality

	Transport Mode SA	**Tunnel Mode SA**
AH	Authenticates IP payload and selected portions of IP header and IPv6 extension headers.	Authenticates entire inner IP packet (inner header plus IP payload) plus selected portions of outer IP header and outer IPv6 extension headers.
ESP	Encrypts IP payload and any IPv6 extension headers following the ESP header.	Encrypts entire inner IP packet.
ESP with Authentication	Encrypts IP payload and any IPv6 extension headers following the ESP header. Authenticates IP payload but not IP header.	Encrypts entire inner IP packet. Authenticates inner IP packet.

9.2   IP SECURITY POLICY

Fundamental to the operation of IPsec is the concept of a security policy applied to each IP packet that transits from a source to a destination. IPsec policy is determined primarily by the interaction of two databases, the **security association database (SAD)** and the **security policy database (SPD)**. This section provides an overview of these two databases and then summarizes their use during IPsec operation. Figure 9.2 illustrates the relevant relationships.

Security Associations

A key concept that appears in both the authentication and confidentiality mechanisms for IP is the security association (SA). An association is a one-way logical connection between a sender and a receiver that affords security services to the traffic carried on it. If a peer relationship is needed for two-way secure exchange, then two security associations are required.

A security association is uniquely identified by three parameters.

- **Security Parameters Index (SPI):** A 32-bit unsigned integer assigned to this SA and having local significance only. The SPI is carried in AH and ESP headers to enable the receiving system to select the SA under which a received packet will be processed.
- **IP Destination Address:** This is the address of the destination endpoint of the SA, which may be an end-user system or a network system such as a firewall or router.
- **Security Protocol Identifier:** This field from the outer IP header indicates whether the association is an AH or ESP security association.

Hence, in any IP packet, the security association is uniquely identified by the Destination Address in the IPv4 or IPv6 header and the SPI in the enclosed extension header (AH or ESP).

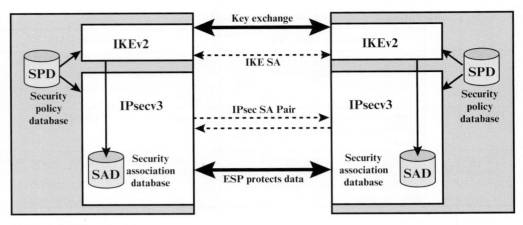

Figure 9.2 IPsec Architecture

Security Association Database

In each IPsec implementation, there is a nominal[2] Security Association Database that defines the parameters associated with each SA. A security association is normally defined by the following parameters in an SAD entry.

- **Security Parameter Index:** A 32-bit value selected by the receiving end of an SA to uniquely identify the SA. In an SAD entry for an outbound SA, the SPI is used to construct the packet's AH or ESP header. In an SAD entry for an inbound SA, the SPI is used to map traffic to the appropriate SA.

- **Sequence Number Counter:** A 32-bit value used to generate the Sequence Number field in AH or ESP headers, described in Section 9.3 (required for all implementations).

- **Sequence Counter Overflow:** A flag indicating whether overflow of the Sequence Number Counter should generate an auditable event and prevent further transmission of packets on this SA (required for all implementations).

- **Anti-Replay Window:** Used to determine whether an inbound AH or ESP packet is a replay, described in Section 9.3 (required for all implementations).

- **AH Information:** Authentication algorithm, keys, key lifetimes, and related parameters being used with AH (required for AH implementations).

- **ESP Information:** Encryption and authentication algorithm, keys, initialization values, key lifetimes, and related parameters being used with ESP (required for ESP implementations).

- **Lifetime of this Security Association:** A time interval or byte count after which an SA must be replaced with a new SA (and new SPI) or terminated, plus an indication of which of these actions should occur (required for all implementations).

---

[2]Nominal in the sense that the functionality provided by a Security Association Database must be present in any IPsec implementation, but the way in which that functionality is provided is up to the implementer.

- **IPsec Protocol Mode:** Tunnel, transport, or wildcard.
- **Path MTU:** Any observed path maximum transmission unit (maximum size of a packet that can be transmitted without fragmentation) and aging variables (required for all implementations).

The key management mechanism that is used to distribute keys is coupled to the authentication and privacy mechanisms only by way of the Security Parameters Index (SPI). Hence, authentication and privacy have been specified independent of any specific key management mechanism.

IPsec provides the user with considerable flexibility in the way in which IPsec services are applied to IP traffic. As we will see later, SAs can be combined in a number of ways to yield the desired user configuration. Furthermore, IPsec provides a high degree of granularity in discriminating between traffic that is afforded IPsec protection and traffic that is allowed to bypass IPsec, as in the former case relating IP traffic to specific SAs.

Security Policy Database

The means by which IP traffic is related to specific SAs (or no SA in the case of traffic allowed to bypass IPsec) is the nominal Security Policy Database (SPD). In its simplest form, an SPD contains entries, each of which defines a subset of IP traffic and points to an SA for that traffic. In more complex environments, there may be multiple entries that potentially relate to a single SA or multiple SAs associated with a single SPD entry. The reader is referred to the relevant IPsec documents for a full discussion.

Each SPD entry is defined by a set of IP and upper-layer protocol field values, called *selectors*. In effect, these selectors are used to filter outgoing traffic in order to map it into a particular SA. Outbound processing obeys the following general sequence for each IP packet.

1. Compare the values of the appropriate fields in the packet (the selector fields) against the SPD to find a matching SPD entry, which will point to zero or more SAs.
2. Determine the SA if any for this packet and its associated SPI.
3. Do the required IPsec processing (i.e., AH or ESP processing).

The following selectors determine an SPD entry:

- **Remote IP Address:** This may be a single IP address, an enumerated list or range of addresses, or a wildcard (mask) address. The latter two are required to support more than one destination system sharing the same SA (e.g., behind a firewall).
- **Local IP Address:** This may be a single IP address, an enumerated list or range of addresses, or a wildcard (mask) address. The latter two are required to support more than one source system sharing the same SA (e.g., behind a firewall).
- **Next Layer Protocol:** The IP protocol header (IPv4, IPv6, or IPv6 Extension) includes a field (Protocol for IPv4, Next Header for IPv6 or IPv6 Extension) that designates the protocol operating over IP. This is an individual protocol number, ANY, or for IPv6 only, OPAQUE. If AH or ESP is used, then this IP protocol header immediately precedes the AH or ESP header in the packet.

Table 9.2 Host SPD Example

Protocol	Local IP	Port	Remote IP	Port	Action	Comment
UDP	1.2.3.101	500	*	500	BYPASS	IKE
ICMP	1.2.3.101	*	*	*	BYPASS	Error messages
*	1.2.3.101	*	1.2.3.0/24	*	PROTECT: ESP intransport-mode	Encrypt intranet traffic
TCP	1.2.3.101	*	1.2.4.10	80	PROTECT: ESP intransport-mode	Encrypt to server
TCP	1.2.3.101	*	1.2.4.10	443	BYPASS	TLS: avoid double encryption
*	1.2.3.101	*	1.2.4.0/24	*	DISCARD	Others in DMZ
*	1.2.3.101	*	*	*	BYPASS	Internet

- **Name:** A user identifier from the operating system. This is not a field in the IP or upper-layer headers but is available if IPsec is running on the same operating system as the user.

- **Local and Remote Ports:** These may be individual TCP or UDP port values, an enumerated list of ports, or a wildcard port.

Table 9.2 provides an example of an SPD on a host system (as opposed to a network system such as a firewall or router). This table reflects the following configuration: A local network configuration consists of two networks. The basic corporate network configuration has the IP network number 1.2.3.0/24. The local configuration also includes a secure LAN, often known as a DMZ, that is identified as 1.2.4.0/24. The DMZ is protected from both the outside world and the rest of the corporate LAN by firewalls. The host in this example has the IP address 1.2.3.10, and it is authorized to connect to the server 1.2.4.10 in the DMZ.

The entries in the SPD should be self-explanatory. For example, UDP port 500 is the designated port for IKE. Any traffic from the local host to a remote host for purposes of an IKE exchange bypasses the IPsec processing.

IP Traffic Processing

IPsec is executed on a packet-by-packet basis. When IPsec is implemented, each outbound IP packet is processed by the IPsec logic before transmission, and each inbound packet is processed by the IPsec logic after reception and before passing the packet contents on to the next higher layer (e.g., TCP or UDP). We look at the logic of these two situations in turn.

OUTBOUND PACKETS Figure 9.3 highlights the main elements of IPsec processing for outbound traffic. A block of data from a higher layer, such as TCP, is passed down to the IP layer and an IP packet is formed, consisting of an IP header and an IP body. Then the following steps occur:

1. IPsec searches the SPD for a match to this packet.
2. If no match is found, then the packet is discarded and an error message is generated.

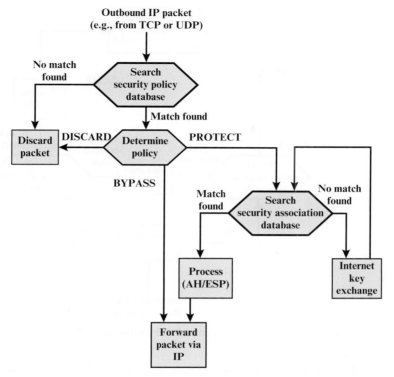

Figure 9.3   Processing Model for Outbound Packets

3. If a match is found, further processing is determined by the first matching entry in the SPD. If the policy for this packet is DISCARD, then the packet is discarded. If the policy is BYPASS, then there is no further IPsec processing; the packet is forwarded to the network for transmission.

4. If the policy is PROTECT, then a search is made of the SAD for a matching entry. If no entry is found, then IKE is invoked to create an SA with the appropriate keys and an entry is made in the SA.

5. The matching entry in the SAD determines the processing for this packet. Either encryption, authentication, or both can be performed, and either transport or tunnel mode can be used. The packet is then forwarded to the network for transmission.

INBOUND PACKETS Figure 9.4 highlights the main elements of IPsec processing for inbound traffic. An incoming IP packet triggers the IPsec processing. The following steps occur:

1. IPsec determines whether this is an unsecured IP packet or one that has ESP or AH headers/trailers, by examining the IP Protocol field (IPv4) or Next Header field (IPv6).

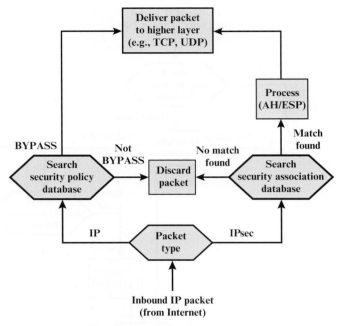

Figure 9.4 Processing Model for Inbound Packets

2. If the packet is unsecured, IPsec searches the SPD for a match to this packet. If the first matching entry has a policy of BYPASS, the IP header is processed and stripped off and the packet body is delivered to the next higher layer, such as TCP. If the first matching entry has a policy of PROTECT or DISCARD, or if there is no matching entry, the packet is discarded.

3. For a secured packet, IPsec searches the SAD. If no match is found, the packet is discarded. Otherwise, IPsec applies the appropriate ESP or AH processing. Then, the IP header is processed and stripped off and the packet body is delivered to the next higher layer, such as TCP.

9.3 ENCAPSULATING SECURITY PAYLOAD

ESP can be used to provide confidentiality, data origin authentication, connectionless integrity, an anti-replay service (a form of partial sequence integrity), and (limited) traffic flow confidentiality. The set of services provided depends on options selected at the time of Security Association (SA) establishment and on the location of the implementation in a network topology.

ESP can work with a variety of encryption and authentication algorithms, including authenticated encryption algorithms such as GCM.

ESP Format

Figure 9.5a shows the top-level format of an ESP packet. It contains the following fields.

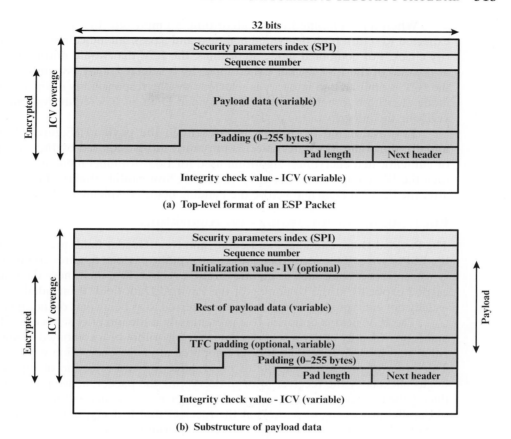

Figure 9.5 ESP Packet Format

- **Security Parameters Index (32 bits):** Identifies a security association.
- **Sequence Number (32 bits):** A monotonically increasing counter value; this provides an anti-replay function, as discussed for AH.
- **Payload Data (variable):** This is a transport-level segment (transport mode) or IP packet (tunnel mode) that is protected by encryption.
- **Padding (0–255 bytes):** The purpose of this field is discussed later.
- **Pad Length (8 bits):** Indicates the number of pad bytes immediately preceding this field.
- **Next Header (8 bits):** Identifies the type of data contained in the payload data field by identifying the first header in that payload (e.g., an extension header in IPv6, or an upper-layer protocol such as TCP).
- **Integrity Check Value (variable):** A variable-length field (must be an integral number of 32-bit words) that contains the Integrity Check Value computed over the ESP packet minus the Authentication Data field.

When any combined mode algorithm is employed, the algorithm itself is expected to return both decrypted plaintext and a pass/fail indication for the integrity check. For combined mode algorithms, the ICV that would normally appear at the end of the ESP packet (when integrity is selected) may be omitted. When the ICV is omitted and integrity is selected, it is the responsibility of the combined mode algorithm to encode within the Payload Data an ICV-equivalent means of verifying the integrity of the packet.

Two additional fields may be present in the payload (Figure 9.5b). An **initialization value (IV)**, or nonce, is present if this is required by the encryption or authenticated encryption algorithm used for ESP. If tunnel mode is being used, then the IPsec implementation may add **traffic flow confidentiality (TFC)** padding after the Payload Data and before the Padding field, as explained subsequently.

Encryption and Authentication Algorithms

The Payload Data, Padding, Pad Length, and Next Header fields are encrypted by the ESP service. If the algorithm used to encrypt the payload requires cryptographic synchronization data, such as an initialization vector (IV), then these data may be carried explicitly at the beginning of the Payload Data field. If included, an IV is usually not encrypted, although it is often referred to as being part of the ciphertext.

The ICV field is optional. It is present only if the integrity service is selected and is provided by either a separate integrity algorithm or a combined mode algorithm that uses an ICV. The ICV is computed after the encryption is performed. This order of processing facilitates rapid detection and rejection of replayed or bogus packets by the receiver prior to decrypting the packet, hence potentially reducing the impact of denial of service (DoS) attacks. It also allows for the possibility of parallel processing of packets at the receiver that is decryption can take place in parallel with integrity checking. Note that because the ICV is not protected by encryption, a keyed integrity algorithm must be employed to compute the ICV.

Padding

The Padding field serves several purposes:

■ If an encryption algorithm requires the plaintext to be a multiple of some number of bytes (e.g., the multiple of a single block for a block cipher), the Padding field is used to expand the plaintext (consisting of the Payload Data, Padding, Pad Length, and Next Header fields) to the required length.

■ The ESP format requires that the Pad Length and Next Header fields be right aligned within a 32-bit word. Equivalently, the ciphertext must be an integer multiple of 32 bits. The Padding field is used to assure this alignment.

■ Additional padding may be added to provide partial traffic-flow confidentiality by concealing the actual length of the payload.

Anti-Replay Service

A **replay attack** is one in which an attacker obtains a copy of an authenticated packet and later transmits it to the intended destination. The receipt of duplicate, authenticated IP packets may disrupt service in some way or may have some other undesired consequence. The Sequence Number field is designed to thwart such attacks. First, we discuss sequence number generation by the sender, and then we look at how it is processed by the recipient.

When a new SA is established, the **sender** initializes a sequence number counter to 0. Each time that a packet is sent on this SA, the sender increments the counter and places the value in the Sequence Number field. Thus, the first value to be used is 1. If anti-replay is enabled (the default), the sender must not allow the sequence number to cycle past $2^{32} - 1$ back to zero. Otherwise, there would be multiple valid packets with the same sequence number. If the limit of $2^{32} - 1$ is reached, the sender should terminate this SA and negotiate a new SA with a new key.

Because IP is a connectionless, unreliable service, the protocol does not guarantee that packets will be delivered in order and does not guarantee that all packets will be delivered. Therefore, the IPsec authentication document dictates that the **receiver** should implement a window of size W, with a default of $W = 64$. The right edge of the window represents the highest sequence number, N, so far received for a valid packet. For any packet with a sequence number in the range from $N - W + 1$ to N that has been correctly received (i.e., properly authenticated), the corresponding slot in the window is marked (Figure 9.6). Inbound processing proceeds as follows when a packet is received:

1. If the received packet falls within the window and is new, the MAC is checked. If the packet is authenticated, the corresponding slot in the window is marked.

2. If the received packet is to the right of the window and is new, the MAC is checked. If the packet is authenticated, the window is advanced so that this sequence number is the right edge of the window, and the corresponding slot in the window is marked.

3. If the received packet is to the left of the window or if authentication fails, the packet is discarded; this is an auditable event.

Transport and Tunnel Modes

Figure 9.7 shows two ways in which the IPsec ESP service can be used. In the upper part of the figure, encryption (and optionally authentication) is provided directly between two hosts. Figure 9.7b shows how tunnel mode operation can be used to set up a **virtual private network**. In this example, an organization has four private networks

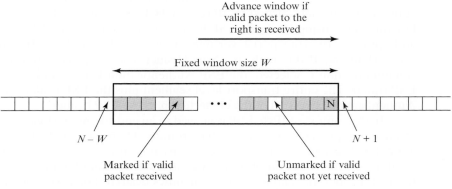

Figure 9.6   Anti-replay Mechanism

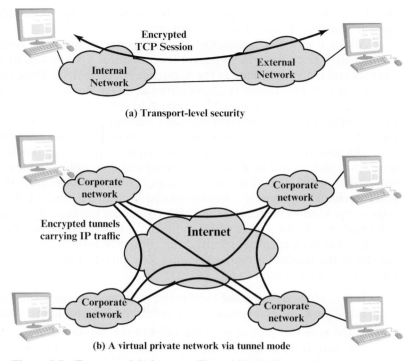

(a) Transport-level security

(b) A virtual private network via tunnel mode

Figure 9.7 Transport-Mode versus Tunnel-Mode Encryptionx

interconnected across the Internet. Hosts on the internal networks use the Internet for transport of data but do not interact with other Internet-based hosts. By terminating the tunnels at the security gateway to each internal network, the configuration allows the hosts to avoid implementing the security capability. The former technique is supported by a transport mode SA, while the latter technique uses a tunnel mode SA.

In this section, we look at the scope of ESP for the two modes. The considerations are somewhat different for IPv4 and IPv6. We use the packet formats of Figure 9.8a as a starting point.

TRANSPORT MODE ESP Transport mode ESP is used to encrypt and optionally authenticate the data carried by IP (e.g., a TCP segment), as shown in Figure 9.8b. For this mode using IPv4, the ESP header is inserted into the IP packet immediately prior to the transport-layer header (e.g., TCP, UDP, ICMP), and an ESP trailer (Padding, Pad Length, and Next Header fields) is placed after the IP packet. If authentication is selected, the ESP Authentication Data field is added after the ESP trailer. The entire transport-level segment plus the ESP trailer are encrypted. Authentication covers all of the ciphertext plus the ESP header.

In the context of IPv6, ESP is viewed as an end-to-end payload; that is, it is not examined or processed by intermediate routers. Therefore, the ESP header appears after the IPv6 base header and the hop-by-hop, routing, and fragment extension headers. The destination options extension header could appear before or after the ESP header, depending on the semantics desired. For IPv6, encryption covers

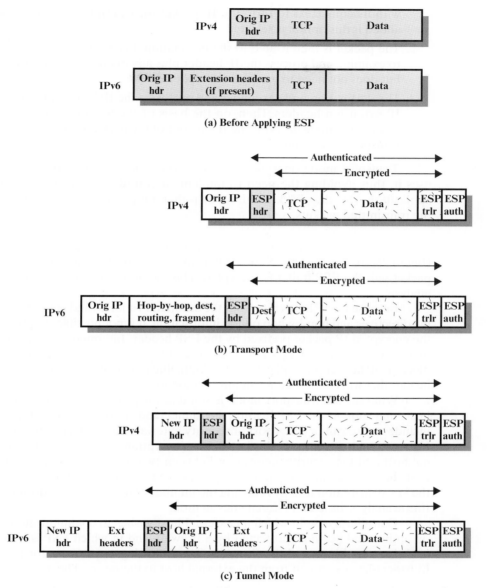

Figure 9.8 Scope of ESP Encryption and Authentication

the entire transport-level segment plus the ESP trailer plus the destination options extension header if it occurs after the ESP header. Again, authentication covers the ciphertext plus the ESP header.

Transport mode operation may be summarized as follows.

1. At the source, the block of data consisting of the ESP trailer plus the entire transport-layer segment is encrypted and the plaintext of this block is replaced

with its ciphertext to form the IP packet for transmission. Authentication is added if this option is selected.

2. The packet is then routed to the destination. Each intermediate router needs to examine and process the IP header plus any plaintext IP extension headers but does not need to examine the ciphertext.

3. The destination node examines and processes the IP header plus any plaintext IP extension headers. Then, on the basis of the SPI in the ESP header, the destination node decrypts the remainder of the packet to recover the plaintext transport-layer segment.

Transport mode operation provides confidentiality for any application that uses it, thus avoiding the need to implement confidentiality in every individual application. One drawback to this mode is that it is possible to do traffic analysis on the transmitted packets.

TUNNEL MODE ESP Tunnel mode ESP is used to encrypt an entire IP packet (Figure 9.8c). For this mode, the ESP header is prefixed to the packet and then the packet plus the ESP trailer is encrypted. This method can be used to counter traffic analysis.

Because the IP header contains the destination address and possibly source routing directives and hop-by-hop option information, it is not possible simply to transmit the encrypted IP packet prefixed by the ESP header. Intermediate routers would be unable to process such a packet. Therefore, it is necessary to encapsulate the entire block (ESP header plus ciphertext plus Authentication Data, if present) with a new IP header that will contain sufficient information for routing but not for traffic analysis.

Whereas the transport mode is suitable for protecting connections between hosts that support the ESP feature, the tunnel mode is useful in a configuration that includes a firewall or other sort of security gateway that protects a trusted network from external networks. In this latter case, encryption occurs only between an external host and the security gateway or between two security gateways. This relieves hosts on the internal network of the processing burden of encryption and simplifies the key distribution task by reducing the number of needed keys. Further, it thwarts traffic analysis based on ultimate destination.

Consider a case in which an external host wishes to communicate with a host on an internal network protected by a firewall, and in which ESP is implemented in the external host and the firewalls. The following steps occur for transfer of a transport-layer segment from the external host to the internal host.

1. The source prepares an inner IP packet with a destination address of the target internal host. This packet is prefixed by an ESP header; then the packet and ESP trailer are encrypted and Authentication Data may be added. The resulting block is encapsulated with a new IP header (base header plus optional extensions such as routing and hop-by-hop options for IPv6) whose destination address is the firewall; this forms the outer IP packet.

2. The outer packet is routed to the destination firewall. Each intermediate router needs to examine and process the outer IP header plus any outer IP extension headers but does not need to examine the ciphertext.

3. The destination firewall examines and processes the outer IP header plus any outer IP extension headers. Then, on the basis of the SPI in the ESP header, the destination node decrypts the remainder of the packet to recover the plaintext inner IP packet. This packet is then transmitted in the internal network.

4. The inner packet is routed through zero or more routers in the internal network to the destination host.

Figure 9.9 shows the protocol architecture for the two modes.

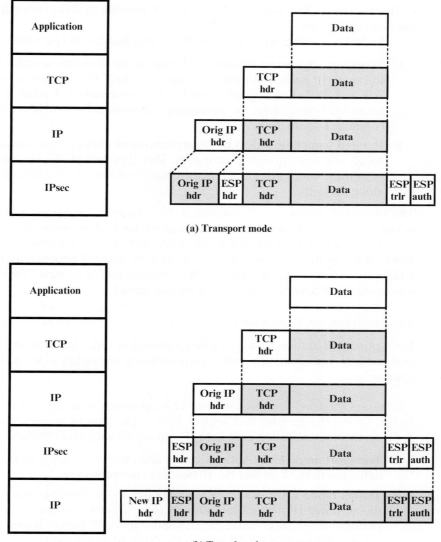

(a) Transport mode

(b) Tunnel mode

Figure 9.9 Protocol Operation for ESP

9.4   COMBINING SECURITY ASSOCIATIONS

An individual SA can implement either the AH or ESP protocol but not both. Sometimes a particular traffic flow will call for the services provided by both AH and ESP. Further, a particular traffic flow may require IPsec services between hosts and, for that same flow, separate services between security gateways, such as firewalls. In all of these cases, multiple SAs must be employed for the same traffic flow to achieve the desired IPsec services. The term *security association bundle* refers to a sequence of SAs through which traffic must be processed to provide a desired set of IPsec services. The SAs in a bundle may terminate at different endpoints or at the same endpoints.

Security associations may be combined into bundles in two ways:

■ **Transport adjacency:** Refers to applying more than one security protocol to the same IP packet without invoking tunneling. This approach to combining AH and ESP allows for only one level of combination; further nesting yields no added benefit since the processing is performed at one IPsec instance: the (ultimate) destination.

■ **Iterated tunneling:** Refers to the application of multiple layers of security protocols effected through IP tunneling. This approach allows for multiple levels of nesting, since each tunnel can originate or terminate at a different IPsec site along the path.

The two approaches can be combined, for example, by having a transport SA between hosts travel part of the way through a tunnel SA between security gateways.

One interesting issue that arises when considering SA bundles is the order in which authentication and encryption may be applied between a given pair of endpoints and the ways of doing so. We examine that issue next. Then we look at combinations of SAs that involve at least one tunnel.

Authentication Plus Confidentiality

Encryption and authentication can be combined in order to transmit an IP packet that has both confidentiality and authentication between hosts. We look at several approaches.

ESP WITH AUTHENTICATION OPTION   This approach is illustrated in Figure 9.8. In this approach, the user first applies ESP to the data to be protected and then appends the authentication data field. There are actually two subcases:

■ **Transport mode ESP:** Authentication and encryption apply to the IP payload delivered to the host, but the IP header is not protected.

■ **Tunnel mode ESP:** Authentication applies to the entire IP packet delivered to the outer IP destination address (e.g., a firewall), and authentication is performed at that destination. The entire inner IP packet is protected by the privacy mechanism for delivery to the inner IP destination.

For both cases, authentication applies to the ciphertext rather than the plaintext.

Transport Adjacency Another way to apply authentication after encryption is to use two bundled transport SAs, with the inner being an ESP SA and the outer being an AH SA. In this case, ESP is used without its authentication option. Because the inner SA is a transport SA, encryption is applied to the IP payload. The resulting packet consists of an IP header (and possibly IPv6 header extensions) followed by an ESP. AH is then applied in transport mode, so that authentication covers the ESP plus the original IP header (and extensions) except for mutable fields. The advantage of this approach over simply using a single ESP SA with the ESP authentication option is that the authentication covers more fields, including the source and destination IP addresses. The disadvantage is the overhead of two SAs versus one SA.

Transport-Tunnel Bundle The use of authentication prior to encryption might be preferable for several reasons. First, because the authentication data are protected by encryption, it is impossible for anyone to intercept the message and alter the authentication data without detection. Second, it may be desirable to store the authentication information with the message at the destination for later reference. It is more convenient to do this if the authentication information applies to the unencrypted message; otherwise the message would have to be reencrypted to verify the authentication information.

One approach to applying authentication before encryption between two hosts is to use a bundle consisting of an inner AH transport SA and an outer ESP tunnel SA. In this case, authentication is applied to the IP payload plus the IP header (and extensions) except for mutable fields. The resulting IP packet is then processed in tunnel mode by ESP; the result is that the entire, authenticated inner packet is encrypted and a new outer IP header (and extensions) is added.

Basic Combinations of Security Associations

The IPsec Architecture document lists four examples of combinations of SAs that must be supported by compliant IPsec hosts (e.g., workstation, server) or security gateways (e.g., firewall, router). These are illustrated in Figure 9.10. The lower part of each case in the figure represents the physical connectivity of the elements; the upper part represents logical connectivity via one or more nested SAs. Each SA can be either AH or ESP. For host-to-host SAs, the mode may be either transport or tunnel; otherwise it must be tunnel mode.

Case 1. All security is provided between end systems that implement IPsec. For any two end systems to communicate via an SA, they must share the appropriate secret keys. Among the possible combinations are

- a. AH in transport mode
- b. ESP in transport mode
- c. ESP followed by AH in transport mode (an ESP SA inside an AH SA)
- d. Any one of a, b, or c inside an AH or ESP in tunnel mode

We have already discussed how these various combinations can be used to support authentication, encryption, authentication before encryption, and authentication after encryption.

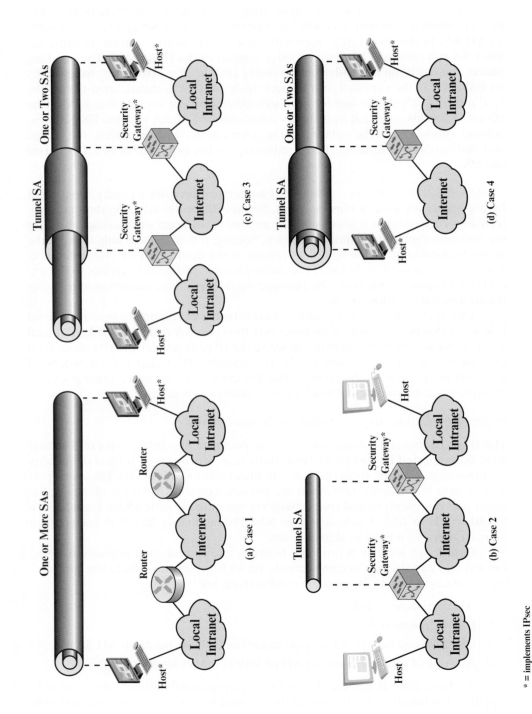

* = implements IPsec

Figure 9.10 Basic Combinations of Security Associations

Case 2. Security is provided only between gateways (routers, firewalls, etc.) and no hosts implement IPsec. This case illustrates simple virtual private network support. The security architecture document specifies that only a single tunnel SA is needed for this case. The tunnel could support AH, ESP, or ESP with the authentication option. Nested tunnels are not required, because the IPsec services apply to the entire inner packet.

Case 3. This builds on case 2 by adding end-to-end security. The same combinations discussed for cases 1 and 2 are allowed here. The gateway-to-gateway tunnel provides either authentication, confidentiality, or both for all traffic between end systems. When the gateway-to-gateway tunnel is ESP, it also provides a limited form of traffic confidentiality. Individual hosts can implement any additional IPsec services required for given applications or given users by means of end-to-end SAs.

Case 4. This provides support for a remote host that uses the Internet to reach an organization's firewall and then to gain access to some server or workstation behind the firewall. Only tunnel mode is required between the remote host and the firewall. As in case 1, one or two SAs may be used between the remote host and the local host.

9.5   INTERNET KEY EXCHANGE

The key management portion of IPsec involves the determination and distribution of secret keys. A typical requirement is four keys for communication between two applications: transmit and receive pairs for both integrity and confidentiality. The IPsec Architecture document mandates support for two types of key management:

- **Manual:** A system administrator manually configures each system with its own keys and with the keys of other communicating systems. This is practical for small, relatively static environments.

- **Automated:** An automated system enables the on-demand creation of keys for SAs and facilitates the use of keys in a large distributed system with an evolving configuration.

The default automated key management protocol for IPsec is referred to as ISAKMP/Oakley and consists of the following elements:

- **Oakley Key Determination Protocol:** Oakley is a key exchange protocol based on the Diffie–Hellman algorithm but providing added security. Oakley is generic in that it does not dictate specific formats.

- **Internet Security Association and Key Management Protocol (ISAKMP):** ISAKMP provides a framework for Internet key management and provides the specific protocol support, including formats, for negotiation of security attributes.

ISAKMP by itself does not dictate a specific key exchange algorithm; rather, ISAKMP consists of a set of message types that enable the use of a variety of key exchange algorithms. Oakley is the specific key exchange algorithm mandated for use with the initial version of ISAKMP.

In IKEv2, the terms Oakley and ISAKMP are no longer used, and there are significant differences from the use of Oakley and ISAKMP in IKEv1. Nevertheless, the basic functionality is the same. In this section, we describe the IKEv2 specification.

Key Determination Protocol

IKE key determination is a refinement of the Diffie–Hellman key exchange algorithm. Recall that Diffie–Hellman involves the following interaction between users A and B. There is prior agreement on two global parameters: q, a large prime number; and α, a primitive root of q. A selects a random integer X_A as its private key and transmits to B its public key $Y_A = \alpha^{X_A} \bmod q$. Similarly, B selects a random integer X_B as its private key and transmits to A its public key $Y_B = \alpha^{X_B} \bmod q$. Each side can now compute the secret session key:

$$K = (Y_B)^{X_A} \bmod q = (Y_A)^{X_B} \bmod q = \alpha^{X_A X_B} \bmod q$$

The Diffie–Hellman algorithm has two attractive features:

■ Secret keys are created only when needed. There is no need to store secret keys for a long period of time, exposing them to increased vulnerability.

■ The exchange requires no pre-existing infrastructure other than an agreement on the global parameters.

However, there are a number of weaknesses to Diffie–Hellman, as pointed out in [HUIT98].

■ It does not provide any information about the identities of the parties.

■ It is subject to a man-in-the-middle attack, in which a third party C impersonates B while communicating with A and impersonates A while communicating with B. Both A and B end up negotiating a key with C, which can then listen to and pass on traffic. The man-in-the-middle attack proceeds as

1. B sends his public key Y_B in a message addressed to A (see Figure 3.14).

2. The enemy (E) intercepts this message. E saves B's public key and sends a message to A that has B's User ID but E's public key Y_E. This message is sent in such a way that it appears as though it was sent from B's host system. A receives E's message and stores E's public key with B's User ID. Similarly, E sends a message to B with E's public key, purporting to come from A.

3. B computes a secret key K_1 based on B's private key and Y_E. A computes a secret key K_2 based on A's private key and Y_E. E computes K_1 using E's secret key X_E and Y_B and computers K_2 using X_E and Y_A.

4. From now on, E is able to relay messages from A to B and from B to A, appropriately changing their encipherment en route in such a way that neither A nor B will know that they share their communication with E.

■ It is computationally intensive. As a result, it is vulnerable to a clogging attack, in which an opponent requests a high number of keys. The victim spends considerable computing resources doing useless modular exponentiation rather than real work.

IKE key determination is designed to retain the advantages of Diffie–Hellman, while countering its weaknesses.

FEATURES OF IKE KEY DETERMINATION The IKE key determination algorithm is characterized by five important features:

1. It employs a mechanism known as cookies to thwart clogging attacks.
2. It enables the two parties to negotiate a *group*; this, in essence, specifies the global parameters of the Diffie–Hellman key exchange.
3. It uses nonces to ensure against replay attacks.
4. It enables the exchange of Diffie–Hellman public key values.
5. It authenticates the Diffie–Hellman exchange to thwart man-in-the-middle attacks.

We have already discussed Diffie–Hellman. Let us look at the remainder of these elements in turn. First, consider the problem of clogging attacks. In this attack, an opponent forges the source address of a legitimate user and sends a public Diffie–Hellman key to the victim. The victim then performs a modular exponentiation to compute the secret key. Repeated messages of this type can *clog* the victim's system with useless work. The **cookie exchange** requires that each side send a pseudorandom number, the cookie, in the initial message, which the other side acknowledges. This acknowledgment must be repeated in the first message of the Diffie–Hellman key exchange. If the source address was forged, the opponent gets no answer. Thus, an opponent can only force a user to generate acknowledgments and not to perform the Diffie–Hellman calculation.

IKE mandates that cookie generation satisfy three basic requirements:

1. The cookie must depend on the specific parties. This prevents an attacker from obtaining a cookie using a real IP address and UDP port and then using it to swamp the victim with requests from randomly chosen IP addresses or ports.
2. It must not be possible for anyone other than the issuing entity to generate cookies that will be accepted by that entity. This implies that the issuing entity will use local secret information in the generation and subsequent verification of a cookie. It must not be possible to deduce this secret information from any particular cookie. The point of this requirement is that the issuing entity need not save copies of its cookies, which are then more vulnerable to discovery, but can verify an incoming cookie acknowledgment when it needs to.
3. The cookie generation and verification methods must be fast to thwart attacks intended to sabotage processor resources.

The recommended method for creating the cookie is to perform a fast hash (e.g., MD5) over the IP Source and Destination addresses, the UDP Source and Destination ports, and a locally generated secret value.

IKE key determination supports the use of different groups for the Diffie–Hellman key exchange. Each group includes the definition of the two global parameters and the identity of the algorithm. The current specification includes the following groups.

■ Modular exponentiation with a 768-bit modulus

$$q = 2^{768} - 2^{704} - 1 + 2^{64} \times (\lfloor 2^{638} \times \pi \rfloor + 149686)$$
$$\alpha = 2$$

■ Modular exponentiation with a 1024-bit modulus

$$q = 2^{1024} - 2^{960} - 1 + 2^{64} \times (\lfloor 2^{894} \times \pi \rfloor + 129093)$$
$$\alpha = 2$$

■ Modular exponentiation with a 1536-bit modulus
  – Parameters to be determined

■ Elliptic curve group over 2^{155}
  – Generator (hexadecimal): $X = 7B, Y = 1C8$
  – Elliptic curve parameters (hexadecimal): $A = 0, Y = 7338F$

■ Elliptic curve group over 2^{185}
  – Generator (hexadecimal): $X = 18, Y = D$
  – Elliptic curve parameters (hexadecimal): $A = 0, Y = 1EE9$

The first three groups are the classic Diffie–Hellman algorithm using modular exponentiation. The last two groups use the elliptic curve analog to Diffie–Hellman.

IKE key determination employs **nonces** to ensure against replay attacks. Each nonce is a locally generated pseudorandom number. Nonces appear in responses and are encrypted during certain portions of the exchange to secure their use.

Three different **authentication** methods can be used with IKE key determination:

■ **Digital signatures:** The exchange is authenticated by signing a mutually obtainable hash; each party encrypts the hash with its private key. The hash is generated over important parameters, such as user IDs and nonces.

■ **Public-key encryption:** The exchange is authenticated by encrypting parameters such as IDs and nonces with the sender's private key.

■ **Symmetric-key encryption:** A key derived by some out-of-band mechanism can be used to authenticate the exchange by symmetric encryption of exchange parameters.

IKEv2 EXCHANGES The IKEv2 protocol involves the exchange of messages in pairs. The first two pairs of exchanges are referred to as the **initial exchanges** (Figure 9.11a). In the first exchange, the two peers exchange information concerning cryptographic algorithms and other security parameters they are willing to use along with nonces and Diffie–Hellman (DH) values. The result of this exchange is to set up a special SA called the IKE SA (see Figure 9.2). This SA defines parameters for a secure channel between the peers over which subsequent message exchanges take place. Thus, all subsequent IKE message exchanges are protected by encryption and message authentication. In the second exchange, the two parties authenticate one another and set up a first IPsec SA to be placed in the SADB and used for

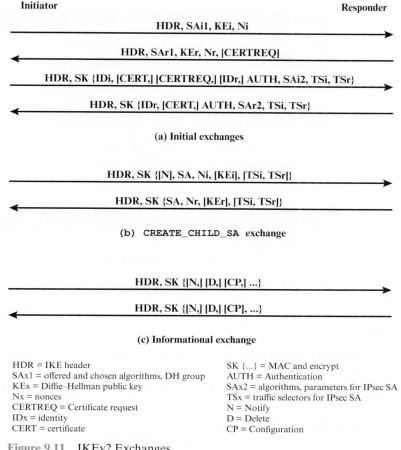

Initiator   Responder

HDR, SAi1, KEi, Ni
→

HDR, SAr1, KEr, Nr, [CERTREQ]
←

HDR, SK {IDi, [CERT,] [CERTREQ,] [IDr,] AUTH, SAi2, TSi, TSr}
→

HDR, SK {IDr, [CERT,] AUTH, SAr2, TSi, TSr}
←

(a) Initial exchanges

HDR, SK {[N], SA, Ni, [KEi], [TSi, TSr]}
→

HDR, SK {SA, Nr, [KEr], [TSi, TSr]}
←

(b) **CREATE_CHILD_SA** exchange

HDR, SK {[N,] [D,] [CP,] ...}
→

HDR, SK {[N,] [D,] [CP], ...}
←

(c) Informational exchange

HDR = IKE header   SK {...} = MAC and encrypt
SAx1 = offered and chosen algorithms, DH group   AUTH = Authentication
KEx = Diffie–Hellman public key   SAx2 = algorithms, parameters for IPsec SA
Nx = nonces   TSx = traffic selectors for IPsec SA
CERTREQ = Certificate request   N = Notify
IDx = identity   D = Delete
CERT = certificate   CP = Configuration

Figure 9.11 IKEv2 Exchanges

protecting ordinary (i.e. non-IKE) communications between the peers. Thus, four messages are needed to establish the first SA for general use.

The **CREATE_CHILD_SA exchange** can be used to establish further SAs for protecting traffic. The **informational exchange** is used to exchange management information, IKEv2 error messages, and other notifications.

Header and Payload Formats

IKE defines procedures and packet formats to establish, negotiate, modify, and delete security associations. As part of SA establishment, IKE defines payloads for exchanging key generation and authentication data. These payload formats provide a consistent framework independent of the specific key exchange protocol, encryption algorithm, and authentication mechanism.

IKE HEADER FORMAT An IKE message consists of an IKE header followed by one or more payloads. All of this is carried in a transport protocol. The specification dictates that implementations must support the use of UDP for the transport protocol.

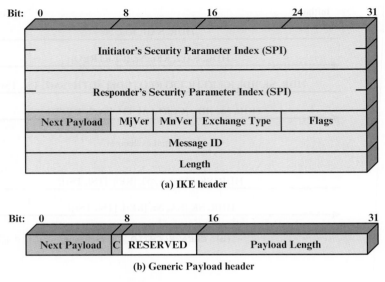

Figure 9.12   IKE Formats

Figure 9.12a shows the header format for an IKE message. It consists of the following fields.

- **Initiator SPI (64 bits):** A value chosen by the initiator to identify a unique IKE security association (SA).
- **Responder SPI (64 bits):** A value chosen by the responder to identify a unique IKE SA.
- **Next Payload (8 bits):** Indicates the type of the first payload in the message; payloads are discussed in the next subsection.
- **Major Version (4 bits):** Indicates major version of IKE in use.
- **Minor Version (4 bits):** Indicates minor version in use.
- **Exchange Type (8 bits):** Indicates the type of exchange; these are discussed later in this section.
- **Flags (8 bits):** Indicates specific options set for this IKE exchange. Three bits are defined so far. The initiator bit indicates whether this packet is sent by the SA initiator. The version bit indicates whether the transmitter is capable of using a higher major version number than the one currently indicated. The response bit indicates whether this is a response to a message containing the same message ID.
- **Message ID (32 bits):** Used to control retransmission of lost packets and matching of requests and responses.
- **Length (32 bits):** Length of total message (header plus all payloads) in octets.

IKE PAYLOAD TYPES All IKE payloads begin with the same generic payload header shown in Figure 9.12b. The Next Payload field has a value of 0 if this is the last payload in the message; otherwise its value is the type of the next payload. The Payload Length field indicates the length in octets of this payload, including the generic payload header.

The critical bit is 0 if the sender wants the recipient to skip this payload if it does not understand the payload type code in the Next Payload field of the previous payload. It is set to 1 if the sender wants the recipient to reject this entire message if it does not understand the payload type.

Table 9.3 summarizes the payload types defined for IKE and lists the fields, or parameters, that are part of each payload. The **SA payload** is used to begin the establishment of an SA. The payload has a complex, hierarchical structure. The payload may contain multiple proposals. Each proposal may contain multiple protocols. Each protocol may contain multiple transforms. And each transform may contain multiple attributes. These elements are formatted as substructures within the payload as follows.

- **Proposal:** This substructure includes a proposal number, a protocol ID (AH, ESP, or IKE), an indicator of the number of transforms, and then a transform substructure. If more than one protocol is to be included in a proposal, then there is a subsequent proposal substructure with the same proposal number.

- **Transform:** Different protocols support different transform types. The transforms are used primarily to define cryptographic algorithms to be used with a particular protocol.

- **Attribute:** Each transform may include attributes that modify or complete the specification of the transform. An example is key length.

Table 9.3   IKE Payload Types

Type	Parameters
Security Association	Proposals
Key Exchange	DH Group #, Key Exchange Data
Identification	ID Type, ID Data
Certificate	Cert Encoding, Certificate Data
Certificate Request	Cert Encoding, Certification Authority
Authentication	Auth Method, Authentication Data
Nonce	Nonce Data
Notify	Protocol-ID, SPI Size, Notify Message Type, SPI, Notification Data
Delete	Protocol-ID, SPI Size, # of SPIs, SPI (one or more)
Vendor ID	Vendor ID
Traffic Selector	Number of TSs, Traffic Selectors
Encrypted	IV, Encrypted IKE payloads, Padding, Pad Length, ICV
Configuration	CFG Type, Configuration Attributes
Extensible Authentication Protocol	EAP Message

The **Key Exchange payload** can be used for a variety of key exchange techniques, including Oakley, Diffie–Hellman, and the RSA-based key exchange used by PGP. The Key Exchange data field contains the data required to generate a session key and is dependent on the key exchange algorithm used.

The **Identification payload** is used to determine the identity of communicating peers and may be used for determining authenticity of information. Typically the ID Data field will contain an IPv4 or IPv6 address.

The **Certificate payload** transfers a public-key certificate. The Certificate Encoding field indicates the type of certificate or certificate-related information, which may include the following:

- PKCS #7 wrapped X.509 certificate
- PGP certificate
- DNS signed key
- X.509 certificate—signature
- X.509 certificate—key exchange
- Kerberos tokens
- Certificate Revocation List (CRL)
- Authority Revocation List (ARL)
- SPKI certificate

At any point in an IKE exchange, the sender may include a **Certificate Request** payload to request the certificate of the other communicating entity. The payload may list more than one certificate type that is acceptable and more than one certificate authority that is acceptable.

The **Authentication** payload contains data used for message authentication purposes. The authentication method types so far defined are RSA digital signature, shared-key message integrity code, and DSS digital signature.

The **Nonce** payload contains random data used to guarantee liveness during an exchange and to protect against replay attacks.

The **Notify** payload contains either error or status information associated with this SA or this SA negotiation. The following table lists the IKE notify messages.

Error Messages	Status Messages
Unsupported Critical Payload	Initial Contact
	Set Window Size
Invalid IKE SPI	Additional TS Possible
Invalid Major Version	IPCOMP Supported
Invalid Syntax	NAT Detection Source IP
Invalid Payload Type	NAT Detection Destination IP
Invalid Message ID	Cookie
Invalid SPI	Use Transport Mode

Error Messages	Status Messages
No Proposal Chosen	HTTP Cert Lookup Supported
Invalid KE Payload	Rekey SA
Authentication Failed	ESP TFC Padding Not Supported
Single Pair Required	Non First Fragments Also
No Additional SAS	
Internal Address Failure	
Failed CP Required	
TS Unacceptable	
Invalid Selectors	

The **Delete** payload indicates one or more SAs that the sender has deleted from its database and that therefore are no longer valid.

The **Vendor ID** payload contains a vendor-defined constant. The constant is used by vendors to identify and recognize remote instances of their implementations. This mechanism allows a vendor to experiment with new features while maintaining backward compatibility.

The **Traffic Selector** payload allows peers to identify packet flows for processing by IPsec services.

The **Encrypted** payload contains other payloads in encrypted form. The encrypted payload format is similar to that of ESP. It may include an IV if the encryption algorithm requires it and an ICV if authentication is selected.

The **Configuration** payload is used to exchange configuration information between IKE peers.

The **Extensible Authentication Protocol (EAP)** payload allows IKE SAs to be authenticated using EAP, which was discussed in Chapter 5.

9.6 CRYPTOGRAPHIC SUITES

The IPsecv3 and IKEv3 protocols rely on a variety of types of cryptographic algorithms. As we have seen in this book, there are many cryptographic algorithms of each type, each with a variety of parameters, such as key size. To promote interoperability, two RFCs define recommended suites of cryptographic algorithms and parameters for various applications.

RFC 4308 defines two cryptographic suites for establishing virtual private networks. Suite VPN-A matches the commonly used corporate VPN security used in older IKEv1 implementations at the time of the issuance of IKEv2 in 2005. Suite VPN-B provides stronger security and is recommended for new VPNs that implement IPsecv3 and IKEv2.

Table 9.4a lists the algorithms and parameters for the two suites. There are several points to note about these two suites. Note that for symmetric cryptography,

Table 9.4   Cryptographic Suites for IPsec

	VPN-A	**VPN-B**
ESP encryption	3DES-CBC	AES-CBC (128-bit key)
ESP integrity	HMAC-SHA1-96	AES-XCBC-MAC-96
IKE encryption	3DES-CBC	AES-CBC (128-bit key)
IKE PRF	HMAC-SHA1	AES-XCBC-PRF-128
IKE Integrity	HMAC-SHA1-96	AES-XCBC-MAC-96
IKE DH group	1024-bit MODP	2048-bit MODP

(a) Virtual private networks (RFC 4308)

	GCM-128	**GCM-256**	**GMAC-128**	**GMAC-256**
ESP encryption/ Integrity	AES-GCM (128-bit key)	AES-GCM (256-bit key)	Null	Null
ESP integrity	Null	Null	AES-GMAC (128-bit key)	AES-GMAC (256-bit key)
IKE encryption	AES-CBC (128-bit key)	AES-CBC (256-bit key)	AES-CBC (128-bit key)	AES-CBC (256-bit key)
IKE PRF	HMAC-SHA-256	HMAC-SHA-384	HMAC-SHA-256	HMAC-SHA-384
IKE Integrity	HMAC-SHA-256-128	HMAC-SHA-384-192	HMAC-SHA-256-128	HMAC-SHA-384-192
IKE DH group	256-bit random ECP	384-bit random ECP	256-bit random ECP	384-bit random ECP

(b) NSA Suite B (RFC 6379)

VPN-A relies on 3DES and HMAC, while VPN-B relies exclusively on AES. Three types of secret-key algorithms are used:

- **Encryption:** For encryption, the cipher block chaining (CBC) mode is used.

- **Message authentication:** For message authentication, VPN-A relies on HMAC with SHA-1 with the output truncated to 96 bits. VPN-B relies on a variant of CMAC with the output truncated to 96 bits.

- **Pseudorandom function:** IKEv2 generates pseudorandom bits by repeated use of the MAC used for message authentication.

RFC 6379 defines four optional cryptographic suites that are compatible with the United States National Security Agency's Suite B specifications. In 2005, the NSA issued Suite B, which defined the algorithms and strengths needed to protect both sensitive but unclassified (SBU) and classified information for use in its Cryptographic Modernization program [LATT09]. The four suites defined in RFC 6379 provide choices for ESP and IKE. The four suites are differentiated by the choice of cryptographic algorithm strengths and a choice of whether ESP is to provide both confidentiality and integrity or integrity only. All of the suites offer greater protection than the two VPN suites defined in RFC 4308.

Table 9.4b lists the algorithms and parameters for the two suites. As with RFC 4308, three categories of secret key algorithms are listed:

- **Encryption:** For ESP, authenticated encryption is provided using the GCM mode with either 128-bit or 256-bit AES keys. For IKE encryption, CBC is used, as it was for the VPN suites.

- **Message authentication:** For ESP, if only authentication is required, then a message authentication algorithm known as GMAC is used. For IKE, message authentication is provided using HMAC with one of the SHA-3 hash functions.

- **Pseudorandom function:** As with the VPN suites, IKEv2 in these suites generates pseudorandom bits by repeated use of the MAC used for message authentication.

For the Diffie–Hellman algorithm, the use of elliptic curve groups modulo a prime is specified. For authentication, elliptic curve digital signatures are listed. The original IKEv2 documents used RSA-based digital signatures. Equivalent or greater strength can be achieved using ECC with fewer key bits.

9.7 KEY TERMS, REVIEW QUESTIONS, AND PROBLEMS

Key Terms

anti-replay service	Internet Security Association	Oakley key determination
Authentication Header (AH)	and Key Management	protocol
Encapsulating Security	Protocol (ISAKMP)	replay attack
Payload (ESP)	IP Security (IPsec)	security association (SA)
Internet Key Exchange	IPv4	transport mode
(IKE)	IPv6	tunnel mode

Review Questions

9.1 List and briefly describe some benefits of IPsec.

9.2 List and briefly define different categories of IPsec documents.

9.3 What parameters identify an SA and what parameters characterize the nature of a particular SA?

9.4 What is the difference between transport mode and tunnel mode?

9.5 What are the types of secret key algorithm used in IPsec?

9.6 Why does ESP include a padding field?

9.7 What are the basic approaches to bundling SAs?

9.8 What are the roles of the Oakley key determination protocol and ISAKMP in IPsec?

Problems

9.1 Describe and explain each of the entries in Table 9.2.

9.2 Draw a figure similar to Figure 9.8 for AH.

9.3 List the major security services provided by AH and ESP, respectively.

9.4 In discussing AH processing, it was mentioned that not all of the fields in an IP header are included in MAC calculation.
   a. For each of the fields in the IPv4 header, indicate whether the field is immutable, mutable but predictable, or mutable (zeroed prior to ICV calculation).
   b. Do the same for the IPv6 header.
   c. Do the same for the IPv6 extension headers.
   In each case, justify your decision for each field.

9.5 Suppose that the current replay window spans from 120 to 530.
   a. If the next incoming authenticated packet has sequence number 340, what will the receiver do with the packet, and what will be the parameters of the window after that?
   b. If instead the next incoming authenticated packet has sequence number 598, what will the receiver do with the packet, and what will be the parameters of the window after that?
   c. If instead the next incoming authenticated packet has sequence number 110, what will the receiver do with the packet, and what will be the parameters of the window after that?

9.6 When tunnel mode is used, a new outer IP header is constructed. For both IPv4 and IPv6, indicate the relationship of each outer IP header field and each extension header in the outer packet to the corresponding field or extension header of the inner IP packet. That is, indicate which outer values are derived from inner values and which are constructed independently of the inner values.

9.7 End-to-end authentication and encryption are desired between two hosts. Draw figures similar to Figure 9.8 that show each of the following.
   a. Transport adjacency with encryption applied before authentication.
   b. A transport SA bundled inside a tunnel SA with encryption applied before authentication.
   c. A transport SA bundled inside a tunnel SA with authentication applied before encryption.

9.8 The IPsec architecture document states that when two transport mode SAs are bundled to allow both AH and ESP protocols on the same end-to-end flow, only one ordering of security protocols seems appropriate: performing the ESP protocol before performing the AH protocol. Why is this approach recommended rather than authentication before encryption?

9.9 For the IKE key exchange, indicate which parameters in each message go in which ISAKMP payload types.

9.10 Where does IPsec reside in a protocol stack?

CHAPTER **10**

MALICIOUS SOFTWARE

LEARNING OBJECTIVES

After studying this chapter, you should be able to:

■ Describe three broad mechanisms malware uses to propagate.

■ Understand the basic operation of viruses, worms, and trojans.

■ Describe four broad categories of malware payloads.

■ Understand the different threats posed by bots, spyware, and rootkits.

■ Describe some malware countermeasure elements.

■ Describe three locations for malware detection mechanisms.

Malicious software, or **malware**, arguably constitutes one of the most significant categories of threats to computer systems. SP 800-83 (*Guide to Malware Incident Prevention and Handling for Desktops and Laptops*, July 2013) defines malware as "a program that is covertly inserted into another program with the intent to destroy data, run destructive or intrusive programs, or otherwise compromise the confidentiality, integrity, or availability of the victim's data, applications, or operating system." Hence, we are concerned with the threat malware poses to application programs, to utility programs, such as editors and compilers, and to kernel-level programs. We are also concerned with its use on compromised or malicious Web sites and servers, or in especially crafted spam e-mails or other messages, which aim to trick users into revealing sensitive personal information.

This chapter[1] examines the wide spectrum of malware threats and countermeasures. We begin with a survey of various types of malware and offer a broad classification based first on the means malware uses to spread or **propagate**, and then on the variety of actions or **payloads** used once the malware has reached a target. Propagation mechanisms include those used by viruses, worms, and trojans. Payloads include system corruption, bots, phishing, spyware, and rootkits. The discussion then includes a review of countermeasure approaches. Finally, distributed denial-of-service (DDoS) attacks are reviewed.

10.1 TYPES OF MALICIOUS SOFTWARE (MALWARE)

The terminology in this area presents problems because of a lack of universal agreement on all of the terms and because some of the categories overlap. Table 10.1 is a useful guide to some of the terms in use.

---

[1] I am indebted to Lawrie Brown of the Australian Defence Force Academy, who contributed substantially to this chapter.

Table 10.1   Terminology for Malicious Software

Name	Description
Virus	Malware that, when executed, tries to replicate itself into other executable code; when it succeeds the code is said to be infected. When the infected code is executed, the virus also executes.
Worm	A computer program that can run independently and can propagate a complete working version of itself onto other hosts on a network.
Logic bomb	A program inserted into software by an intruder. A logic bomb lies dormant until a predefined condition is met; the program then triggers an unauthorized act.
Trojan horse	A computer program that appears to have a useful function, but also has a hidden and potentially malicious function that evades security mechanisms, sometimes by exploiting legitimate authorizations of a system entity that invokes the Trojan horse program.
Backdoor (trapdoor)	Any mechanism that bypasses a normal security check; it may allow unauthorized access to functionality.
Mobile code	Software (e.g., script, macro, or other portable instruction) that can be shipped unchanged to a heterogeneous collection of platforms and execute with identical semantics.
Exploits	Code specific to a single vulnerability or set of vulnerabilities.
Downloaders	Program that installs other items on a machine that is under attack. Usually, a downloader is sent in an e-mail.
Auto-rooter	Malicious hacker tools used to break into new machines remotely.
Kit (virus generator)	Set of tools for generating new viruses automatically.
Spammer programs	Used to send large volumes of unwanted e-mail.
Flooders	Used to attack networked computer systems with a large volume of traffic to carry out a denial-of-service (DoS) attack.
Keyloggers	Captures keystrokes on a compromised system.
Rootkit	Set of hacker tools used after attacker has broken into a computer system and gained root-level access.
Zombie, bot	Program activated on an infected machine that is activated to launch attacks on other machines.
Spyware	Software that collects information from a computer and transmits it to another system.
Adware	Advertising that is integrated into software. It can result in pop-up ads or redirection of a browser to a commercial site.

A Broad Classification of Malware

Although a range of schemes can be used, one useful approach classifies malware into two broad categories, based first on how it spreads or propagates to reach the desired targets and then on the actions or payloads it performs once a target is reached.

Propagation mechanisms include infection of existing executable or interpreted content by viruses that is subsequently spread to other systems; exploit of software vulnerabilities either locally or over a network by worms or drive-by-downloads to allow the malware to replicate; and social engineering attacks that convince users to bypass security mechanisms to install trojans or to respond to phishing attacks.

Earlier approaches to malware classification distinguished between those that need a host program, being parasitic code such as viruses, and those that are independent, self-contained programs run on the system such as worms, trojans, and bots. Another distinction used was between malware that does not replicate, such as trojans and spam e-mail, and malware that does, including viruses and worms.

Payload actions performed by malware once it reaches a target system can include corruption of system or data files; theft of service in order to make the system a zombie agent of attack as part of a botnet; theft of information from the system, especially of logins, passwords, or other personal details by keylogging or spyware programs; and stealthing where the malware hides its presence on the system from attempts to detect and block it.

While early malware tended to use a single means of propagation to deliver a single payload, as it evolved we see a growth of blended malware that incorporates a range of both propagation mechanisms and payloads that increase its ability to spread, hide, and perform a range of actions on targets. A **blended attack** uses multiple methods of infection or propagation, to maximize the speed of contagion and the severity of the attack. Some malware even support an update mechanism that allows it to change the range of propagation and payload mechanisms utilized once it is deployed.

In the following sections, we survey these various categories of malware, and then follow with a discussion of appropriate countermeasures.

Attack Kits

Initially, the development and deployment of malware required considerable technical skill by software authors. This changed with the development of virus-creation toolkits in the early 1990s, and then later of more general attack kits in the 2000s, that greatly assisted in the development and deployment of malware [FOSS10]. These toolkits, often known as **crimeware**, now include a variety of propagation mechanisms and payload modules that even novices can combine, select, and deploy.

They can also easily be customized with the latest discovered vulnerabilities in order to exploit the window of opportunity between the publication of a weakness and the widespread deployment of patches to close it. These kits greatly enlarged the population of attackers able to deploy malware. Although the malware created with such toolkits tends to be less sophisticated than that designed from scratch, the sheer number of new variants that can be generated by attackers using these toolkits creates a significant problem for those defending systems against them.

The Zeus crimeware toolkit is a prominent, recent example of such an attack kit, which was used to generate a wide range of very effective, stealthed malware that facilitates a range of criminal activities, in particular capturing and exploiting banking credentials [BINS10]. Other widely used toolkits include Blackhole, Sakura, and Phoenix [SYMA13].

Attack Sources

Another significant malware development over the last couple of decades is the change from attackers being individuals, often motivated to demonstrate their technical competence to their peers, to more organized and dangerous attack sources. These include politically motivated attackers, criminals, and organized crime; organizations that sell their services to companies and nations; and national government agencies. This has significantly changed the resources available and motivation behind the rise of malware, and indeed has led to development of a large underground economy involving the sale of attack kits, access to compromised hosts, and to stolen information.

10.2 ADVANCED PERSISTENT THREAT

Advanced Persistent Threats (APTs) have risen to prominence in recent years. These are not a new type of malware, but rather the well-resourced, persistent application of a wide variety of intrusion technologies and malware to selected targets, usually business or political. APTs are typically attributed to state-sponsored organizations, with some attacks likely from criminal enterprises as well. We discuss these categories of intruders further in Chapter 11.

APTs differ from other types of attack by their careful target selection, and persistent, often stealthy, intrusion efforts over extended periods. A number of high profile attacks, including Aurora, RSA, APT1, and Stuxnet, are often cited as examples. They are named as a result of these characteristics:

- **Advanced:** Used by the attackers of a wide variety of intrusion technologies and malware, including the development of custom malware if required. The individual components may not necessarily be technically advanced, but are carefully selected to suit the chosen target.

- **Persistent:** Determined application of the attacks over an extended period against the chosen target in order to maximize the chance of success. A variety of attacks may be progressively, and often stealthily, applied until the target is compromised.

- **Threats:** Threats to the selected targets as a result of the organized, capable, and well-funded attackers intent to compromise the specifically chosen targets. The active involvement of people in the process greatly raises the threat level from that due to automated attacks tools and the likelihood of successful attack.

The aim of these attacks varies from theft of intellectual property or security and infrastructure related data, to the physical disruption of infrastructure. Techniques used include social engineering, spear-phishing e-mails, drive-by-downloads from selected compromised Web sites likely to be visited by personnel in the target organization, to infect the target with sophisticated malware with multiple propagation mechanisms and payloads. Once they have gained initial access to systems in the target organization, a further range of attack tools are used to maintain and extend their access.

As a result, these attacks are much harder to defend against due to this specific targeting and persistence. It requires a combination of technical countermeasures, such as we discuss later in this chapter, as well as awareness training to assist personnel to resist such attacks. Even with current best-practice countermeasures, the use of zero-day exploits and new attack approaches means that some of these attacks are likely to succeed [SYMA13, MAND13]. Thus multiple layers of defense are needed, with mechanisms to detect, respond and mitigate such attacks. These may include monitoring for malware command and control traffic, and detection of exfiltration traffic.

10.3 PROPAGATION—INFECTED CONTENT—VIRUSES

The first category of malware propagation concerns parasitic software fragments that attach themselves to some existing executable content. The fragment may be machine code that infects some existing application, utility, or system program, or even the code used to boot a computer system. More recently, the fragment has been some form of scripting code, typically used to support active content within data files such as Microsoft Word documents, Excel spreadsheets, or Adobe PDF documents.

The Nature of Viruses

A computer virus is a piece of software that can "infect" other programs, or indeed any type of executable content, by modifying them. The modification includes injecting the original code with a routine to make copies of the virus code, which can then go on to infect other content.

A computer virus carries in its instructional code the recipe for making perfect copies of itself. The typical virus becomes embedded in a program, or carrier of executable content, on a computer. Then, whenever the infected computer comes into contact with an uninfected piece of code, a fresh copy of the virus passes into the new location. Thus, the infection can spread from computer to computer, aided by unsuspecting users, who exchange these programs or carrier files on disk or USB stick, or who send them to one another over a network. In a network environment, the ability to access documents, applications, and system services on other computers provides a perfect culture for the spread of such viral code.

A virus that attaches to an executable program can do anything that the program is permitted to do. It executes secretly when the host program is run. Once the virus code is executing, it can perform any function, such as erasing files and programs, that is allowed by the privileges of the current user. One reason viruses dominated the malware scene in earlier years was the lack of user authentication and access controls on personal computer systems at that time. This enabled a virus to infect any executable content on the system. The significant quantity of programs shared on floppy disk also enabled its easy, if somewhat slow, spread. The inclusion of tighter access controls on modern operating systems significantly hinders the ease of infection of such traditional, machine-executable code, viruses. This resulted in the development of macro viruses that exploit the active content supported by some document types, such as Microsoft Word or Excel files, or Adobe PDF documents. Such documents are easily modified and shared by users as part of their normal system use and are not protected by the same access controls as programs. Currently, a viral mode of infection is typically one of several propagation mechanisms used by contemporary malware, which may also include worm and Trojan capabilities.

A computer virus, and more generally many contemporary types of malware, includes one or more variants of each of these components:

- **Infection mechanism:** The means by which a virus spreads or propagates, enabling it to replicate. The mechanism is also referred to as the **infection vector**.
- **Trigger:** The event or condition that determines when the payload is activated or delivered, sometimes known as a **logic bomb**.
- **Payload:** What the virus does, besides spreading. The payload may involve damage or benign but noticeable activity.

During its lifetime, a typical virus goes through the following four phases:

- **Dormant phase:** The virus is idle. The virus will eventually be activated by some event, such as a date, the presence of another program or file, or the capacity of the disk exceeding some limit. Not all viruses have this stage.
- **Propagation phase:** The virus places a copy of itself into other programs or into certain system areas on the disk. The copy may not be identical to the propagating version; viruses often morph to evade detection. Each infected program will now contain a clone of the virus, which will itself enter a propagation phase.
- **Triggering phase:** The virus is activated to perform the function for which it was intended. As with the dormant phase, the triggering phase can be caused by a variety of system events, including a count of the number of times that this copy of the virus has made copies of itself.
- **Execution phase:** The function is performed. The function may be harmless, such as a message on the screen, or damaging, such as the destruction of programs and data files.

Most viruses that infect executable program files carry out their work in a manner that is specific to a particular operating system and, in some cases, specific to a particular hardware platform. Thus, they are designed to take advantage of the details and weaknesses of particular systems. Macro viruses, though, target specific document types, which are often supported on a variety of systems.

EXECUTABLE VIRUS STRUCTURE Traditional machine-executable virus code can be prepended or postpended to some executable program, or it can be embedded into the program in some other fashion. The key to its operation is that the infected program, when invoked, will first execute the virus code and then execute the original code of the program.

A very general depiction of virus structure is shown in Figure 10.1a. In this case, the virus code, V, is prepended to infected programs, and it is assumed that the entry point to the program, when invoked, is the first line of the program.

The infected program begins with the virus code and works as follows. The first line of code labels the program, which then begins execution with the main action block of the virus. The second line is a special marker that is used by the virus to determine whether or not a potential victim program has already been infected with this virus. When the program is invoked, control is immediately transferred to the main virus program. The virus program may first seek out uninfected executable files and infect them. Next, the virus may execute its payload if the required trigger

```
program V                              program CV
1234567;                               1234567;

procedure attach-to-program;           procedure attach-to-program;
begin                                  begin
   repeat                                 repeat
      file := get-random-program;           file := get-random-program;
      until first-program-line ≠ 1234567;   until first-program-line ≠ 1234567;
      prepend V to file;                    compress file; (* t₁ *)
end;                                         prepend CV to file; (* t₂ *)
                                       end;
procedure execute-payload;
begin                                  procedure (* main action block *)
   (* perform payload actions *)          if ask-permission then attach-to-program;
end;                                      uncompress rest of this file into tempfile; (* t₃ *)
                                          execute tempfile; (* t₄ *)
procedure trigger-condition;           end;
begin
   (* return true if trigger condition is true *)
end;

begin (* main action block *)
   attach-to-program;
   if trigger-condition then execute-payload;
   goto main;
end;
```

<table>
<tr><td>(a) A simple virus</td><td>(b) A compression virus</td></tr>
</table>

Figure 10.1   Example Virus Logic

conditions, if any, are met. Finally, the virus transfers control to the original program. If the infection phase of the program is reasonably rapid, a user is unlikely to notice any difference between the execution of an infected and an uninfected program.

A virus such as the one just described is easily detected because an infected version of a program is longer than the corresponding uninfected one. A way to thwart such a simple means of detecting a virus is to compress the executable file so that both the infected and uninfected versions are of identical length. Figure 10.1b shows in general terms the logic required. The key lines in this virus are labeled with times, and Figure 10.2 illustrates the operation. We begin at time t_0, with program P_1', which is program P_1 infected with virus CV, and a clean program P_2, which is not infected with CV. When P_1 is invoked, control passes to its virus, which performs the following steps:

t_1: For each uninfected file P_2 that is found, the virus first compresses that file to produce P_2', which is shorter than the original program by the size of the virus CV.

t_2: A copy of CV is prepended to the compressed program.

t_3: The compressed version of the original infected program, P_1' is uncompressed.

t_4: The uncompressed original program P_1 is executed.

In this example, the virus does nothing other than propagate. As previously mentioned, the virus may also include one or more payloads.

Once a virus has gained entry to a system by infecting a single program, it is in a position to potentially infect some or all other executable files on that system

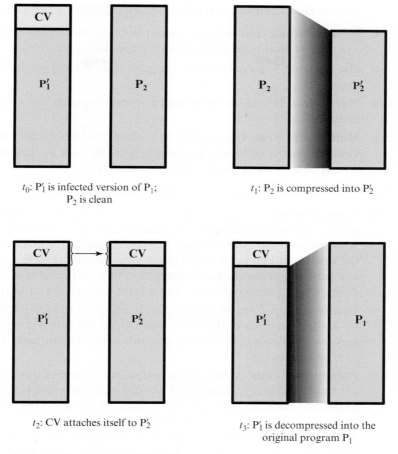

t_0: P_1' is infected version of P_1;
P_2 is clean

t_1: P_2 is compressed into P_2'

t_2: CV attaches itself to P_2'

t_3: P_1' is decompressed into the
original program P_1

Figure 10.2 A Compression Virus

when the infected program executes, depending on the access permissions the infected program has. Thus, viral infection can be completely prevented by blocking the virus from gaining entry in the first place. Unfortunately, prevention is extraordinarily difficult because a virus can be part of any program outside a system. Thus, unless one is content to take an absolutely bare piece of iron and write all one's own system and application programs, one is vulnerable. Many forms of infection can also be blocked by denying normal users the right to modify programs on the system.

Viruses Classification

There has been a continuous arms race between virus writers and writers of antivirus software since viruses first appeared. As effective countermeasures are developed for existing types of viruses, newer types are developed. There is no simple or universally agreed-upon classification scheme for viruses. In this section, we follow [AYCO06] and classify viruses along two orthogonal axes: the type of target the virus tries to infect and the method the virus uses to conceal itself from detection by users and antivirus software.

A virus **classification by target** includes the following categories:

■ **Boot sector infector:** Infects a master boot record or boot record and spreads when a system is booted from the disk containing the virus.

■ **File infector:** Infects files that the operating system or shell consider to be executable.

■ **Macro virus:** Infects files with macro or scripting code that is interpreted by an application.

■ **Multipartite virus:** Infects files in multiple ways. Typically, the multipartite virus is capable of infecting multiple types of files, so that virus eradication must deal with all of the possible sites of infection.

A virus classification by concealment strategy includes the following categories:

■ **Encrypted virus:** A typical approach is as follows. A portion of the virus creates a random encryption key and encrypts the remainder of the virus. The key is stored with the virus. When an infected program is invoked, the virus uses the stored random key to decrypt the virus. When the virus replicates, a different random key is selected. Because the bulk of the virus is encrypted with a different key for each instance, there is no constant bit pattern to observe.

■ **Stealth virus:** A form of virus explicitly designed to hide itself from detection by antivirus software. Thus, the entire virus, not just a payload, is hidden. It may use both code mutation, for example, compression, and rootkit techniques to achieve this.

■ **Polymorphic virus:** A form of virus that creates copies during replication that are functionally equivalent but have distinctly different bit patterns, in order to defeat programs that scan for viruses. In this case, the "signature" of the virus will vary with each copy. To achieve this variation, the virus may randomly insert superfluous instructions or interchange the order of independent instructions. A more effective approach is to use encryption. The strategy of the encryption virus is followed. The portion of the virus that is responsible for generating keys and performing encryption/decryption is referred to as the *mutation engine*. The mutation engine itself is altered with each use.

■ **Metamorphic virus:** As with a polymorphic virus, a metamorphic virus mutates with every infection. The difference is that a metamorphic virus rewrites itself completely at each iteration, increasing the difficulty of detection. Metamorphic viruses may change their behavior as well as their appearance.

Macro and Scripting Viruses

Macro viruses infect scripting code used to support active content in a variety of user document types. Macro viruses are particularly threatening for a number of reasons:

1. A macro virus is platform independent. Many macro viruses infect active content in commonly used applications, such as macros in Microsoft Word documents or other Microsoft Office documents, or scripting code in Adobe PDF

documents. Any hardware platform and operating system that supports these applications can be infected.

2. Macro viruses infect documents, not executable portions of code. Most of the information introduced onto a computer system is in the form of documents rather than programs.

3. Macro viruses are easily spread, as the documents they exploit are shared in normal use. A very common method is by electronic mail.

4. Because macro viruses infect user documents rather than system programs, traditional file system access controls are of limited use in preventing their spread, since users are expected to modify them.

Macro viruses take advantage of support for active content using a scripting or macro language, embedded in a word processing document or other type of file. Typically, users employ macros to automate repetitive tasks and thereby save keystrokes. They are also used to support dynamic content, form validation, and other useful tasks associated with these documents.

Successive releases of MS Office products provide increased protection against macro viruses. For example, Microsoft offers an optional Macro Virus Protection tool that detects suspicious Word files and alerts the customer to the potential risk of opening a file with macros. Various antivirus product vendors have also developed tools to detect and remove macro viruses. As in other types of viruses, the arms race continues in the field of macro viruses, but they no longer are the predominant virus threat.

Another possible host for macro virus–style malware is in Adobe's PDF documents. These can support a range of embedded components, including Javascript and other types of scripting code. Although recent PDF viewers include measures to warn users when such code is run, the message the user is shown can be manipulated to trick them into permitting its execution. If this occurs, the code could potentially act as a virus to infect other PDF documents the user can access on his or her system. Alternatively, it can install a Trojan, or act as a worm, as we discuss later.

10.4 PROPAGATION—VULNERABILITY EXPLOIT—WORMS

A worm is a program that actively seeks out more machines to infect, and then each infected machine serves as an automated launching pad for attacks on other machines. Worm programs exploit software vulnerabilities in client or server programs to gain access to each new system. They can use network connections to spread from system to system. They can also spread through shared media, such as USB drives or optical data disks. E-mail worms spread in macro or script code included in documents attached to e-mail or to instant messenger file transfers. Upon activation, the worm may replicate and propagate again. In addition to propagation, the worm usually carries some form of payload, such as those we discuss later.

To replicate itself, a worm uses some means to access remote systems. These include the following, most of which are still seen in active use [SYMA13]:

- **Electronic mail or instant messenger facility:** A worm e-mails a copy of itself to other systems or sends itself as an attachment via an instant message service, so that its code is run when the e-mail or attachment is received or viewed.

- **File sharing:** A worm either creates a copy of itself or infects other suitable files as a virus on removable media such as a USB drive; it then executes when the drive is connected to another system using the autorun mechanism by exploiting some software vulnerability or when a user opens the infected file on the target system.

- **Remote execution capability:** A worm executes a copy of itself on another system, either by using an explicit remote execution facility or by exploiting a program flaw in a network service to subvert its operations.

- **Remote file access or transfer capability:** A worm uses a remote file access or transfer service to another system to copy itself from one system to the other, where users on that system may then execute it.

- **Remote login capability:** A worm logs onto a remote system as a user and then uses commands to copy itself from one system to the other, where it then executes.

The new copy of the worm program is then run on the remote system where, in addition to any payload functions that it performs on that system, it continues to propagate.

A worm typically uses the same phases as a computer virus: dormant, propagation, triggering, and execution. The propagation phase generally performs the following functions:

- Search for appropriate access mechanisms to other systems to infect by examining host tables, address books, buddy lists, trusted peers, and other similar repositories of remote system access details; by scanning possible target host addresses; or by searching for suitable removable media devices to use.

- Use the access mechanisms found to transfer a copy of itself to the remote system and cause the copy to be run.

The worm may also attempt to determine whether a system has previously been infected before copying itself to the system. In a multiprogramming system, it can also disguise its presence by naming itself as a system process or using some other name that may not be noticed by a system operator. More recent worms can even inject their code into existing processes on the system and run using additional threads in that process, to further disguise their presence.

Target Discovery

The first function in the propagation phase for a network worm is for it to search for other systems to infect, a process known as **scanning** or **fingerprinting**. For such worms, which exploit software vulnerabilities in remotely accessible network services, it must identify potential systems running the vulnerable service, and then infect them. Then, typically, the worm code now installed on the infected machines repeats the same scanning process, until a large distributed network of infected machines is created.

[MIRK04] lists the following types of network address scanning strategies that such a worm can use:

- **Random:** Each compromised host probes random addresses in the IP address space, using a different seed. This technique produces a high volume of Internet traffic, which may cause generalized disruption even before the actual attack is launched.

- **Hit list:** The attacker first compiles a long list of potential vulnerable machines. This can be a slow process done over a long period to avoid detection that an attack is underway. Once the list is compiled, the attacker begins infecting machines on the list. Each infected machine is provided with a portion of the list to scan. This strategy results in a very short scanning period, which may make it difficult to detect that infection is taking place.

- **Topological:** This method uses information contained on an infected victim machine to find more hosts to scan.

- **Local subnet:** If a host is infected behind a firewall, that host then looks for targets in its own local network. The host uses the subnet address structure to find other hosts that would otherwise be protected by the firewall.

Worm Propagation Model

A well-designed worm can spread rapidly and infect massive numbers of hosts. It is useful to have a general model for the rate of worm propagation. Computer viruses and worms exhibit similar self-replication and propagation behavior to biological viruses. Thus we can look to classic epidemic models for understanding computer virus and worm propagation behavior. A simplified, classic epidemic model can be expressed as follows:

$$\frac{dI(t)}{dt} = \beta I(t)S(t)$$

where

$I(t)$ = number of individuals infected as of time t
$S(t)$ = number of susceptible individuals (susceptible to infection but not yet infected) at time t
β = infection rate
N = size of the population, $N = I(t) + S(t)$

Figure 10.3 shows the dynamics of worm propagation using this model. Propagation proceeds through three phases. In the initial phase, the number of hosts increases exponentially. To see that this is so, consider a simplified case in which a worm is launched from a single host and infects two nearby hosts. Each of these

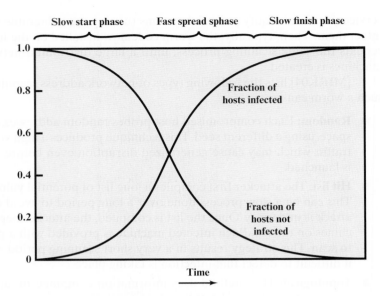

Figure 10.3   Worm Propagation Model

hosts infects two more hosts, and so on. This results in exponential growth. After a time, infecting hosts waste some time attacking already-infected hosts, which reduces the rate of infection. During this middle phase, growth is approximately linear, but the rate of infection is rapid. When most vulnerable computers have been infected, the attack enters a slow finish phase as the worm seeks out those remaining hosts that are difficult to identify.

Clearly, the objective in countering a worm is to catch the worm in its slow start phase, at a time when few hosts have been infected.

Zou and others [ZOU05] describe a model for worm propagation based on an analysis of network worm attacks at that time. The speed of propagation and the total number of hosts infected depend on a number of factors, including the mode of propagation, the vulnerability or vulnerabilities exploited, and the degree of similarity to preceding attacks. For the latter factor, an attack that is a variation of a recent previous attack may be countered more effectively than a more novel attack. Zou's model agrees closely with Figure 10.3.

The Morris Worm

The earliest significant worm infection was released onto the Internet by Robert Morris in 1988 [ORMA03]. The Morris worm was designed to spread on UNIX systems and used a number of different techniques for propagation. When a copy began execution, its first task was to discover other hosts known to this host that would allow entry from this host. The worm performed this task by examining a variety of lists and tables, including system tables that declared which other machines were trusted by this host, users' mail forwarding files, tables by which users gave themselves permission for access to remote accounts, and from a program that reported the status of network connections. For each discovered host, the worm tried a number of methods for gaining access:

1. It attempted to log on to a remote host as a legitimate user. In this method, the worm first attempted to crack the local password file and then used the discovered passwords and corresponding user IDs. The assumption was that many users would use the same password on different systems. To obtain the passwords, the worm ran a password-cracking program that tried

   a. Each user's account name and simple permutations of it

   b. A list of 432 built-in passwords that Morris thought to be likely candidates[2]

   c. All the words in the local system dictionary

4. It exploited a bug in the UNIX finger protocol, which reports the whereabouts of a remote user.

5. It exploited a trapdoor in the debug option of the remote process that receives and sends mail.

If any of these attacks succeeded, the worm achieved communication with the operating system command interpreter. It then sent this interpreter a short bootstrap program, issued a command to execute that program, and then logged off. The bootstrap program then called back the parent program and downloaded the remainder of the worm. The new worm was then executed.

State of Worm Technology

The state of the art in worm technology includes the following:

- **Multiplatform:** Newer worms are not limited to Windows machines but can attack a variety of platforms, especially the popular varieties of UNIX, or exploit macro or scripting languages supported in popular document types.

- **Multiexploit:** New worms penetrate systems in a variety of ways, using exploits against Web servers, browsers, e-mail, file sharing, and other network-based applications, or via shared media.

- **Ultrafast spreading:** Exploit various techniques to optimize the rate of spread of a worm to maximize its likelihood of locating as many vulnerable machines as possible in a short time period.

- **Polymorphic:** To evade detection, skip past filters, and foil real-time analysis, worms adopt the virus polymorphic technique. Each copy of the worm has new code generated on the fly using functionally equivalent instructions and encryption techniques.

- **Metamorphic:** In addition to changing their appearance, metamorphic worms have a repertoire of behavior patterns that are unleashed at different stages of propagation.

- **Transport vehicles:** Because worms can rapidly compromise a large number of systems, they are ideal for spreading a wide variety of malicious payloads,

---

[2]The complete list is provided at this book's Premium Content Web site.

such as distributed denial-of-service bots, rootkits, spam e-mail generators, and spyware.

■ **Zero-day exploit:** To achieve maximum surprise and distribution, a worm should exploit an unknown vulnerability that is only discovered by the general network community when the worm is launched.

Mobile Code

SP 800-28 (*Guidelines on Active Content and Mobile Code*, March 2008) defines mobile code as programs (e.g., script, macro, or other portable instruction) that can be shipped unchanged to a heterogeneous collection of platforms and execute with identical semantics.

Mobile code is transmitted from a remote system to a local system and then executed on the local system without the user's explicit instruction. Mobile code often acts as a mechanism for a virus, worm, or Trojan horse to be transmitted to the user's workstation. In other cases, mobile code takes advantage of vulnerabilities to perform its own exploits, such as unauthorized data access or root compromise. Popular vehicles for mobile code include Java applets, ActiveX, JavaScript, and VBScript. The most common ways of using mobile code for malicious operations on local system are cross-site scripting, interactive and dynamic Web sites, e-mail attachments, and downloads from untrusted sites or of untrusted software.

Client–Side Vulnerabilities and Drive-by-Downloads

Another approach to exploiting software vulnerabilities involves the exploit of bugs in user applications to install malware. One common approach to this exploits browser vulnerabilities so that when the user views a Web page controlled by the attacker, it contains code that exploits the browser bug to download and install malware on the system without the user's knowledge or consent. This is known as a **drive-by-download** and is a common exploit in recent attack kits. In most cases this malware does not actively propagate as a worm does, but rather waits for unsuspecting users to visit the malicious Web page in order to spread to their systems.

In general, drive-by-download attacks are aimed at anyone who visits a compromised site and is vulnerable to the exploits used. Watering-hole attacks are a variant of this used in highly targeted attacks. The attacker researches their intended victims to identify Web sites they are likely to visit and then scans these sites to identify those with vulnerabilities that allow their compromise with a drive-by-download attack. They then wait for one of their intended victims to visit one of the compromised sites. Their attack code may even be written so that it will only infect systems belonging to the target organization and take no action for other visitors to the site. This greatly increases the likelihood of the site compromise remaining undetected.

Malvertising is another technique used to place malware on Web sites without actually compromising them. The attacker pays for advertisements that are highly likely to be placed on their intended target Web sites, and which incorporate malware in them. Using these malicious adds, attackers can infect visitors to sites displaying them. Again, the malware code may be dynamically generated to either reduce the chance of detection or only infect specific systems.

Related variants can exploit bugs in common e-mail clients, such as the Klez mass-mailing worm seen in October 2001, which targeted a bug in the HTML handling in Microsoft's Outlook and Outlook Express programs to automatically run itself. Or, such malware may target common PDF viewers to also download and install malware without the user's consent, when they view a malicious PDF document [STEV11]. Such documents may be spread by spam e-mail or be part of a targeted phishing attack, as we discuss next.

Clickjacking

Clickjacking, also known as a *user-interface (UI) redress attack*, is a vulnerability used by an attacker to collect an infected user's clicks. The attacker can force the user to do a variety of things from adjusting the user's computer settings to unwittingly sending the user to Web sites that might have malicious code. Also, by taking advantage of Adobe Flash or JavaScript, an attacker could even place a button under or over a legitimate button, making it difficult for users to detect. A typical attack uses multiple transparent or opaque layers to trick a user into clicking on a button or link on another page when they were intending to click on the top level page. Thus, the attacker is hijacking clicks meant for one page and routing them to another page, most likely owned by another application, domain, or both.

Using a similar technique, keystrokes can also be hijacked. With a carefully crafted combination of stylesheets, iframes, and text boxes, a user can be led to believe they are typing in the password to their e-mail or bank account but are instead typing into an invisible frame controlled by the attacker.

There is a wide variety of techniques for accomplishing a clickjacking attack, and new techniques are developed as defenses to older techniques are put in place. [NIEM11] and [STON10] are useful discussions.

10.5 PROPAGATION—SOCIAL ENGINEERING—SPAM E-MAIL, TROJANS

The final category of malware propagation we consider involves social engineering, "tricking" users to assist in the compromise of their own systems or personal information. This can occur when a user views and responds to some SPAM e-mail or permits the installation and execution of some Trojan horse program or scripting code.

Spam (Unsolicited Bulk) E-Mail

Unsolicited bulk e-mail, commonly known as spam, imposes significant costs on both the network infrastructure needed to relay this traffic and on users who need to filter their legitimate e-mails out of this flood. In response to the explosive growth in spam, there has been the equally rapid growth of the antispam industry, which provides products to detect and filter spam e-mails. This has led to an arms race between the spammers devising techniques to sneak their content through and the defenders taking efforts to block them. In recent years, the volume of spam e-mail has started to decline. One reason is the rapid growth of attacks, including spam, spread via social media networks. This reflects the rapid growth in use of these networks, which form a new arena for attackers to exploit [SYMA13].

While some spam is sent from legitimate mail servers, most recent spam is sent by botnets using compromised user systems, as we discuss in Section 10.6. A significant portion of spam e-mail content is just advertising, trying to convince the recipient to purchase some product online, or used in scams, such as stock scams or money mule job ads. But spam is also a significant carrier of malware. The e-mail may have an attached document, which, if opened, may exploit a software vulnerability to install malware on the user's system, as we discussed in the previous section. Or, it may have an attached Trojan horse program or scripting code that, if run, also installs malware on the user's system. Some trojans avoid the need for user agreement by exploiting a software vulnerability in order to install themselves, as we discuss next. Finally the spam may be used in a phishing attack, typically directing the user either to a fake Web site that mirrors some legitimate service, such as an online banking site, where it attempts to capture the user's login and password details, or to complete some form with sufficient personal details to allow the attacker to impersonate the user in an identity theft. All of these uses make spam e-mails a significant security concern. However, in many cases it requires the user's active choice to view the e-mail and any attached document or to permit the installation of some program, in order for the compromise to occur.

Trojan Horses

A Trojan horse is a useful, or apparently useful, program or utility containing hidden code that, when invoked, performs some unwanted or harmful function.

Trojan horse programs can be used to accomplish functions indirectly that the attacker could not accomplish directly. For example, to gain access to sensitive, personal information stored in the files of a user, an attacker could create a Trojan horse program that, when executed, scans the user's files for the desired sensitive information and sends a copy of it to the attacker via a Web form or e-mail or text message. The author could then entice users to run the program by incorporating it into a game or useful utility program and making it available via a known software distribution site or app store. This approach has been used recently with utilities that "claim" to be the latest antivirus scanner, or security update, for systems, but which are actually malicious trojans, often carrying payloads such as spyware that searches for banking credentials. Hence, users need to take precautions to validate the source of any software they install.

Trojan horses fit into one of three models:

- Continuing to perform the function of the original program and additionally performing a separate malicious activity
- Continuing to perform the function of the original program but modifying the function to perform malicious activity (e.g., a Trojan horse version of a login program that collects passwords) or to disguise other malicious activity (e.g., a Trojan horse version of a process-listing program that does not display certain processes that are malicious)
- Performing a malicious function that completely replaces the function of the original program

Some trojans avoid the requirement for user assistance by exploiting some software vulnerability to enable their automatic installation and execution. In this they share some features of a worm, but unlike it, they do not replicate. A prominent example of such an attack was the Hydraq Trojan used in Operation Aurora in 2009 and early 2010. This exploited a vulnerability in Internet Explorer to install itself and targeted several high-profile companies [SYMA13]. It was typically distributed either by spam e-mail or via a compromised Web site using a "drive-by-download."

10.6 PAYLOAD—SYSTEM CORRUPTION

Once malware is active on the target system, the next concern is what actions it will take on this system, that is, what payload does it carry. Some malware has a non-existent or nonfunctional payload. Its only purpose, either deliberate or due to accidental early release, is to spread. More commonly, it carries one or more payloads that perform covert actions for the attacker.

An early payload seen in a number of viruses and worms resulted in data destruction on the infected system when certain trigger conditions were met [WEAV03]. A related payload is one that displays unwanted messages or content on the user's system when triggered. More seriously, another variant attempts to inflict real-world damage on the system. All of these actions target the integrity of the computer system's software or hardware, or of the user's data. These changes may not occur immediately, but only when specific trigger conditions are met that satisfy their logic-bomb code.

As an alternative to just destroying data, some malware encrypts the user's data and demands payment in order to access the key needed to recover this information. This is sometimes known as **ransomware**. The PC Cyborg Trojan seen in 1989 was an early example of this. However, around mid-2006 a number of worms and trojans, such as the Gpcode Trojan, that used public-key cryptography with increasingly larger key sizes to encrypt data. The user needed to pay a ransom or to make a purchase from certain sites, in order to receive the key to decrypt this data. While earlier instances used weaker cryptography that could be cracked without paying the ransom, the later versions using public-key cryptography with large key sizes could not be broken this way.

Real-World Damage

A further variant of system corruption payloads aims to cause damage to physical equipment. The infected system is clearly the device most easily targeted. The Chernobyl virus not only corrupts data, it attempts to rewrite the BIOS code used to initially boot the computer. If it is successful, the boot process fails, and the system is unusable until the BIOS chip is either reprogrammed or replaced.

The Stuxnet worm targets some specific industrial control system software as its key payload [CHEN11]. If control systems using certain Siemens industrial control software with a specific configuration of devices are infected, then the worm replaces the original control code with code that deliberately drives the controlled equipment outside its normal operating range, resulting in the failure of the attached equipment. The centrifuges used in the Iranian uranium enrichment program were strongly suspected as the target, with reports of much higher than normal failure rates observed in them over the period when this worm was active. As noted in our earlier discussion, this has raised concerns over the use of sophisticated targeted malware for industrial sabotage.

Logic Bomb

A key component of data-corrupting malware is the logic bomb. The logic bomb is code embedded in the malware that is set to "explode" when certain conditions are met. Examples of conditions that can be used as triggers for a logic bomb are the presence or absence of certain files or devices on the system, a particular day of the week or date, a particular version or configuration of some software, or a particular user running the application. Once triggered, a bomb may alter or delete data or entire files, cause a machine halt, or do some other damage. All of the examples we describe in this section include such code.

10.7 PAYLOAD—ATTACK AGENT—ZOMBIE, BOTS

The next category of payload we discuss is where the malware subverts the computational and network resources of the infected system for use by the attacker. Such a system is known as a bot (robot), zombie, or drone, and secretly takes over another Internet-attached computer and then uses that computer to launch or manage attacks that are difficult to trace to the bot's creator. The bot is typically planted on hundreds or thousands of computers belonging to unsuspecting third parties. The collection of bots often is capable of acting in a coordinated manner; such a collection is referred to as a **botnet**. This type of payload attacks the integrity and availability of the infected system.

Uses of Bots

[HONE05] lists the following uses of bots:

- **Distributed denial-of-service (DDoS) attacks:** A DDoS attack is an attack on a computer system or network that causes a loss of service to users. We examine DDoS attacks in Section 10.10.

- **Spamming:** With the help of a botnet and thousands of bots, an attacker is able to send massive amounts of bulk e-mail (spam).

- **Sniffing traffic:** Bots can also use a packet sniffer to watch for interesting cleartext data passing by a compromised machine. The sniffers are mostly used to retrieve sensitive information like usernames and passwords.

- **Keylogging:** If the compromised machine uses encrypted communication channels (e.g., HTTPS or POP3S), then just sniffing the network packets on the victim's computer is useless because the appropriate key to decrypt the packets is missing. But by using a keylogger, which captures keystrokes on the infected machine, an attacker can retrieve sensitive information.

- **Spreading new malware:** Botnets are used to spread new bots. This is very easy since all bots implement mechanisms to download and execute a file via HTTP or FTP. A botnet with 10,000 hosts that acts as the start base for a worm or mail virus allows very fast spreading and thus causes more harm.

- **Installing advertisement add-ons and browser helper objects (BHOs):** Botnets can also be used to gain financial advantages. This works by setting up a fake Web site with some advertisements: The operator of this Web site negotiates a deal with some hosting companies that pay for clicks on ads. With the help of a botnet, these clicks can be "automated" so that instantly a few thousand bots click on the pop-ups. This process can be further enhanced if the bot hijacks the start-page of a compromised machine so that the "clicks" are executed each time the victim uses the browser.

- **Attacking IRC chat networks:** Botnets are also used for attacks against Internet Relay Chat (IRC) networks. Popular among attackers is the so-called clone attack: In this kind of attack, the controller orders each bot to connect a large number of clones to the victim IRC network. The victim is flooded by service requests from thousands of bots or thousands of channel-joins by these cloned bots. In this way, the victim IRC network is brought down, similar to a DDoS attack.

- **Manipulating online polls/games:** Online polls/games are getting more and more attention and it is rather easy to manipulate them with botnets. Since every bot has a distinct IP address, every vote will have the same credibility as a vote cast by a real person. Online games can be manipulated in a similar way.

Remote Control Facility

The remote control facility is what distinguishes a bot from a worm. A worm propagates itself and activates itself, whereas a bot is controlled from some central facility, at least initially.

A typical means of implementing the remote control facility is on an IRC server. All bots join a specific channel on this server and treat incoming messages as commands. More recent botnets tend to avoid IRC mechanisms and use covert communication channels via protocols such as HTTP. Distributed control mechanisms, using peer-to-peer protocols, are also used, to avoid a single point of failure.

Once a communications path is established between a control module and the bots, the control module can activate the bots. In its simplest form, the control module simply issues command to the bot that causes the bot to execute routines that are already implemented in the bot. For greater flexibility, the control module can issue update commands that instruct the bots to download a file from some Internet location and execute it. The bot in this latter case becomes a more general-purpose tool that can be used for multiple attacks.

10.8 PAYLOAD—INFORMATION THEFT—KEYLOGGERS, PHISHING, SPYWARE

We now consider payloads where the malware gathers data stored on the infected system for use by the attacker. A common target is the user's login and password credentials to banking, gaming, and related sites, which the attacker then uses to impersonate the user to access these sites for gain. Less commonly, the payload may target documents or system configuration details for the purpose of reconnaissance or espionage. These attacks target the confidentiality of this information.

Credential Theft, Keyloggers, and Spyware

Typically, users send their login and password credentials to banking, gaming, and related sites over encrypted communication channels (e.g., HTTPS or POP3S), which protect them from capture by monitoring network packets. To bypass this, an attacker can install a **keylogger**, which captures keystrokes on the infected machine to allow an attacker to monitor this sensitive information. Since this would result in the attacker receiving a copy of all text entered on the compromised machine, keyloggers typically implement some form of filtering mechanism that only returns information close to desired keywords (e.g., "login" or "password" or "paypal.com").

In response to the use of keyloggers, some banking and other sites switched to using a graphical applet to enter critical information, such as passwords. Since these do not use text entered via the keyboard, traditional keyloggers do not capture this information. In response, attackers developed more general **spyware** payloads, which subvert the compromised machine to allow monitoring of a wide range of activity on the system. This may include monitoring the history and content of browsing activity, redirecting certain Web page requests to fake sites controlled by the attacker, dynamically modifying data exchanged between the browser and certain Web sites of interest. All of which can result in significant compromise of the user's personal information.

Phishing and Identity Theft

Another approach used to capture a user's login and password credentials is to include a URL in a spam e-mail that links to a fake Web site controlled by the attacker, but which mimics the login page of some banking, gaming, or similar site. This is normally included in some message suggesting that urgent action is required by the user to authenticate his or her account, to prevent it being locked. If the user is careless, and doesn't realize that he or she is being conned, then following the link and supplying the requested details will certainly result in the attackers exploiting the user's account using the captured credentials.

More generally, such a spam e-mail may direct a user to a fake Web site controlled by the attacker or to complete some enclosed form and return to an e-mail accessible to the attacker, which is used to gather a range of private, personal information on the user. Given sufficient details, the attacker can then "assume" the user's identity for the purpose of obtaining credit or sensitive access to other resources. This is known as a **phishing** attack, which exploits social engineering to leverage user's trust by masquerading as communications from a trusted source [GOLD10].

Such general spam e-mails are typically widely distributed to very large numbers of users, often via a botnet. While the content will not match appropriate trusted sources for a significant fraction of the recipients, the attackers rely on it reaching sufficient users of the named trusted source, a gullible portion of whom will respond, for it to be profitable.

A more dangerous variant of this is the **spear-phishing** attack. This again is an e-mail claiming to be from a trusted source. However, the recipients are carefully researched by the attacker, and each e-mail is carefully crafted to suit its recipient specifically, often quoting a range of information to convince him or her of its authenticity. This greatly increases the likelihood of the recipient responding as desired by the attacker.

Reconnaissance and Espionage

Credential theft and identity theft are special cases of a more general reconnaissance payload, which aims to obtain certain types of desired information and return this to the attacker. These special cases are certainly the most common; however other targets are known. Operation Aurora in 2009 used a Trojan to gain access to and potentially modify source code repositories at a range of high-tech, security, and defense contractor companies [SYMA13]. The Stuxnet worm discovered in 2010 included capture of hardware and software configuration details in order to determine whether it had compromised the specific desired target systems. Early versions of this worm returned this same information, which was then used to develop the attacks deployed in later versions [CHEN11].

10.9 PAYLOAD—STEALTHING—BACKDOORS, ROOTKITS

The final category of payload we discuss concerns techniques used by malware to hide its presence on the infected system and to provide covert access to that system. This type of payload also attacks the integrity of the infected system.

Backdoor

A **backdoor**, also known as a **trapdoor**, is a secret entry point into a program that allows someone who is aware of the backdoor to gain access without going through the usual security access procedures. The backdoor is code that recognizes some special sequence of input or is triggered by being run from a certain user ID or by an unlikely sequence of events.

A backdoor is usually implemented as a network service listening on some nonstandard port that the attacker can connect to and issue commands through to be run on the compromised system.

It is difficult to implement operating system controls for backdoors in applications. Security measures must focus on the program development and software update activities, and on programs that wish to offer a network service.

Rootkit

A rootkit is a set of programs installed on a system to maintain covert access to that system with administrator (or root)[3] privileges, while hiding evidence of its presence to the greatest extent possible. This provides access to all the functions and services of the operating system. The rootkit alters the host's standard functionality in a malicious and stealthy way. With root access, an attacker has complete control of the system and can add or change programs and files, monitor processes, send and receive network traffic, and get backdoor access on demand.

---

[3]On UNIX systems, the administrator, or *superuser*, account is called root; hence the term *root access*.

A rootkit can make many changes to a system to hide its existence, making it difficult for the user to determine that the rootkit is present and to identify what changes have been made. In essence, a rootkit hides by subverting the mechanisms that monitor and report on the processes, files, and registries on a computer.

A rootkit can be classified using the following characteristics:

■ **Persistent:** Activates each time the system boots. The rootkit must store code in a persistent store, such as the registry or file system, and configure a method by which the code executes without user intervention. This means it is easier to detect, as the copy in persistent storage can potentially be scanned.

■ **Memory based:** Has no persistent code and therefore cannot survive a reboot. However, because it is only in memory, it can be harder to detect.

■ **User mode:** Intercepts calls to APIs (application program interfaces) and modifies returned results. For example, when an application performs a directory listing, the return results don't include entries identifying the files associated with the rootkit.

■ **Kernel mode:** Can intercept calls to native APIs in kernel mode.[4] The rootkit can also hide the presence of a malware process by removing it from the kernel's list of active processes.

■ **Virtual machine based:** This type of rootkit installs a lightweight virtual machine monitor and then runs the operating system in a virtual machine above it. The rootkit can then transparently intercept and modify states and events occurring in the virtualized system.

■ **External mode:** The malware is located outside the normal operation mode of the targeted system, in BIOS or system management mode, where it can directly access hardware.

This classification shows a continuing arms race between rootkit authors, who exploit ever more stealthy mechanisms to hide their code, and those who develop mechanisms to harden systems against such subversion or to detect when it has occurred.

10.10 COUNTERMEASURES

Malware Countermeasure Approaches

SP 800-83 lists four main elements of prevention: policy, awareness, vulnerability mitigation, and threat mitigation. Having a suitable policy to address malware prevention provides a basis for implementing appropriate preventative countermeasures.

---

[4]The kernel is the portion of the OS that includes the most heavily used and most critical portions of software. Kernel mode is a privileged mode of execution reserved for the kernel. Typically, kernel mode allows access to regions of main memory that are unavailable to processes executing in a less privileged mode and also enables execution of certain machine instructions that are restricted to the kernel mode.

One of the first countermeasures that should be employed is to ensure all systems are as current as possible, with all patches applied, in order to reduce the number of vulnerabilities that might be exploited on the system. The next is to set appropriate access controls on the applications and data stored on the system, to reduce the number of files that any user can access, and hence potentially infect or corrupt, as a result of them executing some malware code. These measures directly target the key propagation mechanisms used by worms, viruses, and some trojans.

The third common propagation mechanism, which targets users in a social engineering attack, can be countered using appropriate user awareness and training. This aims to equip users to be more aware of these attacks, and less likely to take actions that result in their compromise. SP 800-83 provides examples of suitable awareness issues.

If prevention fails, then technical mechanisms can be used to support the following threat mitigation options:

- **Detection:** Once the infection has occurred, determine that it has occurred and locate the malware.
- **Identification:** Once detection has been achieved, identify the specific malware that has infected the system.
- **Removal:** Once the specific malware has been identified, remove all traces of malware virus from all infected systems so that it cannot spread further.

If detection succeeds but either identification or removal is not possible, then the alternative is to discard any infected or malicious files and reload a clean backup version. In the case of some particularly nasty infections, this may require a complete wipe of all storage, and rebuild of the infected system from known clean media.

To begin, let us consider some requirements for effective malware countermeasures:

- **Generality:** The approach taken should be able to handle a wide variety of attacks.
- **Timeliness:** The approach should respond quickly so as to limit the number of infected programs or systems and the consequent activity.
- **Resiliency:** The approach should be resistant to evasion techniques employed by attackers to hide the presence of their malware.
- **Minimal denial-of-service costs:** The approach should result in minimal reduction in capacity or service due to the actions of the countermeasure software, and should not significantly disrupt normal operation.
- **Transparency:** The countermeasure software and devices should not require modification to existing (legacy) OSs, application software, and hardware.
- **Global and local coverage:** The approach should be able to deal with attack sources both from outside and inside the enterprise network.

Achieving all these requirements often requires the use of multiple approaches. Detection of the presence of malware can occur in a number of locations. It may occur on the infected system, where some host-based "antivirus" program is running, monitoring data imported into the system, and the execution and behavior of programs running on the system. Or, it may take place as part of the perimeter security mechanisms used in an organization's firewall and intrusion detection systems (IDSs). Lastly, detection may use distributed mechanisms that gather data from both host-based and perimeter sensors, potentially over a large number of networks and organizations, in order to obtain the largest scale view of the movement of malware.

Host–Based Scanners

The first location where antivirus software is used is on each end system. This gives the software the maximum access to information not only on the behavior of the malware as it interacts with the targeted system but also on the smallest overall view of malware activity. The use of antivirus software on personal computers is now widespread, in part caused by the explosive growth in malware volume and activity. Advances in virus and other malware technology, and in antivirus technology and other countermeasures, go hand in hand. Early malware used relatively simple and easily detected code, and hence could be identified and purged with relatively simple antivirus software packages. As the malware arms race has evolved, both the malware code and, necessarily, antivirus software have grown more complex and sophisticated.

[STEP93] identifies four generations of antivirus software:

- **First generation:** Simple scanners
- **Second generation:** Heuristic scanners
- **Third generation:** Activity traps
- **Fourth generation:** Full-featured protection

A **first-generation** scanner requires a malware signature to identify the malware. The signature may contain "wildcards" but matches essentially the same structure and bit pattern in all copies of the malware. Such signature-specific scanners are limited to the detection of known malware. Another type of first-generation scanner maintains a record of the length of programs and looks for changes in length as a result of virus infection.

A **second-generation** scanner does not rely on a specific signature. Rather, the scanner uses heuristic rules to search for probable malware instances. One class of such scanners looks for fragments of code that are often associated with malware. For example, a scanner may look for the beginning of an encryption loop used in a polymorphic virus and discover the encryption key. Once the key is discovered, the scanner can decrypt the malware to identify it, and then remove the infection and return the program to service.

Another second-generation approach is integrity checking. A checksum can be appended to each program. If malware alters or replaces some program without changing the checksum, then an integrity check will catch this change. To counter malware that is sophisticated enough to change the checksum when it alters a program, an encrypted hash function can be used. The encryption key is stored separately from the program so that the malware cannot generate a new hash code and encrypt that. By using a hash function rather than a simpler checksum, the malware is prevented from adjusting the program to produce the same hash code as before. If a protected list of programs in trusted locations is kept, this approach can also detect attempts to replace or install rogue code or programs in these locations.

Third-generation programs are memory-resident programs that identify malware by its actions rather than its structure in an infected program. Such programs the advantage that it is not necessary to develop signatures and heuristics for a wide array of malware. Rather, it is necessary only to identify the small set of actions that indicate that malicious activity is being attempted and then to intervene.

Fourth-generation products are packages consisting of a variety of antivirus techniques used in conjunction. These include scanning and activity trap components. In addition, such a package includes access control capability, which limits the ability of malware to penetrate a system and then limits the ability of a malware to update files in order to propagate.

The arms race continues. With fourth-generation packages, a more comprehensive defense strategy is employed, broadening the scope of defense to more general-purpose computer security measures. These include more sophisticated antivirus approaches. We now highlight two of the most important.

HOST-BASED BEHAVIOR-BLOCKING SOFTWARE   Unlike heuristics or fingerprint-based scanners, **behavior-blocking software** integrates with the operating system of a host computer and monitors program behavior in real time for malicious actions [CONR02, NACH02]. The behavior blocking software then blocks potentially malicious actions before they have a chance to affect the system. Monitored behaviors can include the following:

- Attempts to open, view, delete, and/or modify files
- Attempts to format disk drives and other unrecoverable disk operations
- Modifications to the logic of executable files or macros
- Modification of critical system settings, such as start-up settings
- Scripting of e-mail and instant messaging clients to send executable content
- Initiation of network communications

Because a behavior blocker can block suspicious software in real time, it has an advantage over such established antivirus detection techniques as fingerprinting or heuristics. There are literally trillions of different ways to obfuscate and rearrange the instructions of a virus or worm, many of which will evade detection by a fingerprint scanner or heuristic. But eventually, malicious code must make a well-defined request to the operating system. Given that the behavior blocker can intercept all such requests, it can identify and block malicious actions regardless of how obfuscated the program logic appears to be.

Behavior blocking alone has limitations. Because the malicious code must run on the target machine before all its behaviors can be identified, it can cause harm before it has been detected and blocked. For example, a new item of malware might shuffle a number of seemingly unimportant files around the hard drive before modifying a single file and being blocked. Even though the actual modification was blocked, the user may be unable to locate his or her files, causing a loss to productivity or possibly having worse consequences.

SPYWARE DETECTION AND REMOVAL Although general antivirus products include signatures to detect spyware, the threat this type of malware poses, and its use of stealthing techniques, means that a range of spyware specific detection and removal utilities exist. These specialize in the detection and removal of spyware, and provide more robust capabilities. Thus they complement, and should be used along with, more general antivirus products.

ROOTKIT COUNTERMEASURES Rootkits can be extraordinarily difficult to detect and neutralize, particularly so for kernel-level rootkits. Many of the administrative tools that could be used to detect a rootkit or its traces can be compromised by the rootkit precisely so that it is undetectable.

Countering rootkits requires a variety of network- and computer-level security tools. Both network- and host-based IDSs can look for the code signatures of known rootkit attacks in incoming traffic. Host-based antivirus software can also be used to recognize the known signatures.

Of course, there are always new rootkits and modified versions of existing rootkits that display novel signatures. For these cases, a system needs to look for behaviors that could indicate the presence of a rootkit, such as the interception of system calls or a keylogger interacting with a keyboard driver. Such behavior detection is far from straightforward. For example, antivirus software typically intercepts system calls.

Another approach is to do some sort of file integrity check. An example of this is RootkitRevealer, a freeware package from SysInternals. The package compares the results of a system scan using APIs with the actual view of storage using instructions that do not go through an API. Because a rootkit conceals itself by modifying the view of storage seen by administrator calls, RootkitRevealer catches the discrepancy.

If a kernel-level rootkit is detected, the only secure and reliable way to recover is to do an entire new OS install on the infected machine.

Perimeter Scanning Approaches

The next location where antivirus software is used is on an organization's firewall and IDS. It is typically included in e-mail and Web proxy services running on these systems. It may also be included in the traffic analysis component of an IDS. This gives the antivirus software access to malware in transit over a network connection to any of the organization's systems, providing a larger-scale view of malware activity. This software may also include intrusion prevention measures, blocking the flow of any suspicious traffic, thus preventing it reaching and compromising some target system, either inside or outside the organization.

However, this approach is limited to scanning the malware content, as it does not have access to any behavior observed when it runs on an infected system. Two types of monitoring software may be used:

- **Ingress monitors:** These are located at the border between the enterprise network and the Internet. They can be part of the ingress-filtering software of a border router or external firewall or a separate passive monitor. A honeypot can also capture incoming malware traffic. An example of a detection technique for an ingress monitor is to look for incoming traffic to unused local IP addresses.

■ **Egress monitors:** These can be located at the egress point of individual LANs on the enterprise network as well as at the border between the enterprise network and the Internet. In the former case, the egress monitor can be part of the egress-filtering software of a LAN router or switch. As with ingress monitors, the external firewall or a honeypot can house the monitoring software. Indeed, the two types of monitors can be collocated. The egress monitor is designed to catch the source of a malware attack by monitoring outgoing traffic for signs of scanning or other suspicious behavior.

Perimeter monitoring can also assist in detecting and responding to botnet activity by detecting abnormal traffic patterns associated with this activity. Once bots are activated and an attack is underway, such monitoring can be used to detect the attack. However, the primary objective is to try to detect and disable the botnet during its construction phase, using the various scanning techniques we have just discussed, identifying and blocking the malware that is used to propagate this type of payload.

PERIMETER WORM COUNTERMEASURES There is considerable overlap in techniques for dealing with viruses and worms. Once a worm is resident on a machine, antivirus software can be used to detect it, and possibly remove it. In addition, because worm propagation generates considerable network activity, perimeter network activity and usage monitoring can form the basis of a worm defense. Following [JHI07], we list six classes of worm defense that address the network activity it may generate:

A. **Signature-based worm scan filtering:** This type of approach generates a worm signature, which is then used to prevent worm scans from entering/leaving a network/host. Typically, this approach involves identifying suspicious flows and generating a worm signature. This approach is vulnerable to the use of polymorphic worms: Either the detection software misses the worm or, if it is sufficiently sophisticated to deal with polymorphic worms, the scheme may take a long time to react. [NEWS05] is an example of this approach.

B. **Filter-based worm containment:** This approach is similar to class A but focuses on worm content rather than a scan signature. The filter checks a message to determine if it contains worm code. An example is Vigilante [COST05], which relies on collaborative worm detection at end hosts. This approach can be quite effective but requires efficient detection algorithms and rapid alert dissemination.

C. **Payload-classification-based worm containment:** These network-based techniques examine packets to see if they contain a worm. Various anomaly detection techniques can be used, but care is needed to avoid high levels of false positives or negatives. An example of this approach, which looks for exploit code in network flows, is reported in [CHIN05]. This approach does not generate signatures based on byte patterns but rather looks for control and data flow structures that suggest an exploit.

D. **Threshold random walk (TRW) scan detection:** TRW exploits randomness in picking destinations to connect to as a way of detecting if a scanner is in operation [JUNG04]. TRW is suitable for deployment in high-speed, low-cost network devices. It is effective against the common behavior seen in worm scans.

E. **Rate limiting:** This class limits the rate of scanlike traffic from an infected host. Various strategies can be used, including limiting the number of new machines a host can connect to in a window of time, detecting a high connection failure rate, and limiting the number of unique IP addresses a host can scan in a window of time. [CHEN04] is an example. This class of countermeasures may introduce longer delays for normal traffic. This class is also not suited for slow, stealthy worms that spread slowly to avoid detection based on activity level.

F. **Rate halting:** This approach immediately blocks outgoing traffic when a threshold is exceeded either in outgoing connection rate or in diversity of connection attempts [JHI07]. The approach must include measures to quickly unblock mistakenly blocked hosts in a transparent way. Rate halting can integrate with a signature- or filter-based approach so that once a signature or filter is generated, every blocked host can be unblocked. Rate halting appears to offer a very effective countermeasure. As with rate limiting, rate-halting techniques are not suitable for slow, stealthy worms.

Distributed Intelligence Gathering Approaches

The final location where antivirus software is used is in a distributed configuration. It gathers data from a large number of both host-based and perimeter sensors, relays this intelligence to a central analysis system able to correlate and analyze the data, which can then return updated signatures and behavior patterns to enable all of the coordinated systems to respond and defend against malware attacks. A number of such systems have been proposed. We discuss one such approach in the remainder of this section.

Figure 10.4 shows an example of a distributed worm countermeasure architecture (based on [SIDI05]). The system works as follows (numbers in figure refer to numbers in the following list):

1. Sensors deployed at various network locations detect a potential worm. The sensor logic can also be incorporated in IDS sensors.

2. The sensors send alerts to a central server, which correlates and analyzes the incoming alerts. The correlation server determines the likelihood that a worm attack is being observed and the key characteristics of the attack.

3. The server forwards its information to a protected environment, where the potential worm may be sandboxed for analysis and testing.

4. The protected system tests the suspicious software against an appropriately instrumented version of the targeted application to identify the vulnerability.

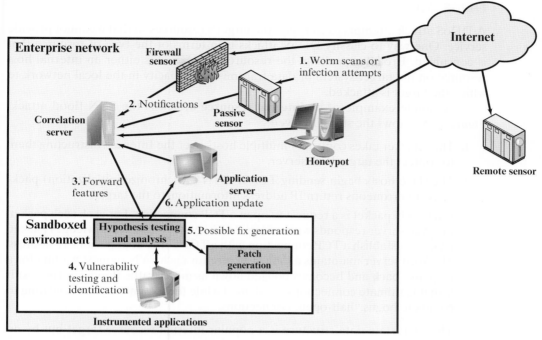

Figure 10.4   Placement of Worm Monitors

5. The protected system generates one or more software patches and tests these.

6. If the patch is not susceptible to the infection and does not compromise the application's functionality, the system sends the patch to the application host to update the targeted application.

10.11 DISTRIBUTED DENIAL OF SERVICE ATTACKS

A denial-of-service (DoS) attack is an attempt to prevent legitimate users of a service from using that service. When this attack comes from a single host or network node, then it is simply referred to as a DoS attack. A more serious threat is posed by a DDoS attack. DDoS attacks make computer systems inaccessible by flooding servers, networks, or even end-user systems with useless traffic so that legitimate users can no longer gain access to those resources. In a typical DDoS attack, a large number of compromised hosts are amassed to send useless packets.

This section is concerned with DDoS attacks. First, we look at the nature and types of attacks. Next, we examine methods by which an attacker is able to recruit a network of hosts for attack launch. Finally, this section looks at countermeasures.

DDoS Attack Description

A DDoS attack attempts to consume the target's resources so that it cannot provide service. One way to classify DDoS attacks is in terms of the type of resource that is consumed. Broadly speaking, the resource consumed is either an internal host resource on the target system or data transmission capacity in the local network to which the target is attacked.

A simple example of an **internal resource attack** is the SYN flood attack. Figure 10.5a shows the steps involved:

1. The attacker takes control of multiple hosts over the Internet, instructing them to contact the target Web server.
2. The slave hosts begin sending TCP/IP SYN (synchronize/initialization) packets, with erroneous return IP address information, to the target.
3. Each SYN packet is a request to open a TCP connection. For each such packet, the Web server responds with a SYN/ACK (synchronize/acknowledge) packet, trying to establish a TCP connection with a TCP entity at a spurious IP address. The Web server maintains a data structure for each SYN request waiting for a response back and becomes bogged down as more traffic floods in. The result is that legitimate connections are denied while the victim machine is waiting to complete bogus "half-open" connections.

The TCP state data structure is a popular internal resource target but by no means the only one. [CERT01] gives the following examples:

1. An intruder may attempt to use up available data structures that are used by the OS to manage processes, such as process table entries and process control information entries. The attack can be quite simple, such as a program that forks new processes repeatedly.
2. An intruder may attempt to allocate to itself large amounts of disk space by a variety of straightforward means. These include generating numerous e-mails, forcing errors that trigger audit trails, and placing files in shareable areas.

Figure 10.5b illustrates an example of an **attack that consumes data transmission resources**. The following steps are involved:

1. The attacker takes control of multiple hosts over the Internet, instructing them to send ICMP ECHO packets[5] with the target's spoofed IP address to a group of hosts that act as reflectors, as described subsequently.
2. Nodes at the bounce site receive multiple spoofed requests and respond by sending echo reply packets to the target site.
3. The target's router is flooded with packets from the bounce site, leaving no data transmission capacity for legitimate traffic.

---

[5]The Internet Control Message Protocol (ICMP) is an IP-level protocol for the exchange of control packets between a router and a host or between hosts. The ECHO packet requires the recipient to respond with an echo reply to check that communication is possible between entities.

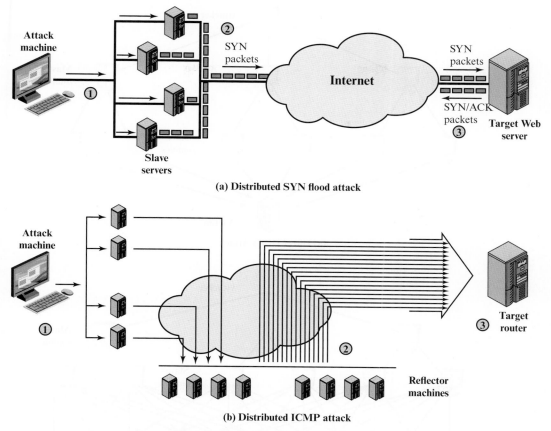

(a) Distributed SYN flood attack

(b) Distributed ICMP attack

Figure 10.5   Examples of Simple DDoS Attacks

Another way to classify DDoS attacks is as either direct or reflector DDoS attacks. In a **direct DDoS attack** (Figure 10.6a), the attacker is able to implant zombie software on a number of sites distributed throughout the Internet. Often, the DDoS attack involves two levels of zombie machines: master zombies and slave zombies. The hosts of both machines have been infected with malicious code. The attacker coordinates and triggers the master zombies, which in turn coordinate and trigger the slave zombies. The use of two levels of zombies makes it more difficult to trace the attack back to its source and provides for a more resilient network of attackers.

A **reflector DDoS attack** adds another layer of machines (Figure 10.6b). In this type of attack, the slave zombies construct packets requiring a response that contain the target's IP address as the source IP address in the packet's IP header. These packets are sent to uninfected machines known as reflectors. The uninfected machines respond with packets directed at the target machine. A reflector DDoS attack can easily involve more machines and more traffic than a direct DDoS attack and hence be more damaging. Further, tracing back the attack or filtering out the attack packets is more difficult because the attack comes from widely dispersed uninfected machines.

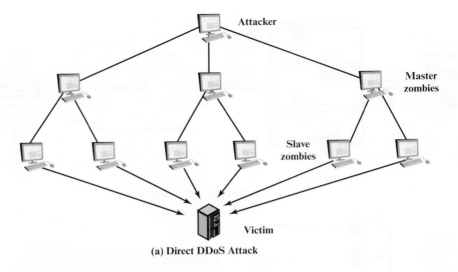

(a) Direct DDoS Attack

(b) Reflector DDoS Attack

Figure 10.6 Types of Flooding-Based DDoS Attacks

Constructing the Attack Network

The first step in a DDoS attack is for the attacker to infect a number of machines with zombie software that will ultimately be used to carry out the attack. The essential ingredients in this phase of the attack are the following:

1. Software that can carry out the DDoS attack. The software must be able to run on a large number of machines, must be able to conceal its existence, must

be able to communicate with the attacker or have some sort of time-triggered mechanism, and must be able to launch the intended attack toward the target.

2. A vulnerability in a large number of systems. The attacker must become aware of a vulnerability that many system administrators and individual users have failed to patch and that enables the attacker to install the zombie software.

3. A strategy for locating vulnerable machines, a process known as scanning.

In the scanning process, the attacker first seeks out a number of vulnerable machines and infects them. Then, typically, the zombie software that is installed in the infected machines repeats the same scanning process, until a large distributed network of infected machines is created. [MIRK04] lists the following types of scanning strategies:

- **Random:** Each compromised host probes random addresses in the IP address space, using a different seed. This technique produces a high volume of Internet traffic, which may cause generalized disruption even before the actual attack is launched.

- **Hit list:** The attacker first compiles a long list of potential vulnerable machines. This can be a slow process done over a long period to avoid detection that an attack is underway. Once the list is compiled, the attacker begins infecting machines on the list. Each infected machine is provided with a portion of the list to scan. This strategy results in a very short scanning period, which may make it difficult to detect that infection is taking place.

- **Topological:** This method uses information contained on an infected victim machine to find more hosts to scan.

- **Local subnet:** If a host is infected behind a firewall, that host then looks for targets in its own local network. The host uses the subnet address structure to find other hosts that would otherwise be protected by the firewall.

DDoS Countermeasures

In general, there are three lines of defense against DDoS attacks [CHAN02]:

- **Attack prevention and preemption (before the attack):** These mechanisms enable the victim to endure attack attempts without denying service to legitimate clients. Techniques include enforcing policies for resource consumption and providing backup resources available on demand. In addition, prevention mechanisms modify systems and protocols on the Internet to reduce the possibility of DDoS attacks.

- **Attack detection and filtering (during the attack):** These mechanisms attempt to detect the attack as it begins and respond immediately. This minimizes the impact of the attack on the target. Detection involves looking for suspicious patterns of behavior. Response involves filtering out packets likely to be part of the attack.

- **Attack source traceback and identification (during and after the attack):** This is an attempt to identify the source of the attack as a first step in preventing future attacks. However, this method typically does not yield results fast enough, if at all, to mitigate an ongoing attack.

The challenge in coping with DDoS attacks is the sheer number of ways in which they can operate. Thus, DDoS countermeasures must evolve with the threat.

10.12 KEY TERMS, REVIEW QUESTIONS, AND PROBLEMS

Key Terms

adware	e-mail virus	reflector DDoS attack
attack kit	flooders	rootkit
backdoor	keyloggers	scanning
behavior-blocking software	logic bomb	spear-phishing
blended attack	macro virus	spyware
boot sector infector	malicious software	stealth virus
bot	malware	trapdoor
botnet	metamorphic virus	Trojan horse
crimeware	mobile code	virus
direct DDoS attack	parasitic virus	worm
distributed denial of service	phishing	zombie
(DDoS)	polymorphic virus	zero-day exploit
downloader	ransomware	
drive-by-download		

Review Questions

10.1   What are three broad mechanisms that malware can use to propagate?

10.2   What is a blended attack?

10.3   What are typical phases of operation of a virus or worm?

10.4   Classify viruses based on the targets they try to infect.

10.5   List the features of macro viruses that enable them to infect scripting codes.

10.6   What functions does a worm perform during the propagation phase?

10.7   Give some examples of client side vulnerabilities that can be exploited by malware?

10.8   What is an "infection vector"?

10.9   Explain the difference between a keylogger and spyware with an example.

10.10 What kind of activities can be performed by an attacker using a rootkit? What makes it difficult to detect a rootkit?

10.11 Describe some malware countermeasure elements.

10.12 List three places malware mitigation mechanisms may be located.

10.13 Briefly describe the four generations of antivirus software.

10.14 List the activities that can be monitored by "behavior-blocking software".

10.15 What is the difference between a reflector DDoS attack and a direct DDoS attack?

Problems

10.1   There is a flaw in the virus program of Figure 10.1a. What is it?

10.2   The question arises as to whether it is possible to develop a program that can analyze a piece of software to determine if it is a virus. Consider that we have a program D that is supposed to be able to do that. That is, for any program P, if we run D(P), the result returned is TRUE (P is a virus) or FALSE (P is not a virus). Now consider the following program:

```
Program CV :=
    { . . .
    main-program :=
        {if D(CV) then goto next:
            else infect-executable;
        }
    next:
    }
```

In the preceding program, infect-executable is a module that scans memory for executable programs and replicates itself in those programs. Determine if D can correctly decide whether CV is a virus.

10.3   The following code fragments show a sequence of virus instructions and a metamorphic version of the virus. Describe the effect produced by the metamorphic code.

Original Code	Metamorphic Code
mov eax, 5	mov eax, 5
add eax, ebx	push edx
call [ebx]	jmp 0x89AB
	swap eax, ebx
	call [ebx]
	nop

10.4   The list of passwords used by the Morris worm is provided at this book's Premium Content Web site.
   a.   The assumption has been expressed by many people that this list represents words commonly used as passwords. Does this seem likely? Justify your answer.
   b.   If the list does not reflect commonly used passwords, suggest some approaches that Morris may have used to construct the list.

10.5   What type of malware is the following code fragment?

```
legitimate code
if data is Friday the 13th;
    crash_computer();
legitimate code
```

10.6   Consider the following situation and identify the type of software attack, if any:

You are the owner of a small business. After you login to your client server application with your credentials, you find that the data is displayed in the form of a jumbled collection of alphabets, numbers, special characters, and symbols. You are unpleasantly surprised and wonder what happened. You get a call after some time, and the person at the other end tells you that your system is hacked, and you can recover the data once you pay him a certain amount of money.

10.7   Assume that you have received an e-mail with an attachment from your friend's e-mail id. You access the e-mail using your work computer, and click on the attachment without screening it for malware. What threats might this pose to your work computer?

10.8 Suppose you observe that your home PC is responding very slowly to information requests from the net. And then you further observe that your network gateway shows high levels of network activity, even though you have closed your e-mail client, Web browser, and other programs that access the net. What types of malware could cause these symptoms? Discuss how the malware might have gained access to your system. What steps can you take to check whether this has occurred? If you do identify malware on your PC, how can you restore it to safe operation?

10.9 Suppose while browsing the Internet, you get a popup window stating that you need to install this software in order to clean your system as it is running low on resources. Since the message seems to be from a genuine OS vendor like Microsoft Windows or Mac iOS, you click the 'OK' button. How could your action harm your system? How can you fix the issue?

10.10 Suppose you have a new smartphone and are excited about the range of apps available for it. You read about a really interesting new game that is available for your phone. You do a quick Web search for it and see that a version is available from one of the free marketplaces. When you download and start to install this app, you are asked to approve the access permissions granted to it. You see that it wants permission to "Send SMS messages" and to "Access your address-book." Should you be suspicious that a game wants these types of permissions? What threat might the app pose to your smartphone? Should you grant these permissions and proceed to install it? What types of malware might it be?

10.11 Assume you receive an e-mail that appears to come from a senior manager of your company, with a subject indicating that it concerns a project that you are currently working on. When you view the e-mail, you see that it asks you to review the attached revised press release, supplied as a PDF document, to check that all details are correct before management releases it. When you attempt to open the PDF, the viewer pops up a dialog labeled "Launch File," indicating that "the file and its viewer application are set to be launched by this PDF file." In the section of this dialog labeled "File" there are a number of blank lines and finally the text "Click the 'Open' button to view this document." You also note that there is a vertical scroll-bar visible for this region. What type of threat might this pose to your computer system should you indeed select the "Open" button? How could you check your suspicions without threatening your system? What type of attack is this type of message associated with? How many people are likely to have received this particular e-mail?

10.12 Assume you work in a financial auditing company. An e-mail arrives in your inbox that appears to be from your chief auditor with the following content:

> "We have identified a few threats which pose potential danger to our information systems. In order to address this, our information security team has decided to ensure proper credentials of all the employees. Please cooperate and complete this process immediately by clicking the given link."

What kind of an attack is this e-mail attempting? How should you respond to such e-mails?

10.13 There are hundreds of unsolicited e-mails in your inbox. What kind of attack is this? Analyze related issues.

10.14 Suggest some methods of attacking the worm countermeasure architecture, discussed in Section 10.9, that could be used by worm creators. Suggest some possible countermeasures to these methods.

CHAPTER 11

INTRUDERS

LEARNING OBJECTIVES

After studying this chapter, you should be able to:

◆ Distinguish among various types of intruder behavior patterns.

◆ Understand the basic principles of and requirements for intrusion detection.

◆ Discuss the key features of intrusion detection systems.

◆ Define the intrusion detection exchange format.

◆ Explain the purpose of honeypots.

◆ Explain the mechanism by which hashed passwords are used for user authentication.

◆ Understand the use of the Bloom filter in password management.

A significant security problem for networked systems is hostile, or at least unwanted, trespass by users or software. User trespass can take the form of unauthorized logon to a machine or, in the case of an authorized user, acquisition of privileges or performance of actions beyond those that have been authorized. Software trespass can take the form of a virus, worm, or Trojan horse.

All these attacks relate to network security because system entry can be achieved by means of a network. However, these attacks are not confined to network-based attacks. A user with access to a local terminal may attempt trespass without using an intermediate network. A virus or Trojan horse may be introduced into a system by means of an optical disc. Only the worm is a uniquely network phenomenon. Thus, system trespass is an area in which the concerns of network security and computer security overlap.

Because the focus of this book is network security, we do not attempt a comprehensive analysis of either the attacks or the security countermeasures related to system trespass. Instead, in this Part we present a broad overview of these concerns.

This chapter covers the subject of intruders. First, we examine the nature of the attack and then look at strategies intended for prevention and, failing that, detection. Next we examine the related topic of password management.

11.1 INTRUDERS

One of the two most publicized threats to security is the intruder (the other is viruses), often referred to as a hacker or cracker. In an important early study of intrusion, Anderson [ANDE80] identified three classes of intruders:

■ **Masquerader:** An individual who is not authorized to use the computer and who penetrates a system's access controls to exploit a legitimate user's account

- **Misfeasor:** A legitimate user who accesses data, programs, or resources for which such access is not authorized, or who is authorized for such access but misuses his or her privileges
- **Clandestine user:** An individual who seizes supervisory control of the system and uses this control to evade auditing and access controls or to suppress audit collection

The masquerader is likely to be an outsider, the misfeasor generally is an insider, and the clandestine user can be either an outsider or an insider.

Intruder attacks range from the benign to the serious. At the benign end of the scale, there are many people who simply wish to explore internets and see what is out there. At the serious end are individuals who are attempting to read privileged data, perform unauthorized modifications to data, or disrupt the system.

[GRAN04] lists the following examples of intrusion:

- Performing a remote root compromise of an e-mail server
- Defacing a Web server
- Guessing and cracking passwords
- Copying a database containing credit card numbers
- Viewing sensitive data, including payroll records and medical information, without authorization
- Running a packet sniffer on a workstation to capture usernames and passwords
- Using a permission error on an anonymous FTP server to distribute pirated software and music files
- Dialing into an unsecured modem and gaining internal network access
- Posing as an executive, calling the help desk, resetting the executive's e-mail password, and learning the new password
- Using an unattended, logged-in workstation without permission

Intruder Behavior Patterns

The techniques and behavior patterns of intruders are constantly shifting, to exploit newly discovered weaknesses and to evade detection and countermeasures. Even so, intruders typically follow one of a number of recognizable behavior patterns, and these patterns typically differ from those of ordinary users. In the following, we look at three broad examples of intruder behavior patterns, to give the reader some feel for the challenge facing the security administrator.

HACKERS Traditionally, those who hack into computers do so for the thrill of it or for status. The hacking community is a strong meritocracy in which status is determined by level of competence. Thus, attackers often look for targets of opportunity and then share the information with others. A typical example is a break-in at a large financial institution reported in [RADC04]. The intruder took advantage of the fact that the corporate network was running unprotected services, some of which were not even needed. In this case, the key to the break-in was the pcAnywhere application. The manufacturer, Symantec, advertises this program as a remote control solution that enables secure connection to remote devices. But the attacker had an easy time gaining access to pcAnywhere; the administrator used the same three-letter username and password for the program. In this case, there was no intrusion detection system on the 700-node corporate network. The intruder was only discovered when a vice-president walked into her office and saw the cursor moving files around on her Windows workstation.

Benign intruders might be tolerable, although they do consume resources and may slow performance for legitimate users. However, there is no way in advance to know whether an intruder will be benign or malign. Consequently, even for systems with no particularly sensitive resources, there is a motivation to control this problem.

Intrusion detection systems (IDSs) and intrusion prevention systems (IPSs) are designed to counter this type of hacker threat. In addition to using such systems, organizations can consider restricting remote logons to specific IP addresses and/or use virtual private network technology.

One of the results of the growing awareness of the intruder problem has been the establishment of a number of computer emergency response teams (CERTs). These cooperative ventures collect information about system vulnerabilities and disseminate it to systems managers. Hackers also routinely read CERT reports. Thus, it is important for system administrators to quickly insert all software patches to discovered vulnerabilities. Unfortunately, given the complexity of many IT systems, and the rate at which patches are released, this is increasingly difficult to achieve without automated updating. Even then, there are problems caused by incompatibilities resulting from the updated software. Hence the need for multiple layers of defense in managing security threats to IT systems.

CRIMINALS Organized groups of hackers have become a widespread and common threat to Internet-based systems. These groups can be in the employ of a corporation or government but often are loosely affiliated gangs of hackers. Typically, these gangs are young, often Eastern European, Russian, or southeast Asian hackers who do business on the Web [ANTE06]. They meet in underground forums with names like DarkMarket.org and theftservices.com to trade tips and data and coordinate attacks. A common target is a credit card file at an e-commerce server. Attackers attempt to gain root access. The card numbers are used by organized crime gangs to purchase expensive items and are then posted to carder sites, where others can access and use the account numbers; this obscures usage patterns and complicates investigation.

Whereas traditional hackers look for targets of opportunity, criminal hackers usually have specific targets, or at least classes of targets in mind. Once a site is penetrated, the attacker acts quickly, scooping up as much valuable information as possible and exiting.

IDSs and IPSs can also be used for these types of attackers, but may be less effective because of the quick in-and-out nature of the attack. For e-commerce sites, database encryption should be used for sensitive customer information, especially credit cards. For hosted e-commerce sites (provided by an outsider service), the e-commerce organization should make use of a dedicated server (not used to support multiple customers) and closely monitor the provider's security services.

INSIDER ATTACKS Insider attacks are among the most difficult to detect and prevent. Employees already have access and knowledge about the structure and content of corporate databases. Insider attacks can be motivated by revenge or simply a feeling of entitlement. An example of the former is the case of Kenneth Patterson, fired from his position as data communications manager for American Eagle Outfitters. Patterson disabled the company's ability to process credit card purchases during five days of the holiday season of 2002. As for a sense of entitlement, there have always been many employees who felt entitled to take extra office supplies for home use, but this now extends to corporate data. An example is that of a vice-president of sales for a stock analysis firm who quit to go to a competitor. Before she left, she copied the customer database to take with her. The offender reported feeling no animus toward her former employee; she simply wanted the data because it would be useful to her.

Although IDS and IPS facilities can be useful in countering insider attacks, other more direct approaches are of higher priority. Examples include the following:

- Enforce least privilege, only allowing access to the resources employees need to do their job.
- Set logs to see what users access and what commands they are entering.
- Protect sensitive resources with strong authentication.
- Upon termination, delete employee's computer and network access.
- Upon termination, make a mirror image of employee's hard drive before reissuing it. That evidence might be needed if your company information turns up at a competitor.

In this section, we look at the techniques used for intrusion. Then we examine ways to detect intrusion.

Intrusion Techniques

The objective of the intruder is to gain access to a system or to increase the range of privileges accessible on a system. Most initial attacks use system or software vulnerabilities that allow a user to execute code that opens a backdoor into the system. Alternatively, the intruder attempts to acquire information that should have been protected. In some cases, this information is in the form of a user password. With knowledge of some other user's password, an intruder can log in to a system and exercise all the privileges accorded to the legitimate user.

Typically, a system must maintain a file that associates a password with each authorized user. If such a file is stored with no protection, then it is an easy matter to gain access to it and learn passwords. The password file can be protected in one of two ways:

- **One-way function:** The system stores only the value of a function based on the user's password. When the user presents a password, the system transforms that password and compares it with the stored value. In practice, the system usually performs a one-way transformation (not reversible), in which the password is used to generate a key for the one-way function and in which a fixed-length output is produced.
- **Access control:** Access to the password file is limited to one or a very few accounts.

If one or both of these countermeasures are in place, some effort is needed for a potential intruder to learn passwords. On the basis of a survey of the literature and interviews with a number of password crackers, [ALVA90] reports the following techniques for learning passwords:

1. Try default passwords used with standard accounts that are shipped with the system. Many administrators do not bother to change these defaults.
2. Exhaustively try all short passwords (those of one to three characters).
3. Try words in the system's online dictionary or a list of likely passwords. Examples of the latter are readily available on hacker bulletin boards.
4. Collect information about users, such as their full names, the names of their spouse and children, pictures in their office, and books in their office that are related to hobbies.
5. Try users' phone numbers, Social Security numbers, and room numbers.
6. Try all legitimate license plate numbers for this state.
7. Use a Trojan horse (described in Chapter 10) to bypass restrictions on access.
8. Tap the line between a remote user and the host system.

The first six methods are various ways of guessing a password. If an intruder has to verify the guess by attempting to log in, it is a tedious and easily countered means of attack. For example, a system can simply reject any login after three password attempts, thus requiring the intruder to reconnect to the host to try again. Under these circumstances, it is not practical to try more than a handful of passwords. However, the intruder is unlikely to try such crude methods. For example, if an intruder can gain access with a low level of privileges to an encrypted password file, then the strategy would be to capture that file and then use the encryption mechanism of that particular system at leisure until a valid password that provided greater privileges was discovered.

Guessing attacks are feasible, and indeed highly effective, when a large number of guesses can be attempted automatically and each guess verified, without the guessing process being detectable. Later in this chapter, we have much to say about thwarting guessing attacks.

The seventh method of attack listed earlier, the Trojan horse, can be particularly difficult to counter. An example of a program that bypasses access controls has been cited in [ALVA90]. A low-privilege user produced a game program and invited the system operator to use it in his or her spare time. The program did indeed play a game, but in the background it also contained code to copy the password file, which was unencrypted but access protected, into the user's file. Because the game was running under the operator's high-privilege mode, it was able to gain access to the password file.

The eighth attack listed, line tapping, is a matter of physical security.

Other intrusion techniques do not require learning a password. Intruders can get access to a system by exploiting attacks such as buffer overflows on a program that runs with certain privileges. Privilege escalation can be done this way as well.

We turn now to a discussion of the two principal countermeasures: detection and prevention. Detection is concerned with learning of an attack, either before or after its success. Prevention is a challenging security goal and an uphill battle at all times. The difficulty stems from the fact that the defender must attempt to thwart all possible attacks, whereas the attacker is free to try to find the weakest link in the defense chain and attack at that point.

11.2 INTRUSION DETECTION

Inevitably, the best intrusion prevention system will fail. A system's second line of defense is intrusion detection, and this has been the focus of much research in recent years. This interest is motivated by a number of considerations, including the following:

1. If an intrusion is detected quickly enough, the intruder can be identified and ejected from the system before any damage is done or any data are compromised. Even if the detection is not sufficiently timely to preempt the intruder, the sooner that the intrusion is detected, the less the amount of damage and the more quickly that recovery can be achieved.

2. An effective intrusion detection system can serve as a deterrent, so acting to prevent intrusions.

3. Intrusion detection enables the collection of information about intrusion techniques that can be used to strengthen the intrusion prevention facility.

Intrusion detection is based on the assumption that the behavior of the intruder differs from that of a legitimate user in ways that can be quantified. Of course, we cannot expect that there will be a crisp, exact distinction between an attack by an intruder and the normal use of resources by an authorized user. Rather, we must expect that there will be some overlap.

Figure 11.1 suggests, in very abstract terms, the nature of the task confronting the designer of an intrusion detection system. Although the typical behavior of an intruder differs from the typical behavior of an authorized user, there is an overlap in these behaviors. Thus, a loose interpretation of intruder behavior, which will catch more intruders, will also lead to a number of **false positives**, or authorized users identified as intruders. On the other hand, an attempt to limit false positives by a tight interpretation of intruder behavior will lead to an increase in **false negatives**, or intruders not identified as intruders. Thus, there is an element of compromise and art in the practice of intrusion detection.

In Anderson's study [ANDE80], it was postulated that one could, with reasonable confidence, distinguish between a masquerader and a legitimate user. Patterns of legitimate user behavior can be established by observing past history, and significant deviation from such patterns can be detected. Anderson suggests that the task of detecting a misfeasor (legitimate user performing in an unauthorized fashion) is more difficult, in that the distinction between abnormal and normal behavior may be small. Anderson concluded that such violations would be undetectable solely through the search for anomalous behavior. However, misfeasor behavior might nevertheless be detectable by intelligent definition of the class of conditions that suggest unauthorized use. Finally, the detection of the clandestine user was felt to

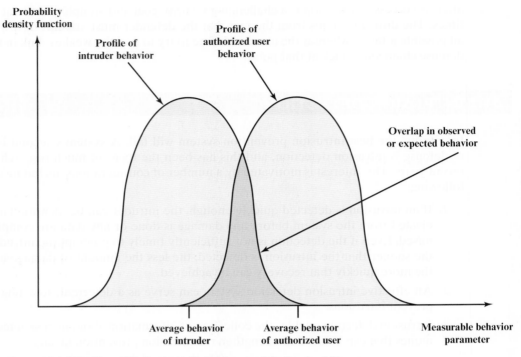

Figure 11.1   Profiles of Behavior of Intruders and Authorized Users

be beyond the scope of purely automated techniques. These observations, which were made in 1980, remain true today.

[PORR92] identifies the following approaches to intrusion detection:

1. **Statistical anomaly detection:**   Involves the collection of data relating to the behavior of legitimate users over a period of time. Then statistical tests are applied to observed behavior to determine with a high level of confidence whether that behavior is not legitimate user behavior.

   a. Threshold detection: This approach involves defining thresholds, independent of user, for the frequency of occurrence of various events.
   b. Profile based: A profile of the activity of each user is developed and used to detect changes in the behavior of individual accounts.

2. **Rule-based detection:**   Involves an attempt to define a set of rules or attack patterns that can be used to decide that a given behavior is that of an intruder. This is often referred to as **signature detection**.

In essence, anomaly approaches attempt to define normal, or expected, behavior, whereas signature-based approaches attempt to define proper behavior.

In terms of the types of attackers listed earlier, statistical anomaly detection is effective against masqueraders, who are unlikely to mimic the behavior patterns of the accounts they appropriate. On the other hand, such techniques may be unable to deal with misfeasors. For such attacks, rule-based approaches may be able to recognize events and sequences that, in context, reveal penetration. In practice, a system may exhibit a combination of both approaches to be effective against a broad range of attacks.

Audit Records

A fundamental tool for intrusion detection is the audit record. Some record of ongoing activity by users must be maintained as input to an intrusion detection system. Basically, two plans are used:

- **Native audit records:** Virtually all multiuser operating systems include accounting software that collects information on user activity. The advantage of using this information is that no additional collection software is needed. The disadvantage is that the native audit records may not contain the needed information or may not contain it in a convenient form.

- **Detection-specific audit records:** A collection facility can be implemented that generates audit records containing only that information required by the intrusion detection system. One advantage of such an approach is that it could be made vendor independent and ported to a variety of systems. The disadvantage is the extra overhead involved in having, in effect, two accounting packages running on a machine.

A good example of detection-specific audit records is one developed by Dorothy Denning [DENN87]. Each audit record contains the following fields:

- **Subject:** A subject initiates actions. A subject could be a user or a process acting on behalf of users or groups of users. Subjects may be grouped into different access classes, and these classes may overlap.

- **Action:** An action initiated by a subject refers to some object; for example, login, read, perform I/O, execute.

- **Object:** Actions are performed on or with objects. Examples include files, programs, messages, records, terminals, printers, and user- or program-created structures. When a subject is the recipient of an action, such as electronic mail, then that subject is considered an object. Objects may be grouped by type. Object granularity may vary by object type and by environment. For example, database actions may be audited for the database as a whole or at the record level.

- **Exception-Condition:** If an exception condition occurs, this field contains identifying information.

- **Resource-Usage:** This is a list, in which each item gives the amount used of some resource (e.g., number of lines printed or displayed, number of records read or written, processor time, I/O units used, session elapsed time).

- **Time-Stamp:** The time stamp specifies the data and time of an action.

Most user operations are made up of a number of elementary actions. For example, a file copy involves the execution of the user command, which includes doing access validation and setting up the copy, plus the read from one file, plus the write to another file. Consider the command

```
COPY GAME.EXE TO <Libray>GAME.EXE
```

issued by Smith to copy an executable file GAME from the current directory to the <Library> directory. The following audit records may be generated:

Smith	execute	<Library>COPY.EXE	0	CPU = 00002	11058721678
Smith	read	<Smith>GAME.EXE	0	RECORDS = 0	11058721679
Smith	execute	<Library>COPY.EXE	write-viol	RECORDS = 0	11058721680

In this case, the copy is aborted because Smith does not have write permission to <Library>.

The decomposition of a user operation into elementary actions has three advantages:

1. Because objects are the protectable entities in a system, the use of elementary actions enables an audit of all behavior affecting an object. Thus, the system can detect attempted subversions of access controls (by noting an abnormality in the number of exception conditions returned) and can detect successful subversions by noting an abnormality in the set of objects accessible to the subject.

2. Single-object, single-action audit records simplify the model and the implementation.

3. Because of the simple, uniform structure of the detection-specific audit records, it may be relatively easy to obtain this information or at least part of it by a straightforward mapping from existing native audit records to the detection-specific audit records.

Statistical Anomaly Detection

As was mentioned, statistical anomaly detection techniques fall into two broad categories: threshold detection and profile-based systems. Threshold detection involves counting the number of occurrences of a specific event type over an interval of time. If the count surpasses what is considered a reasonable number that one might expect to occur, then intrusion is assumed.

Threshold analysis, by itself, is a crude and ineffective detector of even moderately sophisticated attacks. Both the threshold and the time interval must be determined. Because of the variability across users, such thresholds are likely to generate either a lot of false positives or a lot of false negatives. However, simple threshold detectors may be useful in conjunction with more sophisticated techniques.

Profile-based anomaly detection focuses on characterizing the past behavior of individual users or related groups of users and then detecting significant deviations. A profile may consist of a set of parameters, so that deviation on just a single parameter may not be sufficient in itself to signal an alert.

The foundation of this approach is an analysis of audit records. The audit records provide input to the intrusion detection function in two ways. First, the designer must decide on a number of quantitative metrics that can be used to measure user behavior. An analysis of audit records over a period of time can be used to determine the activity profile of the average user. Thus, the audit records serve to define typical behavior. Second, current audit records are the input used to detect intrusion. That is, the intrusion detection model analyzes incoming audit records to determine deviation from average behavior.

Examples of metrics that are useful for profile-based intrusion detection are the following:

- **Counter:** A nonnegative integer that may be incremented but not decremented until it is reset by management action. Typically, a count of certain event types is kept over a particular period of time. Examples include the number of logins by a single user during an hour, the number of times a given command is executed during a single user session, and the number of password failures during a minute.

- **Gauge:** A nonnegative integer that may be incremented or decremented. Typically, a gauge is used to measure the current value of some entity. Examples include the number of logical connections assigned to a user application and the number of outgoing messages queued for a user process.

- **Interval timer:** The length of time between two related events. An example is the length of time between successive logins to an account.

- **Resource utilization:** Quantity of resources consumed during a specified period. Examples include the number of pages printed during a user session and total time consumed by a program execution.

Given these general metrics, various tests can be performed to determine whether current activity fits within acceptable limits. [DENN87] lists the following approaches that may be taken:

- Mean and standard deviation
- Multivariate
- Markov process
- Time series
- Operational

The simplest statistical test is to measure the **mean and standard deviation** of a parameter over some historical period. This gives a reflection of the average behavior and its variability. The use of mean and standard deviation is applicable to a wide variety of counters, timers, and resource measures. But these measures, by themselves, are typically too crude for intrusion detection purposes.

The **mean and standard deviation** of a parameter are simple measures to calculate. Taken over a given period of time, these values provide a measure average behavior and its variability. These two calculations can be applied to a variety of counters, timers, and resource measures. However, these two measures are inadequate, by themselves, for effective intrusion detection.

A **multivariate** calculation determines a correlate between two or more variables. Intruder behavior may be characterized with greater confidence by considering such correlations (for example, processor time and resource usage, or login frequency and session elapsed time).

A **Markov process** estimates transition probabilities among various states. As an example, this model might be used to look at transitions between certain commands.

A **time series** model observes and calculates values based on a sequence of events over time. Such models can be used to detect a series of actions that happens to rapidly or too slowly. A variety of statistical tests can be applied to characterize abnormal timing.

An **operational model** can be used to characterize what is considered abnormal, as opposed to performing an automated analysis of past audit records. Typically, fixed limits are defined and intrusion is suspected for an observation that is outside the limits. This type of approach works best where intruder behavior can be deduced from certain types of activities. For example, a large number of login attempts over a short period suggests an attempted intrusion.

As an example of the use of these various metrics and models, Table 11.1 shows various measures considered or tested for the Stanford Research Institute (SRI) Intrusion Detection System (IDES) [ANDE95, JAVI91] and the follow-on program Emerald [NEUM99].

The main advantage of the use of statistical profiles is that a prior knowledge of security flaws is not required. The detector program learns what is "normal" behavior and then looks for deviations. The approach is not based on system-dependent characteristics and vulnerabilities. Thus, it should be readily portable among a variety of systems.

Rule-Based Intrusion Detection

Rule-based techniques detect intrusion by observing events in the system and applying a set of rules that lead to a decision regarding whether a given pattern of activity is or is not suspicious. In very general terms, we can characterize all approaches as focusing on either anomaly detection or penetration identification, although there is some overlap in these approaches.

Rule-based anomaly detection is similar in terms of its approach and strengths to statistical anomaly detection. With the rule-based approach, historical audit records are analyzed to identify usage patterns and to automatically generate rules that describe those patterns. Rules may represent past behavior patterns of users, programs, privileges, time slots, terminals, and so on. Current behavior is then observed, and each transaction is matched against the set of rules to determine if it conforms to any historically observed pattern of behavior.

As with statistical anomaly detection, rule-based anomaly detection does not require knowledge of security vulnerabilities within the system. Rather, the scheme is based on observing past behavior and, in effect, assuming that the future will be like the past. In order for this approach to be effective, a rather large database of rules will be needed. For example, a scheme described in [VACC89] contains anywhere from 10^4 to 10^6 rules.

Table 11.1   Measures That May Be Used for Intrusion Detection

Measure	Model	Type of Intrusion Detected
Login and Session Activity		
Login frequency by day and time	Mean and standard deviation	Intruders may be likely to log in during off-hours
Frequency of login at different locations	Mean and standard deviation	Intruders may log in from a location that a particular user rarely or never uses
Time since last login	Operational	Break in on a "dead" account
Elapsed time per session	Mean and standard deviation	Significant deviations might indicate masquerader
Quantity of output to location	Mean and standard deviation	Excessive amounts of data transmitted to remote locations could signify leakage of sensitive data
Session resource utilization	Mean and standard deviation	Unusual processor or I/O levels could signal an intruder
Password failures at login	Operational	Attempted break-in by password guessing
Failures to login from specified terminals	Operational	Attempted break-in
Command or Program Execution Activity		
Execution frequency	Mean and standard deviation	May detect intruders, who are likely to use different commands, or a successful penetration by a legitimate user, who has gained access to privileged commands
Program resource utilization	Mean and standard deviation	An abnormal value might suggest injection of a virus or Trojan horse, which performs side-effects that increase I/O or processor utilization
Execution denials	Operational model	May detect penetration attempt by individual user who seeks higher privileges
File Access Activity		
Read, write, create, delete frequency	Mean and standard deviation	Abnormalities for read and write access for individual users may signify masquerading or browsing
Records read, written	Mean and standard deviation	Abnormality could signify an attempt to obtain sensitive data by inference and aggregation
Failure count for read, write, create, delete	Operational	May detect users who persistently attempt to access unauthorized files

Rule-based penetration identification takes a very different approach to intrusion detection. The key feature of such systems is the use of rules for identifying known penetrations or penetrations that would exploit known weaknesses. Rules can also be defined that identify suspicious behavior, even when the behavior is within the bounds of established patterns of usage. Typically, the rules used in these systems are specific to the machine and operating system. The most fruitful approach to developing such rules is to analyze attack tools and scripts collected on the Internet. These rules can be supplemented with rules generated by knowledgeable security personnel. In this latter case, the normal procedure is to interview system administrators and security analysts to collect a suite of known penetration scenarios and key events that threaten the security of the target system.

A simple example of the type of rules that can be used is found in NIDX, an early system that used heuristic rules that can be used to assign degrees of suspicion to activities [BAUE88]. Example heuristics are the following:

1. Suspicious activity: A user accesses the personal directory of another user and attempts to read files in that directory.
2. Suspicious activity: A user accesses the personal directory of another user and attempts to write or create files in that directory.
3. Expected activity: A user logs in after hours and accesses the same file he or she accessed during business hours.
4. Suspicious activity: A user opens a disk devices directly rather than relying on higher-level operating system utilities.
5. Suspicious activity: A user is logged onto one system twice at the same time.
6. Suspicious activity: A user makes copies of system programs.

The penetration identification scheme used in IDES is representative of the strategy followed. Audit records are examined as they are generated, and they are matched against the rule base. If a match is found, then the user's *suspicion rating* is increased. If enough rules are matched, then the rating will pass a threshold that results in the reporting of an anomaly.

The IDES approach is based on an examination of audit records. A weakness of this plan is its lack of flexibility. For a given penetration scenario, there may be a number of alternative audit record sequences that could be produced, each varying from the others slightly or in subtle ways. It may be difficult to pin down all these variations in explicit rules. Another method is to develop a higher-level model independent of specific audit records. An example of this is a state transition model known as USTAT [VIGN02, ILGU95]. USTAT deals in general actions rather than the detailed specific actions recorded by the UNIX auditing mechanism. USTAT is implemented on a SunOS system that provides audit records on 239 events. Of these, only 28 are used by a preprocessor, which maps these onto 10 general actions (Table 11.2). Using just these actions and the parameters that are invoked with each action, a state transition diagram is developed that characterizes suspicious activity. Because a number of different auditable events map into a smaller number of actions, the rule-creation process is simpler. Furthermore, the state transition diagram model is easily modified to accommodate newly learned intrusion behaviors.

The Base–Rate Fallacy

To be of practical use, an intrusion detection system should detect a substantial percentage of intrusions while keeping the false alarm rate at an acceptable level. If only a modest percentage of actual intrusions are detected, the system provides a false sense of security. On the other hand, if the system frequently triggers an alert when there is no intrusion (a false alarm), then either system managers will begin to ignore the alarms or much time will be wasted analyzing the false alarms.

Unfortunately, because of the nature of the probabilities involved, it is very difficult to meet the standard of high rate of detections with a low rate of false alarms. In general, if the actual numbers of intrusions is low compared to the

Table 11.2   USTAT Actions Versus SunOS Event Types

USTAT Action	SunOS Event Type
Read	open_r, open_rc, open_rtc, open_rwc, open_rwtc, open_rt, open_rw, open_rwt
Write	truncate, ftruncate, creat, open_rtc, open_rwc, open_rwtc, open_rt, open_rw, open_rwt, open_w, open_wt, open_wc, open_wct
Create	mkdir, creat, open_rc, open_rtc, open_rwc, open_rwtc, open_wc, open_wtc, mknod
Delete	rmdir, unlink
Execute	exec, execve
Exit	exit
Modify_Owner	chown, fchown
Modify_Perm	chmod, fchmod
Rename	rename
Hardlink	link

number of legitimate uses of a system, then the false alarm rate will be high unless the test is extremely discriminating. This is an example of a phenomenon known as the **base-rate fallacy**. A study of existing intrusion detection systems, reported in [AXEL00], indicated that current systems have not overcome the problem of the base-rate fallacy. See Appendix J for a brief background on the mathematics of this problem.

Distributed Intrusion Detection

Traditionally, work on intrusion detection systems focused on single-system stand-alone facilities. The typical organization, however, needs to defend a distributed collection of hosts supported by a LAN or internetwork. Although it is possible to mount a defense by using stand-alone intrusion detection systems on each host, a more effective defense can be achieved by coordination and cooperation among intrusion detection systems across the network.

Porras points out the following major issues in the design of a distributed intrusion detection system [PORR92]:

- A distributed intrusion detection system may need to deal with different audit record formats. In a heterogeneous environment, different systems will employ different native audit collection systems and, if using intrusion detection, may employ different formats for security-related audit records.

- One or more nodes in the network will serve as collection and analysis points for the data from the systems on the network. Thus, either raw audit data or summary data must be transmitted across the network. Therefore, there is a requirement to assure the integrity and confidentiality of these data. Integrity is required to prevent an intruder from masking his or her activities by altering the transmitted audit information. Confidentiality is required because the transmitted audit information could be valuable.

■ Either a centralized or decentralized architecture can be used. With a centralized architecture, there is a single central point of collection and analysis of all audit data. This eases the task of correlating incoming reports but creates a potential bottleneck and single point of failure. With a decentralized architecture, there are more than one analysis centers, but these must coordinate their activities and exchange information.

A good example of a distributed intrusion detection system is one developed at the University of California at Davis [HEBE92, SNAP91]. A similar approach has been taken for a project at Purdue [SPAF00, BALA98]. Figure 11.2 shows the overall architecture, which consists of three main components:

■ **Host agent module:** An audit collection module operating as a background process on a monitored system. Its purpose is to collect data on security-related events on the host and transmit these to the central manager.

■ **LAN monitor agent module:** Operates in the same fashion as a host agent module except that it analyzes LAN traffic and reports the results to the central manager.

■ **Central manager module:** Receives reports from LAN monitor and host agents, and processes and correlates these reports to detect intrusion.

The scheme is designed to be independent of any operating system or system auditing implementation. Figure 11.3 shows the general approach that is taken. The agent captures each audit record produced by the native audit collection system. A filter is applied that retains only those records that are of security interest. These records are then reformatted into a standardized format referred to as the host audit

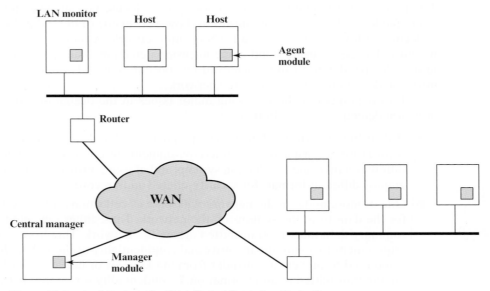

Figure 11.2   Architecture for Distributed Intrusion Detection

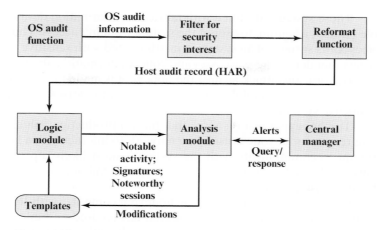

Figure 11.3 Agent Architecture

record (HAR). Next, a template-driven logic module analyzes the records for suspicious activity. At the lowest level, the agent scans for notable events that are of interest independent of any past events. Examples include failed file accesses, accessing system files, and changing a file's access control. At the next higher level, the agent looks for sequences of events, such as known attack patterns (signatures). Finally, the agent looks for anomalous behavior of an individual user based on a historical profile of that user, such as number of programs executed, number of files accessed, and the like.

When suspicious activity is detected, an alert is sent to the central manager. The central manager includes an expert system that can draw inferences from received data. The manager may also query individual systems for copies of HARs to correlate with those from other agents.

The LAN monitor agent also supplies information to the central manager. The LAN monitor agent audits host-host connections, services used, and volume of traffic. It searches for significant events, such as sudden changes in network load, the use of security-related services, and network activities such as *rlogin*.

The architecture depicted in Figures 11.2 and 11.3 is quite general and flexible. It offers a foundation for a machine-independent approach that can expand from stand-alone intrusion detection to a system that is able to correlate activity from a number of sites and networks to detect suspicious activity that would otherwise remain undetected.

Honeypots

A relatively recent innovation in intrusion detection technology is the honeypot. Honeypots are decoy systems that are designed to lure a potential attacker away from critical systems. Honeypots are designed to

- divert an attacker from accessing critical systems
- collect information about the attacker's activity
- encourage the attacker to stay on the system long enough for administrators to respond

These systems are filled with fabricated information designed to appear valuable but that a legitimate user of the system wouldn't access. Thus, any access to the honeypot is suspect. The system is instrumented with sensitive monitors and event loggers that detect these accesses and collect information about the attacker's activities. Because any attack against the honeypot is made to seem successful, administrators have time to mobilize and log and track the attacker without ever exposing productive systems.

The honeypot is a resource that has no production value. There is no legitimate reason for anyone outside the network to interact with a honeypot. Thus, any attempt to communicate with the system is most likely a probe, scan, or attack. Conversely, if a honeypot initiates outbound communication, the system has probably been compromised.

Initial efforts involved a single honeypot computer with IP addresses designed to attract hackers. More recent research has focused on building entire honeypot networks that emulate an enterprise, possibly with actual or simulated traffic and data. Once hackers are within the network, administrators can observe their behavior in detail and figure out defenses.

Honeypots can be deployed in a variety of locations. Figure 11.4 illustrates some possibilities. The location depends on a number of factors, such as the type of information the organization is interested in gathering and the level of risk that organizations can tolerate to obtain the maximum amount of data.

A honeypot outside the external firewall (**location 1**) is useful for tracking attempts to connect to unused IP addresses within the scope of the network. A honeypot at this location does not increase the risk for the internal network. The danger of having a compromised system behind the firewall is avoided. Further, because the honeypot attracts many potential attacks, it reduces the alerts issued by the firewall and by internal IDS sensors, easing the management burden. The disadvantage of an external honeypot is that it has little or no ability to trap internal attackers, especially if the external firewall filters traffic in both directions.

The network of externally available services, such as Web and mail, often called the DMZ (demilitarized zone), is another candidate for locating a honeypot (**location 2**). The security administrator must assure that the other systems in the DMZ are secure against any activity generated by the honeypot. A disadvantage of this location is that a typical DMZ is not fully accessible, and the firewall typically blocks traffic to the DMZ that attempts to access unneeded services. Thus, the firewall either has to open up the traffic beyond what is permissible, which is risky, or limit the effectiveness of the honeypot.

A fully internal honeypot (**location 3**) has several advantages. Its most important advantage is that it can catch internal attacks. A honeypot at this location can also detect a misconfigured firewall that forwards impermissible traffic from the Internet to the internal network. There are several disadvantages. The most serious of these is if the honeypot is compromised so that it can attack other internal systems. Any further traffic from the Internet to the attacker is not blocked by the firewall because it is regarded as traffic to the honeypot only. Another difficulty for this honeypot location is that, as with location 2, the firewall must adjust its filtering to allow traffic to the honeypot, thus complicating firewall configuration and potentially compromising the internal network.

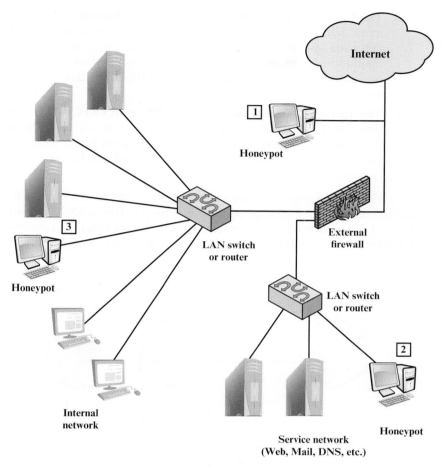

Figure 11.4   Example of Honeypot Deployment

Intrusion Detection Exchange Format

To facilitate the development of distributed intrusion detection systems that can function across a wide range of platforms and environments, standards are needed to support interoperability. Such standards are the focus of the IETF Intrusion Detection Working Group. The purpose of the working group is to define data formats and exchange procedures for sharing information of interest to intrusion detection and response systems and to management systems that may need to interact with them.

The working group issued the following RFCs in 2007:

■ **Intrusion Detection Message Exchange Requirements (RFC 4766):** This document defines requirements for the Intrusion Detection Message Exchange Format (IDMEF). The document also specifies requirements for a communication protocol for communicating IDMEF.

■ **The Intrusion Detection Message Exchange Format (RFC 4765):** This document describes a data model to represent information exported by intrusion detection systems and explains the rationale for using this model. An implementation of the data model in the Extensible Markup Language (XML) is presented, an XML Document Type Definition is developed, and examples are provided.

■ **The Intrusion Detection Exchange Protocol (RFC 4767):** This document describes the Intrusion Detection Exchange Protocol (IDXP), an application-level protocol for exchanging data between intrusion detection entities. IDXP supports mutual authentication, integrity, and confidentiality over a connection-oriented protocol.

Figure 11.5 illustrates the key elements of the model on which the intrusion detection message exchange approach is based. This model does not correspond to any particular product or implementation, but its functional components are the key elements of any IDS. The functional components are as follows:

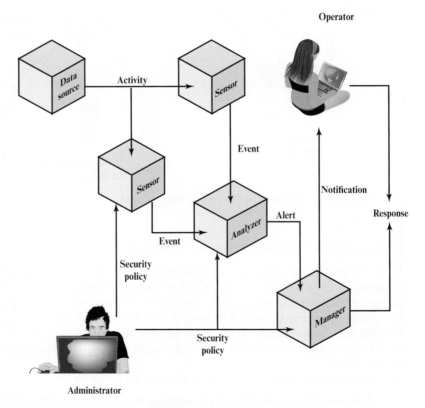

Figure 11.5   Model for Intrusion Detection Message Exchange

- **Data source:** The raw data that an IDS uses to detect unauthorized or undesired activity. Common data sources include network packets, operating system audit logs, application audit logs, and system-generated checksum data.

- **Sensor:** Collects data from the data source. The sensor forwards events to the analyzer.

- **Analyzer:** The ID component or process that analyzes the data collected by the sensor for signs of unauthorized or undesired activity or for events that might be of interest to the security administrator. In many existing IDSs, the sensor and the analyzer are part of the same component.

- **Administrator:** The human with overall responsibility for setting the security policy of the organization, and, thus, for decisions about deploying and configuring the IDS. This may or may not be the same person as the operator of the IDS. In some organizations, the administrator is associated with the network or systems administration groups. In other organizations, it's an independent position.

- **Manager:** The ID component or process from which the operator manages the various components of the ID system. Management functions typically include sensor configuration, analyzer configuration, event notification management, data consolidation, and reporting.

- **Operator:** The human that is the primary user of the IDS manager. The operator often monitors the output of the IDS and initiates or recommends further action.

In this model, intrusion detection proceeds in the following manner. The sensor monitors data sources looking for suspicious **activity**, such as network sessions showing unexpected telnet activity, operating system log file entries showing a user attempting to access files to which he or she is not authorized to have access, and application log files showing persistent login failures. The sensor communicates suspicious activity to the analyzer as an **event**, which characterizes an activity within a given period of time. If the analyzer determines that the event is of interest, it sends an **alert** to the manager component that contains information about the unusual activity that was detected, as well as the specifics of the occurrence. The manager component issues a **notification** to the human operator. A **response** can be initiated automatically by the manager component or by the human operator. Examples of responses include logging the activity; recording the raw data (from the data source) that characterized the event; terminating a network, user, or application session; or altering network or system access controls. The **security policy** is the predefined, formally documented statement that defines what activities are allowed to take place on an organization's network or on particular hosts to support the organization's requirements. This includes, but is not limited to, which hosts are to be denied external network access.

The specification defines formats for event and alert messages, message types, and exchange protocols for communication of intrusion detection information.

11.3 PASSWORD MANAGEMENT

The front line of defense against intruders is the password system. Virtually all multiuser systems require that a user provide not only a name or identifier (ID) but also a password. The password serves to authenticate the ID of the individual logging on to the system. In turn, the ID provides security in the following ways:

- The ID determines whether the user is authorized to gain access to a system. In some systems, only those who already have an ID filed on the system are allowed to gain access.

- The ID determines the privileges accorded to the user. A few users may have supervisory or "superuser" status that enables them to read files and perform functions that are especially protected by the operating system. Some systems have guest or anonymous accounts, and users of these accounts have more limited privileges than others.

- The ID is used in what is referred to as discretionary access control. For example, by listing the IDs of the other users, a user may grant permission to them to read files owned by that user.

The Vulnerability of Passwords

In this subsection, we outline the main forms of attack against password-based authentication and briefly outline a countermeasure strategy. The remainder of Section 11.3 goes into more detail on the key countermeasures.

Typically, a system that uses password-based authentication maintains a password file indexed by user ID. One technique that is typically used is to store not the user's password but a one-way hash function of the password, as described subsequently.

We can identify the following attack strategies and countermeasures:

- **Offline dictionary attack:** Typically, strong access controls are used to protect the system's password file. However, experience shows that determined hackers can frequently bypass such controls and gain access to the file. The attacker obtains the system password file and compares the password hashes against hashes of commonly used passwords. If a match is found, the attacker can gain access by that ID/password combination. Countermeasures include controls to prevent unauthorized access to the password file, intrusion detection measures to identify a compromise, and rapid reissuance of passwords should the password file be compromised.

- **Specific account attack:** The attacker targets a specific account and submits password guesses until the correct password is discovered. The standard countermeasure is an account lockout mechanism, which locks out access to the account after a number of failed login attempts. Typical practice is no more than five access attempts.

- **Popular password attack:** A variation of the preceding attack is to use a popular password and try it against a wide range of user IDs. A user's tendency is to choose a password that is easily remembered; this unfortunately makes the password easy to guess. Countermeasures include policies to inhibit the selection by users of common passwords and scanning the IP addresses of authentication requests and client cookies for submission patterns.

- **Password guessing against single user:** The attacker attempts to gain knowledge about the account holder and system password policies and uses that knowledge to guess the password. Countermeasures include training in and enforcement of password policies that make passwords difficult to guess. Such policies address the secrecy, minimum length of the password, character set, prohibition against using well-known user identifiers, and length of time before the password must be changed.

- **Workstation hijacking:** The attacker waits until a logged-in workstation is unattended. The standard countermeasure is automatically logging the workstation out after a period of inactivity. Intrusion detection schemes can be used to detect changes in user behavior.

- **Exploiting user mistakes:** If the system assigns a password, then the user is more likely to write it down because it is difficult to remember. This situation creates the potential for an adversary to read the written password. A user may intentionally share a password, to enable a colleague to share files, for example. Also, attackers are frequently successful in obtaining passwords by using social engineering tactics that trick the user or an account manager into revealing a password. Many computer systems are shipped with preconfigured passwords for system administrators. Unless these preconfigured passwords are changed, they are easily guessed. Countermeasures include user training, intrusion detection, and simpler passwords combined with another authentication mechanism.

- **Exploiting multiple password use:** Attacks can also become much more effective or damaging if different network devices share the same or a similar password for a given user. Countermeasures include a policy that forbids the same or similar password on particular network devices.

- **Electronic monitoring:** If a password is communicated across a network to log on to a remote system, it is vulnerable to eavesdropping. Simple encryption will not fix this problem, because the encrypted password is, in effect, the password and can be observed and reused by an adversary.

The Use of Hashed Passwords

A widely used password security technique is the use of hashed passwords and a salt value. This scheme is found on virtually all UNIX variants as well as on a number of other operating systems. The following procedure is employed (Figure 11.6a). To load a new password into the system, the user selects or is assigned a password. This password is combined with a fixed-length **salt value** [MORR79]. In older implementations, this value is related to the time at which the password is assigned to the user. Newer implementations use a pseudorandom or random number. The password and salt serve as inputs to a hashing algorithm to produce a fixed-length hash code. The hash algorithm is designed to be slow to execute to thwart attacks. The hashed password is then stored, together with a plaintext copy of the salt, in

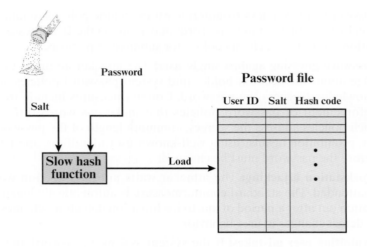

(a) Loading a new password

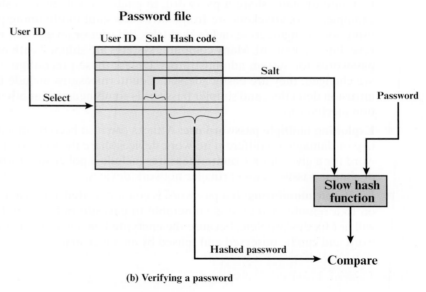

(b) Verifying a password

Figure 11.6 UNIX Password Scheme

the password file for the corresponding user ID. The hashed-password method has been shown to be secure against a variety of cryptanalytic attacks [WAGN00].

When a user attempts to log on to a UNIX system, the user provides an ID and a password (Figure 11.6b). The operating system uses the ID to index into the password file and retrieve the plaintext salt and the encrypted password. The salt and user-supplied password are used as input to the encryption routine. If the result matches the stored value, the password is accepted.

The salt serves three purposes:

- It prevents duplicate passwords from being visible in the password file. Even if two users choose the same password, those passwords will be assigned different salt values. Hence, the hashed passwords of the two users will differ.

- It greatly increases the difficulty of offline dictionary attacks. For a salt of length b bits, the number of possible passwords is increased by a factor of 2^b, increasing the difficulty of guessing a password in a dictionary attack.

- It becomes nearly impossible to find out whether a person with passwords on two or more systems has used the same password on all of them.

To see the second point, consider the way that an offline dictionary attack would work. The attacker obtains a copy of the password file. Suppose first that the salt is not used. The attacker's goal is to guess a single password. To that end, the attacker submits a large number of likely passwords to the hashing function. If any of the guesses matches one of the hashes in the file, then the attacker has found a password that is in the file. But faced with the UNIX scheme, the attacker must take each guess and submit it to the hash function once for each salt value in the dictionary file, multiplying the number of guesses that must be checked.

There are two threats to the UNIX password scheme. First, a user can gain access on a machine using a guest account or by some other means and then run a password guessing program, called a password cracker, on that machine. The attacker should be able to check many thousands of possible passwords with little resource consumption. In addition, if an opponent is able to obtain a copy of the password file, then a cracker program can be run on another machine at leisure. This enables the opponent to run through millions of possible passwords in a reasonable period.

UNIX IMPLEMENTATIONS Since the original development of UNIX, most implementations have relied on the following password scheme. Each user selects a password of up to eight printable characters in length. This is converted into a 56-bit value (using 7-bit ASCII) that serves as the key input to an encryption routine. The hash routine, known as crypt(3), is based on DES. A 12-bit salt value is used. The modified DES algorithm is executed with a data input consisting of a 64-bit block of zeros. The output of the algorithm then serves as input for a second encryption. This process is repeated for a total of 25 encryptions. The resulting 64-bit output is then translated into an 11-character sequence. The modification of the DES algorithm converts it into a one-way hash function. The crypt(3) routine is designed to discourage guessing attacks. Software implementations of DES are slow compared to hardware versions, and the use of 25 iterations multiplies the time required by 25.

This particular implementation is now considered woefully inadequate. For example, [PERR03] reports the results of a dictionary attack using a supercomputer. The attack was able to process over 50 million password guesses in about 80 minutes. Further, the results showed that for about $10,000 anyone should be able to do the same in a few months using one uniprocessor machine. Despite its known weaknesses, this UNIX scheme is still often required for compatibility with existing account management software or in multivendor environments.

There are other, much stronger, hash/salt schemes available for UNIX. The recommended hash function for many UNIX systems, including Linux, Solaris, and FreeBSD (a widely used open source UNIX implementation), is based on the MD5 secure hash algorithm (which is similar to, but not as secure as SHA-1). The MD5 crypt routine uses a salt of up to 48 bits and effectively has no limitations on password length. It produces a 128-bit hash value. It is also far slower than crypt(3). To achieve the slowdown, MD5 crypt uses an inner loop with 1000 iterations.

Probably the most secure version of the UNIX hash/salt scheme was developed for OpenBSD, another widely used open source UNIX. This scheme, reported in [PROV99], uses a hash function based on the Blowfish symmetric block cipher. The hash function, called Bcrypt, is quite slow to execute. Bcrypt allows passwords of up to 55 characters in length and requires a random salt value of 128 bits, to produce a 192-bit hash value. Bcrypt also includes a cost variable; an increase in the cost variable causes a corresponding increase in the time required to perform a Bcyrpt hash. The cost assigned to a new password is configurable, so that administrators can assign a higher cost to privileged users.

PASSWORD CRACKING APPROACHES The traditional approach to password guessing, or password cracking as it is called, is to develop a large dictionary of possible passwords and to try each of these against the password file. This means that each password must be hashed using each available salt value and then compared to stored hash values. If no match is found, then the cracking program tries variations on all the words in its dictionary of likely passwords. Such variations include backwards spelling of words, additional numbers or special characters, or sequence of characters,

An alternative is to trade off space for time by precomputing potential hash values. In this approach the attacker generates a large dictionary of possible passwords. For each password, the attacker generates the hash values associated with each possible salt value. The result is a mammoth table of hash values known as a **rainbow table**. For example, [OECH03] showed that using 1.4 GB of data, he could crack 99.9% of all alphanumeric Windows password hashes in 13.8 seconds. This approach can be countered by using a sufficiently large salt value and a sufficiently large hash length. Both the FreeBSD and OpenBSD approaches should be secure from this attack for the foreseeable future.

User Password Choices

Even the stupendous guessing rates referenced in the preceding section do not yet make it feasible for an attacker to use a dumb brute-force technique of trying all possible combinations of characters to discover a password. Instead, password crackers rely on the fact that some people choose easily guessable passwords.

Some users, when permitted to choose their own password, pick one that is absurdly short. One study at Purdue University [SPAF92a] observed password change choices on 54 machines, representing approximately 7000 user accounts. Almost 3% of the passwords were three characters or fewer in length. An attacker could begin the attack by exhaustively testing all possible passwords of length 3 or fewer. A simple remedy is for the system to reject any password choice of fewer than, say, six characters or even to require that all passwords be exactly eight characters in length. Most users would not complain about such a restriction.

Password length is only part of the problem. Many people, when permitted to choose their own password, pick a password that is guessable, such as their own name, their street name, a common dictionary word, and so forth. This makes the job of password cracking straightforward. The cracker simply has to test the password file against lists of likely passwords. Because many people use guessable passwords, such a strategy should succeed on virtually all systems.

One demonstration of the effectiveness of guessing is reported in [KLEI90]. From a variety of sources, the author collected UNIX password files, containing nearly 14,000 encrypted passwords. The result, which the author rightly characterizes as frightening, is shown in Table 11.3. In all, nearly one-fourth of the passwords were guessed. The following strategy was used:

1. Try the user's name, initials, account name, and other relevant personal information. In all, 130 different permutations for each user were tried.

2. Try words from various dictionaries. The author compiled a dictionary of over 60,000 words, including the online dictionary on the system itself, and various other lists as shown.

3. Try various permutations on the words from step 2. This included making the first letter uppercase or a control character, making the entire word uppercase, reversing the word, changing the letter "o" to the digit "zero," and so on. These permutations added another 1 million words to the list.

4. Try various capitalization permutations on the words from step 2 that were not considered in step 3. This added almost 2 million additional words to the list.

Thus, the test involved in the neighborhood of 3 million words. Using the fastest Thinking Machines implementation listed earlier, the time to encrypt all these words for all possible salt values is under an hour. Keep in mind that such a thorough search could produce a success rate of about 25%, whereas even a single hit may be enough to gain a wide range of privileges on a system.

ACCESS CONTROL One way to thwart a password attack is to deny the opponent access to the password file. If the encrypted password portion of the file is accessible only by a privileged user, then the opponent cannot read it without already knowing the password of a privileged user. [SPAF92a] points out several flaws in this strategy:

■ Many systems, including most UNIX systems, are susceptible to unanticipated break-ins. Once an attacker has gained access by some means, he or she may wish to obtain a collection of passwords in order to use different accounts for different logon sessions to decrease the risk of detection. Or a user with an account may desire another user's account to access privileged data or to sabotage the system.

■ An accident of protection might render the password file readable, thus compromising all the accounts.

Table 11.3 Passwords Cracked from a Sample Set of 13,797 Accounts [KLEI90]

Type of Password	Search Size	Number of Matches	Percentage of Passwords Matched	Cost/Benefit Ratio[a]
User/account name	130	368	2.7%	2.830
Character sequences	866	22	0.2%	0.025
Numbers	427	9	0.1%	0.021
Chinese	392	56	0.4%	0.143
Place names	628	82	0.6%	0.131
Common names	2239	548	4.0%	0.245
Female names	4280	161	1.2%	0.038
Male names	2866	140	1.0%	0.049
Uncommon names	4955	130	0.9%	0.026
Myths & legends	1246	66	0.5%	0.053
Shakespearean	473	11	0.1%	0.023
Sports terms	238	32	0.2%	0.134
Science fiction	691	59	0.4%	0.085
Movies and actors	99	12	0.1%	0.121
Cartoons	92	9	0.1%	0.098
Famous people	290	55	0.4%	0.190
Phrases and patterns	933	253	1.8%	0.271
Surnames	33	9	0.1%	0.273
Biology	58	1	0.0%	0.017
System dictionary	19683	1027	7.4%	0.052
Machine names	9018	132	1.0%	0.015
Mnemonics	14	2	0.0%	0.143
King James bible	7525	83	0.6%	0.011
Miscellaneous words	3212	54	0.4%	0.017
Yiddish words	56	0	0.0%	0.000
Asteroids	2407	19	0.1%	0.007
Total	62727	3340	24.2%	0.053

[a]Computed as the number of matches divided by the search size. The more words that needed to be tested for a match, the lower the cost/benefit ratio.

■ Some of the users have accounts on other machines in other protection domains, and they use the same password. Thus, if the passwords could be read by anyone on one machine, a machine in another location might be compromised.

Thus, a more effective strategy would be to force users to select passwords that are difficult to guess.

Password Selection Strategies

The lesson from the two experiments just described ([SPAF92a], [KLEI90]) is that, left to their own devices, many users choose a password that is too short or too easy to guess. At the other extreme, if users are assigned passwords consisting of eight randomly selected printable characters, password cracking is effectively impossible. But it would be almost as impossible for most users to remember their passwords. Fortunately, even if we limit the password universe to strings of characters that are reasonably memorable, the size of the universe is still too large to permit practical cracking. Our goal, then, is to eliminate guessable passwords while allowing the user to select a password that is memorable. Four basic techniques are in use:

- User education
- Computer-generated passwords
- Reactive password checking
- Proactive password checking

Users can be told the importance of using hard-to-guess passwords and can be provided with guidelines for selecting strong passwords. This **user education** strategy is unlikely to succeed at most installations, particularly where there is a large user population or a lot of turnover. Many users will simply ignore the guidelines. Others may not be good judges of what is a strong password. For example, many users (mistakenly) believe that reversing a word or capitalizing the last letter makes a password unguessable.

Computer-generated passwords also have problems. If the passwords are quite random in nature, users will not be able to remember them. Even if the password is pronounceable, the user may have difficulty remembering it and so be tempted to write it down. In general, computer-generated password schemes have a history of poor acceptance by users. FIPS PUB 181 defines one of the best-designed automated password generators. The standard includes not only a description of the approach but also a complete listing of the C source code of the algorithm. The algorithm generates words by forming pronounceable syllables and concatenating them to form a word. A random number generator produces a random stream of characters used to construct the syllables and words.

A **reactive password checking** strategy is one in which the system periodically runs its own password cracker to find guessable passwords. The system cancels any passwords that are guessed and notifies the user. This tactic has a number of drawbacks. First, it is resource intensive if the job is done right. Because a determined opponent who is able to steal a password file can devote full CPU time to the task for hours or even days, an effective reactive password checker is at a distinct disadvantage. Furthermore, any existing passwords remain vulnerable until the reactive password checker finds them.

The most promising approach to improved password security is a **proactive password checker**. In this scheme, a user is allowed to select his or her own password. However, at the time of selection, the system checks to see if the password is allowable and, if not, rejects it. Such checkers are based on the philosophy that, with sufficient guidance from the system, users can select memorable passwords from a fairly large password space that are not likely to be guessed in a dictionary attack.

The trick with a proactive password checker is to strike a balance between user acceptability and strength. If the system rejects too many passwords, users will complain that it is too hard to select a password. If the system uses some simple algorithm to define what is acceptable, this provides guidance to password crackers to refine their guessing technique. In the remainder of this subsection, we look at possible approaches to proactive password checking.

The first approach is a simple system for rule enforcement. For example, the following rules could be enforced:

- All passwords must be at least eight characters long.
- In the first eight characters, the passwords must include at least one each of uppercase, lowercase, numeric digits, and punctuation marks.

These rules could be coupled with advice to the user. Although this approach is superior to simply educating users, it may not be sufficient to thwart password crackers. This scheme alerts crackers as to which passwords *not* to try but may still make it possible to do password cracking.

Another possible procedure is simply to compile a large dictionary of possible "bad" passwords. When a user selects a password, the system checks to make sure that it is not on the disapproved list. There are two problems with this approach:

- **Space:** The dictionary must be very large to be effective. For example, the dictionary used in the Purdue study [SPAF92a] occupies more than 30 megabytes of storage.
- **Time:** The time required to search a large dictionary may itself be large. In addition, to check for likely permutations of dictionary words, either those words most be included in the dictionary, making it truly huge, or each search must also involve considerable processing.

Bloom Filter

A technique [SPAF92a, SPAF92b] for developing an effective and efficient proactive password checker that is based on rejecting words on a list has been implemented on a number of systems, including Linux. It is based on the use of a Bloom filter [BLOO70]. To begin, we explain the operation of the Bloom filter. A Bloom filter of order k consists of a set of k independent hash functions $H_1(x), H_2(x), \ldots, H_k(x)$, where each function maps a password into a hash value in the range 0 to $N - 1$. That is,

$$H_i(X_j) = y \quad 1 \le i \le k; \quad 1 \le j \le D; \quad 0 \le y \le N - 1$$

where

$X_j = j$th word in password dictionary
D = number of words in password dictionary

The following procedure is then applied to the dictionary:

1. A hash table of N bits is defined, with all bits initially set to 0.

2. For each password, its k hash values are calculated, and the corresponding bits in the hash table are set to 1. Thus, if $H_i(X_j) = 67$ for some (i, j), then the sixty-seventh bit of the hash table is set to 1; if the bit already has the value 1, it remains at 1.

When a new password is presented to the checker, its k hash values are calculated. If all the corresponding bits of the hash table are equal to 1, then the password is rejected. All passwords in the dictionary will be rejected. But there will also be some "false positives" (i.e., passwords that are not in the dictionary but that produce a match in the hash table). To see this, consider a scheme with two hash functions. Suppose that the passwords *undertaker* and *hulkhogan* are in the dictionary, but xG%#jj98 is not. Further suppose that

$$H_1(\text{undertaker}) = 25 \qquad H_1(\text{hulkhogan}) = 83 \qquad H_1(\text{xG\%\#jj98}) = 665$$

$$H_2(\text{undertaker}) = 998 \qquad H_2(\text{hulkhogan}) = 665 \qquad H_2(\text{xG\%\#jj98}) = 998$$

If the password xG%#jj98 is presented to the system, it will be rejected even though it is not in the dictionary. If there are too many such false positives, it will be difficult for users to select passwords. Therefore, we would like to design the hash scheme to minimize false positives. It can be shown that the probability of a false positive can be approximated by:

$$P \approx (1 - e^{kD/N})^k = (1 - e^{k/R})^k$$

or, equivalently,

$$R \approx \frac{-k}{\ln(1 - P^{1/k})}$$

where

$\quad k$ = number of hash functions
$\quad N$ = number of bits in hash table
$\quad D$ = number of words in dictionary
$\quad R$ = N/D, ratio of hash table size (bits) to dictionary size (words)

Figure 11.7 plots P as a function of R for various values of k. Suppose we have a dictionary of 1 million words and we wish to have a 0.01 probability of rejecting a password not in the dictionary. If we choose six hash functions, the required ratio is $R = 9.6$. Therefore, we need a hash table of 9.6×10^6 bits or about 1.2 MBytes of storage. In contrast, storage of the entire dictionary would require on the order of 8 MBytes. Thus, we achieve a compression of almost a factor of 7. Furthermore, password checking involves the straightforward calculation of six hash functions and is independent of the size of the dictionary, whereas with the use of the full dictionary, there is substantial searching.[1]

---

[1] The Bloom filter involves the use of probabilistic techniques. There is a small probability that some passwords not in the dictionary will be rejected. It is often the case in designing algorithms that the use of probabilistic techniques results in a less time-consuming or less complex solution, or both.

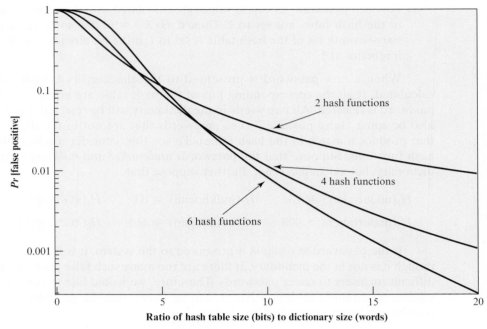

Figure 11.7   Performance of Bloom Filter

11.4 KEY TERMS, REVIEW QUESTIONS, AND PROBLEMS

Key Terms

audit record	intruder	rainbow table
base-rate fallacy	intrusion detection	rule-based intrusion detection
bloom filter	intrusion detection exchange	salt value
distributed intrusion detection	format	signature detection
honeypot	password	statistical anomaly detection

Review Questions

11.1   List and briefly define three classes of intruders.

11.2   Give examples of intrusion.

11.3   List the direct approaches that can be implemented to counter insider attacks.

11.4   Explain how statistical anomaly detection and rule-based intrusion detection are used to detect different types of intruders.

11.5   List the tests that can be performed to determine if a user's current activity is statistically anomalous or whether it is within acceptable parameters.

11.6   What is the base- rate fallacy?

11.7 List the possible locations where a honeypot can be deployed.

11.8 Briefly explain the purposes that a salt serves in the context of UNIX password management.

11.9 Discuss the threats to the UNIX password scheme.

Problems

11.1 In the context of an IDS, we define a false positive to be an alarm generated by an IDS in which the IDS alerts to a condition that is actually benign. A false negative occurs when an IDS fails to generate an alarm when an alert-worthy condition is in effect. Using the following diagram, depict two curves that roughly indicate false positives and false negatives, respectively.

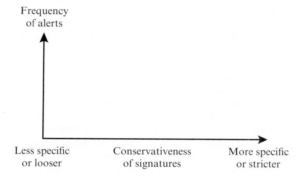

11.2 The overlapping area of the two probability density functions of Figure 11.1 represents the region in which there is the potential for false positives and false negatives. Further, Figure 11.1 is an idealized and not necessarily representative depiction of the relative shapes of the two density functions. Suppose there is 1 actual intrusion for every 1000 authorized users, and the overlapping area covers 1% of the authorized users and 50% of the intruders.

    a. Sketch such a set of density functions and argue that this is not an unreasonable depiction.

    b. Observe, that the overlap region equally covers authorized users and intruders. Does it always mean there is equal probability that events in this region are by authorized users and intruders? Justify your answer.

11.3 An example of a host-based intrusion detection tool is the tripwire program. This is a file integrity checking tool that scans files and directories on the system on a regular basis and notifies the administrator of any changes. It uses a protected database of cryptographic checksums for each file checked and compares this value with that recomputed on each file as it is scanned. It must be configured with a list of files and directories to check, and what changes, if any, are permissible to each. It can allow, for example, log files to have new entries appended, but not for existing entries to be changed. What are the advantages and disadvantages of using such a tool? Consider the problem of determining which files should only change rarely, which files may change more often and how, and which change frequently and hence cannot be checked. Hence consider the amount of work in both the configuration of the program and on the system administrator monitoring the responses generated.

11.4 A taxicab was involved in a fatal hit-and-run accident at night. Two cab companies, the Yellow and the Red, operate in the city. You are told that:

    ■ 85% of the cabs in the city are Yellow and 15% are Red.

    ■ A witness identified the cab as Red.

The court tested the reliability of the witness under the same circumstances that existed on the night of the accident and concluded that the witness was correct in identifying the color of the cab 90% of the time. What is the probability that the cab involved in the incident was Red rather than Yellow?

11.5 Explain the suitability or unsuitability of the following passwords:

<table>
<tr><td>a.</td><td>anu 1998</td><td>e.</td><td>Olympics</td></tr>
<tr><td>b.</td><td>5mimf2a3c (for 5 members in
my family 2 adults 3 children)</td><td>f.</td><td>msk@123</td></tr>
<tr><td></td><td></td><td>g.</td><td>g.0987654</td></tr>
<tr><td>c.</td><td>Coimbatore16</td><td>h.</td><td>iamking</td></tr>
<tr><td>d.</td><td>Windows</td><td></td><td></td></tr>
</table>

11.6 An early attempt to force users to use less predictable passwords involved computer-supplied passwords. The passwords were eight characters long and were taken from the character set consisting of lowercase letters and digits. They were generated by a pseudorandom number generator with 2^{15} possible starting values. Using the technology of the time, the time required to search through all character strings of length 8 from a 36-character alphabet was 112 years. Unfortunately, this is not a true reflection of the actual security of the system. Explain the problem.

11.7 Assume that passwords are selected from five-character combinations of 26 alphabetic characters. Assume that an adversary is able to attempt passwords at a rate of one per second.

   a. Assuming no feedback to the adversary until each attempt has been completed, what is the expected time to discover the correct password?
   b. Assuming feedback to the adversary flagging an error as each incorrect character is entered, what is the expected time to discover the correct password?

11.8 Assume that source elements of length k are mapped in some uniform fashion into a target elements of length p. If each digit can take on one of r values, then the number of source elements is r^k and the number of target elements is the smaller number r^p. A particular source element x_i is mapped to a particular target element y_j.

   a. What is the probability that the correct source element can be selected by an adversary on one try?
   b. What is the probability that a different source element $x_k (x_i \neq x_k)$ that results in the same target element, y_j, could be produced by an adversary?
   c. What is the probability that the correct target element can be produced by an adversary on one try?

11.9 A phonetic password generator picks two segments randomly for each six-letter password. The form of each segment is C9VC (consonant, digit, vowel, consonant), where $V = <$a, e, i, o, u$>$ and $C \neq V$.

   a. What is the total password population?
   b. What is the probability of an adversary guessing a password correctly?

11.10 Assume that passwords are limited to the use of the 95 printable ASCII characters and that all passwords are 12 characters in length. Assume a password cracker with an encryption rate of 6.4 million encryptions per second. How long will it take to test exhaustively all possible passwords on a UNIX system?

11.11 Because of the known risks of the UNIX password system, the SunOS-4.0 documentation recommends that the password file be removed and replaced with a publicly readable file called /etc/publickey. An entry in the file for user A consists of a user's identifier ID_A, the user's public key, PU_a, and the corresponding private key PR_a. This private key is encrypted using DES with a key derived from the user's login password P_a. When A logs in, the system decrypts $E(P_a, PR_a)$ to obtain PR_a.

   a. The system then verifies that P_a was correctly supplied. How?
   b. How can an opponent attack this system?

11.12 The encryption scheme used for UNIX passwords is one way; it is not possible to reverse it. Therefore, would it be accurate to say that this is, in fact, a hash code rather than an encryption of the password?

11.13 It was stated that the inclusion of the salt in the UNIX password scheme increases the difficulty of guessing by a factor of 4096. But the salt is stored in plaintext in the same entry as the corresponding ciphertext password. Therefore, those two characters are known to the attacker and need not be guessed. Why is it asserted that the salt increases security?

11.14 Assuming that you have successfully answered the preceding problem and understand the significance of the salt, here is another question. Wouldn't it be possible to thwart completely all password crackers by dramatically increasing the salt size to, say, 24 or 48 bits?

11.15 Consider the Bloom filter discussed in Section 11.3. Define k = number of hash functions; N = number of bits in hash table; and D = number of words in dictionary.
   a. Show that the expected number of bits in the hash table that are equal to zero is expressed as

$$\phi = \left(1 - \frac{k}{N}\right)^D$$

   b. Show that the probability that an input word, not in the dictionary, will be falsely accepted as being in the dictionary is

$$P = (1 - \phi)^k$$

   c. Show that the preceding expression can be approximated as

$$P \approx (1 - e^{-kD/N})^k$$

11.16 Design a file access system to allow certain users read and write access to files, depending on authorization set up by the system. The instructions should be of the format:

ReadFile(F1, User A):   User A has read access to file F1
WriteFile(F2, User A):   User A has write access to file F2
ExecuteFile(F3, User B):   User B has execute access to file F3

Each file has a *header record,* which contains authorization privileges; that is, a list of users who can read and write. The file is to be encrypted by a key that is not shared by the users but known only to the system.

CHAPTER 12

FIREWALLS

LEARNING OBJECTIVES

After studying this chapter, you should be able to:

◆ Explain the role of firewalls as part of a computer and network security strategy.

◆ List the key characteristics of firewalls.

◆ Discuss the various basing options for firewalls.

◆ Understand the relative merits of various choices for firewall location and configurations.

Firewalls can be an effective means of protecting a local system or network of systems from network-based security threats while at the same time affording access to the outside world via wide area networks and the Internet.

12.1 THE NEED FOR FIREWALLS

Information systems in corporations, government agencies, and other organizations have undergone a steady evolution. The following are notable developments:

■ Centralized data processing system, with a central mainframe supporting a number of directly connected terminals

■ Local area networks (LANs) interconnecting PCs and terminals to each other and the mainframe

■ Premises network, consisting of a number of LANs, interconnecting PCs, servers, and perhaps a mainframe or two

■ Enterprise-wide network, consisting of multiple, geographically distributed premises networks interconnected by a private wide area network (WAN)

■ Internet connectivity, in which the various premises networks all hook into the Internet and may or may not also be connected by a private WAN

Internet connectivity is no longer optional for organizations. The information and services available are essential to the organization. Moreover, individual users within the organization want and need Internet access, and if this is not provided via their LAN, they will use dial-up capability from their PC to an Internet service provider (ISP). However, while Internet access provides benefits to the organization, it enables the outside world to reach and interact with local network assets. This creates a threat to the organization. While it is possible to equip each workstation and server on the premises network with strong security features, such as intrusion protection, this may not be sufficient and in some cases is not cost-effective. Consider a network with hundreds or even thousands of systems, running various operating systems, such as different versions of UNIX and Windows. When a security flaw is discovered, each potentially affected system must be upgraded to fix that flaw. This requires scaleable configuration management and aggressive patching to function effectively. While difficult, this is possible and is necessary if only host-based security is used. A widely accepted alternative or at least complement to host-based security services is the firewall. The firewall is inserted between the premises network and the Internet to establish a controlled link and to erect an outer security wall or perimeter. The aim of this perimeter is to protect the premises network from Internet-based attacks and to provide a single choke point where security and auditing can be imposed. The firewall may be a single computer system or a set of two or more systems that cooperate to perform the firewall function.

The firewall, then, provides an additional layer of defense, insulating the internal systems from external networks. This follows the classic military doctrine of "defense in depth," which is just as applicable to IT security.

12.2 FIREWALL CHARACTERISTICS AND ACCESS POLICY

[BELL94b] lists the following design goals for a firewall:

1. All traffic from inside to outside, and vice versa, must pass through the firewall. This is achieved by physically blocking all access to the local network except via the firewall. Various configurations are possible, as explained later in this chapter.

2. Only authorized traffic, as defined by the local security policy, will be allowed to pass. Various types of firewalls are used, which implement various types of security policies, as explained later in this chapter.

3. The firewall itself is immune to penetration. This implies the use of a hardened system with a secured operating system. Trusted computer systems are suitable for hosting a firewall and often required in government applications.

A critical component in the planning and implementation of a firewall is specifying a suitable access policy. This lists the types of traffic authorized to pass through the firewall, including address ranges, protocols, applications, and content types. This policy should be developed from the organization's information security risk assessment and policy. This policy should be developed from a broad specification of which traffic types the organization needs to support. It is then refined to detail the filter elements we discuss next, which can then be implemented within an appropriate firewall topology.

SP 800-41-1 (*Guidelines on Firewalls and Firewall Policy*, September 2009) lists a range of characteristics that a firewall access policy could use to filter traffic, including:

■ **IP Address and Protocol Values:** Controls access based on the source or destination addresses and port numbers, direction of flow being inbound or outbound, and other network and transport layer characteristics. This type of filtering is used by packet filter and stateful inspection firewalls. It is typically used to limit access to specific services.

- **Application Protocol:** Controls access on the basis of authorized application protocol data. This type of filtering is used by an application-level gateway that relays and monitors the exchange of information for specific application protocols, for example, checking SMTP e-mail for spam, or HTPP Web requests to authorized sites only.

- **User Identity:** Controls access based on the users identity, typically for inside users who identify themselves using some form of secure authentication technology, such as IPSec (Chapter 9).

- **Network Activity:** Controls access based on considerations such as the time or request, for example, only in business hours; rate of requests, for example, to detect scanning attempts; or other activity patterns.

Before proceeding to the details of firewall types and configurations, it is best to summarize what one can expect from a firewall. The following capabilities are within the scope of a firewall:

1. A firewall defines a single choke point that keeps unauthorized users out of the protected network, prohibits potentially vulnerable services from entering or leaving the network, and provides protection from various kinds of IP spoofing and routing attacks. The use of a single choke point simplifies security management because security capabilities are consolidated on a single system or set of systems.

2. A firewall provides a location for monitoring security-related events. Audits and alarms can be implemented on the firewall system.

3. A firewall is a convenient platform for several Internet functions that are not security related. These include a network address translator, which maps local addresses to Internet addresses, and a network management function that audits or logs Internet usage.

4. A firewall can serve as the platform for IPsec. Using the tunnel mode capability described in Chapter 9, the firewall can be used to implement virtual private networks.

Firewalls have their limitations, including the following:

1. The firewall cannot protect against attacks that bypass the firewall. Internal systems may have dial-out capability to connect to an ISP. An internal LAN may support a modem pool that provides dial-in capability for traveling employees and telecommuters.

2. The firewall may not protect fully against internal threats, such as a disgruntled employee or an employee who unwittingly cooperates with an external attacker.

3. An improperly secured wireless LAN may be accessed from outside the organization. An internal firewall that separates portions of an enterprise network cannot guard against wireless communications between local systems on different sides of the internal firewall.

4. A laptop, PDA, or portable storage device may be used and infected outside the corporate network, and then attached and used internally.

12.3 TYPES OF FIREWALLS

A firewall can monitor network traffic at a number of levels, from low-level network packets either individually or as part of a flow, to all traffic within a transport connection, up to inspecting details of application protocols. The choice of which level is appropriate is determined by the desired firewall access policy. It can operate as a positive filter, allowing to pass only packets that meet specific criteria, or as a negative filter, rejecting any packet that meets certain criteria. The criteria implement the access policy for the firewall, that we discussed in the previous section. Depending on the type of firewall, it may examine one or more protocol headers in each packet, the payload of each packet, or the pattern generated by a sequence of packets. In this section, we look at the principal types of firewalls.

Packet Filtering Firewall

A packet filtering firewall applies a set of rules to each incoming and outgoing IP packet and then forwards or discards the packet (Figure 12.1b). The firewall is typically configured to filter packets going in both directions (from and to the internal network). Filtering rules are based on information contained in a network packet:

- **Source IP address:** The IP address of the system that originated the IP packet (e.g., 192.178.1.1)
- **Destination IP address:** The IP address of the system the IP packet is trying to reach (e.g., 192.168.1.2)
- **Source and destination transport-level address:** The transport-level (e.g., TCP or UDP) port number, which defines applications such as SNMP or TELNET
- **IP protocol field:** Defines the transport protocol
- **Interface:** For a firewall with three or more ports, which interface of the firewall the packet came from or which interface of the firewall the packet is destined for

The packet filter is typically set up as a list of rules based on matches to fields in the IP or TCP header. If there is a match to one of the rules, that rule is invoked to determine whether to forward or discard the packet. If there is no match to any rule, then a default action is taken. Two default policies are possible:

- **Default = discard:** That which is not expressly permitted is prohibited.
- **Default = forward:** That which is not expressly prohibited is permitted.

The default discard policy is more conservative. Initially, everything is blocked, and services must be added on a case-by-case basis. This policy is more visible to users, who are more likely to see the firewall as a hindrance. However, this is the policy likely to be preferred by businesses and government organizations. Further, visibility to users diminishes as rules are created. The default forward policy increases ease of use for end users but provides reduced security; the security administrator must, in essence, react to each new security threat as it becomes known. This policy may be used by generally more open organizations, such as universities.

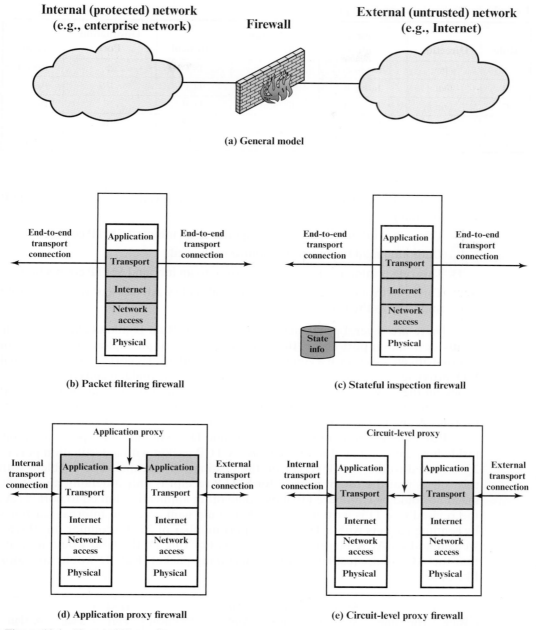

Figure 12.1 Types of Firewalls

Table 12.1 is a simplified example of a ruleset for SMTP traffic. The goal is to allow inbound and outbound e-mail traffic but to block all other traffic. The rules are applied top to bottom to each packet.

Table 12.1 Packet-Filtering Example

Rule	Direction	Source Address	Destination Address	Protocol	Destination Port	Action
A	In	External	Internal	TCP	25	Permit
B	Out	Internal	External	TCP	> 1023	Permit
C	Out	Internal	External	TCP	25	Permit
D	In	External	Internal	TCP	> 1023	Permit
E	Either	Any	Any	Any	Any	Deny

> **A.** Inbound mail from an external source is allowed (port 25 is for SMTP incoming).
> **B.** This rule is intended to allow a response to an inbound SMTP connection.
> **C.** Outbound mail to an external source is allowed.
> **D.** This rule is intended to allow a response to an inbound SMTP connection.
> **E.** This is an explicit statement of the default policy. All rulesets include this rule implicitly as the last rule.

There are several problems with this ruleset. Rule D allows external traffic to any destination port above 1023. As an example of an exploit of this rule, an external attacker can open a connection from the attacker's port 5150 to an internal Web proxy server on port 8080. This is supposed to be forbidden and could allow an attack on the server. To counter this attack, the firewall ruleset can be configured with a source port field for each row. For rules B and D, the source port is set to 25; for rules A and C, the source port is set to > 1023.

But a vulnerability remains. Rules C and D are intended to specify that any inside host can send mail to the outside. A TCP packet with a destination port of 25 is routed to the SMTP server on the destination machine. The problem with this rule is that the use of port 25 for SMTP receipt is only a default; an outside machine could be configured to have some other application linked to port 25. As the revised rule D is written, an attacker could gain access to internal machines by sending packets with a TCP source port number of 25. To counter this threat, we can add an ACK flag field to each row. For rule D, the field would indicate that the ACK flag must be set on the incoming packet. Rule D would now look like this:

Rule	Direction	Source Address	Source Port	Dest Address	Protocol	Dest Port	Flag	Action
D	In	External	25	Internal	TCP	> 1023	ACK	Permit

The rule takes advantage of a feature of TCP connections. Once a connection is set up, the ACK flag of a TCP segment is set to acknowledge segments sent from the other side. Thus, this rule allows incoming packets with a source port number of 25 that include the ACK flag in the TCP segment.

One advantage of a packet filtering firewall is its simplicity. Also, packet filters typically are transparent to users and are very fast. [SP 800-41-1] lists the following weaknesses of packet filter firewalls:

- Because packet filter firewalls do not examine upper-layer data, they cannot prevent attacks that employ application-specific vulnerabilities or functions. For example, a packet filter firewall cannot block specific application commands; if a packet filter firewall allows a given application, all functions available within that application will be permitted.

- Because of the limited information available to the firewall, the logging functionality present in packet filter firewalls is limited. Packet filter logs normally contain the same information used to make access control decisions (source address, destination address, and traffic type).

- Most packet filter firewalls do not support advanced user authentication schemes. Once again, this limitation is mostly due to the lack of upper-layer functionality by the firewall.

- Packet filter firewalls are generally vulnerable to attacks and exploits that take advantage of problems within the TCP/IP specification and protocol stack, such as *network layer address spoofing*. Many packet filter firewalls cannot detect a network packet in which the OSI Layer 3 addressing information has been altered. Spoofing attacks are generally employed by intruders to bypass the security controls implemented in a firewall platform.

- Finally, due to the small number of variables used in access control decisions, packet filter firewalls are susceptible to security breaches caused by improper configurations. In other words, it is easy to accidentally configure a packet filter firewall to allow traffic types, sources, and destinations that should be denied based on an organization's information security policy.

Some of the attacks that can be made on packet filtering firewalls and the appropriate countermeasures are the following:

- **IP address spoofing:** The intruder transmits packets from the outside with a source IP address field containing an address of an internal host. The attacker hopes that the use of a spoofed address will allow penetration of systems that employ simple source address security, in which packets from specific trusted internal hosts are accepted. The countermeasure is to discard packets with an inside source address if the packet arrives on an external interface. In fact, this countermeasure is often implemented at the router external to the firewall.

- **Source routing attacks:** The source station specifies the route that a packet should take as it crosses the Internet, in the hopes that this will bypass security measures that do not analyze the source routing information. The countermeasure is to discard all packets that use this option.

- **Tiny fragment attacks:** The intruder uses the IP fragmentation option to create extremely small fragments and force the TCP header information into a separate packet fragment. This attack is designed to circumvent filtering rules that depend on TCP header information. Typically, a packet filter will make a filtering decision on the first fragment of a packet. All subsequent fragments of that packet are filtered out solely on the basis that they are part of the packet whose first fragment was rejected. The attacker hopes that the filtering firewall examines only the first fragment and that the remaining fragments are passed through. A tiny fragment attack can be defeated by enforcing a rule that the first fragment of a packet must contain a predefined minimum amount of the transport header. If the first fragment is rejected, the filter can remember the packet and discard all subsequent fragments.

Stateful Inspection Firewalls

A traditional packet filter makes filtering decisions on an individual packet basis and does not take into consideration any higher-layer context. To understand what is meant by *context* and why a traditional packet filter is limited with regard to context, a little background is needed. Most standardized applications that run on top of TCP follow a client/server model. For example, for the Simple Mail Transfer Protocol (SMTP), e-mail is transmitted from a client system to a server system. The client system generates new e-mail messages, typically from user input. The server system accepts incoming e-mail messages and places them in the appropriate user mailboxes. SMTP operates by setting up a TCP connection between client and server, in which the TCP server port number, which identifies the SMTP server application, is 25. The TCP port number for the SMTP client is a number between 1024 and 65535 that is generated by the SMTP client.

In general, when an application that uses TCP creates a session with a remote host, it creates a TCP connection in which the TCP port number for the remote (server) application is a number less than 1024 and the TCP port number for the local (client) application is a number between 1024 and 65535. The numbers less than 1024 are the "well-known" port numbers and are assigned permanently to particular applications (e.g., 25 for server SMTP). The numbers between 1024 and 65535 are generated dynamically and have temporary significance only for the lifetime of a TCP connection.

A simple packet filtering firewall must permit inbound network traffic on all these high-numbered ports for TCP-based traffic to occur. This creates a vulnerability that can be exploited by unauthorized users.

A stateful inspection packet firewall tightens up the rules for TCP traffic by creating a directory of outbound TCP connections, as shown in Table 12.2. There is an entry for each currently established connection. The packet filter will now allow incoming traffic to high-numbered ports only for those packets that fit the profile of one of the entries in this directory.

A stateful packet inspection firewall reviews the same packet information as a packet filtering firewall, but also records information about TCP connections (Figure 12.1c). Some stateful firewalls also keep track of TCP sequence numbers to prevent attacks that depend on the sequence number, such as session hijacking. Some even inspect limited amounts of application data for some well-known protocols like FTP, IM and SIPS commands, in order to identify and track related connections.

Table 12.2   Example Stateful Firewall Connection State Table (SP 800-41-1)

Source Address	Source Port	Destination Address	Destination Port	Connection State
192.168.1.100	1030	210.22.88.29	80	Established
192.168.1.102	1031	216.32.42.123	80	Established
192.168.1.101	1033	173.66.32.122	25	Established
192.168.1.106	1035	177.231.32.12	79	Established
223.43.21.231	1990	192.168.1.6	80	Established
2122.22.123.32	2112	192.168.1.6	80	Established
210.922.212.18	3321	192.168.1.6	80	Established
24.102.32.23	1025	192.168.1.6	80	Established
223.21.22.12	1046	192.168.1.6	80	Established

Application-Level Gateway

An application-level gateway, also called an **application proxy**, acts as a relay of application-level traffic (Figure 12.1d). The user contacts the gateway using a TCP/IP application, such as Telnet or FTP, and the gateway asks the user for the name of the remote host to be accessed. When the user responds and provides a valid user ID and authentication information, the gateway contacts the application on the remote host and relays TCP segments containing the application data between the two endpoints. If the gateway does not implement the proxy code for a specific application, the service is not supported and cannot be forwarded across the firewall. Further, the gateway can be configured to support only specific features of an application that the network administrator considers acceptable while denying all other features.

Application-level gateways tend to be more secure than packet filters. Rather than trying to deal with the numerous possible combinations that are to be allowed and forbidden at the TCP and IP level, the application-level gateway need only scrutinize a few allowable applications. In addition, it is easy to log and audit all incoming traffic at the application level.

A prime disadvantage of this type of gateway is the additional processing overhead on each connection. In effect, there are two spliced connections between the end users, with the gateway at the splice point, and the gateway must examine and forward all traffic in both directions.

Circuit-Level Gateway

A fourth type of firewall is the circuit-level gateway or **circuit-level proxy** (Figure 12.1e). This can be a stand-alone system or it can be a specialized function performed by an application-level gateway for certain applications. As with an application gateway, a circuit-level gateway does not permit an end-to-end TCP connection; rather, the gateway sets up two TCP connections, one between itself and a TCP user on an inner host and one between itself and a TCP user on an outside host. Once the two connections are established, the gateway typically relays TCP segments from one connection to the other without examining the contents. The security function consists of determining which connections will be allowed.

A typical use of circuit-level gateways is a situation in which the system administrator trusts the internal users. The gateway can be configured to support application-level or proxy service on inbound connections and circuit-level functions for outbound connections. In this configuration, the gateway can incur the processing overhead of examining incoming application data for forbidden functions but does not incur that overhead on outgoing data.

An example of a circuit-level gateway implementation is the SOCKS package [KOBL92]; version 5 of SOCKS is specified in RFC 1928. The SOCKS protocol provides a framework for client-server applications in both the TCP and UDP domains. It is designed to provide convenient and secure access to a network-level firewall. The protocol occupies a thin layer between the application and either TCP or UDP but does not provide network-level routing services, such as forwarding of ICMP messages.

SOCKS consists of the following components:

- The SOCKS server, which often runs on a UNIX-based firewall. SOCKS is also implemented on Windows systems.
- The SOCKS client library, which runs on internal hosts protected by the firewall.
- SOCKS-ified versions of several standard client programs such as FTP and TELNET. The implementation of the SOCKS protocol typically involves either the recompilation or relinking of TCP-based client applications or the use of alternate dynamically loaded libraries, to use the appropriate encapsulation routines in the SOCKS library.

When a TCP-based client wishes to establish a connection to an object that is reachable only via a firewall (such determination is left up to the implementation), it must open a TCP connection to the appropriate SOCKS port on the SOCKS server system. The SOCKS service is located on TCP port 1080. If the connection request succeeds, the client enters a negotiation for the authentication method to be used, authenticates with the chosen method, and then sends a relay request. The SOCKS server evaluates the request and either establishes the appropriate connection or denies it. UDP exchanges are handled in a similar fashion. In essence, a TCP connection is opened to authenticate a user to send and receive UDP segments, and the UDP segments are forwarded as long as the TCP connection is open.

12.4 FIREWALL BASING

It is common to base a firewall on a stand-alone machine running a common operating system, such as UNIX or Linux. Firewall functionality can also be implemented as a software module in a router or LAN switch. In this section, we look at some additional firewall basing considerations.

Bastion Host

A bastion host is a system identified by the firewall administrator as a critical strong point in the network's security. Typically, the bastion host serves as a platform for an application-level or circuit-level gateway. Common characteristics of a bastion host are as follows:

- The bastion host hardware platform executes a secure version of its operating system, making it a hardened system.

- Only the services that the network administrator considers essential are installed on the bastion host. These could include proxy applications for DNS, FTP, HTTP, and SMTP.

- The bastion host may require additional authentication before a user is allowed access to the proxy services. In addition, each proxy service may require its own authentication before granting user access.

- Each proxy is configured to support only a subset of the standard application's command set.

- Each proxy is configured to allow access only to specific host systems. This means that the limited command/feature set may be applied only to a subset of systems on the protected network.

- Each proxy maintains detailed audit information by logging all traffic, each connection, and the duration of each connection. The audit log is an essential tool for discovering and terminating intruder attacks.

- Each proxy module is a very small software package specifically designed for network security. Because of its relative simplicity, it is easier to check such modules for security flaws. For example, a typical UNIX mail application may contain over 20,000 lines of code, while a mail proxy may contain fewer than 1000.

- Each proxy is independent of other proxies on the bastion host. If there is a problem with the operation of any proxy, or if a future vulnerability is discovered, it can be uninstalled without affecting the operation of the other proxy applications. Also, if the user population requires support for a new service, the network administrator can easily install the required proxy on the bastion host.

- A proxy generally performs no disk access other than to read its initial configuration file. Hence, the portions of the file system containing executable code can be made read only. This makes it difficult for an intruder to install Trojan horse sniffers or other dangerous files on the bastion host.

- Each proxy runs as a nonprivileged user in a private and secured directory on the bastion host.

Host-Based Firewalls

A host-based firewall is a software module used to secure an individual host. Such modules are available in many operating systems or can be provided as an add-on package. Like conventional stand-alone firewalls, host-resident firewalls filter and restrict the flow of packets. A common location for such firewalls is a server. There are several advantages to the use of a server-based or workstation-based firewall:

- Filtering rules can be tailored to the host environment. Specific corporate security policies for servers can be implemented, with different filters for servers used for different application.

- Protection is provided independent of topology. Thus both internal and external attacks must pass through the firewall.

- Used in conjunction with stand-alone firewalls, the host-based firewall provides an additional layer of protection. A new type of server can be added to the network, with its own firewall, without the necessity of altering the network firewall configuration.

Personal Firewall

A personal firewall controls the traffic between a personal computer or workstation on one side and the Internet or enterprise network on the other side. Personal firewall functionality can be used in the home environment and on corporate intranets. Typically, the personal firewall is a software module on the personal computer. In a home environment with multiple computers connected to the Internet, firewall functionality can also be housed in a router that connects all of the home computers to a DSL, cable modem, or other Internet interface.

Personal firewalls are typically much less complex than either server-based firewalls or stand-alone firewalls. The primary role of the personal firewall is to deny unauthorized remote access to the computer. The firewall can also monitor outgoing activity in an attempt to detect and block worms and other malware.

Personal firewall capabilities are provided by the netfilter package on Linux systems, or the pf package on BSD and Mac OS X systems. These packages may be configured on the command-line, or with a GUI front-end. When such a personal firewall is enabled, all inbound connections are usually denied except for those the user explicitly permits. Outbound connections are usually allowed. The list of inbound services that can be selectively re-enabled, with their port numbers, may include the following common services:

- Personal file sharing (548, 427)
- Windows sharing (139)
- Personal Web sharing (80, 427)
- Remote login—SSH (22)
- FTP access (20–21, 1024-65535 from 20–21)
- Printer sharing (631, 515)
- iChat Rendezvous (5297, 5298)
- iTunes Music Sharing (3869)
- CVS (2401)
- Gnutella/Limewire (6346)

- ICQ (4000)
- IRC (194)
- MSN Messenger (6891–6900)
- Network Time (123)
- Retrospect (497)
- SMB (without netbios; 445)
- Timbuktu (407)
- VNC (5900–5902)
- WebSTAR Admin (1080, 1443)

When FTP access is enabled, ports 20 and 21 on the local machine are opened for FTP; if others connect this computer from ports 20 or 21, the ports 1024 through 65535 are open.

For increased protection, advanced firewall features may be configured. For example, stealth mode hides the system on the Internet by dropping unsolicited communication packets, making it appear as though the system is not present. UDP packets can be blocked, restricting network traffic to TCP packets only for open ports. The firewall also supports logging, an important tool for checking on unwanted activity. Other types of personal firewall allow the user to specify that only selected applications, or applications signed by a valid certificate authority, may provide services accessed from the network.

12.5 FIREWALL LOCATION AND CONFIGURATIONS

As Figure 12.1a indicates, a firewall is positioned to provide a protective barrier between an external, potentially untrusted source of traffic and an internal network. With that general principle in mind, a security administrator must decide on the location and on the number of firewalls needed. In this section, we look at some common options.

DMZ Networks

Figure 12.2 suggests the most common distinction, that between an internal and an external firewall. An external firewall is placed at the edge of a local or enterprise network, just inside the boundary router that connects to the Internet or some wide area network (WAN). One or more internal firewalls protect the bulk of the enterprise network. Between these two types of firewalls are one or more networked devices in a region referred to as a DMZ (demilitarized zone) network. Systems that are externally accessible but need some protections are usually located on DMZ networks. Typically, the systems in the DMZ require or foster external connectivity, such as a corporate Web site, an e-mail server, or a DNS (domain name system) server.

The external firewall provides a measure of access control and protection for the DMZ systems consistent with their need for external connectivity. The external

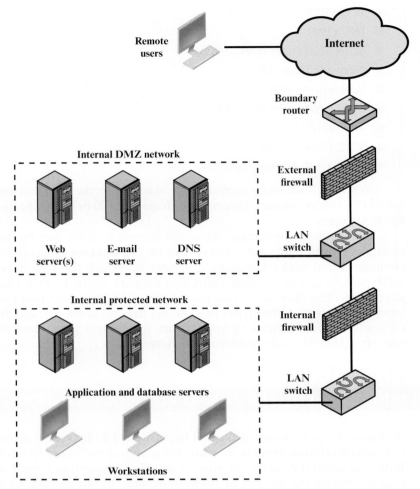

Figure 12.2 Example Firewall Configuration

firewall also provides a basic level of protection for the remainder of the enterprise network. In this type of configuration, internal firewalls serve three purposes:

1. The internal firewall adds more stringent filtering capability, compared to the external firewall, in order to protect enterprise servers and workstations from external attack.

2. The internal firewall provides two-way protection with respect to the DMZ. First, the internal firewall protects the remainder of the network from attacks launched from DMZ systems. Such attacks might originate from worms, rootkits, bots, or other malware lodged in a DMZ system. Second, an internal firewall can protect the DMZ systems from attack from the internal protected network.

3. Multiple internal firewalls can be used to protect portions of the internal network from each other. For example, firewalls can be configured so that internal servers are protected from internal workstations and vice versa. A common practice is to place the DMZ on a different network interface on the external firewall from that used to access the internal networks.

Virtual Private Networks

In today's distributed computing environment, the **virtual private network** (VPN) offers an attractive solution to network managers. In essence, a VPN consists of a set of computers that interconnect by means of a relatively unsecure network and that make use of encryption and special protocols to provide security. At each corporate site, workstations, servers, and databases are linked by one or more local area networks (LANs). The Internet or some other public network can be used to interconnect sites, providing a cost savings over the use of a private network and offloading the wide area network management task to the public network provider. That same public network provides an access path for telecommuters and other mobile employees to log on to corporate systems from remote sites.

But the manager faces a fundamental requirement: security. Use of a public network exposes corporate traffic to eavesdropping and provides an entry point for unauthorized users. To counter this problem, a VPN is needed. In essence, a VPN uses encryption and authentication in the lower protocol layers to provide a secure connection through an otherwise insecure network, typically the Internet. VPNs are generally cheaper than real private networks using private lines but rely on having the same encryption and authentication system at both ends. The encryption may be performed by firewall software or possibly by routers. The most common protocol mechanism used for this purpose is at the IP level and is known as IPsec.

Figure 12.3 (Compare Figure 9.1) is a typical scenario of IPSec usage.[1] An organization maintains LANs at dispersed locations. Nonsecure IP traffic is conducted on each LAN. For traffic off site, through some sort of private or public WAN, IPSec protocols are used. These protocols operate in networking devices, such as a router or firewall, that connect each LAN to the outside world. The IPSec networking device will typically encrypt and compress all traffic going into the WAN and decrypt and uncompress traffic coming from the WAN; authentication may also be provided. These operations are transparent to workstations and servers on the LAN. Secure transmission is also possible with individual users who dial into the WAN. Such user workstations must implement the IPSec protocols to provide security. They must also implement high levels of host security, as they are directly connected to the wider Internet. This makes them an attractive target for attackers attempting to access the corporate network.

A logical means of implementing an IPSec is in a firewall, as shown in Figure 12.3. If IPSec is implemented in a separate box behind (internal to) the firewall, then VPN traffic passing through the firewall in both directions is encrypted. In this case, the firewall is unable to perform its filtering function or other security

---

[1]Details of IPSec are provided in Chapter 9. For this discussion, all that we need to know is that IPSec adds one or more additional headers to the IP packet to support encryption and authentication functions.

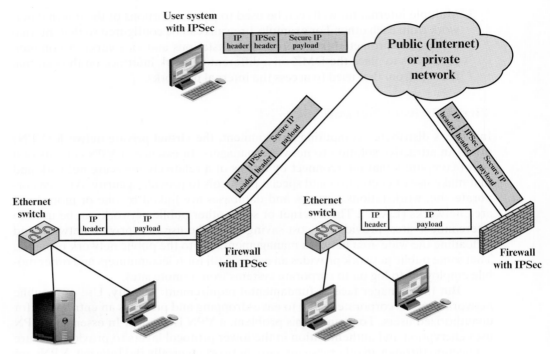

Figure 12.3 A VPN Security Scenario

functions, such as access control, logging, or scanning for viruses. IPSec could be implemented in the boundary router, outside the firewall. However, this device is likely to be less secure than the firewall and thus less desirable as an IPSec platform.

Distributed Firewalls

A distributed firewall configuration involves stand-alone firewall devices plus host-based firewalls working together under a central administrative control. Figure 12.4 suggests a distributed firewall configuration. Administrators can configure host-resident firewalls on hundreds of servers and workstations as well as configure personal firewalls on local and remote user systems. Tools let the network administrator set policies and monitor security across the entire network. These firewalls protect against internal attacks and provide protection tailored to specific machines and applications. Stand-alone firewalls provide global protection, including internal firewalls and an external firewall, as discussed previously.

With distributed firewalls, it may make sense to establish both an internal and an external DMZ. Web servers that need less protection because they have less critical information on them could be placed in an external DMZ, outside the external firewall. What protection is needed is provided by host-based firewalls on these servers.

An important aspect of a distributed firewall configuration is security monitoring. Such monitoring typically includes log aggregation and analysis, firewall statistics, and fine-grained remote monitoring of individual hosts if needed.

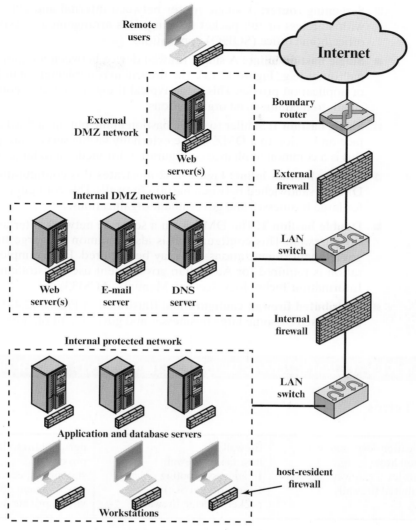

Figure 12.4   Example Distributed Firewall Configuration

Summary of Firewall Locations and Topologies

We can now summarize the discussion from Sections 12.4 and 12.5 to define a spectrum of firewall locations and topologies. The following alternatives can be identified:

- **Host-resident firewall:** This category includes personal firewall software and firewall software on servers. Such firewalls can be used alone or as part of an in-depth firewall deployment.

- **Screening router:** A single router between internal and external networks with stateless or full packet filtering. This arrangement is typical for small office/home office (SOHO) applications.

- **Single bastion inline:** A single firewall device between an internal and external router (e.g., Figure 12.1a). The firewall may implement stateful filters and/or application proxies. This is the typical firewall appliance configuration for small- to medium-sized organizations.

- **Single bastion T:** Similar to single bastion inline but has a third network interface on bastion to a DMZ where externally visible servers are placed. Again, this is a common appliance configuration for medium to large organizations.

- **Double bastion inline:** Figure 12.2 illustrates this configuration, where the DMZ is sandwiched between bastion firewalls. This configuration is common for large businesses and government organizations.

- **Double bastion T:** The DMZ is on a separate network interface on the bastion firewall. This configuration is also common for large businesses and government organizations and may be required. For example, this configuration is required for Australian government use (Australian Government Information Technology Security Manual—ACSI33).

- **Distributed firewall configuration:** Illustrated in Figure 12.4. This configuration is used by some large businesses and government organizations.

12.6 KEY TERMS, REVIEW QUESTIONS, AND PROBLEMS

Key Terms

application-level gateway	firewall	personal firewall
bastion host	host-based firewall	proxy
circuit-level gateway	IP address spoofing	stateful inspection firewall
distributed firewalls	IP security (IPSec)	tiny fragment attack
DMZ	packet filtering firewall	virtual private network (VPN)

Review Questions

12.1 List three design goals for a firewall.

12.2 List four techniques used by firewalls to control access and enforce a security policy.

12.3 When does a packet filtering firewall resort to default actions? List these default policies.

12.4 What are some weaknesses of a packet filtering firewall?

12.5 Explain three attacks that can be made on packet filtering firewalls. What measures can be taken to counter these attacks?

12.6 What is an application-level gateway?

12.7 What is a circuit-level gateway?

12.8 What are the differences among the firewalls of Figure 12.1?

12.9 What are the common characteristics of a bastion host?

12.10 Why is it useful to have host-based firewalls?

12.11 What is a virtual private network? How does it ensure a secure connection?

12.12 Describe the spectrum of firewall locations and topologies.

Problems

12.1 As was mentioned in Section 12.3, one approach to defeating the tiny fragment attack is to enforce a minimum length of the transport header that must be contained in the first fragment of an IP packet. If the first fragment is rejected, all subsequent fragments can be rejected. However, the nature of IP is such that fragments may arrive out of order. Thus, an intermediate fragment may pass through the filter before the initial fragment is rejected. How can this situation be handled?

12.2 In an IPv4 packet, the size of the payload in the first fragment, in octets, is equal to Total Length $-$ (4 $\times$ IHL). If this value is less than the required minimum (8 octets for TCP), then this fragment and the entire packet are rejected. Suggest an alternative method of achieving the same result using only the Fragment Offset field.

12.3 RFC 791, the IPv4 protocol specification, describes a reassembly algorithm that results in new fragments overwriting any overlapped portions of previously received fragments. Given such a reassembly implementation, an attacker could construct a series of packets in which the lowest (zero-offset) fragment would contain innocuous data (and thereby be passed by administrative packet filters), and in which some subsequent packet having a non-zero offset would overlap TCP header information (destination port, for instance) and cause it to be modified. The second packet would be passed through most filter implementations because it does not have a zero fragment offset. Suggest a method that could be used by a packet filter to counter this attack.

12.4 Table 12.3 shows a sample of a packet filter firewall ruleset for an imaginary network of IP address that range from 192.168.1.0 to 192.168.1.254. Describe the effect of each rule.

12.5 SMTP (Simple Mail Transfer Protocol) is the standard protocol for transferring mail between hosts over TCP. A TCP connection is set up between a user agent and a server program. The server listens on TCP port 25 for incoming connection requests. The user end of the connection is on a TCP port number above 1023. Suppose you wish to build a packet filter ruleset allowing inbound and outbound SMTP traffic. You generate the following ruleset:

Table 12.3 Sample Packet Filter Firewall Ruleset

	Source Address	Source Port	Dest Address	Dest Port	Action
1	Any	Any	192.168.1.0	> 1023	Allow
2	192.168.1.1	Any	Any	Any	Deny
3	Any	Any	192.168.1.1	Any	Deny
4	192.168.1.0	Any	Any	Any	Allow
5	Any	Any	192.168.1.2	SMTP	Allow
6	Any	Any	192.168.1.3	HTTP	Allow
7	Any	Any	Any	Any	Deny

Rule	Direction	Src Addr	Dest Addr	Protocol	Dest Port	Action
A	In	External	Internal	TCP	25	Permit
B	Out	Internal	External	TCP	>1023	Permit
C	Out	Internal	External	TCP	25	Permit
D	In	External	Internal	TCP	>1023	Permit
E	Either	Any	Any	Any	Any	Deny

a. Describe the effect of each rule.

b. Your host in this example has IP address 172.16.1.1. Someone tries to send e-mail from a remote host with IP address 192.168.3.4. If successful, this generates an SMTP dialogue between the remote user and the SMTP server on your host consisting of SMTP commands and mail. Additionally, assume that a user on your host tries to send e-mail to the SMTP server on the remote system. Four typical packets for this scenario are as shown:

Packet	Direction	Src Addr	Dest Addr	Protocol	Dest Port	Action
1	In	192.168.3.4	172.16.1.1	TCP	25	?
2	Out	172.16.1.1	192.168.3.4	TCP	1234	?
3	Out	172.16.1.1	192.168.3.4	TCP	25	?
4	In	192.168.3.4	172.16.1.1	TCP	1357	?

Indicate which packets are permitted or denied and which rule is used in each case.

c. Someone from the outside world (10.1.2.3) attempts to open a connection from port 5150 on a remote host to the Web proxy server on port 8080 on one of your local hosts (172.16.3.4), in order to carry out an attack. Typical packets are as follows:

Packet	Direction	Src Addr	Dest Addr	Protocol	Dest Port	Action
5	In	10.1.2.3	172.16.3.4	TCP	8080	?
6	Out	172.16.3.4	10.1.2.3	TCP	5150	?

Will the attack succeed? Give details.

12.6 To provide more protection, the ruleset from the preceding problem is modified as follows:

Rule	Direction	Src Addr	Dest Addr	Protocol	Src Port	Dest Port	Action
A	In	External	Internal	TCP	>1023	25	Permit
B	Out	Internal	External	TCP	25	>1023	Permit
C	Out	Internal	External	TCP	>1023	25	Permit
D	In	External	Internal	TCP	25	>1023	Permit
E	Either	Any	Any	Any	Any	Any	Deny

a. Describe the change.

b. Apply this new ruleset to the same six packets of the preceding problem. Indicate which packets are permitted or denied and which rule is used in each case.

12.7   A hacker uses port 25 as the client port on his or her end to attempt to open a connection to your Web proxy server.

   a.   The following packets might be generated:

Packet	Direction	Src Addr	Dest Addr	Protocol	Src Port	Dest Port	Action
7	In	10.1.2.3	172.16.3.4	TCP	25	8080	?
8	Out	172.16.3.4	10.1.2.3	TCP	8080	25	?

    Explain why this attack will succeed, using the ruleset of the preceding problem.

   b.   When a TCP connection is initiated, the ACK bit in the TCP header is not set. Subsequently, all TCP headers sent over the TCP connection have the ACK bit set. Use this information to modify the ruleset of the preceding problem to prevent the attack just described.

12.8   A common management requirement is that "all external Web traffic must flow via the organization's Web proxy." However, that requirement is easier stated than implemented. Discuss the various problems and issues, possible solutions, and limitations with supporting this requirement. In particular consider issues such as identifying exactly what constitutes "Web traffic" and how it may be monitored, given the large range of ports and various protocols used by Web browsers and servers.

12.9   Consider the threat of "theft/breach of proprietary or confidential information held in key data files on the system." One method by which such a breach might occur is the accidental/deliberate e-mailing of information to a user outside of the organization. A possible countermeasure to this is to require all external e-mail to be given a sensitivity tag (classification if you like) in its subject and for external e-mail to have the lowest sensitivity tag. Discuss how this measure could be implemented in a firewall and what components and architecture would be needed to do this.

12.10   You are given the following "informal firewall policy" details to be implemented using a firewall like that in Figure 12.2:

   1.   E-mail may be sent using SMTP in both directions through the firewall, but it must be relayed via the DMZ mail gateway that provides header sanitization and content filtering. External e-mail must be destined for the DMZ mail server.

   2.   Users inside may retrieve their e-mail from the DMZ mail gateway, using either POP3 or POP3S, and authenticate themselves.

   3.   Users outside may retrieve their e-mail from the DMZ mail gateway, but only if they use the secure POP3 protocol, and authenticate themselves.

   4.   Web requests (both insecure and secure) are allowed from any internal user out through the firewall but must be relayed via the DMZ Web proxy, which provides content filtering (noting this is not possible for secure requests), and users must authenticate with the proxy for logging.

   5.   Web requests (both insecure and secure) are allowed from anywhere on the Internet to the DMZ Web server.

   6.   DNS lookup requests by internal users allowed via the DMZ DNS server, which queries to the Internet.

   7.   External DNS requests are provided by the DMZ DNS server.

   8.   Management and update of information on the DMZ servers is allowed using secure shell connections from relevant authorized internal users (may have different sets of users on each system as appropriate).

   9.   SNMP management requests are permitted from the internal management hosts to the firewalls, with the firewalls also allowed to send management traps (i.e., notification of some event occurring) to the management hosts.

Design suitable packet filter rulesets (similar to those shown in Table 12.1) to be implemented on the "External Firewall" and the "Internal Firewall" to satisfy the aforementioned policy requirements.

APPENDIX A

SOME ASPECTS OF NUMBER THEORY

A.1 Prime and Relatively Prime Numbers

Divisors
Prime Numbers
Relatively Prime Numbers

A.2 Modular Arithmetic

In this appendix, we provide some background on two concepts referenced in this book: prime numbers and modular arithmetic.

A.1 PRIME AND RELATIVELY PRIME NUMBERS

In this section, unless otherwise noted, we deal only with nonnegative integers. The use of negative integers would introduce no essential differences.

Divisors

We say that $b \neq 0$ divides a if $a = mb$ for some m, where a, b, and m are integers. That is, b divides a if there is no remainder on division. The notation $b|a$ is commonly used to mean b divides a. Also, if $b|a$, we say that b is a *divisor* of a. For example, the positive divisors of 24 are 1, 2, 3, 4, 6, 8, 12, and 24.

The following relations hold:

- If $a|1$, then $a = \pm 1$
- If $a|b$ and $b|a$, then $a = \pm b$
- Any $b \neq 0$ divides 0
- If $b|g$ and $b|h$, then $b|(mg + nh)$ for arbitrary integers m and n

To see this last point, note that

If $b|g$, then g is of the form $g = b \times g_1$ for some integer g_1.
If $b|h$, then h is of the form $h = b \times h_1$ for some integer h_1.

So

$$mg + nh = mbg_1 + nbh_1 = b \times (mg_1 + nh_1)$$

and therefore b divides $mg + nh$.

Prime Numbers

An integer $p > 1$ is a prime number if its only divisors are ± 1 and $\pm p$. Prime numbers play a critical role in number theory and in the techniques discussed in Chapter 3.

Any integer $a > 1$ can be factored in a unique way as

$$a = p_1^{a_1} \times p_2^{a_2} \times \ldots \times p_t^{a_t}$$

where $p_1 < p_2 < \ldots < p_t$ are prime numbers and where each a_i is a positive integer. For example, $91 = 7 \times 13$ and $11011 = 7 \times 11^2 \times 13$.

It is useful to cast this another way. If P is the set of all prime numbers, then any positive integer can be written uniquely in the following form:

$$a = \prod_{p \in P} p^{a_p} \quad \text{where each } a_p \geq 0$$

The right-hand side is the product over all possible prime numbers p; for any particular value of a, most of the exponents a_p will be 0.

The value of any given positive integer can be specified by simply listing all the nonzero exponents in the foregoing formulation. Thus, the integer 12 is represented by $\{a_2 = 2, a_3 = 1\}$, and the integer 18 is represented by $\{a_2 = 1, a_3 = 2\}$. Multiplication of two numbers is equivalent to adding the corresponding exponents:

$$k = mn \quad \rightarrow \quad k_p = m_p + n_p \quad \text{for all } p$$

What does it mean, in terms of these prime factors, to say that $a|b$? Any integer of the form p^k can be divided only by an integer that is of a lesser or equal power of the same prime number, p^j with $j \leq k$. Thus, we can say

$$a|b \quad \rightarrow \quad a_p \leq b_p \quad \text{for all } p$$

Relatively Prime Numbers

We will use the notation $\gcd(a, b)$ to mean the **greatest common divisor** of a and b. The positive integer c is said to be the greatest common divisor of a and b if

1. c is a divisor of a and of b.
2. Any divisor of a and b is a divisor of c.

An equivalent definition is the following:

$$\gcd(a, b) = \max[k, \text{ such that } k|a \text{ and } k|b]$$

Because we require that the greatest common divisor be positive, $\gcd(a, b) = \gcd(a, -b) = \gcd(-a, b) = \gcd(-a, -b)$. In general, $\gcd(a, b) = \gcd(|a|, |b|)$. For example, $\gcd(60, 24) = \gcd(60, -24) = 12$. Also, because all nonzero integers divide 0, we have $\gcd(a, 0) = |a|$.

It is easy to determine the greatest common divisor of two positive integers if we express each integer as the product of primes. For example,

$$300 = 2^2 \times 3^1 \times 5^2$$
$$18 = 2^1 \times 3^2$$
$$\gcd(18, 300) = 2^1 \times 3^1 \times 5^0 = 6$$

In general,

$$k = \gcd(a, b) \quad \rightarrow \quad k_p = \min(a_p, b_p) \quad \text{for all } p$$

Determining the prime factors of a large number is no easy task, so the preceding relationship does not directly lead to a way of calculating the greatest common divisor.

The integers a and b are relatively prime if they have no prime factors in common, that is, if their only common factor is 1. This is equivalent to saying that a and b are relatively prime if $\gcd(a, b) = 1$. For example, 8 and 15 are relatively prime because the divisors of 8 are 1, 2, 4, and 8, and the divisors of 15 are 1, 3, 5, and 15, so 1 is the only number on both lists.

A.2 MODULAR ARITHMETIC

Given any positive integer n and any nonnegative integer a, if we divide a by n, we get an integer quotient q and an integer remainder r that obey the following relationship:

$$a = qn + r \qquad 0 \le r < n; \ q = \lfloor a/n \rfloor$$

where $\lfloor x \rfloor$ is the largest integer less than or equal to x.

   Figure A.1 a demonstrates that, given a and positive n, it is always possible to find q and r that satisfy the preceding relationship. Represent the integers on the number line; a will fall somewhere on that line (positive a is shown, a similar demonstration can be made for negative a). Starting at 0, proceed to n, $2n$, up to qn such that $qn \le a$ and $(q + 1)n > a$. The distance from qn to a is r, and we have found the unique values of q and r. The remainder r is often referred to as a **residue**.

   If a is an integer and n is a positive integer, we define a mod n to be the remainder when a is divided by n. Thus, for any integer a, we can always write:

$$a = \lfloor a/n \rfloor \times n + (a \bmod n)$$

   Two integers a and b are said to be **congruent modulo** n, if $(a \bmod n) = (b \bmod n)$. This is written $a \equiv b \bmod n$. For example, $73 \equiv 4 \bmod 23$ and $21 \equiv -9 \bmod 10$. Note that if $a \equiv 0 \bmod n$, then $n \mid a$.

   The modulo operator has the following properties:

1. $a \equiv b \bmod n$ if $n \mid (a - b)$
2. $(a \bmod n) = (b \bmod n)$ implies $a \equiv b \bmod n$

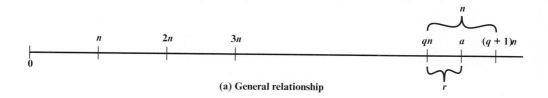

(a) General relationship

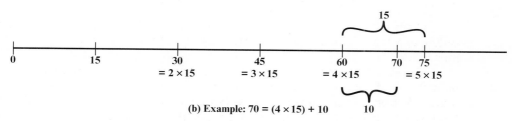

(b) Example: 70 = (4 × 15) + 10

Figure A.1   The Relationship $a = qn + r$; $0 \le r < n$

3. $a \equiv b \bmod n$ implies $b \equiv a \bmod n$.

4. $a \equiv b \bmod n$ and $b \equiv c \bmod n$ imply $a \equiv c \bmod n$.

To demonstrate the first point, if $n|(a - b)$, then $(a - b) = kn$ for some k. So we can write $a = b + kn$. Therefore, $(a \bmod n) =$ (remainder when $b + kn$ is divided by n) = (remainder when b is divided by n) = ($b \bmod n$). The remaining points are as easily proved.

The (mod n) operator maps all integers into the set of integers $\{0, 1, \ldots, (n - 1)\}$. This suggests the question: Can we perform arithmetic operations within the confines of this set? It turns out that we can; the technique is known as **modular arithmetic**.

Modular arithmetic exhibits the following properties:

1. $[(a \bmod n) + (b \bmod n)] \bmod n = (a + b) \bmod n$

2. $[(a \bmod n) - (b \bmod n)] \bmod n = (a - b) \bmod n$

3. $[(a \bmod n) \times (b \bmod n)] \bmod n = (a \times b) \bmod n$

We demonstrate the first property. Define $(a \bmod n) = r_a$ and $(b \bmod n) = r_b$. Then we can write $a = r_a + jn$ for some integer j and $b = r_b + kn$ for some integer k. Then

$$(a + b) \bmod n = (r_a + jn + r_b + kn) \bmod n$$
$$= (r_a + r_b + (k + j)n) \bmod n$$
$$= (r_a + r_b) \bmod n$$
$$= [(a \bmod n) + (b \bmod n)] \bmod n$$

The remaining properties are as easily proved.

APPENDIX B

PROJECTS FOR TEACHING NETWORK SECURITY

Many instructors believe that research or implementation projects are crucial to the clear understanding of network security. Without projects, it may be difficult for students to grasp some of the basic concepts and interactions among components. Projects reinforce the concepts introduced in the book, give the student a greater appreciation of how a cryptographic algorithm or protocol works, and can motivate students and give them confidence that they are capable of not only understanding but implementing the details of a security capability.

In this text, I have tried to present the concepts of network security as clearly as possible and have provided numerous homework problems to reinforce those concepts. However, many instructors will wish to supplement this material with projects. This appendix provides some guidance in that regard and describes support material available in the **Instructor's Resource Center (IRC)** for this book, accessible to instructors from Pearson Education. The support material covers nine types of projects:

1. Research projects
2. Hacking project
3. Programming projects
4. Laboratory exercises
5. Practical security assessments
6. Firewall projects
7. Case studies
8. Writing assignments
9. Reading/report assignments

B.1   RESEARCH PROJECTS

An effective way of reinforcing basic concepts from the course and for teaching students research skills is to assign a research project. Such a project could involve a literature search as well as an Internet search of vendor products, research lab activities, and standardization efforts. Projects could be assigned to teams or, for smaller projects, to individuals. In any case, it is best to require some sort of project proposal early in the term, giving the instructor time to evaluate the proposal for appropriate topic and appropriate level of effort. Student handouts for research projects should include the following:

■ A format for the proposal
■ A format for the final report
■ A schedule with intermediate and final deadlines
■ A list of possible project topics

The students can select one of the topics listed in the instructor's manual or devise their own comparable project. The IRC includes a suggested format for the proposal and final report as well as a list of fifteen possible research topics.

B.2 HACKING PROJECT

The aim of this project is to hack into a corporation's network through a series of steps. The Corporation is named Extreme In Security Corporation. As the name indicates, the corporation has some security holes in it, and a clever hacker is able to access critical information by hacking into its network. The IRC includes what is needed to set up the Web site. The student's goal is to capture the secret information about the price on the quote the corporation is placing next week to obtain a contract for a governmental project.

The student should start at the Web site and find his or her way into the network. At each step, if the student succeeds, there are indications as to how to proceed on to the next step as well as the grade until that point.

The project can be attempted in three ways:

1. Without seeking any sort of help
2. Using some provided hints
3. Using exact directions

The IRC includes the files needed for this project:

1. Web Security project
2. Web Hacking exercises (XSS and Script-attacks) covering client-side and server-side vulnerability exploitations, respectively
3. Documentation for installation and use for the above
4. A PowerPoint file describing Web hacking. This file is crucial to understanding how to use the exercises since it clearly explains the operation using screen shots.

This project was designed and implemented by Professor Sreekanth Malladi of Dakota State University.

B.3 PROGRAMMING PROJECTS

The programming project is a useful pedagogical tool. There are several attractive features of stand-alone programming projects that are not part of an existing security facility.

1. The instructor can choose from a wide variety of cryptography and network security concepts to assign projects.
2. The projects can be programmed by the students on any available computer and in any appropriate language; they are platform and language independent.
3. The instructor need not download, install, and configure any particular infrastructure for stand-alone projects.

There is also flexibility in the size of projects. Larger projects give students more sense of achievement, but students with less ability or fewer organizational skills can be left behind. Larger projects usually elicit more overall effort from the best students. Smaller projects can have a higher concepts-to-code ratio, and because more of them can be assigned, the opportunity exists to address a variety of different areas.

Again, as with research projects, the students should first submit a proposal. The student handout should include the same elements listed in Section B.1. The IRC includes a set of twelve possible programming projects.

The following individuals have supplied the research and programming projects suggested in the instructor's manual: Henning Schulzrinne of Columbia University; Cetin Kaya Koc of Oregon State University; and David M. Balenson of Trusted Information Systems and George Washington University.

B.4 LABORATORY EXERCISES

Professor Sanjay Rao and Ruben Torres of Purdue University have prepared a set of laboratory exercises that are part of the IRC. These are implementation projects designed to be programmed on Linux but could be adapted for any Unix environment. These laboratory exercises provide realistic experience in implementing security functions and applications.

B.5 PRACTICAL SECURITY ASSESSMENTS

Examining the current infrastructure and practices of an existing organization is one of the best ways of developing skills in assessing its security posture. The IRC contains a list of such activities. Students, working either individually or in small groups, select a suitable small-to-medium-sized organization. They then interview some key personnel in that organization in order to conduct a suitable selection of security risk assessment and review tasks as it relates to the organization's IT infrastructure and practices. As a result, they can then recommend suitable changes, which can improve the organization's IT security. These activities help students develop an appreciation of current security practices and the skills needed to review these and recommend changes.

Lawrie Brown of the Australian Defence Force Academy developed these projects.

B.6 FIREWALL PROJECTS

The implementation of network firewalls can be a difficult concept for students to grasp initially. The IRC includes a Network Firewall Visualization tool to convey and teach network security and firewall configuration. This tool is intended to teach and reinforce key concepts including the use and purpose of a perimeter firewall, the use of separated subnets, the purposes behind packet filtering, and the shortcomings of a simple packet filter firewall.

The IRC includes a .jar file that is fully portable and a series of exercises. The tool and exercises were developed at U.S. Air Force Academy.

B.7 CASE STUDIES

Teaching with case studies engages students in active learning. The IRC includes case studies in the following areas:

- Disaster recovery
- Firewalls
- Incidence response
- Physical security
- Risk
- Security policy
- Virtualization

Each case study includes learning objectives, case description, and a series of case discussion questions. Each case study is based on real-world situations and includes papers or reports describing the case.

The case studies were developed at North Carolina A&T State University.

B.8 WRITING ASSIGNMENTS

Writing assignments can have a powerful multiplier effect in the learning process in a technical discipline such as cryptography and network security. Adherents of the Writing Across the Curriculum (WAC) movement (http://wac.colostate.edu/) report substantial benefits of writing assignments in facilitating learning. Writing assignments lead to more detailed and complete thinking about a particular topic. In addition, writing assignments help to overcome the tendency of students to pursue a subject with a minimum of personal engagement—just learning facts and problem-solving techniques without obtaining a deep understanding of the subject matter.

The IRC contains a number of suggested writing assignments, organized by chapter. Instructors may ultimately find that this is an important part of their approach to teaching the material. I would greatly appreciate any feedback on this area and any suggestions for additional writing assignments.

B.9 READING/REPORT ASSIGNMENTS

Another excellent way to reinforce concepts from the course and to give students research experience is to assign papers from the literature to be read and analyzed. The IRC includes a suggested list of papers, one or two per chapter, to be assigned. A PDF copy of each of the papers is available at https://app.box.com/netsec6e. The IRC also includes a suggested assignment wording.

REFERENCES

ABBREVIATIONS

ACM   Association for Computing Machinery
IBM   International Business Machines Corporation
IEEE Institute of Electrical and Electronics Engineers
NIST National Institute of Standards and Technology

ALVA90   Alvare, A. "How Crackers Crack Passwords or What Passwords to Avoid." *Proceedings, UNIX Security Workshop II*, August 1990.

ANDE80   Anderson, J. *Computer Security Threat Monitoring and Surveillance.* Fort Washington, PA: James P. Anderson Co., April 1980.

ANDE95   Anderson, D., et al. *Detecting Unusual Program Behavior Using the Statistical Component of the Next-generation Intrusion Detection Expert System (NIDES).* Technical Report SRI-CSL-95-06, SRI Computer Science Laboratory, May 1995. www.csl.sri.com/programs/intrusion.

ANTE06   Ante, S., and Grow, B. "Meet the Hackers." *Business Week*, May 29, 2006.

AROR12   Arora, M. "How Secure is AES against Brute-Force Attack?" *EE Times*, May 7, 2012.

AXEL00   Axelsson, S. "The Base-Rate Fallacy and the Difficulty of Intrusion Detection." *ACM Transactions and Information and System Security*, August 2000.

AYCO06   Aycock, J. *Computer Viruses and Malware.* New York: Springer, 2006.

BALA98   Balasubramaniyan, J., et al. "An Architecture for Intrusion Detection Using Autonomous Agents." *Proceedings, 14th Annual Computer Security Applications Conference*, 1998.

BARD12   Bardou, R., et al. "Efficient Padding Oracle Attacks on Cryptographic Hardware," INRIA, Rapport de recherche RR-7944, Apr. 2012. http://hal.inria.fr/hal-00691958.

BASU12   Basu, A. *Intel AES-NI Performance Testing over Full Disk Encryption.* Intel Corp. May 2012.

BAUE88   Bauer, D., and Koblentz, M. "NIDX—An Expert System for Real-Time Network Intrusion Detection." *Proceedings, Computer Networking Symposium*, April 1988.

BELL90   Bellovin, S., and Merritt, M. "Limitations of the Kerberos Authentication System." *Computer Communications Review*, October 1990.

BELL94a   Bellare, M., and Rogaway, P. "Optimal Asymmetric Encryption—How to Encrypt with RSA." *Proceedings, Eurocrypt '94*, 1994.

BELL94b   Bellovin, S., and Cheswick, W. "Network Firewalls." *IEEE Communications Magazine*, September 1994.

BELL96a   Bellare, M.; Canetti, R.; and Krawczyk, H. "Keying Hash Functions for Message Authentication." *Proceedings, CRYPTO '96*, August 1996; published by Springer-Verlag. An expanded version is available at http://www-cse.ucsd.edu/users/mihir.

BELL96b   Bellare, M.; Canetti, R.; and Krawczyk, H. "The HMAC Construction." *CryptoBytes*, Spring 1996.

BINS10   Binsalleeh, H., et al. "On the Analysis of the Zeus Botnet Crimeware Toolkit." *Proceedings of the 8th Annual International Conference on Privacy, Security and Trust*, IEEE, September 2010.

BLEI98   Bleichenbacher, D. "Chosen Ciphertext Attacks against Protocols Based on the RSA Encryption Standard PKCS #1," *CRYPTO '98*, 1998.

BLOO70   Bloom, B. "Space/time Trade-offs in Hash Coding with Allowable Errors." *Communications of the ACM*, July 1970.

BRYA88   Bryant, W. *Designing an Authentication System: A Dialogue in Four Scenes.* Project Athena document, February 1988. Available at http://web.mit.edu/kerberos/www/dialogue.html.

CERT01   CERT Coordination Center. "Denial of Service Attacks." June 2001. http://www.cert. org/tech_tips/denial_of_service.html.

CHAN02   Chang, R. "Defending against Flooding-Based Distributed Denial-of-Service Attacks: A Tutorial." *IEEE Communications Magazine*, October 2002.

CHEN04   Chen, S., and Tang, T. "Slowing Down Internet Worms," *Proceedings of the 24th International Conference on Distributed Computing Systems*, 2004.

CHEN11   Chen, T., and Abu-Nimeh, S. "Lessons from Stuxnet." *IEEE Computer*, 44(4), pp. 91–93, April 2011.

CHIN05   Chinchani, R., and Berg, E. "A Fast Static Analysis Approach to Detect Exploit Code Inside Network Flows." *Recent Advances in Intrusion Detection, 8th International Symposium*, 2005.

CHOI08   Choi, M., et al. "Wireless Network Security: Vulnerabilities, Threats and Countermeasures." *International Journal of Multimedia and Ubiquitous Engineering*, July 2008.

COMP06   Computer Associates International. *The Business Value of Identity Federation*. White Paper, January 2006.

CONR02   Conry-Murray, A. "Behavior-Blocking Stops Unknown Malicious Code." *Network Magazine*, June 2002.

COST05   Costa, M., et al. "Vigilante: End-to-End Containment of Internet Worms." *ACM Symposium on Operating Systems Principles*, 2005.

CSA10   Cloud Security Alliance. *Top Threats to Cloud Computing V1.0*. CSA Report, March 2010.

CSA11a   Cloud Security Alliance. *Security Guidance for Critical Areas of Focus in Cloud Computing V3.0*. CSA Report, 2011.

CSA11b   Cloud Security Alliance. *Security as a Service (SecaaS)*. CSA Report, 2011.

DAMI03   Damiani, E., et al. "Balancing Confidentiality and Efficiency in Untrusted Relational Databases." *Proceedings, Tenth ACM Conference on Computer and Communications Security*, 2003.

DAMI05   Damiani, E., et al. "Key Management for Multi-User Encrypted Databases." *Proceedings, 2005 ACM Workshop on Storage Security and Survivability*, 2005.

DAVI89   Davies, D., and Price, W. *Security for Computer Networks*. New York: Wiley, 1989.

DAWS96   Dawson, E., and Nielsen, L. "Automated Cryptoanalysis of XOR Plaintext Strings." *Cryptologia*, April 1996.

DENN87   Denning, D. "An Intrusion-Detection Model." *IEEE Transactions on Software Engineering*, February 1987.

DIFF76   Diffie, W., and Hellman, M. "Multiuser Cryptographic Techniques." *IEEE Transactions on Information Theory*, November 1976.

DIFF79   Diffie, W., and Hellman, M. "Privacy and Authentication: An Introduction to Cryptography." *Proceedings of the IEEE*, March 1979.

DIMI07   Dimitriadis, C. "Analyzing the Security of Internet Banking Authentication Mechanisms." *Information Systems Control Journal*, Vol. 3, 2007.

EFF98   Electronic Frontier Foundation. *Cracking DES: Secrets of Encryption Research, Wiretap Politics, and Chip Design*. Sebastopol, CA: O'Reilly, 1998.

ENIS09   European Network and Information Security Agency. *Cloud Computing: Benefits, Risks and Recommendations for Information Security*. ENISA Report, November 2009.

FEIS73   Feistel, H. "Cryptography and Computer Privacy." *Scientific American*, May 1973.

FLUH00   Fluhrer, S., and McGrew, D. "Statistical Analysis of the Alleged RC4 Key Stream Generator." *Proceedings, Fast Software Encryption 2000*, 2000.

FLUH01   Fluhrer, S.; Mantin, I.; and Shamir, A. "Weakness in the Key Scheduling Algorithm of RC4." *Proceedings, Workshop in Selected Areas of Cryptography*, 2001.

FORD95   Ford, W. "Advances in Public-Key Certificate Standards." *ACM SIGSAC Review*, July 1995.

FOSS10   Fossi, M., et al. "Symantec Report on Attack Kits and Malicious Websites." Symantec, 2010.

FRAN07   Frankel, S., et al. *Establishing Wireless Robust Security Networks: A Guide to IEEE 802.11i.* NIST Special Publication 800-97, February 2007.

GARD77   Gardner, M. "A New Kind of Cipher That Would Take Millions of Years to Break." *Scientific American*, August 1977.

GOLD10   Gold, S. "Social Engineering Today: Psychology, Strategies and Tricks." *Network Security*, November 2010.

GOOD11   Goodin, D. "Hackers Break SSL Encryption Used by Millions of Sites." *The Register*, September 19, 2011.

GOOD12a   Goodin, D. "Why Passwords Have Never Been Weaker—and Crackers Have Never Been Stronger." *Ars Technica*, August 20, 2012.

GOOD12b   Goodin, D. "Crack in Internet's Foundation of Trust Allows HTTPS Session Hijacking." *Ars Technica*, September 13, 2012.

GRAN04   Grance, T.; Kent, K.; and Kim, B. *Computer Security Incident Handling Guide.* NIST Special Publication 800-61, January 2004.

HACI02   Hacigumus, H., et al. "Executing SQL over Encrypted Data in the Database-Service-Provider Model." *Proceedings, 2002 ACM SIGMOD International Conference on Management of Data*, 2002.

HEBE92   Heberlein, L.; Mukherjee, B.; and Levitt, K. "Internetwork Security Monitor: An Intrusion-Detection System for Large-Scale Networks." *Proceedings, 15th National Computer Security Conference,* October 1992.

HILT06   Hiltgen, A.; Kramp, T.; and Wiegold, T. "Secure Internet Banking Authentication." *IEEE Security and Privacy*, Vol. 4, No. 2, 2006.

HONE05   The Honeynet Project. "Knowing Your Enemy: Tracking Botnets." *Honeynet White Paper*, March 2005. http://honeynet.org/papers/bots.

HOWA03   Howard, M.; Pincus, J.; and Wing, J. "Measuring Relative Attack Surfaces." *Proceedings, Workshop on Advanced Developments in Software and Systems Security*, 2003.

HUIT98   Huitema, C. *IPv6: The New Internet Protocol.* Upper Saddle River, NJ: Prentice Hall, 1998.

IANS90   I'Anson, C., and Mitchell, C. "Security Defects in CCITT Recommendation X.509 – The Directory Authentication Framework." *Computer Communications Review*, April 1990.

ILGU95   Ilgun, K.; Kemmerer, R.; and Porras, P. "State Transition Analysis: A Rule-Based Intrusion Detection Approach." *IEEE Transaction on Software Engineering,* March 1995.

JANS11   Jansen, W., and Grance, T. *Guidelines on Security and Privacy in Public Cloud Computing.* NIST Special Publication 800-144, January 2011.

JAVI91   Javitz, H., and Valdes, A. "The SRI IDES Statistical Anomaly Detector." *Proceedings, 1991 IEEE Computer Society Symposium on Research in Security and Privacy*, May 1991.

JHI07   Jhi, Y., and Liu, P. "PWC: A Proactive Worm Containment Solution for Enterprise Networks." *Third International Conference on Security and Privacy in Communications Networks*, 2007.

JUEN85   Jueneman, R.; Matyas, S.; and Meyer, C. "Message Authentication." *IEEE Communications Magazine*, September 1988.

JUNG04   Jung, J., et al. "Fast Portscan Detection Using Sequential Hypothesis Testing," *Proceedings, IEEE Symposium on Security and Privacy*, 2004.

KLEI90   Klein, D. "Foiling the Cracker: A Survey of, and Improvements to, Password Security." *Proceedings, UNIX Security Workshop II*, August 1990.

KNUD98   Knudsen, L., et al. "Analysis Method for Alleged RC4." *Proceedings, ASIACRYPT '98*, 1998.

KOBL92   Koblas, D., and Koblas, M. "SOCKS." *Proceedings, UNIX Security Symposium III*, September 1992.

KOHL89   Kohl, J. "The Use of Encryption in Kerberos for Network Authentication." *Proceedings, Crypto '89*, 1989; published by Springer-Verlag.

KOHL94   Kohl, J.; Neuman, B.; and Ts'o, T. "The Evolution of the Kerberos Authentication Service." In Brazier, F., and Johansen, D. eds., *Distributed Open Systems*. Los Alamitos, CA: IEEE Computer Society Press, 1994. Available at http://web.mit.edu/kerberos/www/papers.html.

KUMA97   Kumar, I. *Cryptology*. Laguna Hills, CA: Aegean Park Press, 1997.

KUMA11   Kumar, M. "The Hacker's Choice Releases SSL DOS Tool." The *Hacker News*, October 24, 2011. http://thehackernews.com/2011/10/hackers-choice-releases-ssl-ddos-tool.html#.

LATT09   Lattin, B. "Upgrade to Suite B Security Algorithms." *Network World*, June 1, 2009.

LEUT94   Leutwyler, K. "Superhack." *Scientific American*, July 1994.

LINN06   Linn, J. "Identity Management." In Bidgoli, H., ed., *Handbook of Information Security*. New York: Wiley, 2006.

LIPM00   Lipmaa, H.; Rogaway, P.; and Wagner, D. "CTR Mode Encryption." *NIST First Modes of Operation Workshop*, October 2000. http://csrc.nist.gov/encryption/modes.

MA10   Ma, D., and Tsudik, G. "Security and Privacy in Emerging Wireless Networks." *IEEE Wireless Communications*, October 2010.

MANA11   Manadhata, P., and Wing, J. "An Attack Surface Metric." *IEEE Transactions on Software Engineering*, Vol. 37, No. 3, 2011.

MAND13   Mandiant "APT1: Exposing One of China's Cyber Espionage Units," 2013. http://intelreport.mandiant.com.

MAUW05   Mauw, S., and Oostdijk, M. "Foundations of Attack Trees." *International Conference on Information Security and Cryptology*, 2005.

MEYE13   Meyer, C.; Schwenk, J.; and Gortz, H. "Lessons Learned from Previous SSL/TLS Attacks A Brief Chronology of Attacks and Weaknesses." *Cryptology ePrint Archive*, 2013. http://eprint.iacr.org/2013/.

MILL88   Miller, S.; Neuman, B.; Schiller, J.; and Saltzer, J. "Kerberos Authentication and Authorization System." *Section E.2.1, Project Athena Technical Plan*, M.I.T. Project Athena, Cambridge, MA, 27 October 1988.

MIRK04   Mirkovic, J., and Relher, P. "A Taxonomy of DDoS Attack and DDoS Defense Mechanisms." *ACM SIGCOMM Computer Communications Review*, April 2004.

MITC90   Mitchell, C.; Walker, M.; and Rush, D. "CCITT/ISO Standards for Secure Message Handling." *IEEE Journal on Selected Areas in Communications*, May 1989.

MOOR01   Moore, A.; Ellison, R.; and Linger, R. "Attack Modeling for Information Security and Survivability." *Carnegie-Mellon University Technical Note CMU/SEI-2001-TN-001*, March 2001.

MORR79   Morris, R., and Thompson, K. "Password Security: A Case History." *Communications of the ACM*, November 1979.

NACH02   Nachenberg, C. "Behavior Blocking: The Next Step in Anti-Virus Protection." *White Paper*, SecurityFocus.com, March 2002.

NCAE13   National Centers of Academic Excellence in Information Assurance/Cyber Defense. *NCAE IA/CD Knowledge Units*. June 2013.

NEUM99   Neumann, P., and Porras, P. "Experience with EMERALD to Date." *Proceedings, 1st USENIX Workshop on Intrusion Detection and Network Monitoring*, April 1999.

NEWS05   Newsome, J.; Karp, B.; and Song, D. "Polygraph: Automatically Generating Signatures for Polymorphic Worms." *IEEE Symposium on Security and Privacy*, 2005.

NIST95   National Institute of Standards and Technology. *An Introduction to Computer Security: The NIST Handbook*. Special Publication 800-12. October 1995.

OECH03   Oechslin, P. "Making a Faster Cryptanalytic Time-Memory Trade-Off." *Proceedings, Crypto 03*, 2003.

ORMA03   Orman, H. "The Morris Worm: A Fifteen-Year Perspective." *IEEE Security and Privacy*, September/October 2003.

PARZ06   Parziale, L., et al. *TCP/IP Tutorial and Technical Overview, 2006.* ibm.com/redbooks.

PELT07   Peltier, J. "Identity Management." *SC Magazine*, February 2007.

PERR03   Perrine, T. "The End of Crypt () Passwords . . . Please?" *;login:*, December 2003.

POIN02   Pointcheval, D. "How to Encrypt Properly with RSA." *CryptoBytes*, Winter/Spring 2002. http://www.rsasecurity.com/rsalabs.

PORR92   Porras, P. *STAT: A State Transition Analysis Tool for Intrusion Detection.* Master's Thesis, University of California at Santa Barbara, July 1992.

PROV99   Provos, N., and Mazieres, D. "A Future-Adaptable Password Scheme." *Proceedings of the 1999 USENIX Annual Technical Conference*, 1999.

RADC04   Radcliff, D. "What Are They Thinking?" *Network World*, March 1, 2004.

RIVE78   Rivest, R.; Shamir, A.; and Adleman, L. "A Method for Obtaining Digital Signatures and Public Key Cryptosystems." *Communications of the ACM*, February 1978.

ROBS95a   Robshaw, M. *Stream Ciphers.* RSA Laboratories Technical Report TR-701, July 1995.

ROBS95b   Robshaw, M. *Block Ciphers.* RSA Laboratories Technical Report TR-601, August 1995.

ROS06   Ros, S. "Boosting the SOA with XML Networking." *The Internet Protocol Journal*, December 2006. cisco.com/ipj.

SALT75   Saltzer, J., and Schroeder, M. "The Protection of Information in Computer Systems." *Proceedings of the IEEE*, September 1975.

SCHN99   Schneier, B. "Attack Trees: Modeling Security Threats." *Dr. Dobb's Journal*, December 1999.

SEAG08   Seagate Technology. *128-Bit Versus 256-Bit AES Encryption.* Seagate Technology Paper, 2008.

SIDI05   Sidiroglou, S., and Keromytis, A. "Countering Network Worms Through Automatic Patch Generation." *IEEE Security and Privacy*, November-December 2005.

SING99   Singh, S. *The Code Book: The Science of Secrecy from Ancient Egypt to Quantum Cryptography.* New York: Anchor Books, 1999.

SNAP91   Snapp, S., et al. "A System for Distributed Intrusion Detection." *Proceedings, COMPCON Spring '91*, 1991.

SPAF92a   Spafford, E. "Observing Reusable Password Choices." *Proceedings, UNIX Security Symposium III*, September 1992.

SPAF92b   Spafford, E. "OPUS: Preventing Weak Password Choices." *Computers and Security*, No. 3, 1992.

SPAF00   Spafford, E., and Zamboni, D. "Intrusion Detection Using Autonomous Agents." *Computer Networks*, October 2000.

STAL15   Stallings, W., and Brown, L. *Computer Security.* Upper Saddle River, NJ: Pearson, 2015.

STAL16   Stallings, W. *Cryptography and Network Security: Principles and Practice, Seventh Edition.* Upper Saddle River, NJ: Pearson, 2016.

STAL16b

STEI88   Steiner, J.; Neuman, C.; and Schiller, J. "Kerberos: An Authentication Service for Open Networked Systems." *Proceedings of the Winter 1988 USENIX Conference*, February 1988.

STEP93   Stephenson, P. "Preventive Medicine." *LAN Magazine*, November 1993.

STEV11   Stevens, D. "Malicious PDF Documents Explained," *IEEE Security & Privacy*, January/February 2011.

SYMA13   Symantec, "Internet Security Threat Report, Vol. 18." April 2013.

TSUD92   Tsudik, G. "Message Authentication with One-Way Hash Functions." *Proceedings, INFOCOM '92*, May 1992.

VACC89   Vaccaro, H., and Liepins, G. "Detection of Anomalous Computer Session Activity." *Proceedings of the IEEE Symposium on Research in Security and Privacy*, May 1989.

VANO94 van Oorschot, P., and Wiener, M. "Parallel Collision Search with Application to Hash Functions and Discrete Logarithms." *Proceedings, Second ACM Conference on Computer and Communications Security*, 1994.

VIGN02 Vigna, G.; Cassell, B.; and Fayram, D. "An Intrusion Detection System for Aglets." *Proceedings of the International Conference on Mobile Agents*, October 2002.

WAGN00 Wagner, D., and Goldberg, I. "Proofs of Security for the UNIX Password Hashing Algorithm." *Proceedings, ASIACRYPT '00*, 2000.

WANG05 Wang, X.; Yin, Y.; and Yu, H. "Finding Collisions in the Full SHA-1." *Proceedings, Crypto '05*, 2005; published by Springer-Verlag.

WEAV03 Weaver, N., et al. "A Taxonomy of Computer Worms." *The First ACM Workshop on Rapid Malcode (WORM)*, 2003.

WOOD10 Wood, T., et al. "Disaster Recovery as a Cloud Service Economic Benefits & Deployment Challenges." *Proceedings, USENIX HotCloud '10*, 2010.

XU10 Xu, L. *Securing the Enterprise with Intel AES-NI*. Intel White Paper, September 2010.

ZOU05 Zou, C., et al. "The Monitoring and Early Detection of Internet Worms." *IEEE/ACM Transactions on Networking*, October 2005.

CREDITS

Page 20: Definition From An Introduction to Computer Security: The NIST Handbook by Barbara Guttman and Edward A. Roback, U.S. Department of Commerce, 1995.

Page 20–21: Three Objectives in Terms of Requirements and the Definition From Standards for Security Categorization of Federal Information and Information Systems. Published by U.S. Department of Commerce, © 2004.

Page 21–22: From Standards for Security Categorization of Federal Information and Information Systems, U.S. Department of Commerce, 2004.

Page 28: From Data Communication Networks: Open Systems Interconnection (OSI); Security, Structure and Applications. Copyright © International Telecommunication Union. Used by permission of International Telecommunication Union.

Page 29: Two specific authentication From Data Communication Networks: Open Systems Interconnection (OSI); Security, Structure and Applications. Used by permission of International Telecommunication Union.

Page 31: From Data Communication Networks: Open Systems Interconnection (OSI); Security, Structure and Applications. Copyright © International Telecommunication Union. Used by permission of International Telecommunication Union.

Page 32: From Data Communication Networks: Open Systems Interconnection (OSI); Security, Structure and Applications. Copyright © International Telecommunication Union. Used by permission of International Telecommunication Union.

Page 32: From 2013 National Centers of Academic Excellence in Information Assurance Designees Announced, National Security Agency, 2013.

Page 51: Feistel, H. "Cryptography and Computer Privacy." Scientific American, Vol 228, No 5 pp 15–23 May 1973.

Page 64: From Cryptology: System Identification and Key-Clustering by I. J. Kumar. Published by Aegean Park Press, © 1997.

Page 72–73: Comments to NIST concerning AES Modes of Operations: CTR-Mode Encryption, National Institute of Standards and Technology (NIST), National Institute of Standards and Technology, 2000.

Page 80: From Security for Computer Networks: An Introduction to Data Security in Teleprocessing and Electronic Funds Transfer, 02e by D. W. Davies and W. L. Price. Published by Wiley, © 1989.

Page 82: From "Message Authentication with One-Way Hash Functions" by Gene Tsudik from ACM SIGCOMM Computer Communication Review, Volume: 22, Issue: 05, pp: 29–38. Published by ACM, Inc., © 1992.

Page 91: Lists From HMAC: Keyed-Hashing for Message Authentication by H. Krawczyk, M. Bellare and R. Canetti. Published by Internet Engineering Task Force, © 1997.

Page 134: X.509 Hierarchy: A Hypothetical Example from Series X: Data Networks, Open System Communications And Security X.509 -International Standard Iso/Iec 9594-8. Used by permission of International Telecommunication Union.

Page 143: From The NIST Definition of Cloud Computing: Recommendations of the National Institute of Standards and Technology by Peter Mell and Timothy Grance, U.S. Department of Commerce, 2011.

Page 165: From The EAP-TLS Authentication Protocol by D. Simon, B. Aboba, R. Hurst. Published by Internet Engineering Task Force, © 2008.

Page 174: From NIST Cloud Computing Reference Architecture: Recommendations of the National Institute of Standards and Technology by Fang Liu, Jin Tong, Jian Mao, Robert Bohn, John Messina, Lee Badger and Dawn Leaf. Published by U.S. Department of Commerce, © 2011.

Page 179: Table 01 Security and Privacy Issues and Recommendations from Guidelines on Security and Privacy in Public Cloud Computing by Wayne Jansen and Timothy Grance, U.S. Department of Commerce, 2011.

Page 180–181: From "Executing SQL Over Encrypted Data in the Database-Service-Provider Model" by Hakan Hacigümüs, Bala Iyer, Chen Li and Sharad Mehrotra from A Proceeding SIGMOD '02 Proceedings of the 2002 ACM SIGMOD International Conference on Management of Data, pp: 216–227. Published by ACM Inc., © 2002.

Page 182: From SecaaS: Defined Categories of Service 2011. Published by Cloud Security Alliance, © 2011.

Page 182: Following SecaaS Categories of Service from SecaaS: Defined Categories of Service 2011. Published by Cloud Security Alliance, © 2011.

Page 243: From Establishing Wireless Robust Security Networks: A Guide to IEEE 802.11i: Recommendations of the National Institute of Standards and Technology by Sheila Frankel, Bernard Eydt, Les Owens and Karen Scarfone, U.S. Department of Commerce, 2007.

Page 244: From Establishing Wireless Robust Security Networks: A Guide to IEEE 802.11i: Recommendations of the National Institute of Standards and Technology by Sheila Frankel, Bernard Eydt, Les Owens and Karen Scarfone. U.S. Department of Commerce, 2007.

Page 245: From Establishing Wireless Robust Security Networks: A Guide to IEEE 802.11i: Recommendations of the National Institute of Standards and Technology by Sheila Frankel, Bernard Eydt, Les Owens and Karen Scarfone, U.S. Department of Commerce, 2007.

Page 259–260: From TCP/IP Tutorial and Technical Overview by Lydia Parziale, David T. Britt, Chuck Davis, Jason Forrester, Wei Liu, Carolyn Matthews and Nicolas Rosselot. Published by IBM Corporation, © 2006.

Page 262–263: Excerpt from Multipurpose Internet Mail Extensions (MIME) Part Two by Ned Freed and Nathaniel S Borenstein. Published by Internet Engineering Task Force, © 1996.

Page 264–265: From Multipurpose Internet Mail Extensions (MIME) Part Five: Conformance Criteria and Examples by Ned Freed and Nathaniel S Borenstein. Published by Internet Engineering Task Force, © 1996.

Page 266: From DRAFT NIST Special Publication 800-177: Trustworthy Email by SRamaswamy Chandramouli, Simson Garfinkel, Stephen Nightingale and Scott Rose, U.S. Department of Commerce, 2015.

Page 267: From DRAFT NIST Special Publication 800-177: Trustworthy Email by SRamaswamy Chandramouli, Simson Garfinkel, Stephen Nightingale and Scott Rose, U.S. Department of Commerce, 2015.

Page 273: From Secure/Multipurpose Internet Mail Extensions (S/MIME) Version 3.2 Message Specification by B. Ramsdell and S. Turner. Published by Internet Engineering Task Force, © 2010.

Page 283: From Resource Records for the DNS Security Extensions by R. Arends, R. Austein, M. Larson, D. Massey and S. Rose. Published by Internet Engineering Task Force, © 2005.

Page 306: From IPv6: The New Internet Protocol by Christian Huitema. Published by Pearson, © 1998.

Page 306: The Document From IP Security (IPsec) and Internet Key Exchange (IKE) Document Roadmap by S. Frankel and S. Krishnan. Published by Internet Engineering Task Force, © 2011.

Page 307: From Security Architecture for the Internet Protocol by S. Kent and K. Seo. Published by Network Working Group, © 2005.

Page 326: From IPv6: The New Internet Protocol by Christian Huitema. Published by Pearson, © 1998.

Page 334: From Cryptographic Suites for Ipsec by P. Hoffman. Published by Network Working Group, © 2005.

Page 338: NIST Special Publication 800-83 Revision 1: Guide to Malware Incident Prevention and Handling for Desktops and Laptops, U.S. Department of Commerce.

Page 348: Most of Which are Still Seen in Active Use from Internet Security Threat Report 2013, Volume 18. Published by Symantec Corporation, © 2013.

Page 356: From Know your Enemy: Tracking Botnets by Paul Bacher, Thorsten Holz , Markus Kötter and Georg Wicherski. Published by The Honeynet Project, © 2005.

Page 362: LAN Magazine.

Page 365–366: Security and Privacy in Communications Networks and the Workshops, IEEE.

Page 371: IEEE Communications Magazine.

Page 377: From Computer Security Incident Handling Guide by Karen Kent and Brian Kim, National Institute of Standards and Technology, 2004.

Page 380: De Alvare, A. "How Crackers Crack Passwords or What Passwords to Avoid." Proceedings, UNIX Security Workshop II, August 1980; US Department of Commerce.

Page 382: Technical Report : STAT -- A State Transition Analysis Tool For Intrusion Detection, ACM.

Page 385: From "An Intrusion-Detection Model" by Dorothy E. Denning in IEEE Transactions on Software Engineering, Volume: 13, Issue: 02, pp: 222–232. Published by IEEE, © 1987.

Page 393: From Intrusion Detection Message Exchange Requirements by M. Wood and M. Erlinger. Published by Network Working Group, © 2007.

Page 394: From The Intrusion Detection Message Exchange Format (IDMEF) by H. Debar, D. Curry and B. Feinstein. Published by Network Working Group, © 2007.

Page 394: From The Intrusion Detection Exchange Protocol (IDXP) by B. Feinstein and G. Matthews. Published by Network Working Group, © 2007.

Page 397: From Guidelines on Firewalls and Firewall Policy: Recommendations of the National Institute of Standards and Technology by Karen Scarfone and Paul Hoffman, U.S. Department of Commerce, 2009.

Page 402–403: Adapted from on Spafford, Eugene. "Observing Reusable Password Choices." Proceedings, UNIX Security Symposium III. September 1992. Accessed at http://docs.lib.purdue.edu/cgi/viewcontent.cgi?article=1969&context=cstech.

Page 417: Lists of Following Weaknesses of Packet Filter Firewalls from Guidelines on Firewalls and Firewall Policy: Recommendations of the National Institute of Standards and Technology by Karen Scarfone and Paul Hoffman. Published by U.S. Department of Commerce, © 2009.

Page 419: From SOCKS Protocol Version 5 by M. Leech, M. Ganis, Y. Lee, R. Kuris, D. Koblas and L. Jones. Published by Network Working Group, © 1996.

INDEX

THE WILLIAM STALLINGS BOOKS ON COMPUTER

DATA AND COMPUTER COMMUNICATIONS, TENTH EDITION

A comprehensive survey that has become the standard in the field, covering (1) data communications, including transmission, media, signal encoding, link control, and multiplexing; (2) communication networks, including wired and wireless WANs and LANs; (3) the TCP/IP protocol suite, including IPv6, TCP, MIME, and HTTP, as well as a detailed treatment of network security. **Received the 2007 Text and Academic Authors Association (TAA) award for the best Computer Science and Engineering Textbook of the year.**

WIRELESS COMMUNICATION NETWORKS AND SYSTEMS
(WITH CORY BEARD)

A comprehensive, state-of-the art survey. Covers fundamental wireless communications topics, including antennas and propagation, signal encoding techniques, spread spectrum, and error correction techniques. Examines satellite, cellular, wireless local loop networks and wireless LANs, including Bluetooth and 802.11. Covers wireless mobile networks and applications.

COMPUTER SECURITY, THIRD EDITION
(WITH LAWRIE BROWN)

A comprehensive treatment of computer security technology, including algorithms, protocols, and applications. Covers cryptography, authentication, access control, database security, cloud security, intrusion detection and prevention, malicious software, denial of service, firewalls, software security, physical security, human factors, auditing, legal and ethical aspects, and trusted systems. **Received the 2008 TAA award for the best Computer Science and Engineering Textbook of the year.**

OPERATING SYSTEMS, EIGHTH EDITION

A state-of-the art survey of operating system principles. Covers fundamental technology as well as contemporary design issues, such as threads, SMPs, multicore, real-time systems, multiprocessor scheduling, embedded OSs, distributed systems, clusters, security, and object-oriented design. **Third, fourth and sixth editions received the TAA award for the best Computer Science and Engineering Textbook of the year.**

AND DATA COMMUNICATIONS TECHNOLOGY

FOUNDATIONS OF MODERN NETWORKING:
SDN, NFV, QOE, IOT, AND CLOUD

An in-depth up-to-date survey and tutorial on Software Defined Networking, Network Functions Virtualization, Quality of Experience, Internet of Things, and Cloud Computing and Networking. Examines standards, technologies, and deployment issues. Also treats security and career topics.

CRYPTOGRAPHY AND NETWORK SECURITY, SEVENTH EDITION

A tutorial and survey on network security technology. Each of the basic building blocks of network security, including conventional and public-key cryptography, authentication, and digital signatures, are covered. Provides a thorough mathematical background for such algorithms as AES and RSA. The book covers important network security tools and applications, including S/MIME, IP Security, Kerberos, SSL/TLS, network access control, and Wi-Fi security. In addition, methods for countering hackers and viruses are explored. **Second edition received the TAA award for the best Computer Science and Engineering Textbook of 1999.**

BUSINESS DATA COMMUNICATIONS, SEVENTH EDITION
(WITH TOM CASE)

A comprehensive presentation of data communications and telecommunications from a business perspective. Covers voice, data, image, and video communications and applications technology and includes a number of case studies. Topics covered include data communications, TCP/IP, cloud computing, Internet protocols and applications, LANs and WANs, network security, and network management.

COMPUTER ORGANIZATION AND ARCHITECTURE,
TENTH EDITION

A unified view of this broad field. Covers fundamentals such as CPU, control unit, microprogramming, instruction set, I/O, and memory. Also covers advanced topics such as multicore, superscalar, and parallel organization. **Five-time winner of the TAA award for the best Computer Science and Engineering Textbook of the year.**

Variation across speech and writing

Douglas Biber

Department of English, Northern Arizona University

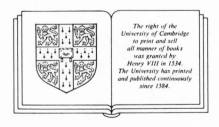

The right of the
University of Cambridge
to print and sell
all manner of books
was granted by
Henry VIII in 1534.
The University has printed
and published continuously
since 1584.

CAMBRIDGE UNIVERSITY PRESS
Cambridge
New York   Port Chester
Melbourne   Sydney

Published by the Press Syndicate of the University of Cambridge
The Pitt Building, Trumpington Street, Cambridge CB2 1RP
40 West 20th Street, New York, NY 10011–4211, USA
10 Stamford Road, Oakleigh, Victoria, 3166, Australia

First published 1988
First paperback edition 1991

Printed in Great Britain at
the University Press, Cambridge

British Library cataloguing in publication data

Biber, Douglas
Variation across speech and writing.
1. spoken language related to written language.
I. Title
001.54

Library of Congress cataloguing in publication data

Biber, Douglas.
Variation across speech and writing / Douglas Biber.
    p.   cm.
Bibliography.
Includes index.
ISBN 0 521 32071 2
1. Language and languages – Variation.   2. Oral communication.
3. Written communication. I. Title.
P120.V37B54 1988
001.54–dc19   87–38213

ISBN 0 521 32071 2 hardback
ISBN 0 521 42556 5 paperback

VN

For my parents,
Martha and Herb Biber

Contents

Contents

Figures

Tables

Acknowledgments

I first became interested in the relationship between speech and writing during my dissertation research, and several of the methodological tools used in the present study were developed at that time. More recently, my dissertation advisors have become my academic colleagues, so that I owe them thanks for both their earlier guidance and their continuing criticism and support. In particular, Edward Finegan, Elinor Ochs, Edward Purcell, and June Shoup have helped me from the earliest stages of this research. Ed Finegan deserves special thanks, since he has been intimately involved in all stages of the research study presented here. As my dissertation chair, he helped conceptualize the methodological approach used here; for example, Ed was the first to suggest that I use computational tools to analyze spoken and written texts, and he went to considerable effort to help obtain computerized text corpora for analysis. He has worked with me on numerous papers and research studies, and his criticisms have ranged from writing style and rhetorical organization to theoretical interpretation and conceptual presentation of results. Finally, over the last several years Ed and I have collaborated on many related studies of variation in English. It is not possible to isolate individual effects of these contributions; they have all influenced the final form of the present study.

Several other colleagues helped directly with the present book. Pat Clancy and Gunnel Tottie both read the manuscript and made especially detailed and helpful comments. Bill Grabe and Niko Besnier helped me through numerous conversations as well as their comments on the manuscript. Larry Ploetz answered numerous computer-related questions during the development of the linguistic analysis programs used here.

Other colleagues at U.S.C. did not help directly with this book but offered their friendship and support; of these, I want to single out Steve Krashen, Larry Hyman, and Joseph Aoun.

Finally, this book would not have been possible without the continued support and understanding of my wife, Teresa, and my children, David and Martha. Although their contributions are less tangible, they are in many ways greater than any of the others.

Part I: Background concepts and issues

1 Introduction: textual dimensions and relations

1.1 Introduction

A considerable body of research in the humanities and social sciences has dealt with the similarities and differences between speech and writing. Work in history, sociology, anthropology, psychology, education, comparative literature, and linguistics has described ways in which the choice between speech and writing is closely related to developments in other social institutions. For example, the development of widespread alphabetic literacy in ancient Greece was probably a catalyst for other social and intellectual developments there. Widespread literacy enabled a fuller understanding and participation by citizens in the workings of government, which might have promoted a democratic form of government in which citizens play a relatively active role. Literacy enabled a permanent, accurate record of ideas and the possibility of knowledge without a living 'knower'. As such it probably aided in the transition from 'myth' to 'history' and the development of critical attitudes towards knowledge. Prior to literacy and a permanent record of beliefs and knowledge, a society can alter its beliefs and not be faced with the possibility of a contradiction; competing ideas which evolve slowly over generations will be accepted as equally factual when there is no contradictory record of earlier ideas. Written records, however, force us to acknowledge the contradictory ideas of earlier societies and thus to regard knowledge with a critical and somewhat skeptical attitude. For example, we know that earlier societies believed that the earth was flat, because these beliefs are permanently recorded in writing. The permanency of writing thus confronts us with the incorrect 'knowledge' of earlier generations and thereby fosters a generally critical attitude towards knowledge.

The permanency of writing also enables the dissection of texts, so that ideas can be critically examined in the abstract and the logical relations among ideas can be discussed. Literacy enables language itself to be the object of inquiry. These possibilities helped foster the development of philosophy as we know it. Similarly, the use of literacy aided the development of new literary forms. Oral literature tends to be poetic, because poetic forms are more easily memorized and transmitted from one generation to the next. The permanency of written texts enables an accurate transmission of any literary form, enabling experimentation with non-poetic types. Although the transition to literacy did not by itself cause any of these intellectual or social developments, it seems to have been an important catalyst.[1]

The transition to literacy seems to have important consequences for individuals as well as societies. Some researchers have claimed that radically different thought processes are enabled by literacy. In particular, it has been claimed that abstract, 'decontextualized' thought depends on literacy, so that non-literate individuals can think in only concrete, contextualized ways. This claim is difficult to evaluate because literacy in Western culture is always confounded with formal education, and thus intellectual differences between literate and non-literate individuals might be due to either the acquisition of literacy or the educational process itself. Research in West Africa by Scribner and Cole (1981) has helped to isolate the effects of literacy from those of formal schooling. The Vai people, who live in Liberia, have developed an indigenous writing system that is used only for traditional, non-academic purposes. Vai literates are taught how to write on an individual basis apart from any other formal schooling. Other members of this tribe become literate in Arabic to study the Quran, or in English by attendance at government schools. Scribner and Cole found that there are specific intellectual abilities which are enhanced by each type of literacy, depending on the particular functions served. For example, Quranic literacy among the Vai greatly enhances memorization abilities because beginning students learn to 'read' the Quran without understanding, and they use their readings to help memorize large portions of the text. Consequences of this type are minor and quite specific to different types of literacy; Scribner and Cole found no global intellectual consequences of literacy apart from the influence of formal schooling.

Although the primary intellectual consequences of literacy are subsumed under those of formal education, there is obviously a very close relationship between school success and literacy. Children who fail at

---

[1] See Goody and Watt (1963), Goody (1977), Stubbs (1980), Ong (1982), and Street (1984) for further discussion of the social and cultural consequences of literacy.

reading and writing fail at school; children who fail at school don't learn how to read. It is difficult to establish a causal relationship here, but schooling is inextricably bound to literacy in Western culture. Several researchers have investigated the acquisition of literacy, and its relation to school success, in Western societies. Some studies describe the problems caused by reliance on spoken language strategies in the compositions of basic writers. Other researchers, such as Heath and Wells, emphasize that many successful students acquire the language-use strategies associated with literacy long before they can actually read and write, and that these strategies are crucially important to literacy acquisition and the types of language use required for school tasks. These patterns of language use can be conveyed by reading to children in the home, but they are further developed by decontextualized spoken interactions; for example, hypothetical discussion of what a storybook character might have done in a particular situation. Students who begin school 'literate', in the sense that they already realize that language can be used for abstract, decontextualized purposes, are the ones who adapt most easily to the requirements of Western education.

Studies similar to these, which look for social or intellectual correlates of writing as distinct from speaking, are found throughout the humanities and social sciences. Given this wide range of interest, it might be expected that the linguistic characteristics of spoken and written language have been thoroughly analyzed. There have, in fact, been many linguistic studies of speech and writing, but there is little agreement on the salient characteristics of the two modes. The general view is that written language is structurally elaborated, complex, formal, and abstract, while spoken language is concrete, context-dependent, and structurally simple. Some studies, though, have found almost no linguistic differences between speech and writing, while others actually claim that speech is more elaborated and complex than writing.

There has also been considerable disagreement concerning the need for a linguistic comparison of speech and writing. Historically, academics have regarded writing, in particular literary works, as the true form of language, while speech has been considered to be unstable, degenerate and not worthy of study. In the nineteenth century this situation began to change when linguists such as Grimm in Germany began to study speech in its own right. The development of phonetics as a separate discipline in Britain, primarily through the work of Henry Sweet and Daniel Jones, further encouraged linguists to study speech. These research trends, however, did not result in linguistic comparisons of speech and writing. Rather, by the early twentieth century, linguists uniformly regarded speech as primary and writing as a secondary form of language derived from speech; thus only speech was considered worth serious linguistic analysis. This bias can be traced from the time of Sapir up to the present, for example:

Sapir: *writing is 'visual speech symbolism' (1921:19–20)*

Bloomfield: *'writing is not language, but merely a way of recording language by visible marks' (1933:21)*

Hall: *'speech is fundamental and writing . . . only a secondary derivative' (1964:8–9)*

Postal: *'writing is a crude way of representing linguistic structure rather than a sign system with a direct relation to the world' (1966:91, n. 20)*

Fillmore: *written communication is 'derivative of the face-to-face conversational norm' (1981:153)*

Aronoff: *notes 'the undoubtedly correct observation that spoken language is "true" language, while written language is an artifact' (1985:28)*

Assuming this secondary, derivative nature of written language, there was no motivation within structural linguistics for comparison of speech and writing.

Although the bias that speech is primary over writing has been extremely important in guiding research efforts within linguistics, it has not been widely accepted outside of linguistics. In fact, the historical view that written, literary language is true language continues as the dominant lay perception to the present time. Our children need to study English at school, which includes written composition and the prescriptive rules of writing, not speech. We criticize immigrant children for not knowing 'English' when they are relatively fluent in a conversation; the problem is that they are not literate in English. We expect our grammars and dictionaries to present the correct forms of written language; when dictionaries present both literate and colloquial vocabulary, they are severely criticized for destroying the standards of English, as happened to

Webster's Third, which has been described as a 'disappointment', 'a scandal and a disaster' (see discussion in Finegan 1980). In our business, legal, and political systems, written commitments are binding and 'real' while spoken commitments are often ignored. As teachers, we explain to children that words like *know* have a silent [k], and words like *doubt* have a silent [b]. Sometimes we even change our pronunciation to reflect an unusual spelling; for example, *often* is now frequently pronounced with a [t], and *palm* with an [l], although these segments were not pronounced at some earlier stages of English. Thus, although speech is claimed to have linguistic primacy, writing is given social priority by most adults in Western cultures.[2]

Even within structural linguistics, researchers have not been entirely consistent regarding the primacy of speech. In particular, there has been a gap between theory and practice in recent syntactic research. In theory, writing is disregarded as secondary and derivative from speech. In practice, however, speech is also disregarded as unsystematic and not representative of the true linguistic structure of a language. This view is especially prominent within the generative-transformationalist paradigm, where grammatical intuitions are the primary data to be analyzed. Although these intuitions are typically collected by means of verbal elicitation, they are in many respects more like writing than speech. Thus the data for analysis within this paradigm deliberately exclude performance errors of 'actual speech', dialect, and register variation, and any linguistic features that depend on a discourse or situational context for interpretation. Although these data are not taken from actual speech or actual writing, they are much closer to stereotypical writing than speech in their form.

All of these perspectives regard either speech or writing as primary and representative of 'true' language; none grants independent status to both speech and writing. However, given the range of arguments on both sides of this issue, it might well be the case that neither speech nor writing is primary; that they are rather different systems, both deserving careful analysis. This is in fact the view advocated by Hymes and other researchers studying communicative competence. That is, in addition to the knowledge that all speakers have about the grammatical structure of

[2] The discussion here owes much to Stubbs (1980). Other works dealing with the primacy of speech or writing include Householder (1971), Vachek (1973), Basso (1974), Schafer (1981), Akinnaso (1982), and Stubbs (1982).

their language, speakers also have extensive knowledge about the use of their language. The former knowledge is grammatical competence, which includes the traditional areas of phonology, syntax, and semantics. The latter knowledge is known as 'communicative competence', and includes formal knowledge of the range of speech-act variation, dialect variation, and register variation, as well as knowledge of when these different linguistic forms are appropriate. Grammatical competence is concerned with the linguistic structure of 'grammatical' utterances; communicative competence is concerned with the form and use of all language – both speech and writing. Within this framework, neither speech nor writing needs to be considered primary to the exclusion of the other. Rather, both require analysis, and the linguistic comparison of the two modes becomes an important question.

Of course, in terms of human development, speech has primary status. Culturally, humans spoke long before they wrote, and individually, children learn to speak before they read or write. All children learn to speak (barring physical disabilities); many children do not learn to read and write. All cultures make use of spoken communication; many languages do not have a written form. From a historical and developmental perspective, speech is clearly primary.

Once a culture has developed written communication, however, there is no reason to regard writing as secondary within that context. It has long been known that cultures exploit variation in linguistic form for functional purposes. For example, variation between lexical items such as *lorry* and *truck* functions to mark geographical differences; variation between pronunciations such as [ka:] versus [kar] and [ðis] versus [dis] functions to mark social differences; variation in address terms, such as *Dr. Jones* versus *Sue*, functions to mark the formality of the situation and the social role relationship between speaker and listener. Similarly, once a culture develops a written form in addition to a spoken form, the two modes come to be exploited for different communicative purposes. Although either speech or writing *can* be used for almost any communicative need, we do not in fact use the two forms interchangeably. Rather, depending on the situational demands of the communicative task, we readily choose one mode over the other. Usually this choice is unconscious, since only one of the modes is suitable or practical. For example, we have no trouble choosing between leaving a note for someone or speaking to the person face-to-face; the situation dictates the mode of communication. Similarly, we have no problem deciding between writing an academic exposition for an audience and addressing the audience by means of a spoken lecture. We could in fact write a lecture or a note to a physically present audience, but this would take more effort and time than required, and it would fail to take advantage of the opportunities for interaction. Conversely, speaking a lecture or a note to an addressee who is separated by time or place is usually not possible at all; apart from the use of telephones and tape recorders, the written mode is required in situations of this type. These simple examples illustrate the fact that the two modes of communication have quite different strengths and weaknesses, and they therefore tend to be used in complementary situations. From this perspective, neither can be said to be primary; they are simply different. The linguistic characteristics of each mode deserve careful attention, and the relationship between the two modes must be investigated empirically rather than assumed on an a priori basis.

1.2 Dimensions and relations

In the present book, spoken and written texts are compared along 'dimensions' of linguistic variation. Researchers have considered texts to be related along particular situational or functional parameters, such as formal/informal, interactive/non-interactive, literary/colloquial, restricted/elaborated. These parameters can be considered as dimensions because they define continuums of variation rather than discrete poles. For example, although it is possible to describe a text as simply formal or informal, it is more accurate to describe it as more or less formal; formal/informal can be considered a continuous dimension of variation.

I will illustrate the concept of 'dimension' in this section by analysis of a few linguistic features in four texts. This illustration greatly over-simplifies the linguistic character of the dimensions actually found in English. Chapters 5–8 present a full analysis based on the distribution of 67 linguistic features in 481 texts. The discussion here thus provides a conceptual description of dimensions, rather than actually describing the complex patterns of variation in English speech and writing.

Following are two quite distinct text samples, which differ along several dimensions. Readers should identify some of the differences between them before proceeding to the following discussion.

Text 1.1: Conversation – comparing home-made beer to other brands

A:	**I had a bottle of ordinary Courage's light ale, which I**	1
	always used to like, and still don't dislike, at Simon	2
	Hale's the other day –	3
	simply because I'm, mm, going through a lean period at	4
	the moment waiting for this next five gallons to be ready,	5
	you know.	6
B:	**mm**	7
A:	**It's just in the bottle stage. You saw it the other night.**	8
B:	**yeah**	9
A:	**and, mm I mean, when you get used to that beer, which**	10
	at its best is simply, you know, superb, it really is.	11
B:	**mm**	12
A:	**you know, I've really got it now, really, you know, got**	13
	it to a T.	14
B:	**yeah**	15
A:	**and mm, oh, there's no, there's no comparison. It tasted**	16
	so watery, you know, lifeless.	17
B:	**mm**	18

Text 1.2: Scientific exposition

Evidence has been presented for a supposed randomness in   1
the movement of plankton animals. If valid, this implies that   2
migrations involve kineses rather than taxes (Chapter 10).   3
However, the data cited in support of this idea comprise   4
without exception observations made in the laboratory.   5

Text 1.1 is taken from an ordinary, face-to-face conversation between friends. It represents the type of communication that we all experience every day. Text 1.2 is much more specialized, coming from a scientific exposition. In contrast to the conversation, relatively few speakers of English commonly read texts like 1.2, and an extremely small proportion are expected to write texts of this type. We might thus distinguish texts 1.1 and 1.2 on a dimension of common versus specialized.

These texts might also be contrasted on a dimension of unplanned versus planned. In text 1.1, speaker A talks without careful planning. At one point he switches topic in the middle of a sentence – in line 10, he begins a thought with *when you get used to that beer*, and two utterances later, in line 16, he completes the sentence with *there's no comparison*; in between these two utterances he notes that his homemade beer is superb when made properly (lines 10–11), and that he really knows how to make the brew now (lines 13–14). Text 1.2 is quite different, having a very careful logical progression indicating careful planning. An idea is presented in lines 1–2, implications of the idea are given in line 3, and the idea is qualified in lines 4–5. This logical progression continues in the rest of text 1.2.

There are several other dimensions that these two texts could be compared along. For example, text 1.1 is interactive while text 1.2 is not; in text 1.1, speaker A refers directly to himself and to speaker B (*I* and *you*), and speaker B responds to A. Text 1.1 is dependent on the immediate situation to a greater extent than text 1.2; in text 1.1, speaker A assumes that B can identify *Simon Hale's* (line 3), *the other day* (line 3), *this next five gallons* (line 5), and *the other night* (line 8). The speaker in text 1.1 displays his feelings enthusiastically and emphatically, while the feelings of the writer in text 1.2 are less apparent; speaker A in text 1.1 repeatedly emphasizes his point with *really*, *simply*, and *you know* (lines 4, 6, 11, 13, 17).

When only two texts are compared, these parameters seem to be dichotomies. If we add a third text, however, we begin to see that these parameters define continuous dimensions. Thus, consider text 1.3 below:

Text 1.3: Panel discussion – discussing corporal punishment as a deterrent to crime

W: **But Mr. Nabarro, we know that you believe this.**

L: **quite**

W: **The strange fact is, that you still haven't given us a reason for it. The only reason you've given for us is, if I may spell it out to you once more, is the following:**
the only crime for which this punishment was a punishment, after its abolition, decreased for eleven years.

> **You base on this the inference that if it had been applied**
> **to crimes it never had been applied to, they wouldn't have**
> **increased.**
> **Now this seems to me totally tortuous.**

Text 1.3 is intermediate between texts 1.1 and 1.2 with respect to the dimensions outlined above. Text 1.3 is certainly not a common everyday communication like text 1.1, but it is not as specialized as text 1.2; text 1.3 is relatively unplanned, but it is more carefully organized than text 1.1; text 1.3 is interactive, but not to the extent of text 1.1; text 1.3 shows little dependence on the immediate situation, but more so than text 1.2; and for the most part, the main speaker in text 1.3 does not reveal his own feelings, although they are more apparent than those of the writer in text 1.2. Text 1.3 is more like text 1.1 with respect to some of these dimensions, and more like text 1.2 with respect to others. However, it has an intermediate characterization with respect to texts 1.1 and 1.2 on each dimension, indicating that these are continuous parameters rather than simple dichotomies.

To this point, we have discussed the notion of dimension from a situational or functional point of view. It is also possible to discuss this notion from a strictly linguistic perspective. In the same way that texts can be described and compared in terms of their situational characterization, there are dimensions that compare texts in terms of their linguistic characterization, e.g., nominal versus verbal, or structurally complex versus structurally simple. Thus consider texts 1.1, 1.2, and 1.3 again. A general impression of text 1.1 is that it is verbal rather than nominal (i.e., many verbs, few nouns) and that it is structurally simple (e.g., little phrasal or clausal elaboration). Text 1.2, on the other hand, seems to be extremely nominal and structurally complex, while text 1.3 seems to have a linguistic characterization between these two. Several questions arise, though: (1) What evidence can we give to support these linguistic impressions? (2) Do these characterizations represent a single linguistic dimension, or two dimensions, or more than two? How can a researcher determine how many linguistic dimensions are required to account for the variation among a set of texts? (3) Are there other linguistic dimensions that are not represented by the above linguistic impressions? If so, how can they be discovered?

I develop an overall empirical approach in the present book that addresses these questions (cf. Section 1.3, Section 3.5, and Chapter 4).

The raw data of this approach are frequency counts of particular linguistic features. Frequency counts give an exact, quantitative characterization of a text, so that different texts can be compared in very precise terms. By themselves, however, frequency counts cannot identify linguistic dimensions. Rather, a linguistic dimension is determined on the basis of a consistent co-occurrence pattern among features. That is, when a group of features consistently co-occur in texts, those features define a linguistic dimension. It should be noted that the direction of analysis here is opposite from that typically used in studies of language use. Most analyses begin with a situational or functional distinction and identify linguistic features associated with that distinction as a second step. For example, researchers have given priority to functional dimensions such as formal/informal, restricted/elaborated, or involved/detached, and subsequently they have identified the linguistic features associated with each dimension. In this approach, the groupings of features are identified in terms of shared function, but they do not necessarily represent linguistic dimensions in the above sense; that is these groupings of features do not necessarily represent those features that co-occur frequently in texts. The opposite approach is used here: quantitative techniques are used to identify the groups of features that actually co-occur in texts, and afterwards these groupings are interpreted in functional terms. The linguistic dimension rather than functional dimension is given priority.

This approach is based on the assumption that strong co-occurrence patterns of linguistic features mark underlying functional dimensions. Features do not randomly co-occur in texts. If certain features consistently co-occur, then it is reasonable to look for an underlying functional influence that encourages their use. In this way, the functions are not posited on an a priori basis; rather they are required to account for the observed co-occurrence patterns among linguistic features.

In fact, there are several unaddressed issues surrounding dimensions identified on functional bases. Although many functional dimensions have been proposed in recent years, few researchers have attempted to relate them to one another or rank them in importance. Consider the following partial list of functional dimensions: informal/formal, restricted/elaborated, contextualized/decontextualized, involved/detached, integrated/fragmented, abstract/concrete, colloquial/literary. Are these all separate dimensions? Do some of them overlap? Are they all equally important? Are they all well-defined in terms of their linguistic characterization? The approach used here begins to answer these questions. By defining 'dimension' from a strictly linguistic perspective, it is possible to identify the set of dimensions required to account for the linguistic variation within a set of texts. Each dimension comprises an independent group of co-occurring linguistic features, and each co-occurrence pattern can be interpreted in functional terms. The result is an empirical assessment of how many independent dimensions there are; an assessment of which functions are independent and which are associated with the same dimension; and an assessment of the relative importance of different dimensions.

The discussion can be made more concrete by considering some frequency counts in texts 1.1, 1.2, and 1.3. In Table 1.1, I list the frequencies for four linguistic features: passive constructions (including post-nominal modifiers, e.g., *the data [which are] cited*), nominalizations, first and second person pronouns, and contractions. The table includes the raw frequency count and the frequency per 100 words; I use the frequency counts normalized to a text of 100 words to compare the three texts.[3]

The conversational text (1.1) and scientific text (1.2) are quite different with respect to these linguistic features. The scientific text has almost seven passives per 100 words and eleven nominalizations per 100 words; the conversation has no passives and less than one nominalization per 100 words. Assuming that these two texts are representative of their kind, their frequency counts indicate that passives and nominalizations tend to co-occur and thus belong to the same linguistic dimension – when a text has many passives, it also has many nominalizations, as in the scientific text; when a text has few passives, it also has few nominalizations, as in the conversational text. Similarly, these two texts indicate that first and second person pronouns and contractions belong to the same dimension – when a text has many first and second person pronouns, it also has many contractions, as in the conversational text; when a text has few first and

---

[3] Raw frequency counts cannot be used for comparison across texts because they are not all the same length. That is, long texts will tend to have higher frequencies simply because there is more opportunity for a feature to occur; in these cases, the higher count does not indicate a more frequent use of the feature. Comparing the frequency per 100 words eliminates this bias. These normalized frequencies are computed as follows:

(actual frequency count ÷ total words in text) × 100

For example, the normalized frequency of contractions in text 1.1 is:

(6 ÷ 118) × 100 = 5.1

Table 1.1 *Frequency counts for texts 1.1, 1.2, and 1.3 (raw frequency count followed by normalized count per 100 words)*

	passives	nominal-izations	1st & 2nd person pronouns	contrac-tions
conversation	0 / 0	1 / .84	12 / 10.2	6 / 5.1
sci. prose	3 / 6.8	5 / 11.4	0 / 0	0 / 0
panel disc.	2 / 2.2	4 / 4.3	10 / 10.8	3 / 3.2

second person pronouns, it also has few contractions, as in the scientific text.

In addition, we might conclude from these two texts that the passive–nominalization dimension and the pronoun–contraction dimension were in fact parts of the same dimension, because there is a consistent co-occurrence pattern between them. That is, when a text has many passives, it has many nominalizations as well as markedly few pronouns and contractions; conversely, when a text has few passives, it has few nominalizations as well as markedly many pronouns and contractions. For these two texts, knowing the frequency of any single feature allows the researcher to predict the frequencies of the other three features, indicating that they comprise a unified dimension. Passives/ nominalizations and pronouns/contractions are not independently related in these two texts – a marked presence of the one set predicts a marked absence of the other. In this sense, dimensions encompass features that consistently occur together and those that consistently complement one another.

Consideration of the panel discussion (text 1.3), however, indicates that passives/nominalizations and pronouns/contractions belong to two separate dimensions. Unlike either the conversation or the scientific text, the panel discussion has high frequencies of all four features. This text confirms the existence of two basic co-occurrence patterns – when a text has many passives, it has many nominalizations; when a text has many first and second person pronouns, it has many contractions. But, the panel discussion shows that these two co-occurrence patterns do not have a consistent relation to one another. It is possible for a text to have many passives/nominalizations and few pronouns/contractions (e.g., the scientific text); it is possible to have many pronouns/contractions and few passives/nominalizations (the conversation); and it is also possible to have many occurrences of both sets of features (the panel discussion). In fact, it is possible for a text to have few passives/nominalizations and few pronouns/contractions, as the following text sample from a novel shows:

Text 1.4: Fiction – K 4

> **She became aware that the pace was slackening; now the coach stopped. The moment had come. Upon the ensuing interview the future would depend. Outwardly she was calm, but her heart was beating fast, and the palms of her hands were damp.**

This text has no passives, no nominalizations, no first or second person pronouns, and no contractions. While this distribution further confirms the two basic co-occurrence patterns identified above – passives co-occurring with nominalizations and pronouns co-occurring with contractions – it also confirms the conclusion that these two patterns belong to two independent dimensions. These two dimensions can be plotted to illustrate their independent status, as in Figures 1.1, 1.2, and 1.3. Figure 1.1 shows that conversation and fiction are alike with respect to the passive/nominalization dimension, as are the scientific text and panel discussion. Figure 1.2 shows a different pattern for the dimension comprising first and second person pronouns and contractions: the conversation and panel discussion are alike, as are the scientific and fictional text. The pattern defined by these two dimensions together is shown in Figure 1.3.

Other linguistic dimensions comprise different sets of co-occurring features. For example, in the above four text samples past tense verbs and third person personal pronouns seem to represent a third co-occurrence pattern. Table 1.2 shows that the scientific text has no past tense verbs and no third person pronouns, that the conversation and panel discussion have a few past tense verbs and no third person pronouns, and that the fiction text has a very frequent number of both past tense verbs and third person pronouns. This co-occurrence pattern is independent from the above two patterns, as shown by Figure 1.4.

Once the linguistic co-occurrence patterns are identified, the resulting dimensions can be interpreted in functional terms. The co-occurrence patterns by themselves are not very interesting. Instead, we want to know why these particular sets of features co-occur in texts; we want to know

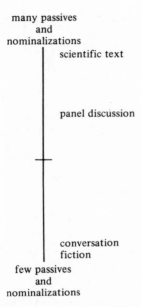

Figure 1.1 *One-dimensional plot of four genres: nominalizations and passives*

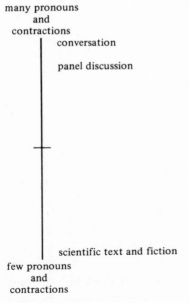

Figure 1.2 *One-dimensional plot of four genres: first and second person pronouns and contractions*

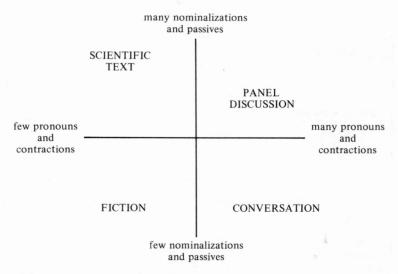

Figure 1.3 *Two-dimensional plot of four genres*

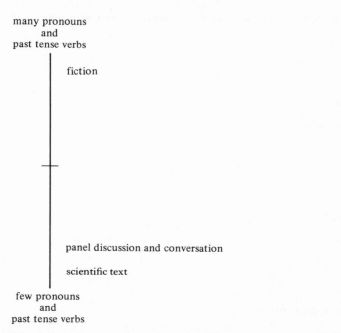

Figure 1.4 *One-dimensional plot of four genres: third person pronouns and past tense verbs*

Table 1.2 *Additional frequency counts for texts 1.1, 1.2, 1.3, and 1.4 (raw frequency count followed by normalized count per 100 words)*

	past tense	3rd person pronouns
conv.	2 / 2.1	0 / 0
sci. prose	0 / 0	0 / 0
panel disc.	3 / 2.5	0 / 0
fiction	6 / 14.3	4 / 9.5

what functional or situational parameters relate to the co-occurring sets of features, influencing their systematic use across a range of texts. For example, from a functional perspective, contractions and first and second person pronouns share a colloquial, informal flavor. They are used in interactive situations that require or permit rapid language production. In the present case, they are used frequently in the conversation and the panel discussion, which are both interactive situations. The linguistic dimension of first and second person pronouns and contractions might thus be interpreted as the surface manifestation of an underlying interactive functional dimension.

The other dimensions could be interpreted through a similar process. The co-occurrence pattern between passives and nominalizations can be interpreted as representing an underlying abstract or informational focus. The co-occurrence pattern between past tense verbs and third person pronouns can be interpreted as representing an underlying narrative focus. Any interpretations need to be verified and refined by analysis of the co-occurring features in particular texts. Through this approach, though, we can proceed from the linguistic features that are in fact used systematically in texts to an account of the underlying functional dimensions of English. In this way, we can identify the functional dimensions that are important enough to be systematically marked, and we will be able to specify the extent to which different discourse functions are independent or overlapping.

Once linguistic dimensions are identified and interpreted, they can be used to specify the 'textual relations' among different kinds of texts in English. Each text can be given a precise quantitative characterization with respect to each dimension, in terms of the frequencies of the co-occurring features that constitute the dimension. This characterization enables a direct comparison of any two texts with respect to each dimension. The textual relations between two texts are defined by a simultaneous comparison of the texts with respect to all dimensions.

Comparison of texts with respect to any single dimension gives an incomplete, and sometimes misleading, picture. For example, consider texts 1.1–1.4 again. If we considered only the passive/nominalization dimension, we would conclude that the fiction text and conversation are linguistically similar and that the scientific text and panel discussion are similar; and that the first two are quite different from the second two. If we considered only the first and second person pronouns/contractions dimension, we would arrive at a quite different set of conclusions: that conversations and panel discussions are quite similar, fiction and academic prose are quite similar, and these two sets of texts are quite different from each other. Finally, considering only the past tense/third person pronouns dimension would lead us to conclude that fiction is very different from the three other texts, which are in turn quite similar to one another. All of these conclusions regarding similarities and differences among texts are inadequate, because the relations among texts cannot be defined unidimensionally. Fiction is not simply similar to or different from scientific prose; rather, it is more or less similar or different with respect to each dimension. Given that the linguistic variation among texts comprises several dimensions, it is no surprise that the relations among texts must be conceptualized in terms of a multi-dimensional space.

The example discussed in this section is extremely simplistic and intended to be illustrative only. To uncover the strong co-occurrence patterns that actually define linguistic dimensions in English, we need to analyze much longer texts, a much larger number of texts taken from many genres, and frequency counts of many linguistic features. Those features that co-occur in different texts across several genres are the ones that define the basic linguistic dimensions of English. A representative selection of texts and linguistic features for analysis is thus a crucial prerequisite to this type of analysis; the range of possible variation must be represented in the texts chosen for analysis, and the range of possible co-occurrence patterns must be represented in the features chosen for analysis. These prerequisites are discussed fully in Chapter 4.

1.3   Theoretical bases for the notion of 'dimension'

The notion that linguistic variation must be analyzed in terms of sets of co-occurring features has been proposed in several places. Ervin-Tripp (1972) and Hymes (1974) discuss co-occurrence relations among linguistic features in terms of 'speech styles,' a variety or register that is characterized by a set of co-occurring linguistic features. Brown and Fraser (1979:38–9) emphasize that:

> it is often difficult, or indeed misleading, to concentrate on specific, isolated [linguistic] markers without taking into account systematic variations which involve the cooccurrence of sets of markers. A reasonable assumption is that socially significant linguistic variations normally occur as varieties or styles, not as individual markers, and it is on those varieties that we should focus.

Although the theoretical importance of co-occurrence patterns among linguistic features has been well established by these researchers, the empirical identification of salient co-occurrence patterns in English discourse has proven to be difficult. One of the few studies to propose specific sets of co-occurring features is Chafe (1982). This study focuses on two fundamental differences between typical speaking and writing – that speaking is faster than writing, and that speakers interact with their audiences to a greater extent than writers – and it proposes an underlying dimension associated with each of these situational differences: integration/fragmentation and detachment/involvement. Along the integration/fragmentation dimension, integration is marked by features that function to pack information into a text, such as nominalizations, participles, attributive adjectives, and series of prepositional phrases; fragmentation is marked by clauses in succession without connectives or joined by coordinating conjunctions. Along the detachment/involvement dimension, detachment is marked by passives and nominalizations; involvement by first person pronouns, emphatic particles, and hedges. Chafe describes conversational texts as fragmented and involved, showing that they have many loosely joined clauses and many involved features such as first person pronouns and emphatics. He describes academic texts as integrated and detached, showing that they have many features like participles, attributive adjectives, nominalizations, and passives. This study is exemplary in that it recognizes the need to discuss linguistic variation among texts in terms of co-occurring features and actually to identify two dimensions of such variation.

Several other researchers have looked at the distribution of linguistic features across social groups and situations: Bernstein (1970) describes restricted versus elaborated codes; Ervin-Tripp (1972) and Irvine (1979) discuss variation between formal and informal registers; Ferguson (1959) describes the differences between high and low varieties (and standard versus non-standard dialects); Ochs (1979) presents differences between planned and unplanned discourse; and several researchers have described linguistic differences between speech and writing. All of these studies describe functional ways in which groups of features co-occur in particular types of texts.

The notion of linguistic co-occurrence patterns is thus well-established in sociolinguistic theory. There are, however, three fundamental differences between earlier conceptualizations and the notion of dimension that I use here. First, most previous studies analyze linguistic variation in terms of a single parameter, while the present study is based on the assumption that linguistic variation in any language is too complex to be analyzed in terms of any single dimension. The simple fact that such a large number of distinctions have been proposed by researchers indicates that no single dimension is adequate in itself. In addition to the distinctions listed above, such as restricted versus elaborated and formal versus informal, linguistic features vary across age, sex, social class, occupation, social role, politeness, purpose, topic, etc. From a theoretical point of view, we thus have every expectation that the description of linguistic variation in a given language will be multi-dimensional, and this expectation forms the basis of the present study.

A second way in which the notion of dimension used here differs from previous conceptualizations relates to their characterization as continuous parameters of variation. Most previous studies have treated linguistic variation in terms of dichotomous distinctions rather than continuous scales. There is no reason, however, to expect that dimensions of variation should be dichotomous. Hymes (1974:41) points out that 'the fact that present taxonomic dimensions consist so largely of dichotomies . . . shows how preliminary is the stage at which we work'. This situation has changed little in the decade since Hymes wrote. In the present study, dimensions are identified as *continuous* quantifiable parameters of variation, i.e., as continuous scales. These scales are labelled in terms of their poles, but a continuous range of texts can be characterized along each dimension. That is, styles, registers, genres, and text types are not related in terms of dichotomous differences; rather they are similar (or different) to differing extents with respect to each dimension. In the approach used in the present study, each text is assigned a precise quantitative characterization with respect to each dimension. The statistical techniques used to compute the dimensions are described in later chapters; the point to note here is that the notion of dimension is quantitative and permits description of a continuous range of variation.

The third difference in the conceptualization of dimension is also a consequence of the quantitative approach adopted here. Previous studies have relied on functional analysis to identify a set of linguistic features that distinguishes among registers. This approach groups together features that are claimed to be functionally similar, but there is no independent check on the extent to which these features actually co-occur in texts. In fact, there are likely to be several overlapping co-occurrence patterns within any set of linguistic features, making it extremely difficult to identify the dimensions of co-occurring features using only functional criteria. In the present analysis, quantitative statistical techniques are used to achieve this goal. Based on the frequencies of features in texts, these techniques provide a precise quantitative specification of the co-occurrence patterns within a set of features. As noted above, these statistical techniques are discussed in later chapters; the point here is that dimensions comprise those features that actually co-occur, rather than a set of features that the researcher expects to co-occur given a particular functional interpretation.

Arguments for or against a parameter of variation that has been proposed on functional grounds are typically presented in terms of the plausibility of the interpretation underlying the grouping of linguistic features. Neither the original analyses nor the criticisms of such studies are based on identification of the actual co-occurrence patterns of linguistic features, because the tools required to identify such patterns have not been readily available to linguists. Thus, for example, Bernstein's distinction between elaborated and restricted codes proposes a group of features that are functionally associated with elaboration and a group of features that are functionally associated with restricted code; and this distinction has been criticized on the grounds that the functional interpretation is not valid. Neither analysts nor critics have determined whether the associated features in fact co-occur in texts.[4] The approach

---

[4] The analyses by Poole (1973) and Poole and Field (1976) analyze the relation between restricted and elaborated codes in terms of continuous dimensions.

adopted here enables a direct consideration of the co-occurrence patterns among features in texts, and thus provides a solid empirical foundation for the identification of underlying dimensions. This approach does not replace functional analysis; it merely changes the order of analysis. Previously, functional analyses were conducted first, in order to identify sets of related linguistic features. In contrast, the present approach first identifies groups of co-occurring features and subsequently interprets them in functional terms.

In summary, the notion of dimension developed here has three distinctive characteristics: (1) no single dimension will be adequate in itself to account for the range of linguistic variation in a language; rather, a multi-dimensional analysis is required; (2) dimensions are continuous scales of variation rather than dichotomous poles; and (3) the co-occurrence patterns underlying dimensions are identified empirically rather than being proposed on an a priori functional basis.

1.4   Is there a spoken/written dimension?

Describing the variation among texts in terms of textual dimensions and relations has important implications for the study of speech and writing. We have seen that situational dimensions such as formality versus informality have no a priori linguistic validity. Similarly, there is no reason to assume that the situational difference between speech and writing constitutes a linguistic dimension in English. This is rather an empirical question: is there a linguistic dimension of co-occurring features that distinguishes between spoken and written texts? That is, if there is a spoken/written dimension, then there will be a set of co-occurring linguistic features that functions to distinguish all written texts from all spoken texts. This question cannot be answered by consideration of a few texts and a few linguistic features. Rather it requires analysis of the distribution of many linguistic features in many different types of speech and writing in English. This book identifies several of the basic linguistic dimensions of variation among spoken and written texts in English, and it specifies the multi-dimensional relations among several different kinds of speech and writing. It shows that the variation among texts within speech and writing is often as great as the variation across the two modes. No absolute spoken/written distinction is identified in the study. Rather, the relations among spoken and written texts are complex and associated with a variety of different situational, functional, and processing considerations. The goal of the study is to specify the multi-dimensional relations among the many different types of speech and writing in English. As a by-product of this analysis, the issue of an absolute spoken/written distinction is addressed and put aside as not central to the relations among spoken and written texts.

1.5 Outline of the book

The remainder of Part I presents other background notions and research. Chapter 2 presents a preliminary typology of 'functions' (communicative purposes served by particular linguistic features in texts) and 'situations' (configurations of cultural, physical, temporal, and psychological features that define the situational context of texts). This typology provides the theoretical foundation required for the interpretation of the quantitative results given in later chapters. Chapter 2 also includes a discussion of the major situational and functional parameters distinguishing among typical spoken and written genres.

In Chapter 3, I present an overview of previous linguistic research on speech and writing in English. I divide studies into quantitative and non-quantitative approaches, and I discuss some of the methodological restrictions that have been shared by both approaches. In a concluding section, I introduce the multi-feature/multi-dimensional approach to textual variation, which is designed to avoid these methodological restrictions, and I summarize the major research findings to date using this approach.

Part II of the book deals with methodological issues. In Chapter 4, I show the necessity of both micro and macro approaches to textual variation, summarize the linguistic features and multivariate statistical analyses used in the study, and describe the particular texts used in some detail. Chapter 5 presents a fairly detailed introduction to factor analysis. It describes the steps involved in doing a factor analysis and presents the particular factor analysis that forms the basis of the present study. Sections 5.2–5.5 are relatively technical; they are not prerequisites to understanding the theoretical results presented in Chapters 6–8.

Part III, which comprises Chapters 6, 7, and 8, constitutes the heart of the study. In Chapter 6, I interpret the factors described in Chapter 5. Six primary factors are identified by the analysis, and the textual dimension underlying each of them is interpreted in functional terms. Then in Chapter 7, the relations among spoken and written genres are identified and interpreted in terms of this six-dimensional space. That is, each of the dimensions identifies a set of similarities and differences among the genres, and consideration of all six dimensions enables a rich assessment of the relations among genres in English. This chapter first considers the relations among genres with respect to each dimension separately, analyzing representative text samples from particular genres in some detail. Then, an overall account of the relations among genres with respect to all six dimensions is given. This chapter addresses the extent to which there is an absolute spoken/written difference in English. It shows that no dimension defines a dichotomous distinction between speech and writing, although several dimensions distinguish among oral and literate genres in different respects.

Chapter 8 extends this description by showing that spoken and written genres differ in their internal coherence; that the texts within some genres differ greatly from one another, while the texts within other genres are highly similar to one another. Some of this variation reflects the extent to which the cultural norms for particular genres are highly constrained. For example, face-to-face conversations can vary considerably in their form and still be considered representative of their genre; official documents, on the other hand, tolerate much less variation in their form. In addition, some genres, such as academic prose and press reportage, permit considerable internal variation because they are composed of several distinct sub-genres, which differ in both their communicative purposes and linguistic form. Relations among sub-genres within academic prose, press reportage, editorials, broadcasts, and telephone conversations are examined with respect to the six textual dimensions.

Finally, Chapter 9 summarizes the major research findings of the book and identifies several applications of the model of textual relations developed here. Applications to dialect, discourse, stylistic, historical, and cross-linguistic comparisons are discussed. In conclusion, the development of a typology of texts is identified as a remaining major research goal. Research conducted towards this goal is described, and it is shown how the description of textual relations among spoken and written genres provides the necessary foundation for a more complete typology.

Four appendices are included in the book. Appendices I, II, and IV support the methodological discussion of Part II, and Appendix III presents descriptive data in support of the analyses in Part III. Appendix I lists the specific texts used in the study. Appendix II gives a detailed description of the linguistic features used in the study, including the algorithms for their automatic identification and their characteristic communicative functions. The appendix begins with an overview of the computational techniques used for the automatic identification of linguistic features. It describes in broad terms the programs used to 'tag' words in texts for their grammatical category and to identify occurrences of particular syntactic constructions. The appendix then discusses, for each feature, the algorithm for automatic identification and the discourse functions associated with the feature in previous studies. Appendix IV presents a correlation matrix of all linguistic features used in the study, which forms the basis of the factor analysis.

Appendix III presents mean frequency counts of all linguistic features for each of the 23 genres used in the study. This appendix is included to support the analyses in Part III and to enable further micro-analyses of particular features (cf. Section 4.5).

2 *Situations and functions*

This study is based on both macroscopic and microscopic analyses of textual variation (see Section 4.1). Macroscopic analyses identify the dimensions of variation among texts and specify the overall relations among genres with respect to those dimensions. Microscopic analyses describe the functions of linguistic features in relation to the speech situations of individual texts. Linguistic features mark particular components of the situation, in addition to their functions as markers of relations within a text. In this chapter, I describe the salient components of the speech situation and provide a brief overview of the major communicative functions served by linguistic features. I then turn to the situational and functional differences between 'typical' speaking and writing and propose a framework for comparing more or less typical genres in terms of their situational characteristics.

2.1 Components of the speech situation

There are several studies that catalog the components of the speech situation, which provides the situational context for 'speech events'. One of the earliest and most complete descriptions is presented in Hymes's (1974:53ff) components of speech, which include message form, message content, speaker, hearer, purposes, key, channels, and norms of interaction. This description is further elaborated by Duranti (1985). Fishman (1972) identifies three primary components of the situation of language use: (1) the participants and the relationship among them, (2) the topic, and (3) the setting. Halliday (1978) also distinguishes among three components of the communicative situation: (1) the type of social action (the 'field'), (2) the role relationships (the 'tenor'), and (3) the symbolic organization (or 'mode'). Brown and Fraser (1979) present a thorough discussion of the components of situation, distinguishing among the three primary components of purpose, setting, and particip-

28

ants, each of which has several sub-components. The discussion below draws heavily on Brown and Fraser (1979) and Hymes (1974, Chapter 2).

Based on these earlier studies, I distinguish eight components of the speech situation, several of them having sub-components: (1) participant roles and characteristics, (2) relations among the participants, (3) setting, (4) topic, (5) purpose, (6) social evaluation, (7) relations of participants to the text, and (8) channel. These components are summarized in Table 2.1.

'Participant roles and characteristics' refers to the communicative roles of participants plus the individual characteristics of each participant, including their own personal characteristics and those characteristics determined by group membership. It is necessary to distinguish at least three groups of participants: addressor(s), addressee(s), and audience. The addressor produces the message (Hymes further distinguishes a sender, who conveys the message); the addressee is the intended recipient of the message; and the audience are participants who hear or overhear the message but are not usually the intended recipients. Although 'speaker' refers strictly to speech, I will use the terms 'speaker' and 'addressor' interchangeably throughout this study.

Participants also have personal characteristics that influence their language use. These characteristics can be stable (e.g., personality, interests, beliefs) or temporary (e.g., mood, emotions). These personal characteristics are presumably the primary influence on a person's personal style, but this is an area that has not been much studied from a linguistic point of view. In addition to personal characteristics, participants can be characterized by their group membership, i.e., a characterization in terms of social class, ethnic group, sex, age, occupation, etc. There has been considerable research relating linguistic use to these group characteristics.

'Relations among the participants' has several facets. First of all, it refers to the social role relations among participants, that is, their relations in terms of relative social power, status, etc. It also refers to the more exclusively personal relationship between participants, that is, whether they like each other, respect each other, etc. The relationship between the addressor(s) and addressee(s) can differ in terms of the amount of specific and cultural/world knowledge they share. Intimate friends will share considerable specific knowledge about one another; business associates will share little specific personal knowledge but much cultural knowledge; participants from different cultures might share little

Table 2.1 *Components of the speech situation*

I. Participant roles and characteristics

   A. Communicative roles of participants

      1. addressor(s)
      2. addressee(s)
      3. audience

   B. Personal characteristics

      1. stable: personality, interests, beliefs, etc.
      2. temporary: mood, emotions, etc.

   C. Group characteristics

      1. social class, ethnic group, gender, age, occupation, education, etc.

II. Relations among participants

   A. Social role relations: relative social power, status, etc.

   B. Personal relations: like, respect, etc.

   C. Extent of shared knowledge

      1. cultural world knowledge
      2. specific personal knowledge

   D. 'Plurality' of participants

III - IV - V. Scene: the interaction of components III, IV, and V

III. Setting

   A. Physical context

   B. Temporal context

   C. Superordinate activity type

   D. Extent to which space and time are shared by participants

IV. Topic

V. Purpose

   A. Conventional goals

   B. Personal goals

Table 2.1 (*cont.*)

VI.   Social evaluation

   A.   Evaluation of the communicative event

      1.   values shared by whole culture

      2.   values held by sub-cultures or individuals

   B.   Speaker's attitudes towards content

      1.   feelings, judgements, attitudinal 'stance'

      2.   key: tone or manner of speech

      3.   degree of commitment towards the content,
          epistemological 'stance'

VII.   Relations of participants to the text

VIII.   Channel

   A.   Primary channel: speech, writing, drums, signs, etc.

   B.   Number of sub-channels available

---

specific or cultural knowledge. The relations among participants will differ depending on the plurality of speaker and addressee. Addressing a large class of people is very different from addressing an individual; similarly, a group production of a message is very different from the more typical individual production. Finally, relations among participants can differ in the extent of interaction possible or appropriate, although this factor will be influenced by the physical/temporal setting and the purpose of communication.

'Setting' refers to the different aspects of the physical and temporal context. Where the communication takes place, when it takes place, and what larger activity it is part of are all components of the setting. The extent to which participants share time and space is an important component of the setting. In addition, the presence or absence of an audience might be considered part of the setting.

The 'topic' is simply what the message is about. This component is closely related to the fifth component, the 'purpose', which refers to the outcomes that participants hope for, expect, or intend from the communicative event. Hymes distinguishes between conventionally recognized outcomes (e.g., participants expect a bargaining session to result in a business agreement) and the specific goals of each participant (e.g., to make a friend, further one's own interests). The setting, topic, and purpose combine to determine the 'scene', which is the psychological setting of communication. That is, as purpose and topic shift within a given setting, the perception of the speech activity also shifts. Similarly, a move to a new setting, holding topic and purpose the same, might cause a shift in the perception of scene. For example, an instructor and students can sit in a classroom before class having an informal conversation. As the time for class passes, the instructor can begin to teach, causing the perception of communicative activity to shift from an informal conversation to a more formal lecture or class discussion. The participants and the physical and temporal setting remain constant, but the perception of the scene changes. Because it is derivative from the components of setting, topic, and purpose, I have not included scene as a separate component in the scheme presented here. The notion of scene, however, is crucial to understanding the differences among communicative situations.

'Social evaluation' refers to the attitudes of the participants, and of the culture at large, to the communicative event and the specific content of the message. In different cultures, some types of language are valued more highly than others. For example, in Western culture schooled language tends to be valued more highly than nonschooled language, and writing tends to be valued more highly than speech. In traditional Somali culture, oral poetry is valued more highly than either schooled language or writing. Values of this type can be shared within a culture or they can be restricted to sub-groups. For example, some groups in American culture frequently use an argumentative style and place high value on argumentative speech events, while other groups avoid an argumentative style at all costs, having a quite negative attitude towards this type of discourse (see Kochman 1981; Schiffrin 1984b). The participants' attitudes towards the content should also be considered here. These attitudes involve expression of the speaker's feelings, judgments, or attitudinal stance. Hymes uses the term 'key' to refer to the tone or manner of speech, for instance serious or sarcastic. Finally, the degree of commitment towards the content, or epistemological stance, can also be considered as part of this component; that is, to what extent is the speaker certain of the truthfulness of the message.

'Relations of participants to the text' is a component of the situation that has not been much discussed. Chafe (1982) notes that one of the key differences between typical speaking and writing relates to the ability of the communicative participants to interact with the text: the writer can write as slowly and carefully as (s)he wishes; the reader can read as quickly or as slowly as (s)he wishes; but speakers and listeners must produce and comprehend language 'on-line', with little opportunity for interaction with the text. Thus, relation to the text is an additional important component of the situation.

Finally, 'channel' refers to the medium of the message. Two aspects need to be distinguished here. The first concerns the primary channel of communication. This is typically either speech or writing, but might also be drums, sign language, telegraph, etc. In addition, the number of sub-channels available for communication must be considered. For example, in typical speaking three sub-channels are available: (1) the lexical/syntactic, (2) prosodic, and (3) paralinguistic (gestures, etc.). In contrast, writing is typically restricted to the lexical/syntactic sub-channel.

All of these components are important in the specification of the situational context of communication. Describing the situation is a precursor to functional descriptions of language use. That is, identification of the salient components of the situation enables an interpretation of the roles played by particular linguistic features within that context. To these functions we turn next.

2.2 Linguistic functions

The notion of function is closely associated with the notion of situation. A primary motivation for analysis of the components of situation is the desire to link the functions of particular linguistic features to variation in the communicative situation. Much work of this type has been under-taken with respect to the phonological markers that distinguish among speakers of different social dialects in different situations (e.g., Labov 1972). This research shows that linguistic form varies systematically with the social category of the speaker and the formality of the situation, so that different linguistic forms function as markers of social category and formality. There has been less research on the ways in which linguistic form varies with other differences in the situation. Such work has typically been done as part of the analysis of 'register', linguistic variation associated with differences in use rather than group differences associated with the user (e.g. Halliday 1968; Ferguson 1977, 1983). Brown and Fraser (1979) discuss the functions of linguistic features as markers of situation, that is, the ways in which linguistic features function to distinguish different aspects of the communicative situation (see also Hymes 1974:22ff; Halliday 1978).

I distinguish here among seven major functions that can be served by linguistic features. Each of these functions identifies a type of information that is marked in discourse. The seven functional categories are: (1) ideational, (2) textual, (3) personal, (4) interpersonal, (5) contextual, (6) processing, and (7) aesthetic. These functions are summarized in Table 2.2.

Ideational functions refer to the ways in which linguistic form is used to convey propositional or referential content. Although most linguists have regarded this as the primary function of language, researchers such as Halliday and Hymes claim instead that this is merely one of several important functions. Certain types of language (e.g., typical face-to-face conversation) have a very low focus on informational content, and, as is shown in Chapter 7, these same types of language have few of the linguistic features that are functionally important for conveying propositional content (such as frequent nouns and prepositional phrases, or a highly varied vocabulary). The ideational function of linguistic features is important, but the present analysis shows that it is only one of several functions determining the linguistic structure of texts.

Textual functions are of two types: to mark information structure or to mark cohesion. Information structure refers to the way in which a text is packaged, including the marking of focus, topic–comment constructions, and theme, by features such as clefts, pseudo-clefts, extraposed clauses, and passives. Cohesion, on the other hand, refers to surface features that mark the ways in which the sentences of a text are referentially related, for example, through the use of pronominal reference, demonstratives, lexical substitution (e.g., 'do' for a verb phrase), and ellipsis (Halliday and Hasan 1976).

The ideational and textual functions are strictly linguistic; they deal respectively with clause structure and text-internal structure. The remaining functions are ways in which linguistic form can serve to mark information outside of the text itself. Personal functions include markers of group membership, personal style, and attitudes towards the communicative event or towards the content of the message. In contrast, interpersonal functions are those that depend on some aspect of the

Table 2.2 *Functions of linguistic features*

I.   Ideational functions

    A. Presentation of propositional meaning
    B. Informational density

II.   Textual functions

    A. Different ways of marking informational structure and prominence
    B. Different ways of marking cohesion
    C. The extent to which informational structure, prominence, and cohesion are marked

III. Personal functions

    A. To mark group membership of addressor
    B. To mark idiosyncratic characteristics of addressor
    C. To express attitudes towards the communicative event or content

IV.   Interpersonal functions

    A. To mark role relations
    B. To express attitudes towards particular participants

V.   Contextual functions

    A. To mark physical or temporal setting
    B. To mark purpose
    C. To mark the psychological 'scene'

VI.   Processing functions: caused by or in consideration of the production and comprehension demands of the communicative event

VII. Aesthetic functions: personal and cultural attitudes towards form

    A. To conform to grammatical prescriptions
    B. To conform to "good style"

---

relationship between participants: role relationships, overtly expressed attitudes towards participants, the extent of shared knowledge, and the interactional possibilities of the communicative event.

Contextual functions are those relating to the physical and temporal setting of communication (actual space and time, and the extent to which place and time are shared), the purposes of communication, and the perception of the scene. Processing functions are those relating to the production and comprehension demands of the communicative event. These can reflect differences in production constraints, or they can reflect the addressor's concern for producing text that is readily understood. Finally, aesthetic functions are those relating to personal or cultural attitudes about the preferred forms of language. These include grammatical prescriptions established by language academies and other linguistic 'guardians' as well as individual notions about 'good' style and rhetorical effect.

Although there are probably other functions served by linguistic features, these seven seem to be the most important. In Appendix II, I describe the specific communicative functions that have been associated with each of the linguistic features used in the present study. In Chapters 6–7, I show that a group of features can share a common, underlying function; that texts are systematically related by their exploitations of those functions; and that textual dimensions can be interpreted by determining the most widely shared functions underlying a group of co-occurring features. As background to the analysis in those chapters, the remainder of the present chapter describes the salient situational and functional distinctions between 'typical' speaking and writing.

2.3   Situational and functional differences between 'typical' speaking and writing

2.3.1   The notion of typical speech and writing

One of the central findings of the present study is that there is no linguistic or situational characterization of speech and writing that is true of all spoken and written genres. On the one hand, some spoken and written genres are very similar to one another (e.g., public speeches and written exposition). On the other hand, some spoken genres are quite different from one another (e.g., conversation and public speeches), as are some written genres (e.g., personal letters and academic exposition). The relations among these genres are systematic but must be specified in a multi-dimensional space.

Despite the fact that speech and writing are not homogeneous types, I find it useful to use the notion of typical speech and writing to refer to the unmarked genre in each mode. From one perspective, this notion refers to the most frequent or common type of speech and writing. From another perspective, this notion refers to the types of speech and writing that have the stereotypical characteristics of their mode. In terms of its situational characteristics, stereotypical speech is interactive, and dependent on shared space, time, and background knowledge; stereotypical writing has the opposite characteristics (see Section 2.3.4). In terms of its linguistic characteristics, stereotypical speech is structurally simple, fragmented, concrete, and dependent on exophoric (situation-dependent) reference; again, stereotypical writing has the opposite characteristics (see Section 3.1). These stereotypical descriptions are based on consideration of the most frequent or common types of speech and writing, so that these two perspectives dovetail into one. Both perspectives indicate face-to-face conversation as typical speech and informational exposition as typical writing. I adopt the notions of typical speech and writing here to make sense out of previous research. In later chapters, I return to this notion to examine the extent to which conversation and exposition are in fact typical of their mode when considered from a multi-dimensional perspective.

2.3.2 Situational differences

Analysis of the situational differences between typical speaking and writing has been undertaken in several places. Rubin (1980) provides an overall taxonomy of these differences, but useful discussions can also be found in Kay (1977), Olson (1977), Olson and Torrance (1981), Green and Morgan (1981), Akinnaso (1982), Stubbs (1982), Heath (1982a,b), Lakoff (1982a,b), Rader (1982), Gumperz *et al.* (1984), and Tannen (1985). These studies are concerned with the particular components of the situational context that are important in distinguishing between speech and writing. Other studies, and the discussion in the first part of this chapter, attempt to identify the full range of components defining the situational context of a discourse. Many components that are important to a full specification of situational context are not highly relevant to the contextual differences between typical speech and writing. These other components include social categories (e.g., class, ethnic group, sex, and age), individual personality characteristics of the speaker and addressee, and the social role relationship (e.g., power and status) between speaker and addressee. The present section does not include discussion of these components; it is limited to the situational components that are central to the distinctions between speaking and writing.

Table 2.3 outlines six situational components identified from previous research as major distinctions between typical speaking and writing; I have divided these components into sixteen situational parameters. Although these parameters might be considered as dichotomies, the poles do not characterize all speaking and writing situations. Rather, these dichotomies describe typical speaking and writing, commonly represented by face-to-face conversation and expository prose. Certain situational characteristics are commonly associated with speaking and others with writing, but none of these characteristics (except the physical mode distinction) is associated exclusively with speaking or writing situations. This point is illustrated in Section 2.3.4.

1.   Physical channel
     refers to the choice of the spoken or written mode as the primary channel, and the total number of sub-channels available for communication.
          a. 'spoken or written channel' merely marks the fact that speaking uses the auditory channel and writing the visual channel. Even an obvious statement like this must be qualified: writing can be produced to be spoken (a speech or dramatic play); speech can be produced to be written (dictating a letter).
          b. 'prosodic and paralinguistic sub-channels available or not' refers to the restriction of writing to the lexical/syntactic channel (i.e., morphemes and their arrangement), as opposed to the multi-channel nature of speech (including prosody, gestures, etc.). It has been claimed that this difference causes writing to be more linearly explicit than speech, since the information structure of written texts must be marked entirely in the grammatical channel, whereas spoken texts can utilize several channels. Sometimes writing uses channels other than the strictly grammatical channel. For example, printed writing can use underlining, bold face, italics, and other fonts (Vachek 1979; Lakoff 1982a). Notes left on the kitchen table can use arrows to point to the immediate context, almost as a paralinguistic gesture. Speaking, on the other hand, can be restricted in the number of available channels; for example, neither a conversation in a dark room nor a tape-recorded speech can use paralinguistic gestures.

2.   Cultural use
     refers to differences between speaking and writing due to the attitudes

Table 2.3 *List of major situational parameters distinguishing between typical speaking and writing*

1. Physical channel

    a. spoken or written channel
    b. prosodic and paralinguistic sub-channels available or not

2. Cultural use

    a. home-acquisition or school-acquisition
    b. high or low social evaluation
    c. maintenance of social status

3. Relation of communicative participants to each other

    a. extent of interaction
    b. extent of shared knowledge about each other
    c. degree of goal negotiability
    d. effort expended to maintain relationship
    e. extent of shared cultural world-knowledge

4. Relation of communicative participants to the external context

    a. extent of shared time
    b. extent of shared space

5. Relation of communicative participants to the text

    a. degree of permanence of the text; opportunity for
       interaction with the text in production (planning or
       revising) and in comprehension
    b. speed of production
    c. speed of comprehension

6. Primary purpose of communication

    a. ideational or interactional

towards and use of each within a given society. These differences change from one cultural group to the next (see Stubbs 1982; Heath 1982a,b).

a. 'home-acquisition versus school-acquisition' refers to the fact that in Western society, literacy is explicitly taught and learned in the schools, while speech is naturally acquired in the home. This results in literacy taking on the decontextualized and formal aspects of educational institutions.

b. 'social evaluation' refers to the attitude that writing is more valuable than speech. This evaluation is by no means a cultural universal (e.g., Philips 1983). In Western societies, however, where writing is considered to represent the 'correct' form of the language, this factor will exert an important influence on the amount of attention paid to speech versus writing.

c. 'maintenance of social status' refers to the tendency of speakers from the upper socio-economic classes, speakers in formal situations, and writers to resist phonological and syntactic reductions as a means of maintaining social distance from other social classes or speech situations (Kroch 1978; Kroch and Small 1978; Finegan and Biber 1986a; and Finegan 1987). This tendency is claimed to result in a closer form–meaning correspondence, and can perhaps be seen as a source of the prescriptive rules common in composition textbooks, which generally advocate a one-to-one correspondence between form and meaning.[1]

3.   Relation of communicative participants to each other

refers to the differences related to the addressee as an active, individual listener in typical speaking versus addressee as a passive group of readers in writing (where 'active' and 'passive' refer to interaction with the speaker, not interaction with the text). I have divided this component into five categories:

a. 'extent of interaction' refers to the listener's unique opportunities to respond directly in speaking situations. These responses can present additional information or opinions, can request clarification of earlier statements, or can simply indicate understanding and continued interest. Readers cannot provide direct feedback of this type, and typically they do not have opportunity to provide any response at all.

b. 'extent of shared knowledge about each other' refers to the speaker/writer's knowledge of the addressees' backgrounds, e.g., their personalities, beliefs, knowledge, interests, etc. In speech, such knowledge is variable, although often intimate, while in writing it is often minimal or

[1] It is interesting to note that these distinctions can be in conflict with one another. For example, teachers of composition in Western schools normally advocate the use of an active style. Society in general, however, attaches a more 'learned' value to a nominal/passive style. Thus, schools and society at large have different expectations concerning good literate style. Williams (1980) describes an experiment in which composition teachers rated essays written in a nominal style more highly than similar essays written in an active style, despite their professed preference for the latter. In actual practice, the values of society at large seem to dominate in this case.

irrelevant. This dimension is influential because a speaker (as opposed to a writer) can reduce the informational content of an utterance on the basis of shared personal knowledge and still expect to be understood.

c. 'negotiability of communicative goal and topic' refers to the on-going negotiation of purpose and topic in typical speech, versus the impossibility of such negotiation in writing. Recently several authors have pointed out that the reading process must also be viewed as an interactive one. For example, Widdowson (1979:174) writes: 'In this view, reading is regarded not as reaction to a text but as interaction between writer and reader mediated through the text' (see also Dillon 1981). Reading is necessarily an interactive process in this sense; readers approach a text with different communicative goals, and come away with different understandings of the meaning. But this interaction takes place between the reader and the text, and it does not influence the form of the text in any way. The writer of a text is concerned only with the general interests of the intended audience, not with the specific interests of individual potential readers. Thus, individual readers must simply decide if the stated goal is agreeable or not – with no recourse to negotiation.

d. 'effort required to maintain relationship' refers to the fact that, in speech, communication crucially depends on the establishment and subsequent maintenance of a focused social relationship between participants, while in writing this necessity does not exist (Olson and Torrance 1981). If a social rapport is not established at the start of a spoken encounter, the encounter is likely to end prematurely (e.g., when the listener leaves, turns to address a third party, or simply stops paying attention). Further, once a relationship has been established between speaker and listener, there must be a continual monitoring of the other party to ensure its maintenance.

The social relationship between reader and writer is also important. In this case, however, the relationship is established a priori, and the reader must decide to either accept or reject that relationship. This decision will be influenced by the writer's stance towards the intended audience and subject-matter. However, in contrast to speech, once a writer takes a given stance, there is no tendency to modify that stance in order to maintain a relationship with a specific addressee. This factor is important in causing speech to be highly concerned with the metacommunicative functions, and writing to be much less concerned with those functions, so that it is free to focus on the ideational functions.

e. 'extent of shared cultural world-knowledge' refers to the general cultural background that writers and speakers assume in their addressees. Rader (1982) has shown that this type of shared knowledge is important in written imaginative fiction as well as in speech. However, the extent of shared cultural background knowledge is in general greater in speech than in writing. That is, in speech the addressee interacts directly with the speaker, and therefore her/his cultural background is usually known (or readily apparent), whereas writing is typically addressed to a broader range of cultural backgrounds. Despite this claim, it is apparent that cultural background knowledge does not represent an absolute distinction between the modes: nothing inherent in writing causes it to be intended for all cultures, just as nothing inherent in speech automatically overcomes the problems of interethnic communication.

4.   Relation of the communicative participants to the external context refers to the spatial and temporal contexts of speech and writing.

   a. 'extent of shared space' refers to the fact that speaker and listener normally share a physical context, while writer and reader typically do not and thus do not refer to the physical surroundings.

   b. 'extent of shared time' refers to the fact that speaker and listener typically share a temporal context, while writer and reader are usually separated by a considerable period of time.

5.   Relation of communicative participants to the text

   a. 'degree of permanence' refers to the temporary nature of speech in contrast to the permanence of writing. Especially with respect to the development of written discourse within Western society, this distinction has been crucial. For instance, the permanence of writing enables a prolonged visual inspection of the text, and the associated activities of planning, organizing, and revision, plus the general high attention to form associated with writing. These activities enable the maximally explicit, highly integrated texts which are associated with writing (Chafe 1982).

   b. 'speed of production and comprehension' refers to the fact that the production of speech is much faster than that of writing, while the speed of comprehension is potentially reversed in the two modes. That is, the reader is free to comprehend at his/her leisure, or to skim an entire text in a few seconds; the listener must comprehend language as it is produced.

6.   Purpose

   refers to the fact that writing is typically for ideational purposes, to convey propositional information, while speaking is more often for personal, interpersonal, and contextual purposes in addition to, or instead of, ideational purposes. Conversational participants often speak to express their personal feelings, or to establish or reaffirm their interpersonal relationship, rather than to convey propositional information.

2.3.3 Functional differences

There are several functional differences between typical speech and writing, which are associated with the typical situational characteristics of the two modes. For example, linguistic features are used for informational elaboration and explicit, situation-independent reference in typical writing, while other features function to mark interaction, expression of personal feelings, and direct reference to the external situation in typical speech.

Chafe (1982, 1985; Chafe and Danielewicz 1986) proposes four functional notions that are particularly useful in the interpretation of the textual dimensions identified in the present study: 'integration', 'fragmentation', 'involvement', and 'detachment'. Each of these functions relates to a particular aspect of the speech or writing situation, and each is marked by several linguistic features.

Integration refers to the way in which a large amount of information is packed into relatively few words in typical writing, because the writer operates under few time constraints and can therefore construct a carefully packaged text. Similarly, the reader, who can read as quickly or slowly as (s)he pleases, is able to take advantage of a highly integrated text. In contrast, typical speech cannot be highly integrated because it is produced and comprehended on-line. Features that are used to integrate information into a text include attributive adjectives, prepositional phrase series, phrasal coordination, and careful word choice.

Fragmentation refers to the linguistic characteristics of texts produced under severe time constraints, the case for typical speech. Under these conditions, information cannot be carefully incorporated into the text, and the resulting structure is much looser, or fragmented. Linguistic features associated with a fragmented text include clauses strung together with simple conjunctions (e.g., *and*) or with no connectives at all.

Involvement refers to those linguistic features which reflect the fact that speaker and listener typically interact with one another, while writer and reader typically do not. Due to this interaction, speakers often make direct reference to the listener (by use of second person pronouns, questions, imperatives, etc.), and they are typically concerned with the expression of their own thoughts and feelings (e.g., marked by use of first person pronouns, affective forms such as emphatics and amplifiers, and cognitive verbs such as *think* and *feel*). As a result of this concern, speech often has a distinctly non-informational and imprecise character (marked by hedges, pronoun *it*, and other forms of reduced or generalized content). These features can be considered together as the characteristics of involved text. In contrast, detachment refers to the characteristics of typical writing which result from the fact that writer and reader usually do not interact (e.g., marked by agentless passives and nominalizations).

These functional notions are useful in the interpretation of the textual dimensions (Chapters 6 and 7), although no dimension corresponds in a one-to-one fashion to any particular notion. For example, one dimension identified in the present analysis indicates that involved texts are also typically fragmented in certain respects; and that these texts are markedly not integrated. Another dimension indicates that certain types of structural elaboration reflect a type of fragmentation; that is, in informational texts produced under strict time constraints, information seems to be tacked on as additional dependent clauses, in a fragmented manner, rather than being tightly integrated into the text. The actual co-occurrence patterns among linguistic features identified in the present study differ from those proposed on functional grounds in some other studies; but the functional notions developed elsewhere provide an important aid to the interpretation of the textual dimensions and to the explanation of the relations found among spoken and written genres.

2.3.4 A situational comparison of four genres

As noted throughout this discussion, the situational differences described here are characteristic of typical speaking and writing. Only two of these characterizations approach absolute distinctions between speaking and writing: (1) the channel difference (many sub-channels available in speaking; only the lexical–syntactic sub-channel available in writing), and (2) the opportunity for interaction with the text (no real-time constraints in writing; severe real-time constraints in speech). Even these two differences are not absolute. Features such as underlining, bold-face, and certain punctuation marks can be used to represent prosodic or paralinguistic sub-channels in writing. Tape-recorded speech bypasses some of the real-time constraints of speech, more so in comprehension than in production. In-class compositions represent writing under severe real-time constraints, although much less so than in speaking. Thus, although each of the parameters listed on Table 2.3 is useful as a distinction between many speaking and writing situations, none of them is an absolute situational distinction between the two modes of communication.

Although these situational distinctions are true only of typical speaking and writing, they can be used to characterize non-typical situations. Following Tannen (1982a, 1985), I use the term 'oral' to refer to typical speaking and 'literate' to refer to typical writing. The differences listed in Table 2.3 can be taken as characteristics of oral and literate situations. Later chapters will discuss the linguistic characteristics of oral and literate genres, specifying how they are typically spoken or written in their linguistic characteristics. It is also possible to classify the communicative situations of particular genres as oral or literate. As noted in Section 2.3.1, I am using face-to-face conversation to represent typical speaking and expository prose to represent typical writing. In Figure 2.1, I compare the situational characteristics of these two typical genres to the characteristics of academic lectures and personal letters, to illustrate the fact that there is no one-to-one correspondence between speaking and writing on the one hand and oral and literate situational characteristics on the other.

In Figure 2.1, face-to-face conversation is presented as a typical speaking situation: for each of the situational dichotomies presented in Table 2.3, ordinary conversation shows the value typical of the speaking situation. Similarly, academic expository prose is presented as a typical writing situation. The characterization of academic lectures and personal letters is more interesting. Academic lectures are spoken but show literate situational characteristics for school acquisition, social value, shared personal knowledge among participants, and information load. In many respects, therefore, lectures can be classified as a literate situation. The opposite characterization is seen for personal letters. Although they are written, they show oral situational characteristics for shared personal knowledge, effort expended to maintain the relationship, and informational load, and intermediate situational characteristics with respect to most of the other differences. Only with respect to physical channel and opportunity for interaction with the text do they show literate values. Thus, personal letters can be classified as having relatively oral situational characteristics although they are written.

These four genres were singled out because they show widely different situational characteristics. They illustrate the fact that there is no simple correspondence between speaking/writing and oral/literate characteristics. Face-to-face conversation is a spoken genre with highly oral situational characteristics; academic prose is a written genre with highly literate situational characteristics; academic lectures represent a spoken genre with relatively literate situational characteristics; and personal letters represent a written genre with relatively oral situational characteristics. In Chapter 7, a similar disparity between the linguistic characterization of genres as spoken/written and oral/literate is shown.

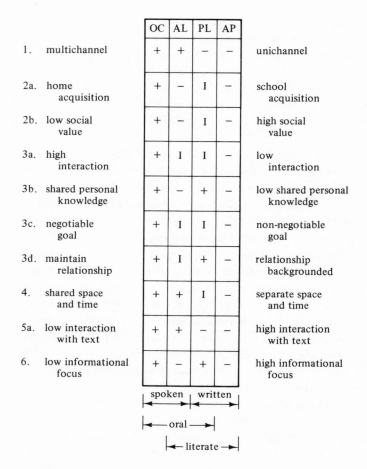

		OC	AL	PL	AP	
1.	multichannel	+	+	−	−	unichannel
2a.	home acquisition	+	−	I	−	school acquisition
2b.	low social value	+	−	I	−	high social value
3a.	high interaction	+	I	I	−	low interaction
3b.	shared personal knowledge	+	−	+	−	low shared personal knowledge
3c.	negotiable goal	+	I	I	−	non-negotiable goal
3d.	maintain relationship	+	I	+	−	relationship backgrounded
4.	shared space and time	+	+	I	−	separate space and time
5a.	low interaction with text	+	+	−	−	high interaction with text
6.	low informational focus	+	−	+	−	high informational focus

|←— spoken —→|←— written —→|
|←——— oral ———→|
|←— literate —→|

Figure 2.1 *Oral and literate situational characteristics of four genres Key: OC = ordinary conversation, AL = academic lectures, PL = personal letters, AP = academic prose. '+' marks an oral situational value, '−' marks a literate situational value, 'I' marks an intermediate situational value.*

3 Previous linguistic research on speech and writing

3.1 Overall linguistic generalizations

There is a long history of research on the linguistic characterization of speech and writing. Although a variety of approaches has been adopted, the shared goal of most previous studies has been to identify specific linguistic features that distinguish between the two modes. Many studies also offer overall linguistic characterizations of speech and writing. In general, writing is claimed to be:

1. more structurally complex and elaborate than speech, indicated by features such as longer sentences or T-units and a greater use of subordination (O'Donnell *et al.* 1967; O'Donnell 1974; Kroll 1977; Chafe 1982; Akinnaso 1982; Tannen 1982a, 1985; Gumperz *et al.* 1984);
2. more explicit than speech, in that it has complete idea units with all assumptions and logical relations encoded in the text (DeVito 1966; 1967; Olson 1977);
3. more decontextualized, or autonomous, than speech, so that it is less dependent on shared situation or background knowledge (Kay 1977; Olson 1977);
4. less personally involved than speech and more detached and abstract than speech (Blankenship 1974; Chafe 1982; Chafe and Danielewicz 1986);
5. characterized by a higher concentration of new information than speech (Stubbs 1980; Kroch and Hindle 1982; Brown and Yule 1983); and
6. more deliberately organized and planned than speech (Ochs 1979; Rubin 1980; Akinnaso 1982; Brown and Yule 1983; Gumperz *et al.* 1984).

As is often the case with broad generalizations, the characterizations listed here do not adequately describe the details of the relations between speech and writing. None of these generalizations is true of all spoken and written genres, and while most of them are characterizations of typical speech and typical writing, some do not seem adequate even in that regard.

The generalization that writing is decontextualized, while speech is

47

contextualized, is based on the perception that speech maximally depends on a shared situation and background while writing does not depend on such a shared context. Tannen (1982a, 1985) notes that this characterization is true of the linguistic differences between conversation and expository prose, the two genres most frequently used to represent speech and writing, but it is not true of speech and writing in general. Spoken genres such as academic lectures do not show a high dependence on a shared context, while written genres such as personal letters or office memos do show such a dependence. Rader (1982) shows that imaginative fiction, which might be regarded as highly literate and therefore decontextualized, depends crucially on background information supplied by the reader and an active role on the part of the reader in the creation of an imagined world. Finally, Prince (1981) raises questions concerning the adequacy of this generalization for even academic prose and face-to-face conversation. In a comparison of a written academic article and a spoken narrative, she finds many more evoked entities (previously mentioned or physically present in the situational context) in the spoken text, but many more inferable entities (reference that is dependent on logical or plausible reasoning by the addressee) in the written text. From this perspective, conversation is contextualized in that it refers directly to the physical speech situation and participants; but academic prose is contextualized in that it crucially depends on shared (academic) background knowledge for understanding.

The claims that writing is more complex, elaborate, and explicit than speech are the most widely accepted of the above characterizations. This greater complexity is generally attributed to two distinctive characteristics of writing: the lack of strict time constraints during production, and the need to establish cohesion strictly through the lexical–syntactic channel. Thus, Chafe (1982:37) notes that 'in writing we have time to mold a succession of ideas into a more complex, coherent, integrated whole', whereas speech, because it is produced on-line, is more fragmented. Tannen (1982a:3) notes that 'cohesion is established in spoken discourse through paralinguistic and non-verbal channels (such as intonation, gesture, and eye-gaze), while cohesion is established in writing through lexicalization and complex syntactic structures which make connectives explicit'. Similar characterizations are offered by Akinnaso (1982), and Gumperz *et al.* (1984). This generalization, however, is not universally accepted. In particular, two studies claim that speech is more structurally complex than writing (Poole and Field 1976;

Halliday 1979), and Blankenship (1962) concludes that t
important linguistic differences between the two modes. '
study investigates the adequacy of this generalization furth
that elaboration and structural complexity are not homoge
structs and that there is no single characterization of speech a.... wiiung
with respect to them.

The remaining characterizations listed above, concerning personal
involvement, concentration of new information, and overall organization, are similarly inadequate as absolute differences between speech
and writing. The present study shows that each of these generalizations
holds for some spoken and written genres, but they are not adequate as
proposals concerning general linguistic differences between the two
modes.

3.2 Previous quantitative studies

To support the generalizations listed in the last section, researchers have
looked at the distribution of specific linguistic features in spoken and
written texts. For example, structural complexity and elaboration have
been measured by the frequency of different subordinate constructions,
prepositional phrase series, adjectives, etc.; complex texts are claimed to
make frequent use of these features. Explicitness has been measured by
features such as word length and type/token ratio, which is the ratio of the
number of different words to total number of words. Detachment and
decontextualization have been measured by the frequency of passives,
nominalizations, noun series, etc. Personal involvement has been
measured by frequency of personal pronouns, questions, exclamations,
and similar features.

I noted in the last section that none of the overall generalizations about
speech and writing are uniformly accepted. In the same way, more
specific disagreements among studies are common. In a few cases, the
cause of the disagreement may simply be definitional. For example,
Blankenship (1962, 1974) found sentence length in speech and writing to
be nearly the same, while other researchers (e.g., O'Donnell 1974; Poole
and Field 1976) have found the mean length of sentences, clauses, or T-
units to be considerably longer in writing. A major problem here
concerns the definition of 'sentence' in speech (in English), and since
most studies do not define their particular use of the term, there is no
basis for comparison. A similar example is the description of speech in

Horowitz and Newman (1964) as containing more ideas and subordinate ideas, and being more elaborated, than writing, in contrast to the generally accepted view that writing is more elaborated than speech. The problem with this study concerns the definition of 'idea', which is conceptualized as a cognitive entity rather than a syntactic unit. This study thus does not describe linguistic complexity or elaboration at all; rather, it shows that, given the same amount of time, a speaker can verbalize more 'ideas' than a writer.

Other contradictions are more difficult to explain. The most striking of these relates to the extent of subordination in the two modes. Most studies have found that writing has a much higher degree of subordination than speech, reflecting its greater structural complexity (O'Donnell 1974; Kroll 1977; Kay 1977; Chafe 1982; and Brown and Yule 1983). Other studies, though, do not support these results, finding little difference in the overall number of subordinate clauses between speech and writing (Blass and Siegman 1975; Cayer and Sacks 1979). In fact, some studies have found the opposite. Poole and Field (1976) found a higher index of embedding in speech, Price and Graves (1980) found a higher ratio of dependent clauses in speech, and Halliday (1979) found more 'complex sentence structures' (i.e., more clauses) in speech. Beaman (1984) presents a careful analysis of subordination in spoken and written narratives; she notes that previous studies have been overly simplistic and that different subordinate constructions may have differing communicative functions.

Another striking contradiction involves the frequency of passive constructions in the two modes. Passives have been associated with decontextualization or detachment and therefore claimed to be characteristic of writing to a greater extent than speech (e.g., Chafe 1982; Brown and Yule 1983). In contrast, Blankenship (1962) found only slightly more passives in writing than speech, while Poole and Field (1976) found few passives in either mode.

Other contradictions may be less striking, because the measures involved are less stereotypically associated with one or the other mode, but they are equally confusing. For instance, with respect to degree of elaboration, Cayer and Sacks (1979) and Stubbs (1980) found more adverbs in writing; Blankenship (1974) found no significant difference in the frequencies of adverbs; and Poole and Field (1976) and Tottie (1984) found more adverbs in speech. The findings are more consistent with respect to adjectives, with Poole and Field, Cayer and Sacks, and Chafe

finding more in writing. Blankenship (1974), though, found no significant difference between the modes, but she did find this to be a useful
measure for distinguishing among genres within both speech and
writing.

Beaman (1984) is one of the few researchers using a quantitative
approach who addresses these widespread contradictory findings. She
notes that the failure to control for differences in register, purpose, degree
of formality, and planning contributes to the confusing picture emerging
from previous quantitative studies. Other researchers have abandoned
quantitative approaches altogether for these same reasons. In the next
section, some non-quantitative studies of speech and writing are
discussed.

3.3 Non-quantitative approaches

Researchers like Akinnaso (1982) and Gumperz *et al.* (1984) claim that
quantitative studies have not addressed the important issues relating to
speech and writing, and that they are perhaps unable to do so. Thus,
Akinnaso questions the validity of previous generalizations regarding the
overall relationships between speech and writing:

> comparative studies of spoken and written language have emphasized
> general, rather than specific, consequences of writing on language
> structure, the working assumption being that written language is
> generally more complex than spoken language. Yet contradictions occur
> when different studies are compared on specific findings. (1982:110)

Akinnaso goes on to conclude that the very attempt to quantify the
relations between speech and writing is at the root of these contradictory
findings. He notes, for example, that a central problem of previous
studies is

> their quantitative orientation, each researcher deciding on what and
> how to count. It is commonplace in social science that statistical counts
> usually capture only 'etic' rather than 'emic' categories, thereby
> ignoring the underlying logic behind surface behavior. (1982:110)

In contrast to the quantitative approach of earlier studies, Akinnaso
and Gumperz propose to study speech and writing from the perspective
of thematic cohesion, an analysis of the ways in which surface structure
elements in a text are connected to mark their unified function in
developing a common theme (Halliday and Hasan 1976). By investigating the ways in which thematic cohesion is achieved in each mode, these

researchers attempt to uncover the underlying differences between speech and writing.

Several other researchers have also opted for a non-quantitative approach. Tannen (1982a) analyzes two texts in detail with respect to linguistic features of integration and involvement. Rader (1982) analyzes a written narrative in detail to show that writing as well as speech can rely heavily on context. These and other researchers have chosen a non-quantitative approach for the greater detail and depth of analysis possible when the linguistic characteristics of a text are directly interpreted in terms of their function(s) in the communicative interaction.

In the present study, I use both quantitative and non-quantitative analyses because the two approaches have complementary strengths and weaknesses (see Chapter 4). Quantitative analyses give a solid empirical foundation to the findings; non-quantitative analyses are required for the interpretation. Either type of analysis in isolation gives an incomplete description. The research results of this combined approach argue against the assessment that quantitative analyses are sterile and invalid. Rather, I claim here that other major restrictions in experimental design, found in both quantitative and non-quantitative studies, have been the cause of the inadequate and contradictory conclusions reached in many previous studies. We now turn to these restrictions and the general design requirements of any study intending to reach valid generalizations concerning speech and writing.

3.4   Requirements for global conclusions concerning speech and writing

The research designs of many previous studies have three major restrictions, and it is these restrictions, rather than a quantitative or non-quantitative approach, that limit the extent to which they can provide global conclusions regarding the linguistic relations among spoken and written genres. Studies with restricted research designs can contribute valuable analyses of individual linguistic features in individual texts and genres, but they do not provide an adequate foundation for global conclusions concerning speech and writing. The three restrictions are:

1.   assigning undue weight to individual texts – because most studies have been based on few texts, an unusual or idiosyncratic text can have a major influence on the analysis;

2.   assigning undue weight to the genres chosen for analysis – most studies

have compared only two genres, one spoken and one written, and many of these have not controlled for the communicative task represented by those genres;

3. assigning undue weight to particular linguistic features – although most studies have considered only a few linguistic features, they have considered a differential distribution in any individual feature to be important evidence.[1]

Schafer (1981:12) notes similar restrictions and finds it 'frustrating' that although previous studies 'are based on texts produced in particular circumstances by only a few subjects . . . speaking and writing in only one situation, this doesn't prevent researchers from offering their results as accurate generalizations of universal differences between speaking and writing'. These restrictions can be found in both quantitative and non-quantitative studies.

First, nearly all previous studies analyze only a few texts. It is very time-consuming to analyze a large number of texts, but the potential influence of idiosyncratic texts on global conclusions must be recognized in studies where it is not possible to analyze a large sample.

The second restriction involves two parts: many studies compare only two genres, and they do not control for the communicative task represented by those genres. The problems resulting from the failure to control for communicative task have been noted by several recent researchers (Akinnaso 1982; Tannen 1982a, 1985; Beaman 1984; Gumperz *et al.* 1984). That is, several earlier studies find striking differences between speech and writing because they compare very different communicative tasks, such as face-to-face conversation and academic prose; other studies find speech and writing to be nearly the same because they compare similar communicative tasks in the two modes, such as expository articles and public speeches. When attempting to reconcile these studies, it is very difficult to determine whether observed dif-

---

[1] There is actually a fourth restriction, in that previous studies have assigned undue weight to the choice of speaker/writer and the choice of language. That is, most studies have taken the speech and writing of middle-class academics to be representative of the English-speaking community as a whole. This decision has been pragmatic, in that it is relatively easy to collect data in academic contexts, but it represents a serious limitation on our general knowledge of speech and writing in English. Further, although most studies have examined only English, they tend to generalize their findings to 'speech' and 'writing', as if the relations among spoken and written genres were the same in all languages. This is particularly not true in the case of non-Western language and cultures, where both the functions and form of spoken and written genres vary considerably from Western norms (Besnier 1986a).

ferences are due to the mode distinction or to some other difference in communicative purpose or situation. To remedy this problem, researchers like Beaman, Tannen, and Gumperz recommend comparing the same communicative task across the two modes: Beaman and Tannen compare written and spoken narratives, and Gumperz compares a written and spoken exposition. Such a comparison guarantees that any observed difference is indeed attributable to differences in the production channel.

A pair-wise comparison of genres, however, cannot determine the overall relations among texts in speech and writing. That is, the final goal in all of these studies is an overall description of the similarities and differences among the full range of spoken and written genres in English. We would like to know, for all spoken and written genres, the ways in which they are similar, the ways in which they are different, and some measure of the extent of their similarities and differences. Such a goal cannot be achieved by a restricted comparison of a few genres, whether they represent the same task in the two modes or not. Rather, it requires comparison of the full range of genres in a single analysis.

Finally, previous studies have focused on relatively few linguistic features as the crucial discriminators among spoken and written texts. Earlier quantitative studies focused on the number of subordinate clauses, passives, etc.; non-quantitative researchers focus on features like thematic cohesion. The analyses presented in Chapters 6–8 of the present book, however, demonstrate that no single linguistic feature can adequately account for the full range of variation among spoken and written texts. Research in sociolinguistics conducted over the last twenty years has shown natural language variation to be quite complex, giving every reason to expect multiple dimensions of variation among spoken and written genres. Work by Hymes, Labov, Gumperz, and others has described systematic linguistic variation across a wide range of social and situational parameters, including the social class and ethnic group of participants, the social and situational relationship between the participants, the setting, and the purpose of communication (Brown and Fraser 1979). The picture emerging from this research is one of a complex coupling of linguistic features and functions, with single features serving many functions and single functions being marked by many features. Thus, the expectation that multiple linguistic features and multiple dimensions will be required for an adequate description of linguistic variation among genres is supported by our general knowledge of language use in society. It is this expectation which forms the basis of the present study.

The discussion in earlier sections has shown that the relations among spoken and written genres are highly complex and still not well-understood. The present section has shown that this is due, at least in part, to the restricted research designs often adopted in earlier studies. An approach is needed that can combine a much broader perspective with an adequate empirical analysis of the linguistic measures involved.

3.5 A new approach: multi-feature/multi-dimensional analysis

The present study is based on the assumption that there are few, if any, absolute differences between speech and writing, and that there is no single parameter of linguistic variation that distinguishes among spoken and written genres. It seeks to systematically describe the linguistic characteristics of the range of genres in English, whether typically spoken, typically written, or other. For each genre we need to know the particular ways in which it is oral and the ways in which it is literate. Thus the present study attempts to identify the linguistic parameters along which genres vary, so that any individual genre can be located within an 'oral' and 'literate' space, specifying both the nature and the extent of the differences and similarities between that genre and the range of other genres in English.

The two key notions of this framework, textual dimension and textual relation, have been described in Chapter 1. Dimensions are bundles of linguistic features that co-occur in texts because they work together to mark some common underlying function. Relations are defined in terms of the dimensions; they specify the ways in which any two genres are linguistically similar and the extent to which they are similar. Both dimensions and relations can be specified quantitatively using computational tools, while careful microscopic analyses of texts are required to interpret the functions underlying the dimensions and to explain the observed relations among genres. These tools are described in detail in Chapters 4–5; the important point here is that the co-occurrence patterns underlying dimensions are identified empirically and quantitatively, rather than on the basis of informed intuitions about texts.

The multi-feature/multi-dimensional (MF/MD) approach to linguistic variation (Biber 1985, 1986a) has been developed to describe the textual relations among spoken and written genres. This approach uses standardized computer-based text corpora and automatic identification techniques to compute the frequencies of salient lexical and syntactic features. The co-occurrence patterns among these features are analyzed through multivariate statistical techniques to identify the functional dimensions of linguistic variation among texts and to provide an overall description of relations among genres with respect to these dimensions.

Research designs using an MF/MD approach avoid the three restrictions identified in the last section. First, large-scale text corpora are used to provide a data base of several hundred text samples. Secondly, texts representing several major genres, such as conversation, broadcast, public speeches, academic prose, and fiction are included in the analysis. The large number of texts precludes a confounding influence from idiosyncratic variation, and inclusion of several genres insures that the analysis will adequately represent the range of variation among texts in spoken and written English.

Thirdly, an MF/MD approach analyzes the distribution of many lexical and syntactic features representing a broad range of the communicative functions served in speech and writing, such as content elaboration and interaction of communicative participants. The frequency of each feature is counted in each of the texts, and statistical techniques are used to empirically group the linguistic features into clusters that co-occur with a high frequency in texts.

Studies using an MF/MD approach show that quantitative approaches are not inherently narrow or theoretically uninteresting. This approach takes advantage of the strengths of both quantitative and non-quantitative approaches while avoiding the restrictions shared by previous studies. The MF/MD approach adopts the notion that co-occurrence patterns are central to register variation from earlier sociolinguistic theory, and it uses computational tools to identify dimensions quantitatively based on these co-occurrence patterns. For all of the above reasons, an MF/MD analysis is well-suited to the description of the global relations among spoken and written genres in a language.

3.6 Summary of the textual dimensions identified to date

Several previous studies have used an MF/MD approach to identify textual dimensions in speech and writing (Biber 1984, 1986a, 1986b; Finegan and Biber 1986b). To date, this research has identified three primary dimensions of linguistic variation among texts in English (see especially Biber 1986a). To reflect their underlying functions, these dimensions are tentatively labelled as follows:

Dimension I: Interactive versus Edited Text
Dimension II: Abstract versus Situated Content
Dimension III: Reported versus Immediate Style

Each dimension represents a group of linguistic features that co-occur in texts, identified by computational analyses. Dimension I is characterized linguistically by features like questions and first and second person pronouns versus word length and more varied vocabulary. Dimension II is characterized by features like nominalizations and passives versus place and time adverbs. Dimension III is characterized by past tense versus present tense features.

These studies have consistently shown that the relations among genres are complex and that no single dimension adequately captures the similarities and differences among genres; rather, a multi-dimensional model is required. This finding can be illustrated by consideration of the relations among four genres, academic prose, professional letters, broadcast, and conversation, along the first two dimensions listed above. With respect to Dimension I (Interactive versus Edited Text), conversation and academic prose are at opposite extremes; conversation is characterized as highly interactive and not edited; academic prose is highly edited but not interactive. These characterizations are precisely quantifiable in terms of the frequencies of co-occurring linguistic features in the genres. Along this same dimension, professional letters, although written, are more similar to conversation than to academic prose, while broadcast, although spoken, is more similar to academic prose than to conversation.

With respect to Dimension II (Abstract versus Situated Content), the relations among these four genres are quite different. Conversation and academic prose are again at opposite poles: conversation highly situated, academic prose highly abstract. Contrary to their positions with respect to one another along Dimension I, however, broadcast is very similar to conversation with respect to Dimension II: both are highly situated. Similarly, both professional letters and academic prose are highly abstract with respect to this dimension.

While consideration of the distribution of texts along any individual dimension is informative, a fuller picture of the relations among these four genres results from a joint consideration of Dimensions I and II: conversation is interactive and situated; professional letters are interactive and abstract; broadcast is situated but not markedly interactive or markedly edited; academic prose is edited and abstract. In these earlier studies, analysis of the similarities and differences among spoken and written genres with respect to all three dimensions enabled a first approximation of a model of textual relations in English.

Taking these earlier studies as its departure point, the present book greatly extends prior research findings and develops a comprehensive model of textual relations among spoken and written genres in English. Many additional linguistic features are included here, as are some additional genres, enabling identification of additional dimensions. In all, six textual dimensions are identified and interpreted in the present study, and the relations among spoken and written genres are analyzed with respect to this six-dimensional model.

Part II: Methodology

4 Methodological overview of the study

4.1 Macroscopic and microscopic approaches to textual variation

Within the broad framework of investigation into the psychological and sociological underpinnings of linguistic variation, researchers have investigated textual variation through macroscopic and microscopic analyses. Macroscopic analysis attempts to define the overall dimensions of variation in a language. Microscopic analysis, on the other hand, provides a detailed description of the communicative functions of particular linguistic features (e.g., clefts as markers of informational prominence, or first person pronouns as markers of personal involvement).

Much of the previous work analyzing linguistic variation in texts falls into the category of microscopic analysis. For instance, Schiffrin (1981) looks at the different functions of past tense and present tense forms in referring to past events in narrative. Aijmer (1986) and Stenström (1986) study the functions of *actually* and *really* respectively in conversational texts. Thompson (1983) studies the functions of detached participial clauses in descriptive texts. And Tannen (1982a) contrasts the level of imageability in written and spoken narratives to illustrate the use of oral strategies in written discourse. These and other studies are characterized by their detailed attention to the functions of specific features in representative texts.

Macroscopic analyses identify the overall parameters of linguistic variation within a given 'domain', e.g., spoken and written texts in English or the range of expository prose in English; they are based on the notions of textual dimension and textual relation. There are few previous examples of macroscopic analyses using quantitative statistical techniques. One of the earliest studies was by Carroll (1960), who examines written prose in English to uncover six dimensions of style, labelled:

General Stylistic Evaluation, Personal Affect, Ornamentation, Abstractness, Seriousness, and Characterization. In a similar study, Marckworth and Baker (1974) uncover three dimensions of style in non-fictional prose in English; they do not propose labels for their dimensions. Poole (1973) identifies six underlying dimensions of restricted and elaborated code variation. In a series of studies at the University of Southern California, a MF/MD approach to macroscopic variation has been used to examine relations among spoken and written texts in English (Biber 1984, 1986a, 1986b), relations among spoken and written texts in Nukulaelae Tuvaluan (Besnier 1986a), relations among American and British written genres (Biber 1987), dimensions of discourse complexity (Finegan and Biber 1986b), dimensions of sociolinguistic prestige (Finegan and Biber 1986a), dimensions of literary and expository style (Biber and Finegan 1988b, 1988c; Grabe 1984a), styles of 'stance' (Biber and Finegan 1988a, forthcoming), and a typology of English texts (Biber and Finegan 1986; Biber forthcoming). Biber (1985) presents a methodological overview of the multi-feature/multi-dimensional approach to textual variation.

Micro and macro approaches to text analysis have complementary strengths and weaknesses. Microscopic text analysis is necessary to pinpoint the exact communicative functions of individual linguistic features. It complements macroscopic analysis in two ways: (1) it identifies the potentially important linguistic features and genre distinctions to be included in a macro-analysis, and (2) it provides detailed functional analyses of individual linguistic features, which enable interpretation of the textual dimension in functional terms. Microscopic analysis, however, is not able to identify the overall parameters of linguistic variation within a set of texts because it is restricted to analysis of few linguistic features in individual texts.

In contrast, macroscopic analyses are needed to identify the underlying textual dimensions in a set of texts, enabling an overall account of linguistic variation among those texts and providing a framework for discussion of the similarities and differences among particular texts and genres. Macro-analysis is restricted in that it overlooks relatively minor parameters of textual variation and relies on form-to-function correlations established in micro-analyses.

These two approaches to text analysis are mutually dependent. Macro-analysis depends on micro-analysis for the identification and functional interpretation of potentially important linguistic features, while micro-analysis benefits from the overall theoretical framework provided by macro-analysis; that is, the choice of texts and linguistic features deserving detailed micro-analysis will be influenced by knowledge of the underlying textual dimensions within a set of texts. The analysis of speech and writing presented here depends on both approaches: it uses a macroscopic approach to analyze the co-occurrence patterns among 67 linguistic features in 481 texts, identifying seven textual dimensions; and it uses microscopic analyses to interpret these dimensions in functional terms.

4.2 Methodological overview of the study

The distinctive methodological characteristics of the present study are: (1) the use of computer-based text corpora, providing a standardized data base and ready access to a wide range of variation in communicative situations and purposes; (2) the use of computer programs to count the frequency of certain linguistic features in a wide range of texts, enabling analysis of the distribution of many linguistic features across many texts and genres; (3) the use of multivariate statistical techniques, especially factor analysis, to determine co-occurrence relations among the linguistic features; and (4) the use of microscopic analyses to interpret the functional parameters underlying the quantitatively identified co-occurrence patterns.

Table 4.1 summarizes the methodological steps of the analysis, which is based on the MF/MD approach to textual variation (Biber 1985). The initial steps involve the choice of texts and linguistic features for analysis. This is followed by the quantitative steps: computational identification of linguistic features in texts, analysis of co-occurrence patterns using factor analysis, and comparison of texts with respect to the dimensions based on computed factor scores. Functional analyses are used to interpret the dimensions identified by the factor analysis and to interpret the relations among texts specified by the factor scores.

A more complete description of factor analysis and factor scores is given in Chapter 5; here I will only summarize the essential concepts. Factor analysis uses frequency counts of linguistic features to identify sets of features that co-occur in texts. As noted in Chapter 1, the use of this technique to identify underlying textual dimensions is based on the assumption that frequently co-occurring linguistic features have at least one shared communicative function. It is claimed here that there are relatively few primary linguistic functions in English, and that the

Table 4.1 *Steps in the analysis*

Preliminary analyses:

    -- review of previous research to identify potentially
        important linguistic features
    -- collection of texts and conversion to machine-readable
        form; review previous research to insure that all
        important situational distinctions are included
        in the text sample
    -- count occurrence of features in the texts (through the
        use of computer programs written in PL/1)

Step 1: Factor analysis:

    -- clustering of linguistic features into groups of
        features that co-occur with a high frequency in texts
    -- interpretation of the factors as textual dimensions
        through assessment of the communicative function(s)
        most widely shared by the features constituting each
        factor

Step 2: Factor scores as operational representatives of the
        textual dimensions:

    -- for each factor, compute a factor score for each text
    -- compute an average factor score for the texts within
        each genre
    -- comparison of the average factor scores for each genre
    -- further interpretation of the textual dimensions in
        light of the relations among genres with respect
        to the factor scores

---

frequent co-occurrence of a group of linguistic features in texts is indicative of an underlying function shared by those features. Working from this assumption, it is possible to decipher a unified dimension underlying each set of co-occurring linguistic features. In this sense, I am using factor analysis as it is commonly used in other social and behavioral sciences: to summarize the interrelationships among a large group of variables in a concise fashion; to build underlying dimensions (or constructs) that are conceptually clearer than the many linguistic measures considered individually.

Although factor analysis enables quantitative identification of underlying dimensions within a set of texts, it cannot be employed usefully apart from a theoretically-motivated research design. That is, before performing a factor analysis, the range of communicative situations and purposes available in a language must be determined, and texts representing that range of variation must be collected. In the same way, linguistic features that are potentially important indicators of variation within the domain must be identified in advance and measured in each of the texts. Inadequate preparation or skewing in these theoretical prerequisites can invalidate the results of a factor analysis (Gorsuch 1983:336ff). That is, factor analysis provides the primary analytical tool, but is dependent on the theoretical foundation provided by an adequate data base of texts and inclusion of multiple linguistic features.

4.3 Text selection

In selecting the texts to be used in a macroscopic textual analysis, care must be taken to include a broad range of the possible situational, social, and communicative task variation occurring in the language. Factor analysis identifies sets of features that co-vary, but if the texts to be analyzed do not represent the full range of situational variation, then neither will the dimensions. The first step in the analysis, then, is to identify the range of situational variation in English and to collect texts representing that range. As noted in earlier chapters, texts can vary along several situational parameters, including their reliance on context, their processing constraints, their communicative purposes, and their relationships among communicative participants.

In English, the task of collecting texts representing the range of situational possibilities is relatively easy due to the availability of standard computerized text corpora, which provide a large number of texts taken from a wide range of genres. A standard corpus enables the verification of results and the direct comparison of results from one study to the next. The use of a computerized corpus also enables automatic identification of linguistic features in a very large collection of texts. In a factor analysis, the data base should include five times as many texts as linguistic features to be analyzed (Gorsuch 1983:332). In addition, simply representing the range of situational and processing possibilities in English requires a large number of texts. To analyze this number of texts without the aid of computational tools would require several years;

computerized corpora enable storage and analysis of a large number of texts in an efficient manner.

Two major text corpora are used for the present analysis. The first is the Lancaster–Oslo–Bergen Corpus of British English, known as the LOB Corpus (see Johansson *et al.* 1978 and Johansson 1982). This corpus is drawn exclusively from printed sources published in 1961. It comprises 500 text samples of about 2,000 words each, taken from fifteen genres: press reportage, editorials, press reviews, religion, popular lore, skills and hobbies, biographies and essays, official documents, learned writings, fiction (including general, mystery, adventure, science, and romance), and humor. The total corpus contains approximately one million words of running text.

The second corpus is the London–Lund Corpus of Spoken English (Svartvik and Quirk 1980; Johansson 1982). This corpus is a collection of 87 spoken British English texts of about 5,000 words each. The total corpus contains approximately 500,000 words, representing six major speech situations: private conversations, public conversations (including interviews and panel discussions), telephone conversations, radio broadcasts, spontaneous speeches, and prepared speeches.

A third corpus, the Brown University corpus of written American English (see Francis and Kucera 1982), has been used in previous studies but is not used here. This is the oldest of the three corpora, and is probably the first large-scale computer-based corpus to be compiled. The LOB corpus is a direct replication of the Brown corpus, so that parallel text samples exist for British and American written English. To avoid any confounding influences from a comparison of British and American English (Biber 1987), the analyses in the present book do not use the Brown corpus.

Since the standard corpora do not include non-published written texts, I have added a collection of professional and personal letters. The professional letters were written in academic contexts but deal with administrative rather than intellectual matters. They are formal and directed to individuals, but their purposes are both informational and interactional.[1] The personal letters are written to friends or relatives; they range from intimate to friendly. Most of the letters are written by Americans, but some of them are written by Canadian or British writers.

Table 4.2 lists the 23 genres used in the study. These genres represent

---

[1] The professional letters were collected by William Grabe.

Table 4.2 *Distribution of texts across 23 genres*

GENRE	# OF TEXTS
Written -- genres 1-15 from the LOB corpus	
1. Press reportage	44
2. Editorials	27
3. Press reviews	17
4. Religion	17
5. Skills and hobbies	14
6. Popular lore	14
7. Biographies	14
8. Official documents	14
9. Academic prose	80
10. General fiction	29
11. Mystery fiction	13
12. Science fiction	6
13. Adventure fiction	13
14. Romantic fiction	13
15. Humor	9
16. Personal letters	6
17. Professional letters	10
Spoken -- from the London-Lund corpus	
18. Face-to-face conversation	44
19. Telephone conversation	27
20. Public conversations, debates, and interviews	22
21. Broadcast	18
22. Spontaneous speeches	16
23. Planned speeches	14
Total:	481
Approximate number of words:	960,000

the full range of situational possibilities available in the corpora: fifteen written genres from the LOB corpus, six spoken genres from the London–Lund corpus, plus the two types of letters. These texts were analyzed by computer to identify occurrences of the relevant linguistic features. The computational analysis involved two steps: automatic grammatical analysis by computer programs (described in Appendix II), and editing the computer results by hand to check for errors. Because the editing was quite time-consuming, not all of the texts in the corpora were used, although all genres in the corpora are represented. A list of the specific texts from the corpora used in the study is given as Appendix I.

The composition of some of these genres requires elaboration because some of the genre categories comprise several sub-genres. Table 4.3 lists these sub-genre distinctions. Press includes several sub-classes: political, sports, society, spot news, financial, and cultural. Editorials includes institutional and personal editorials as well as letters to the editor. Popular lore contains texts about politics, history, health, etc., taken from popular magazines and books (e.g., *Punch, Woman's Mirror, Wine and Food*). Official documents are primarily government documents, but also foundation reports, industry reports, and a section from a university catalog. Academic prose combines several sub-classes: natural sciences, medicine, mathematics, social and behavioral sciences, political science/law/education, humanities, and technology/engineering. Public conversations, debates, and interviews represent public, relatively formal interactions (e.g., on radio talk shows). Spontaneous speeches are unprepared public monologues, for example, from a court case, dinner speech, or speeches in the House of Commons. One of these texts (a court case) includes some dialogic exchanges also. Prepared speeches are planned but without a written text, and are taken from sermons, university lectures, court cases, etc. Finally, broadcast is composed of radio sports broadcasting and other radio commentary on non-sports events. The other text categories are self-explanatory. For the LOB corpus, Johansson *et al.* (1978) further describe the kinds of texts in each genre and give bibliographic references for each of the texts. For the London–Lund corpus, some further information about the genre classes and the speakers can be found in Svartvik and Quirk (1980).

I use the term 'genre' to refer to text categorizations made on the basis of external criteria relating to author/speaker purpose. The genre categories in the present study are adopted from the distinctions used in the corpora. Some of these categories are complex and might be considered to be a combination of several genres. For example, prepared speeches comprise sermons, university lectures, final statements in court, and political speeches, all of which can be considered as different genres. In these cases, the general category (e.g., prepared speeches) might be considered as a 'way of speaking' (Hymes 1974), representing a super-ordinate category, while the specific categories might be considered as the 'genres'. Although this more specific use of the term might be theoreti-

Table 4.3 *List of sub-genres used in the study*

Press:
      political
      sports
      society
      spot news
      financial
      cultural

Editorials:
      institutional
      personal
      letters to the editor

Official documents:
      government documents
      foundation reports
      industry reports
      college catalog
      industry house organ

Academic prose:
      natural sciences
      medicine
      mathematics
      social and behavioral sciences
      political science, law, and education
      humanities
      technology and engineering

Broadcasts (radio):
      sports
      non-sports

Spontaneous speeches:
      case in court
      dinner speech
      radio essays
      speeches in House of Commons

Prepared speeches:
      sermons
      university lectures
      cases in court
      political speech
      popular lecture

---

cally preferable, in the present study I use the term 'genre' for the general categories distinguished in the LOB and London–Lund corpora. In Chapter 8, however, I consider the relations among several of the more specific 'sub-genre' categories included in the corpora and listed in Table 4.3.

Texts can differ by subject-matter, purpose, rhetorical structure, and style in addition to situational parameters such as the relation between the communicative participants, the relation of the participants to the external context, and the relation of the participants to the text itself. As noted above, I use the term 'genre' to refer to categorizations assigned on the basis of external criteria. I use the term 'text type', on the other hand, to refer to groupings of texts that are similar with respect to their linguistic form, irrespective of genre categories (similar to the 'speech styles' discussed by Ervin-Tripp 1972 and Hymes 1974). For example, a science fiction text represents a genre of fiction (relating to author's purpose), but it might represent an abstract and technical text type (in terms of its linguistic form), similar to some types of academic exposition and different from most other fictional texts. In a fully developed typology of texts, genres and text types must be distinguished, and the relations among them identified and explained (see Biber and Finegan 1986; Biber forthcoming). The present study deals only with the relations among spoken and written genres, but the model developed here provides the basis for a typology of texts as well.

The makers of the corpora do not provide a great deal of information concerning the writers and speakers. As the written texts have all been published (except for the private collections of letters), it can be assumed that all writers are educated and probably from the middle-class. The speakers in the London–Lund corpus are more diverse. They range in age from 20 to 87 years, and they include academics, students, secretaries, housewives, engineers, doctors, bankers, clerks, electricians, broadcasters, MPs, ministers, and judges.

The genres used in the present study represent a broad range of the situational possibilities of speaking and writing in English, discussed in Chapter 2. Among the written genres, press is directed towards a more general audience than academic prose, involves considerable effort towards maintaining a relationship with its audience, and is concerned with temporal and physical situations in addition to abstract information. Editorial letters are less concerned about offending potential readers, but make greater assumptions concerning specific shared background knowledge (e.g., concerning particular social issues or past articles appearing in the press). Professional letters are structured like academic prose, often stating a thesis with several supporting arguments, but they are directed towards individuals, require concern for the interpersonal relationship, and enable a relatively high degree of interaction between participants and reliance on shared background. Fiction is directed to a very broad audience but requires a considerable amount of shared cultural assumptions and builds its own internal shared physical and temporal context. Finally, personal letters are informal and directed to individuals, they deal with truly personal matters, and they assume a high degree of shared background knowledge between writer and reader.

Among the spoken genres, public speeches are directed towards broad audiences and thus permit little interaction and relatively little dependence on shared knowledge. Spontaneous and planned speeches differ in the amount of time permitted for production, although both allow little time for comprehension in comparison to written genres. Broadcast is directed towards an extremely broad audience, while at the same time being highly dependent on the temporal and physical contexts being reported. In contrast, interviews show little concern for the temporal/physical context but have a high interactional focus, often involving only two direct communicative participants plus a broad audience of passive participants. Finally, in face-to-face and, to a lesser extent, telephone conversation the interactional focus is primary, usually overshadowing the informational focus. Conversation is characterized by a high degree of interaction and goal negotiability, considerable effort at maintaining a relationship, and considerable shared background knowledge. Both face-to-face and telephone conversation share a temporal context, but the shared physical context is more important in face-to-face conversation.

Other genres not included in the present study differ in further ways. Written notes left on the kitchen table, dialogues conducted across a computer network, and tape-recorded 'letters' are three such genres. The genres included in this study, though, represent a broad range of situational possibilities across the written and spoken modes.

4.4 Selection of the linguistic features

Prior to any comparison of texts, a principled decision must be made concerning the linguistic features to be used. For the purposes of this study, previous research was surveyed to identify potentially important linguistic features – those that have been associated with particular communicative functions and therefore might be used to differing extents in different types of texts. No a priori commitment is made concerning the importance of an individual linguistic feature or the validity of a previous functional interpretation during the selection of features. Rather, the goal is to include the widest possible range of *potentially* important linguistic features.

A survey of previous research on spoken/written differences identified the 67 linguistic features used in the present study. Table 4.4 lists these features, organized by their grammatical class; the features fall into sixteen major grammatical categories: (A) tense and aspect markers, (B) place and time adverbials, (C) pronouns and pro-verbs, (D) questions, (E) nominal forms, (F) passives, (G) stative forms, (H) subordination features, (I) prepositional phrases, adjectives, and adverbs, (J) lexical specificity, (K) lexical classes, (L) modals, (M) specialized verb classes, (N) reduced forms and dispreferred structures, (O) coordination, and (P) negation. Although the organization of Table 4.4 reflects the grammatical function of each feature rather than its discourse function, each of these features has been described as a functional marker in texts. The present study is based on the functional aspects of these features, represented by their co-occurrence distributions in texts. These 67 features represent several form–function pairings; features from the same grammatical category can have different functions, and features from different grammatical categories can have a shared function. As such, these features provide a solid basis for determining the underlying functional dimensions in English.

Appendix II gives a detailed description of these features. This appendix provides two types of information. The first concerns the computer programs used for the automatic identification of linguistic features in texts. The appendix sketches the broad outlines of these programs and provides the specific algorithms used for each feature. I have included this information for readers interested in programming applications and for readers who want to know exactly which forms were counted for each feature. The second part of Appendix II presents, for each feature, a summary of the functions proposed in previous research and a list of relevant studies. The functional analyses summarized in this appendix form the basis for the dimension interpretations offered in Chapters 6–8. Further, this information should be useful to readers undertaking microscopic analyses of particular linguistic features.

Table 4.4 *Features used in the analysis*

A. Tense and aspect markers

    1. past tense
    2. perfect aspect
    3. present tense

B. Place and time adverbials

    4. place adverbials (e.g., above, beside, outdoors)
    5. time adverbials (e.g., early, instantly, soon)

C. Pronouns and pro-verbs

    6. first person pronouns
    7. second person pronouns
    8. third person personal pronouns (excluding it)
    9. pronoun it
    10. demonstrative pronouns (that, this, these, those as pronouns)
    11. indefinite pronouns (e.g., anybody, nothing, someone)
    12. pro-verb do

D. Questions

    13. direct WH-questions

E. Nominal forms

    14. nominalizations (ending in -tion, -ment, -ness, -ity)
    15. gerunds (participial forms functioning as nouns)
    16. total other nouns

F. Passives

    17. agentless passives
    18. by-passives

G. Stative forms

    19. be as main verb
    20. existential there

H. Subordination features

    21. that verb complements (e.g., I said that he went.)
    22. that adjective complements (e.g., I'm glad that you like it.)
    23. WH clauses (e.g., I believed what he told me.)
    24. infinitives
    25. present participial clauses (e.g., Stuffing his mouth with
            cookies, Joe ran out the door.)

Table 4.4 (*cont.*)

26. past participial clauses (e.g., <u>Built in a single week, the</u>
    <u>house would stand for fifty years.</u>)
27. past participial WHIZ deletion relatives (e.g., <u>the solution</u>
    <u>produced by this process</u>)
28. present participial WHIZ deletion relatives (e.g., <u>the</u>
    <u>event causing this decline is...</u>)
29. <u>that</u> relative clauses on subject position (e.g., <u>the dog</u>
    <u>that bit me</u>)
30. <u>that</u> relative clauses on object position (e.g., <u>the dog</u>
    <u>that I saw</u>)
31. WH relatives on subject position (e.g., <u>the man who likes</u>
    <u>popcorn</u>)
32. WH relatives on object position (e.g., <u>the man who Sally</u>
    <u>likes</u>)
33. pied-piping relative clauses (e.g., <u>the manner in which he</u>
    <u>was told</u>)
34. sentence relatives (e.g., <u>Bob likes fried mangoes, which is</u>
    <u>the most disgusting thing I've ever heard of</u>)
35. causative adverbial subordinators (<u>because</u>)
36. concessive adverbial subordinators (<u>although, though</u>)
37. conditional adverbial subordinators (<u>if, unless</u>)
38. other adverbial subordinators (e.g., <u>since, while, whereas</u>)

I. Prepositional phrases, adjectives, and adverbs

39. total prepositional phrases
40. attributive adjectives (e.g., <u>the big horse</u>)
41. predicative adjectives (e.g., <u>the horse is big</u>)
42. total adverbs

J. Lexical specificity

43. type/token ratio
44. mean word length

K. Lexical classes

45. conjuncts (e.g., <u>consequently, furthermore, however</u>)
46. downtoners (e.g., <u>barely, nearly, slightly</u>)
47. hedges (e.g., <u>at about, something like, almost</u>)
48. amplifiers (e.g., <u>absolutely, extremely, perfectly</u>)
49. emphatics (e.g., <u>a lot, for sure, really</u>)
50. discourse particles (e.g., sentence initial <u>well, now,</u>
    <u>anyway</u>)
51. demonstratives

L. Modals

52. possibility modals (<u>can, may, might, could</u>)
53. necessity modals (<u>ought, should, must</u>)
54. predictive modals (<u>will, would, shall</u>)

Table 4.4 *(cont.)*

M. Specialized verb classes

    55. public verbs (e.g., <u>assert</u>, <u>declare</u>, <u>mention</u>, <u>say</u>)
    56. private verbs (e.g., <u>assume</u>, <u>believe</u>, <u>doubt</u>, <u>know</u>)
    57. suasive verbs (e.g., <u>command</u>, <u>insist</u>, <u>propose</u>)
    58. <u>seem</u> and <u>appear</u>

N. Reduced forms and dispreferred structures

    59. contractions
    60. subordinator <u>that</u> deletion (e.g., <u>I think</u> [that] <u>he went</u>)
    61. stranded prepositions (e.g., <u>the candidate that I was</u>
           <u>thinking of</u>)
    62. split infinitives (e.g., <u>he wants to convincingly prove</u>
           <u>that</u> ...)
    63. split auxiliaries (e.g., <u>they are objectively shown to</u> ...)

O. Coordination

    64. phrasal coordination (NOUN <u>and</u> NOUN; ADJ <u>and</u> ADJ; VERB <u>and</u>
          VERB; ADV <u>and</u> ADV)
    65. independent clause coordination (clause initial <u>and</u>)

P. Negation

    66. synthetic negation (e.g., <u>no answer is good enough for</u>
          <u>Jones</u>)
    67. analytic negation (e.g., <u>that's not likely</u>)

4.5 Frequency counts of the linguistic features

The frequency counts of all linguistic features are normalized to a text length of 1,000 words (except for type/token ratio and word length – see discussion in Appendix II). This normalization is crucial for any comparison of frequency counts across texts, because text length can vary widely. A comparison of non-normalized counts will give an inaccurate assessment of the frequency distribution in texts. For example, suppose that there were three texts in a comparison, text A with 1,000 words, text B with 2,000 words, and text C with 1,330 words; and that text A had 20 adjectives, text B had 30, and text C had 20. From the raw frequencies, we would conclude that texts A and C had the same frequency of adjectives, but that text B had a third more adjectives than the other texts, a quite substantial difference. However, the total of 30 adjectives in text B is based on a count of the number of adjectives per 2,000 words of text, which provides twice as many opportunities for adjectives to occur than in the 1,000 words of text A. Similarly, the total of 20 adjectives in text C is based on a count per 1,330 words of text. Thus, these counts are raw *totals*, but they do not represent comparable *frequencies* of occurrence. By normalizing the total counts to a text length of 1,000 words – that is, computing how many adjectives *would* occur if the text had been 1,000 words long – the frequencies can be compared directly. In the present example, the frequency counts would be:

Text A:
(20 (adjs.) ÷ 1,000 (length of text)) × 1,000 = 20 (adjs.)

Text B:
(30 (adjs.) ÷ 2,000 (length of text)) × 1,000 = 15 (adjs.)

Text C:
(20 (adjs.) ÷ 1,330 (length of text)) × 1,000 = 15 (adjs.)

That is, when the counts are normalized so that they represent frequencies per 1,000 words, we see that text B uses adjectives less frequently than text A, and that texts B and C use adjectives with the same frequency, in marked contrast to the relations indicated by the raw counts.

Table 4.5 presents descriptive statistics for the frequencies of the linguistic features in the entire corpus of texts. Included are: (1) the mean frequency, (2) the maximum and minimum frequencies, that is, the maximum and minimum occurrences in any text, (3) the 'range', that is, the difference between the maximum and the minimum values, and (4) the 'standard deviation', a measure of the spread of the distribution – 68% of the texts in the corpus have frequency values within the spread of plus or minus one standard deviation from the mean score. This table does not enable characterization of particular genres, but it provides an assessment of the overall distribution of particular features in English texts. Some features occur very frequently, for example, nouns with a mean of 180 per 1,000 words; other features occur very infrequently, for example, causative adverbial subordinators with a mean of 1 per 1,000 words. The variability in the frequency of features also differs from one feature to the next; some features are rather evenly distributed across the

Table 4.5 *Descriptive statistics for the corpus as a whole*

Linguistic feature	Mean	Minimum value	Maximum value	Range	Standard deviation
past tense	40.1	0.0	119.0	119.0	30.4
perfect aspect verbs	8.6	0.0	40.0	40.0	5.2
present tense	77.7	12.0	182.0	170.0	34.3
place adverbials	3.1	0.0	24.0	24.0	3.4
time adverbials	5.2	0.0	24.0	24.0	3.5
first person pronouns	27.2	0.0	122.0	122.0	26.1
second person pronouns	9.9	0.0	72.0	72.0	13.8
third person pronouns	29.9	0.0	124.0	124.0	22.5
pronoun IT	10.3	0.0	47.0	47.0	7.1
demonstrative pronouns	4.6	0.0	30.0	30.0	4.8
indefinite pronouns	1.4	0.0	13.0	13.0	2.0
DO as pro-verb	3.0	0.0	22.0	22.0	3.5
WH questions	0.2	0.0	4.0	4.0	0.6
nominalizations	19.9	0.0	71.0	71.0	14.4
gerunds	7.0	0.0	23.0	23.0	3.8
nouns	180.5	84.0	298.0	214.0	35.6
agentless passives	9.6	0.0	38.0	38.0	6.6
BY passives	0.8	0.0	8.0	8.0	1.3
BE as main verb	28.3	7.0	72.0	65.0	9.5
existential THERE	2.2	0.0	11.0	11.0	1.8
THAT verb complements	3.3	0.0	20.0	20.0	2.9
THAT adj. complements	0.3	0.0	3.0	3.0	0.6
WH clauses	0.6	0.0	7.0	7.0	1.0
infinitives	14.9	1.0	36.0	35.0	5.6
present participial clauses	1.0	0.0	11.0	11.0	1.7
past participial clauses	0.1	0.0	3.0	3.0	0.4
past prt. WHIZ deletions	2.5	0.0	21.0	21.0	3.1
present prt. WHIZ deletions	1.6	0.0	11.0	11.0	1.8
THAT relatives: subj. position	0.4	0.0	7.0	7.0	0.8
THAT relatives: obj. position	0.8	0.0	7.0	7.0	1.1
WH relatives: subj. position	2.1	0.0	15.0	15.0	2.0
WH relatives: obj. position	1.4	0.0	9.0	9.0	1.7
WH relatives: pied pipes	0.7	0.0	7.0	7.0	1.1
sentence relatives	0.1	0.0	3.0	3.0	0.4
adv. subordinator - cause	1.1	0.0	11.0	11.0	1.7
adv. sub. - concession	0.5	0.0	5.0	5.0	0.8
adv. sub. - condition	2.5	0.0	13.0	13.0	2.2
adv. sub. - other	1.0	0.0	6.0	6.0	1.1
prepositions	110.5	50.0	209.0	159.0	25.4
attributive adjectives	60.7	16.0	115.0	99.0	18.8
predicative adjectives	4.7	0.0	19.0	19.0	2.6
adverbs	65.6	22.0	125.0	103.0	17.6
type/token ratio	51.1	35.0	64.0	29.0	5.2
word length	4.5	3.7	5.3	1.6	0.4
conjuncts	1.2	0.0	12.0	12.0	1.6
downtoners	2.0	0.0	10.0	10.0	1.6
hedges	0.6	0.0	10.0	10.0	1.3
amplifiers	2.7	0.0	14.0	14.0	2.6
emphatics	6.3	0.0	22.0	22.0	4.2
discourse particles	1.2	0.0	15.0	15.0	2.3
demonstratives	9.9	0.0	22.0	22.0	4.2

Table 4.5 (*cont.*)

Linguistic feature	Mean	Minimum value	Maximum value	Range	Standard deviation
possibility modals	5.8	0.0	21.0	21.0	3.5
necessity modals	2.1	0.0	13.0	13.0	2.1
predictive modals	5.6	0.0	30.0	30.0	4.2
public verbs	7.7	0.0	40.0	40.0	5.4
private verbs	18.0	1.0	54.0	53.0	10.4
suasive verbs	2.9	0.0	36.0	36.0	3.1
SEEM/APPEAR	0.8	0.0	6.0	6.0	1.0
contractions	13.5	0.0	89.0	89.0	18.6
THAT deletion	3.1	0.0	24.0	24.0	4.1
stranded prepositions	2.0	0.0	23.0	23.0	2.7
split infinitives	0.0	0.0	1.0	1.0	0.0
split auxiliaries	5.5	0.0	15.0	15.0	2.5
phrasal coordination	3.4	0.0	12.0	12.0	2.7
non-phrasal coordination	4.5	0.0	44.0	44.0	4.8
synthetic negation	1.7	0.0	8.0	8.0	1.6
analytic negation	8.5	0.0	32.0	32.0	6.1

corpus, for example, split infinitives have a maximum frequency of 1 per 1,000 words and a minimum frequency of 0 per 1,000 words; other features show large differences, for example, first person pronouns occur 122 times in some texts but not at all in other texts.

Appendix III provides descriptive statistics of the frequency of each linguistic feature in each genre; it includes a table with the same format as Table 4.5 for each of the genres. This appendix provides a wealth of information concerning the distributions of individual features among the genres. It enables a characterization of each genre and comparison of genres with respect to individual linguistic features. Consideration of the frequencies of individual features, however, cannot provide a comprehensive description of the dimensions of textual variation or the textual relations among genres. For these purposes, multivariate statistical techniques provide an invaluable research tool, and we turn next to a description of these techniques as applied to the analysis of textual variation.

5 *Statistical analysis*

5.1 Factor analysis: introduction

Factor analysis is the primary statistical tool of the multi-feature/multi-dimensional approach to textual variation. In a factor analysis, a large number of original variables, in this case the frequencies of linguistic features, are reduced to a small set of derived variables, the 'factors'. Each factor represents some area in the original data that can be summarized or generalized. That is, each factor represents an area of high shared variance in the data, a grouping of linguistic features that co-occur with a high frequency. The factors are linear combinations of the original variables, derived from a correlation matrix of all variables. For instance, if the linguistic features in an analysis were first person pronouns, questions, passives, and nominalizations, the correlation matrix for these features might look like this:

	1st pers. pro.	*questions*	*passives*	*nominal-izations*
1st pers. pro.	*1.00*			
questions	*.85*	*1.00*		
passives	*−.15*	*−.21*	*1.00*	
nominal-izations	*.08*	*−.17*	*.90*	*1.00*

The size of a correlation (whether positive or negative) indicates the extent to which two linguistic features vary together. A large negative correlation indicates that two features covary in a systematic, complementary fashion, i.e., the presence of the one is highly associated with the absence of the other. A large positive correlation indicates that the two features systematically occur together. Squaring the correlation coef-

79

ficient (R-squared) provides a measure of the percentage of variance shared by any two variables, indicating directly the importance of the relationship between them. For example, in the above hypothetical matrix, first person pronouns and questions have a high correlation of .85, which translates into an R-squared of 72%; that is, 72% of the variance in the frequency values for first person pronouns and questions is shared. In concrete terms, a correlation of this magnitude shows that when first person pronouns occur in a text, it is highly likely that questions will occur to a similar extent, and when first person pronouns are absent from a text it is likely that questions will be absent also.

Overall, the correlations shown in the above matrix form a clear pattern: first person pronouns and questions are highly correlated, and passives and nominalizations are highly correlated; while the other four correlations (between passives and first person pronouns, passives and questions, nominalizations and first person pronouns, and nominalizations and questions) are all quite low. Intuitively, two distinct factors can be identified from this matrix, Factor A having first person pronouns and questions, and Factor B having passives and nominalizations. The matrix also indicates that these two factors are relatively independent or uncorrelated with one another, since the linguistic features on Factor A show low correlations with the features on Factor B.

This example is simplistic, but indicative of the way in which factors are computed. They are defined by correlations among the frequency counts of linguistic features. When several linguistic features are highly correlated, showing that they frequently co-occur, then a factor is defined. A factor analysis of the above correlation matrix might produce the following two factors:

Factor A =   .82 (1st pers. pro.) + .82 (questions)
*   + .11 (nominalizations) − .23 (passives)*

Factor B = − .16 (1st pers. pro.) − .19 (questions)
*   + .91 (passives) + .76 (nominalizations)*

The numbers in front of the linguistic features on each factor are referred to as factor 'loadings' or 'weights'. There is no one-to-one correspondence between these loadings and the correlation coefficients, but they both indicate the same pattern: one factor representing a strong co-occurrence relationship between first person pronouns and questions (Factor A), and another factor representing a strong co-occurrence relationship between passives and nominalizations (Factor B). Factor loadings indicate the degree to which one can generalize from a given factor to an individual linguistic feature. The further from 0.0 a factor loading is, the more one can generalize from that factor to the linguistic feature in question. Thus, features with higher loadings on a factor are better representatives of the dimension underlying the factor, and when interpreting the nature of a factor, the features with large loadings are given priority. In the above two fictitious factors, first person pronouns and questions are the important loadings on Factor A (i.e., first person pronouns and questions are features strongly representative of the dimension underlying Factor A) and passives and nominalizations are the important loadings on Factor B.

Multivariate statistical techniques such as factor analysis are not practical without the aid of computers. A factor analysis involves many lengthy computations using matrix algebra. The starting-point for a factor analysis is a simple correlation matrix of all variables, yet a small study of twenty variables would require calculation of nearly 200 correlation coefficients, a task that would take many hours in itself if done by hand. To compute an entire factorial structure by hand might require several weeks of work. Fortunately, factor analysis routines are usually included as part of the standard statistical packages (e.g., SAS, SPSS, SPSSX) available on computers at most academic institutions. This computational tool makes possible a new range of linguistic research, but the proper use of factor analysis requires understanding of several technical points, including a grasp of the theoretical prerequisites, the differences among the various extraction and rotation techniques, the nature of the resulting factors, and the nature of the final interpretations. An overview of these points is presented in the following sections, and fuller details can be found in any standard reference work on factor analysis (e.g., Gorsuch 1983). The discussion in the following sections is relatively technical; the information given here enables a relatively complete understanding of the research methodology used in the study. The research results presented in Chapters 6 and 7, however, can be understood without reading the technical descriptions given here.

5.2 Factor analysis: technical description

The first step in a factor analysis is to choose a method for extracting the factors. Because the use of factor analysis in linguistics is usually exploratory (rather than confirmatory), a principal factor solution should be used (Gorsuch 1983 – Chapter 6). There are several options available, but the most widely used is known as 'common factor analysis' or 'principal factor analysis'.[1] This procedure extracts the maximum amount of shared variance among the variables for each factor. Thus, the first factor extracts the maximum amount of shared variance, i.e., the largest grouping of co-occurrences in the data; the second factor then extracts the maximum amount of shared variance from the tokens left over after the first factor has been extracted, and so on. In this way, each factor is extracted so that it is uncorrelated with the other factors.

Once a method of extraction has been chosen, the best number of factors in a solution must be determined (Gorsuch 1983 – Chapter 8). As noted above, the purpose of factor analysis is to reduce the number of observed variables to a relatively small number of underlying constructs. A factor analysis will continue extracting factors until all of the shared variance among the variables has been accounted for; but only the first few factors are likely to account for a nontrivial amount of shared variance and therefore be worth further consideration. There is no mathematically exact method for determining the number of factors to be extracted. There are, however, several guidelines for this decision. One of the simplest is to examine a plot of the eigenvalues, which are direct indices of the amount of variance accounted for by each factor. Such a plot is called a scree plot, and will normally show a characteristic break indicating the point at which additional factors contribute little to the overall analysis.

The first eleven eigenvalues for the factor analysis used in the present study are given in Table 5.1, and the scree plot corresponding to these values is given in Figure 5.1. As shown in Table 5.1, the eigenvalues can be used to indicate the percentage of shared variance that is accounted for by each factor. Thus, in the present analysis, Factor 1 accounts for 26.8% of the shared variance, Factor 2 for an additional 8%, etc.

Both the table and the scree plot show that the first factor accounts for the greatest proportion of variance by far. As noted above, the scree plot can also be used to indicate the optimal number of factors. The clearest

---

[1] Another commonly used factoring procedure is principal components. The primary difference between principal factor analysis (PFA) and principal components analysis (PCA) is that a PCA attempts to account for *all* of the variance in the data while a PFA attempts to account for only the *shared* variance. In PCA, unique and error variance get treated as if they were shared variance, which can result in factor loadings that are inflated. The solutions produced by PFA are thus more accurate and have been preferred in recent social science research (see Farhady 1983).

Table 5.1 *First 11 eigenvalues of the unrotated factor analysis*

Factor number	Eigenvalue	% of shared variance
1	17.67	26.8%
2	5.33	8.1%
3	3.45	5.2%
4	2.29	3.5%
5	1.92	2.9%
6	1.84	2.8%
7	1.69	2.6%
8	1.43	2.2%
9	1.32	2.0%
10	1.27	1.9%
11	1.23	1.9%

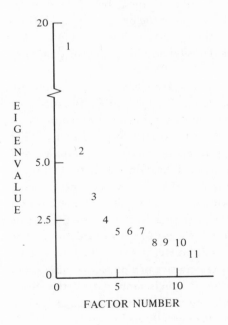

Figure 5.1 *Scree plot of eigenvalues*

Table 5.2 *Inter-factor correlations*

	FACT1	FACT2	FACT3	FACT4	FACT5	FACT6	FACT7
FACTOR1	1.00						
FACTOR2	0.24	1.00					
FACTOR3	-0.49	-0.34	1.00				
FACTOR4	0.17	0.12	0.12	1.00			
FACTOR5	-0.23	-0.21	0.30	0.16	1.00		
FACTOR6	0.16	-0.24	0.01	0.00	0.05	1.00	
FACTOR7	-0.01	-0.01	-0.10	0.24	-0.05	-0.09	1.00

break in the plot occurs between the fourth and fifth factor, but a second break occurs between the seventh and eighth factor. When faced with a choice between a larger or smaller number of factors, the more conservative procedure is to extract the larger number and then discard any unnecessary factors (Gorsuch 1983; Farhady 1983). Extracting too few factors will result in loss of information, because the constructs underlying the excluded factors will be overlooked; it might also distort the factorial structure of the remaining factors, because multiple constructs are collapsed into a single factor. In the present case, solutions for 4, 5, 6, 7, and 8 factors were examined, and the 7-factor solution was settled on as optimal; I discuss this decision and illustrate the danger of under-factoring in Section 5.3.

A final, and very important, step in a factor analysis before interpretation is rotation of the factors (Gorsuch 1983 – Chapter 9). Because each factor in a principal factor analysis accounts for the maximum amount of variance, it is often difficult to interpret a factorial solution directly. That is, the first factor accounts for the greatest proportion of the variance, and thus a majority of the linguistic features will load on this factor instead of subsequent factors – a representation that hides the theoretically interesting constructs underlying the other factors. To compensate for this problem, various techniques have been devised to rotate the factors to a simple structure, a solution in which each feature loads on as few factors as possible. In such a rotated solution, each factor is characterized by the few features that are most representative of a particular amount of shared variance. The rotated solution is much simpler than the initial extraction (which allows many small, but not trivial, loadings on each of the factors), and this simplified structure greatly facilitates the interpretation of the constructs underlying each factor.

There are several different methods of rotation, many of them available as part of the standard statistical packages. Two of these are used commonly: Varimax and Promax. These two rotation methods differ in that Varimax maintains orthogonal structure, requiring the assumption that the factors are uncorrelated, while Promax permits oblique structure, that is, it permits minor correlations among the factors. In the description of textual variation, where the factors represent underlying textual dimensions, there is no reason to assume that the factors are completely uncorrelated, and therefore a Promax rotation is recommended.[2] In the present case, the intercorrelations among the factors are small, shown in Table 5.2: the largest inter-factor correlations are between Factors 1 and 3 ($-.49$), Factors 2 and 3 ($-.34$), and Factors 3 and 5 (.30).

5.3 The factorial structure

The final rotated factor pattern for the present study is given as Table 5.3. This factorial structure is based on analysis of 67 linguistic features counted in 481 spoken and written text samples.[3] In the last section, I pointed out that the factorial structure is derived from a correlation matrix of all variables; the correlation matrix for the present analysis, including a key to the abbreviations, is given as Appendix IV.

In the final factor solution, seven factors were extracted using a principal factors solution, and the factors were subsequently rotated using a Promax rotation. Table 5.3 presents the factor loadings for each of the linguistic features on each of the factors. As noted above, a factor loading indicates the extent to which one can generalize from a factor to a particular linguistic feature, or the extent to which a given feature is representative of the dimension underlying a factor. The loading of a feature on a factor reflects the extent to which the variation in the frequency of that feature correlates with the overall variation of the factor; it indicates the strength of the co-occurrence relationship between

[2] In fact, oblique solutions might be generally preferable in studies of language use and acquisition, since it is unlikely that orthogonal, uncorrelated factors actually occur as components of the communication process. That is, from a theoretical perspective, all aspects of language use appear to be interrelated to at least some extent, and thus there is no reason to expect mathematically uncorrelated factors representing those aspects (see Hinofotis 1983).
[3] Table 3 shows factor loadings for only 66 linguistic features – split infinitives were dropped from the analysis because they occur very infrequently (see p. 78).

Table 5.3   *Rotated factor pattern for the 7 factor solution* (*Promax rotation*)

LX FEATURE	FACTOR1	FACTOR2	FACTOR3	FACTOR4	FACTOR5	FACTOR6	FACTOR7
PRO1	0.744	0.088	0.025	0.026	-0.089	0.008	-0.098
PRO2	0.860	-0.043	-0.018	0.016	0.007	-0.168	-0.064
PRO3	-0.053	0.727	-0.074	-0.018	-0.167	-0.076	0.138
PANY	0.618	0.046	0.011	0.085	-0.094	-0.085	-0.032
PDEM	0.756	-0.166	-0.001	-0.108	0.004	0.306	-0.077
PERFECTS	0.051	0.480	0.049	-0.016	-0.101	0.146	0.143
PASTTNSE	-0.083	0.895	0.002	-0.249	-0.049	-0.052	0.021
N	-0.799	-0.280	-0.091	-0.045	-0.294	-0.076	-0.213
N_NOM	-0.272	-0.237	0.357	0.179	0.277	0.129	-0.019
N_VBG	-0.252	-0.127	0.216	0.177	0.087	-0.052	0.052
PREP	-0.540	-0.251	0.185	-0.185	0.234	0.145	-0.008
ADVS	0.416	-0.001	-0.458	-0.020	-0.156	0.053	0.314
CONJNCTS	-0.141	-0.160	0.064	0.108	0.481	0.180	0.217
SUB_COS	0.661	-0.080	0.110	0.023	-0.061	0.078	-0.076
SUB_CON	0.006	0.092	0.100	-0.071	0.010	-0.056	0.300
SUB_CND	0.319	-0.076	-0.206	0.466	0.120	0.103	-0.007
SUB_OTHR	-0.109	0.051	-0.018	0.008	0.388	0.102	0.109
INF	-0.071	0.059	0.085	0.760	-0.274	-0.005	-0.074
PRO_DO	0.821	0.004	0.071	0.049	-0.057	-0.077	-0.056
SEEM	0.054	0.128	0.160	-0.010	0.015	0.045	0.348
DOWNTONE	-0.084	-0.008	0.021	-0.080	0.066	0.113	0.325
AMPLIFR	0.563	-0.156	-0.028	-0.124	-0.124	0.225	-0.018
PL_ADV	-0.417	-0.060	-0.492	-0.094	-0.067	-0.018	-0.023
TM_ADV	-0.199	-0.062	-0.604	-0.020	-0.290	0.116	-0.046
TH_CL	0.045	0.228	0.125	0.265	0.053	0.558	-0.122
ADJ_CL	-0.124	0.066	-0.080	0.123	0.171	0.360	0.183
CONTRAC	0.902	-0.100	-0.141	-0.138	-0.002	-0.057	-0.032
TYPETOKN	-0.537	0.058	0.002	-0.005	-0.311	-0.228	0.219
SYNTHNEG	-0.232	0.402	0.046	0.133	-0.057	0.176	0.110
NOT_NEG	0.778	0.149	0.017	0.125	0.019	0.001	0.037
BE_STATE	0.713	0.056	0.075	0.008	0.014	0.292	0.180
POS_MOD	0.501	-0.123	0.044	0.367	0.122	-0.022	0.115
NEC_MOD	-0.007	-0.107	-0.015	0.458	0.102	0.135	0.042
PRD_MOD	0.047	-0.056	-0.054	0.535	-0.072	0.063	-0.184
PUB_VB	0.098	0.431	0.163	0.135	-0.030	0.046	-0.279
PRV_VB	0.962	0.160	0.179	-0.054	0.084	-0.049	0.106
SUA_VB	-0.240	-0.035	-0.017	0.486	0.051	0.016	-0.237
PRTCLE	0.663	-0.218	-0.128	-0.029	-0.096	0.165	-0.140
GEN_HDG	0.582	-0.156	-0.051	-0.087	-0.022	-0.145	0.096
GEN_EMPH	0.739	-0.216	0.015	-0.027	-0.188	-0.087	0.210
SENT_REL	0.550	-0.086	0.152	-0.118	-0.025	0.048	-0.041
WH_QUES	0.523	-0.024	0.117	-0.111	-0.032	0.036	-0.094
P_AND	-0.253	-0.091	0.355	-0.066	-0.046	-0.324	0.126
O_AND	0.476	0.041	-0.052	-0.161	-0.139	0.218	-0.125
WHIZ_VBN	-0.382	-0.336	-0.071	-0.137	0.395	-0.128	-0.103
WHIZ_VBG	-0.325	-0.114	0.080	-0.169	0.212	-0.070	-0.093
CL_VBN	-0.025	-0.154	0.029	-0.050	0.415	-0.142	-0.059
CL_VBG	-0.211	0.392	-0.142	-0.076	0.268	-0.217	0.121
EX_THERE	0.262	0.108	0.113	-0.124	-0.004	0.318	0.017
DEM	0.040	-0.062	0.113	0.010	0.132	0.478	0.153
WRDLNGTH	-0.575	-0.314	0.270	-0.009	0.023	0.028	0.081

Table 5.3 *(cont.)*

LX FEATURE	FACTOR1	FACTOR2	FACTOR3	FACTOR4	FACTOR5	FACTOR6	FACTOR7
REL_SUBJ	-0.087	-0.067	0.453	-0.027	-0.174	0.228	0.047
REL_OBJ	-0.072	0.049	0.627	-0.060	-0.083	0.302	0.165
REL_PIPE	-0.029	0.026	0.606	-0.144	0.046	0.280	0.192
THTREL_S	0.051	-0.036	0.021	0.019	-0.058	0.184	0.033
THTREL_O	-0.047	0.053	0.201	0.223	-0.125	0.457	-0.065
WH_CL	0.467	0.143	0.221	0.032	-0.050	-0.044	-0.027
IT	0.706	-0.021	-0.038	-0.034	-0.038	0.022	0.060
ADJ_PRED	0.187	0.076	-0.089	0.248	0.311	-0.012	0.210
ADJ_ATTR	-0.474	-0.412	0.176	-0.055	-0.038	-0.064	0.299
THAT_DEL	0.909	0.036	0.098	-0.059	-0.005	-0.178	-0.081
SPL_AUX	-0.195	0.040	0.012	0.437	0.043	0.120	0.239
FINLPREP	0.426	0.007	-0.124	-0.210	0.023	0.340	-0.100
PRES	0.864	-0.467	-0.008	0.229	-0.006	0.011	0.011
BY_PASV	-0.256	-0.189	0.065	-0.124	0.413	-0.089	-0.045
AGLS_PSV	-0.388	-0.145	0.109	0.060	0.430	0.063	-0.057

the feature in question and the factor as a whole. There are several techniques for determining the required magnitude of statistically significant loadings, that is, the loadings not due to random patterns of variation. Most of these techniques depend on the number of observations in the analysis (Gorsuch 1983:208ff), but loadings having an absolute value less than .30 are generally excluded as unimportant even if they are statistically significant. Only the important, or 'salient', loadings should be interpreted as part of each factor.

For example, Factor 2 on Table 5.3 shows the following salient loadings having weights larger than .30: past tense (.895), third person personal pronouns (.727), perfect aspect (.480), public verbs (.431), synthetic negation (.402), present participial clauses (.392), present tense (− .467), attributive adjectives (− .412), past participial WHIZ deletions (− .336), and word length (− .314). These loadings are not equally large, and therefore these features are not equally representative of the dimension underlying Factor 2. Past tense and third person pronouns show quite large loadings; present tense, perfect aspect, and public verbs all have large loadings; word length and past participial WHIZ deletions have minimally salient loadings. In the interpretation of each factor, greater attention is given to those features with the largest loadings.

A positive or negative sign does not influence the importance of a loading; for example, present tense (− .467) has a larger loading on Factor 2 than public verbs (.431). Rather than indicating differences in importance, positive and negative loadings show groups of features that are distributed in texts in a complementary pattern. That is, with respect to Factor 2, the features with positive weights (past tense, third person pronouns, perfect aspect, public verbs, etc.) all co-occur with a high frequency in texts; the features with negative weights (present tense, adjectives, etc.) mark a similar group of co-occurring features; and these two groups of linguistic features have a special relationship to each other: they occur in a largely complementary pattern. Thus, when past tense, third person pronouns, and perfect aspect verbs occur with a high frequency in a text, present tense verbs and adjectives are likely to be notably absent from that text, and vice versa. In the interpretations of the factors, both the negative and positive cluster of features must be taken into consideration.

Table 5.4 summarizes the salient positive and negative loadings on each of the factors of the present analysis. The decision to extract seven factors was based on consideration of these salient loadings. It will be remembered from Section 5.2 that a scree plot of the eigenvalues provides a first indication of the optimal number of factors. The scree plot in Figure 5.1 shows a sharp break between Factors 4 and 5, and a lesser break between Factors 7 and 8. The solutions for 4, 5, 6, 7, and 8 factors were therefore examined to determine how well the factors were represented in each case. In the 4 factor solution, each factor was represented by at least eleven salient loadings; in the 5, 6, and 7 factor solutions, each factor was represented by at least five salient loadings; in the 8 factor solution, one of the factors was represented by only two salient loadings. In general, five salient loadings are required for a meaningful interpretation of the construct underlying a factor. Thus, the eight factor solution was excluded as over-factoring. Similarly, since all of the factors in the 5, 6, and 7 factor solutions were sufficiently represented for interpretation, the 4 factor solution was excluded as obviously under-factoring.

I noted in the last section that it is generally preferable to extract too many rather than too few factors, once the choice has been narrowed down to two or three different solutions. If too many factors are extracted, it might be necessary to exclude some of them from interpretation because they are not theoretically well-defined. If too few factors are extracted, however, certain constructs will not be represented in the final factorial structure, and a confused picture of the other constructs might result because factors have been collapsed. In the present analysis,

Table 5.4 *Summary of the factorial structure (features in parentheses were not used in the computation of factor scores – see discussion in Section 5.5)*

FACTOR 1		FACTOR 2	
private verbs	.96	past tense verbs	.90
THAT deletion	.91	third person pronouns	.73
contractions	.90	perfect aspect verbs	.48
present tense verbs	.86	public verbs	.43
2nd person pronouns	.86	synthetic negation	.40
DO as pro-verb	.82	present participial	
analytic negation	.78	clauses	.39
demonstrative			
pronouns	.76	-------------------------	
general emphatics	.74		
1st person pronouns	.74	(present tense verbs	-.47)
pronoun IT	.71	(attributive adjs.	-.41)
BE as main verb	.71	(past participial	
causative		WHIZ deletions	-.34)
subordination	.66	(word length	-.31)
discourse particles	.66		
indefinite pronouns	.62		
general hedges	.58		
amplifiers	.56		
sentence relatives	.55		
WH questions	.52		
possibility modals	.50		
non-phrasal			
coordination	.48	FACTOR 3	
WH clauses	.47		
final prepositions	.43	WH relative clauses on	
(adverbs	.42)	object positions	.63
(conditional		pied piping	
subordination	.32)	constructions	.61
		WH relative clauses on	
-------------------------		subject positions	.45
		phrasal coordination	.36
nouns	-.80	nominalizations	.36
word length	-.58		
prepositions	-.54	-------------------------	
type/token ratio	-.54		
attributive adjs.	-.47	time adverbials	-.60
(place adverbials	-.42)	place adverbials	-.49
(agentless passives	-.39)	adverbs	-.46
(past participial			
WHIZ deletions	-.38)		
(present participial			
WHIZ deletions	-.32)		

Table 5.4 (*cont.*)

FACTOR 4		FACTOR 5	
infinitives	.76	conjuncts	.48
prediction modals	.54	agentless passives	.43
suasive verbs	.49	past participial	
conditional		clauses	.42
subordination	.47	BY-passives	.41
necessity modals	.46	past participial	
split auxiliaries	.44	WHIZ deletions	.40
(possibility modals	.37)	other adverbial	
		subordinators	.39
		(predicative adjs.)	.31

------------------------- (FACTOR 4)

-- no negative features --

------------------------- (FACTOR 5)

(type/token ratio   -.31)

FACTOR 6		FACTOR 7	
THAT clauses as		SEEM/APPEAR	.35
verb complements	.56	(downtoners	.33)
demonstratives	.55	(adverbs	.31)
THAT relative clauses		(concessive	
on object positions	.46	subordination	.30)
THAT clauses as		(attributive adjs.	.30)
adj. complements	.36		
(final prepositions	.34)		
(existential THERE	.32)		
(demonstrative			
pronouns	.31)		
(WH relative clauses			
on object positions	.30)		

------------------------- (FACTOR 6)   ------------------------- (FACTOR 7)

(phrasal coordination   -.32)   -- no negative features --

the 7 factor solution was thus chosen over the 5 and 6 factor solutions. It turns out that all seven factors in the final solution seem to be theoretically well-defined, which further supports the decision to extract seven factors.

A brief comparison of the 6 and 7 factor solutions illustrates the danger of under-factoring. The first, second, fourth, and fifth factors in the 7 factor solution correspond directly to factors in the 6 factor solution, having the same features with salient weights. The third and sixth factors from the 7 factor solution, however, have been collapsed in the 6 factor solution. That is, the third factor in the 6 factor solution, shown in Table 5.5, has the following major loadings: *that* clauses as verb complements

Table 5.5 *Factor 3 of the 6 factor solution*

```
    FACTOR 3

THAT clauses as
   verb complements    .57
THAT relative clauses
   on object positions .51
demonstratives          .46
WH relative clauses
   on object positions .39
pied piping
   constructions        .35
(WH relative clauses
   on subject position .33)
(existential THERE      .32)
(THAT clauses as
   adj. complements     .31)
(final prepositions    .30)


-------------------------

-- no negative features --
```

(.57), *that* relative clauses on object position (.51), demonstratives (.46), WH relative clauses on object position (.39), pied piping constructions (.35), WH relative clauses on subject position (.33), and *that* clauses as adjective complements (.31). Comparing Table 5.4 and Table 5.5 shows that this third factor in the 6 factor solution combines the major loadings from Factor 3 and Factor 6 of the 7 factor solution. If we based our final interpretation on the 6 factor solution, we would miss the finding that *that* complements, *that* relative clauses, and demonstratives function as part of a different construct from WH relative clauses and pied-piping constructions.

5.4 Interpretation of the factors

In the interpretation of a factor, an underlying functional dimension is sought to explain the co-occurrence pattern among features identified by the factor. That is, it is claimed that a cluster of features co-occur frequently in texts because they are serving some common function in those texts. At this point, micro-analyses of linguistic features become crucially important. Functional analyses of individual features in texts enable identification of the shared function underlying a group of features in a factor analysis. It must be emphasized, however, that while the co-occurrence patterns are derived quantitatively through factor analysis, interpretation of the dimension underlying a factor is tentative and requires confirmation, similar to any other interpretive analysis.

With this caution in mind, we can proceed to a brief discussion of the considerations involved in factor interpretation. Table 5.4 lists the salient features on each of the seven factors in the present analysis. The linguistic features grouped on each factor can be interpreted as a textual dimension through an assessment of the communicative functions most widely shared by the features. The complementary relationship between positive and negative loadings must also be considered in the interpretation.

For example, consider Factor 2. The features with salient positive loadings are past tense, third person personal pronouns, perfect aspect, public verbs, present participial clauses, and synthetic negation. These features can all be used for narrative purposes: past tense and perfect aspect verbs are used to refer to actions in the past; third person personal pronouns are used to refer to animate, usually human, individuals who are not participating in the immediate communicative interaction; public verbs are used frequently for reported speech; and present participial clauses are used for depictive discourse. The two major features with negative loadings are present tense and attributive adjectives, which are used for more immediate reference. Thus, a preliminary interpretation of the dimension underlying this factor would describe it as distinguishing texts with a primary narrative emphasis, marked by considerable reference to past events and removed situations, from texts with non-narrative emphases (descriptive, expository, or other), marked by little reference to a removed situation but by high reference to a present situation. A full interpretation of each of the factors is presented in Chapter 6.

As noted above, interpretations of the factors are tentative until confirmed by further research. One technique used to confirm a factor interpretation uses scores computed from the factors as operational representatives of the hypothesized dimensions; these scores are known as 'factor scores'. In the present case, the factor scores represent textual dimensions. A factor score, or dimension score, can be computed for each text, and the similarities and differences among genres (the textual 'relations') can be analyzed with respect to these scores to support or refute hypothesized interpretations. I discuss the computation of factor scores in Section 5.5 and analyze the relations among genres with respect to the factor scores in Chapter 7. A second technique used to validate hypothesized factor interpretations is confirmatory factor analysis. In this type of analysis, additional features are included in a subsequent analysis, and predictions are made concerning the factors that these features should load on, if the interpretations in question are correct. To the extent that these additional variables load on factors as hypothesized, the interpretation is confirmed. Many additional variables that were not included in Biber (1986a) have been added to the present analysis; in Chapter 6, I discuss the extent to which the interpretations presented in the 1986 analysis are confirmed by the distribution of these additional features.

5.5 Factor scores

In the same way that the frequency of passives in a text might be called the passive score of that text, factor scores are computed for each text to characterize the text with respect to each factor. A factor score is computed by summing, for each text, the number of occurrences of the features having salient loadings on that factor. Due to the large number of features loading on most of the factors in the present analysis, I use a conservative cut-off of .35 for those features to be included in the computation of factor scores. Seven features did not have a weight larger than .35 on any factor and were therefore dropped from the analysis at this point, viz., predicative adjectives, gerunds, concessive subordination, downtoners, present participial WHIZ deletions, existential *there*, and *that* relativization on subject position.

Some features have salient loadings on more than one of the factors (e.g., present tense on Factors 1 and 2); to assure the experimental independence of the factor scores, each feature was included in the computation of only one factor score (Gorsuch 1983:268). Thus, each linguistic feature is included in the factor score of the factor on which it has the highest loading (in terms of absolute magnitude, ignoring plus or minus sign). Salient loadings not used in the computation of the factor scores are given in parentheses on Table 5.4. For example, present tense has a loading of .86 on Factor 1 and −.47 on Factor 2, and therefore it is included in the factor score for Factor 1.

To illustrate the computation of factor scores, consider Factor 2 on Table 5.4. The factor score representing Factor 2 is computed by adding together the frequencies of past tense forms, perfect aspect forms, third person pronouns, public verbs, present participial clauses, and synthetic negation – the features with positive loadings – for each text. No frequencies are subtracted in this case, because the two features with negative loadings larger than .35 – present tense and attributive adjectives – both have higher loadings on Factor 1. For example, one of the general fiction texts in this study (text K:6 from the LOB corpus) has 113 past tense forms, 124 third person personal pronouns, 30 perfect aspect forms, 14 public verbs, 5 present participial clauses, and 3 occurrences of synthetic negation, resulting in the following factor score for Factor 2:

$$(113 + 124 + 30 + 14 + 5 + 3) = 289$$

In the present study, all frequencies were standardized to a mean of 0.0 and a standard deviation of 1.0 before the factor scores were computed.[4] The means and standard deviations of each feature are listed in Table 4.5. The mean is a measure of the central frequency of a feature; the standard deviation is a measure of the spread of frequency values of a feature: 68% of the texts in the corpus have frequency values within the range of plus or minus one standard deviation from the mean score. When the frequency values are standardized, they are translated to a new scale. For example, consider past tense verbs. Table 4.5 shows that this feature has a mean value of 40.1 and a standard deviation of 30.4. Thus, if a text had 40 past tense verbs, it would have a standardized score of 0.0 for this feature, because its frequency equals the mean; the standardized score of 0.0 indicates that this text is unmarked with respect to past tense verbs. If, on the other hand, a text had a frequency of 113 past tense verbs, as in the above example, it would have a standardized score of 2.4, that is,

$$113 = (2.4 \times 30.4) + 40.1$$

The score of 113 is 2.4 standard deviations more than the mean of 40.1, and the standard score of 2.4 shows that this text is quite marked with respect to past tense verbs.

This procedure prevents those features that occur very frequently from having an inordinate influence on the computed factor score. For example, in the above factor score of 289 for text K:6, the frequencies for past tense and third person pronouns have a much larger influence than those for perfect aspect verbs, public verbs, etc. Frequencies standardized to a standard deviation of 1.0 retain the range of variation for each linguistic feature while standardizing the absolute magnitudes of those

---

[4] This standardization procedure should not be confused with the normalization of frequencies to a text length of 1,000 words (Section 4.5). That is, all frequencies are both normalized to a text length of 1,000 words, so that the frequency values for different *texts* are comparable, and they are standardized to a mean of 0.0 and standard deviation of 1.0, so that the values of *features* are comparable because they are translated to a single scale.

frequencies to a single scale. For comparison, the factor score of the above text (K:6) is computed using standardized frequencies:

(2.4 + 4.2 + 4.1 + 1.5 + 2.3 + 1.4) = 15.9

(i.e., 2.4 past tense forms, 4.2 third person personal pronouns, 4.1 perfect aspect forms, 1.5 public verbs, 2.3 present participial clauses, 1.4 occurrences of synthetic negation).

This method of computation shows that the frequencies of all of these features are markedly high in this text, most of them more than 2 standard deviations above the corpus mean. A standardized score can be negative also, if the frequency of a feature in a text is markedly less than the mean frequency for the entire corpus. For example, the standardized score for present tense in the above text is -1.1, reflecting the fact that there are fewer present tense forms in this text than the mean number of present tense forms in the corpus as a whole. The effect of this method of computation is to give each linguistic feature a weight in terms of the range of its *variation* rather than in terms of its absolute frequency in texts. Thus, in the above example, perfect aspect verbs occur only 30 times in this text sample, but this absolute frequency is four standard deviations above the corpus mean for perfects, showing that this is a very frequent use of perfects in relation to their use in the corpus as a whole. This standardized value, reflecting the magnitude of a frequency with respect to the range of possible variation, is a more adequate representation for the purposes of the present study.

The relations among spoken and written genres can be considered through plots of the mean values of the factor scores, representing the underlying textual dimensions, for each genre. That is, a factor score for each factor is computed for each text, as illustrated above. Then, the mean of each factor score for each genre is computed. For example, if there were only three fiction texts, having factor scores for Factor 2 of 16.6, 12.0, and 10.4, the mean score for fiction on Dimension 2 (Factor Score 2) would be:

(16.6 + 12.0 + 10.4) ÷ 3 = 13.0

To illustrate, Figure 5.2 presents the mean scores of Factor Score 2 for each genre, showing the relations among the genres along that dimension. A statistical procedure called General Linear Models[5] can be used to test if there are significant differences among the genres with respect to each factor score. In the present case, the F and p values reported at the bottom

---

[5] General Linear Models is an ANOVA/Regression type procedure that does not depend on the presence of balanced cells. It is one of the multivariate procedures available in SAS, a computational package for statistical analysis.

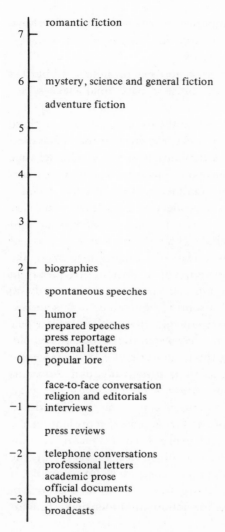

Figure 5.2 *Mean scores of Dimension 2 for each of the genres Dimension 2 (F = 32.30, p < .0001, R*R = 60.8%)*

of Figure 5.2 show that there are significant differences; a p value smaller than .05 indicates a statistically significant relationship. The R*R value presented at the bottom of Figure 5.2 gives the squared multiple correlation coefficient, which indicates the *importance* of the factor score, that is, the percentage of variance in the factor score accounted for by knowing the genre distinctions. The R*R value of 60.8% shows that Factor Score 2 is quite important, in addition to being a statistically significant discriminator among genres.

A full interpretation of a textual dimension is made possible by considering: (1) the factor score means of each genre, (2) the situational and processing parameters associated with the distribution of factor scores, and (3) the linguistic features constituting the factor score. Consider briefly the plot of genres along Textual Dimension 2 shown in Figure 5.2. The fictional genres have the highest values, reflecting high frequencies of past tense verbs, third person personal pronouns, etc. Public speeches, biographies, humor, press reportage, and personal letters have intermediate values; and genres like broadcast, academic prose, and official documents have the lowest values, reflecting very low frequencies of past tense verbs, third person pronouns, etc. in these genres. This distribution confirms the interpretation of a dimension that distinguishes among texts according to their focus on narrative concerns versus non-narrative concerns. Fictional texts are largely narrative; public speeches, biographies, humor, press reportage, and personal letters include both narrative and non-narrative portions and thus have intermediate scores on this dimension; broadcasts, academic prose, and official documents are largely non-narrative and so have quite low scores on this dimension. The distribution of genres along the other dimensions can be examined in a similar way, to further refine the factor interpretations and to specify the relations among genres. The distribution of texts along each dimension is discussed fully in Chapter 7.

5.6 Summary of Chapter 5

This chapter has presented a technical overview of factor analysis and a discussion of the factorial structure of the present analysis, including the rationale for the extraction of seven factors, an overview of the factor interpretation process, and a discussion of the computation and use of factor scores. The following two chapters use these methodologies to develop a comprehensive description of textual variation among spoken and written texts in English. Chapter 6 presents the factor interpretations, describing the textual dimensions uncovered in the present study; Chapter 7 presents a comparison of spoken and written genres with respect to their dimension scores and an overall discussion of the textual relations among genres with respect to all seven dimensions.

Part III: Dimensions and relations in English

6 Textual dimensions in speech and writing

6.1 Summary of factor interpretation principles

In this chapter we turn to an interpretation of the factors presented in Chapter 5, to identify the construct or dimension underlying each factor. Recall that the factor analysis identifies groups of linguistic features that co-occur frequently in texts. The interpretation of the factors is based on the theoretical assumption that these co-occurrence patterns indicate an underlying communicative function shared by the features; that is, it is assumed that linguistic features co-occur frequently in texts because they are used for a shared set of communicative functions in those texts. The interpretation of each factor thus involves an assessment of the communicative function(s) most widely shared by the co-occurring features. Functional analyses of individual features in texts are crucially important in the interpretation process, since they provide the foundation for determining the function(s) underlying a set of features. In the present case, functional interpretations from previous research are summarized in Appendix II, and micro-analyses of features in particular texts are further discussed in Chapter 7. The interpretations presented here are based both on the findings of previous research and the analyses given in Chapter 7.

Table 5.4 (in Chapter 5), which summarizes the final factorial structure, is repeated here for convenience as Table 6.1. This table presents the important linguistic features comprising each factor. I pointed out in Chapter 5 that the features with positive and negative weights on a factor have a special relationship to one another: the features with positive weights co-occur in texts; the features with negative weights co-occur in texts; and these two groups of features occur in a largely complementary distribution. That is, when a text has several occurrences of the features with negative weights it will likely have few of the features with positive weights, and vice versa. In assessing the shared function

Table 6.1   *Summary of the factorial structure*

FACTOR 1		FACTOR 2	
private verbs	.96	past tense verbs	.90
THAT deletion	.91	third person pronouns	.73
contractions	.90	perfect aspect verbs	.48
present tense verbs	.86	public verbs	.43
2nd person pronouns	.86	synthetic negation	.40
DO as pro-verb	.82	present participial	
analytic negation	.78	clauses	.39
demonstrative			
pronouns	.76	-------------------------	
general emphatics	.74		
1st person pronouns	.74	(present tense verbs	-.47)
pronoun IT	.71	(attributive adjs.	-.41)
BE as main verb	.71	(past participial	
causative		WHIZ deletions	-.34)
subordination	.66	(word length	-.31)
discourse particles	.66		
indefinite pronouns	.62		
general hedges	.58		
amplifiers	.56		
sentence relatives	.55		
WH questions	.52		
possibility modals	.50		
non-phrasal			
coordination	.48	FACTOR 3	
WH clauses	.47		
final prepositions	.43	WH relative clauses on	
(adverbs	.42)	object positions	.63
(conditional		pied piping	
subordination	.32)	constructions	.61
		WH relative clauses on	
-------------------------		subject positions	.45
		phrasal coordination	.36
nouns	-.80	nominalizations	.36
word length	-.58		
prepositions	-.54	-------------------------	
type/token ratio	-.54		
attributive adjs.	-.47	time adverbials	-.60
(place adverbials	-.42)	place adverbials	-.49
(agentless passives	-.39)	adverbs	-.46
(past participial			
WHIZ deletions	-.38)		
(present participial			
WHIZ deletions	-.32)		

Table 6.1 *(cont.)*

FACTOR 4		FACTOR 5	
infinitives	.76	conjuncts	.48
prediction modals	.54	agentless passives	.43
suasive verbs	.49	past participial	
conditional		clauses	.42
subordination	.47	BY-passives	.41
necessity modals	.46	past participial	
split auxiliaries	.44	WHIZ deletions	.40
(possibility modals	.37)	other adverbial	
		subordinators	.39
		(predicative adjs.)	.31

FACTOR 4: -- no negative features --

FACTOR 5: (type/token ratio   -.31)

FACTOR 6		FACTOR 7	
THAT clauses as		SEEM/APPEAR	.35
verb complements	.56	(downtoners	.33)
demonstratives	.55	(adverbs	.31)
THAT relative clauses		(concessive	
on object positions	.46	subordination	.30)
THAT clauses as		(attributive adjs.	.30)
adj. complements	.36		
(final prepositions	.34)		
(existential THERE	.32)		
(demonstrative			
pronouns	.31)		
(WH relative clauses			
on object positions	.30)		

FACTOR 7: -- no negative features --

FACTOR 6: (phrasal coordination -.32)

underlying a factor, the researcher must consider the reasons for the complementary distribution of these two groups of features as well as the reasons for the co-occurrence patterns of positive and negative features.

6.2   Interpretation of the factors as textual dimensions

6.2.1   Interpretation of Factor 1

Consider Factor 1, on Table 6.1. This is obviously a very powerful factor: 34 linguistic features have weights larger than .30 on this factor; 24 features have weights larger than .50. In an unrotated factor solution, it would not be surprising to find such a powerful first factor (see Section 5.2). In the present case, however, the factors have been rotated, so that each linguistic feature tends to load on only one factor, and each factor is characterized by those relatively few features that are most representative of the underlying construct. Thus, the structure of Factor 1 is not an artifact of the factor extraction technique. This is rather an extremely powerful factor representing a very basic dimension of variation among spoken and written texts in English.

To interpret this dimension, we must assess the functions shared by these co-occurring features. There are relatively few features with negative weights, and their interpretation is relatively straightforward. Nouns, word length, prepositional phrases, type/token ratio, and attributive adjectives all have negative weights larger than .45 and none of these features have larger weights on another factor. High frequencies of all of these features can be associated with a high informational focus and a careful integration of information in a text. Nouns are the primary bearers of referential meaning in a text, and a high frequency of nouns thus indicates great density of information. Prepositional phrases also serve to integrate high amounts of information into a text. Word length and type/token ratio similarly mark high density of information, but they further mark very precise lexical choice resulting in an exact presentation of informational content. A high type/token ratio results from the use of many different lexical items in a text, and this more varied vocabulary reflects extensive use of words that have very specific meanings. Chafe and Danielewicz (1986) find that precise lexical choice is a very difficult production task and is thus rarely accomplished in speech. Longer words also convey more specific, specialized meanings than shorter words; Zipf

(1949) shows that shorter words are more frequently used and correspondingly more general in meaning. Attributive adjectives are used to further elaborate nominal information. They are a more integrated form of nominal elaboration than predicative adjectives or relative clauses, since they pack information into relatively few words and structures. Together, these five features are used to integrate high amounts of information into a text; to present information as concisely and precisely as possible. These features are associated with communicative situations that require a high informational focus and provide ample opportunity for careful integration of information and precise lexical choice.

The other features with negative weights are place adverbials, past participial WHIZ deletions, agentless passives, and present participial WHIZ deletions. These features are less important in the interpretation of Factor 1: they all have weights less than .42, and most of them have larger weights on some other factor. They are all informational in one way or another, often marking highly abstract types of information. WHIZ deletions are used to modify nouns, further elaborating the nominal content. Passives are associated with a static, nominal style. The co-occurrence of place adverbials with these other features is surprising, but might be due to text internal deixis in highly informational texts (e.g., *It is shown here*; *It was shown above*). Thus, these less important features share the same highly informational functions as nouns, prepositional phrases, type/token ratio, word length, and attributive adjectives.

The features with positive weights on Factor 1 are more complex. All of them can be associated in one way or another with an involved, non-informational focus, due to a primarily interactive or affective purpose and/or to highly constrained production circumstances. These features can be characterized as verbal, interactional, affective, fragmented, reduced in form, and generalized in content.

Private verbs and present tense forms are among the features with largest weights on this factor, indicating a verbal, as opposed to nominal, style. These features can also be considered interactive or involved. Present tense refers to actions occurring in the immediate context of interaction; although informational prose can also be written in the present tense, it uses relatively few verbs. Private verbs (e.g., *think, feel*) are used for the overt expression of private attitudes, thoughts, and emotions. First and second person pronouns, which also have large weights on this factor, refer directly to the addressor and addressee and are thus used frequently in highly interactive discourse. Similarly WH-questions, which have a lower weight, are used primarily in interactive discourse where there is a specific addressee present to answer questions. Emphatics and amplifiers both mark heightened feeling, and sentence relatives are used for attitudinal comments by the speaker (e.g., *He went to the store today, which I think is ridiculous*). All of these features are used for involved discourse, marking high interpersonal interaction or high expression of personal feelings.

Other features with positive weights on Factor 1 mark a reduced surface form, a generalized or uncertain presentation of information, and a generally fragmented production of text. Reduced surface form is marked by *that*-deletions (e.g., *I think* [*that*] *I'll go*), contractions, pro-verb *do*, which substitutes for a fuller verb phrase or clause, and the pronominal forms, *it*, demonstrative pronouns, and indefinite pronouns, which substitute for fuller noun phrases. Final (stranded) prepositions mark a surface disruption in form–meaning correspondence (e.g., *that's the person I talked to*). In most of these cases, a reduction in surface form also results in a more generalized, uncertain content. Thus, contractions result in homophonous expressions, for example, [its] can mean *it is*, *it has*, or *it*-possessive; *it*, demonstrative pronouns, and indefinite pronouns all stand for unspecified nominal referents; and *do* stands for an unspecified verbal referent. In addition, hedges and possibility modals are used to flag uncertainty or lack of precision in the presentation of information. Analytic negation, *be* as main verb, and non-phrasal coordination can all be associated with a fragmented presentation of information, resulting in a low informational density. Analytic negation (*not*) is an alternative to the more integrative synthetic negation (*no*, *neither*). Non-phrasal *and* is used to string clauses together in a loose, logically unspecified manner, instead of integrating the information into fewer units through the use of prepositional phrases, relative clauses, adjectives, etc. *Be* as main verb is typically used to modify a noun with a predicative expression, instead of integrating the information into the noun phrase itself; for example, *the house is big* versus *the big house*. Discourse particles (e.g., *well*, *anyway*) are generalized markers of informational relations in a text. They help to maintain textual coherence when a text is fragmented and would otherwise be relatively incoherent.

Four subordination features are included among the features with positive weights on this factor: causative subordination (*because*), sentence relatives, WH-clauses, and conditional subordination. The co-occurrence of these features with a variety of involved and generalized-content features, and in a complementary pattern to highly informational features, is surprising. This distribution disagrees with the expectations of O'Donnell (1974), Kay (1977), and others – that subordination marks greater elaboration and thus should be characteristic of informational discourse – but it agrees with the findings of Poole and Field (1976) and Halliday (1979) that subordination is associated with the production constraints characteristic of speech. In the present study, subordination features are found on all seven factors, showing the theoretical in-adequacy of any proposal that attempts to characterize subordination as a functionally unified construct. The subordination features grouped on Factor 1 seem to be associated with the expression of information under real-time production constraints, when there is little opportunity to elaborate through precise lexical choice. These features also seem to have a primary affective function. A major function of sentence relatives is to express attitudinal comments. WH-clauses provide a way to 'talk about' questions (Winter 1982). Causative and conditional subordination can also be considered as markers of affect or stance, that is, as justification for actions or beliefs (*because*) or conditions for actions or beliefs (*if*, *unless*). These subordination features thus seem to be associated with a relatively loose presentation of information due to real-time production con-straints, and they seem to mark a range of affective functions relating to the elaboration of personal attitudes or feelings.

In summary, Factor 1 represents a dimension marking high inform-ational density and exact informational content versus affective, interac-tional, and generalized content. Two separate communicative parameters seem to be involved here: (1) the primary purpose of the writer/speaker: informational versus interactive, affective, and involved; and (2) the production circumstances: those circumstances characterized by careful editing possibilities, enabling precision in lexical choice and an integrated textual structure, versus circumstances dictated by real-time constraints, resulting in generalized lexical choice and a generally fragmented presentation of information. Reflecting both of these parameters, I propose the interpretive label 'Informational versus Involved Produc-tion' for the dimension underlying this factor.

The distribution of features seen on Factor 1 shows that these two parameters are highly related. That is, discourse characterized by strict production constraints typically has an involved, interactive purpose, and vice versa. This is not surprising, since it represents a natural evolution of discourse purposes in accordance with production possibilities. Discourse produced under real-time conditions will be constrained in its lexical precision and informational density; it is therefore not surprising that such discourse is associated with non-informational purposes. Conversely, as society has developed the need for highly informational texts, it is not surprising that we have turned to those production circumstances that enable precise lexical choice and high informational density. In fact, in some cases these two concerns seem to have an immediate influence on one another. For example, personal letters would appear to contradict the above generalization, being produced without time constraints and yet being involved in focus. However, despite the opportunity for careful production, many personal letters are produced under strict self-imposed time constraints, perhaps reflecting an assessment of the amount of attention deserved by involved discourse. That is, in the case of personal letters, the affective and interactive purposes of the writer seem to result in self-imposed constraints on production opportunity.

It was noted above that the large number of features grouped on this factor identify it as a very important, fundamental dimension of linguistic variation among texts. This dimension has many of the features that have been associated previously with basic discourse dichotomies, for example, nominal versus verbal styles (Wells 1960) and oral versus literate discourse (Tannen 1982a, 1985). This dimension combines features from Chafe's (1982) two dimensions of integration–fragmentation and detachment–involvement. Although the overall interpretation given here is not in terms of oral and literate discourse, this dimension indicates that there is a fundamental parameter of variation among texts that marks the extent to which they are oral or literate in terms of their production characteristics and primary communicative purposes.

6.2.2   Interpretation of Factor 2

Factor 2 was used throughout Chapter 5 to illustrate the methodology of factor analysis. The interpretation of this factor is more straightforward than for Factor 1. There are seven features with weights larger than .40 on Factor 2. The features with positive weights – past tense verbs, third person personal pronouns, perfect aspect verbs, public verbs, synthetic negation, and present participial clauses (.39) – can be considered as markers of narrative action. Past tense and perfect aspect verbs describe past events. Third person personal pronouns mark reference to animate, typically human, referents apart from the speaker and addressee. Narrative discourse depends heavily on these two features, presenting a sequential description of past events involving specific animate participants. Public verbs are apparently used frequently with these other forms because they function as markers of indirect, reported speech (e.g., *admit, assert, declare, hint, report, say*). In addition, one subordination feature, present participial clauses, is grouped with these narrative-marking features. Thompson (1983) characterizes these participial clauses as detached in their syntactic form and shows how they are used to create vivid images in depictive discourse. The grouping of features seen on this factor thus indicates that narrative discourse is often depictive; that the narration of past events is often framed by the vivid imagery provided by present participial clauses. The grouping of synthetic negation with these other features needs further analysis, although it might be due to a high frequency of denials and rejections in the reported reasoning processes of narrative participants. Tottie (1983a) further notes that synthetic negation is more literary than analytic negation and so would be preferred in literary narrative; this might be related to the stronger emphatic force of synthetic negation (e.g., *he said nothing* versus *he did not say anything*).

Only two features have large negative weights on Factor 2: present tense and attributive adjectives. Present tense has a very large weight on Factor 1 in addition to its weight on Factor 2, and attributive adjectives have a slightly larger weight on Factor 1 than Factor 2. The complementary distribution of present and past tense verbs on Factor 2 is intuitively transparent: a discourse typically reports events in the past or deals with more immediate matters, but does not mix the two. The cooccurrence of attributive adjectives and present tense verbs apparently reflects a more frequent use of elaborated nominal referents in nonnarrative types of discourse than in narrative discourse.

Overall, this dimension can be considered as distinguishing narrative discourse from other types of discourse. It might also be considered as distinguishing between active, event-oriented discourse and more static, descriptive or expository types of discourse. This dimension can thus be interpretively labelled 'Narrative versus Non-narrative Concerns': narrative concerns marked by considerable reference to past time, third person animate referents, reported speech, and depictive details; non-narrative concerns, whether expository, descriptive, or other, marked by immediate time and attributive nominal elaboration.

6.2.3   Interpretation of Factor 3

Three different forms of relative clauses are grouped as the primary positive features on Factor 3: WH relative clauses on object positions, WH relative clauses on subject positions, and pied piping constructions. In addition, phrasal coordination and nominalizations have smaller positive weights on this factor. The three forms of WH relative clauses can all be considered as devices for the explicit, elaborated identification of referents in a text. Several researchers have noted functional differences among these forms (Kroch and Hindle 1982; Frawley 1982; Beaman 1984), but their grouping on a single factor indicates that these differences are minor in comparison to the shared function of referential explicitness. The co-occurrence of phrasal coordination and nominalizations with these relativization features indicates that referentially explicit discourse also tends to be integrated and informational.

Three features have large negative weights on Factor 3: time adverbials, place adverbials, and other adverbs. Place and time adverbials are used for locative and temporal reference (e.g., *above, behind*; *earlier, soon*). They can be used for text-internal referents, but they are more commonly used for reference to places and times outside of the text itself. In fact, these forms often serve as deictics that can only be understood by reference to an external physical and temporal situation. The class 'other adverbs' has a much broader range of functions, which includes time and place reference in addition to specification of manner, etc.

Considering both positive and negative features, the dimension underlying Factor 3 seems to distinguish between highly explicit, context-independent reference and nonspecific, situation-dependent reference. WH relative clauses are used to specify the identity of referents within a text in an explicit and elaborated manner, so that the addressee will have no doubt as to the intended referent. Time and place adverbials, on the other hand, crucially depend on referential inferences by the addressee: for text-internal references (e.g., *see above*; *discussed later*), the addressee must infer where and when in the text *above* and *later* refer to; in the much more common text-external references, the addressee must identify the intended place and time referents in the actual physical context of the discourse. This dimension thus corresponds closely to the distinction between endophoric and exophoric reference (Halliday and Hasan 1976). Overall, the label 'Explicit versus Situation-Dependent Reference' can be suggested for this dimension.

6.2.4   Interpretation of Factor 4

Factor 4 has only features with positive weights: infinitives, prediction modals, suasive verbs, conditional subordination, necessity modals, split auxiliaries, and possibility modals. Looking ahead to the microanalysis of these features in texts, presented in Section 7.2.4, it is possible to suggest here that they function together to mark persuasion: either explicit marking of the speaker's own persuasion (the speaker's own point of view) or argumentative discourse designed to persuade the addressee. Prediction modals are direct pronouncements that certain events *will* occur; necessity modals are pronouncements concerning the obligation or necessity of certain events, that they *should* occur; possibility modals are pronouncements concerning the ability or possibility of certain events occurring, that they *can* or *might* occur. Suasive verbs (e.g., *command*, *demand*, *instruct*) imply intentions to bring about certain events in the future, while conditional subordination specifies the conditions that are required in order for certain events to occur. Although infinitives can have other functions, they are most commonly used as adjective and verb complements; in these constructions, the head adjective or verb frequently encodes the speaker's attitude or stance towards the proposition encoded in the infinitival clause (e.g., *happy to do it*; *hoped to see it*). Split auxiliaries occur when adverbs are placed between auxiliaries and their main verb; the fact that these auxiliaries are often modals probably accounts for the co-occurrence of split auxiliaries with these other features. Considering the function shared by these different features, I propose the interpretive label 'Overt Expression of Persuasion'. That is, this dimension marks the degree to which persuasion is marked overtly, whether overt marking of the speaker's own point of view, or an assessment of the advisability or likelihood of an event presented to persuade the addressee.

6.2.5   Interpretation of Factor 5

The features with positive weights on Factor 5 are conjuncts, agentless passives, adverbial past participial clauses, *by*-passives, past participial WHIZ deletions, other adverbial subordinators, and predicative adjectives with a relatively small weight. The frequency counts of agentless passives, past participial clauses, *by*-passives, and past participial WHIZ deletions are all independent; that is, the counts of *by* and agentless passives include only those passive forms *not* counted as past participial WHIZ deletions or clauses. From one point of view, *by* and agentless passives serve different thematic functions (Thompson 1982; Weiner and Labov 1983), but the strong co-occurrence of these two passive types on Factor 5 reflects the importance of a more basic function shared by these forms. Similarly, the co-occurrence of passive subordinate clauses (adverbial and WHIZ) with main clause passive forms shows that the passive function is more important here than any subordinate/main clause distinction. These forms are all used to present propositions with reduced emphasis on the agent, either demoting the agent to object position or eliding the agent altogether. They are used to give prominence to the patient of the verb, the entity acted upon, which is typically a non-animate referent and is often an abstract concept rather than a concrete referent. Passives are frequently used in procedural discourse, where the same agent is presupposed across several clauses and the specific agent of a clause is not important to the discourse purpose. Discourse with very frequent passive constructions is typically abstract and technical in content, and formal in style. Apparently conjuncts and adverbial subordinators frequently co-occur with passive forms to mark the complex logical relations among clauses that characterize this type of discourse.

No feature has a large negative weight on Factor 5, although the negative weight for type/token ratio ($-.31$) is interesting. That is, the distribution of high lexical variety, represented by type/token ratio, in a complementary pattern to passives, conjuncts, etc. is quite surprising, since both sets of features have been associated with discourse having a highly informational focus. This distribution indicates that abstract, technical discourse, marked by frequent use of passives and conjuncts, has a relatively low lexical variety when compared to other types of informational discourse. Apparently technical discourse repeatedly uses a small set of precise technical vocabulary to refer to the exact concepts and entities intended (Grabe 1984a). Other texts can be highly inform- ational but not technical in this sense. The high loading of type/token ratio on Factor 1 indicates that all informational discourse, technical or not, has a high lexical variety in contrast to interactive, affective types of discourse; the lesser loading of type/token ratio here on Factor 5 indicates that non-technical informational discourse has a markedly higher lexical variety than abstract, technical discourse.

Overall, the dimension underlying this factor seems to mark informational discourse that is abstract, technical, and formal versus other types of discourse, suggesting the label 'Abstract versus Non-Abstract Information'. As with the other factors, this interpretation is further supported by the analysis of these co-occurring features in particular texts, presented in Section 7.2.5.

6.2.6 Interpretation of Factor 6

Three subordination features have high positive weights on Factor 6: *that* complements to verbs, *that* complements to adjectives, and *that* relative clauses on object positions. In addition, demonstratives have a large positive weight on Factor 6, while final prepositions, existential *there*, demonstrative pronouns, and WH relative clauses on object positions have smaller weights. The only feature with a salient negative weight on this factor is phrasal coordination, which is described by Chafe (1982; Chafe and Danielewicz 1986) as a device for idea unit expansion and informational integration.

The distributional pattern shown on Factor 6 runs counter to previous theoretical expectations: several subordination measures that are typically associated with informational elaboration co-occur here with demonstratives, final prepositions, and demonstrative pronouns, which are associated with informal, unplanned types of discourse; while all of these features occur in a largely complementary distribution to phrasal coordination, which is used to integrate information into idea units. The co-occurrence of these subordination features with features such as stranded prepositions suggests that they function to mark informational elaboration in relatively unplanned types of discourse, an interpretation that is supported by Halliday (1979) and Biber (1986a). Halliday's description of the structural complexity associated with speech has been noted previously; that is, because spoken language is produced and comprehended as an on-going process, it is characterized by 'an intricacy of movement [and by] complex sentence structures with low lexical density (more clauses, but fewer high-content words per clause)'. The subordination features grouped on Factor 6 apparently mark informational elaboration that is produced under strict real-time constraints, resulting in a fragmented presentation of information accomplished by tacking on additional dependent clauses, rather than an integrated presentation that packs information into fewer constructions containing more high-content words and phrases (as on Factor 1).

In addition, *that* complements to verbs and adjectives can be used for elaboration of information relative to the personal stance of the speaker, introducing an affective component into this dimension (e.g., *I wish that . . .; it is amazing that . . .; I am happy that . . .*). The co-occurrence of demonstratives with the other features having positive weights on Factor 6 needs further investigation, because the frequency count of demonstratives does not distinguish among text-internal and text-external functions. It can only be suggested here that cohesion in unplanned informational discourse relies heavily on demonstratives.

. Overall, the dimension underlying Factor 6 seems to distinguish discourse that is informational but produced under real-time conditions from other types of discourse. The label 'On-line Informational Elaboration' is suggested here, but the interpretation of this dimension will be considered in greater detail in Section 7.2.6.

6.2.7   Interpretation of Factor 7

Factor 7 has no loadings over .40, it has only five features with weights larger than .30, and most of these features have larger weights on some other factor. Any interpretation of this factor is thus extremely tentative. Despite this caution, the few features grouped on this factor seem to be theoretically coherent, enabling an initial interpretation. That is, the function underlying these features seems to be that of academic hedging, to qualify the extent to which an assertion is 'known' in academic discourse. *Seem* and *appear* mark perception (Quirk *et al.* 1985:1183) rather than bald assertion of fact; downtoners indicate the degree of probability of an assertion, as opposed to hedges which load on Factor 1 and simply mark an assertion as uncertain; concessive subordination indicates that an assertion is true within the bounds of some other, possibly contrasting, assertion (*although* ASSERTION 2, ASSERTION 1). One of the functions of adverbs is to indicate possibility or generalization (e.g., *possibly, generally, approximately*), and it is probably in this function that total *-ly* adverbs co-occur with these other features. Similarly, adjectives can function to mark qualification or possibility (e.g., *a possible explanation*). Thus, the dimension underlying this factor seems to mark academic qualification or hedging. Future research is required to confirm or deny the existence of a dimension with this function; the factorial structure of Factor 7 is not strong enough for a firm interpretation, and this factor will therefore not be considered further in the present study.

6.2.8   Summary of the textual dimensions

The first six factors in this analysis have strong factorial structures, and the features grouped on each factor are functionally coherent and can be readily interpreted on the basis of prior microscopic research. I have suggested interpretive labels for each factor, to describe the underlying functional dimension.

Dimension 1 is labelled 'Informational versus Involved Production'. The poles of this dimension represent discourse with interactional, affective, involved purposes, associated with strict real-time production and comprehension constraints, versus discourse with highly informational purposes, which is carefully crafted and highly edited. This dimension is very strong and represents a fundamental parameter of variation among texts in English.

Dimension 2 is labelled 'Narrative versus Non-Narrative Concerns'. It distinguishes discourse with primary narrative purposes from discourse with non-narrative purposes (expository, descriptive, or other). Dimension 3 is labelled 'Explicit versus Situation-Dependent Reference' and distinguishes between discourse that identifies referents fully and explicitly through relativization, and discourse that relies on nonspecific deictics and reference to an external situation for identification purposes. Dimension 4 is labelled 'Overt Expression of Persuasion'; the features on this dimension are associated with the speaker's expression of own point of view or with argumentative styles intended to persuade the addressee.

Dimension 5 is labelled 'Abstract Non-Abstract Information' and distinguishes between texts with a highly abstract and technical informational focus and those with non-abstract focuses. Dimension 6 is labelled 'On-line Informational Elaboration'. It distinguishes between informational discourse produced under highly constrained conditions, in which the information is presented in a relatively loose, fragmented manner, and other types of discourse, whether informational discourse that is highly integrated or discourse that is not informational. Factor 7 seems to mark academic hedging or qualification but is not sufficiently represented for a full interpretation.

6.3   Comparison to the 1986 analysis

In my 1986 analysis of spoken and written textual dimensions (Biber 1986a), three primary dimensions are identified and interpreted. These dimensions are labelled 'Interactive versus Edited Text', 'Abstract versus Situated Content', and 'Reported versus Immediate Style'. In this section, I will discuss the extent to which the 1986 factorial structure is replicated by the present analysis and the extent to which the interpretations proposed in that earlier analysis are confirmed here.

The factorial structure of the 1986 analysis is summarized in Table 6.2. There are striking similarities between the first three factors of the 1986 analysis, which were the only factors interpreted, and Factors 1, 2, and 5 of the present analysis. Factor 1 of the present analysis corresponds directly to Factor 1.1986; Factor 2 corresponds to Factor 3.1986; and Factor 5 corresponds to Factor 2.1986. All five of the features with large weights on Factor 3.1986 load on Factor 2 in the present analysis (past tense, third person personal pronouns, and perfect aspect with positive weights; present tense and adjectives with negative weights). A majority of the features with large weights on Factor 1.1986 load on Factor 1 in the present analysis (pro-verb *do*, contractions, first and second person pronouns, hedges, WH clauses, WH questions, pronoun *it*, emphatics, and present tense with positive weights; word length and type/token ratio with negative weights). Two other features on Factor 1.1986 have split off to group with additional features as Factor 6 in the present analysis (*that* verb complements and final prepositions). Finally, three of the most important features on Factor 2.1986 load on Factor 5 of the present analysis (conjuncts, agentless passives, and *by*-passives). In addition, nominalizations and prepositions, which have high weights on Factor 2.1986, have notable weights on Factor 5 of the present analysis (.28 and .23 respectively), although they both have higher weights on other factors. Place and time adverbials, which grouped as two of the primary features with negative weights on Factor 2.1986, have split off with nominalizations (one of the primary features with a positive weight) to group with other features forming Factor 3 of the present analysis.

Overall, the factorial structure of the 1986 analysis is closely replicated by the present analysis. The major differences between the two analyses are due to the addition of several linguistic features in the present analysis, which enables identification of additional dimensions that were collapsed in the earlier analysis; thus, two features from Factor 1.1986 have split off to group with additional features as part of Factor 6 in the present analysis, and two features have split off from Factor 2.1986 to group with additional features as part of Factor 3 in the present analysis.

Given this replication of the factorial structure, it is reasonable to consider the extent to which the interpretations proposed in the 1986

Table 6.2 *Summary of the factorial structure of 41 linguistic features, taken from Biber (1986a)*

FACTOR 1		FACTOR 2	
questions	.79	nominalizations	.74
THAT-clauses	.76	prepositions	.61
final prepositions	.68	specific conjuncts	.61
pro-verb DO	.67	agentless passives	.60
contractions	.67	BY-passives	.47
first and second		IT-clefts	.45
person pronouns	.62	split auxiliaries	.42
general hedges	.61	word length	.40
IF-clauses	.56	attitudinal disjuncts	.35
WH-questions	.52		
pronoun IT	.49	-------	
other subordinators	.48		
specific emphatics	.46	place adverbs	-.57
demonstrative BE	.42	time adverbs	-.55
present tense	.42	relative pronoun	
WH-clauses	.41	deletion	-.50
general emphatics	.41	THAT deletion	-.42
infinitives	.35	third person	
		pronouns	-.35
-------			
word length	-.71		
type / token ratio	-.65		

FACTOR 3

past tense	.89
third person pronouns	.61
perfect aspect	.47
-------	
present tense	-.62
adjectives	-.40

analysis have been confirmed by the present analysis. In a confirmatory factor analysis (see Section 5.4), additional linguistic features are included in the analysis to see if they load as hypothesized. To the extent that features with certain functions load on the factors hypothesized to have the same functions, those functional interpretations of the factors are confirmed. To greater or lesser extents, the interpretations for the first five factors of the present analysis represent confirmations of the hypothesized interpretations in the 1986 analysis.

The easiest case to consider is Factor 3.1986, labelled 'Reported versus Immediate Style'. This factor is completely replicated by Factor 2 in the present analysis. In addition, three new features added to the present analysis are grouped with the previous features. One of these, public verbs, has a primary function of marking reported speech, which agrees fully with the interpretation of a dimension marking reported, narrative discourse. The second new feature, present participial clauses, extends the earlier interpretation to include depictive details as part of this reported style. The third additional feature, synthetic negation, in no way disconfirms the hypothesized interpretation, but it is not obvious how it fits into this dimension. Together, these features confirm the interpretation of a dimension marking a 'removed' or narrative style.

Factor 1 in the 1986 analysis was hypothesized to differentiate between texts 'produced under conditions of high personal involvement and real-time constraints (marked by low explicitness in the expression of meaning, high subordination, and interactive features) as opposed to texts produced under conditions permitting considerable editing and high explicitness in the lexical content, but little interaction or personal involvement' (1986a:395). Several additional features in the present analysis group on Factor 1 in a way that confirms the basic outlines of the above interpretation. Three of these features, demonstrative pronouns, indefinite pronouns, and discourse particles, mark reduced lexical content and interpersonal involvement, confirming that aspect of the interpretation. Three other features, private verbs, sentence relatives, and possibility modals, emphasize the affective aspect of personal involvement. Finally, a count of all nouns (excluding nominalizations) was added to the present analysis, and this feature groups with word length and type/token ratio (marking lexical content elaboration and specificity) as expected.

Other aspects of the interpretation of Factor 1.1986 are extended by the present analysis, being identified as belonging to a separate dimension (Factor 6). Thus, it was hypothesized in the 1986 interpretation of Factor 1 that discourse produced under real-time constraints has its own complexities, marked by *that* clauses, *if* clauses, and other adverbial clauses. The addition of *that* adjectival complements and *that* relative clauses to the present analysis confirmed the existence of this complexity, but showed that it functions as part of a separate dimension: one marking informational (rather than interactional) discourse produced under real-time constraints, viz. the dimension underlying Factor 6.

Finally, Dimension 2.1986 was labelled 'Abstract versus Situated Content' and was interpreted as distinguishing discourse with highly abstract, formal content (marked by passives, conjuncts, nominalizations, etc.) from discourse with concrete, situation-dependent content (marked by place and time adverbials, etc.). The existence of a hypothesized dimension marking abstract, formal content is confirmed by the features with positive weights on Factor 5 in the present analysis. These features include the new features of adverbial past participle clauses and past participial WHIZ deletions, which mark abstract information and have large weights on this factor. The existence of a dimension marking situation-dependent content is also confirmed by the present analysis, but not as part of the same dimension. That is, the addition of relative clause features in the present analysis shows that abstract and situated content are not best analyzed as opposite poles of the same dimension. Rather, the features associated with situated content (primarily place and time adverbials) are shown to be part of a referential dimension in the present analysis, marking explicit versus situation-dependent reference (Factor 3). This extended interpretation is enabled by the three WH relative clause features added to the present analysis, which are found to occur in a complementary pattern to the situated content features from the 1986 analysis.

In summary, the major aspects of the 1986 dimensions are replicated and confirmed by the present analysis. Specifically, in both analyses there are three major dimensions that mark (1) interactive, involved discourse versus edited, informational discourse; (2) formal, abstract information versus non-abstract types of information; and (3) reported, narrative discourse versus non-narrative types of discourse. In addition, the present analysis extends the 1986 interpretation, identifying additional aspects of the earlier dimensions or showing that some aspects actually function as part of additional dimensions. These extensions include: (1) the importance of affect as part of interpersonal involvement on Factor 1; (2) the importance of depictive details in narrative discourse (Factor 2); (3) the fact that abstract, technical discourse is relatively low in lexical diversity (Factor 5); (4) the separation of informational discourse produced under real-time constraints (Factor 6) from involved discourse produced under real-time constraints (Factor 1); and (5) the separation of a dimension marking situation-dependent reference versus highly explicit reference (Factor 3) from a dimension marking non-abstract information versus abstract information (Factor 5).

Comparison of these two analyses provides a relatively solid foundation to the interpretations of Dimensions 1–3 and 5–6 in the present analysis. Dimension 4 is not a confirmation of any earlier study and thus is more speculative. As noted above, the dimension underlying Factor 7 is not sufficiently well-represented to warrant further interpretation. The remaining analyses in this book will use the first six dimensions described here to compare the relations among spoken and written genres.

7 Textual relations in speech and writing

7.1 Factor scores and textual relations

The primary goal of this study is specification of the textual relations in English speech and writing, that is, the linguistic similarities and differences among English texts. To this point, six parameters of variation have been identified through a factor analysis and interpreted as underlying textual dimensions. In the present chapter, the similarities and differences among genres are considered with respect to each of these dimensions, and the overall relations among genres in speech and writing are specified by consideration of all dimensions simultaneously. Genres can be similar with respect to some dimensions but quite different with respect to others; the textual relations among genres are determined by the joint assessment of similarities and differences with respect to all dimensions.

Genres can be compared along each dimension by computing factor scores (see Section 5.5). To recapitulate, factor scores are computed by summing the frequency of each of the features on a factor, for each text; for example, the factor score of a text for Factor 2 might equal 23 past tense + 50 third person pronouns + 10 perfect aspect verbs + etc. The factor scores for each text can be averaged across all texts in a genre to compute a mean dimension score for the genre, and these mean dimension scores can be compared to specify the relations among genres.

Table 7.1 presents the dimension scores of each genre. This table presents, for each of the dimensions, the mean score for each genre, the minimum and maximum dimension scores within the genre, the range, which is the difference between the minimum and maximum scores, and the standard deviation, which measures the spread of the distribution – 68% of the texts in a genre have dimension scores that are plus or minus one standard deviation from the mean dimension score for the genre. Large standard deviations show that the texts in a genre are widely

Table 7.1 *Descriptive dimension statistics for all genres*

Dimension 1: 'Involved versus Informational Production'
Dimension 2: 'Narrative versus Non-Narrative Concerns'
Dimension 3: 'Explicit versus Situation-Dependent Reference'
Dimension 4: 'Overt Expression of Persuasion'
Dimension 5: 'Abstract versus Non-Abstract Information'
Dimension 6: 'On-Line Informational Elaboration'

Dimension	Mean	Minimum value	Maximum value	Range	Standard deviation
------------------------------ Press Reportage -------------------------
Dimension 1	-15.1	-24.1	-3.1	21.0	4.5
Dimension 2	0.4	-3.2	7.7	10.9	2.1
Dimension 3	-0.3	-6.2	6.5	12.7	2.9
Dimension 4	-0.7	-6.0	5.7	11.7	2.6
Dimension 5	0.6	-4.4	5.5	9.9	2.4
Dimension 6	-0.9	-4.0	3.9	8.0	1.8
------------------------------ Press Editorials ------------------------
Dimension 1	-10.0	-18.0	1.6	19.5	3.8
Dimension 2	-0.8	-3.5	1.8	5.3	1.4
Dimension 3	1.9	-2.9	5.4	8.3	2.0
Dimension 4	3.1	-1.8	9.3	11.2	3.2
Dimension 5	0.3	-2.4	4.5	6.9	2.0
Dimension 6	1.5	-1.8	5.7	7.5	1.6
------------------------------ Press Reviews ---------------------------
Dimension 1	-13.9	-20.5	-8.6	11.8	3.9
Dimension 2	-1.6	-4.3	2.7	7.0	1.9
Dimension 3	4.3	-1.8	10.3	12.2	3.7
Dimension 4	-2.8	-6.5	1.5	8.1	2.0
Dimension 5	0.8	-3.1	5.8	9.0	2.1
Dimension 6	-1.0	-3.7	3.9	7.6	1.9
------------------------------ Religion --------------------------------
Dimension 1	-7.0	-17.2	16.5	33.7	8.3
Dimension 2	-0.7	-4.4	5.5	9.9	2.7
Dimension 3	3.7	-0.6	9.8	10.4	3.3
Dimension 4	0.2	-2.9	6.2	9.1	2.7
Dimension 5	1.4	-2.4	5.2	7.6	2.4
Dimension 6	1.0	-2.0	6.5	8.4	2.4
------------------------------ Hobbies ---------------------------------
Dimension 1	-10.1	-18.8	-2.0	16.9	5.0
Dimension 2	-2.9	-4.8	1.6	6.4	1.9
Dimension 3	0.3	-5.7	10.0	15.7	3.6
Dimension 4	1.7	-5.8	11.0	16.8	4.6
Dimension 5	1.2	-3.6	13.0	16.6	4.2
Dimension 6	-0.7	-3.0	2.5	5.5	1.8

Table 7.1 (*cont.*)

Dimension	Mean	Minimum value	Maximum value	Range	Standard deviation
--------------------------- Popular Lore ---------------------------
Dimension 1	-9.3	-24.7	9.9	34.5	11.3
Dimension 2	-0.1	-4.7	9.2	13.9	3.7
Dimension 3	2.3	-2.1	11.5	13.6	3.5
Dimension 4	-0.3	-4.4	13.3	17.8	4.8
Dimension 5	0.1	-3.9	3.0	6.9	2.3
Dimension 6	-0.8	-3.8	3.8	7.6	1.8
--------------------------- Biographies ---------------------------
Dimension 1	-12.4	-21.4	7.5	28.9	7.5
Dimension 2	2.1	-1.5	8.0	9.5	2.5
Dimension 3	1.7	-2.4	8.8	11.2	3.5
Dimension 4	-0.7	-3.9	1.8	5.7	1.6
Dimension 5	-0.5	-3.5	6.0	9.5	2.5
Dimension 6	-0.3	-3.3	3.6	6.9	2.2
--------------------------- Official Documents ---------------------------
Dimension 1	-18.1	-26.3	-9.1	17.2	4.8
Dimension 2	-2.9	-5.4	-1.5	3.9	1.2
Dimension 3	7.3	2.1	13.4	11.3	3.6
Dimension 4	-0.2	-8.4	8.7	17.1	4.1
Dimension 5	4.7	0.6	9.4	8.8	2.4
Dimension 6	-0.9	-3.8	2.7	6.5	2.0
--------------------------- Academic Prose ---------------------------
Dimension 1	-14.9	-26.5	7.1	33.6	6.0
Dimension 2	-2.6	-6.2	5.3	11.5	2.3
Dimension 3	4.2	-5.8	18.6	24.3	3.6
Dimension 4	-0.5	-7.1	17.5	24.6	4.7
Dimension 5	5.5	-2.4	16.8	19.2	4.8
Dimension 6	0.5	-3.3	9.2	12.5	2.7
--------------------------- General Fiction ---------------------------
Dimension 1	-0.8	-19.6	22.3	41.9	9.2
Dimension 2	5.9	1.2	15.6	14.3	3.2
Dimension 3	-3.1	-8.2	1.0	9.2	2.3
Dimension 4	0.9	-3.2	7.2	10.3	2.6
Dimension 5	-2.5	-4.8	1.5	6.3	1.6
Dimension 6	-1.6	-4.3	2.7	6.9	1.9
--------------------------- Mystery Fiction ---------------------------
Dimension 1	-0.2	-15.4	12.6	28.0	8.5
Dimension 2	6.0	0.7	10.3	9.7	3.0
Dimension 3	-3.6	-7.2	4.8	12.0	3.4
Dimension 4	-0.7	-5.6	4.2	9.7	3.3
Dimension 5	-2.8	-4.5	-0.4	4.1	1.2
Dimension 6	-1.9	-4.3	-0.2	4.1	1.3

Table 7.1 (*cont.*)

Dimension	Mean	Minimum value	Maximum value	Range	Standard deviation
------------------------ Science Fiction ------------------------					
Dimension 1	-6.1	-12.1	-1.7	10.4	4.6
Dimension 2	5.9	2.4	8.7	6.3	2.5
Dimension 3	-1.4	-6.0	3.8	9.8	3.7
Dimension 4	-0.7	-3.0	1.8	4.8	1.7
Dimension 5	-2.5	-3.6	-1.7	1.8	0.8
Dimension 6	-1.6	-3.5	0.4	3.9	1.6
------------------------ Adventure Fiction ------------------------					
Dimension 1	-0.0	-11.9	11.1	23.1	6.3
Dimension 2	5.5	2.2	10.5	8.3	2.7
Dimension 3	-3.8	-7.8	-1.6	6.2	1.7
Dimension 4	-1.2	-5.0	5.6	10.6	2.8
Dimension 5	-2.5	-4.5	-0.8	3.7	1.2
Dimension 6	-1.9	-4.0	1.8	5.8	1.7
------------------------ Romantic Fiction ------------------------					
Dimension 1	4.3	-6.5	15.3	21.9	5.6
Dimension 2	7.2	1.4	11.7	10.3	2.8
Dimension 3	-4.1	-6.4	-1.2	5.2	1.6
Dimension 4	1.8	-1.1	7.2	8.2	2.7
Dimension 5	-3.1	-4.2	-1.5	2.7	0.9
Dimension 6	-1.2	-3.8	2.1	5.9	2.2
------------------------ Humor ------------------------					
Dimension 1	-7.8	-13.7	7.6	21.3	6.7
Dimension 2	0.9	-2.0	3.0	5.0	1.8
Dimension 3	-0.8	-3.5	4.2	7.7	2.6
Dimension 4	-0.3	-4.8	3.8	8.6	2.7
Dimension 5	-0.4	-3.0	1.2	4.2	1.4
Dimension 6	-1.5	-3.6	1.3	4.8	1.7
------------------------ Personal Letters ------------------------					
Dimension 1	19.5	13.8	27.0	13.2	5.4
Dimension 2	0.3	-0.9	1.7	2.6	1.0
Dimension 3	-3.6	-6.6	-1.3	5.3	1.8
Dimension 4	1.5	-1.6	6.4	8.0	2.6
Dimension 5	-2.8	-4.8	0.5	5.4	1.9
Dimension 6	-1.4	-3.7	0.3	4.0	1.6
------------------------ Professional Letters ------------------------					
Dimension 1	-3.9	-17.1	24.8	41.9	13.7
Dimension 2	-2.2	-6.9	4.6	11.5	3.5
Dimension 3	6.5	1.4	12.4	11.0	4.2
Dimension 4	3.5	-5.3	11.0	16.3	4.7
Dimension 5	0.4	-3.5	4.4	7.9	2.4
Dimension 6	1.5	-3.6	9.6	13.2	3.6

Table 7.1 (*cont.*)

Dimension	Mean	Minimum value	Maximum value	Range	Standard deviation

-------------------------- Face-to-face Conversations --------------

Dimension	Mean	Minimum value	Maximum value	Range	Standard deviation
Dimension 1	35.3	17.7	54.1	36.4	9.1
Dimension 2	-0.6	-4.4	4.0	8.4	2.0
Dimension 3	-3.9	-10.5	1.6	12.1	2.1
Dimension 4	-0.3	-5.2	6.5	11.7	2.4
Dimension 5	-3.2	-4.5	0.1	4.6	1.1
Dimension 6	0.3	-3.6	6.5	10.1	2.2

------------------------- Telephone Conversations -----------------

Dimension 1	37.2	7.2	52.9	45.8	9.9
Dimension 2	-2.1	-4.2	4.7	8.9	2.2
Dimension 3	-5.2	-10.1	2.3	12.5	2.9
Dimension 4	0.6	-4.9	8.4	13.3	3.6
Dimension 5	-3.7	-4.8	0.1	4.9	1.2
Dimension 6	-0.9	-4.8	3.3	8.1	2.1

------------------------- Interviews -----------------------------

Dimension 1	17.1	3.5	36.0	32.5	10.7
Dimension 2	-1.1	-5.0	2.7	7.8	2.1
Dimension 3	-0.4	-6.3	8.3	14.7	4.0
Dimension 4	1.0	-3.4	6.1	9.5	2.4
Dimension 5	-2.0	-4.1	0.4	4.5	1.3
Dimension 6	3.1	-1.4	10.5	11.9	2.6

------------------------- Broadcasts -----------------------------

Dimension 1	-4.3	-19.6	16.9	36.6	10.7
Dimension 2	-3.3	-5.2	-0.6	4.6	1.2
Dimension 3	-9.0	-15.8	-2.2	13.6	4.4
Dimension 4	-4.4	-6.9	-0.3	6.5	2.0
Dimension 5	-1.7	-4.7	5.4	10.0	2.8
Dimension 6	-1.3	-3.6	1.7	5.3	1.6

------------------------- Spontaneous Speeches --------------------

Dimension 1	18.2	-2.6	33.1	35.7	12.3
Dimension 2	1.3	-3.8	9.4	13.2	3.6
Dimension 3	1.2	-5.4	9.7	15.1	4.3
Dimension 4	0.3	-5.5	7.4	12.9	4.4
Dimension 5	-2.6	-4.5	0.7	5.1	1.7
Dimension 6	2.6	-2.4	10.6	13.0	4.2

------------------------- Prepared Speeches ----------------------

Dimension 1	2.2	-7.3	14.8	22.1	6.7
Dimension 2	0.7	-4.9	6.1	11.0	3.3
Dimension 3	0.3	-5.6	6.1	11.6	3.6
Dimension 4	0.4	-4.4	11.2	15.5	4.1
Dimension 5	-1.9	-3.9	1.0	5.0	1.4
Dimension 6	3.4	-0.8	7.5	8.3	2.8

scattered around the mean score; small standard deviations show that the texts are tightly grouped around the mean score.

For example, the first set of dimension scores on Table 7.1 are for the genre press reportage. The mean dimension score for Dimension 1 is -15.1, reflecting the fact that the texts in this genre have high frequencies of nouns and prepositions, long words, and high type/token ratios (the features with negative weights on Factor 1) combined with low frequencies of private verbs, present tense verbs, contractions, first and second person pronouns, emphatics, etc. (the features with positive weights on Factor 1). Press reportage texts are not tightly grouped around this mean score, however. Table 7.1 shows that the lowest dimension score for a press text on Dimension 1 is -24.1, while the highest is -3.1, giving a spread, or range, of 21.0. The standard deviation of 4.5 shows that 68% of the press reportage texts have dimension scores between -19.6 and -10.6; i.e., the mean score (-15.1) plus or minus one standard deviation. This spread is not overly large, but it indicates that there is diversity within the genre press reportage (see further discussion in Chapter 8).

Table 7.2 presents overall F and correlation values for each dimension. These values were computed using a General Linear Models procedure. The F value is a test of statistical significance, indicating whether a dimension can distinguish among genres to a significant extent. The p value shows the probability that the F value is significant, based on the size of the F score and the number of texts being considered; values of p smaller than .05 indicate that there is a statistically significant relationship. Because statistical significance is tied closely to the number of texts in a study, it is possible in very large studies to have significant relationships that are not very important and therefore not very interesting from a theoretical point of view. In contrast, the values of R*R, the squared multiple correlation coefficient, indicate the *importance* of each dimension in distinguishing among the genres, and thus they are more useful in evaluating the overall predictive power of a dimension. R*R values directly indicate the percentage of variance in the dimension scores that can be predicted by knowing the genre distinctions; that is, the R*R value indicates the percentage of variation in the dimension scores of texts that can be accounted for by knowing the genre category of the texts.

For example, Table 7.2 shows that Dimension 1 ('Informational versus Involved Production') has an F score of 111.9, which is significant at

Table 7.2 *F and correlation scores for the six textual dimensions*

Dimension 1: 'Involved versus Informational Production'
Dimension 2: 'Narrative versus Non-Narrative Concerns'
Dimension 3: 'Explicit versus Situation-Dependent Reference'
Dimension 4: 'Overt Expression of Persuasion'
Dimension 5: 'Abstract versus Non-Abstract Information'
Dimension 6: 'On-Line Informational Elaboration'

Dimension	F value	Probability (p)	R*R
1	111.9	p < .0001	84.3%
2	32.3	p < .0001	60.8%
3	31.9	p < .0001	60.5%
4	4.2	p < .0001	16.9%
5	28.8	p < .0001	58.0%
6	8.3	p < .0001	28.5%

$p < .0001$; that is, Dimension 1 is a significant predictor of genre differences. More interestingly, the R*R value of Dimension 1 is 84.3% ; that is, 84% of the variation in values for Dimension Score 1 can be accounted for by knowing the genre categories of texts. There is thus an extremely strong correlation between the genre distinctions and the values of Dimension Score 1.

In fact, Table 7.2 shows that all of the dimensions have strong relationships with the genre distinctions, although there are large differences in their predictive power. The distinctions among genres with respect to each dimension are significant at $p < .0001$. Four of the six dimensions have R*R values greater than 50% , while a fifth (Dimension 6) has an R*R of 29% . Only Dimension 4 shows a relatively small R*R of 17% , which is still large enough to be noteworthy. Overall, these values show that the dimensions identified in the present study are very powerful predictors of the differences among spoken and written genres.

The textual relations among genres can be further considered by plotting the mean dimension score for each genre, as in Figures 7.1–7.6. These plots are graphic presentations of the mean dimension scores given in Table 7.1. For example, Figure 7.1 presents the mean dimension score

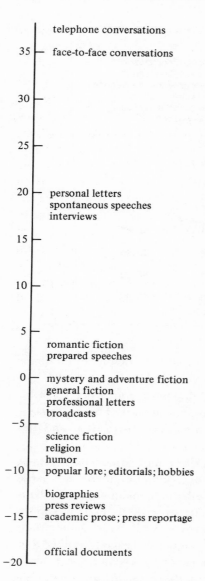

Figure 7.1 *Mean scores of Dimension 1 for each of the genres Dimension 1: 'Involved versus Informational Production'*

of each genre for Dimension 1, situating the genres with respect to one another along a continuous parameter of variation that has been labelled 'Informational versus Involved Production'. To more fully interpret each dimension, it is necessary to consider: (1) the similarities and differences among genres with respect to their mean dimension scores, summarized in Figures 7.1–7.6; (2) the linguistic features constituting the dimension, summarized in Table 6.1; and (3) the underlying functional parameter(s) (situational, processing, or other) associated with the dimension. As noted elsewhere, the interplay between micro- and macro-analyses is crucial for an overall description of the relations among genres. In Chapter 6, micro-analyses of individual features provided the foundation for the initial interpretations of the factors as dimensions. In the present chapter, macro-analysis determines the overall relations of genres relative to one another, while micro-analyses of text samples from particular genres are used to seek fuller functional interpretations of the dimensions. I first discuss the similarities and differences among genres with respect to each dimension in turn, and then I assess the overall relations among genres with respect to this six-dimensional model.

7.2   Relations along Dimensions

7.2.1   Relations along Dimension 1

The relations among genres with respect to Dimension 1 are summarized in Figure 7.1: a plot of the mean of Dimension Score 1 for each genre. This figure shows that face-to-face and telephone conversation have very high mean scores on Dimension 1, while biographies, press reviews, academic prose, press reportage, and official documents have very low scores. Personal letters, spontaneous speeches, and interviews have moderately high scores, while science fiction, religion, humor, popular lore, editorials, and hobbies all have moderately low scores. From Chapter 6, we know that the genres with high mean scores on Dimension 1 are characterized by frequent occurrences of private verbs, *that*-deletions, present tense, contractions, second person pronouns, etc. (the features with positive weights on Factor 1), together with markedly infrequent occurrences of nouns, prepositions, long words, more varied vocabulary, and attributive adjectives (the features with negative weights on Factor 1). Genres with low scores on this dimension have the opposite characteristics. These characteristics can be illustrated by the following two text samples – one from a telephone conversation, with a very high

score on this dimension, and the other from an official document, with a
low dimension score.[1]

Text 7.1: Telephone conversation (LL:7,3,f)

B: *anyway #*
       how did you get on [pause] skiing #

A: *skiing # [pause]*
       skiing was good fun actually #

B: *oh #*

A: *mm # [pause]*
       I I I enjoyed actually skiing #
       and it was [pause] really quite funny #
       being with [short pause] thrust together with #
       sort of sixteen other people for a fortnight and # [pause]
       and

B: *oh #*
       I'd love a fortnight's holiday where you can relax #

A: *well it's it's fantastic #*
       because it's [pause] so completely different from anything
         that you [short pause] you know #
       would ever get yourself to do otherwise #

B: *yes #*
       yes #

A: *I think #*

B: *yes*

[1] Texts are labelled as follows:
CORPUS:GENRE,TEXT-NUMBER,SUBTEXT
For example, text 7.1 is labelled LL:7,3,f, because it is from the London–Lund Corpus,
genre 7 (telephone conversation), text no. 3 within that genre, and subtext f within that
text – see Appendix I for details.

Text 7.2: Official document (LOB:H,26 – Royal College of Surgeons of England, Annual Report for 1960–1)

> **The restoration of a further volume of the collection of Hunterian drawings has been completed at the British Museum. A selection from the collection of Pharmacy Jars was lent to The Times Book Shop in connexion with their Royal Society Tercentenary Exhibition. Two coloured engravings of the College in the early nineteenth century were presented to the Royal Australasian College of Surgeons by the President when he visited Melbourne.**

Text 7.1 illustrates many of the linguistic characteristics of texts having high scores on Dimension 1: a high level of interaction and personal affect, shown by many references to *I* and *you*, private verbs (e.g., *think, love*), emphatics (e.g., *really, so completely different*), WH questions (e.g., *how did . . .*), and causative subordination (e.g., *because*); and a generalized and fragmented presentation of content, shown by hedges (e.g., *sort of*), discourse particles (e.g., *anyway, well*), contractions (e.g., *I'd, it's*), non-phrasal *and*, *be* as main verb, pro-verb *do*, and pronoun *it*. Even though the topic deals with past events, much of the text is in the present tense, emphasizing the immediacy of the interaction (e.g., *it's fantastic, it's so completely different*). In addition to frequent occurrences of the features listed above, text 7.1 is characterized by the relative absence of the features with negative weights on Dimension 1: markedly few nouns and prepositions, relatively short words, and much repetition of vocabulary (a low type/token ratio). Thus, text 7.1 is highly involved, interactive, and affective. It packages information in general rather than specific terms, and it focuses on interpersonal and affective content rather than strictly informational content.

In contrast, text 7.2 is highly informational and shows almost no concern for interpersonal or affective content. This text shows a very high frequency of nouns and prepositions (e.g., *of a further volume of the collection of Hunterian drawings*), while it has only four verbs in the entire passage. There are many quite long words and a careful selection of vocabulary, resulting in a high type/token ratio (e.g., *restoration, collection, engravings, century*). None of the involved or generalized types of features that characterize text 7.1 are found in text 7.2.

In Chapter 6, Dimension 1 was interpreted as distinguishing between texts having an informational focus and texts having an involved focus.

The dimension was further interpreted as distinguishing between texts produced under conditions permitting careful word choice and high informational density versus texts produced under strict real-time constraints resulting in generalized lexical content and lower informational densities. Official documents, illustrated by text 7.2, and conversations, illustrated by text 7.1, clearly represent these two opposite communicative concerns and production circumstances.

A cursory examination of Dimension 1 on Figure 7.1 might suggest that this parameter identifies a dichotomy between spoken and written texts: spoken genres like face-to-face and telephone conversation have very high scores, and written genres like biographies, press reviews, academic prose, press reportage, and official documents all have very low scores. A closer examination shows that this interpretation is not adequate; personal letters have a score higher than all non-conversational spoken genres, romantic fiction has an intermediate score which is higher than the scores for prepared speeches and broadcasts, while broadcasts have a score in the lower half of this scale, directly among the majority of written genres. This distribution of texts in no way corresponds to a spoken–written distinction. It can be understood, however, in terms of the interpretation of involved real-time production versus informational, edited production.

Personal letters, for example, are written but have an involved focus. In addition, they are typically produced under self-imposed time constraints, and thus do not show careful word choice or a high informational density. These characteristics are illustrated by text 7.3:

Text 7.3: Personal letter (private corpus, no. 2)

> *How you doing? I'm here at work waiting for my appointment to get here, it's Friday. Thank goodness, but I still have tomorrow, but this week has flown by, I guess because I've been staying busy, getting ready for Christmas and stuff. Have you done your Christmas shopping yet? I'm pretty proud of myself. I'm almost finished. Me and L went shopping at Sharpstown last Monday and I got a lot done, I just have a few little things to get. Thanks for the poster, I loved it, I hung it in my room last night, sometimes I feel like that's about right.*

This written passage shows many of the same interactive and affective characteristics as conversation. There is a high frequency of the pronouns

I and *you*, WH questions, contractions, and private verbs (e.g., *feel, love*). The letter is written primarily in the present tense, although writer and reader do not share time. It shows little lexical variety, few long words, and few nouns or prepositions; rather, it relies heavily on forms that are not at all precise in their informational content, for example, pronoun *it*, demonstrative pronouns (e.g., *that's about right*), pro-verb *do*, and hedges. The fact that personal letters are written has little bearing on their characterization with respect to Dimension 1; rather, their affective, interactional purpose and the relatively little attention given to production are the important functional parameters to be considered here.

Professional letters, although similar to personal letters in that they are written from one individual to another, differ with respect to the functions underlying Dimension 1. They are written for informational purposes and only acknowledge interpersonal relations in a secondary manner. Further, they are written with considerable care, sometimes even being revised and rewritten, and thus they can show considerable lexical variety and informational density. Thus consider text 7.4:

Text 7.4: Professional letter (private corpus, no. 8)

> **We felt that we needed a financial base on which to work, but the goals which we indicated for I. are also included in the goals of L., including of course the occasional papers . . . In the meantime, we are going ahead with plans to establish three language resource institutes resource centers in ESL, which will have three functions: (1) to be a resource center with a reading library of ESL materials and directors who are competent ESL professionals, (2) as a funnel for consultant activities both outward using local expertise needed in other areas where we have L and inward bringing into the area needed expertise and including workshops, mini-conferences, and seminars, and finally (3) to offer educational programs.**

This text portion shows that interpersonal communication can be highly informational. There are few features that refer directly to personal emotions or the interaction between reader and writer, while there are frequent nouns and prepositions, and a relatively varied vocabulary. Letters of this type are interactive (shown, e.g., by the use of first and second person pronouns), but their primary focus is informational rather than involved.

Finally, the dimension score of broadcasts is noteworthy with respect to Dimension 1. Broadcasts are not typically reckoned among the literate genres: they directly report events in progress rather than conceptual information. It is thus surprising that broadcasts have a low mean score and appear to be quite similar to the majority of written genres with respect to Dimension 1. In the case of this genre, however, the low score for Dimension 1 marks the absence of an affective or interactive focus rather than the presence of a highly informational focus *per se*. That is, broadcasts have neither a primary involved focus nor a primary informational focus, because they deal almost exclusively with reportage of events in progress.[2] Text 7.5 illustrates these characteristics:

Text 7.5: Broadcast of state funeral (LL:10,5)

> **B:**   *flanked* ‡
>   *by its escort of the Royal Air Force* ‡
>   *the gun carriage* ‡
>   *bearing the coffin* ‡ *[pause]*
>   *draped with the Union Jack* ‡ *[pause]*
>   *on it* ‡
>   *the gold* ‡
>   *and enamel* ‡
>   *of the insignia of the Garter* ‡ *[pause]*
>   *and as it breasts* ‡
>   *the slight rise* ‡ *[pause]*
>   *the naval crew that draws it* ‡
>   *presents* ‡
>   *an overwhelming impression* ‡
>   *of strength* ‡
>   *and solidarity* ‡ *[pause]*

Text 7.5 illustrates the specialized characteristics of Broadcasts with respect to Dimension 1. The grammatical structure of these texts is very reduced, but there are relatively many different words, and frequent

---

[2] More recent forms of radio and television broadcasts have developed in different ways. For example, sports broadcasts presently seem to include more affective commentary (opinions of plays and players), interpersonal interaction (between multiple commentators), and propositional information (concerning fine points of the game) than the broadcasts in the London–Lund corpus.

nouns and prepositions. The focus is event-oriented. Despite this event orientation, however, there are relatively few verbs, because many of the verbs are deleted due to time constraints, or to give the impression of action that moves so fast that there is no time for a full description (Ferguson 1983). The few verbs found in these texts are in the present tense, describing action that is on-going at the time of discourse production. The surprising fact that broadcasts have a more literate score than spontaneous and prepared speeches with respect to Dimension 1 might be explained by the reduced grammatical structure common in texts of this genre, leaving, essentially, only noun phrases and pre-positional phrases. Speeches, on the other hand, depend on elaborated grammatical structure, and thus they are more typical of informational discourse. In addition, speeches are addressed to specific, physically-present audiences, permitting some interaction and affective content, whereas broadcasts are directed to an unseen, relatively unknown, audience. Thus, broadcasts are a specialized genre, which is spoken and produced in real-time, but has the characteristics of informational production.

Overall, we have seen that the interpretation of Dimension 1 as 'Informational versus Involved Production' fits the relations among genres defined by this dimension. Highly interactive, affective discourse produced under real-time constraints, whether spoken or written, has a high score on this dimension; highly informational discourse produced without time constraints has a markedly low score on this dimension. Although the linguistic features co-occurring on this dimension can be associated with a basic oral/literate distinction, the relations among genres seen here in no way correspond to speech versus writing. Rather, the underlying communicative functions associated with this dimension cut directly across any distinction between the written and spoken modes.

7.2.2 Relations along Dimension 2

Figure 7.2 shows the relations among genres with respect to Dimension 2, 'Narrative versus Non-narrative Concerns'. The fiction genres have by far the highest mean scores on this dimension, while broadcasts, professional letters, academic prose, hobbies, and official documents all have very low scores. Table 6.1 shows that the genres with high scores on Dimension 2 are characterized by frequent occurrences of past tense and perfect aspect verbs, third person pronouns, public verbs, present

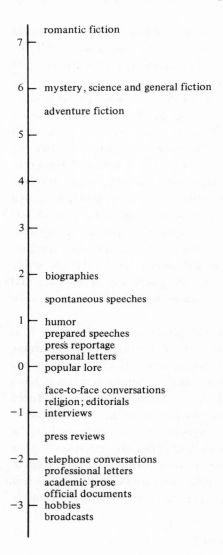

Figure 7.2 *Mean scores of Dimension 2 for each of the genres*
Dimension 2: 'Narrative versus Non-Narrative Concerns'

participial clauses, and synthetic negation, together with markedly infrequent occurrences of present tense verbs and attributive adjectives. Genres with low scores on Dimension 2 have the opposite characteristics. The large separation of the fiction genres from all other genres seen on

Figure 7.2 indicates that the proposed interpretation of a narrative versus non-narrative dimension is an accurate description of the underlying function here. Text 7.6 illustrates the characteristics of texts with high scores on Dimension 2:

Text 7.6: General fiction (LOB:K,6)

> *It was difficult to tell whether he was unable to speak or whether he could see no point. Sometimes he started to say things in a hoarse whisper, looking ahead as if there might be people to either side who would stop him, but never got further than one or two words. Most of the time he lay on his back with his eyes open. After three days there seemed nothing Martin could do and he went to the office again.*
>
> *They had given the speech to Burridge. They would be able, later, when time had become a little confused, to explain his failure by his father's illness, if they wanted to.*

This text sample is straight narrative. It is written throughout in the past tense, to report past events, and it uses past perfects (e.g., *had given*, *had become*) to mark past events with continuing results (e.g., *They had given the speech to Burridge*, and he still had it at the present time). There are frequent third person personal pronouns, referring to the story participants. There are frequent public verbs of speaking (e.g., *tell, speak, say, explain*), even though there is no dialogue in this sample. In addition, this text illustrates the use of present participial clauses for depictive imagery (e.g., *looking ahead as if there might be people . . .*). Text 7.6 is representative of all five fiction genres, which have high narrative concerns and use the linguistic features on Dimension 2 to develop narrative structures.

In contrast, the genres with low scores on Dimension 2 are similar to one another only in that they do not have narrative concerns. That is, the frequent use of past tense, third person pronouns, etc., can be considered as the marked value of Dimension 2, being reserved for narrative discourse, while the frequent use of present tense and adjectives, coupled with infrequent use of past tense, etc., can be considered as the unmarked value of Dimension 2, which is associated with any of several different communicative purposes. These non-narrative purposes include (1) the presentation of expository information, which has few verbs and few animate referents; (2) the presentation of procedural information, which uses many imperative and infinitival verb forms to give a step-by-step description of what to do, rather than what somebody else has done; and (3) description of actions actually in progress, that is, action in the present tense. These three non-narrative purposes are illustrated by texts 7.7–7.9, taken from official documents, hobbies, and broadcasts, respectively:

Text 7.7: Official document (LOB:H,3 – government report)

> **In order to give a more detailed appraisal of the work done in modern language courses, it is convenient to consider separately the different facets of language study. Nevertheless it must be emphasized that, if language teaching is to be successful, there can be no question of dividing up the work into rigid compartments . . .**
>
> **The initial oral training is too rarely continued and developed in the later stages and many pupils do not progress beyond the standard of speech they had reached by the end of the second year. Many teachers feel that they cannot afford the time necessary for the development of oral work, but in most cases it is not additional time which is required so much as more systematic and purposeful training in the correct use of more difficult speech forms.**

Text 7.8: Hobbies (LOB:E,2)

> **A great deal of modern furniture has tapered legs, and in reproduction period pieces they are frequently used. The simpler varieties are extremely easy to work, the four sides being simply planed to give the required taper . . .**
>
> **When a leg has a simple taper the procedure of making it is straightforward. The wood is first planed parallel to the largest section, and pencil lines marking the beginning of the taper squared round on to all four sides. At the bottom end the extent of the taper is gauged in, again on all four sides . . .**
>
> **For convenience in handling it is convenient to work the hollow moulding before planing the taper of the toe. Mark in with pencil the depth of the hollow, using the pencil and finger as a gauge, and cut a chamfer with a keen chisel on all four sides as at (D). Cut**

inwards with the chisel from each side so that the far corner does
not splinter . . .

Text 7.9: Broadcasts (LL:10,7,c – scientific demonstration)

right #
so what I'm going to demonstrate here #
is the difference #
between #
transverse wave #
and a longitudinal wave #
and I'm going to use this gadget#
which some of you may know #
and may have played with #
in your younger days # [pause]
which is called a slinky # [pause]
it's in effect #
a special kind of spring #
and it has rather nice properties #
you can stand it up # [pause]
on end #
rather like that # [pause]
and then if you bring the other end over # [pause]
then the whole lot will just turn itself #
from one side to the other # [pause] . . .
so we've got a system here #
which can transmit a wave #
and if it's a transverse one #
then it's like this #
I can just send a pulse down # [long pause]
that sort # [pause]

Text 7.7, taken from an official document, is expository, presenting a straightforward and concise packaging of information. There are relatively few verbs, and those that do exist are often infinitival or passive constructions. Throughout, if tense is marked, it is in the present, emphasizing that this is a description of current findings or the current state of affairs (e.g., *training is too rarely continued; teachers feel; more systematic training is required*). There are many attributive adjectives in this type of discourse, which provide descriptive details that elaborate and specify the exact nature of the nominal referents (e.g., *detailed appraisal*; *modern language*; *rigid compartments*; *initial oral training*; *systematic and purposeful training*). Overall, discourse of this type is nominal, and descriptive or argumentative, rather than verbal and narrative.

Text 7.8 is taken from a hobbies magazine. It describes the procedure for making a certain type of table leg. This text has both descriptive and procedural portions, although most of the text is procedural. Descriptive portions are consistently in the present tense (e.g., *modern furniture has tapered legs*), while the procedural portions use either present passive forms (e.g., *wood is first planed*; *extent of the taper is gauged in*) or imperative forms (e.g., *mark in with pencil*; *cut a chamfer*; *cut inwards*). Attributive adjectives are used throughout to specify the particular referent intended (e.g., *the largest section*; *the bottom end*; *the hollow moulding*). Procedural discourse differs from expository discourse in that it is event-driven and concrete rather than conceptual and abstract, but with respect to Dimension 2 these two types of discourse are similar in that they frequently use non-past verbal forms and attributive adjectives rather than past tense forms, third person animate referents, etc.

Broadcasts illustrate yet another non-narrative concern. Text 7.9 is from a scientific demonstration, and thus it represents informational broadcast, while text 7.5 (discussed in Section 7.2.1) illustrates a broadcast with a non-informational focus, the more typical case. In either case, broadcasts report events actually in progress, and they thus have strictly non-narrative concerns. In Section 7.2.1, I noted that text 7.5 has few verbs, but those that do occur are exclusively in the present tense (e.g., *as it breasts the slight rise*; *the naval crew that draws it presents an overwhelming impression*). The attributive adjectives in this case are not so much for exact identification, as in the official document and procedural text, but for a more vivid description of the events (e.g., *slight rise*; *overwhelming impression*). Text 7.9 has a greater informational focus, but still reports events in progress in that it informs by demonstrating. Throughout, it uses present tense and present progressive forms, emphasizing the on-going nature of the events. There are no animate referents and thus no third person personal pronouns. Attributive adjectives are used for both identificatory and descriptive purposes (e.g., *transverse wave*; *longitudinal wave*; and *younger days*; *special kind*; *nice properties*). Thus, broadcasts have low scores on Dimension 2 because they report events actually in progress, whether for informational or entertainment purposes. They are grouped with official documents and procedural texts on this dimension because they have non-narrative concerns, although each of these genres is 'immediate' in a different sense.

In addition to these two poles on Dimension 2, several genres have intermediate values, indicating both narrative and non-narrative concerns. These genres include prepared and spontaneous speeches, biographies, personal letters, humor, face-to-face conversation, and press reportage. Text 7.10, from a spontaneous speech, illustrates the mixing of narrative and non-narrative concerns:

Text 7.10: Spontaneous speech (LL:11,3,d)

D: *well #*
       I shall have to [pause] take you to a period of my life #
           [pause]
       which I'm not very proud of actually # [pause]
       when I was a professional Scrabble player #[pause]
       mm [pause]
       it happened #
       at a small hotel in Sussex #
       where I happened to be staying #
       after dinner #
       they used to all go in the lounge #
       and all play Scrabble #
       like crazy #
       and as I got in through the doors #
       a strange woman #
       rushed up to me #
       and said you're just the man I want # [pause]

Text 7.10 is taken from a spontaneous speech in which the speaker presents a personal narrative. The narrative is framed in terms of the present interaction between speaker and audience (*I shall have to take you; I'm not very proud of*). As the speaker begins his story, however, he switches to the past tense (*when I was a professional Scrabble player; it happened*), and the story itself uses the linguistic features characteristic of narrative discourse: past tense (e.g., *I got in; woman rushed up to me and said*), third person personal pronouns (e.g., *they*), and public verbs (e.g., *said*). The other genres with intermediate values on Dimension 2, such as biographies and personal letters, combine narrative and non-narrative concerns in similar ways.

Overall, Dimension 2 distinguishes between narrative and non-narrative discourse. The imaginative fiction genres are the only texts included in the present study with an extreme narrative concern. The dialogue portions in fiction are subordinate to the narrative purpose rather than marking a separate interactional purpose. Other genres, such as official documents, hobbies, and broadcasts, have strictly non-narrative concerns, but they differ from one another as to their specific purpose. Finally, genres such as public speeches, personal letters, and conversation have both narrative and non-narrative concerns. In these cases, narratives are typically framed within some larger interactive or expository discourse, and thus the narrative is in some sense subordinate to a larger purpose, although the text can be described as having both narrative and non-narrative emphases.

7.2.3   Relations along Dimension 3

Figure 7.3 shows the relations among genres with respect to Dimension 3, 'Explicit versus Situation-Dependent Reference'. Official documents and professional letters have the highest scores, while broadcasts have by far the lowest score. Press reviews, academic prose, and religion have moderately high scores on this dimension, and the conversational genres, fiction genres, and personal letters have moderately low scores. From the interpretation of Dimension 3 in Chapter 6, it will be recalled that texts with high scores on this dimension are characterized by frequent occurrences of WH relative clauses, pied-piping constructions, phrasal coordination, and nominalizations, together with infrequent occurrences of place and time adverbials and other adverbs; texts with low scores on this dimension have the opposite characteristics. I interpreted this distribution of features as representing a dimension that distinguishes highly explicit and elaborated, endophoric reference from situation-dependent, exophoric reference. The overall distribution of genres seen in Figure 3 supports this interpretation; genres such as official documents, professional letters, and academic prose require highly explicit, text-internal reference, while genres such as broadcasts and conversation

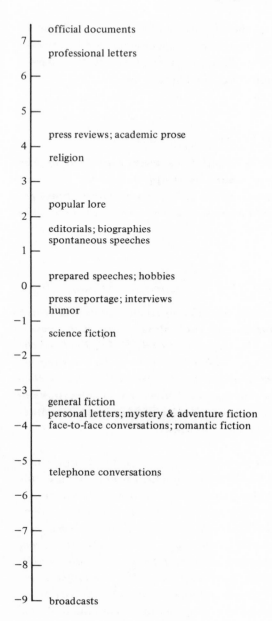

Figure 7.3 *Mean scores of Dimension 3 for each of the genres Dimension 3: 'Explicit versus Situation-Dependent Reference'*

permit extensive reference to the physical and temporal situation of discourse. Texts 7.11 and 7.12, from official documents, and 7.4, from a professional letter (discussed in Section 7.2.1), illustrate the characteristics of genres having high scores for Dimension 3:

Text 7.11: Official document (LOB:H, 26 – annual report)

> **During the past year 347 candidates were examined by the Surgical Section, 321 of whom were approved, and 352 were examined by the Dental Section, 230 of whom were approved, making a total of 230 candidates who were awarded the Licence in Dental Surgery.**

Text 7.12: Official document (LOB:H,29 – university bulletin)

> **Students must follow throughout the terms the courses for which they are registered and attend such classes and such examinations as required by the University and by the Heads of the Departments concerned . . . Students must enter on their registration form particulars of any external examinations which they propose to take during the session. University examinations of any kind will in all cases take priority over any other examinations which a student wishes to take.**

Text 7.11 is taken from the same document as text 7.2 (in Section 7.2.1). In text 7.11, WH relative clauses are used for nominal identification and elaboration. Relative clauses pack information into noun phrases instead of expressing the information as separate, independent clauses (e.g., *347 candidates were examined . . ., 321 of whom were approved* could be expressed as *347 candidates were examined . . ., and 320 of them were approved*; similarly, *making a total of 230 candidates who were awarded the Licence* could be expressed as *in total, 230 candidates were awarded the Licence*). Text 7.12 shows a similar use of WH relative clauses for explicit and elaborated identification of nominal referents (e.g., *the courses for which they are registered*; *any external examinations which they propose to take*; *any other examination which a student wishes to take*). Text 7.4, which is from a professional letter, further illustrates these uses of

WH relative clauses. This sample uses pied-piping constructions (e.g., *a financial base on which to work*), WH relatives on subject position (e.g., *directors who are competent . . .*), and WH relatives on object positions (e.g., *the goals which we indicated; other areas where we have L*). In all of these cases, WH relative clauses are used for elaborated, explicit identification of nominal referents.

In addition, text 7.12 shows the use of phrasal coordination to integrate information into a text (e.g., *such classes and such examinations; by the University and by the Heads*). This use of phrasal coordination is further illustrated by text 7.13, from a press review:

Text 7.13: Press reviews (LOB:C,10)

> **Somewhere in the middle of all this – the clowning and the prettiness, the slapstick and whimsy and phantasmagoria – Verdi's simplicity and honesty have fallen by the wayside . . . Mr. Evans continues to ripen and improve his distinguished Falstaff, but we cannot expect to see this impersonation at its best until it figures within a less confusing framework.**

This text sample shows extreme use of phrasal coordination, to pack high amounts of information into each phrase and clause (e.g., *the clowning and the prettiness, the slapstick and whimsy and phantasmagoria; simplicity and honesty; to ripen and improve*). In addition, both texts 7.12 and 7.13 illustrate relatively frequent use of nominalizations, emphasizing the prominence of informational, nominal content in these texts (text 7.12: *examinations, departments, registration;* text 7.13: *prettiness, simplicity, honesty, impersonation*). Taken together these texts illustrate informational discourse that is highly elaborated and explicit in its nominal reference.

In contrast, broadcasts report events actually in progress, thus encouraging direct reference to the physical and temporal situation of discourse. In the London–Lund corpus, these texts are recorded from radio broadcasts, and therefore the speaker and listener do not actually share the same physical situation. The speaker's physical surroundings, however, are well-known to the listener and therefore can be referred to directly. The extent of this exophoric reference is illustrated by text 7.14, from a sports broadcast:

Text 7.14: Sports broadcast (LL:10,2 – soccer match)

just over ten minutes gone # [*pause*]
into this second half # [*pause*]
and still #
nil nil #
the situation of the game # [*pause*]
as from the hands of Stepney the ball comes out onto this near side #
and from the foot of Hemsley #
the ball into touch #
just below us here # [*pause*]
a throw to be taken by Alan Gowling # [*pause*]
used to be reckoned #
a strike forward #
but of course now turned #
by manager O'Farrell #
as indeed Willy Morgan has been #
into a midfield player # [*pause*]
a free kick given #
a little bit of argybargy #
quickly taken by Brian Kydd #
Kydd now #
to number seven #
that's Willy Morgan # [*pause*]
Morgan to # [*pause*]
aaa Bobby Charlton #
Charlton flicking it even more laterally #
away from us #
to his left fullback #
that's Tony Dunn #
Dunn #
down the line now #
aiming for Best #
or Aston #
missed them both #
and it's Derby that take up the count #
with Curry #
on the far side of the field #
chips the ball forward # [*pause*]

This sample illustrates extensive reference to the physical situation of discourse. In order to understand this text, the listener must construct a mental map of the playing field. Phrases such as *flicking it even more laterally* and *down the line* make direct reference to the physical layout of the playing field. Phrases such as *this near side, just below us here, away from us*, and *on the far side of the field* require placement of the broadcaster's booth on the listener's mental map, with events occurring relative to that position. Throughout, the reference is situation-dependent and cannot be understood unless the listener is physically present or able to construct a mental map of the situation. Even the personal referents are context dependent: proper names are used throughout, assuming familiarity with the players and their positions. Because the purpose of sports broadcast is to report on-going events within a constrained physical situation, contextualized reference is extremely high in these texts.

Such reference is found in informational broadcast as well. For example, text 7.9, the scientific demonstration discussed in Section 7.2.2, has an informational focus but is highly dependent on the physical and temporal situation of discourse production. It makes extensive reference to the physical situation of discourse (e.g., *I'm going to demonstrate here; you can stand it up on end; from one side to the other; we've got a system here; send a pulse down*), and the speaker commonly uses deictics to refer to physical objects or actions (e.g., *this gadget; it; like that; like this; the other end*). Again, a listener must construct a mental map of the situation in order to understand this text. The situated nature of broadcast, whether for informational or entertainment purposes, results in extensive reference to the situation of discourse.

Conversation, fiction, and personal letters also include considerable reference to the physical and temporal situation of discourse production, even though it is only in conversation that speaker and addressee actually share this situation. In fact, in the case of personal letters, reader and writer share neither physical nor temporal context; yet familiarity with both is often assumed. For example, consider again text 7.3 (in Section 7.2.1), which makes extensive reference to the writer's situational context: temporal (e.g., *Friday; tomorrow; this week; last Monday; last night*) and physical (e.g., *I'm here at work; in my room*). Thus, in personal letters as in broadcasts and conversations, the speaker/writer assumes familiarity with the production situation.

The case of fiction is somewhat different, since reference is made to a text-internal physical and temporal situation. In its form, this reference appears to be exophoric because it refers directly to the situation of events; but, in this case, the context of discourse production is not the same as the context of events – rather, there is a fictional situation that is referred to directly in the text. For example, consider again text 7.6 (discussed in Section 7.2.2). This sample marks direct reference to both physical context (e.g., *looking ahead*; *to either side*) and temporal context (e.g., *after three days*). The reader understands this reference in terms of the internal physical and temporal situation developed in the text rather than any actually existing external context.

Overall this dimension distinguishes between informational texts that mark referents in an elaborated and explicit manner, and situated texts that depend on direct reference to, or extensive knowledge of, the physical and temporal situation of discourse production for understanding.

7.2.4. Relations along Dimension 4

In Chapter 6, Dimension 4 was interpreted as marking persuasion. The features grouped on this dimension are prediction modals, necessity modals, possibility modals, conditional clauses, suasive verbs, infinitives, and split auxiliaries. These features often simply mark the speaker's persuasion, that is, the speaker's own assessment of likelihood or advisability. Prediction and possibility modals mark intention when used with a first person agent (e.g., *I will go*; *I might do it*), and they can mark assessment of likelihood in other cases (e.g., *he will come*; *it might rain*). Other features, such as necessity modals and suasive verbs, can mark the speaker's attempts to persuade the addressee that certain events are desirable or probable (e.g., *you should go*). These functions can all be considered as overt markers of persuasion in one way or another.

The distribution of genres shown in Figure 7.4 lends support to the above interpretation. Professional letters and editorials are the two genres with high scores on Dimension 4, while broadcasts and press reviews have markedly low scores. Both professional letters and editorials are opinionated genres intended to persuade the reader. They are argumentative in that they consider several different possibilities but seek to convince the reader of the advisability or likelihood of one of them. For example, consider text 7.15 from an editorial, and text 7.16 from a professional letter:

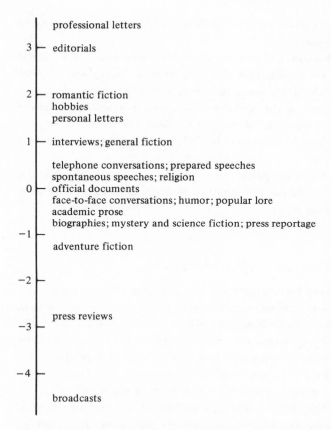

professional letters

3 ⊢ editorials

2 ⊢ romantic fiction
hobbies
personal letters

1 ⊢ interviews; general fiction

telephone conversations; prepared speeches
spontaneous speeches; religion
0 ⊢ official documents
face-to-face conversations; humor; popular lore
academic prose
biographies; mystery and science fiction; press reportage

−1 ⊢

adventure fiction

−2 ⊢

press reviews
−3 ⊢

−4 ⊢

broadcasts

Figure 7.4 *Mean scores of Dimension 4 for each of the genres*
Dimension 4: 'Overt Expression of Persuasion'

Text 7.15: Editorial (B,1 – Daily Herald, March 6, 1961)

> **Prime Minister after Prime Minister speaks out in revulsion
> against the South African Government's policy of apartheid as we
> wait for the curtain to rise on the Commonwealth Conference in
> London.**
>
> **Will it end with South Africa's exclusion from the Com-
> monwealth? The issue is touch and go.**
>
> **There is a possibility that it will not be settled at this conference.
> It may be agreed to wait until South Africa actually becomes a
> republic later in the year.**

But if a final decision is to be faced now, on which side do the strongest arguments lie?

The Archbishop of Capetown has shown that the matter is not clear-cut. The Archbishop has long been a courageous fighter against apartheid. He must be heard with attention.

On purely practical grounds he holds that it would be a mistake to expel South Africa, weakening the whites who are working for a change of policy. In his view it would also be against the interests of the Africans.

He holds that more pressure can be put on South Africa while she remains in the Commonwealth than could be exercised were she cut off from it.

Text 7.16: Professional letter (private corpus, no. 1)

This resolution text is far from ideal. The parliamentarian can help you phrase it more clearly, and I'm sure you can do a lot with it yourself; my intent is only to suggest a vehicle for getting the notion in front of the membership. Furthermore, it would really be inappropriate for me to put words in your mouth. In short, you should really take the format of the resolution and put in your own thoughts . . . Please understand that while I am sympathetic to what you are trying to achieve, and that while I understand that certain N populations are more severely impacted than others, I am not at present entirely in sympathy with the notion.

Text 7.15 illustrates the features of a typical argumentative text written to persuade the reader. Several perspectives are considered, with arguments for and against them, but the overall discourse builds towards a final conclusion and attempts to convince the reader that this conclusion is superior to any other. Predictive modals are used to refer to the future, to consider events that will or will not occur (e.g., *will it end*; *it will not be settled*; *it would be a mistake to . . .*; *it would also be against the interests of the Africans*); possibility modals and conditional clauses are used to consider different perspectives on the issue (e.g., *it may be agreed*; *more pressure can be put . . . than could be exercised*; *if a final decision is to be faced now, on which side do the strongest arguments lie?*; see also *there is a possibility that*); necessity modals are directly persuasive (e.g., *he must be heard with attention*). Similar features are seen in text 7.16. This sample illustrates the expression of possibility (e.g., *the parliamentarian can help you*), direct expression of author's own intentions or persuasion (e.g., *my intent is only to suggest*; *it would really be inappropriate for me to put . . .*), and direct persuasion (e.g., *you should really take . . .*). Both of these samples have an overall persuasive tone, and particular aspects of this persuasion are marked by the features grouped on Dimension 4.

In contrast, broadcasts and press reviews are not persuasive. Broadcasts are a simple reportage of events and thus do not involve opinion or argumentation at all (see texts 7.5, 7.9, and 7.14). Press reviews are opinionated, but not intended to persuade. That is, the author's purpose in press reviews does not involve consideration of alternative points of view or argumentation that one point of view is superior to others. Rather, press reviews present directly the author's opinion as such, to be accepted or rejected as the reader wishes (see, e.g., text 7.13).

Overall, Dimension 4 distinguishes between persuasive and non-persuasive discourse. Figure 7.4 shows, however, that the genres are relatively undistinguished along this dimension. Four genres stand out: editorials and professional letters as persuasive, and broadcasts and press reviews as non-persuasive. With respect to most of the other genres, there is no general characterization as persuasive or not; rather, certain texts within these genres are persuasive, while others are not (see Chapter 8).

7.2.5   Relations along Dimension 5

Figure 7.5 plots the mean scores of the genres with respect to Dimension 5, 'Abstract versus Non-Abstract Information'. Academic prose and official documents have by far the highest scores on this dimension, while the fiction genres, personal letters, and the conversational genres have very low scores. Returning to Table 6.1, we can see that genres with high scores for Dimension 5 make frequent use of conjuncts, agentless and *by* passives, past participial clauses, WHIZ deletions, and certain types of adverbial subordination. Genres with low scores on Dimension 5 have the opposite characteristics. I interpret this dimension in Chapter 6 as distinguishing genres with an abstract and technical focus from the other genres; the separation of academic prose and official documents from the other genres seen on Figure 7.5 supports this interpretation. The characteristics of texts with high scores on this dimension are illustrated by texts 7.2 and 7.7 (discussed in Sections 7.2.1 and 7.2.2 respectively) and text 7.17 below. The former text portions are taken from official documents, while the latter is from an academic engineering text.

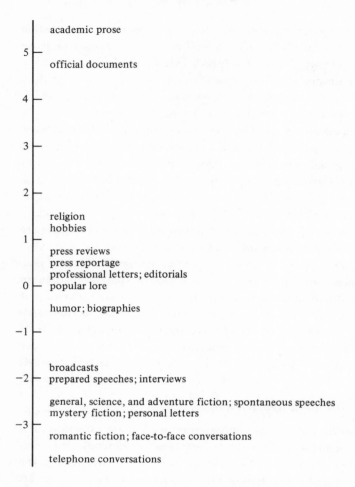

Figure 7.5 *Mean scores of Dimension 5 for each of the genres*
Dimension 5: 'Abstract versus Non-Abstract Information'

Text 7.17: Academic prose (LOB:J,75 – engineering report)

> *It follows that the performance of down-draught systems can be*
> *improved by the influence of cross draughts only if the thermal*
> *currents are blown into exhaust air streams at higher velocities*
> *than the cross draughts, so that the resultant direction of all dust-*
> *bearing air streams is towards the grid . . .*
> *The exhaust air volume required by the 6-ft. × 4-ft. grid with the*

*8-in. deep hot and cold moulds and the 16-in. deep cold moulds
tested in the absence of appreciable cross draughts exceeded the
volumes required by the 4-ft. 6-in. × 3-ft. 6-in. grid by between 25
and 40 per cent.*

Text 7.17 is strictly informational; any human agents are quite
incidental to the purpose of this text. Thus, several verbs are given
without any agent specified (independent clauses such as *thermal currents
are blown*, and WHIZ deletions such as *cold moulds tested in* . . .). When
an agent is specified in a *by* phrase, it is typically inanimate and less closely
tied to the discourse topic than the promoted patient (e.g., *performance . . . can be improved by the influence of cross-draughts*; *air volume
required by the . . . grid*). Although this text sample is informational, there
is considerable repetition of vocabulary because of the exact technical
meanings associated with particular terms (e.g., *draught, stream, grid,
mould*). In addition, although this text sample refers to some concrete
entities (e.g., *grids* and *moulds*), the overall topic is conceptual and
abstract rather than concrete, dealing with notions such as *performance*
and the *exhaust air volume*. The Dimension 5 score for this text reflects its
abstract conceptual focus.

Texts 7.2 and 7.7 show similar characteristics. Text 7.2 is an
informational report of completed activities; the purpose is to document
the annual activities undertaken by the Royal College of Surgeons. The
human agents associated with these activities are largely unimportant to
this purpose; in the first two clauses, the agent is irrelevant (e.g., *has been
completed*) or can be inferred (e.g., *was lent*, probably by the College); in
the third clause, the agent is important (e.g., *presented . . . by the
President*), but it is still subordinate to the report of the activity itself. In
text 7.7, a government document on language teaching, all passives are
agentless; the agent is inferable as the author (e.g., *it must be emphasized*)
or teachers (e.g., *the work done in modern language courses*; *initial oral
training is too rarely continued and developed*), and in all cases, the agent is
subordinate to the discourse topic, which is conceptual in nature (viz., *a
more detailed appraisal of the work done in modern language courses*). In all
of these texts, passives and other past participial clauses are used to
emphasize abstract conceptual information over more concrete or active
content.

Conversational and fiction genres have markedly low scores on
Dimension 5, indicating an absence of the abstract and technical

emphases found in academic prose and official documents. Text 7.1 (Section 7.2.1) from a conversation and text 7.6 (Section 7.2.2) from a fiction text illustrate the concrete, active emphases in these genres. Conversation is interactive and usually deals with immediate concerns, while fiction is carefully integrated and deals with narrative concerns; these two genres are similar with respect to Dimension 5 in that they both deal with active, human participants and concrete topics.

Overall, Dimension 5 distinguishes between highly abstract, technical discourse and non-abstract types of discourse. It can be seen from Figure 7.5 that many genres have intermediate scores on this dimension, indicating a mixture of the two content types. For example, hobby texts such as text 7.8 (Section 7.2.2) deal primarily with concrete referents (*table legs*, *pencils*, *chisels*, etc.) and concrete actions (*planing*, *gauging*, *marking*, *cutting*, etc.), yet no human agent is important to the discourse topic because the reader is the inferable agent throughout. Rather, the patient, the object being acted upon, is most central to the discourse topic, and therefore these texts use passive constructions relatively frequently (e.g., *wood is first planed*; *extent of the taper is first gauged in*). Similarly, press reportage, press reviews, and editorials show intermediate values on this dimension due to the twin purposes of these genres: reportage of events involving concrete, often human, referents; and abstract discussion of the implications of those events in conceptual terms. Overall, then, genres have high values on Dimension 5 to the extent that they focus on abstract, conceptual or technical subject matter.

7.2.6   Relations along Dimension 6

The co-occurrence pattern among linguistic features associated with Dimension 6, discussed in Section 6.2.6, is surprising: features with informational functions are included among both the positive and negative loadings, and subordination features co-occur with colloquial features such as final prepositions and demonstrative pronouns. The features with large positive weights on this dimension are *that* complements to verbs, *that* complements to adjectives, *that* relatives on object positions, and demonstratives (all with positive weights). Features with lesser positive weights are final prepositions, existential *there*, demonstrative pronouns, and WH relatives on object positions. The only feature with a negative weight is phrasal coordination, with a relatively small loading of −.32. The three subordination features with positive

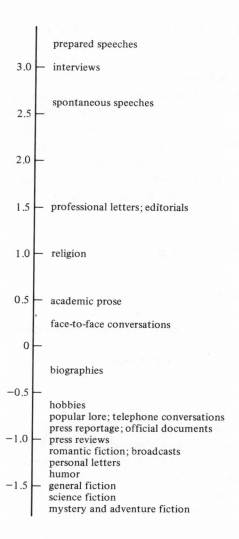

Figure 7.6 *Mean scores of Dimension 6 for each of the genres Dimension 6: 'On-Line Informational Elaboration'*

weights are all used for informational elaboration, and the co-occurrence pattern found on Dimension 6 was interpreted as indicating a dimension marking informational elaboration under strict real-time conditions.

The distribution of genres along Dimension 6, shown in Figure 7.6, largely supports this interpretation. Three genres stand out as having high scores on this dimension: prepared speeches, interviews, and spontaneous speeches. They all have an informational focus, but in all of them, the speaker must contend with real-time production constraints. The genre with the highest mean score for Dimension 6 is prepared speeches. Texts 7.18 and 7.19, taken from a political speech and a judge's final statement respectively, illustrate the characteristics of texts having high scores on this dimension:

Text 7.18: Prepared speech (LL:12, 5 – political speech)

A: *does anyone believe* ‡
     that we would have accepted for the seventies ‡
     a degree of freedom of capital movement ‡
     that would have aggravated that power of speculative attack
         on sterling ‡
     which we had to fight in the sixties ‡ [*pause*] . . .
     George Brown and I ‡
     were reasonably satisfied ‡
     that the permissive society ‡
     they then described to us ‡
     very intent on saying what a permissive society it was ‡
     would allow a Labour government to carry out the regional
         policies we regarded as essential ‡ . . .
     and let me make clear ‡ [*pause*]
     that we have to be utterly vigilant ‡
     about new Common Market development ‡

Text 7.19: Prepared speech (LL:12,4,a – judge's statement)

A: *the plaintiff says* ‡
     that the defendant ‡
     came up from behind ‡
     notwithstanding the warning ‡
     that he the plaintiff gave ‡

that he was about to go across #
from his own side of the road #
towards the entrance of Hill Morris's factory # [*pause*]
and struck the plaintiff's cycle #
in such a way #
as to break the plaintiff's right leg # [*pause*]
the defendant says #
that there was and had been #
for some time before the accident #
a motor car #
ahead of him # [*pause*]
driving in the same direction #
as that in which the defendant was driving # [*pause*]
and that # [*pause*]
the [*short pause*] *that motor car* # [*pause*]
pulled out slightly #
to pass #
what proved to be the plaintiff on his cycle # [*pause*]
that the defendant #
followed the motor car #
in doing the same thing # [*pause*]
and that when # [*pause*]
the defendant was some thirty or forty yards #
before behind the plaintiff #
on his bicycle #
the plaintiff #
put out his hand # [*pause*]
and without more ado # [*pause*]
pulled # [*pause*]
across the main road # [*pause*]

Texts 7.18 and 7.19 are both highly informational, and both are produced under strict real-time constraints. The extreme use of pauses in text 7.19 reflects the planning required by the judge to express his final statement as carefully as possible. In both cases, *that* complements are used for informational elaboration in a way that does not integrate information tightly into the text. In text 7.18, *that* clauses are further used for indirect expressions of attitude (e.g., *does anyone believe that* . . .; *we were reasonably satisfied that* . . .; *let me make clear that* . . .). In text 7.19, *that* clauses are used primarily for reported speech, which is the primary linguistic device used by the judge to present the facts of the case. For example, the judge states: *the defendant says that there was . . . and that the* [pause] *that motor car pulled out slightly . . . that the defendant followed the motor car . . . and that when the defendant was . . .* – each of these *that* clauses reports further details of the defendant's statement, further elaborating the background facts of the case. Text 7.19 also illustrates the use of *that*-relatives for nominal elaboration (e.g., *the warning that he the plaintiff gave*). In both texts 7.18 and 7.19, *that* complements to verbs and adjectives, and *that* relatives, are used for informational elaboration in such a way that each additional piece of information is tacked on rather than integrated tightly into the text.

Similar use of these features is seen in interview texts. Thus, consider text 7.20:

Text 7.20: Interview (LL:5,2 – panel discussion)

F is the discussion moderator

**Question: How did men think before speech was
        formed? . . .**

M: *and I believe* ‡
        that in Japanese and in Chinese ‡
        that the [*short pause*] *when the Japanese took the
        Chinese script* ‡
        they attached their own words ‡
        to the [*short pause*] *the* [*short pause*] *id* [*short pause*] *id*
        [*pause*] *id* [*short pause*] *id id id id ideographs* ‡
        . . .

Question: a
        when one thinks of the thousands of ancestors who've had a hand n
        in our making we ought not be unduly surprised when our r
        children do not resemble us in appearance or character   t
        *couldn't the genealogist be of service here to the biologist and the
        psychologist* . . .

F: *Moncreiffe* ‡

M: *could I br* [*gap*] *it's a long interest of mine* ‡
        and I've never been able to corner a biologist ‡
        over this ‡ *pause*]

> **but you know that what makes you a man #**
> **is that your father gives you a Y chromosome #**
> **mm and that only your father can**

F: *yes #*

M: *give that # [pause]*
    now it's quite obvious that certain things can be sexlinked
    to the Y chromosome #

In text 7.20, *that* complements are used for the elaboration of personal feelings or opinions (e.g., *I believe that . . .; you know that . . . and that . . .; it's quite obvious that . . .*). In fact, throughout texts 7.18–7.20, *that* complements to verbs and adjectives are used to express informational attitudes, opinions, or statements attributed to individuals or groups of people. In those cases where there is no explicit agent, the speaker can be inferred as the individual holding the stated opinion (e.g., *it's quite obvious that . . .*). Thus, the features grouped on this dimension enable a direct encoding of attitude or stance in addition to their use for informational elaboration.

It is seemingly for this reason that professional letters, editorials, and religion have moderately high scores on this dimension. Since these genres are not produced under real-time constraints, the interpretation given in Chapter 6 would not predict the relatively high scores shown for them on Figure 7.6. The information presented in these genres, however, is often given in relation to the attitudes, opinions, or statements of specific individuals, resulting in a moderately high use of the features on this dimension. For example, consider again text 7.15, from an editorial (in Section 7.2.4), and texts 7.4 and 7.16, from professional letters (in Sections 7.2.1 and 7.2.4 respectively). In the editorial, *that* complements are used to attribute certain arguments to the Archbishop of Capetown, adding weight to them because of his claimed expertise (e.g., *The Archbishop . . . has shown that*; *he holds that*). In the professional letters, the writers use *that* complements to express their feelings (7.4: *we felt that we needed . . .*) and to express an 'understanding' attitude (7.16: *please understand that while I am . . ., and that while I understand that . . .*).

We are now in a position to offer a fuller interpretation of the functions underlying this dimension. The primary use of *that* complements, to both verbs and adjectives, and *that* relative clauses on object position seems to be for informational elaboration under real-time production constraints. An important secondary use of these features, however, seems to be for the expression of opinions, attitudes, or personal statements of individuals. This finding indicates that those discourse tasks which involve the explicit marking of an individual's stance are frequently also tasks that demand informational production under real-time constraints. Thus, public speeches and interviews, which have especially high scores on this dimension, typically present high amounts of information in relation to an individual's beliefs or attitudes, framed in real-time; and the features grouped on this dimension are apparently well-suited to this combination of communicative demands. In the case of professional letters and editorials, there are no real-time production constraints, but since these genres often present information relative to the stance of the author or some other authority, they tend to have the characteristic features of this dimension.

7.3 Speech and writing; orality and literacy

Given these six dimensions of linguistic variation and the relations among genres with respect to each of them, it is possible now to return to the issues raised in Chapters 1 and 3 concerning the nature and extent of linguistic differences between speech and writing. The present study makes no simple two-way distinction between texts produced as speaking and those produced as writing, and it does not directly test overall or average differences between the two modes. That is, no a priori decision is made that all spoken texts should be grouped together as opposed to all written texts. Rather, the study includes a wide variety of genres from each mode and describes the relations among them. If the relations along any dimension distinguish between all written and spoken genres, then we have uncovered a true linguistic distinction between speech and writing. If no dimension makes an absolute distinction between all written and spoken genres, then it is reasonable to question the existence of an absolute linguistic difference between the two modes in English. In the present study, no absolute difference is observed; with respect to each dimension, written and spoken texts overlap. There do, however, seem to be some differences in the potential form of speech and writing, due to the different cognitive constraints on speakers and writers. I will return to this issue below.

Reviewing Figures 7.1–7.6, it can be seen that there is considerable overlap among written and spoken genres with respect to every dimension. Speech and writing are relatively well-distinguished along Dimensions 1, 3, and 5; but even in these cases, there is considerable overlap. Along Dimension 1, the spoken genres tend to have high scores (involved production), and the written genres tend to have low scores (informational production); but among the written genres, personal letters have a quite high score and the fiction genres have relatively high scores, while among the spoken genres, prepared speeches have a relatively low score and broadcasts have a quite low score. Along Dimension 3, written genres tend to have high scores (explicit reference) and spoken genres tend to have low scores (situation-dependent reference), but public speeches and interviews have relatively high scores while the fiction genres have relatively low scores. Along Dimension 5, written genres tend to have high scores (abstract information) and spoken genres tend to have low scores (non-abstract information), but the fiction genres and personal letters are among the lowest scores. Thus, no dimension defines an absolute spoken/written distinction.

This lack of an absolute difference between speech and writing shows that it is possible, within each mode, to override the salient situational characteristics of the mode. Speakers typically share space, time, and high amounts of knowledge with listeners, and they are typically constrained by real-time production considerations, but none of these characteristics prohibits production of dense, elaborated, or abstract discourse. Similarly, writing is well-suited to highly informational communicative tasks, because of the production and comprehension advantages of writers and readers over speakers and listeners, and it is not well-suited to interactional, attitudinal, or other involved purposes, because reader and writer do not typically share space, time, or intimate knowledge; but none of these characteristics require writing to be highly integrated and informational. In both cases, speakers and writers sometimes thwart the situational forces operating in each mode and produce discourse that is atypical for that mode.

Despite this fact, it is meaningful to discuss the typical or expected types of discourse in each mode, associated with the typical situational characteristics of speaking and writing. In Chapter 2, I use the term 'oral' discourse to refer to language produced in situations that are typical or expected for speaking, and the term 'literate' discourse to refer to language produced in situations that are typical for writing. From this point of view, face-to-face conversation is a stereotypically oral genre, having the characteristic situational features that are most typical of speech, while academic expository prose is considered one of the most literate genres, because it has the situational features most typically expected in writing.

Given this working definition of oral and literate discourse, it is possible to consider Dimensions 1, 3, and 5 of the present study as oral/literate dimensions. With respect to each of these dimensions, viz., 'Informational versus Involved Production', 'Explicit versus Situation-Dependent Reference', and 'Abstract versus Non-Abstract Information', the poles characterize academic exposition and conversation respectively (see Figures 7.1, 7.3, and 7.5). However, these three dimensions are by no means equivalent: each is defined by a different set of co-occurring linguistic features, and each defines a different set of relations among genres. For example, consider the relations among spontaneous speeches, fiction, professional letters, and broadcasts with respect to these three dimensions. Dimension I is composed of involved and generalized content features versus features indicating highly careful and precise lexical content; with respect to Dimension 1, spontaneous speeches are relatively involved and therefore oral, and the fiction genres, professional letters, and broadcasts all have similar, intermediate values not markedly oral or literate. Dimension 3 is composed of features marking explicit, elaborated reference, versus features marking situation-dependent reference. With respect to this dimension, the same four genres have quite different relations to one another and to the oral and literate poles: professional letters have one of the highest, most literate scores, marking highly explicit, elaborated reference; broadcasts have the lowest score by far, marking reference that is extremely situation-dependent and therefore oral; while spontaneous speeches have a moderately high, literate score, and the fiction genres have moderately low, oral scores. Finally, Dimension 5 is composed of abstract informational features such as passives and past participial clauses. This dimension shows yet another set of relations among these four genres: none of the four is abstract and therefore literate; professional letters has an intermediate score, while broadcasts, spontaneous speeches, and fiction all have non-abstract, oral values. Dimensions 1, 3, and 5 each distinguish between oral and literate discourse in some sense, but together they show that there is no single dimension of orality versus literacy. That is, even the notions of 'oral' and 'literate' texts, taken to represent typical speech and writing, are multi-dimensional constructs. The present analysis characterizes 'oral' discourse as involved production, situation-dependent reference, and non-abstract content, and

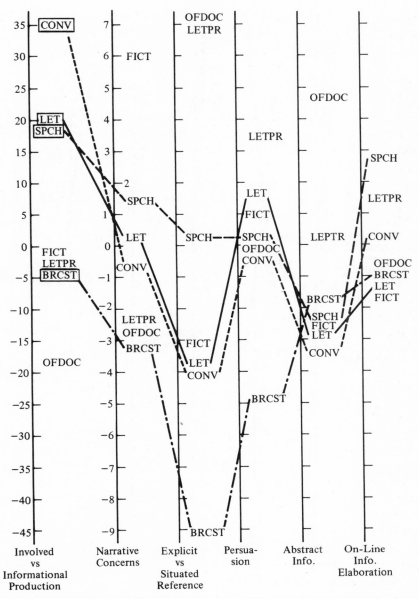

Figure 7.7 *Plot of the textual relations among seven genres, highlighting face-to-face conversation (– – – –), personal letters (————), spontaneous speeches (— — — — —), and broadcasts (—— . ——). (Key: CONV = face-to-face conversation; LET = personal letters; LETPR = professional letters; SPCH = spontaneous speeches; FICT = general fiction; BRCST = broadcasts; OFDOC = official documents)*

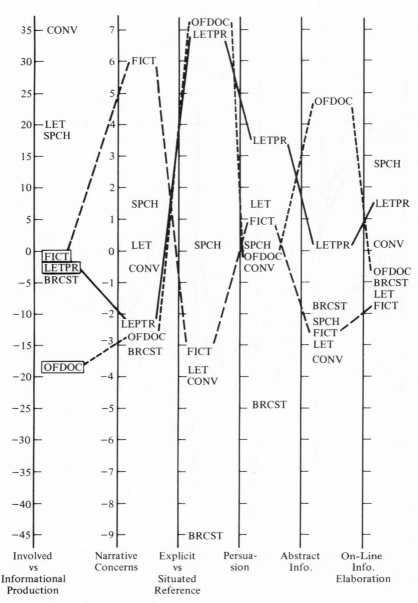

Figure 7.8 *Plot of the textual relations among seven genres, highlighting official documents* (– – – –), *professional letters* (————), *and general fiction* (— — — —).

(Key: CONV = face-to-face conversation; LET = personal letters; LETPR = professional letters; SPCH = spontaneous speeches; FICT = general fiction; BRCST = broadcasts; OFDOC = official documents)

dimensions; that is, it is not marked with respect to narrative concerns (Dimension 2), expression of persuasion (Dimension 4), or on-line informational elaboration (Dimension 6). Personal letters are quite similar to conversation, being involved, situation-dependent, and non-abstract, and not having markedly high or low scores on the other dimensions. Spontaneous speeches are also similar to conversation in some respects, being relatively involved (Dimension 1), non-abstract (Dimension 5), and unmarked for persuasion (Dimension 4). Spontaneous speeches differ from conversation in that they have a moderately high score on Dimension 2, indicating a certain amount of narrative as well as non-narrative subject matter; they have an intermediate score on Dimension 3, indicating some use of both explicit, elaborated reference and situation-dependent reference; and they have the highest score on Dimension 6, marking a dependence on on-line elaboration strategies for the production of informational discourse.

At the other end of the spectrum are official documents. They are characterized by informational production (Dimension 1), a marked non-narrative concern (Dimension 2), highly explicit and elaborated reference (Dimension 3), highly abstract information (Dimension 5), and unmarked scores with respect to Dimensions 4 and 6. In some respects, professional letters are similar to official documents; on Dimension 2 they show a marked non-narrative concern, and on Dimension 3 they are characterized by markedly explicit and elaborated reference. They have intermediate scores on Dimension 1, indicating aspects of both involved and informational production, and on Dimension 5, indicating a certain amount of abstract information. Professional letters differ from official documents primarily on Dimensions 4 and 6. On Dimension 4, professional letters are characterized as the most persuasive genre, and on Dimension 6, they show a relatively high use of on-line informational elaboration for marking stance or associating particular statements with other individuals.

The remaining two genres, general fiction and broadcasts, are unlike any of the other genres. Fiction stands out as having a marked narrative concern (Dimension 2). It is non-abstract (Dimension 5) and depends on situation-dependent reference (Dimension 3), despite the fact that it has an intermediate score on Dimension 1, indicating characteristics of both informational and involved production. It has an unmarked score on Dimension 4 (persuasion), and it makes very little use of the informational elaboration devices associated with Dimension 6. Broadcasts have an intermediate score on Dimension 1, indicating an absence of either informational or involved production characteristics. They are highly marked with respect to Dimensions 2, 3, and 4, being the most non-narrative and non-persuasive genre, and depending the most on situated reference. They are not abstract (Dimension 5) and make little use of the informational elaboration features associated with Dimension 6.

The relation between any two genres is based on consideration of all six dimensions. If we considered only Dimension 1, which has been shown to be a very important and fundamental distinction between oral and literate types of discourse, we would conclude that personal letters and spontaneous speeches are relatively similar to conversation, and that fiction, professional letters, and broadcasts are quite similar to one another and relatively similar to official documents. If we considered only Dimension 3, on the other hand, we would conclude that broadcasts are unlike any other genre, that fiction, conversations, and personal letters are similar to one another, that official documents and professional letters are very similar to each other and very different from the other genres, and that spontaneous speeches are quite distinct from any of these genres. If we were to consider any of the other dimensions in isolation, we would develop yet another set 'of conclusions regarding the relations among these genres. But characterizations of similarity or difference with respect to any single dimension are inadequate, and often they are inaccurate. Comparisons along a single dimension are inaccurate when they lead to false conclusions of how two genres differ. For example, it is simply not correct to conclude that fiction and conversation are very different, as they are with respect to Dimensions 1 and 2, or that they are very similar, as they are with respect to Dimensions 3 and 5; rather, these two genres are similar in some respects and quite different in other respects. Further, even in cases where two genres have nearly the same relation with respect to all dimensions, as in the case of conversation and personal letters, it is still not adequate to simply describe the two genres as similar with respect to a single dimension. Rather, according to the model developed here, two genres are 'similar' to the extent that they are similarly characterized with respect to all dimensions; they are 'different' to the extent that they are distinguished along all dimensions. The relations among any two genres in this sense will be a relatively complex comparison of the genres with respect to all dimensions. This comparison will not be simple or easy to report, because the textual relations among genres are not simple. The dimensions given here enable comparison of spoken and written genres in terms of six basic parameters of variation. Each dimension is associated with a different set of underlying communicative functions, and each defines a different set of similarities and differences among genres. Consideration of all dimensions is required for an adequate description of the relations among spoken and written texts.

7.5 A note on simplicity of analysis

A fundamental tenet of recent American linguistics is that the linguistic structure of a language is best described by a small number of general, underlying rules or principles. This is the case in formal grammatical studies as well as in many sociolinguistic and discourse studies. The present study is also based on this approach, but it puts the goal of descriptive adequacy above the goal of simplicity. The resulting analysis is relatively complex. There is no simple dimension of variation posited here to account for the linguistic differences among texts; rather, six independent dimensions of variation are identified, each of which defines a different set of relations among texts. This degree of complexity is required to characterize adequately the relations among genres in English; as shown in the preceding sections, a simpler analysis would be misleading with respect to the overall relations among at least some genres.

The present analysis does, however, strive for the goal of simplicity of analysis. The six dimensions identified here are general, underlying parameters of variation. These dimensions do not represent all of the differences defined by the original 67 linguistic features. Rather the dimensions are abstractions, describing the underlying parameters of variation in relatively global terms. Consideration of the 67 features in isolation would not enable accurate generalizations concerning the relations among genres. Reducing these features to their underlying dimensions does enable such generalizations, resulting in an overall description of the textual relations among spoken and written genres in English.

8 Extending the description: variation within genres

8.1 Genres and text types

Genre categories are determined on the basis of external criteria relating to the speaker's purpose and topic; they are assigned on the basis of use rather than on the basis of form. It is also possible to consider groupings of texts that are derived on the basis of linguistic form. In other work (Biber forthcoming) I distinguish 'genres' from 'text types': genres characterize texts on the basis of external criteria, while text types represent groupings of texts that are similar in their linguistic form, irrespective of genre. For example, an academic article on Asian history represents formal, academic exposition in terms of the author's purpose, but its linguistic form might be narrative-like and more similar to some types of fiction than to scientific or engineering academic articles. The genre of such a text would be academic exposition, but its text type might be academic narrative.

Genres are not equally coherent in their linguistic characterizations. Some genres have several sub-classes which are quite different from one another; for example, academic prose includes engineering articles, political and historical analyses, and literary discussions. The linguistic form of texts in other genres is simply not highly constrained, and thus these genres permit a relatively wide range of variation; for example, the linguistic characteristics of face-to-face conversation in private academic settings, public social settings, and intimate settings are all different. In an analysis of text types, texts from different genres are grouped together when they are similar in their linguistic form; texts from a single genre might represent several different text types. It is beyond the scope of the present study to identify underlying text types in English; here I consider only the extent to which genre categories are internally coherent and the relations among several sub-genres.

8.2 Internal coherence of the genre categories

Figures 8.1–8.6 plot the range of dimension scores found within twelve of the genres used in the present study. These figures plot the maximum, minimum, and mean scores for each genre, taken from Table 7.1. For example, Figure 8.1 plots the range of scores on Dimension 1, 'Informational versus Involved Production'. The first column on this plot represents the range of scores in face-to-face conversation. It shows that the minimum score for a conversational text is around 18, the highest score for a conversational text is around 54, and the mean score for conversational texts is about 35; the actual scores (minimum: 17.7; maximum: 54.1; mean: 35.3) are given on Table 7.1.

A quick look at Figures 8.1–8.6 shows considerable variation in the score ranges. There are much greater ranges on some dimensions than others; for example, there are relatively large ranges on Dimensions 1 and 4, and a relatively small range on Dimension 5. In addition, some genres show much wider ranges than others; compare, for example, academic prose, which has a large range on every dimension, with personal letters, which has relatively small ránges. The range of scores indicates the internal coherence of a genre category – that is, the range of variation possible within a genre.[1] For example, Figures 8.1–8.6 show that academic prose texts can be quite different from one another and still be considered representative of their genre; personal letters are apparently much more similar to one another in their linguistic form.

Differences within genres can be considered from two perspectives. First, some of the genres used here include several well-defined sub-genres, and the variation within the genre is due in part to variation among the sub-genres. For example, in the LOB corpus, academic prose is divided into seven sub-categories: natural science, medical, mathematics, social science, politics/education, humanities, and technology/engineering. Due to the differences among these sub-genres, the dimension scores for academic prose have quite large ranges. Some other genres, however, are simply not well-constrained or defined. For example, conversation shows large ranges on most of the dimensions, even though there are no clear-cut sub-genre distinctions within conversation.

[1] Maximum and minimum scores plot the total range of variation within a genre; plots of the standard deviations would indicate how tightly the scores within a genre are grouped around the mean score; see Table 7.1 and the discussion in Section 7.1.

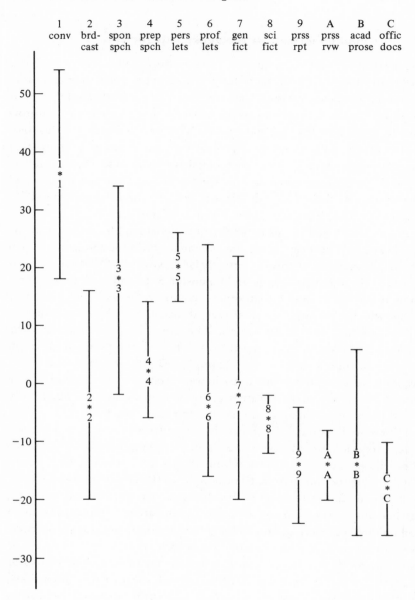

Figure 8.1 *Spread of scores along Dimension 1 ('Informational versus Involved Production') for selected genres (* marks the mean score of each genre)*

(*Key: conv = face-to-face conversation; brdcast = broadcasts; spon spch = spontaneous speeches; prep spch = prepared speeches; pers lets = personal letters; prof lets = professional letters; gen fict = general fiction; sci fict = science fiction; prss rpt = press reportage; prss rvw = press reviews; acad prose = academic prose; offic docs = official documents.*)

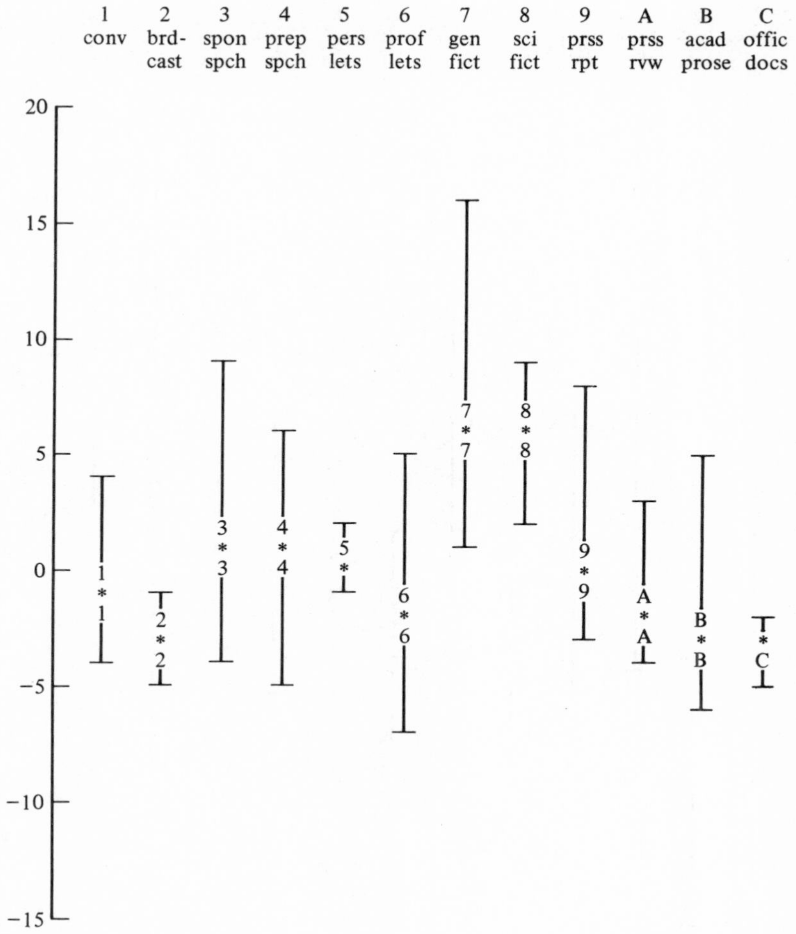

Figure 8.2 *Spread of scores along Dimension 2 ('Narrative versus Non-Narrative Concerns') for selected genres (* marks the mean score of each genre)*

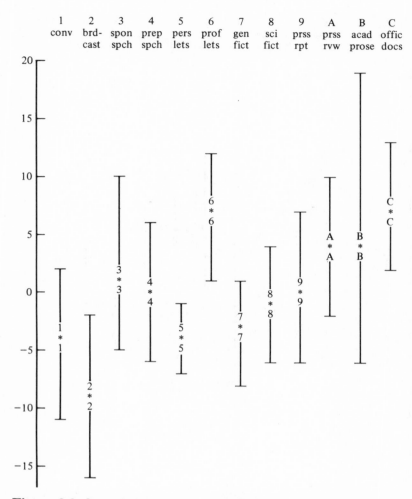

Figure 8.3 *Spread of scores along Dimension 3 ('Explicit versus Situation-Dependent Reference') for selected genres (* marks the mean score of each genre)*

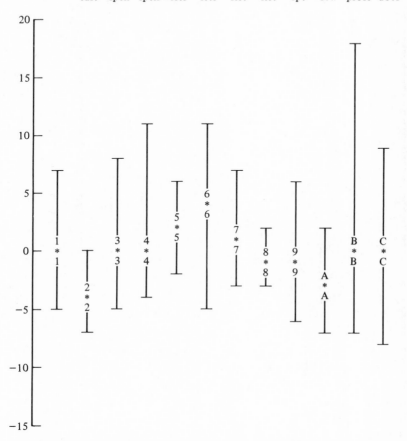

Figure 8.4 *Spread of scores along Dimension 4 ('Overt Expression of Persuasion') for selected genres (* marks the mean score of each genre)*

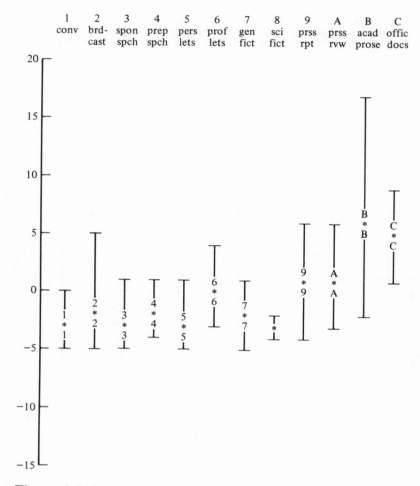

Figure 8.5 *Spread of scores along Dimension 5 ('Abstract versus Non-Abstract Information') for selected genres (* marks the mean score of each genre)*

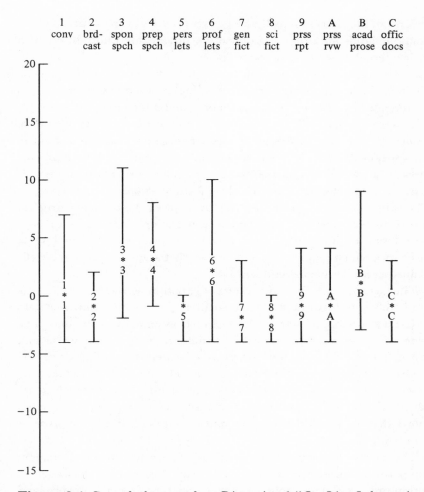

Figure 8.6 *Spread of scores along Dimension 6 ('On-Line Informational Elaboration') for selected genres (* marks the mean score of each genre)*

Some of the distributions shown in Figures 8.1–8.6 are surprising. For example, academic prose and official documents are quite different in their internal coherence, although they are quite similar with respect to their mean dimension scores. Official documents actually include several distinguishable discourse types, including government reports, legal documents and treaties, business reports, and a university bulletin; yet this genre is markedly constrained in linguistic form compared to academic prose. The difference between these genres is apparently due to the freedom for personal expression and a personal style in academic prose, whereas official documents are in some sense truly faceless (there is often no acknowledged author) and conform to a much more rigid form. The wide range of scores for academic prose texts is nevertheless surprising and contrary to popular expectation; many studies have considered academic prose to be a stereotypical example of literate discourse, which requires the assumption that academic prose is a well-defined and highly coherent genre.

The fact that there is a wide range of variation within conversation is intuitively sensible, but it is again surprising in relation to the characterization of particular conversational texts as stereotypically oral. The wide range of variation possible within both academic prose and conversation is disconcerting when we consider studies that use a few academic prose texts to represent writing and a few conversational texts to represent speech. I have shown in earlier chapters that no single genre adequately represents writing or speech; the present chapter further shows that no individual text adequately represents academic prose or conversation.

The consistently wide range of variation seen for press reportage in comparison to press reviews is apparently due to the range of sub-genres within press reportage (politics, sports, society, spot news, finance, and cultural events). Broadcasts show a wide range of variation on several dimensions because this genre includes coverage of sports events, non-sports events (such as a funeral and a wedding), and scientific demonstrations. On Dimension 2, 'Narrative versus Non-Narrative Concerns', there is very little variation among broadcast texts because they all report events actually in progress.

General fiction shows a considerably greater range of variation than science fiction. In this case, the small sample size for science fiction (only six texts) biases the comparison, since there is less opportunity for variation within that genre. However, the comparison also indicates that science fiction is more constrained than general fiction; that general fiction apparently deals with a broader range of topics and uses a broader range of styles than science fiction.

Both prepared speeches and spontaneous speeches include political and legal speeches. In addition, prepared speeches include sermons and a university lecture. Despite the greater range of purposes included in the category of prepared speeches, spontaneous speeches consistently show a greater range of scores. This difference might relate to the planning opportunities in the two genres, but it might also simply indicate a greater freedom for personal variation in spontaneous speeches.

Finally, the comparison of personal letters and professional letters is noteworthy: professional letters consistently have a much greater range of scores than personal letters. This is surprising, given the intuitive impression that personal letters are similar to conversation in being relatively unconstrained, and that professional letters are highly constrained. The actual distribution of texts in these two genres indicates that the opposite is the case: personal letters are apparently quite constrained in their linguistic form while professional letters show considerable variation. This generalization is based on only twenty letters, but the difference between these two genres is quite striking. The personal letters studied here have strictly interactional, affective purposes, and they therefore tolerate little variation in linguistic form. Professional letters, on the other hand, have both interactional and informational purposes, and apparently these two concerns can be weighted quite differently from one professional letter to the next, resulting in considerable variation within this genre.

The above characterizations consider the extent of variation possible within particular genres. We can also consider the extent of variation possible with respect to each dimension. Genres show the least internal variation with respect to Dimension 5, indicating that they are relatively uniform in their characterization as abstract or non-abstract. Academic prose is the only genre to show a wide range of variation on this dimension. The range of variation within most genres is also small with respect to Dimension 2, indicating that genres are relatively uniform in their characterization as narrative or non-narrative. Several genres, however, do show considerable ranges on Dimension 2; surprisingly, general fiction shows one of the largest score spreads on this dimension, perhaps due to variation in the amount of dialogue and description in these texts. The other dimensions show greater ranges within the genres.

On Dimension 1, only personal letters, science fiction, press reviews, and official documents show relatively small ranges. On Dimension 4, only broadcasts and science fiction show small ranges.

The standard deviations of the genre scores, which are also presented in Table 7.1, provide a different perspective on the coherence of the genre categories. The standard deviation shows how tightly a majority of texts are grouped around the genre mean score. A genre can have a small standard deviation, showing that a majority of texts in the genre are grouped tightly around the mean, yet have a large range, showing that at least some of the texts in the genre are quite different from the mean. This is in fact the case with respect to most of the genres studied here; Table 7.1 shows that most genres have relatively small standard deviations, but Figures 8.1–8.6 show that some texts in many of the genres differ greatly from the mean score, indicating that considerable variation is tolerated within most of these genres.

8.3   Relations among sub-genres

It was noted in the last section that the large range of variation within some genres is due to the inclusion of several sub-genres. In the present section, I consider the relations among some of these more specific genre categories.[2] Within the genre 'press reportage', the following sub-types of reportage are considered: political, sports, society, spot news, financial, and cultural; within the genre 'editorials', three sub-types are considered: institutional editorials, personal editorials, and letters to the editor; within the genre 'academic prose', seven sub-genres are considered: natural science, medical, mathematics, social science, politics/education/law, humanities, and technology/engineering; two types of 'broadcasts' are considered: sports and non-sports; and finally, three classes of 'telephone conversations' are considered: personal, between business associates, and between disparates.

Table 8.1 presents descriptive statistics for the dimension scores of each of these sub-genres. Similar to Table 7.1, this table presents the mean score, minimum and maximum scores, range, and standard deviation of each dimension score for each sub-genre. The data presented in this table thus enable comparison of the mean scores for different sub-genres as well as consideration of the internal coherence of the sub-genre

---

[2] The sub-genres considered here include all of the major sub-category distinctions made in the LOB or London–Lund corpus.

Table 8.1 *Descriptive statistics for specialized sub-genres*

Dimension 1: 'Involved versus Informational Production'
Dimension 2: 'Narrative versus Non-Narrative Concerns'
Dimension 3: 'Explicit versus Situation-Dependent Reference'
Dimension 4: 'Overt Expression of Persuasion'
Dimension 5: 'Abstract versus Non-Abstract Information'
Dimension 6: 'On-Line Informational Elaboration'

Dimension	Mean	Minimum value	Maximum value	Range	Standard deviation
---------------------- Political Press Reportage -------------------					
Dimension 1	-17.1	-22.6	-11.9	10.7	3.2
Dimension 2	0.8	-2.6	2.6	5.2	1.5
Dimension 3	-0.9	-6.2	5.6	11.7	3.5
Dimension 4	0.6	-3.4	3.4	6.7	2.0
Dimension 5	0.6	-1.6	2.8	4.5	1.7
Dimension 6	0.4	-2.8	3.9	6.7	1.9
---------------------- Sports Press Reportage ---------------------					
Dimension 1	-14.7	-22.7	-10.2	12.4	4.1
Dimension 2	-0.4	-2.0	1.1	3.0	1.2
Dimension 3	-1.2	-4.1	1.6	5.7	2.1
Dimension 4	-0.5	-4.9	2.5	7.4	2.7
Dimension 5	0.1	-3.3	3.6	6.9	2.2
Dimension 6	-1.5	-3.1	0.8	3.9	1.4
---------------------- Society Press Reportage --------------------					
Dimension 1	-16.1	-22.4	-8.3	14.1	7.2
Dimension 2	-0.4	-2.5	1.0	3.5	1.9
Dimension 3	1.0	-2.1	6.5	8.6	4.8
Dimension 4	-2.1	-4.6	1.3	5.9	3.1
Dimension 5	-0.9	-1.6	0.3	2.0	1.1
Dimension 6	-2.1	-4.0	0.8	4.9	2.6
---------------------- Spot News Reportage ------------------------					
Dimension 1	-13.9	-18.7	-7.6	11.1	3.7
Dimension 2	2.1	-0.4	7.7	8.1	2.5
Dimension 3	0.4	-3.7	4.4	8.0	3.0
Dimension 4	-1.2	-3.7	5.7	9.4	2.9
Dimension 5	1.6	-1.4	5.0	6.5	2.4
Dimension 6	-1.6	-3.6	0.6	4.2	1.4
---------------------- Financial Press Reportage -------------------					
Dimension 1	-17.6	-24.1	-12.4	11.7	4.9
Dimension 2	-2.0	-2.7	-1.3	1.3	0.5
Dimension 3	-0.2	-1.7	1.7	3.3	1.7
Dimension 4	-1.1	-6.0	3.4	9.5	4.0
Dimension 5	2.7	-1.5	5.5	7.0	3.1
Dimension 6	-0.8	-3.2	1.1	4.4	2.2

Table 8.1 (*cont.*)

Dimension	Mean	Minimum value	Maximum value	Range	Standard deviation
-----------------------	Cultural Press Reportage	--------------------			
Dimension 1	-11.7	-18.8	-3.1	15.7	5.5
Dimension 2	-0.4	-3.2	3.3	6.6	2.1
Dimension 3	0.3	-1.6	3.9	5.5	2.2
Dimension 4	-2.0	-5.5	0.7	6.2	2.1
Dimension 5	-0.6	-4.4	4.8	9.1	2.9
Dimension 6	-1.2	-3.1	0.2	3.3	1.4
-----------------------	Institutional Editorials	--------------------			
Dimension 1	-9.1	-14.7	1.6	16.2	4.6
Dimension 2	-0.6	-2.7	1.6	4.4	1.3
Dimension 3	1.8	-2.9	5.4	8.3	2.3
Dimension 4	4.0	-1.2	9.3	10.6	3.1
Dimension 5	0.1	-2.2	3.9	6.1	1.8
Dimension 6	1.9	0.3	5.7	5.4	1.7
-----------------------	Personal Editorials	------------------------			
Dimension 1	-11.0	-18.0	-7.4	10.6	3.5
Dimension 2	-0.4	-3.2	1.8	4.9	1.6
Dimension 3	1.5	-0.4	4.5	4.9	1.7
Dimension 4	1.6	-1.8	7.4	9.3	3.2
Dimension 5	0.6	-2.2	4.5	6.8	2.2
Dimension 6	1.1	-1.8	3.6	5.4	1.6
-----------------------	Letters to the Editor	-----------------------			
Dimension 1	-9.9	-13.0	-6.0	7.0	2.8
Dimension 2	-1.6	-3.5	0.2	3.7	1.3
Dimension 3	2.5	-0.1	5.1	5.3	2.1
Dimension 4	3.8	-0.8	9.2	10.0	3.2
Dimension 5	0.4	-2.4	3.2	5.6	2.1
Dimension 6	1.5	-1.0	3.2	4.2	1.5
-----------------------	Natural Science Academic Prose	--------------			
Dimension 1	-18.2	-22.9	-11.2	11.7	3.9
Dimension 2	-2.6	-5.1	0.9	6.0	1.8
Dimension 3	2.7	-5.8	7.7	13.5	3.7
Dimension 4	-2.1	-7.1	4.4	11.4	3.0
Dimension 5	8.8	3.0	16.8	13.8	4.5
Dimension 6	-0.8	-3.1	4.1	7.2	2.4
-----------------------	Medical Academic Prose	--------------------			
Dimension 1	-17.0	-22.5	-12.9	9.7	4.4
Dimension 2	-1.3	-5.9	0.5	6.3	2.6
Dimension 3	4.1	1.4	6.5	5.2	2.0
Dimension 4	-1.9	-6.8	3.9	10.7	4.6
Dimension 5	7.3	2.3	11.5	9.2	3.9
Dimension 6	1.1	-2.5	3.8	6.3	2.4

Table 8.1 (*cont.*)

Dimension	Mean	Minimum value	Maximum value	Range	Standard deviation
---------------------	Mathematics Academic Prose				--------------------
Dimension 1	-4.4	-12.9	1.6	14.5	6.4
Dimension 2	-3.1	-4.9	-1.0	3.9	1.7
Dimension 3	3.7	0.8	5.5	4.7	2.0
Dimension 4	-0.2	-4.4	1.6	6.0	2.8
Dimension 5	7.6	5.0	11.3	6.3	2.6
Dimension 6	3.6	0.1	9.2	9.0	4.1
---------------------	Social Science Academic Prose				---------------
Dimension 1	-14.0	-21.3	-3.5	17.8	4.6
Dimension 2	-2.8	-6.1	1.5	7.7	2.2
Dimension 3	5.1	-1.0	18.6	19.6	4.9
Dimension 4	-1.8	-5.8	3.9	9.6	2.9
Dimension 5	3.4	-1.4	12.6	14.1	4.7
Dimension 6	0.7	-3.1	6.1	9.2	3.0
---------------------	Politics/Education Academic Prose				-----------
Dimension 1	-15.3	-26.5	-2.5	23.9	5.4
Dimension 2	-2.8	-5.3	0.4	5.7	1.7
Dimension 3	4.9	-0.4	10.3	10.6	3.6
Dimension 4	2.6	-6.0	14.8	20.8	5.1
Dimension 5	3.7	-2.4	10.6	13.0	3.1
Dimension 6	0.9	-3.1	5.4	8.5	2.7
---------------------	Humanities Academic Prose				--------------------
Dimension 1	-14.9	-22.8	7.1	29.9	7.9
Dimension 2	-1.5	-5.5	5.3	10.8	2.8
Dimension 3	3.8	-2.3	11.9	14.1	3.7
Dimension 4	-0.7	-6.2	17.5	23.6	6.3
Dimension 5	2.8	-1.6	15.2	16.9	4.1
Dimension 6	0.1	-3.3	6.9	10.2	2.5
------------------	Technology/Engineering Academic Prose				------------
Dimension 1	-14.3	-21.3	-9.2	12.1	3.4
Dimension 2	-4.1	-6.2	0.3	6.6	1.8
Dimension 3	4.7	0.3	8.5	8.2	2.6
Dimension 4	-0.3	-4.8	6.6	11.5	3.6
Dimension 5	9.7	2.7	15.5	12.8	4.0
Dimension 6	0.2	-2.1	4.4	6.5	2.1
---------------------	Sports Broadcasts				-------------------------
Dimension 1	-3.0	-16.0	7.0	23.0	7.0
Dimension 2	-3.0	-4.7	-0.6	4.1	1.3
Dimension 3	-11.4	-15.8	-3.7	12.1	4.1
Dimension 4	-4.8	-6.4	-2.1	4.3	1.5
Dimension 5	-1.5	-4.7	5.4	10.0	3.6
Dimension 6	-1.2	-3.6	1.7	5.3	1.7

Table 8.1 (*cont.*)

Dimension	Mean	Minimum value	Maximum value	Range	Standard deviation
---------------------- Non-Sports Broadcasts ----------------------					
Dimension 1	-6.0	-19.6	16.9	36.6	14.4
Dimension 2	-3.7	-5.2	-2.3	2.9	1.2
Dimension 3	-6.2	-11.3	-2.2	9.1	2.8
Dimension 4	-3.8	-6.9	-0.3	6.5	2.4
Dimension 5	-2.0	-3.4	0.1	3.5	1.2
Dimension 6	-1.5	-2.8	1.2	4.0	1.5
------------ Telephone Conversations / Personal Friends -------------					
Dimension 1	40.8	25.7	52.9	27.2	8.6
Dimension 2	-1.7	-4.1	4.7	8.8	2.5
Dimension 3	-6.2	-10.1	-3.8	6.4	2.2
Dimension 4	0.3	-4.9	8.4	13.3	3.7
Dimension 5	-3.8	-4.8	0.1	4.9	1.4
Dimension 6	-1.5	-4.8	3.3	8.1	2.4
------------ Telephone Conversations / Business Associates ----------					
Dimension 1	37.2	32.9	48.3	15.4	5.1
Dimension 2	-1.7	-3.2	1.7	4.9	1.8
Dimension 3	-4.3	-9.1	2.3	11.5	4.1
Dimension 4	1.0	-4.1	5.3	9.4	3.5
Dimension 5	-3.1	-4.2	-1.4	2.8	1.1
Dimension 6	-0.8	-3.7	1.2	5.0	1.7
------------ Telephone Conversations / Disparates --------------------					
Dimension 1	29.3	7.2	45.3	38.2	13.8
Dimension 2	-3.4	-4.2	-1.6	2.6	1.1
Dimension 3	-4.1	-7.5	-1.9	5.6	1.9
Dimension 4	0.8	-4.9	6.8	11.8	4.0
Dimension 5	-4.2	-4.7	-3.5	1.2	0.5
Dimension 6	0.4	-1.8	2.6	4.4	1.7

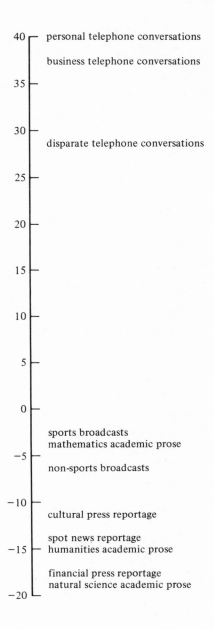

Figure 8.7 *Mean scores of Dimension 1 for selected sub-genres Dimension 1: 'Involved versus Informational Production'*

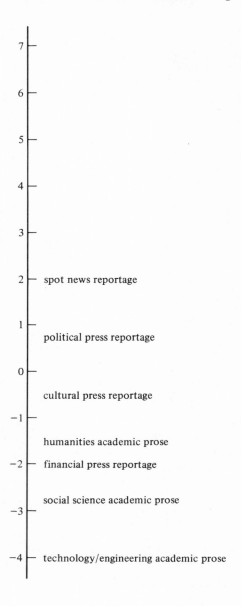

Figure 8.8 *Mean scores of Dimension 2 for selected sub-genres*
Dimension 2: 'Narrative versus Non-Narrative Concerns'

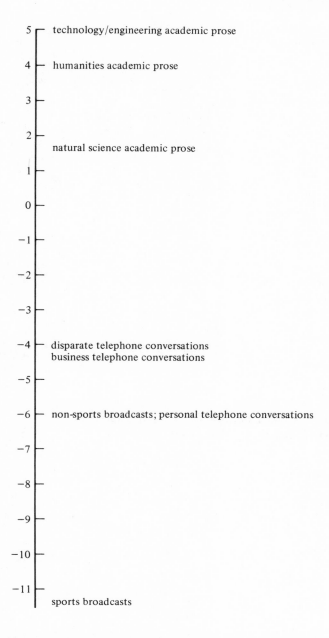

Figure 8.9 *Mean scores of Dimension 3 for selected sub-genres Dimension 3: 'Explicit versus Situation-Dependent Reference'*

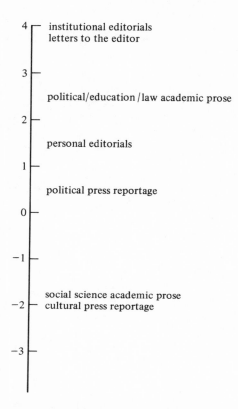

Figure 8.10 *Mean scores of Dimension 4 for selected sub-genres*
Dimension 4: 'Overt Expression of Persuasion'

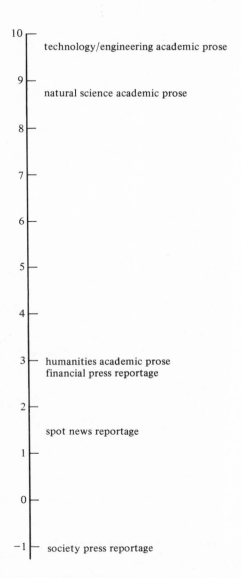

Figure 8.11 *Mean scores of Dimension 5 for selected sub-genres*
Dimension 5: 'Abstract versus Non-Abstract Information'

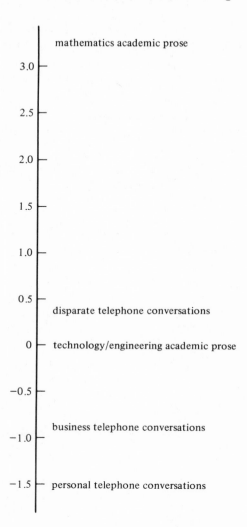

Figure 8.12 *Mean scores of Dimension 6 for selected sub-genres Dimension 6: 'On-Line Informational Elaboration'*

categories. Figures 8.7–8.12 plot the mean dimension scores for some of these sub-genres. Although Table 8.1 gives descriptive statistics for all sub-genre categories, Figures 8.7–8.12 plot the mean scores of only a few sub-genres, to illustrate the major differences within genres on each dimension. These plots show that there are systematic patterns of variation within the major genre categories of press reportage, academic prose, editorials, broadcasts, and telephone conversations. In the following sections, I discuss each of these genres in turn.

8.3.1 Press reportage sub-genres

There are interesting differences among press reportage sub-genres with respect to Dimensions 1, 2, 4, and 5. Figure 8.7 plots the differences among cultural press reportage, spot news, and financial press reportage with respect to Dimension 1 ('Involved versus Informational Production'); the mean scores for the other press sub-genres on Dimension 1 are given in Table 8.1. Figure 8.7 shows that some types of press reportage are more colloquial, affective, and involved than other types. Cultural press reportage (e.g., reportage of theatre or music events) is the most involved type of reportage; financial reportage is the least involved; spot news, along with the other types of reportage not plotted here, have intermediate scores. In relation to the total range of genres on Dimension 1, none of the press sub-genres are involved, but among themselves there are small yet systematic differences with respect to this dimension.

Figure 8.8 plots the mean scores of spot news, political press, cultural press, and financial press along Dimension 2 ('Narrative versus Non-narrative Concerns'); again, the scores for the other press sub-genres are given in Table 8.1. Along Dimension 2, we see relatively large differences among the press reportage sub-genres with respect to their narrative concerns. Spot news has a markedly high narrative focus, presumably because this type of reportage deals primarily with the description of past events. Political, sports, society, and cultural reportage have intermediate scores on Dimension 2, indicating the presence of both narrative and non-narrative text portions; that is, these sub-genres typically include news analysis as well as description of past events. Finally, financial reportage has a markedly non-narrative focus, dealing almost exclusively with the analysis and current implications of past events and processes.

Press reportage is reputed to be a direct, factual reportage of information, suggesting that there should be little difference among press texts along the dimension 'Overt Expression of Persuasion' (Dimension 4). Figure 8.10, however, shows that there is considerable variation among press texts along this dimension. Political reportage has a relatively high score, indicating a substantial amount of persuasion and argumentation, while cultural reportage has a markedly low mean score. Table 8.1 shows that there is also considerable variation within each of the sub-genres along this dimension. Thus, for example, spot news has a maximum score of 5.7 on Dimension 4, and a minimum score of -3.7, making a range of 9.4. This distribution is quite surprising; it shows that spot news can vary considerably in its purpose, ranging from a strictly informational and factual presentation of past events to a more argumentative or persuasive consideration of possibilities. A quick look at almost any newspaper confirms this range of discourse purposes, but it disagrees with the stereotype of press reportage as factual, decontextualized, informational discourse.

Finally, Figure 8.11 shows that press texts differ considerably in their degree of abstractness (Dimension 5). Financial reportage has a high score along this dimension, indicating a considerable amount of abstract information. Spot news also has a relatively high score on this dimension. These two sub-genres are quite different from each other – financial reportage deals with primarily conceptual, abstract topics, while spot news deals with concrete events and human agents – but they are relatively similar in their characterization along this dimension. In financial reportage, an abstract form is used because there are few active agents, due to the nature of the subject matter. In spot news, on the other hand, the use of passives and other past participial constructions apparently reflects the greater topical relevance of 'patients' and events over agents, who are held constant throughout much of a typical news story. Most of the other press sub-genres have intermediate or low scores on this dimension, reflecting a more active, concrete presentation of information. (There are no striking differences among press sub-genres with respect to Dimensions 3 or 6.)

8.3.2 Academic prose sub-genres

Table 8.1 and Figures 8.7–8.12 show that the seven sub-genres of academic prose have systematic, and often large, differences among themselves. With respect to Dimension 1 ('Involved versus Informational Production'; Figure 8.7), these differences are relatively small;

except for mathematics, all academic sub-genres are characterized by the features of highly informational production (frequent nouns, pre-positions, attributive adjectives, long words, and high lexical variety). Mathematics texts have a somewhat higher score, apparently because their subject matter is technical and sometimes non-linguistic, using mathematical expressions instead.

Like press reportage, academic prose texts show considerable variation in the extent to which they use narrative as a means of expression (Dimension 2; Figure 8.8). Humanities prose has a relatively high score on this dimension, showing a topical concern for concrete events and participants, while technology/engineering prose shows a markedly low score on this dimension, reflecting its concern with abstract concepts and findings rather than events in the past. Table 8.1 shows that the other academic sub-genres have intermediate scores between humanities and technology/engineering prose. This table also shows the range of scores possible within some of the sub-genres. In particular, humanities academic prose can be markedly narrative in focus (with a maximum score of 5.3) or markedly non-narrative (with a minimum score of −5.5). This range seems to reflect the differences between historical and biographical studies, which describe and analyze events in the past, and philosophical and analytical studies, which deal exclusively with abstract, conceptual information.

Although all academic prose sub-genres have high scores on Dimension 3 ('Explicit versus Situation-Dependent Reference'), Figure 8.9 shows that there are some differences among them; further, Table 8.1 shows that there is considerable variation within some of the sub-genres with respect to this dimension. Technology/engineering prose has a very high mean score on Dimension 3, indicating a highly explicit and elaborated identification of referents, while natural science prose has a relatively low mean score. The range of texts within natural science is even more striking: the maximum score is 7.7, similar to the typical scores for technology/engineering, medical, and mathematics texts, but the minimum score is −5.8, which is comparable to the mean scores for non-sports broadcasts and personal telephone conversations. These low scores for certain natural science texts seem to reflect situation-dependent reference rather than inexplicit reference. These texts are taken from disciplines such as geology, meteorology, and biology, which deal with specific aspects of the physical environment and thus make extensive reference to that environment. 'Situation-dependent reference' in these texts is not in relation to the situation of text production, but to the physical environment being analyzed as the discourse topic.

Along Dimension 4 ('Overt Expression of Persuasion'; Figure 8.10), we see considerable variation among academic texts in the extent to which they argue for a particular point of view, rather than simply presenting informational findings. Political/education/law academic prose is quite persuasive relative to the other academic sub-genres, while social science prose is more typical of academic exposition in being non-persuasive. In fact, Table 8.1 shows that some political/education/law texts and some humanities texts are extremely persuasive or argumentative in purpose: the political/education/law sub-genre shows a maximum of 14.8 and a minimum of − 6.0; humanities shows a maximum of 17.5 and a minimum of − 6.2. The differences within these sub-genres reflect both personal style and purpose; these scores indicate the extent to which an author considers alternative points of view and argues persuasively for a particular perspective. Studies that depend on logical development and argumentation, such as political, legal, or philosophical analyses, make considerable use of this style of argumentation; studies that are more experimental or empirical in nature (natural sciences, social sciences, etc.) depend less on the logical comparison of alternatives and the use of persuasive form.

Figure 8.11 shows that there are large differences among academic prose sub-genres with respect to Dimension 5, marking abstract, technical information. Sub-genres such as technology/engineering, natural science, and mathematics prose have extremely high scores on this dimension, while sub-genres such as humanities, social science, and political prose have considerably lower scores. A primary distinction here seems to be between those sub-genres that are strictly technical and abstract, and therefore do not deal with specific participants or events, and those that are less technical in nature. The extremely abstract form for scientific and engineering prose might also reflect the linguistic norms that are explicitly taught to scientists and engineers: that empirical studies are factual, and therefore faceless and agentless. Conversely, humanists are taught (and teach) that passives are dispreferred constructions and that good writing is active. In fact, all academic prose sub-genres are quite abstract in form when compared to the full range of English genres, but technical and scientific prose represents extreme use of these forms.

Finally, on Dimension 6 ('On-Line Informational Elaboration';

Figure 8.12), mathematics prose is distinguished from the other sub-genres of academic prose, similar to the distribution along Dimension 1. In the interpretation of this dimension, I suggested that features like *that* complements to verbs, *that* complements to adjectives, and *that* relative clauses are used for informational elaboration in discourse that cannot be carefully planned and integrated; and that these features are also used to mark stance in those same types of discourse. The relatively high score for mathematics prose reflects primarily the use of *that* complements to mark logical development or emphasis. Logical development is marked by constructions such as: *it follows that* . . .; *this shows that* . . .; *if we* . . ., *we find that* . . .; emphasis is marked by constructions such as *note that* . . . The extremely dense use of mathematical formulas and argumentation in this type of prose apparently makes it difficult to integrate the marking of logical relations, resulting in a relatively frequent use of these features. In fact, all academic prose sub-genres use these features to some extent. The interpretation of Dimension 6 as on-line informational elaboration was not meant to exclude the use of these features in other types of discourse, but rather indicates a primary use of these features in genres such as public speeches and interviews, which are informational but must be produced in an on-line manner.

8.3.3 Editorial sub-genres

Overall, editorials are relatively homogeneous, but the sub-genres within this category show interesting differences along Dimension 4 ('Overt Expression of Persuasion'; Figure 8.10). All three editorial sub-genres are persuasive when compared to the other major genres in this study, but institutional editorials and letters to the editor are even more persuasive in focus than personal editorials. Institutional editorials, which are the official opinions of a newspaper, generally make no attempt at objectivity; they are overt expressions of opinion intended to persuade readers. Letters to the editor are also highly opinionated and persuasive. They are reactions to a previous news article or editorial and thus, like institutional editorials, assume no obligation to discuss all sides of an issue; rather they present a personal opinion written to persuade potential readers. Personal editorials are also persuasive, but approach the task more covertly, considering a broad range of perspectives on a given issue, and arguing for the superiority of one perspective on logical grounds. In form, personal editorials are therefore less opinionated and persuasive than the other two editorial sub-genres. However, as with most other genres, Table 8.1 shows that the scores within all three editorial types vary considerably on Dimension 4. For institutional editorials, the maximum score is 9.3, the minimum score is −1.2; for personal editorials, the maximum is 7.4, the minimum is −1.8; for letters to the editor, the maximum is 9.2, the minimum is −0.8. Thus, in all three sub-genres, texts can range from extremely persuasive and argumentative to markedly non-persuasive.

8.3.4   Broadcast sub-genres

Broadcasts are divided into two groups, sports broadcasts and non-sports broadcasts. The latter includes coverage of non-sports public events, such as weddings or parades, as well as informational broadcasts, such as scientific demonstrations. On most dimensions, the two types of broadcasts are quite similar, but there is a noteworthy difference along Dimension 1 and a quite large difference along Dimension 3. With respect to Dimension 1 ('Involved versus Informational Production'; Figure 8.7), both sports and non-sports broadcasts have a relatively low score because they lack a specific addressee and are focused on external events; they are therefore not highly interactive, affective, or involved, although they are not highly informational either. The slightly higher score for sports broadcasts on this dimension indicates greater involvement in this sub-genre than in non-sports broadcasts. Table 8.1 shows, however, that there is a very large range of variation within non-sports broadcasts. The maximum score for a non-sports broadcast on Dimension 1 is 16.9, compared to a maximum of 7.0 for sports broadcasts; the minimum score for non-sports broadcasts is −19.6, compared to a minimum of −16.0 for sports broadcasts. This extremely high amount of variation within non-sports broadcasts with respect to Dimension 1 probably reflects the difference between involved reportage of events that have very high emotional import, such as a wedding or funeral, and the more detached reportage of informational broadcasts.

With respect to Dimension 3 ('Explicit versus Situation-Dependent Reference'; Figure 8.9), both sub-genres of broadcasts are highly situated in their reference, but sports broadcasts show extreme dependence on the external situation. These texts are produced under severe real-time constraints, because of the rapid succession of events in a typical sports situation (Ferguson 1983). In the reportage of sports such as boxing, where events actually occur at a relatively slow pace, broadcasters often package the reportage in a way that gives the impression of strict time constraints and a high level of excitement. There is thus not time, or desire, for elaborated, explicit reference in these broadcasts; and due to the fact that the situation of reference is constrained to the playing-field, sports broadcasters can make extreme use of situation-dependent reference. Some non-sports broadcasts also make a very high use of situation-dependent reference. For example, the referential frame for a wedding in a well-known church is constrained in a similar way to a playing-field for a sports event. In general, though, non-sports broadcasts depend less on the production situation than do sports broadcasts.

8.3.5 Telephone conversation sub-genres

Three types of telephone conversations are included in the London–Lund corpus, which are ranked along scales of intimacy and formality: conversations between personal friends (the most intimate and least formal), between business acquaintances, and between disparates (the least intimate and most formal). These three types of conversation have similar speech situations in most respects; they differ primarily in the social role relations between participants, the amount of background knowledge shared by participants, and the purpose of communication (affective versus informational). Although these situational differences are relatively minor in relation to the possible differences among genres, they are associated with systematic linguistic differences on Dimensions 1, 3, and 6.

On Dimension 1 ('Involved versus Informational Production'; Figure 8.7), personal telephone conversations are the most involved, followed by conversations with business acquaintances and those with disparates. Conversations with disparates are considerably less involved than the other two types, reflecting a lesser expression of affect and a greater informational emphasis in those texts. All three types of conversation are equally constrained by real-time production, but the social relations between participants differ in each case and seem to be the major influence on the differences among these sub-genres with respect to Dimension 1.

On Dimension 3 ('Explicit versus Situation-Dependent Reference'; Figure 8.9), personal conversations are markedly more situated in reference than disparate or business conversations. On Dimension 6

('On-Line Informational Elaboration'; Figure 8.12), conversations between disparates show considerably higher scores than business or
personal conversations. In both cases, this distribution seems to be
related to two factors: (1) the greater amounts of specific background
knowledge shared by personal friends in comparison to business associates or disparates, and (2) the more formal and informational
purposes of disparate conversations compared to conversations between
business associates and personal friends. High amounts of shared
background knowledge and an informal, non-informational purpose, as
in personal telephone conversations, permit highly situated reference (on
Dimension 3), even when participants do not share physical space; the
opposite characteristics of less shared background knowledge and a more
formal, informational purpose, as in conversations between disparates,
result in more on-line informational elaboration (Dimension 6). Thus,
with respect to Dimensions 1, 3, and 6, we see that social role relations are
also associated with systematic differences in linguistic form.

8.3.6   Summary of sub-genre variation

Sub-genre differences account for a considerable amount of the variation
existing within the major genre categories. This is especially the case with
respect to academic prose: Figures 8.1–8.6 show that academic prose
taken as a single genre has a large range of variation on all six dimensions,
and Figures 8.7–8.12 show that the seven academic sub-genres are quite
different from one another with respect to each of the six dimensions.
With respect to some of the dimensions, however, consideration of sub-
genre categories is not very helpful in explaining the range of variation
within genres. Dimension 4 in particular does not distinguish neatly
among genres or sub-genres; the range of scores within sub-genres on
Dimension 4 is usually larger than the differences among the sub-genre
mean scores. In these cases, textual distinctions other than those captured
by traditional genre categories seem to be at work. For example, the
difference between persuasive prose and factual prose seems to cut
directly across traditional genre categories. Future research is required to
investigate the salient groupings of texts with respect to dimensions like
Dimension 4.

9 Afterword: applying the model

9.1 Overview of the study

The analysis presented here was undertaken to describe the relationship between speech and writing in English. Previous studies have offered a wide range of conclusions concerning this relationship; some studies conclude that speech and writing are not very different from a linguistic perspective, while others conclude that they are fundamentally different; some studies conclude that the differences between speech and writing are due to one set of features, while others focus on a different set of features. The present study sorts out these contradictory findings and arrives at an overall account of the textual relations in spoken and written English. To accomplish this task, the study analyzes the distribution of many functionally diverse linguistic features in many different types of spoken and written texts. This analysis shows that there is no single, absolute difference between speech and writing in English; rather there are several dimensions of variation, and particular types of speech and writing are more or less similar with respect to each dimension. In all, six dimensions of variation are identified here, which are interpreted in functional terms and labelled: Dimension 1: 'Involved versus Informational Production', Dimension 2: 'Narrative versus Non-Narrative Concerns', Dimension 3: 'Explicit versus Situation-Dependent Reference', Dimension 4: 'Overt Expression of Persuasion', Dimension 5: 'Abstract versus Non-Abstract Information', and Dimension 6: 'On-Line Informational Elaboration'.

Each dimension defines a different set of relations among texts. For example, on Dimension 1 conversation and personal letters are involved, and official documents and press reportage are informational; on Dimension 2, fiction is highly narrative, while telephone conversations and official documents are both non-narrative; on Dimension 3, official documents and professional letters both use highly explicit and elaborated forms of reference, while broadcasts are by far the most situation-dependent in reference; on Dimension 4, professional letters and editorials are both persuasive, while broadcasts and press reviews are not (even though the reviews are opinionated); on Dimension 5, academic prose and official documents are extremely abstract, while fiction and conversations are markedly non-abstract; finally, on Dimension 6, prepared speeches and interviews have frequent features of on-line informational elaboration, fiction and personal letters have markedly few of these features, and academic prose is similar to face-to-face conversation in having an intermediate score.

Although this study began as an investigation of speech and writing, the final analysis presents an overall description of the relations among texts in English, and it can therefore be used as a basis for the investigation of several related issues. That is, since the texts used in this study cover many of the possible discourse types in English, and the linguistic features used here cover many of the communicative functions marked by surface features in English, the resulting dimensions are not strictly parameters of variation between speech and writing; rather they are fundamental parameters of linguistic variation among English texts. As such, the dimensions can be used to specify the relations among many different types of texts, for example, texts from different historical periods, texts from different social dialects, or texts from student writers of differing abilities. Similarly, the general MF/MD approach to textual variation, which I apply here to the relations among spoken and written texts in English, can be used to investigate a number of other discourse issues. In particular, this approach can be used to specify the relations among texts in other languages and provide a basis for cross-linguistic comparisons of text types. In the concluding sections of this book, I discuss several specific applications of the model of textual relations developed here and the MF/MD approach in general: dialect comparisons (Section 9.2), discourse, stylistic, and historical comparisons (Section 9.3), composition research (Section 9.4), comparison of stance types (Section 9.5), cross-linguistic textual comparisons (Section 9.6), and a typology of English texts (Section 9.7).

9.2 Dialect comparisons

Most studies of dialect variation, whether social or regional, have been restricted to analysis of phonological differences. In contrast, the textual dimensions identified here enable comparison of English dialects at a textual level, in terms of systematic variation among lexical and syntactic features. I illustrate the value of this approach in a comparison of nine written genres from British and American English (Biber 1987). The findings of that study show that there are highly systematic differences between British and American written texts with respect to two underlying textual dimensions: American written genres are consistently more colloquial and involved than British written genres, while at the same time American written genres are consistently more nominal and jargony than British genres. I suggest that these two patterns reflect a single underlying functional priority, relating to a greater influence of grammatical and stylistic prescriptions in British writing and editing. With respect to the first dimension, the prescriptions restrict the use of interactional and colloquial features in British writing; with respect to the second dimension, prescriptions discourage the use of a heavily nominal style in British writing. These proposed explanations need further confirmation, but the relations among British and American genres along these two dimensions are highly systematic, indicating that this analysis captures significant differences between the British and American dialects at a textual level.

Similar analyses can be undertaken with respect to social dialect comparisons or gender comparisons. Although mainstream work on social dialect variation (e.g. Labov 1972) has focused on phonological features, some previous research on 'code elaboration' examines social dialects from a textual perspective (see Labov 1969; Bernstein 1970; Poole 1973; Poole and Field 1976). The six dimensions identified here can be used to gain new insights into the textual relations among social dialects. This would require analysis of spoken and written texts from several genres produced by speakers and writers of different social dialects. Dimension scores for each genre in each dialect could be computed, enabling specification of the relations among the genres and dialects. The results of the present study predict that the relations among social dialects will not be simple or unidimensional; rather, each dimension potentially defines a different set of relations.

Many studies of gender differences in English have been restricted in similar ways to previous research on speech and writing; they typically consider only a few linguistic features in a few texts that represent only one or two speaking situations. The MF/MD approach can enable new insights into this area of research by providing overall characterizations of male and female speech as well as comparison of female–female, male–male, female–male, and male–female interactions. Similar to other text-related issues, an MF/MD analysis of gender differences would be based on consideration of texts from several speaking and writing situations, with special emphasis on the different role relations between men and women.

9.3   Discourse, stylistic, and historical comparisons

Several studies have investigated discourse issues using an MF/MD approach. For example, Finegan and Biber (1986b) show that the notion of 'discourse complexity' is not a unified construct; rather, it comprises at least two relatively independent dimensions. The first dimension shows that certain types of structural elaboration, represented by subordination features such as *that*-complements to verbs, WH-clauses, and *if*-clauses, occur in a largely complementary pattern to complexity and elaboration in lexical content, represented by high type/token ratio and frequent long words. Public speeches and conversations make frequent use of the structural elaboration associated with this dimension, while more planned, written genres such as official documents, academic prose, and fiction depend on lexical elaboration. Both positive and negative features on this dimension have been taken as markers of discourse complexity in other research; the fact that they occur in a largely complementary pattern shows that there are different types of complexity, and that it is not adequate to simply characterize particular genres as complex or not – rather, different genres are complex in different ways to different extents. The discourse complexity of spoken informational genres takes the form of structural elaboration, while the complexity of planned, written genres takes the form of lexical elaboration and precision. (The second dimension in this study identifies yet another aspect of discourse complexity relating to abstractness of content.)

Other discourse issues can be addressed using this approach as well. Finegan and Biber (1986a) identify two dimensions of sociolinguistic prestige using an MF/MD approach. The one dimension is associated with differences between speech and writing; the other dimension seems to be associated with differences in formality. Grabe (1984a) uses an MF/MD approach to analyze the salient text type distinctions within English expository prose. This study analyzes exposition from social sciences, humanities, and engineering texts, including both introductory textbooks as well as advanced academic articles.

In other studies, the model of textual relations developed here has been used for stylistic comparisons (Biber and Finegan 1988b, 1988c). These studies have two major emphases. In the one case, they focus on the stylistic distinctiveness of particular authors by considering the position of an author's works relative to the range of texts in the same genre – this can be done simply by plotting the factor score of particular texts on Figures 8.1–8.6. For example, on Dimension 1 Mark Twain's fiction is relatively colloquial and involved relative to the range of twentieth-century general fiction; D.H. Lawrence's fiction is informational and non-involved relative to the same range. By considering particular authors, and particular works, relative to all six dimensions, we achieve a macroscopic analysis of an author's stylistic distinctiveness. The second major emphasis of these stylistic studies is to trace the historical evolution of written texts in English. By comparing fiction and exposition from the eighteenth, nineteenth, and twentieth centuries with respect to the six dimensions, we achieve a macroscopic description of the historical shifts in discourse style over the last three centuries. This analysis indicates that the discourse norms for fictional narrative and expository essays are relatively independent; for example, on Dimension 3 fiction has shifted to less explicit, more situation-dependent forms of reference, while essays have remained essentially constant; on Dimension 5, both fiction and essays have shifted to less abstract, passive forms of presentation.

9.4 Application to composition research

A discourse issue that has received much attention concerns the comparison of student compositions and an assessment of the linguistic characteristics of 'good' and 'poor' writing (Hillocks 1986). Some previous analyses note that compositions from different genres must be studied separately; that is, since the linguistic characteristics of narrative, exposition, argumentation, and description are all different, the com-position tasks used in any particular study must be considered when evaluating the results and conclusions. An MF/MD approach is ideally suited to research issues of this type, because it enables a comparison of good and poor writing from several different composition tasks in a single, coherent analysis. Grabe and Biber (1987) use the model of textual relations developed here in a pilot study of the linguistic characteristics of good and poor essays written by native and non-native writers of English. That study finds almost no difference between native and non-native essays and only small differences between good and poor essays. The most striking result, however, is that student essays are unlike any of the published genres of English; they use the surface forms of academic writing (e.g., passives), but they are relatively non-informational and involved, and they are extremely persuasive in form. This finding indicates that compositions do not have a well-defined discourse norm in English.

The research issues surrounding written compositions are quite complex, including differences due to composition task, planning opportunities, classroom practices, amount of in-class and out-of-class writing, amount of in-class and out-of-class reading, extent and type of comments given on compositions, and the social background and home culture of the student. In addition, the relation of good compositions to different types of published exposition is crucially important. MF/MD analyses can help provide a macroscopic characterization of student compositions with respect to these different parameters.

9.5   Comparison of stance types

In other studies I have used an MF/MD approach for the analysis of stance types, that is, the ways in which an author or speaker overtly expresses attitudes, feelings, judgments, or commitment concerning the message. Biber and Finegan (1988a) focus exclusively on the adverbial marking of stance, analyzing the distribution of six classes of adverbials (such as *surely* adverbials, *actually* adverbials, and *maybe* adverbials) in order to group texts into text types that are similar in the ways that they mark stance. Biber and Finegan (forthcoming) extend this research to include verbs and adjectives as markers of stance. Both of these studies use a multivariate statistical technique called cluster analysis to group together texts that are similar in their linguistic form, irrespective of their genre classification. The resulting clusters of texts are interpreted as stance styles by considering the characteristic linguistic features in each cluster, the particular kinds of texts grouped in each cluster, and micro-analyses of the stance features in particular texts. In the interpretation, functional labels are proposed for the different styles; for example, in Biber and Finegan (1988a), eight stance styles are identified and given labels such as 'Cautious', 'Secluded from Dispute', and 'Faceless'.

9.6 Cross-linguistic textual comparisons

The approach to macroscopic textual variation developed here is not restricted to English language studies. For example, Besnier (1986a) uses an MF/MD approach to analyse textual variation in Nukulaelae Tuvaluan, a Polynesian language. From a mechanical point of view, the application of an MF/MD approach is identical from one language to the next. However, analyses of other languages often require considerable research into the range of speech situations and the functions of linguistic features before attempting a macroscopic analysis. Thus, Besnier undertook a careful ethnographic analysis to determine the situational characteristics of each genre according to the patterns of usage in Tuvaluan, rather than assuming a set of situational characteristics from English. Similarly, he determined the communicative functions served by particular linguistic features in Tuvaluan, independently of the functions of seemingly similar features in English. For example, Tuvaluan participants in conversation rarely express affect towards one another or concerning themselves. In contrast, writers of personal letters in Tuvaluan often express intimate feelings and display affect towards the recipient. Thus, in this sense personal letters are more intimate and interactive than face-to-face conversation in Tuvaluan, so that the situational characterization of these genres is different from the characterization commonly assumed for the closest equivalent in English.

Not surprisingly, Besnier found that the situational contrasts between conversations and personal letters are associated with different linguistic characterizations in Tuvaluan and English. Similar to the present study of English, Besnier finds that no dimension of variation in Tuvaluan correlates with a simple spoken/written contrast. For instance, with respect to the first dimension identified by Besnier, which is associated with the extent of involvement (e.g., first and second person pronouns, emphatic particles), both the most involved and the least involved texts are from written genres, while the spoken genres all have intermediate scores. That is, personal letters are by far the most involved genre in Tuvaluan, while written sermon notes are by far the least involved. Conversation is the most involved of the spoken genres on this dimension, but is far less involved than personal letters. Similar relations are shown with respect to the two other dimensions identified in Besnier's study. In general, the dimensions of variation identified in Tuvaluan are quite similar to the dimensions identified in English, but the relations among genres are quite different due to the differing situational characterizations of genres in English and Tuvaluan. Besnier's study on Tuvaluan is the first to analyze the overall textual relations among spoken and written genres in a non-Western language. It makes a very important contribution to the study of speech and writing, showing that Western sociolinguistic norms cannot be assumed to prevail in other cultures; the study thus paves the way for cross-linguistic comparisons of textual variation.

9.7   Towards a typology of English texts

In all of the above applications, different types of discourse are compared from different theoretical perspectives. One of the final goals of this line of research is the development of an overall typology of texts that can be used to specify the interrelations existing among texts in terms of their exploitation of linguistic features for functional purposes. Such a typology is required as a foundation for discourse research, which typically undertakes analyses of particular sets of texts without specifying their relations to other kinds of texts, often making the unwarranted assumption that findings can be generalized to discourse as a whole. We have seen earlier that discourse researchers have often undertaken comparisons of spoken and written texts without adequate consideration of the genres chosen for analysis in relation to other genres. Researchers in discourse comprehension have overgeneralized in a similar way, often analyzing only the comprehension of stories but generalizing their findings to all discourse processing. In fact, any research issue that involves particular types of text in relation to other texts (for example, any of the research areas discussed in Sections 9.2–9.6) requires a typology of texts to place findings in their proper perspective with respect to the possible types of discourse.

Discourse types can be considered from at least two perspectives. In the present study, I use the term 'genre' for classes of texts that are determined on the basis of external criteria relating to author's or speaker's purpose. In other studies (e.g., Biber forthcoming), I use the term 'text type' to refer to classes of texts that are grouped on the basis of similarities in linguistic form, irrespective of their genre classifications. For example, particular texts from press reportage, biographies, and academic prose might be very similar in having a narrative linguistic form, and they would thus be grouped together as a single text type, even though they represent three different genres. In a fully developed typology of texts, genres and text types will be distinguished, and the relations among and between them will be identified and explained.

The present study has identified six dimensions of variation among texts in English, and it has specified the relations among genres with respect to those dimensions.

The present study has identified six dimensions of variation among texts in English, and it has specified the relations among genres with respect to those dimensions. Biber (forthcoming) uses a cluster analysis to develop a typology of English texts in terms of these same dimensions. The 'types' are identified empirically such that the texts grouped in each type are maximally similar in their linguistic characterizations (with respect to the dimensions). In all, eight text types are identified. The types are interpreted by considering the salient linguistic characteristics of each type together with the shared situational, communicative, and processing characteristics of the texts grouped in each type. The typology identifies several interesting differences among English texts. For example, there is no single interactive text type. Rather, two major types are identified: 'Intimate Interpersonal Interaction' and 'Informational Interaction'. Similarly, there is no single expository text type; rather, the analysis distinguishes among 'Scientific Exposition', 'Learned Exposition', and 'General Narrative Exposition'. The other three types in the analysis are labelled 'Imaginative Narrative', 'Situated Reportage', and 'Involved Persuasion'. Overall, this typology provides a theoretical basis for a variety of discourse comparisons in English.

Additional research is required concerning the relations among texts with respect to other linguistic systems, such as the marking of cohesion, coherence, and information structure. However, the present model of variation, as well as the approach to variation developed here, should continue to prove useful to the investigation of many related discourse issues in English, and it is hoped that it will provide a foundation for cross-linguistic research to identify universal dimensions of variation among texts.

APPENDIX I

Texts used in the study

As noted in Chapter 4, not all texts from the London–Lund and LOB corpora were included in the study, because of the time involved in editing the tagged texts. All genres included in the corpora, however, are represented in the study.

In addition, many of the text samples in the London–Lund corpus were divided. Texts were divided for one of two reasons. The first is that many of these texts, which are 5,000 words long, actually comprise two or more shorter texts. For example, a typical telephone 'text' consists of several conversations which are juxtaposed so that the total number of words in the text sample exceeds 5,000. In these cases, each conversation (or speech, broadcast, etc.) was separated and treated as a distinct text. If a text thus separated was shorter than 400 words, it was excluded from the analysis. (For this same reason, several of the letters that had been collected were excluded.)

Text samples that did not consist of several different texts were divided to obtain two samples of approximately 2,500 (continuous) words each. For this reason, these are not 'texts' in the sense that they are not bounded and do not contain all of the structural (textual) properties of a text. Many of the 2,000-word samples in the LOB corpus are of this type also; the text samples do not represent entire books, articles, or even chapters, and so do not represent entire 'texts'. Rather they are representative 2,000-word (continuous) samples from those texts. In the same way, it was felt that dividing the 5,000 word spoken text samples into two portions would not alter the validity of these samples. In the case of some of these samples, the original text was not bounded in the first place. (For example, it is difficult to determine when a conversation begins and ends; rather participants come and go, topics gradually shift, but the conversation continues for long periods.) In all cases where a sample was divided, it was done at a turn boundary, and, when possible, it was done at a place where there seemed to be some kind of topic shift also.

The LOB and London–Lund corpora have specific identifiers for each of the genres, and, within each genre, the texts are numbered consecutively. The following list identifies the individual texts used in the present study.

Press reportage: all texts in LOB category A
Editorials: all texts in LOB category B
Press reviews: all texts in LOB category C
Religion: all texts in LOB category D
Skills and hobbies: the first 30,000 words (texts 1–14) from LOB category E
Popular lore: the first 30,000 words (texts 1–14) from LOB category F
Biographies: the first 30,000 words (texts 1–14) from LOB category G
Official documents: texts 1–6 (government reports), 13–14 (acts and treaties), 25–30 (other official reports and documents) from LOB category H
Academic prose: all texts in LOB category J
General fiction: all texts in LOB category K
Mystery fiction: the first 30,000 words (texts 1–14) from LOB category L
Science fiction: all texts in LOB category M
Adventure and western fiction: the first 30,000 words (texts 1–14) from LOB category N
Romance fiction: the first 30,000 words (texts 1–14) from LOB category P
Humor: all texts in LOB category R
Face-to-face conversation: from the London–Lund corpus, texts 1.1 (divided), 1.2 (4 sub-texts), 1.3 (divided), 1.4 (divided), 1.5 (divided), 1.6 (divided), 1.7 (divided), 1.8 (divided), 1.9 (divided), 1.10 (divided), 1.11 (2 sub-texts), 1.12 (divided), 1.13 (divided), 1.14 (2 sub-texts), 3.1 (3 sub-texts), 3.2 (3 sub-texts), 3.3 (divided), 3.4 (divided), 3.5 (2 sub-texts), 3.6 (divided)
Telephone conversation: from the London–Lund corpus (texts shorter than 400 words are excluded), texts 7.1 (5 sub-texts), 7.2 (5 sub-texts), 7.3 (3 sub-texts), 8.1 (3 sub-texts), 8.2 (1 sub-text), 8.3 (3 sub-texts), 8.4 (1 sub-text), 9.1 (3 sub-texts), 9.2 (2 sub-texts), 9.3 (1 sub-text)
Public conversations, debates, interviews: from the London–Lund corpus, 5.1 (divided), 5.2 (divided), 5.3 (divided), 5.5 (divided), 5.6 (divided), 5.7 (divided), 6.1 (3 sub-texts), 6.3 (divided), 6.4a (1 sub-text), 6.5 (divided), 6.6 (divided) – texts 5.8–5.11, 6.2, and 6.4b are excluded because they are not public conversations – 5.4 was excluded accidentally – 6.6 is actually a narrative monologue
Broadcasts: from the London–Lund corpus, 10.1 (divided), 10.2 (divided), 10.3 (divided), 10.4 (4 sub-texts), 10.5 (divided), 10.6 (2 sub-texts), 10.7 (3 sub-texts), 10.8 (1 sub-text – 1 sub-text excluded because it was too short)

Spontaneous speeches: from the London–Lund corpus, 11.1 (divided), 11.2 (divided), 11.3 (7 sub-texts), 11.4 (divided), 11.5 (divided)

Prepared speeches: from the London–Lund corpus, 12.1 (4 sub-texts), 12.2 (2 sub-texts), 12.3 (divided), 12.4 (2 sub-texts), 12.5 (divided), 12.6 (divided)

Linguistic features: algorithms and functions

II.1 Development of computer programs for grammatical analysis

One of the distinctive characteristics of the present study is inclusion of a large number of linguistic features representing the range of functional possibilities in English. Further, these features are counted in a large number of texts and genres, to exclude idiosyncratic variation and to insure inclusion of the range of situational and linguistic variation existing within speaking and writing in English.

The use of computerized text corpora and computer programs for the automatic identification of linguistic features made it possible to carry out a study of this scope. The programs, which are written in PL/1, use the untagged versions of the LOB and London–Lund corpora as input. In a tagged corpus, such as the Brown corpus, the words in a text are all marked, or 'tagged', for their grammatical category, greatly facilitating automatic syntactic analysis. A tagged version of the LOB corpus became available during the course of the present study, but it was not used because there is no comparable version of the London–Lund corpus (the spoken texts). That is, programs that took advantage of the grammatical tagging in the LOB corpus would identify features with a greater accuracy than could be identified in the London–Lund corpus, thus skewing the comparison of spoken and written genres. Therefore, the untagged versions of both corpora were used, and a single set of programs was developed for the analysis of both.

There are two major steps involved in the automatic identification of linguistic features. The first is to identify, or tag, the grammatical category of each word, as a noun, verb, adjective, preposition, WH pronoun, etc. This step requires a computerized dictionary, so that the program can 'look up' words in the dictionary and find their grammatical category. The tags resulting from this procedure provide the basis for the second step, which identifies particular sequences of words as instances of a linguistic feature. For example, if a noun is followed by a WH pronoun and not preceded by the verb *tell* or *say*, it can be identified as a relative clause; the sequence *tell/say* + noun phrase + WH pronoun might be either a relative clause or a WH clause (e.g., *Tell the man who came that I'm not home* versus *Tell the man who came last night*).

Work on the programs used for the frequency counts, which was spread over the years 1983–6, progressed in two major stages. Programs resulting from the first stage provided the basis for the analyses in Biber (1984, 1986a). These earlier programs were hampered by the lack of a dictionary; to identify linguistic constructions, they relied on small lists of words built into the program structure itself. These lists included prepositions, conjuncts, pronominal forms, auxiliary forms, the 120 most common adjectives occurring in the Brown corpus, and the 150 most common verbs in the Brown corpus. Since these word lists were relatively restricted, the grammatical category of many words in texts could not be accurately identified, and therefore these programs did not identify all of the occurrences of some linguistic features. The programs were designed to avoid skewing the frequency counts of features in one genre or another, so that the relative frequencies were accurate. The main disadvantage of this earlier approach was that certain linguistic features could not be counted at all. For example, there was no way to compute a simple frequency count for the total nouns in a text, because nouns could not be identified. For these reasons, a second set of programs was developed.

The second stage of program development took place during the year 1985–6. The approach used in this stage differed from that of the first stage. First, a general tagging program to identify the grammatical category of each word in a text was developed. The goal at this point was to develop a program that was general enough to be used for tagging both written and spoken texts; thus, for example, the program could not depend on upper case letters or sentence punctuation.

This goal is achieved by using a large-scale dictionary together with a number of context-dependent disambiguating algorithms. Because the Brown corpus exists in a tagged version (i.e., each word in this corpus has an identifier marking the grammatical category of the word in its context), it was sorted into alphabetical order and used as a dictionary. Duplicate entries (the same lexical entry with the same grammatical tag) were deleted, and the resulting dictionary contains 50,624 lexical entries from the four major categories of noun, verb, adjective, and adverb. The closed grammatical categories (e.g., prepositions, pronouns, conjuncts, auxiliaries) are identified directly by the tagging program. Using the dictionary and the word-lists of closed category items built into the program, the initial identification of most words in the LOB and London–Lund corpora was relatively straightforward.

The major problem that had to be solved was that many of the most common words in English are ambiguous as to their grammatical category. Words like *account* can be either nouns or verbs; words like *absent* can be either adjectives or verbs; words like *acid* can be either nouns or adjectives; words like *abstract* can function as a noun, adjective, or verb. There are 3,440 such words in the dictionary compiled from the Brown corpus. In addition, all past and present participial forms can function as noun (gerund), adjective, or verb. A simple word like *that* can function as a demonstrative, demonstrative pronoun, relative pronoun, complementizer, or adverbial subordinator. Using Quirk *et al.* (1985) as a grammatical reference, I developed algorithms to disambiguate occurrences of these (and other) words, depending on their surrounding contexts. For example, a participial form preceded by an article, demonstrative, quantifier, numeral, adjective, or possessive pronoun is functioning as a noun or adjective (i.e., it is not functioning as a verb in this context); given this preceding context, if the form is followed by a noun or adjective then it will be tagged as an adjective; if it is followed by a verb or preposition, then it will be tagged as a noun.

Tagged texts enable automatic identification of a broad range of linguistic features that are important for distinguishing among genres in English. The tagged texts are subsequently used as input to other programs that count the frequencies of certain tagged items (e.g., nouns, adjectives, adverbs) and compute the frequencies of particular syntactic constructions (e.g., relativization on subject versus non-subject position). This approach enables a higher degree of accuracy than the approach used in my earlier analyses, plus it enables inclusion of many features that could not be accurately identified by the previous set of programs. The resulting analysis is thus considerably more complete than earlier analyses.

In section II.2, I describe the major outlines of the tagging program used for the present analysis. In section II.3, then, I describe the particular algorithm used for each linguistic feature. In addition, the primary functions that have been associated with each feature are presented in this section, providing the background for the factor interpretations in Chapter 6.

II.2   General description of the tagging program

The tagging program operates in two steps: (1) initial identification of the grammatical category of each word, and (2) in cases where the dictionary lists more than one possible grammatical category for a word, resolution of ambiguities. There is not space here for a complete description of this program, but I will briefly summarize the major components.

The program first identifies words belonging to any of the following closed grammatical categories:

DO: *do, does, did, don't, doesn't, didn't, doing, done*
HAVE: *have, has, had, having, -'ve#, -'d#, haven't, hasn't, hadn't*
BE: *am, is, are, was, were, being, been -'m #, -'ve #, isn't, aren't, wasn't, weren't*
MODAL: *can, may, shall, will, -'ll#, could, might, should, would, must, can't, won't, couldn't, mightn't, shouldn't, wouldn't, mustn't*
AUX: MODAL/DO/HAVE/BE/-'s
Subject pronouns: *I, we, he, she, they* (plus contracted forms)
Object pronouns: *me, us, him, them* (plus contracted forms)
Possessive pronouns: *my, our, your, his, their, its* (plus contracted forms)
Reflexive pronouns: *himself, themselves, herself, itself*
Other personal pronouns: *you, her, it* (plus contracted forms)
Subordinators (e.g., *since, while, because*)
Prepositions (e.g., *at, among*)
Conjuncts (e.g., *furthermore, therefore*)
Amplifiers (e.g., *absolutely, greatly*)
Downtoners (e.g., *almost, nearly*)
Place adverbials (e.g., *beneath, downstairs*)
Time adverbials (e.g., *early, tonight*)
WH pronouns: *who, whom, whose, which*
Other WH words: *what, where, when, how, whether, why, whoever, whomever, whichever, wherever, whenever, whatever, however*
Nominalizations: all words ending in *-tion#, -ment#, -ness#,* or *-ity#* (plus plurals)
Articles: *a, an, the, (dhi)*
Demonstratives: *this, that, these, those*
Quantifiers: *each, all, every, many, much, few, several, some, any*
Numerals: *one . . . twenty, hundred, thousand*
Ordinal numerals: *first . . . tenth*
Quantifier pronouns: *everybody, somebody, anybody, everyone, someone, anyone, everything, something, anything*
Titles: *mr, ms, miss, mrs, dr*
Clause punctuation (Cl-P): '.', '!', '?', ':', ';', '—'

Failing to match a word with one of these closed categories, the program then attempts to locate the word in the dictionary, which contains nouns, verbs, adjectives, and adverbs. If there is a single entry for the lexical item in the dictionary, then it is simply tagged. If there are multiple entries, then the item must be disambiguated. If the lexical item is not found in the dictionary, and if it is longer than six letters, there is one final check: if the word ends in *ing*, it is tagged as a present participle; if it ends in *ly*, it is tagged as an adverb; if it ends in *ed*, it is tagged as a past tense form of a verb. Words that match none of the above criteria are left untagged.

There is a separate disambiguating algorithm for each possible ambiguity: adjective–noun (e.g., *assistant*, *kind*), adjective–verb (e.g., *appropriate*, *approximate*), noun–verb (e.g., *abuse*, *acts*), adjective–noun–verb (e.g., *abstract*, *average*, *base*), adverb–adjective (e.g., *late*, *long*), adverb–noun (e.g., *more*), adverb–adjective–verb (e.g., *close*, *clean*, *slow*), adverb–adjective–noun (e.g., *flat*, *high*), and adverb–adjective–verb–noun (e.g., *fine*, *light*). In addition, present and past participial forms are disambiguated according to their function as noun, verb, or adjective.

For example, noun–verb–adjective forms are disambiguated as follows:

(1)   if the preceding word is a form of the verb *be*, *seem*, or *appear*, then tag the item as an adjective;
(2)   else (having not met condition 1), if the preceding word is an article, demonstrative, quantifier, numeral, adjective, possessive noun or pronoun, preposition, or verb, then do the following:
      (2a) if (having met condition 2), the following word is an adjective, noun, or an ambiguity of the types ADJ–N, N–V, or ADJ–N–V, then tag the item as an adjective;
      (2b) else (having met condition 2 but not 2a), tag the item as a noun;
(3)   else (having not met conditions 1 or 2), if the preceding word is a subject pronominal form, the pronoun *you* or *it*, a modal, or a form of the verb *do*, then tag the item as a verb;
(4)   else (having not met conditions 1, 2, or 3), if the following word is unambiguously a noun or adjective, tag the item as an adjective;
(5)   else (having not met conditions 1, 2, 3, or 4), if the following word is a verb, auxiliary, or participial form, then tag the item as a noun;
(6)   else (having failed to meet any of the above conditions), if the preceding word is a WH pronoun or a subject pronoun, or the following word is an object pronoun, possessive pronoun, reflexive pronoun, quantifier pronoun, *it*, *you*, article, demonstrative, quantifier, numeral, or adverb, then tag the item as a verb;
(7)   else (having failed the above conditions), if the following word is *of* then tag the item as a noun;
(8)   else, failing to meet each of these conditions, the item remains untagged.

Similar algorithms have been developed for the other ambiguities (some of them even more complex than this one). In addition to the basic categories listed above, several other lexical and syntactic features are marked by the tagging program. These include: demonstrative pronouns, passives, perfect aspect, past tense, present tense, infinitives, participial and non-participial adjectives in attributive versus predicative positions, nominalizations, gerunds, causative subordinators, conditional subordinators, concessive subordinators, *that* complements to verbs and adjectives, contractions, analytic and synthetic negation, *be* as main verb, necessity modals, possibility modals, prediction modals, public verbs, private verbs, suasive verbs, discourse particles, hedges, emphatics, sentence relatives, WH questions, phrasal coordination, non-phrasal coordination, WHIZ deletions, participial clauses, and existential *there*. More details of the algorithms for specific features are given in the next section. An example of the output of the tagging program is given as Table II.1. This example is from the tagged version of text K–13, where K is the genre identifier for general fiction and 13 marks this as text no. 13 in that genre.

The tagging of some lexical items was so problematic that they were systematically excluded. For example, the item *as* can function as an adverb, preposition, conjunction, particle, subordinator, or even relative, and it is very difficult to decide among these functions (even for a human analyst!). This lexical item was thus not tagged, to avoid producing incorrectly tagged items in texts. In addition, I carried out some hand-editing of the tagged texts to correct certain inaccuracies. For example, in the spoken texts a *that* immediately following an intonation unit boundary was ambiguous because there was no way to determine if it was clause-initial or clause-internal; it was not possible to automatically decide whether *that* in this position was functioning as a demonstrative, complementizer, or relative pronoun. All occurrences of *that* in this position were therefore checked by hand. Similarly, it was not possible to determine automatically whether *which* following an intonation unit boundary or a comma was functioning as a relative pronoun modifying a specific noun or as a sentence relative pronoun; these items were also checked by hand. Finally, past and present participial forms were checked by hand. Although the tagging program includes elaborate algorithms to distinguish among gerunds, participial adjectives, WHIZ deletions, participial clauses, passives and perfects (in the case of past participles), and main active verbs (present or past), a high percentage of these forms was incorrectly tagged. For example, it is extremely difficult, without the aid of semantic content, to distinguish between active past tense forms and passive WHIZ deletions in constructions such as: (1) . . .

the Americans ranked close in importance . . .; (2) . . . *the woman asked for her fare* . . .; versus (3) . . . *the equation solved in the last section* . . . As human readers, we expect human referents to be agents of verbs and abstract referents to be patients of verbs. Thus, the verb form in example no. 3 is unambiguously a past participle WHIZ deletion construction, and in example nos. 1 and 2 the verb forms are most straightforwardly past tense active verbs, although they can also be past participle heads of WHIZ deletion constructions. To a computer program without access to semantic information, however, there is no difference between these constructions, and thus at least one of the two cases will be tagged incorrectly. Similar problems were found in attempting to disambiguate the other functions of present and past participial forms; as a result, all participial forms were checked by hand.

Spot checks of the tagged texts indicate that the accuracy of the tagging program is quite good. To provide a quantitative assessment of the accuracy, after the hand-editing described above, I examined the tags in twelve randomly selected 100-word passages: three from each of conversation, prepared speeches, general fiction, and academic prose. (The sample output in Table II.1 is taken from one of these general fiction passages.) Out of the 1,200 words examined, five items were incorrectly tagged and 56 items were left untagged (twelve of these were in a single sample). Translating these figures into percentages, the program incorrectly tagged less than one per cent of the items in these text samples, and left untagged approximately five per cent. It is not possible to claim that these twelve samples are representative of the entire corpus used in the study, but even a conservative interpretation of these results indicates that the tagging program (plus editing of participial forms, etc.) achieves coverage of 90 per cent or better.

A general survey of the corpus and analysis of the specific mistags and untagged items in the twelve sample texts indicates that the errors are relatively idiosyncratic or specialized; that there is no serious skewing of results in one genre or another; and that the major features used in the present study are identified with a very high accuracy. The incorrectly tagged items in the sample texts are distributed one in each of five text samples: one of the conversation samples, two of the fiction samples, and two of the academic prose samples. In the conversational mistag, the program failed to recognize *one* in the form *one's* as a pronoun, and instead tagged the form as a possessive noun on the basis of the *'s* ending. In one of the academic prose mistags, the item *a* was tagged as an article when in fact it was simply a label (*classes a and b*). The remaining three mistags are more problematic. In two of them (from two of the fictional samples), a *that* following a noun is incorrectly classified as a relative pronoun. In one

Table II.1 *Sample output from the tagging program, taken from general fiction (genre 'K'), text no. 13 (*** marks incorrectly tagged items)*

k 13	his	p3p				
k 13	short		adj			
k 13	speech		nn			
k 13	which		whp			
k 13	followed	vbn	vbd			
k 13	,					
k 13	showed	vbn	vbd	prv	v	
k 13	clearly		adv	rb		
k 13	where		who			
k 13	his	p3p				
k 13	sympathies		nns			
k 13	lay	vbn	vbd			
k 13	.		clp			
k 13	the		art			
k 13	burgomaster's		n			
k 13	question		n	nom		
k 13	had		vbd	hv	aux	
k 13	come	prf	vbn		v	
k 13	as					
k 13	no		qan	neg		
k 13	surprise		nn			
k 13	to		pp			
k 13	him	p3o				
k 13	;		clp			
k 13	he	p3s				
k 13	had		vbd	hv	aux	
k 13	been	prf	vbn	be	aux	
k 13	warned	psv	vbn	pub	v	
k 13	before		adv	rb		
k 13	the		art			
k 13	reception		n	nom		
k 13	that		tht	rel		***
k 13	he	p3s				
k 13	would		prd	mod	aux	
k 13	be		vb	be	aux	
k 13	challenged	psv	vbn		v	
k 13	,					
k 13	and		hand			
k 13	vicky		np			
k 13	,					
k 13	who		whp			
k 13	was		vbd	be	v	

Table II.1 *(cont.)*

k 13	with		pp		
k 13	him	p3o			
k 13	,				
k 13	had		vbd	hv	aux
k 13	implored	prf	vbn		v
k 13	him	3po			
k 13	to		inf		
k 13	make		vb		
k 13	his	p3p			
k 13	position		n	nom	
k 13	plain		adj		
k 13	.		clp		
k 13	they	p3s			
k 13	had		vbd	hv	v
k 13	their	p3p			
k 13	own		adj		
k 13	following	vbg	n		
k 13	,				
k 13	she	p3s			
k 13	argued	vbn	vbd	pub	
k 13	,				
k 13	though		sub	con	
k 13	it	it			
k 13	might		pos	mod	aux
k 13	be		vb	be	v
k 13	a		art		
k 13	minority		n	nom	
k 13	following	vbg	n		
k 13	,				
k 13	and		hand		
k 13	fritz		np		
k 13	owed	vbn	vbd		
k 13	it	it			
k 13	to		pp		
k 13	them	p3o			
k 13	to		inf		
k 13	show		vb	prv	
k 13	that		tht	thcl	
k 13	he	p3s			
k 13	was		vbd	be	aux
k 13	not	not			adv
k 13	involved	psv	vbn		v

case, the *that* is rather the head of a clefted clause, and in the other case, the *that* is the complementizer of a displaced *that*-clause (*he had been warned before the reception that* . . .; where *that* is complementizer to the verb *warned*). In both of these cases, the tagging program analyzed a NOUN + *that* sequence as a relative clause when in fact the *that* was associated with some other more distant entity. The final mistag is from another of the academic prose samples, in which a noun–verb ambiguity was incorrectly analyzed as a verb (*change* in the phrase *free energy change per mole*). None of these mistags represents a fundamental problem in the tagging program; rather, they all represent specialized ambiguities that cannot be readily disambiguated by an automated analysis.

The untagged items are similarly very specialized. A large number of these items are proper nouns that do not occur in the dictionary, because they do not occur in the Brown corpus. These include *Gibraltar, Pompidou, Duffield, Stoke Poges*, and *Gilliatt*; some of these items occur multiple times in a single sample. Other untagged items were archaic forms, unusual spellings, or British spellings, such as *thou, shouldest, wilful*, and *colour*. Some of the untagged items were simply uncommon nouns, such as *centurion, hominem, frigates, churchwarden, cricketers, gas-constant*, and *diabetics*. The program made no attempt to tag numerals and dates (e.g., 1959, 25, 54, etc.), because they are not needed to identify any of the relevant linguistic features. For the reasons noted above, occurrences of *as* were not tagged. Finally, a few of the untagged items are due to ambiguities that could not be resolved. Three occurrences of *it's* could not be resolved between *it has* and *it is* and so were tagged only as *it* plus auxiliary. Three occurrences of *this* or *that* were tagged as demonstratives but not identified as pronominal in their function. The sequence *appropriate values*, in which both items are ambiguous as to their class, was not resolved and both items were left untagged.

Overall, these results indicate that the tagging program is quite accurate. First, there are very few mistags; the majority of 'errors' are untagged items, which do not introduce misleading analyses, and even untagged items are relatively uncommon. Secondly, there is no serious skewing of mistags in any particular genre so that the results are accurate in relative terms; that is, the results enable accurate comparisons across texts because the same word types are left untagged in all texts. Finally, the few mistags and untagged items that do exist are of a very specialized or idiosyncratic nature, and often these items have no bearing on the linguistic features counted for the analysis of textual dimensions. The tagged texts produced by this program thus provide a good basis for the automatic identification of linguistic features. As discussed in Chapter 4, only the potentially important linguistic features are actually counted, those features that have been associated with particular communicative functions in previous research. The grammatical tags on each word enable identification of these linguistic features, and we turn now to a discussion of the particular algorithm used for each feature and the communicative functions that have been associated with each feature in previous research.

II.3   Discussion of the individual linguistic features

To this point, the linguistic features used in the present study have been discussed in only general terms. The earlier part of this appendix indicates the algorithms for their automatic identification but does not present specific details. Similarly, Chapters 2 and 4 indicate some of the functions that have been associated with linguistic features but present no details about particular features. This section provides these additional details; for each linguistic feature, this section gives the algorithm for its automatic identification, a description of the functions associated with the feature, and a list of previous studies that discuss the feature in functional terms or as a marker of situational differences among genres. The algorithms are given so that interested readers can determine exactly which forms were counted as instances of each feature. The functional discussion is given as the background to the dimension interpretations in Chapters 6–8.

Many linguistic features are included in the present study that are not used in my earlier investigations of speech and writing (Biber 1984, 1986a). Most of these features could not be identified without the use of a tagging program and large-scale dictionary. The additional features include: gerunds, total other nouns, existential *there*, *be* as main verb, *that* adjective complements, present and past participial clauses, relativization on different positions and *that* versus WH relatives, WHIZ deletion constructions, subclasses of adverbial subordination (causative, concessive), participial adjectives, attributive versus predicative adjectives, phrasal and independent clause coordination, synthetic and analytic negation, sub-classes of modals (possibility, necessity, and predictive), verb sub-classes (public, private, and suasive), demonstrative pronouns, *any* and *none* as pronouns, and demonstratives. In addition, some linguistic features that were included in earlier studies have been excluded here, because I determined that they cannot be accurately identified by automatic analysis in spoken texts where there is no sentence or clause punctuation. Excluded features include: *it*-clefts, WH-clefts, fronted *that*-clauses, fronted prepositional phrases, relative pronoun deletions, and direct questions. In all, the 67 linguistic features listed in

Table 4.4 were counted. These features include all features that: (1) have been assigned distinctive functions by previous research, and (2) can be automatically identified in spoken and written texts. Each of these features is discussed in turn here.

The following notation is used in the descriptions of the algorithms:

+: used to separate constituents
(): marks optional constituents
/: marks disjunctive options
xxx: stands for any word
#: marks a word boundary
T#: marks a 'tone unit' boundary, as defined in Quirk *et al.* (1972: 937–8) for use in the London–Lund corpus.[1]
DO: *do, does, did, don't, doesn't, didn't, doing, done*
HAVE: *have, has, had, having, -'ve#, -'d#, haven't, hasn't, hadn't*
BE: *am, is, are, was, were, being, been -'m#, -'re#, isn't, aren't, wasn't, weren't*
MODAL: *can, may, shall, will, -'ll#, could, might, should, would, must, can't, won't, couldn't, mightn't, shouldn't, wouldn't, mustn't*
AUX: MODAL/DO/HAVE/BE/-'s
SUBJPRO: *I, we, he, she, they* (plus contracted forms)
OBJPRO: *me, us, him, them* (plus contracted forms)
POSSPRO: *my, our, your, his, their, its* (plus contracted forms)
REFLEXPRO: *myself, ourselves, himself, themselves, herself, yourself, yourselves, itself*
PRO: SUBJPRO/OBJPRO/POSSPRO/REFLEXPRO/*you/her/it*
PREP: prepositions (e.g. *at, among* – see no. 39)
CONJ: conjuncts (e.g. *furthermore, therefore* – see no. 45)
ADV: adverbs (see no. 42)
ADJ: adjectives (see nos. 40, 41)
N: nouns (see nos. 14, 15, 16)
VBN: any past tense or irregular past participial verb
VBG: *-ing* form of verb
VB: base form of verb
VBZ: third person, present tense form of verb
PUB: 'public' verbs (see no. 55)
PRV: 'private' verbs (see no. 56)
SUA: 'suasive' verbs (see no. 57)
V: any verb

In general, a tone unit corresponds to a simple sentence, unless: (1) it begins with a phrasal or clausal adverbial element, (2) it contains a medial phrase or clause (such as a non-restrictive relative clause), (3) it contains a vocative, disjunct, or polysyllabic conjunct, (4) it has a clause or long noun phrase as subject, (5) it contains clausal coordination. In these cases, the structure in question often constitutes an additional tone unit.

WHP: WH pronouns – *who, whom, whose, which*
WHO: other WH words – *what, where, when, how, whether, why, whoever, whomever, whichever, wherever, whenever, whatever, however*
ART: articles – *a, an, the, (dhi)*
DEM: demonstratives – *this, that, these, those*
QUAN: quantifiers – *each, all, every, many, much, few, several, some, any*
NUM: numerals – *one . . . twenty, hundred, thousand*
DET: ART/DEM/QUAN/NUM
ORD: ordinal numerals – *first . . . tenth*
QUANPRO: quantifier pronouns – *everybody, somebody, anybody, everyone, someone, anyone, everything, something, anything*
TITLE: address titles
CL-P: clause punctuation ('.', '!', '?', ':', ';', '–')
ALL-P: all punctuation (CL-P plus ',')

In the following discussion, the 67 linguistic features have been grouped into sixteen major categories: (A) tense and aspect markers, (B) place and time adverbials, (C) pronouns and pro-verbs, (D) questions, (E) nominal forms, (F) passives, (G) stative forms, (H) subordination features, (I) adjectives and adverbs, (J) lexical specificity, (K) specialized lexical classes, (L) modals, (M) specialized verb classes, (N) reduced or dispreferred forms, (O) coordination, and (P) negation. The order of discussion here follows that of Tables 4.4 and 4.5.

(A) TENSE AND ASPECT MARKERS (nos. 1–3)
1. **past tense**
Any past tense form that occurs in the dictionary, or any word not otherwise identified that is longer than six letters and ends in *ed♯*. Past tense forms have been edited by hand to distinguish between those forms with past participial functions and those with past tense functions.

Past tense forms are usually taken as the primary surface marker of narrative. Schiffrin (1981) describes alternations between past tense forms and the historical present within narratives. Studies that use frequency counts of past tense verbs in register comparisons include Blankenship (1962), Marckworth and Baker (1974), Biber (1986a).
2. **perfect aspect**
(a) HAVE + (ADV) + (ADV) + VBN
(b) HAVE + N/PRO + VBN (questions)
(includes contracted forms of HAVE)
Perfect aspect forms mark actions in past time with 'current relevance' (Quirk *et al.* 1985:189ff). They have been associated with narrative/descriptive texts and with certain types of academic writing

(Feigenbaum 1978). Biber (1986a) and Marckworth and Baker (1974) find that perfect aspect forms co-occur frequently with past tense forms as markers of narrative.

3. **present tense**
All VB (base form) or VBZ (third person singular present) verb forms in the dictionary, excluding infinitives.

Present tense verbs deal with topics and actions of immediate relevance. They can also be used in academic styles to focus on the information being presented and remove focus from any temporal sequencing. In contrast, use of the past tense places focus on the temporal sequence, even when used for informational purposes. Ochs (1979) associates the more ready use of present tense forms in unplanned speech styles with the fact that they are acquired before past or future tense forms in English. Weber (1985) notes that cognitive verbs (verbs describing the speaker's mental processes) typically occur in the present tense. Biber (1986a) and Grabe (1986) describe present tense forms as a marker of immediate, as opposed to removed, situations.

(B) PLACE AND TIME ADVERBIALS (nos. 4–5)
mark direct reference to the physical and temporal context of the text, or in the case of fiction, to the text-internal physical and temporal world. Chafe and Danielewicz (1986) include place and time adverbials as markers of involvement. Biber (1986a) interprets their distribution as marking situated, as opposed to abstract, textual content.

4. **place adverbials**
aboard, above, abroad, across, ahead, alongside, around, ashore, astern, away, behind, below, beneath, beside, downhill, downstairs, downstream, east, far, hereabouts, indoors, inland, inshore, inside, locally, near, nearby, north, nowhere, outdoors, outside, overboard, overland, overseas, south, underfoot, underground, underneath, uphill, upstairs, upstream, west

This list is taken from Quirk *et al.* (1985:514ff). Items with other major functions, for example, *in, on*, which often mark logical relations in a text, have been excluded from the list.

5. **time adverbials**
afterwards, again, earlier, early, eventually, formerly, immediately, initially, instantly, late, lately, later, momentarily, now, nowadays, once, originally, presently, previously, recently, shortly, simultaneously, soon, subsequently, today, tomorrow, tonight, yesterday

This list is taken from Quirk *et al.* (1985:526ff). Items with other major functions, for example, *last, next*, which often mark logical relations within a text, have been excluded from the list.

(C) PRONOUNS AND PRO-VERBS (nos. 6–12)

Some studies have grouped all pronominal forms together as a single category which is interpreted as marking a relatively low informational load, a lesser precision in referential identification, or a less formal style (e.g., Kroch and Hindle 1982; Brainerd 1972). Other studies have grouped all personal pronouns into a single category, and interpret that category as marking interpersonal focus (Carroll 1960; Poole 1973; Poole and Field 1976). In the present analysis, I separate personal and impersonal pronominal forms, as well as each of the persons within the personal pronouns.

(C1) PERSONAL PRONOUNS

6. **first person pronouns**

I, me, we, us, my, our, myself, ourselves
(plus contracted forms)

First person pronouns have been treated as markers of ego-involvement in a text. They indicate an interpersonal focus and a generally involved style (Chafe 1982, 1985). Weber (1985) points out that the subjects of cognitive verbs are usually first person pronouns, indicating that discussion of mental processes is a personal matter often associated with high ego-involvement. Numerous studies have used first person pronouns for comparison of spoken and written registers (Poole 1973; Poole and Field 1976; Blankenship 1974; Hu 1984; Chafe and Danielewicz 1986; Biber 1986a).

7. **second person pronouns**

you, your, yourself, yourselves (plus contracted forms)

Second person pronouns require a specific addressee and indicate a high degree of involvement with that addressee (Chafe 1985). They have been used as a marker of register differences by Hu (1984), Finegan (1982), and Biber (1986a).

8. **third person personal pronouns**

she, he, they, her, him, them, his, their, himself, herself, themselves (plus contracted forms)

Third person personal pronouns mark relatively inexact reference to persons outside of the immediate interaction. They have been used in register comparisons by Poole and Field (1976) and Hu (1984). Biber (1986a) finds that third person pronouns co-occur frequently with past tense and perfect aspect forms, as a marker of narrative, reported (versus immediate) styles.

(C2) IMPERSONAL PRONOUNS

9. **pronoun *it***

It is the most generalized pronoun, since it can stand for referents ranging from animate beings to abstract concepts. This pronoun can be substituted for nouns, phrases, or whole clauses. Chafe and Danielewicz (1986) and Biber (1986a) treat a frequent use of this pronoun as marking a relatively inexplicit lexical content due to strict time constraints and a non-informational focus. Kroch and Hindle (1982) associate greater generalized pronoun use with the limited amounts of information that can be produced and comprehended in typical spoken situations.

10. **demonstrative pronouns** (e.g., *this is ridiculous*)
(a) *that/this/these/those* + V/AUX/CL-P/T♯/WHP/*and*
     (where *that* is not a relative pronoun)
(b) *that's*
(c) *T♯* + *that*
     (*that* in this last context was edited by hand to distinguish among demonstrative pronouns, relative pronouns, complementizers, etc.)

Demonstrative pronouns can refer to an entity outside the text, an exophoric referent, or to a previous referent in the text itself. In the latter case, it can refer to a specific nominal entity or to an inexplicit, often abstract, concept (e.g., *this shows . . .*). Chafe (1985; Chafe and Danielewicz 1986) characterizes those demonstrative pronouns that are used without nominal referents as errors typically found in speech due to faster production and the lack of editing. Demonstrative pronouns have also been used for register comparisons by Carroll (1960) and Hu (1984).

11. **indefinite pronouns**
anybody, anyone, anything, everybody, everyone, everything, nobody, none, nothing, nowhere, somebody, someone, something (Quirk *et al.* 1985:376ff)

These forms have not been used frequently for register comparison. They are included here as markers of generalized pronominal reference, in a similar way to *it* and the demonstrative pronouns.

(C3) PRO-VERBS
12. **pro-verb *do*** (e.g., *the cat did it*)
DO when NOT in the following constructions:
DO + (ADV) + V   (DO as auxiliary)
ALL-P/T♯/WHP + DO   (DO as question)

This feature was included in Biber (1986a) as a marker of register differences. *Do* as pro-verb substitutes for an entire clause, reducing the informational density of a text and indicating a lesser informational focus, due to processing constraints or a higher concern with interpersonal matters.

(D) QUESTIONS (no. 13)

Questions, like second person pronouns, indicate a concern with interpersonal functions and involvement with the addressee (Marckworth and Baker 1974; Biber 1986a). *Yes/no* questions were excluded from the present analysis because they could not be accurately identified by automatic analysis in formal spoken genres, where every phrase tends to be a separate intonation unit; that is, many intonation units begin with an auxiliary and therefore are identical in form to direct questions.

13. **direct WH-questions**

CL-P/T♯ + WHO + AUX

(where AUX is not part of a contracted form)

(E) NOMINAL FORMS (nos. 14–16)

The overall nominal characterization of a text and the distinction between nominal and verbal styles is identified as one of the most fundamental distinctions among registers by Wells (1960) and Brown and Fraser (1979). A high nominal content in a text indicates a high (abstract) informational focus, as opposed to primarily interpersonal or narrative foci. Nominalizations, including gerunds, have particularly been taken as markers of conceptual abstractness.

14. **nominalizations**

All words ending in *-tion*♯, *-ment*♯, *-ness*♯, or *-ity*♯ (plus plural forms).

Nominalizations have been used in many register studies. Chafe (1982, 1985, and Danielewicz 1986) focuses on their use to expand idea units and integrate information into fewer words. Biber (1986a) finds that they tend to co-occur with passive constructions and prepositions and thus interprets their function as conveying highly abstract (as opposed to situated) information. Janda (1985) shows that nominalizations are used during note-taking to reduce full sentences to more compact and efficient series of noun phrases. Other references: Carroll (1960), DeVito (1967), Marckworth and Baker (1974), Grabe (1984a).

15. **gerunds**

All participle forms serving nominal functions – these are edited by hand.

Gerunds (or verbal nouns) are verbal forms serving nominal functions. As such, they are closely related to nominalizations in their functions. Some researchers (e.g., Chafe 1982) do not distinguish among the different participial functions, treating gerunds, participial adjectives (nos. 40–1), and participial clauses (nos. 25–8) as a single feature. In the present study, these functions are treated separately. Studies that have used gerunds as a distinguishing marker of register are Carroll (1960) and O'Donnell (1974).

16. **total other nouns**
All nouns included in the dictionary, excluding those forms counted as
nominalizations or gerunds.

This count provides an overall nominal assessment of a text.
Nominalizations and gerunds are excluded from the total noun count
so that the three features will be statistically independent. In addition
to Wells (1960), overall noun counts have been used by Carroll (1960)
and Blankenship (1974).

(F) PASSIVES (nos. 17–18)
Passives have been taken as one of the most important surface markers
of the decontextualized or detached style that stereotypically characterizes writing. In passive constructions, the agent is demoted or
dropped altogether, resulting in a static, more abstract presentation of
information. Passives are also used for thematic purposes (Thompson
1982; Finegan 1982; Weiner and Labov 1983; Janda 1985). From this
perspective, agentless passives are used when the agent does not have a
salient role in the discourse; *by*-passives are used when the
patient is more closely related to the discourse theme than the patient.
Studies that have used passives for register comparisons include
Carroll (1960), Blankenship (1962), Poole (1973), Poole and Field
(1976), O'Donnell (1974), Marckworth and Baker (1974), Ochs
(1979), Brown and Yule (1983), Young (1985), Chafe (1982, 1985),
Chafe and Danielewicz (1986), Biber (1986a), and Grabe (1984a).
17. **agentless passives**   18. ***by*-passives***
(a) BE + (ADV) + (ADV) + VBN + (*by*)**
(b) BE + N/PRO + VBN + (*by*)**   (question form)
(** no. 18 with the *by*-phrase)

(G) STATIVE FORMS (nos. 19–20)
Only a few studies have used stative forms for register comparisons.
These forms might be considered as markers of the static, informational style common in writing, since they preclude the presence of an
active verb. Conversely, they can be considered as non-complex
constructions with a reduced informational load, and therefore might
be expected to be more characteristic of spoken styles. Kroch and
Hindle (1982) analyze existential *there* as being used to introduce a new
entity while adding a minimum of other information. Janda (1985)
notes that stative or predicative constructions (X *be* Y) are used
frequently in note-taking, although the *be* itself is often dropped.
Predicative constructions with *be*-ellipsis are also common in sports
announcer talk (Ferguson 1983). These predicative constructions
might be characterized as fragmented, because they are typically

alternatives to more integrated attributive constructions (e.g., *the house is big* versus *the big house*). *Be* as main verb is used for register comparisons by Carroll (1960) and Marckworth and Baker (1974).

19. ***be* as main verb**
BE + DET/POSSPRO/TITLE/PREP/ADJ
20. **existential *there*** (e.g., *there are several explanations* . . .)
(a) *there* + (xxx) + BE
(b) *there's*

(H) SUBORDINATION (nos. 21–38)

Subordination has perhaps been the most discussed linguistic feature used for register comparisons. It has generally been taken as an index of structural complexity and therefore supposed to be more commonly used in typical writing than typical speech. Some researchers, though, have found higher use of subordination in speech than writing (e.g., Poole and Field 1976). Halliday (1979) claims that even conversational speech has more subordination than written styles, because the two modes have different types of complexities: spoken language, because it is created and perceived as an on-going process, is characterized by 'an intricacy of movement [and by] complex sentence structures with low lexical density (more clauses, but fewer high-content words per clause)'; written language, in which the text is created and perceived as an object, is characterized by 'a denseness of matter [and by] simple sentence structures with high lexical density (more high-content words per clause, but fewer clauses)'.

Thompson (1983, 1984, 1985; Thompson and Longacre 1985; Ford and Thompson to appear) has carried out some of the most careful research into the discourse functions of subordination. She distinguishes between dependent clauses (complementation and relative clauses) and other types of subordination (e.g., adverbial clauses) that function to frame discourse information in different ways. Her studies have focused on the discourse functions of detached participial clauses, adverbial clauses in general, purpose clauses, and conditional clauses (see below). In all of these studies, Thompson emphasizes that subordination is not a unified construct, that different types of structural dependency have different discourse functions, and that particular subordination features are therefore used to different degrees in different types of discourse.

Beaman (1984) and Biber (1986a) also find that different subordination forms are distributed differently. Based on an analysis of spoken and written narratives, Beaman observes that there are more finite nominal clauses (*that*-clauses and WH-clauses) in speech and more non-finite nominal clauses (infinitives and participial clauses) in writing. She also discusses the distribution of relative and adverbial clauses in these texts (see below). In my own earlier studies, I find that *that*-clauses, WH-clauses, and adverbial subordinators co-occur frequently with interpersonal and reduced-content features such as first and second person pronouns, questions, contractions, hedges, and emphatics. These types of subordination occur frequently in spoken genres, both interactional (conversation) and informational (speeches), but they occur relatively infrequently in informational written genres. Relative clauses and infinitive were found to have a separate distribution from the other types of subordination, but they did not form a strong enough co-occurrence pattern for interpretation. These same features are discussed from the perspective of discourse complexity in Finegan and Biber (1986b).

These studies by Thompson and Beaman, and my own earlier studies, all show that different types of subordination function in different ways. Based on these analyses, I have divided the subordination features used in the present study into four sub-classes: complementation (H1), participial forms (H2), relative clauses (H3), and adverbial clauses (H4). Each of these is now discussed in turn.

(H1) COMPLEMENTATION (nos. 21–4)
21.   ***that* verb complements** (e.g., *I said that he went*)
(a) *and/nor/but/or/also*/ALL-P + *that* +
DET/PRO/*there*/plural noun/proper noun/TITLE
(these are *that*-clauses in clause-initial positions)
(b) PUB/PRV/SUA/SEEM/APPEAR + *that* + xxx
(where xxx is NOT: V/AUX/CL-P/T#/*and*)
   (*that*-clauses as complements to verbs which are not included in the above verb classes are not counted – see Quirk *et al.* 1985:1179ff.)
(c) PUB/PRV/SUA + PREP + xxx + N + *that*
(where xxx is any number of words, but NOT = N)
   (This algorithm allows an intervening prepositional phrase between a verb and its complement.)
(d) T# + *that*
(This algorithm applies only to spoken texts. Forms in this context are checked by hand, to distinguish among *that* complements, relatives, demonstrative pronouns and subordinators.)
   Chafe (1982, 1985) identifies *that*-complements as one of the indices of integration, used for idea-unit expansion in typical writing. Ochs (1979) describes complementation as a relatively complex construction used to a greater extent in planned than unplanned discourse. In contrast, Beaman (1984) finds more *that* complementation in her

spoken than written narratives. Biber (1986a) finds that *that*-complements co-occur frequently with interactive features such as first and second person pronouns and questions, and that all of these features are more common in spoken than written genres. In that paper and in Finegan and Biber (1986b), this distribution is interpreted in a similar way to Halliday's characterization: that this type of structural complexity is used in typical speech, where there is little opportunity for careful production or revision, while other types of linguistic complexity, notably lexical variety and density, are used in typical academic writing, which provides considerable opportunity for production and revision.

Other studies that have used *that*-complements for register comparisons include Carroll (1960), O'Donnell (1974), Frawley (1982), and Weber (1985). Winter (1982) notes that both verb and adjective *that*-complements provide a way to talk about the information in the dependent clause, with the speaker's evaluation (commitment, etc.) being given in the main clause and the propositional information in the *that*-clause.

Some verb complements do not have an overt complementizer (e.g., *I think he went*); these are counted as a separate feature (no. 60).

22. ***that* adjective complements** (e.g., *I'm glad that you like it*)
ADJ + (T♯) + *that*
(complements across intonation boundaries were edited by hand)

Most studies of *that*-clauses consider only verb complements. Winter (1982) points out, however, that verb and adjective complements seem to have similar discourse functions, and so both should be important for register comparisons. Because there is no a priori way to know if *that* verb and adjective complements are distributed in the same way among genres, they are included as separate features here. Householder (1964) has compiled a list of adjectives that occur before *that*-clauses; Quirk *et al.* (1985:1222–5) give a grammatical and discourse description of these constructions.

23. **WH-clauses** (e.g., *I believed what he told me*)
PUB/PRV/SUA + WHP/WHO + xxx
(where xxx is NOT = AUX – this excludes WH questions)

This algorithm captures only those WH clauses that occur as object complements to the restricted verb classes described below in nos. 55–7; see Quirk *et al.* 1985:1184–5. Other WH clauses could not be identified reliably by automatic analysis and so were not counted.

Similar to *that*-clauses, WH-clauses are complements to verbs. Chafe (1985) analyzes them as being used for idea unit expansion, and thus they should be more frequent in typical writing. Beaman (1984) did not find WH-clauses in her written narratives; she writes that they resemble questions and serve interpersonal functions in discourse, accounting for their use in spoken but not written narratives. Winter (1982) notes that WH complements provide a way to talk about questions in the same way that *that*-complements provide a way to talk about statements, that is, with the speaker's evaluation, commitment, etc. provided in the main clause. Biber (1986a) finds WH-clauses to be distributed in a similar pattern to *that*-clauses, both of which co-occur frequently with interpersonal features such as first and second person pronouns and questions.

24. **infinitives**

to + (ADV) + VB

Infinitives are the final form of complementation to be included in the present study. The algorithm above groups together all infinitival forms: complements to nouns, adjectives, and verbs, as well as 'purpose' adverbial clauses (see below). The distribution and discourse functions of infinitives seem to be less marked than that of other types of subordination. Chafe (1982, 1985) includes infinitives as one of the devices used to achieve integration and idea-unit expansion in typical writing. Beaman (1984) finds that infinitives co-occur with other non-finite nominal clauses (especially participial clauses), and that they are more common in written than spoken narratives. Biber (1986a) finds a weak co-occurrence relationship between infinitives and relative clauses. Finally, Thompson (1985) carefully distinguishes between those infinitives functioning as complements and those functioning as adverbial purpose clauses, and she analyzes the thematic discourse functions of the latter in some detail. Although this is an important functional distinction, it is not made here because of the limitations of the automatic analysis. Other references include: Carroll (1960), O'Donnell (1974), and Dubuisson *et al.* (1983).

(H2) PARTICIPIAL FORMS (nos. 25-8)

Participles are among the most difficult forms to analyze. They can function as nouns, adjectives, or verbs, and within their use as verbs, they can function as main verbs (present progressive, perfect, or passive), complement clauses, adjectival clauses, or adverbial clauses. Some studies do not distinguish among these functions, counting all participial forms (excluding main verbs) as a single feature (e.g., Chafe 1982; Beaman 1984). Many studies also do not distinguish between present and past participial clauses, or they count only present participle forms. In the present analysis, each of the different grammatical functions of participles is treated as a separate linguistic feature, since these grammatical functions are likely to be associated with different discourse functions.

Studies that consider participles typically find that they occur more frequently in writing than in speech; the usual interpretation associated with this distribution is that participles are used for integration or structural elaboration. References include Carroll (1960), O'Donnell (1974), Winter (1982), Chafe (1985), Young (1985), Chafe and Danielewicz (1986), Bäcklund (1986), Quirk *et al.* (1985).

Thompson (1983) distinguishes syntactically detached participial clauses (e.g., *Stuffing his mouth with cookies, Joe ran out the door*) from other participial functions. She shows how these clauses are used for depictive functions, that is, for discourse that describes by creating an image. No. 25 and no. 26 below are algorithms for detached participial clauses (present and past). These forms were edited by hand to exclude participial forms not having an adverbial function. Participial clauses functioning as reduced relatives, also known as WHIZ deletions, are treated separately (nos. 27 and 28). Janda (1985) notes the use of these forms in note-taking to replace full relative clauses, apparently because they are more compact and integrated and therefore well-suited to the production of highly informational discourse under severe time constraints. In the present analysis, these forms were also edited by hand to distinguish between subordinate clause functions and other functions; in particular, past participles following a noun can represent either a simple past tense form or the head of a reduced relative clause, and these forms thus needed to be checked by hand. Finally, participles functioning as nouns and adjectives were distinguished (nos. 15 and 40–1 respectively); these forms were also edited by hand to verify their grammatical function.

25. present participial clauses
(e.g., *Stuffing his mouth with cookies, Joe ran out the door*)
T♯/ALL-P + VBG + PREP/DET/WHP/WHO/PRO/ADV
(these forms were edited by hand)

26. past participial clauses
(e.g., *Built in a single week, the house would stand for fifty years.*)
T♯/ALL-P + VBN + PREP/ADV
(these forms were edited by hand)

27. past participial WHIZ deletion relatives
(e.g., *the solution produced by this process*)
N/QUANPRO + VBN + PREP/BE/ADV
(these forms were edited by hand)

28. present participial WHIZ deletion relatives
(e.g., *the event causing this decline is . . .*)
N + VBG
(these forms were edited by hand)

(H3) RELATIVES (nos. 29–34)

Relative clauses have been used frequently as a marker of register differences. Relatives provide a way to talk about nouns, either for identification or simply to provide additional information (Winter 1982; Beaman 1984). Ochs (1979) notes that referents are marked differently in planned and unplanned discourse: simple determiners are preferred in unplanned discourse while relative clauses are used for more exact and explicit reference in planned discourse. Chafe (1982, 1985) states that relative clauses are also used as a device for integration and idea unit expansion. Other references include Carroll (1960), Poole (1973), Poole and Field (1976), O'Donnell (1974), Kroll (1977), Frawley (1982), Dubuisson *et al.* (1983), Biber (1986a), and Grabe (1984a).

In general, these studies find that relative clauses occur more frequently in writing than in speech. Some studies, however, do not treat all relative clauses as a single feature and consequently do not find a uniform distribution. Kroch and Hindle (1982) and Beaman (1984) provide two of the fullest discussions. Beaman analyzes *that* relatives separately from WH relatives and finds more *that* relatives in her spoken narratives but more WH relatives in her written narratives; further, she finds more relativization on subject position in her spoken narratives versus more relativization on object positions in her written narratives. In contrast, Kroch and Hindle find more relativization on subject position in their written texts and more relativization on object position in their spoken texts. They attribute this to a greater use of pronouns in subject position in speech, making this position unavailable for relativization. Both of these studies also analyze pied-piping constructions separately, finding more in written than in spoken texts. In the present analysis, I separate *that* from WH relatives, and relativization on subject position from relativization on object position. Pied-piping constructions are also treated separately.

29.   *that* relative clauses on subject position
(e.g., *the dog that bit me*)
N + (T#) + *that* + (ADV) + AUX/V
(*that* relatives across intonation boundaries are identified by hand.)

30.   *that* relative clauses on object position
(e.g., *the dog that I saw*)
N + (T#) + *that* + DET / SUBJPRO / POSSPRO / *it* / ADJ / plural noun / proper noun / possessive noun / TITLE
(This algorithm does not distinguish between *that* complements to nouns and true relative clauses.)

(In spoken texts, *that* relatives sometimes span two intonation units; these are identified by hand.)

31. **WH relative clauses on subject position**
(e.g., *the man who likes popcorn*)
xxx + yyy + N + WHP + (ADV) + AUX/V
(where xxx is NOT any form of the verbs ASK or TELL; to exclude indirect WH questions like *Tom asked the man who went to the store*)

32. **WH relative clauses on object positions**
(e.g., *the man who Sally likes*)
xxx + yyy + N + WHP + zzz
(where xxx is NOT any form of the verbs ASK or TELL, to exclude indirect WH questions, and zzz is not ADV, AUX or V, to exclude relativization on subject position)

33. **pied-piping relative clauses**
(e.g., *the manner in which he was told*)
PREP + WHP

34. **sentence relatives**
(e.g., *Bob likes fried mangoes, which is the most disgusting thing I've ever heard of*)
T#/, + *which*
(These forms are edited by hand to exclude non-restrictive relative clauses.)

Sentence relatives do not have a nominal antecedent, referring instead to the entire predication of a clause (Quirk *et al.* 1985:1118–20). They function as a type of comment clause, and they are not used for identificatory functions in the way that other relative clauses are. A preliminary analysis of texts suggested that these constructions were considerably more frequent in certain spoken genres than in typical writing, and they are therefore included here as a separate feature.

(H4) ADVERBIAL CLAUSES (nos. 35–8)
Adverbial clauses appear to be an important device for indicating informational relations in a text. Overall, Thompson (1984) and Biber (1986a) find more adverbial clauses in speech than in writing. Several studies, though, separate preposed from postposed adverbial clauses, and find that these two types have different scopes, functioning to mark global versus local topics, and that they have different distributions (Winter 1982; Chafe 1984a; Thompson 1985; Thompson and Longacre 1985; Ford and Thompson 1986). Other references include Carroll (1960), O'Donnell (1974), Marckworth and Baker (1974), Beaman (1984), Chafe (1985), Altenberg (1984, 1986), and Grabe (1984a).

There are several subclasses of adverbial clauses, including condition, reason/cause, purpose, comparison, and concession (Quirk *et al.* 1985:1077–18; Tottie 1986; Smith and Frawley 1983). The most common types, causative, concessive, and conditional adverbials, can be identified unambiguously by machine (nos. 35–7); the other subordinators are grouped together as a general category (no. 38).

35. causative adverbial subordinators: *because*

Because is the only subordinator to function unambiguously as a causative adverbial. Other forms, such as *as*, *for*, and *since*, can have a range of functions, including causative. Most researchers find more causative adverbials in speech (Beaman 1984; Tottie 1986), although the functional reasons for this distribution are not clear. Tottie (1986) and Altenberg (1984) both provide detailed analyses of these subordination constructions. For example, Tottie notes that while there is more causative subordination overall in speech, the form *as* is used as a causative subordinator more in writing. Other references: Smith and Frawley (1983), Schiffrin (1985b).

36. concessive adverbial subordinators: *although, though*

Following a general pattern for adverbial clauses, concessive adverbials can also be used for framing purposes or to introduce background information, and they have different functions in pre- and post-posed positions (McClure and Geva 1983; Altenberg 1986). Both Altenberg and Tottie (1986) find more concessive subordination overall in writing.

37. conditional adverbial subordinators: *if, unless*

Conditional clauses are also used for discourse framing and have differing functions when they are in pre- or post-posed position (Ford and Thompson 1986). Finegan (1982) finds a very frequent use of conditional clauses in legal wills, due to the focus on the possible conditions existing when the will is executed. Several researchers have found more conditional clauses in speech than in writing (Beaman 1984; Tottie 1986; Biber 1986a; Ford and Thompson 1986), but the functional reasons for this distribution are not clear.

38. other adverbial subordinators: (having multiple functions)

since, while, whilst, whereupon, whereas, whereby, such that, so that xxx, such that xxx, inasmuch as, forasmuch as, insofar as, insomuch as, as long as, as soon as
(where xxx is NOT: N/ADJ)

(I1) PREPOSITIONAL PHRASES (no. 39)

39. total prepositional phrases

against, amid, amidst, among, amongst, at, besides, between, by, despite, during, except, for, from, in, into, minus, notwithstanding, of, off, on, onto, opposite, out, per, plus, pro, re, than, through, throughout, thru, to, toward, towards, upon, versus, via, with, within, without

This list of prepositions is taken from Quirk *et al.* (1985:665–7), excluding those lexical items that have some other primary function, such as place or time adverbial, conjunct, or subordinator (e.g., *down, after, as*).

Prepositions are an important device for packing high amounts of information into academic nominal discourse. Chafe (1982, 1985; and Danielewicz 1986) describes prepositions as a device for integrating information into idea units and expanding the amount of information contained within an idea unit. Biber (1986a) finds that prepositions tend to co-occur frequently with nominalizations and passives in academic prose, official documents, professional letters, and other informational types of written discourse. Other references include: Carroll (1960), Blankenship (1974), Marckworth and Baker (1974), and Dubuisson *et al.* (1983).

(I2) ADJECTIVES AND ADVERBS (nos. 40-2)
Adjectives and adverbs also seem to expand and elaborate the information presented in a text. Chafe (1982, 1985; and Danielewicz 1986) groups adjectives together with prepositional phrases and subordination constructions as devices used for idea unit integration and expansion. However, the descriptive kinds of information presented by adjectives and adverbs do not seem equivalent to the logical, nominal kinds of information often presented in prepositional phrases. In my earlier work (e.g., Biber 1986a), I find that prepositions, subordination features, adjectives, and adverbs are all distributed differently; for example, prepositional phrases occur frequently in formal, abstract styles, while many types of subordination occur frequently in highly interactive, unplanned discourse; adjectives and adverbs are distributed in yet other ways. All of these features elaborate information in one way or another, but the type of information being elaborated is apparently different in each case. Other relevant studies include: Carroll (1960), Drieman (1962), Poole (1973), Poole and Field (1976), Blankenship (1974), O'Donnell (1974), Marckworth and Baker (1974), Dubuisson *et al.* (1983), Tottie (1986), and Grabe (1984a).

Some studies distinguish between attributive and predicative adjectives (e.g., Drieman, O'Donnell, and Chafe). Attributive adjectives are highly integrative in their function, while predicative adjectives might be considered more fragmented. In addition, predicative adjectives are frequently used for marking stance (as heads of *that* or *to* complements; see Winter 1982). The present analysis distinguishes between attributive and predicative adjectives, including both participial and non-participial forms.

40. **attributive adjectives** (e.g., *the big horse*)

ADJ + ADJ/N

(+ any ADJ not identified as predicative – no. 41)

41. **predicative adjectives** (e.g., *the horse is big*)

(a) BE + ADJ + xxx

(where xxx is NOT ADJ, ADV, or N)

(b) BE + ADJ + ADV + xxx

(where xxx is NOT ADJ or N)

42. **total adverbs**

Any adverb form occurring in the dictionary, or any form that is longer than five letters and ends in *-ly*. The count for total adverbs excludes those adverbs counted as instances of hedges, amplifiers, downtoners, amplifiers, place adverbials, and time adverbials.

(J) LEXICAL SPECIFICITY (nos. 43–4)

Two measures of lexical specificity or diversity are commonly used: type/token ratio and word length. Unlike structural elaboration, differences in lexical specificity seem to truly correlate with the production differences between speaking and writing; the high levels of lexical diversity and specificity that are found in formal academic writing are apparently not possible in spoken texts due to the restrictions of on-line production (Chafe and Danielewicz 1986; Biber 1986a). Type/token ratio (the number of different words per text) was a favorite measure of psychologists and researchers in communication studying linguistic differences between speech and writing (Osgood 1960; Drieman 1962; Horowitz and Newman 1964; Gibson *et al*. 1966; Preston and Gardner 1967; Blankenship 1974). Longer words also convey more specific, specialized meanings than shorter ones; Zipf (1949) has shown that words become shorter as they are more frequently used and more general in meaning. Osgood, Drieman and Blankenship include measures of word length in their studies. These two features are found to co-occur frequently in planned written genres by Biber (1986a), and this distributional pattern is interpreted as marking a highly exact presentation of information, conveying maximum content in the fewest words.

43. **type/token ratio**

the number of different lexical items in a text, as a percentage

This feature is computed by counting the number of different lexical items that occur in the first 400 words of each text, and then dividing by four; texts shorter than 400 words are not included in the present analysis. In a preliminary version of the computer programs used here, I computed this feature by counting the number of different lexical items in a text, dividing by the total number of words in the text, and then multiplying by 100. If the texts in the analysis were all nearly the same length, these two methods of computing type/token ratio would give nearly equivalent results. If text length varies widely, however, these two methods will give quite different results, because the relation between the number of 'types' (different lexical items) and the total number of words in a text is not linear. That is, a large number of the different words used in the first 100 words of a text will be repeated in each successive 100-word chunk of text. The result is that each additional 100 words of text adds fewer and fewer additional types. In a comparison of very short texts and very long texts, the type/token ratio computed over the entire text will thus appear to be much higher in the short texts than in the long texts. To avoid this skewing, the present study computes the number of types in the first 400 words of each text, regardless of the total text length.

44. **word length**
mean length of the words in a text, in orthographic letters

(K) LEXICAL CLASSES (nos. 45–51)
45. **conjuncts**
alternatively, altogether, consequently, conversely, eg, e.g., else, furthermore, hence, however, i.e., instead, likewise, moreover, namely, nevertheless, nonetheless, notwithstanding, otherwise, rather, similarly, therefore, thus, viz.

  *in + comparison/contrast/particular/addition/conclusion/consequence
/sum/summary/any event/any case/other words*
  for + example/instance
  by + contrast/comparison
  as a + result/consequence
  on the + contrary/other hand
  ALL-P/T# + *that is/else/altogether* + T#/,
  ALL-P/T# + *rather* + T#/,/xxx
  (where xxx is NOT: ADJ/ADV)

Conjuncts explicitly mark logical relations between clauses, and as such they are important in discourse with a highly informational focus. Quirk *et al.* (1985:634–6) list the following functional classes of conjuncts: listing, summative, appositive, resultive, inferential, contrastive, and transitional. Despite their importance in marking logical relations, few register comparisons have analysed the distribution of conjuncts. Ochs (1979) notes that they are more formal and therefore more common in planned discourse than unplanned. Biber (1986a) finds that they co-occur frequently with prepositions, passives, and nominalizations in highly informational genres such as academic prose, official documents, and professional letters. Altenberg (1986) looks at concessive and antithetic conjuncts and finds that they are generally more common in writing than speech.

46. downtoners

almost, barely, hardly, merely, mildly, nearly, only, partially, partly, practically, scarcely, slightly, somewhat

Downtoners 'have a general lowering effect on the force of the verb' (Quirk *et al.*, 1985:597–602). Chafe and Danielewicz (1986) characterize these forms as 'academic hedges', since they are commonly used in academic writing to indicate probability. Chafe (1985) notes that downtoners are among those evidentials used to indicate reliability. Holmes (1984) notes that these forms can mark politeness or deference towards the addressee in addition to marking uncertainty towards a proposition.

47. hedges

*at about/something like/more or less/almost/maybe/*xxx *sort of/*xxx *kind of* (where xxx is NOT: DET/ADJ/POSSPRO/WHO – excludes *sort* and *kind* as true nouns)

Hedges are informal, less specific markers of probability or uncertainty. Downtoners give some indication of the degree of uncertainty; hedges simply mark a proposition as uncertain. Chafe (1982) discusses the use of these forms to mark fuzziness in involved discourse, and Chafe and Danielewicz (1986) state that the use of hedges in conversational discourse indicates an awareness of the limited word choice that is possible under the production restrictions of speech. Biber (1986a) finds hedges co-occurring with interactive features (e.g., first and second person pronouns and questions) and with other features marking reduced or generalized lexical content (e.g., general emphatics, pronoun *it*, contractions). Other references include Aijmer (1984), Schourup (1985), and Grabe (1984a).

48. amplifiers

absolutely, altogether, completely, enormously, entirely, extremely, fully, greatly, highly, intensely, perfectly, strongly, thoroughly, totally, utterly, very

Amplifiers have the opposite effect of downtoners, boosting the force of the verb (Quirk *et al.* 1985:590–7). They are used to indicate, in positive terms, the reliability of propositions (Chafe 1985). Holmes (1984) notes that, similar to downtoners, amplifiers can be used for non-propositional functions; in particular, they can signal solidarity with the listener in addition to marking certainty or conviction towards the proposition.

49. emphatics
for sure/a lot/such a/real + ADJ/*so* + ADJ/DO + V/*just/really/most /more*

The relation between emphatics and amplifiers is similar to that between hedges and downtoners: emphatics simply mark the presence (versus absence) of certainty while amplifiers indicate the degree of certainty towards a proposition. Emphatics are characteristic of informal, colloquial discourse, marking involvement with the topic (Chafe 1982, 1985). As noted above, Biber (1986a) finds emphatics and hedges co-occurring frequently in the conversational genres. Labov (1984) discusses forms of this type under the label of 'intensity': the 'emotional expression of social orientation toward the linguistic proposition'. Other studies of emphatics include Stenström's (1986) analysis of *really* and Aijmer's (1985) analysis of *just*.

50. discourse particles
CL-P/T# + *well/now/anyway/anyhow/anyways*

Discourse particles are used to maintain conversational coherence (Schiffrin 1982, 1985a). Chafe (1982, 1985) describes their role as 'monitoring the information flow' in involved discourse. They are very generalized in their functions and rare outside of the conversational genres. Other studies include: Hu (1984), Schourup (1985), and Perera (1986).

51. demonstratives
that/this/these/those

(This count excludes demonstrative pronouns (no. 10) and *that* as relative, complementizer, or subordinator.)

Demonstratives are used for both text-internal deixis (Kurzon 1985) and for exophoric, text-external, reference. They are an important device for marking referential cohesion in a text (Halliday and Hasan 1976). Ochs (1979) notes that demonstratives are preferred to articles in unplanned discourse.

(L) MODALS (nos. 52–4)
It is possible to distinguish three functional classes of modals: (1) those marking permission, possibility, or ability; (2) those marking obligation or necessity; and (3) those marking volition or prediction (Quirk *et al.* 1985:219–36; Coates 1983; Hermeren 1986). Tottie (1985; Tottie and Overgaard 1984) discusses particular aspects of. modal usage, including the negation of necessity modals and the use of *would*. Chafe (1985) includes possibility modals among the evidentials that mark reliability, and necessity modals among those evidentials that mark some aspect of the reasoning process.

52. possibility modals
can/may/might/could (+ contractions)

53. **necessity modals**
ought/should/must (+ contractions)
54. **predictive modals**
will/would/shall (+ contractions)

(M) SPECIALIZED VERB CLASSES (nos. 55–8)
Certain restricted classes of verbs can be identified as having specific functions. Several researchers refer to 'verbs of cognition', those verbs that refer to mental activities (Carroll 1960; Weber 1985). Chafe (1985) discusses the use of 'sensory' verbs (e.g., *see, hear, feel*) to mark knowledge from a particular kind of evidence. In the present analysis, I distinguish four specialized classes of verbs: public, private, suasive, and *seem/appear*. Public verbs involve actions that can be observed publicly; they are primarily speech act verbs, such as *say* and *explain*, and they are commonly used to introduce indirect statements. Private verbs express intellectual states (e.g., *believe*) or nonobservable intellectual acts (e.g., *discover*); this class corresponds to the 'verbs of cognition' used in other studies. Suasive verbs imply intentions to bring about some change in the future (e.g., *command, stipulate*). All present and past tense forms of these verbs are included in the counts.

55. **public verbs**
(e.g., *acknowledge, admit, agree, assert, claim, complain, declare, deny, explain, hint, insist, mention, proclaim, promise, protest, remark, reply, report, say, suggest, swear, write*)

This class of verbs is taken from Quirk *et al.* (1985:1180–1).

56. **private verbs**
(e.g., *anticipate, assume, believe, conclude, decide, demonstrate, determine, discover, doubt, estimate, fear, feel, find, forget, guess, hear, hope, imagine, imply, indicate, infer, know, learn, mean, notice, prove, realize, recognize, remember, reveal, see, show, suppose, think, understand*)

This class of verbs is taken from Quirk *et al.* (1985:1181–2).

57. **suasive verbs**
(e.g., *agree, arrange, ask, beg, command, decide, demand, grant, insist, instruct, ordain, pledge, pronounce, propose, recommend, request, stipulate, suggest, urge*)

This class of verbs is taken from Quirk *et al.* (1985:1182–3).

58. *seem/appear*
These are 'perception' verbs (Quirk *et al.* 1985:1033, 1183). They can be used to mark evidentiality with respect to the reasoning process (Chafe 1985), and they represent another strategy used for academic hedging (see the discussion of downtoners – no. 46).

(N) REDUCED FORMS AND DISPREFERRED STRUCTURES (nos. 59–63)

Several linguistic constructions, such as contractions, stranded prepositions, and split infinitives, are dispreferred in edited writing. Linguists typically disregard the prescriptions against these constructions as arbitrary. Finegan (1980, 1987; Finegan and Biber 1986a), however, shows that grammatical prescriptions tend to be systematic if considered from a strictly linguistic point of view: they tend to disprefer those constructions that involve a mismatch between surface form and underlying representation, resulting in either a reduced surface form (due to contraction or deletion) or a weakened isomorphism between form and meaning (e.g., split infinitives). Biber (1986a) finds that these features tend to co-occur frequently with interactive features (e.g., first and second person pronouns) and with certain types of subordination. Chafe (1984b) discusses the linguistic form of grammatical prescriptions and analyzes the historical evolution of certain prescriptions in speech and writing. Features 59–63 are all dispreferred in edited writing; nos. 59–60 involve surface reduction of form and nos. 61–3 involve a weakened isomorphism between form and meaning.

59. **contractions**

(1) all contractions on pronouns
(2) all contractions on auxiliary forms (negation)
(3) 's suffixed on nouns is analyzed separately (to exclude possessive forms):

N's + V/AUX/ADV+V/ADV+AUX/DET/POSSPRO/
PREP/ADJ+CL-P/ADJ+T#

Contractions are the most frequently cited example of reduced surface form. Except for certain types of fiction, they are dispreferred in formal, edited writing; linguists have traditionally explained their frequent use in conversation as being a consequence of fast and easy production. Finegan and Biber (1986a), however, find that contractions are distributed as a cline: used most frequently in conversation; least frequently in academic prose; and with intermediate frequencies in broadcast, public speeches, and press reportage. Biber (1987) finds that contractions are more frequent in American writing than in British writing, apparently because of greater attention to grammatical prescriptions by British writers. Chafe and Danielewicz (1986) also find that there is no absolute difference between speech and writing in the use of contractions. Thus, the use of contractions seems to be tied to appropriateness considerations as much as to the differing production circumstances of speech and writing. Other references include: Marckworth and Baker (1974), Chafe (1985), and Biber (1986a).

60. **subordinator-*that* deletion**

(e.g., *I think* [*that*] *he went to . . .*)

(1) PUB/PRV/SUA + (T♯) + demonstrative pro/SUBJPRO

(2) PUB/PRV/SUA + PRO/N + AUX/V

(3) PUB/PRV/SUA + ADJ/ADV/DET/POSSPRO + (ADJ) + N + AUX/V

While contractions are a form of phonological (or orthographic) reduction, subordinator-*that* deletion is a form of syntactic reduction. There are very few of these deletions in edited writing, even though few explicit prescriptions prohibit this form. Apparently the concern for elaborated and explicit expression in typical edited writing is the driving force preventing this reduction. Studies that discuss the distribution of *that*-deletions include Frawley (1982), Finegan and Biber (1986a), Elsness (1984), Beaman (1984), Weber (1985), and Biber (1986a).

61. **stranded prepositions**

(e.g., *the candidate that I was thinking of*)

PREP + ALL-P/T♯

Stranded prepositions represent a mismatch between surface and underlying representations, since the relative pronoun and the preposition belong to the same phrase in underlying structure. Chafe (1985) cites these forms as an example of spoken 'errors' due to the production constraints of speech.

62. **split infinitives**

(e.g., *he wants to convincingly prove that . . .*)

to + ADV + (ADV) + VB

Split infinitives are the most widely cited prescription against surface–underlying mismatches. This notoriety suggests that writers *would* use split infinitives if it were not for the prescriptions against them, but these forms in fact seem to be equally uncommon in spoken and written genres (Biber 1986a; Chafe 1984b). This feature did not co-occur meaningfully with the other features included in the present study, and it was therefore dropped from the factor analysis (Chapter 5).

63. **split auxiliaries**

(e.g., *they are objectively shown to . . .*)

AUX + ADV + (ADV) + VB

Split auxiliaries are analogous to split infinitives, but they have not received much attention from prescriptive grammarians. They are actually more common in certain written genres than in typical conversation; Biber (1986a) finds that they frequently co-occur with passives, prepositions, and nominalizations.

(O) COORDINATION (nos. 64–5)

Phrase and clause coordination have complementary functions, so that any overall count of coordinators would be hopelessly confounded. *And* as a clause coordinator is a general purpose connective that can mark many different logical relations between two clauses. Chafe (1982, 1985) relates the fragmented style resulting from this simple chaining of ideas to the production constraints of speech. *And* as a phrase coordinator, on the other hand, has an integrative function and is used for idea unit expansion (Chafe 1982, 1985; Chafe and Danielewicz 1986). Other studies that analyze the distribution and uses of *and* include Marckworth and Baker (1974), Schiffrin (1982), and Young (1985). The algorithms used in the present study identify only those uses of *and* that are clearly phrasal or clausal connectives.

64. **phrasal coordination**

xxxx1 + *and* + xxxx2

(where xxx1 and xxx2 are both: ADV/ADJ/V/N)

65. **independent clause coordination**

(a) T#/, + *and* + *it/so/then/you/there*+BE/demonstrative pronoun /SUBJPRO

(b) CL-P + *and*

(c) *and* + WHP/WHO/adverbial subordinator (nos. 35–8)/discourse particle (no. 50)/conjunct (no. 45)

(P) NEGATION (nos. 66–7)

There is twice as much negation overall in speech as in writing, a distribution that Tottie (1981, 1982, 1983b) attributes to the greater frequency of repetitions, denials, rejections, questions, and mental verbs in speech. Tottie (1983a) distinguishes between synthetic and analytic negation. Synthetic negation is more literary, and seemingly more integrated; analytic negation is more colloquial and seems to be more fragmented.

66. **synthetic negation**

(a) *no* + QUANT/ADJ/N

(b) *neither, nor*

(excludes *no* as a response)

67. **analytic negation: *not***

(also contracted forms)

Mean frequency counts of all features in each genre

This appendix presents descriptive statistics for the frequency count of each linguistic feature in each genre. The frequency counts are all normalized to a text length of 1,000 words (except for type/token ratio and word length – see Appendix II). Further discussion of the normalization procedure is given in Section 4.5.

Mean frequencies for Press Reportage

Linguistic feature	Mean	Minimum value	Maximum value	Range	Standard deviation
past tense	45.1	7.0	110.0	103.0	21.6
perfect aspect verbs	8.0	3.0	14.0	11.0	2.8
present tense	55.8	22.0	82.0	60.0	15.9
place adverbials	4.7	0.0	24.0	24.0	4.5
time adverbials	6.5	1.0	13.0	12.0	3.1
first person pronouns	9.5	0.0	32.0	32.0	8.7
second person pronouns	1.1	0.0	5.0	5.0	1.4
third person pronouns	28.7	5.0	57.0	52.0	13.2
pronoun IT	5.8	1.0	13.0	12.0	2.9
demonstrative pronouns	1.6	0.0	5.0	5.0	1.2
indefinite pronouns	0.6	0.0	6.0	6.0	1.0
DO as pro-verb	1.3	0.0	5.0	5.0	1.3
WH questions	0.0	0.0	1.0	1.0	0.2
nominalizations	19.2	5.0	43.0	38.0	9.3
gerunds	7.8	3.0	16.0	13.0	3.2
nouns	220.5	186.0	273.0	87.0	18.5
agentless passives	11.0	2.0	22.0	20.0	4.6
BY passives	1.6	0.0	5.0	5.0	1.2
BE as main verb	20.7	10.0	38.0	28.0	5.6
existential THERE	1.8	0.0	5.0	5.0	1.3
THAT verb complements	3.3	0.0	10.0	10.0	2.4
THAT adj. complements	0.1	0.0	1.0	1.0	0.3
WH clauses	0.4	0.0	2.0	2.0	0.5
infinitives	13.8	5.0	22.0	17.0	4.3
present participial clauses	0.6	0.0	3.0	3.0	0.7
past participial clauses	0.2	0.0	1.0	1.0	0.4
past prt. WHIZ deletions	3.1	0.0	14.0	14.0	2.3
present prt. WHIZ deletions	2.5	0.0	6.0	6.0	1.4
THAT relatives: subj. position	0.2	0.0	1.0	1.0	0.4
THAT relatives: obj. position	0.8	0.0	3.0	3.0	0.9
WH relatives: subj. position	2.0	0.0	4.0	4.0	1.0
WH relatives: obj. position	1.0	0.0	3.0	3.0	1.0
WH relatives: pied pipes	0.6	0.0	3.0	3.0	0.8
sentence relatives	0.0	0.0	0.0	0.0	0.0
adv. subordinator - cause	0.5	0.0	3.0	3.0	0.8
adv. sub. - concession	0.4	0.0	2.0	2.0	0.5
adv. sub. - condition	1.4	0.0	5.0	5.0	1.3
adv. sub. - other	1.0	0.0	3.0	3.0	0.8
prepositions	116.6	90.0	148.0	58.0	13.1
attributive adjectives	64.5	30.0	90.0	60.0	14.0
predicative adjectives	3.0	0.0	8.0	8.0	1.8
adverbs	52.8	27.0	83.0	56.0	12.2
type/token ratio	55.3	46.0	63.0	17.0	4.4
word length	4.7	4.2	4.9	0.7	0.2
conjuncts	0.6	0.0	4.0	4.0	1.0
downtoners	1.6	0.0	5.0	5.0	1.4
hedges	0.2	0.0	1.0	1.0	0.4
amplifiers	0.9	0.0	4.0	4.0	1.1
emphatics	4.2	1.0	10.0	9.0	2.1
discourse particles	0.0	0.0	1.0	1.0	0.2
demonstratives	7.4	2.0	16.0	14.0	2.8
possibility modals	3.2	0.0	8.0	8.0	1.8
necessity modals	1.7	0.0	8.0	8.0	1.6
predictive modals	6.1	1.0	13.0	12.0	2.8
public verbs	12.0	2.0	28.0	26.0	6.5
private verbs	10.4	3.0	23.0	20.0	4.1
suasive verbs	3.0	0.0	7.0	7.0	1.8
SEEM/APPEAR	0.5	0.0	2.0	2.0	0.7
contractions	1.8	0.0	10.0	10.0	3.1
THAT deletion	2.0	0.0	9.0	9.0	2.0
stranded prepositions	0.5	0.0	3.0	3.0	0.8
split infinitives	0.0	0.0	0.0	0.0	0.0
split auxiliaries	5.4	1.0	10.0	9.0	2.2
phrasal coordination	4.1	0.0	8.0	8.0	2.0
non-phrasal coordination	2.3	0.0	6.0	6.0	1.7
synthetic negation	1.5	0.0	6.0	6.0	1.3
analytic negation	4.7	0.0	9.0	9.0	2.2

Mean frequencies for Press Editorials

Linguistic feature	Mean	Minimum value	Maximum value	Range	Standard deviation
past tense	18.1	3.0	61.0	58.0	12.2
perfect aspect verbs	9.7	5.0	16.0	11.0	3.0
present tense	81.8	49.0	104.0	55.0	12.6
place adverbials	4.0	1.0	13.0	12.0	2.7
time adverbials	4.2	1.0	7.0	6.0	1.9
first person pronouns	11.2	2.0	34.0	32.0	7.6
second person pronouns	1.6	0.0	10.0	10.0	2.6
third person pronouns	21.9	8.0	58.0	50.0	10.8
pronoun IT	9.3	4.0	17.0	13.0	3.2
demonstrative pronouns	2.9	0.0	7.0	7.0	1.6
indefinite pronouns	0.6	0.0	2.0	2.0	0.8
DO as pro-verb	1.9	0.0	4.0	4.0	1.2
WH questions	0.3	0.0	2.0	2.0	0.6
nominalizations	27.6	14.0	45.0	31.0	7.9
gerunds	7.4	3.0	14.0	11.0	2.7
nouns	201.0	178.0	233.0	55.0	16.6
agentless passives	11.7	7.0	19.0	12.0	2.9
BY passives	0.8	0.0	4.0	4.0	0.9
BE as main verb	28.9	17.0	43.0	26.0	5.8
existential THERE	3.2	1.0	7.0	6.0	1.8
THAT verb complements	3.9	0.0	8.0	8.0	2.1
THAT adj. complements	0.4	0.0	1.0	1.0	0.5
WH clauses	0.4	0.0	2.0	2.0	0.6
infinitives	17.6	9.0	25.0	16.0	3.6
present participial clauses	0.3	0.0	2.0	2.0	0.6
past participial clauses	0.1	0.0	1.0	1.0	0.3
past prt. WHIZ deletions	2.9	1.0	5.0	4.0	1.3
present prt. WHIZ deletions	2.0	0.0	6.0	6.0	1.5
THAT relatives: subj. position	0.4	0.0	2.0	2.0	0.6
THAT relatives: obj. position	1.4	0.0	4.0	4.0	0.9
WH relatives: subj. position	3.1	1.0	7.0	6.0	1.5
WH relatives: obj. position	1.6	0.0	4.0	4.0	1.4
WH relatives: pied pipes	0.7	0.0	4.0	4.0	0.9
sentence relatives	0.1	0.0	1.0	1.0	0.3
adv. subordinator - cause	0.7	0.0	4.0	4.0	1.0
adv. sub. - concession	0.3	0.0	2.0	2.0	0.6
adv. sub. - condition	2.7	0.0	6.0	6.0	1.8
adv. sub. - other	0.8	0.0	3.0	3.0	0.8
prepositions	116.3	101.0	138.0	37.0	8.4
attributive adjectives	74.4	47.0	89.0	42.0	8.9
predicative adjectives	5.6	3.0	10.0	7.0	1.9
adverbs	60.4	46.0	77.0	31.0	8.5
type/token ratio	54.4	48.0	62.0	14.0	3.3
word length	4.7	4.4	4.9	0.6	0.1
conjuncts	1.6	0.0	6.0	6.0	1.6
downtoners	2.6	0.0	6.0	6.0	1.6
hedges	0.3	0.0	2.0	2.0	0.7
amplifiers	1.1	0.0	3.0	3.0	0.8
emphatics	5.9	2.0	12.0	10.0	2.3
discourse particles	0.2	0.0	2.0	2.0	0.5
demonstratives	11.7	7.0	17.0	10.0	2.4
possibility modals	6.4	2.0	10.0	8.0	2.1
necessity modals	4.0	0.0	8.0	8.0	2.4
predictive modals	7.7	3.0	21.0	18.0	3.7
public verbs	6.8	2.0	12.0	10.0	2.8
private verbs	11.4	6.0	17.0	11.0	2.8
suasive verbs	4.0	1.0	11.0	10.0	2.3
SEEM/APPEAR	0.7	0.0	4.0	4.0	1.0
contractions	0.8	0.0	7.0	7.0	1.9
THAT deletion	0.8	0.0	4.0	4.0	1.1
stranded prepositions	0.3	0.0	3.0	3.0	0.7
split infinitives	0.0	0.0	0.0	0.0	0.0
split auxiliaries	7.2	2.0	11.0	9.0	2.0
phrasal coordination	4.4	2.0	9.0	7.0	1.7
non-phrasal coordination	2.1	0.0	6.0	6.0	1.6
synthetic negation	2.8	1.0	6.0	5.0	1.2
analytic negation	6.6	2.0	10.0	8.0	2.2

Mean frequencies for Press Reviews

Linguistic feature	Mean	Minimum value	Maximum value	Range	Standard deviation
past tense	18.2	2.0	39.0	37.0	11.4
perfect aspect verbs	6.8	3.0	11.0	8.0	2.4
present tense	70.9	45.0	91.0	46.0	12.9
place adverbials	1.9	0.0	4.0	4.0	1.1
time adverbials	4.3	2.0	8.0	6.0	1.8
first person pronouns	7.5	1.0	20.0	19.0	5.7
second person pronouns	1.2	0.0	6.0	6.0	1.7
third person pronouns	33.6	15.0	62.0	47.0	12.1
pronoun IT	7.9	4.0	17.0	13.0	3.3
demonstrative pronouns	1.9	0.0	6.0	6.0	1.6
indefinite pronouns	1.0	0.0	3.0	3.0	1.0
DO as pro-verb	1.1	0.0	3.0	3.0	1.1
WH questions	0.0	0.0	0.0	0.0	0.0
nominalizations	21.6	11.0	36.0	25.0	7.6
gerunds	8.2	4.0	13.0	9.0	2.9
nouns	208.3	180.0	250.0	70.0	21.5
agentless passives	8.6	5.0	12.0	7.0	2.1
BY passives	1.4	0.0	4.0	4.0	1.2
BE as main verb	25.5	13.0	36.0	23.0	6.4
existential THERE	1.2	0.0	3.0	3.0	0.9
THAT verb complements	1.8	0.0	6.0	6.0	1.4
THAT adj. complements	0.1	0.0	1.0	1.0	0.3
WH clauses	0.4	0.0	1.0	1.0	0.5
infinitives	11.6	8.0	17.0	9.0	2.7
present participial clauses	0.5	0.0	2.0	2.0	0.7
past participial clauses	0.2	0.0	1.0	1.0	0.4
past prt. WHIZ deletions	3.8	1.0	6.0	5.0	1.4
present prt. WHIZ deletions	2.5	0.0	5.0	5.0	1.5
THAT relatives: subj. position	0.6	0.0	2.0	2.0	0.8
THAT relatives: obj. position	0.9	0.0	3.0	3.0	0.8
WH relatives: subj. position	3.5	1.0	6.0	5.0	1.5
WH relatives: obj. position	2.6	0.0	5.0	5.0	1.6
WH relatives: pied pipes	1.5	0.0	4.0	4.0	1.2
sentence relatives	0.0	0.0	0.0	0.0	0.0
adv. subordinator - cause	0.2	0.0	1.0	1.0	0.4
adv. sub. - concession	0.7	0.0	2.0	2.0	0.8
adv. sub. - condition	1.1	0.0	3.0	3.0	0.9
adv. sub. - other	0.8	0.0	3.0	3.0	1.0
prepositions	119.3	102.0	141.0	39.0	12.3
attributive adjectives	82.3	62.0	100.0	38.0	12.5
predicative adjectives	3.2	0.0	7.0	7.0	1.9
adverbs	60.8	34.0	77.0	43.0	12.1
type/token ratio	56.5	49.0	64.0	15.0	4.4
word length	4.7	4.5	4.9	0.5	0.1
conjuncts	1.2	0.0	4.0	4.0	1.2
downtoners	2.3	0.0	4.0	4.0	1.2
hedges	0.4	0.0	1.0	1.0	0.5
amplifiers	2.0	0.0	4.0	4.0	1.2
emphatics	6.5	2.0	9.0	7.0	1.9
discourse particles	0.2	0.0	1.0	1.0	0.4
demonstratives	8.7	3.0	13.0	10.0	3.1
possibility modals	3.5	1.0	7.0	6.0	1.7
necessity modals	1.1	0.0	4.0	4.0	1.2
predictive modals	3.0	1.0	13.0	12.0	2.9
public verbs	4.9	1.0	10.0	9.0	2.8
private verbs	11.3	7.0	14.0	7.0	2.5
suasive verbs	1.9	0.0	4.0	4.0	1.3
SEEM/APPEAR	1.4	0.0	4.0	4.0	1.1
contractions	1.9	0.0	13.0	13.0	3.6
THAT deletion	0.5	0.0	2.0	2.0	0.6
stranded prepositions	0.5	0.0	2.0	2.0	0.7
split infinitives	0.0	0.0	0.0	0.0	0.0
split auxiliaries	4.8	1.0	9.0	8.0	2.2
phrasal coordination	6.5	2.0	12.0	10.0	2.4
non-phrasal coordination	1.8	0.0	4.0	4.0	1.0
synthetic negation	2.0	0.0	5.0	5.0	1.5
analytic negation	6.0	1.0	13.0	12.0	3.0

Mean frequencies for Religion

Linguistic feature	Mean	Minimum value	Maximum value	Range	Standard deviation
past tense	26.1	4.0	85.0	81.0	19.1
perfect aspect verbs	6.1	1.0	12.0	11.0	3.4
present tense	79.4	30.0	106.0	76.0	20.3
place adverbials	2.2	0.0	11.0	11.0	2.7
time adverbials	3.1	0.0	6.0	6.0	2.0
first person pronouns	16.6	0.0	35.0	35.0	12.5
second person pronouns	2.9	0.0	20.0	20.0	5.4
third person pronouns	22.5	5.0	60.0	55.0	13.1
pronoun IT	9.6	5.0	15.0	10.0	3.6
demonstrative pronouns	3.6	0.0	10.0	10.0	2.4
indefinite pronouns	0.9	0.0	5.0	5.0	1.4
DO as pro-verb	2.2	0.0	10.0	10.0	3.1
WH questions	0.1	0.0	1.0	1.0	0.3
nominalizations	26.8	11.0	50.0	39.0	10.8
gerunds	9.3	3.0	19.0	16.0	4.6
nouns	187.7	149.0	225.0	76.0	22.4
agentless passives	14.6	8.0	25.0	17.0	5.1
BY passives	1.1	0.0	3.0	3.0	1.1
BE as main verb	30.4	19.0	44.0	25.0	6.2
existential THERE	2.5	0.0	7.0	7.0	1.9
THAT verb complements	4.3	1.0	10.0	9.0	2.3
THAT adj. complements	0.2	0.0	1.0	1.0	0.4
WH clauses	0.8	0.0	5.0	5.0	1.2
infinitives	14.9	6.0	33.0	27.0	7.4
present participial clauses	0.4	0.0	2.0	2.0	0.6
past participial clauses	0.1	0.0	1.0	1.0	0.2
past prt. WHIZ deletions	3.4	0.0	7.0	7.0	2.3
present prt. WHIZ deletions	1.4	0.0	4.0	4.0	1.3
THAT relatives: subj. position	0.6	0.0	4.0	4.0	1.1
THAT relatives: obj. position	0.6	0.0	3.0	3.0	0.9
WH relatives: subj. position	2.8	0.0	7.0	7.0	1.9
WH relatives: obj. position	2.3	0.0	7.0	7.0	1.9
WH relatives: pied pipes	0.9	0.0	3.0	3.0	1.1
sentence relatives	0.0	0.0	0.0	0.0	0.0
adv. subordinator - cause	0.6	0.0	3.0	3.0	0.9
adv. sub. - concession	0.4	0.0	2.0	2.0	0.7
adv. sub. - condition	2.1	0.0	9.0	9.0	2.7
adv. sub. - other	0.8	0.0	3.0	3.0	1.2
prepositions	117.7	83.0	135.0	52.0	15.3
attributive adjectives	59.5	31.0	97.0	66.0	16.6
predicative adjectives	5.2	2.0	12.0	10.0	2.7
adverbs	54.1	32.0	84.0	52.0	14.5
type/token ratio	50.1	44.0	55.0	11.0	3.3
word length	4.5	4.2	5.0	0.8	0.2
conjuncts	1.9	0.0	5.0	5.0	1.5
downtoners	2.6	0.0	6.0	6.0	1.6
hedges	0.0	0.0	0.0	0.0	0.0
amplifiers	1.5	0.0	4.0	4.0	1.2
emphatics	4.0	1.0	10.0	9.0	2.1
discourse particles	0.1	0.0	1.0	1.0	0.2
demonstratives	13.5	6.0	21.0	15.0	4.4
possibility modals	5.4	2.0	12.0	10.0	2.8
necessity modals	2.2	0.0	7.0	7.0	1.8
predictive modals	6.0	2.0	15.0	13.0	4.0
public verbs	9.4	4.0	25.0	21.0	5.5
private verbs	14.5	7.0	24.0	17.0	5.7
suasive verbs	2.9	0.0	7.0	7.0	2.2
SEEM/APPEAR	0.5	0.0	4.0	4.0	1.1
contractions	1.8	0.0	30.0	30.0	7.3
THAT deletion	0.9	0.0	4.0	4.0	1.2
stranded prepositions	0.5	0.0	2.0	2.0	0.6
split infinitives	0.0	0.0	0.0	0.0	0.0
split auxiliaries	5.9	2.0	9.0	7.0	2.2
phrasal coordination	5.0	0.0	12.0	12.0	3.0
non-phrasal coordination	2.9	0.0	12.0	12.0	2.9
synthetic negation	2.8	0.0	7.0	7.0	2.2
analytic negation	7.0	3.0	21.0	18.0	4.6

Mean frequencies for Hobbies

Linguistic feature	Mean	Minimum value	Maximum value	Range	Standard deviation
past tense	17.6	0.0	54.0	54.0	16.8
perfect aspect verbs	5.6	1.0	11.0	10.0	3.1
present tense	79.7	46.0	102.0	56.0	18.1
place adverbials	3.4	0.0	9.0	9.0	2.5
time adverbials	4.4	1.0	9.0	8.0	2.5
first person pronouns	14.9	0.0	59.0	59.0	15.2
second person pronouns	4.2	0.0	16.0	16.0	5.3
third person pronouns	14.1	4.0	44.0	40.0	10.9
pronoun IT	7.6	2.0	14.0	12.0	3.8
demonstrative pronouns	3.2	0.0	8.0	8.0	2.2
indefinite pronouns	0.8	0.0	2.0	2.0	0.6
DO as pro-verb	1.2	0.0	6.0	6.0	1.7
WH questions	0.0	0.0	0.0	0.0	0.0
nominalizations	13.1	8.0	20.0	12.0	4.1
gerunds	10.4	5.0	17.0	12.0	3.4
nouns	199.1	174.0	237.0	63.0	20.5
agentless passives	15.4	8.0	30.0	22.0	6.9
BY passives	0.8	0.0	2.0	2.0	0.9
BE as main verb	24.0	13.0	32.0	19.0	6.1
existential THERE	1.5	0.0	4.0	4.0	1.2
THAT verb complements	2.7	1.0	6.0	5.0	1.3
THAT adj. complements	0.2	0.0	1.0	1.0	0.4
WH clauses	0.1	0.0	1.0	1.0	0.3
infinitives	18.3	9.0	27.0	18.0	5.3
present participial clauses	1.6	0.0	3.0	3.0	0.9
past participial clauses	0.2	0.0	3.0	3.0	0.8
past prt. WHIZ deletions	2.7	0.0	6.0	6.0	2.0
present prt. WHIZ deletions	1.6	0.0	5.0	5.0	1.7
THAT relatives: subj. position	0.4	0.0	1.0	1.0	0.5
THAT relatives: obj. position	0.4	0.0	3.0	3.0	0.8
WH relatives: subj. position	1.6	0.0	4.0	4.0	1.1
WH relatives: obj. position	1.6	0.0	9.0	9.0	2.4
WH relatives: pied pipes	0.9	0.0	5.0	5.0	1.3
sentence relatives	0.0	0.0	0.0	0.0	0.0
adv. subordinator - cause	0.5	0.0	3.0	3.0	0.9
adv. sub. - concession	0.6	0.0	2.0	2.0	0.8
adv. sub. - condition	2.5	0.0	9.0	9.0	2.6
adv. sub. - other	1.0	0.0	3.0	3.0	1.1
prepositions	114.6	106.0	132.0	26.0	7.8
attributive adjectives	72.0	55.0	87.0	32.0	10.6
predicative adjectives	5.4	2.0	12.0	10.0	2.4
adverbs	62.1	38.0	89.0	51.0	14.5
type/token ratio	53.2	44.0	59.0	15.0	4.4
word length	4.5	4.2	4.8	0.6	0.2
conjuncts	1.3	0.0	5.0	5.0	1.4
downtoners	2.2	0.0	6.0	6.0	1.8
hedges	0.4	0.0	2.0	2.0	0.8
amplifiers	2.3	0.0	6.0	6.0	1.8
emphatics	6.1	2.0	13.0	11.0	3.4
discourse particles	0.2	0.0	1.0	1.0	0.4
demonstratives	10.2	3.0	17.0	14.0	3.7
possibility modals	6.8	1.0	14.0	13.0	3.9
necessity modals	3.1	0.0	9.0	9.0	3.0
predictive modals	5.7	0.0	12.0	12.0	3.0
public verbs	3.3	0.0	9.0	9.0	2.4
private verbs	10.3	6.0	15.0	9.0	3.3
suasive verbs	2.9	0.0	8.0	8.0	2.2
SEEM/APPEAR	0.6	0.0	3.0	3.0	1.1
contractions	1.4	0.0	11.0	11.0	2.9
THAT deletion	0.5	0.0	3.0	3.0	0.9
stranded prepositions	0.9	0.0	5.0	5.0	1.3
split infinitives	0.0	0.0	0.0	0.0	0.0
split auxiliaries	6.6	2.0	12.0	10.0	3.2
phrasal coordination	4.4	2.0	9.0	7.0	2.2
non-phrasal coordination	2.6	0.0	7.0	7.0	2.2
synthetic negation	1.1	0.0	4.0	4.0	1.4
analytic negation	4.3	0.0	9.0	9.0	2.6

Mean frequencies for Popular Lore

Linguistic feature	Mean	Minimum value	Maximum value	Range	Standard deviation
past tense	40.0	1.0	87.0	86.0	28.1
perfect aspect verbs	8.0	2.0	28.0	26.0	6.7
present tense	65.9	22.0	127.0	105.0	32.6
place adverbials	2.8	0.0	5.0	5.0	1.7
time adverbials	3.4	1.0	9.0	8.0	2.3
first person pronouns	11.7	0.0	55.0	55.0	16.9
second person pronouns	12.0	0.0	67.0	67.0	23.5
third person pronouns	33.9	15.0	70.0	55.0	15.6
pronoun IT	8.4	3.0	15.0	12.0	3.7
demonstrative pronouns	2.1	0.0	5.0	5.0	1.7
indefinite pronouns	1.0	0.0	4.0	4.0	1.1
DO as pro-verb	1.5	0.0	4.0	4.0	1.1
WH questions	0.1	0.0	1.0	1.0	0.3
nominalizations	21.8	4.0	49.0	45.0	12.3
gerunds	9.6	5.0	13.0	8.0	3.1
nouns	195.4	161.0	229.0	68.0	23.2
agentless passives	10.6	2.0	18.0	16.0	5.1
BY passives	0.9	0.0	4.0	4.0	1.3
BE as main verb	24.3	12.0	35.0	23.0	6.0
existential THERE	1.6	0.0	4.0	4.0	1.4
THAT verb complements	2.7	0.0	8.0	8.0	2.6
THAT adj. complements	0.2	0.0	1.0	1.0	0.4
WH clauses	0.6	0.0	3.0	3.0	0.9
infinitives	17.3	11.0	30.0	19.0	5.7
present participial clauses	1.0	0.0	3.0	3.0	1.0
past participial clauses	0.0	0.0	0.0	0.0	0.0
past prt. WHIZ deletions	3.7	0.0	12.0	12.0	3.3
present prt. WHIZ deletions	2.6	0.0	7.0	7.0	2.1
THAT relatives: subj. position	0.4	0.0	1.0	1.0	0.5
THAT relatives: obj. position	1.1	0.0	3.0	3.0	1.0
WH relatives: subj. position	3.0	0.0	6.0	6.0	1.8
WH relatives: obj. position	1.5	0.0	5.0	5.0	1.3
WH relatives: pied pipes	1.0	0.0	4.0	4.0	1.2
sentence relatives	0.0	0.0	0.0	0.0	0.0
adv. subordinator - cause	0.5	0.0	3.0	3.0	0.9
adv. sub. - concession	0.7	0.0	3.0	3.0	1.1
adv. sub. - condition	2.1	0.0	10.0	10.0	2.9
adv. sub. - other	0.6	0.0	2.0	2.0	0.8
prepositions	114.8	92.0	148.0	56.0	16.0
attributive adjectives	68.5	40.0	96.0	56.0	17.1
predicative adjectives	4.1	1.0	7.0	6.0	2.0
adverbs	57.6	37.0	76.0	39.0	10.4
type/token ratio	53.7	47.0	58.0	11.0	3.8
word length	4.6	4.1	5.3	1.2	0.3
conjuncts	1.6	0.0	4.0	4.0	1.3
downtoners	1.7	0.0	4.0	4.0	1.1
hedges	0.6	0.0	3.0	3.0	0.9
amplifiers	1.6	0.0	3.0	3.0	1.0
emphatics	5.4	1.0	11.0	10.0	2.7
discourse particles	0.1	0.0	1.0	1.0	0.3
demonstratives	6.6	3.0	10.0	7.0	2.2
possibility modals	4.4	1.0	10.0	9.0	3.3
necessity modals	1.6	0.0	11.0	11.0	2.9
predictive modals	5.4	0.0	13.0	13.0	4.2
public verbs	6.1	2.0	13.0	11.0	2.8
private verbs	17.3	7.0	33.0	26.0	8.0
suasive verbs	2.4	0.0	8.0	8.0	2.2
SEEM/APPEAR	0.6	0.0	1.0	1.0	0.5
contractions	2.6	0.0	12.0	12.0	4.5
THAT deletion	1.9	0.0	7.0	7.0	2.2
stranded prepositions	0.6	0.0	2.0	2.0	0.7
split infinitives	0.0	0.0	0.0	0.0	0.0
split auxiliaries	5.1	2.0	10.0	8.0	2.3
phrasal coordination	4.4	1.0	9.0	8.0	2.3
non-phrasal coordination	2.9	0.0	10.0	10.0	3.0
synthetic negation	2.0	0.0	6.0	6.0	2.0
analytic negation	5.1	1.0	13.0	12.0	3.4

Mean frequencies for Biographies

Linguistic feature	Mean	Minimum value	Maximum value	Range	Standard deviation
past tense	68.4	35.0	94.0	59.0	16.4
perfect aspect verbs	10.6	1.0	29.0	28.0	6.7
present tense	35.9	17.0	90.0	73.0	18.2
place adverbials	2.0	0.0	5.0	5.0	1.5
time adverbials	5.0	1.0	10.0	9.0	2.3
first person pronouns	22.1	0.0	80.0	80.0	24.1
second person pronouns	0.6	0.0	3.0	3.0	0.9
third person pronouns	34.3	9.0	85.0	76.0	20.2
pronoun IT	7.6	4.0	12.0	8.0	2.7
demonstrative pronouns	0.9	0.0	3.0	3.0	0.9
indefinite pronouns	1.0	0.0	4.0	4.0	1.1
DO as pro-verb	1.2	0.0	5.0	5.0	1.4
WH questions	0.0	0.0	0.0	0.0	0.0
nominalizations	20.6	5.0	33.0	28.0	9.6
gerunds	6.9	3.0	11.0	8.0	2.2
nouns	192.4	144.0	226.0	82.0	20.7
agentless passives	9.9	5.0	15.0	10.0	3.1
BY passives	0.9	0.0	2.0	2.0	0.8
BE as main verb	24.2	15.0	37.0	22.0	6.0
existential THERE	1.9	0.0	4.0	4.0	1.2
THAT verb complements	2.5	0.0	5.0	5.0	1.6
THAT adj. complements	0.3	0.0	2.0	2.0	0.6
WH clauses	0.6	0.0	7.0	7.0	1.9
infinitives	16.9	7.0	23.0	16.0	4.1
present participial clauses	1.3	0.0	3.0	3.0	1.3
past participial clauses	0.0	0.0	0.0	0.0	0.0
past prt. WHIZ deletions	1.8	0.0	6.0	6.0	1.7
present prt. WHIZ deletions	1.6	0.0	4.0	4.0	1.2
THAT relatives: subj. position	0.4	0.0	4.0	4.0	1.2
THAT relatives: obj. position	0.6	0.0	2.0	2.0	0.6
WH relatives: subj. position	2.5	0.0	7.0	7.0	2.0
WH relatives: obj. position	1.9	0.0	5.0	5.0	1.6
WH relatives: pied pipes	1.0	0.0	3.0	3.0	1.0
sentence relatives	0.0	0.0	0.0	0.0	0.0
adv. subordinator - cause	0.3	0.0	2.0	2.0	0.6
adv. sub. - concession	0.3	0.0	2.0	2.0	0.6
adv. sub. - condition	0.9	0.0	3.0	3.0	0.9
adv. sub. - other	1.1	0.0	3.0	3.0	1.1
prepositions	122.6	105.0	149.0	44.0	13.8
attributive adjectives	66.4	49.0	90.0	41.0	12.1
predicative adjectives	3.1	0.0	6.0	6.0	1.8
adverbs	65.9	43.0	100.0	57.0	14.2
type/token ratio	55.2	51.0	60.0	9.0	2.6
word length	4.5	4.2	4.8	0.6	0.2
conjuncts	1.0	0.0	5.0	5.0	1.5
downtoners	1.7	0.0	4.0	4.0	1.1
hedges	0.1	0.0	1.0	1.0	0.4
amplifiers	2.7	0.0	7.0	7.0	2.1
emphatics	4.2	1.0	8.0	7.0	2.2
discourse particles	0.0	0.0	0.0	0.0	0.0
demonstratives	10.7	6.0	22.0	16.0	4.3
possibility modals	4.0	1.0	7.0	6.0	1.7
necessity modals	1.3	0.0	3.0	3.0	1.1
predictive modals	3.3	0.0	7.0	7.0	1.8
public verbs	7.1	2.0	14.0	12.0	3.3
private verbs	13.6	8.0	22.0	14.0	3.5
suasive verbs	3.2	0.0	8.0	8.0	2.3
SEEM/APPEAR	0.8	0.0	2.0	2.0	0.8
contractions	0.9	0.0	3.0	3.0	1.3
THAT deletion	1.2	0.0	6.0	6.0	2.0
stranded prepositions	0.6	0.0	3.0	3.0	0.9
split infinitives	0.0	0.0	0.0	0.0	0.0
split auxiliaries	6.6	4.0	12.0	8.0	2.0
phrasal coordination	4.9	2.0	9.0	7.0	1.8
non-phrasal coordination	2.4	0.0	8.0	8.0	2.2
synthetic negation	2.6	0.0	6.0	6.0	1.8
analytic negation	6.2	2.0	13.0	11.0	2.9

Mean frequencies for Official Documents

Linguistic feature	Mean	Minimum value	Maximum value	Range	Standard deviation
past tense	16.2	0.0	44.0	44.0	15.1
perfect aspect verbs	7.9	2.0	18.0	16.0	5.1
present tense	59.1	21.0	84.0	63.0	19.1
place adverbials	2.1	0.0	6.0	6.0	1.9
time adverbials	3.4	0.0	9.0	9.0	2.5
first person pronouns	10.0	0.0	38.0	38.0	15.0
second person pronouns	1.4	0.0	10.0	10.0	3.0
third person pronouns	10.1	3.0	16.0	13.0	4.4
pronoun IT	3.2	0.0	6.0	6.0	1.9
demonstrative pronouns	1.1	0.0	5.0	5.0	1.4
indefinite pronouns	0.2	0.0	1.0	1.0	0.4
DO as pro-verb	0.6	0.0	2.0	2.0	0.8
WH questions	0.0	0.0	0.0	0.0	0.0
nominalizations	39.8	14.0	69.0	55.0	17.7
gerunds	10.6	2.0	16.0	14.0	4.1
nouns	206.5	183.0	257.0	74.0	23.2
agentless passives	18.6	8.0	31.0	23.0	6.5
BY passives	2.1	0.0	5.0	5.0	1.4
BE as main verb	16.5	7.0	27.0	20.0	6.8
existential THERE	2.0	0.0	5.0	5.0	1.5
THAT verb complements	1.4	0.0	4.0	4.0	1.3
THAT adj. complements	0.2	0.0	1.0	1.0	0.4
WH clauses	0.2	0.0	1.0	1.0	0.4
infinitives	13.4	2.0	24.0	22.0	6.0
present participial clauses	0.3	0.0	1.0	1.0	0.5
past participial clauses	0.5	0.0	3.0	3.0	0.9
past prt. WHIZ deletions	7.5	4.0	11.0	7.0	2.3
present prt. WHIZ deletions	4.0	0.0	9.0	9.0	2.7
THAT relatives: subj. position	0.2	0.0	1.0	1.0	0.4
THAT relatives: obj. position	0.7	0.0	2.0	2.0	0.6
WH relatives: subj. position	2.7	0.0	5.0	5.0	1.6
WH relatives: obj. position	3.0	1.0	6.0	5.0	1.5
WH relatives: pied pipes	2.0	0.0	4.0	4.0	1.4
sentence relatives	0.1	0.0	1.0	1.0	0.3
adv. subordinator - cause	0.1	0.0	1.0	1.0	0.4
adv. sub. - concession	0.4	0.0	3.0	3.0	0.9
adv. sub. - condition	1.0	0.0	3.0	3.0	1.0
adv. sub. - other	0.9	0.0	3.0	3.0	0.9
prepositions	150.9	109.0	209.0	100.0	25.3
attributive adjectives	77.9	52.0	110.0	58.0	16.7
predicative adjectives	4.3	2.0	11.0	9.0	2.3
adverbs	43.7	22.0	66.0	44.0	10.5
type/token ratio	47.8	38.0	55.0	17.0	5.7
word length	4.9	4.5	5.1	0.6	0.2
conjuncts	1.2	0.0	3.0	3.0	1.0
downtoners	1.9	0.0	7.0	7.0	2.0
hedges	0.0	0.0	0.0	0.0	0.0
amplifiers	0.9	0.0	3.0	3.0	1.1
emphatics	4.0	0.0	15.0	15.0	4.7
discourse particles	0.0	0.0	0.0	0.0	0.0
demonstratives	9.6	2.0	18.0	16.0	4.1
possibility modals	5.0	0.0	14.0	14.0	4.2
necessity modals	2.2	0.0	13.0	13.0	3.4
predictive modals	4.9	0.0	16.0	16.0	5.0
public verbs	4.9	1.0	12.0	11.0	3.3
private verbs	7.8	2.0	13.0	11.0	3.7
suasive verbs	5.2	0.0	13.0	13.0	3.3
SEEM/APPEAR	0.4	0.0	2.0	2.0	0.6
contractions	0.0	0.0	0.0	0.0	0.0
THAT deletion	0.8	0.0	4.0	4.0	1.2
stranded prepositions	0.3	0.0	1.0	1.0	0.5
split infinitives	0.0	0.0	0.0	0.0	0.0
split auxiliaries	5.7	1.0	11.0	10.0	2.6
phrasal coordination	7.3	1.0	12.0	11.0	3.0
non-phrasal coordination	1.2	0.0	6.0	6.0	1.8
synthetic negation	1.5	0.0	3.0	3.0	1.3
analytic negation	3.4	0.0	8.0	8.0	2.2

Mean frequencies for Academic Prose

Linguistic feature	Mean	Minimum value	Maximum value	Range	Standard deviation
past tense	21.9	0.0	84.0	84.0	21.1
perfect aspect verbs	4.9	0.0	16.0	16.0	3.5
present tense	63.7	12.0	114.0	102.0	23.1
place adverbials	2.4	0.0	21.0	21.0	3.3
time adverbials	2.8	0.0	10.0	10.0	2.1
first person pronouns	5.7	0.0	29.0	29.0	7.4
second person pronouns	0.2	0.0	13.0	13.0	1.5
third person pronouns	11.5	0.0	46.0	46.0	10.6
pronoun IT	5.9	1.0	16.0	15.0	3.4
demonstrative pronouns	2.5	0.0	9.0	9.0	1.9
indefinite pronouns	0.2	0.0	10.0	10.0	1.2
DO as pro-verb	0.7	0.0	9.0	9.0	1.3
WH questions	0.0	0.0	0.0	0.0	0.0
nominalizations	35.8	11.0	71.0	60.0	13.3
gerunds	8.5	2.0	23.0	21.0	4.2
nouns	188.1	84.0	242.0	158.0	24.0
agentless passives	17.0	7.0	38.0	31.0	7.4
BY passives	2.0	0.0	8.0	8.0	1.7
BE as main verb	23.8	11.0	49.0	38.0	6.7
existential THERE	1.8	0.0	11.0	11.0	1.7
THAT verb complements	3.2	0.0	10.0	10.0	2.4
THAT adj. complements	0.4	0.0	3.0	3.0	0.7
WH clauses	0.3	0.0	4.0	4.0	0.8
infinitives	12.8	4.0	34.0	30.0	6.0
present participial clauses	1.3	0.0	7.0	7.0	1.5
past participial clauses	0.4	0.0	3.0	3.0	0.7
past prt. WHIZ deletions	5.6	0.0	21.0	21.0	3.8
present prt. WHIZ deletions	2.5	0.0	9.0	9.0	2.2
THAT relatives: subj. position	0.2	0.0	3.0	3.0	0.5
THAT relatives: obj. position	0.8	0.0	5.0	5.0	1.0
WH relatives: subj. position	2.6	0.0	10.0	10.0	2.1
WH relatives: obj. position	2.0	0.0	9.0	9.0	1.7
WH relatives: pied pipes	1.3	0.0	7.0	7.0	1.2
sentence relatives	0.0	0.0	0.0	0.0	0.0
adv. subordinator - cause	0.3	0.0	4.0	4.0	0.7
adv. sub. - concession	0.5	0.0	2.0	2.0	0.7
adv. sub. - condition	2.1	0.0	9.0	9.0	2.1
adv. sub. - other	1.8	0.0	6.0	6.0	1.5
prepositions	139.5	95.0	185.0	90.0	16.7
attributive adjectives	76.9	32.0	115.0	83.0	16.1
predicative adjectives	5.0	1.0	11.0	10.0	2.1
adverbs	51.8	30.0	77.0	47.0	10.3
type/token ratio	50.6	39.0	62.0	23.0	5.2
word length	4.8	4.0	5.3	1.3	0.2
conjuncts	3.0	0.0	12.0	12.0	2.1
downtoners	2.5	0.0	10.0	10.0	1.8
hedges	0.2	0.0	2.0	2.0	0.5
amplifiers	1.4	0.0	6.0	6.0	1.5
emphatics	3.6	0.0	10.0	10.0	2.3
discourse particles	0.0	0.0	2.0	2.0	0.2
demonstratives	11.4	4.0	22.0	18.0	4.6
possibility modals	5.6	0.0	14.0	14.0	3.1
necessity modals	2.2	0.0	11.0	11.0	2.3
predictive modals	3.7	0.0	14.0	14.0	3.4
public verbs	5.7	0.0	28.0	28.0	4.7
private verbs	12.5	2.0	30.0	28.0	5.8
suasive verbs	4.0	0.0	36.0	36.0	5.8
SEEM/APPEAR	1.0	0.0	4.0	4.0	1.2
contractions	0.1	0.0	4.0	4.0	0.6
THAT deletion	0.4	0.0	3.0	3.0	0.7
stranded prepositions	1.1	0.0	23.0	23.0	2.9
split infinitives	0.0	0.0	0.0	0.0	0.0
split auxiliaries	5.8	1.0	11.0	10.0	2.5
phrasal coordination	4.2	0.0	10.0	10.0	2.4
non-phrasal coordination	1.9	0.0	6.0	6.0	1.4
synthetic negation	1.3	0.0	6.0	6.0	1.3
analytic negation	4.3	0.0	15.0	15.0	3.0

Mean frequencies for General Fiction

Linguistic feature	Mean	Minimum value	Maximum value	Range	Standard deviation
past tense	85.6	41.0	113.0	72.0	15.7
perfect aspect verbs	12.3	4.0	30.0	26.0	5.5
present tense	53.4	25.0	100.0	75.0	18.8
place adverbials	4.4	1.0	14.0	13.0	3.2
time adverbials	5.8	2.0	10.0	8.0	2.0
first person pronouns	32.0	1.0	83.0	82.0	23.5
second person pronouns	11.1	0.0	35.0	35.0	9.1
third person pronouns	67.2	21.0	124.0	103.0	26.3
pronoun IT	11.5	5.0	24.0	19.0	4.6
demonstrative pronouns	2.1	0.0	7.0	7.0	1.8
indefinite pronouns	1.5	0.0	5.0	5.0	1.6
DO as pro-verb	3.3	0.0	12.0	12.0	2.5
WH questions	0.1	0.0	1.0	1.0	0.4
nominalizations	10.0	3.0	25.0	22.0	5.5
gerunds	6.5	2.0	11.0	9.0	2.0
nouns	160.7	112.0	216.0	104.0	25.7
agentless passives	5.7	0.0	12.0	12.0	3.2
BY passives	0.2	0.0	1.0	1.0	0.4
BE as main verb	25.6	15.0	35.0	20.0	5.7
existential THERE	1.7	0.0	4.0	4.0	1.2
THAT verb complements	2.1	0.0	7.0	7.0	1.9
THAT adj. complements	0.1	0.0	1.0	1.0	0.3
WH clauses	0.9	0.0	4.0	4.0	1.0
infinitives	16.6	6.0	26.0	20.0	4.7
present participial clauses	2.7	0.0	7.0	7.0	2.1
past participial clauses	0.0	0.0	0.0	0.0	0.0
past prt. WHIZ deletions	0.7	0.0	3.0	3.0	0.8
present prt. WHIZ deletions	1.1	0.0	4.0	4.0	1.3
THAT relatives: subj. position	0.3	0.0	2.0	2.0	0.6
THAT relatives: obj. position	0.4	0.0	2.0	2.0	0.6
WH relatives: subj. position	1.0	0.0	3.0	3.0	1.0
WH relatives: obj. position	0.9	0.0	4.0	4.0	1.2
WH relatives: pied pipes	0.2	0.0	2.0	2.0	0.5
sentence relatives	0.0	0.0	0.0	0.0	0.0
adv. subordinator - cause	0.4	0.0	3.0	3.0	0.8
adv. sub. - concession	1.1	0.0	5.0	5.0	1.3
adv. sub. - condition	2.6	0.0	6.0	6.0	1.9
adv. sub. - other	0.9	0.0	4.0	4.0	1.0
prepositions	92.8	67.0	134.0	67.0	15.8
attributive adjectives	50.7	31.0	80.0	49.0	9.9
predicative adjectives	5.3	2.0	12.0	10.0	2.3
adverbs	74.1	49.0	108.0	59.0	13.2
type/token ratio	52.7	46.0	61.0	15.0	3.8
word length	4.2	3.8	4.7	0.9	0.2
conjuncts	0.5	0.0	3.0	3.0	0.8
downtoners	2.1	0.0	8.0	8.0	1.7
hedges	0.4	0.0	4.0	4.0	0.9
amplifiers	1.7	0.0	5.0	5.0	1.4
emphatics	4.9	0.0	12.0	12.0	2.9
discourse particles	0.2	0.0	2.0	2.0	0.6
demonstratives	7.8	2.0	13.0	11.0	3.2
possibility modals	5.2	1.0	13.0	12.0	2.7
necessity modals	1.9	0.0	4.0	4.0	1.3
predictive modals	6.2	0.0	14.0	14.0	2.9
public verbs	10.3	2.0	23.0	21.0	5.1
private verbs	20.6	10.0	36.0	26.0	6.9
suasive verbs	2.5	0.0	7.0	7.0	1.6
SEEM/APPEAR	1.1	0.0	4.0	4.0	1.2
contractions	11.2	0.0	42.0	42.0	11.4
THAT deletion	3.0	0.0	9.0	9.0	2.5
stranded prepositions	1.3	0.0	5.0	5.0	1.3
split infinitives	0.0	0.0	0.0	0.0	0.0
split auxiliaries	7.0	2.0	15.0	13.0	3.0
phrasal coordination	3.4	0.0	6.0	6.0	1.6
non-phrasal coordination	3.6	0.0	8.0	8.0	2.2
synthetic negation	2.7	0.0	8.0	8.0	2.0
analytic negation	10.4	3.0	17.0	14.0	3.9

Mean frequencies for Mystery Fiction

Linguistic feature	Mean	Minimum value	Maximum value	Range	Standard deviation
past tense	93.6	72.0	116.0	44.0	12.4
perfect aspect verbs	14.9	2.0	29.0	27.0	7.7
present tense	46.4	22.0	66.0	44.0	16.3
place adverbials	4.8	1.0	13.0	12.0	3.7
time adverbials	5.6	1.0	9.0	8.0	2.2
first person pronouns	29.2	4.0	89.0	85.0	24.3
second person pronouns	10.5	0.0	26.0	26.0	8.1
third person pronouns	57.8	5.0	81.0	76.0	20.5
pronoun IT	13.9	6.0	29.0	23.0	5.7
demonstrative pronouns	3.2	0.0	7.0	7.0	1.7
indefinite pronouns	2.7	0.0	6.0	6.0	2.3
DO as pro-verb	3.5	0.0	5.0	5.0	1.7
WH questions	0.0	0.0	0.0	0.0	0.0
nominalizations	8.3	3.0	13.0	10.0	3.7
gerunds	4.9	2.0	7.0	5.0	1.6
nouns	165.7	127.0	212.0	85.0	25.7
agentless passives	4.9	1.0	12.0	11.0	3.4
BY passives	0.1	0.0	1.0	1.0	0.3
BE as main verb	28.0	19.0	43.0	24.0	7.5
existential THERE	2.5	0.0	7.0	7.0	1.9
THAT verb complements	1.8	0.0	5.0	5.0	1.6
THAT adj. complements	0.0	0.0	0.0	0.0	0.0
WH clauses	0.6	0.0	3.0	3.0	0.9
infinitives	14.5	7.0	24.0	17.0	4.7
present participial clauses	2.8	0.0	11.0	11.0	3.0
past participial clauses	0.0	0.0	0.0	0.0	0.0
past prt. WHIZ deletions	1.0	0.0	6.0	6.0	1.7
present prt. WHIZ deletions	1.3	0.0	4.0	4.0	1.4
THAT relatives: subj. position	0.8	0.0	3.0	3.0	0.9
THAT relatives: obj. position	0.7	0.0	3.0	3.0	0.9
WH relatives: subj. position	1.1	0.0	4.0	4.0	1.3
WH relatives: obj. position	0.6	0.0	5.0	5.0	1.4
WH relatives: pied pipes	0.4	0.0	4.0	4.0	1.1
sentence relatives	0.0	0.0	0.0	0.0	0.0
adv. subordinator - cause	0.2	0.0	1.0	1.0	0.4
adv. sub. - concession	0.5	0.0	2.0	2.0	0.8
adv. sub. - condition	3.2	0.0	6.0	6.0	2.0
adv. sub. - other	0.8	0.0	3.0	3.0	1.1
prepositions	93.0	68.0	132.0	64.0	15.8
attributive adjectives	50.4	32.0	73.0	41.0	13.3
predicative adjectives	5.4	2.0	10.0	8.0	2.4
adverbs	73.6	55.0	94.0	39.0	11.1
type/token ratio	53.2	47.0	59.0	12.0	3.7
word length	4.2	3.8	4.5	0.7	0.2
conjuncts	0.3	0.0	2.0	2.0	0.6
downtoners	2.2	0.0	4.0	4.0	1.2
hedges	0.7	0.0	4.0	4.0	1.1
amplifiers	1.1	0.0	3.0	3.0	1.2
emphatics	5.1	0.0	11.0	11.0	2.8
discourse particles	0.2	0.0	1.0	1.0	0.4
demonstratives	6.6	2.0	11.0	9.0	2.6
possibility modals	6.1	1.0	14.0	13.0	4.1
necessity modals	1.6	0.0	4.0	4.0	1.3
predictive modals	4.5	0.0	10.0	10.0	3.3
public verbs	8.3	1.0	16.0	15.0	5.3
private verbs	19.2	10.0	33.0	23.0	6.0
suasive verbs	2.5	0.0	8.0	8.0	2.3
SEEM/APPEAR	0.7	0.0	4.0	4.0	1.3
contractions	18.1	1.0	31.0	30.0	10.2
THAT deletion	3.2	0.0	8.0	8.0	2.2
stranded prepositions	1.9	0.0	4.0	4.0	1.3
split infinitives	0.0	0.0	0.0	0.0	0.0
split auxiliaries	4.5	1.0	10.0	9.0	2.8
phrasal coordination	2.4	0.0	6.0	6.0	1.7
non-phrasal coordination	2.0	0.0	6.0	6.0	1.6
synthetic negation	2.8	1.0	7.0	6.0	2.0
analytic negation	9.4	2.0	16.0	14.0	3.7

Mean frequencies for Science Fiction

Linguistic feature	Mean	Minimum value	Maximum value	Range	Standard deviation
past tense	74.2	63.0	89.0	26.0	11.2
perfect aspect verbs	8.8	7.0	12.0	5.0	2.1
present tense	51.2	31.0	64.0	33.0	10.9
place adverbials	4.5	3.0	7.0	4.0	1.4
time adverbials	5.3	2.0	8.0	6.0	2.2
first person pronouns	22.2	8.0	57.0	49.0	17.6
second person pronouns	7.3	0.0	18.0	18.0	6.3
third person pronouns	44.5	25.0	66.0	41.0	14.6
pronoun IT	11.3	7.0	14.0	7.0	3.0
demonstrative pronouns	1.8	0.0	5.0	5.0	1.8
indefinite pronouns	0.7	0.0	1.0	1.0	0.5
DO as pro-verb	3.3	0.0	8.0	8.0	2.7
WH questions	0.0	0.0	0.0	0.0	0.0
nominalizations	14.0	7.0	24.0	17.0	6.0
gerunds	7.0	1.0	12.0	11.0	3.7
nouns	171.7	153.0	188.0	35.0	14.5
agentless passives	5.8	4.0	9.0	5.0	2.1
BY passives	0.0	0.0	0.0	0.0	0.0
BE as main verb	25.2	21.0	32.0	11.0	3.9
existential THERE	1.5	0.0	3.0	3.0	1.2
THAT verb complements	1.5	1.0	4.0	3.0	1.2
THAT adj. complements	0.2	0.0	1.0	1.0	0.4
WH clauses	0.3	0.0	1.0	1.0	0.5
infinitives	12.5	9.0	15.0	6.0	2.1
present participial clauses	6.7	4.0	10.0	6.0	2.3
past participial clauses	0.0	0.0	0.0	0.0	0.0
past prt. WHIZ deletions	1.8	0.0	5.0	5.0	1.8
present prt. WHIZ deletions	1.5	0.0	3.0	3.0	1.4
THAT relatives: subj. position	0.8	0.0	2.0	2.0	1.0
THAT relatives: obj. position	0.2	0.0	1.0	1.0	0.4
WH relatives: subj. position	1.3	0.0	4.0	4.0	1.4
WH relatives: obj. position	1.3	0.0	4.0	4.0	1.8
WH relatives: pied pipes	0.7	0.0	3.0	3.0	1.2
sentence relatives	0.0	0.0	0.0	0.0	0.0
adv. subordinator - cause	0.3	0.0	2.0	2.0	0.8
adv. sub. - concession	1.2	0.0	2.0	2.0	0.8
adv. sub. - condition	2.5	0.0	5.0	5.0	2.1
adv. sub. - other	0.8	0.0	2.0	2.0	0.8
prepositions	94.3	74.0	110.0	36.0	14.5
attributive adjectives	62.8	46.0	86.0	40.0	14.0
predicative adjectives	4.0	1.0	9.0	8.0	2.7
adverbs	70.5	57.0	80.0	23.0	7.8
type/token ratio	55.2	47.0	61.0	14.0	4.7
word length	4.4	4.2	4.6	0.4	0.1
conjuncts	0.2	0.0	1.0	1.0	0.4
downtoners	1.7	0.0	4.0	4.0	1.6
hedges	0.3	0.0	1.0	1.0	0.5
amplifiers	1.7	0.0	6.0	6.0	2.4
emphatics	4.7	1.0	8.0	7.0	2.3
discourse particles	0.3	0.0	1.0	1.0	0.5
demonstratives	9.2	4.0	14.0	10.0	3.8
possibility modals	5.2	1.0	10.0	9.0	3.4
necessity modals	1.8	0.0	3.0	3.0	1.3
predictive modals	4.0	1.0	9.0	8.0	2.8
public verbs	8.7	5.0	13.0	8.0	3.0
private verbs	17.5	13.0	23.0	10.0	3.9
suasive verbs	3.8	1.0	6.0	5.0	1.7
SEEM/APPEAR	1.2	0.0	3.0	3.0	1.5
contractions	6.5	0.0	14.0	14.0	5.8
THAT deletion	1.7	0.0	4.0	4.0	1.5
stranded prepositions	2.0	0.0	6.0	6.0	2.2
split infinitives	0.0	0.0	0.0	0.0	0.0
split auxiliaries	5.2	1.0	9.0	8.0	2.7
phrasal coordination	4.2	0.0	10.0	10.0	3.3
non-phrasal coordination	3.3	1.0	7.0	6.0	2.3
synthetic negation	2.8	0.0	6.0	6.0	2.4
analytic negation	7.5	4.0	12.0	8.0	2.7

Mean frequencies for Adventure Fiction

Linguistic feature	Mean	Minimum value	Maximum value	Range	Standard deviation
past tense	84.8	67.0	119.0	52.0	14.2
perfect aspect verbs	12.2	3.0	21.0	18.0	4.8
present tense	55.2	29.0	81.0	52.0	16.0
place adverbials	5.0	1.0	11.0	10.0	2.9
time adverbials	5.2	2.0	9.0	7.0	2.2
first person pronouns	35.2	11.0	67.0	56.0	19.4
second person pronouns	13.1	2.0	27.0	25.0	8.3
third person pronouns	55.2	32.0	79.0	47.0	15.4
pronoun IT	10.8	5.0	19.0	14.0	3.4
demonstrative pronouns	2.0	0.0	6.0	6.0	1.7
indefinite pronouns	1.7	0.0	5.0	5.0	1.5
DO as pro-verb	3.5	0.0	8.0	8.0	2.4
WH questions	0.1	0.0	1.0	1.0	0.3
nominalizations	7.8	3.0	13.0	10.0	3.8
gerunds	6.0	2.0	11.0	9.0	2.5
nouns	165.6	133.0	194.0	61.0	17.3
agentless passives	4.6	1.0	9.0	8.0	2.3
BY passives	0.1	0.0	1.0	1.0	0.3
BE as main verb	25.7	18.0	36.0	18.0	5.0
existential THERE	2.1	0.0	4.0	4.0	1.3
THAT verb complements	1.8	0.0	5.0	5.0	1.5
THAT adj. complements	0.2	0.0	1.0	1.0	0.4
WH clauses	1.2	0.0	4.0	4.0	1.1
infinitives	15.3	10.0	26.0	16.0	5.4
present participial clauses	3.2	0.0	8.0	8.0	2.7
past participial clauses	0.0	0.0	0.0	0.0	0.0
past prt. WHIZ deletions	0.3	0.0	1.0	1.0	0.5
present prt. WHIZ deletions	1.1	0.0	4.0	4.0	1.3
THAT relatives: subj. position	0.5	0.0	4.0	4.0	1.1
THAT relatives: obj. position	0.1	0.0	1.0	1.0	0.3
WH relatives: subj. position	1.2	0.0	3.0	3.0	1.2
WH relatives: obj. position	0.4	0.0	4.0	4.0	1.1
WH relatives: pied pipes	0.1	0.0	1.0	1.0	0.3
sentence relatives	0.0	0.0	0.0	0.0	0.0
adv. subordinator - cause	0.4	0.0	2.0	2.0	0.8
adv. sub. - concession	0.5	0.0	3.0	3.0	1.0
adv. sub. - condition	2.3	0.0	6.0	6.0	1.7
adv. sub. - other	1.3	0.0	3.0	3.0	1.1
prepositions	94.3	73.0	112.0	39.0	13.9
attributive adjectives	46.5	38.0	58.0	20.0	7.1
predicative adjectives	5.2	1.0	9.0	8.0	2.4
adverbs	69.8	59.0	88.0	29.0	8.5
type/token ratio	52.8	48.0	59.0	11.0	3.5
word length	4.1	3.9	4.5	0.6	0.2
conjuncts	0.5	0.0	2.0	2.0	0.8
downtoners	1.5	0.0	5.0	5.0	1.5
hedges	0.5	0.0	3.0	3.0	1.0
amplifiers	0.9	0.0	2.0	2.0	1.0
emphatics	5.8	3.0	10.0	7.0	2.1
discourse particles	0.2	0.0	1.0	1.0	0.4
demonstratives	7.5	2.0	13.0	11.0	3.6
possibility modals	6.1	4.0	10.0	6.0	2.0
necessity modals	1.8	0.0	5.0	5.0	1.8
predictive modals	4.2	1.0	9.0	8.0	2.4
public verbs	10.0	4.0	20.0	16.0	5.6
private verbs	18.8	11.0	31.0	20.0	5.9
suasive verbs	2.3	0.0	6.0	6.0	1.8
SEEM/APPEAR	0.8	0.0	3.0	3.0	1.1
contractions	17.5	4.0	30.0	26.0	8.5
THAT deletion	1.8	0.0	4.0	4.0	1.4
stranded prepositions	2.2	0.0	6.0	6.0	1.7
split infinitives	0.0	0.0	0.0	0.0	0.0
split auxiliaries	4.1	1.0	9.0	8.0	2.4
phrasal coordination	2.0	0.0	5.0	5.0	1.7
non-phrasal coordination	2.4	0.0	5.0	5.0	1.9
synthetic negation	2.7	0.0	7.0	7.0	2.1
analytic negation	9.2	3.0	17.0	14.0	4.3

Mean frequencies for Romantic Fiction

Linguistic feature	Mean	Minimum value	Maximum value	Range	Standard deviation
past tense	83.7	64.0	105.0	41.0	11.1
perfect aspect verbs	13.6	8.0	30.0	22.0	5.5
present tense	65.8	46.0	90.0	44.0	11.8
place adverbials	3.6	0.0	8.0	8.0	2.3
time adverbials	6.8	3.0	10.0	7.0	2.3
first person pronouns	32.4	18.0	56.0	38.0	11.4
second person pronouns	18.6	9.0	31.0	22.0	7.2
third person pronouns	78.5	49.0	102.0	53.0	13.9
pronoun IT	9.8	6.0	16.0	10.0	2.9
demonstrative pronouns	2.6	1.0	5.0	4.0	1.4
indefinite pronouns	2.3	0.0	5.0	5.0	1.6
DO as pro-verb	3.7	2.0	8.0	6.0	1.5
WH questions	0.2	0.0	2.0	2.0	0.6
nominalizations	8.5	5.0	15.0	10.0	2.9
gerunds	5.8	3.0	9.0	6.0	1.8
nouns	146.8	119.0	173.0	54.0	17.6
agentless passives	5.0	4.0	7.0	3.0	1.1
BY passives	0.0	0.0	0.0	0.0	0.0
BE as main verb	28.1	23.0	33.0	10.0	3.2
existential THERE	1.5	0.0	4.0	4.0	1.5
THAT verb complements	2.5	0.0	7.0	7.0	2.5
THAT adj. complements	0.4	0.0	2.0	2.0	0.7
WH clauses	0.5	0.0	2.0	2.0	0.7
infinitives	19.0	14.0	27.0	13.0	3.3
present participial clauses	4.5	0.0	9.0	9.0	2.8
past participial clauses	0.1	0.0	1.0	1.0	0.3
past prt. WHIZ deletions	0.1	0.0	1.0	1.0	0.3
present prt. WHIZ deletions	0.5	0.0	3.0	3.0	1.0
THAT relatives: subj. position	0.3	0.0	1.0	1.0	0.5
THAT relatives: obj. position	0.2	0.0	1.0	1.0	0.4
WH relatives: subj. position	0.8	0.0	3.0	3.0	1.0
WH relatives: obj. position	0.4	0.0	1.0	1.0	0.5
WH relatives: pied pipes	0.1	0.0	1.0	1.0	0.3
sentence relatives	0.0	0.0	0.0	0.0	0.0
adv. subordinator - cause	0.2	0.0	2.0	2.0	0.6
adv. sub. - concession	0.4	0.0	2.0	2.0	0.7
adv. sub. - condition	3.2	0.0	8.0	8.0	2.0
adv. sub. - other	0.8	0.0	2.0	2.0	0.8
prepositions	82.0	69.0	97.0	28.0	8.5
attributive adjectives	41.9	36.0	56.0	20.0	5.9
predicative adjectives	7.0	4.0	11.0	7.0	1.7
adverbs	78.4	65.0	93.0	28.0	10.0
type/token ratio	52.9	47.0	59.0	12.0	3.5
word length	4.1	3.9	4.3	0.3	0.1
conjuncts	0.1	0.0	1.0	1.0	0.3
downtoners	1.8	0.0	4.0	4.0	1.1
hedges	0.1	0.0	1.0	1.0	0.3
amplifiers	2.2	0.0	5.0	5.0	1.4
emphatics	6.8	2.0	11.0	9.0	2.6
discourse particles	0.0	0.0	0.0	0.0	0.0
demonstratives	7.3	4.0	12.0	8.0	2.4
possibility modals	6.5	3.0	11.0	8.0	2.4
necessity modals	1.9	0.0	6.0	6.0	2.1
predictive modals	8.5	4.0	17.0	13.0	3.5
public verbs	8.6	3.0	15.0	12.0	4.0
private verbs	24.2	12.0	31.0	19.0	5.4
suasive verbs	2.6	0.0	8.0	8.0	2.3
SEEM/APPEAR	0.8	0.0	3.0	3.0	0.9
contractions	19.0	4.0	41.0	37.0	11.3
THAT deletion	5.2	2.0	14.0	12.0	3.1
stranded prepositions	1.5	0.0	5.0	5.0	1.3
split infinitives	0.0	0.0	0.0	0.0	0.0
split auxiliaries	6.0	2.0	9.0	7.0	1.8
phrasal coordination	3.2	1.0	7.0	6.0	1.8
non-phrasal coordination	2.8	0.0	7.0	7.0	1.8
synthetic negation	2.5	0.0	7.0	7.0	2.4
analytic negation	12.7	7.0	20.0	13.0	4.2

Mean frequencies for Humor

Linguistic feature	Mean	Minimum value	Maximum value	Range	Standard deviation
past tense	56.1	6.0	89.0	83.0	30.4
perfect aspect verbs	8.0	4.0	12.0	8.0	2.4
present tense	59.8	32.0	112.0	80.0	27.9
place adverbials	3.2	1.0	7.0	6.0	2.2
time adverbials	5.3	0.0	10.0	10.0	3.2
first person pronouns	29.7	5.0	58.0	53.0	18.3
second person pronouns	8.7	0.0	24.0	24.0	8.0
third person pronouns	33.0	9.0	53.0	44.0	13.2
pronoun IT	8.2	2.0	14.0	12.0	4.2
demonstrative pronouns	1.9	1.0	3.0	2.0	0.9
indefinite pronouns	1.3	0.0	3.0	3.0	1.1
DO as pro-verb	1.8	0.0	4.0	4.0	1.2
WH questions	0.3	0.0	2.0	2.0	0.7
nominalizations	12.1	6.0	17.0	11.0	3.4
gerunds	7.3	3.0	12.0	9.0	3.0
nouns	190.2	142.0	243.0	101.0	29.1
agentless passives	7.8	6.0	10.0	4.0	1.4
BY passives	0.3	0.0	2.0	2.0	0.7
BE as main verb	26.3	17.0	43.0	26.0	7.7
existential THERE	1.9	0.0	5.0	5.0	2.0
THAT verb complements	2.1	0.0	5.0	5.0	1.7
THAT adj. complements	0.0	0.0	0.0	0.0	0.0
WH clauses	0.4	0.0	2.0	2.0	0.7
infinitives	16.3	10.0	24.0	14.0	4.5
present participial clauses	1.7	0.0	3.0	3.0	0.9
past participial clauses	0.2	0.0	1.0	1.0	0.4
past prt. WHIZ deletions	2.8	1.0	5.0	4.0	1.4
present prt. WHIZ deletions	1.4	0.0	3.0	3.0	1.1
THAT relatives: subj. position	0.1	0.0	1.0	1.0	0.3
THAT relatives: obj. position	0.4	0.0	3.0	3.0	1.0
WH relatives: subj. position	2.1	0.0	3.0	3.0	1.1
WH relatives: obj. position	1.3	0.0	4.0	4.0	1.2
WH relatives: pied pipes	0.7	0.0	3.0	3.0	1.0
sentence relatives	0.0	0.0	0.0	0.0	0.0
adv. subordinator - cause	0.4	0.0	2.0	2.0	0.7
adv. sub. - concession	0.2	0.0	1.0	1.0	0.4
adv. sub. - condition	2.0	1.0	4.0	3.0	1.3
adv. sub. - other	0.7	0.0	3.0	3.0	1.0
prepositions	111.7	96.0	127.0	31.0	10.0
attributive adjectives	65.0	55.0	81.0	26.0	7.6
predicative adjectives	4.1	2.0	6.0	4.0	1.5
adverbs	68.2	55.0	84.0	29.0	11.8
type/token ratio	55.3	49.0	59.0	10.0	3.2
word length	4.5	4.3	4.6	0.4	0.1
conjuncts	1.6	0.0	5.0	5.0	1.4
downtoners	2.2	0.0	5.0	5.0	1.6
hedges	0.1	0.0	1.0	1.0	0.3
amplifiers	1.6	0.0	3.0	3.0	1.1
emphatics	4.8	1.0	12.0	11.0	3.3
discourse particles	0.3	0.0	2.0	2.0	0.7
demonstratives	8.9	4.0	14.0	10.0	3.3
possibility modals	4.4	2.0	9.0	7.0	2.2
necessity modals	1.1	0.0	3.0	3.0	0.9
predictive modals	5.7	0.0	15.0	15.0	4.2
public verbs	6.6	3.0	12.0	9.0	3.4
private verbs	13.8	10.0	20.0	10.0	3.5
suasive verbs	2.7	0.0	7.0	7.0	2.2
SEEM/APPEAR	0.9	0.0	2.0	2.0	0.8
contractions	6.1	0.0	16.0	16.0	6.5
THAT deletion	1.1	0.0	2.0	2.0	0.6
stranded prepositions	2.0	0.0	5.0	5.0	1.7
split infinitives	0.0	0.0	0.0	0.0	0.0
split auxiliaries	5.9	3.0	11.0	8.0	2.3
phrasal coordination	3.6	1.0	6.0	5.0	1.7
non-phrasal coordination	2.4	1.0	4.0	3.0	1.0
synthetic negation	2.1	1.0	4.0	3.0	1.3
analytic negation	7.8	4.0	14.0	10.0	3.4

Mean frequencies for Personal Letters

Linguistic feature	Mean	Minimum value	Maximum value	Range	Standard deviation
past tense	43.8	14.0	65.0	51.0	19.9
perfect aspect verbs	11.2	6.0	20.0	14.0	5.5
present tense	127.7	103.0	143.0	40.0	16.0
place adverbials	2.0	0.0	5.0	5.0	1.8
time adverbials	8.3	3.0	14.0	11.0	4.0
first person pronouns	62.0	37.0	91.0	54.0	22.5
second person pronouns	20.2	5.0	43.0	38.0	13.4
third person pronouns	52.8	28.0	75.0	47.0	19.7
pronoun IT	11.0	6.0	16.0	10.0	3.6
demonstrative pronouns	3.7	0.0	6.0	6.0	2.1
indefinite pronouns	2.3	0.0	6.0	6.0	2.2
DO as pro-verb	4.3	0.0	8.0	8.0	2.9
WH questions	0.2	0.0	1.0	1.0	0.4
nominalizations	5.2	2.0	8.0	6.0	2.8
gerunds	3.5	1.0	6.0	5.0	1.6
nouns	156.7	124.0	195.0	71.0	26.1
agentless passives	2.8	0.0	6.0	6.0	2.3
BY passives	0.0	0.0	0.0	0.0	0.0
BE as main verb	39.3	35.0	49.0	14.0	5.2
existential THERE	1.2	0.0	3.0	3.0	1.3
THAT verb complements	1.3	0.0	4.0	4.0	1.5
THAT adj. complements	0.2	0.0	1.0	1.0	0.4
WH clauses	1.0	1.0	1.0	0.0	0.0
infinitives	19.8	16.0	23.0	7.0	2.6
present participial clauses	0.2	0.0	1.0	1.0	0.4
past participial clauses	0.0	0.0	0.0	0.0	0.0
past prt. WHIZ deletions	0.2	0.0	1.0	1.0	0.4
present prt. WHIZ deletions	0.0	0.0	0.0	0.0	0.0
THAT relatives: subj. position	0.0	0.0	0.0	0.0	0.0
THAT relatives: obj. position	0.5	0.0	1.0	1.0	0.5
WH relatives: subj. position	0.7	0.0	2.0	2.0	0.8
WH relatives: obj. position	0.2	0.0	1.0	1.0	0.4
WH relatives: pied pipes	0.2	0.0	1.0	1.0	0.4
sentence relatives	0.2	0.0	1.0	1.0	0.4
adv. subordinator - cause	2.7	0.0	4.0	4.0	1.4
adv. sub. - concession	1.7	0.0	4.0	4.0	1.6
adv. sub. - condition	3.5	0.0	9.0	9.0	3.4
adv. sub. - other	1.7	0.0	6.0	6.0	2.3
prepositions	72.0	54.0	82.0	28.0	10.3
attributive adjectives	44.2	36.0	54.0	18.0	6.4
predicative adjectives	8.3	6.0	13.0	7.0	2.5
adverbs	80.7	70.0	89.0	19.0	6.7
type/token ratio	52.5	50.0	56.0	6.0	2.6
word length	3.9	3.8	4.0	0.2	0.1
conjuncts	0.2	0.0	1.0	1.0	0.4
downtoners	1.2	0.0	2.0	2.0	0.8
hedges	3.3	0.0	7.0	7.0	2.7
amplifiers	2.2	0.0	5.0	5.0	1.9
emphatics	11.2	4.0	17.0	13.0	5.1
discourse particles	1.2	0.0	4.0	4.0	1.6
demonstratives	9.0	3.0	16.0	13.0	5.0
possibility modals	9.0	4.0	16.0	12.0	4.8
necessity modals	1.5	0.0	5.0	5.0	2.1
predictive modals	9.8	3.0	16.0	13.0	4.4
public verbs	6.7	3.0	11.0	8.0	3.2
private verbs	27.2	20.0	33.0	13.0	5.0
suasive verbs	1.0	0.0	3.0	3.0	1.3
SEEM/APPEAR	2.2	0.0	6.0	6.0	2.3
contractions	22.2	12.0	48.0	36.0	13.9
THAT deletion	12.8	8.0	21.0	13.0	4.4
stranded prepositions	1.3	0.0	3.0	3.0	1.0
split infinitives	0.2	0.0	1.0	1.0	0.4
split auxiliaries	5.5	3.0	7.0	4.0	1.6
phrasal coordination	5.7	1.0	11.0	10.0	4.3
non-phrasal coordination	6.3	2.0	11.0	9.0	4.2
synthetic negation	0.7	0.0	2.0	2.0	0.8
analytic negation	12.0	3.0	19.0	16.0	5.6

Mean frequencies for Professional Letters

Linguistic feature	Mean	Minimum value	Maximum value	Range	Standard deviation
past tense	10.1	0.0	20.0	20.0	6.7
perfect aspect verbs	10.3	0.0	24.0	24.0	8.7
present tense	94.7	71.0	123.0	52.0	16.8
place adverbials	1.6	0.0	6.0	6.0	2.0
time adverbials	2.0	0.0	4.0	4.0	1.7
first person pronouns	40.9	16.0	68.0	52.0	14.8
second person pronouns	15.2	0.0	42.0	42.0	13.8
third person pronouns	8.7	0.0	24.0	24.0	9.1
pronoun IT	7.1	1.0	28.0	27.0	8.1
demonstrative pronouns	2.4	0.0	10.0	10.0	3.1
indefinite pronouns	1.1	0.0	8.0	8.0	2.5
DO as pro-verb	2.6	0.0	12.0	12.0	3.6
WH questions	0.0	0.0	0.0	0.0	0.0
nominalizations	44.2	24.0	60.0	36.0	12.0
gerunds	11.7	4.0	23.0	19.0	6.3
nouns	172.6	143.0	221.0	78.0	22.8
agentless passives	7.3	1.0	15.0	14.0	4.3
BY passives	0.6	0.0	2.0	2.0	0.8
BE as main verb	27.0	13.0	45.0	32.0	10.2
existential THERE	0.7	0.0	4.0	4.0	1.3
THAT verb complements	4.3	0.0	14.0	14.0	4.3
THAT adj. complements	0.5	0.0	3.0	3.0	1.1
WH clauses	1.0	0.0	5.0	5.0	1.8
infinitives	24.1	12.0	32.0	20.0	6.0
present participial clauses	0.3	0.0	2.0	2.0	0.7
past participial clauses	0.2	0.0	1.0	1.0	0.4
past prt. WHIZ deletions	1.3	0.0	3.0	3.0	1.2
present prt. WHIZ deletions	2.5	0.0	11.0	11.0	3.4
THAT relatives: subj. position	0.7	0.0	3.0	3.0	1.1
THAT relatives: obj. position	1.1	0.0	7.0	7.0	2.2
WH relatives: subj. position	3.4	0.0	15.0	15.0	4.6
WH relatives: obj. position	2.9	0.0	9.0	9.0	3.4
WH relatives: pied pipes	0.9	0.0	3.0	3.0	1.1
sentence relatives	0.0	0.0	0.0	0.0	0.0
adv. subordinator - cause	2.9	0.0	11.0	11.0	3.8
adv. sub. - concession	0.5	0.0	4.0	4.0	1.3
adv. sub. - condition	2.0	0.0	6.0	6.0	2.3
adv. sub. - other	1.4	0.0	4.0	4.0	1.7
prepositions	118.9	96.0	157.0	61.0	21.8
attributive adjectives	76.5	56.0	101.0	45.0	17.1
predicative adjectives	7.4	1.0	19.0	18.0	5.3
adverbs	49.8	36.0	74.0	38.0	12.6
type/token ratio	53.0	45.0	60.0	15.0	4.2
word length	4.8	4.5	5.1	0.6	0.2
conjuncts	2.5	0.0	10.0	10.0	3.1
downtoners	1.6	0.0	7.0	7.0	2.1
hedges	0.3	0.0	2.0	2.0	0.7
amplifiers	1.9	0.0	8.0	8.0	2.6
emphatics	7.8	1.0	20.0	19.0	6.3
discourse particles	0.2	0.0	2.0	2.0	0.6
demonstratives	12.0	2.0	22.0	20.0	5.2
possibility modals	7.7	1.0	20.0	19.0	5.6
necessity modals	2.2	0.0	6.0	6.0	2.3
predictive modals	11.9	0.0	30.0	30.0	10.1
public verbs	9.2	0.0	26.0	26.0	8.1
private verbs	17.1	11.0	30.0	19.0	6.3
suasive verbs	3.7	0.0	10.0	10.0	3.9
SEEM/APPEAR	1.0	0.0	4.0	4.0	1.3
contractions	4.7	0.0	26.0	26.0	8.1
THAT deletion	1.9	0.0	7.0	7.0	2.7
stranded prepositions	0.1	0.0	1.0	1.0	0.3
split infinitives	0.0	0.0	0.0	0.0	0.0
split auxiliaries	6.0	2.0	10.0	8.0	2.9
phrasal coordination	5.8	0.0	12.0	12.0	4.3
non-phrasal coordination	1.5	0.0	4.0	4.0	1.6
synthetic negation	1.0	0.0	3.0	3.0	1.3
analytic negation	7.2	0.0	14.0	14.0	4.4

Mean frequencies for Face-to-face Conversations

Linguistic feature	Mean	Minimum value	Maximum value	Range	Standard deviation
past tense	37.4	10.0	72.0	62.0	17.3
perfect aspect verbs	10.4	3.0	22.0	19.0	3.6
present tense	128.4	66.0	182.0	116.0	22.2
place adverbials	2.0	0.0	14.0	14.0	2.2
time adverbials	5.1	1.0	8.0	7.0	1.9
first person pronouns	57.9	28.0	86.0	58.0	13.5
second person pronouns	30.8	10.0	55.0	45.0	11.2
third person pronouns	29.2	4.0	70.0	66.0	16.0
pronoun IT	20.0	6.0	42.0	36.0	7.7
demonstrative pronouns	13.1	5.0	28.0	23.0	4.5
indefinite pronouns	3.9	1.0	9.0	8.0	2.1
DO as pro-verb	9.0	1.0	18.0	17.0	3.6
WH questions	0.7	0.0	4.0	4.0	1.0
nominalizations	9.2	2.0	25.0	23.0	5.3
gerunds	4.7	1.0	13.0	12.0	2.2
nouns	137.4	110.0	164.0	54.0	15.6
agentless passives	4.2	1.0	11.0	10.0	2.1
BY passives	0.1	0.0	1.0	1.0	0.3
BE as main verb	39.5	24.0	65.0	41.0	7.2
existential THERE	2.8	0.0	10.0	10.0	1.9
THAT verb complements	4.0	0.0	8.0	8.0	2.0
THAT adj. complements	0.1	0.0	2.0	2.0	0.4
WH clauses	1.3	0.0	3.0	3.0	1.0
infinitives	13.8	7.0	22.0	15.0	3.7
present participial clauses	0.0	0.0	1.0	1.0	0.2
past participial clauses	0.0	0.0	0.0	0.0	0.0
past prt. WHIZ deletions	0.1	0.0	2.0	2.0	0.4
present prt. WHIZ deletions	0.4	0.0	2.0	2.0	0.6
THAT relatives: subj. position	0.4	0.0	2.0	2.0	0.5
THAT relatives: obj. position	0.9	0.0	3.0	3.0	0.9
WH relatives: subj. position	0.9	0.0	4.0	4.0	1.0
WH relatives: obj. position	0.5	0.0	3.0	3.0	0.7
WH relatives: pied pipes	0.2	0.0	2.0	2.0	0.5
sentence relatives	0.7	0.0	3.0	3.0	0.9
adv. subordinator - cause	3.5	1.0	8.0	7.0	1.7
adv. sub. - concession	0.3	0.0	3.0	3.0	0.7
adv. sub. - condition	3.9	0.0	8.0	8.0	2.1
adv. sub. - other	0.8	0.0	4.0	4.0	1.0
prepositions	85.0	64.0	112.0	48.0	12.4
attributive adjectives	40.8	30.0	68.0	38.0	7.9
predicative adjectives	4.2	0.0	9.0	9.0	1.9
adverbs	86.0	62.0	115.0	53.0	11.6
type/token ratio	46.1	39.0	60.0	21.0	3.6
word length	4.1	3.8	4.3	0.5	0.1
conjuncts	0.3	0.0	3.0	3.0	0.7
downtoners	1.5	0.0	5.0	5.0	1.3
hedges	2.1	0.0	10.0	10.0	2.1
amplifiers	6.0	2.0	12.0	10.0	2.3
emphatics	12.2	4.0	20.0	16.0	3.7
discourse particles	3.9	0.0	8.0	8.0	2.0
demonstratives	11.1	5.0	20.0	15.0	3.9
possibility modals	7.9	2.0	21.0	19.0	3.4
necessity modals	1.9	0.0	7.0	7.0	1.5
predictive modals	5.8	1.0	16.0	15.0	3.5
public verbs	8.8	3.0	19.0	16.0	4.0
private verbs	35.4	22.0	53.0	31.0	8.0
suasive verbs	1.5	0.0	8.0	8.0	1.6
SEEM/APPEAR	0.4	0.0	2.0	2.0	0.6
contractions	46.2	27.0	71.0	44.0	10.8
THAT deletion	9.6	3.0	23.0	20.0	4.0
stranded prepositions	4.8	1.0	13.0	12.0	2.4
split infinitives	0.0	0.0	0.0	0.0	0.0
split auxiliaries	4.8	1.0	9.0	8.0	1.7
phrasal coordination	1.3	0.0	5.0	5.0	1.3
non-phrasal coordination	9.5	4.0	20.0	16.0	4.4
synthetic negation	0.9	0.0	4.0	4.0	0.9
analytic negation	18.5	8.0	32.0	24.0	5.1

Mean frequencies for Telephone Conversations

Linguistic feature	Mean	Minimum value	Maximum value	Range	Standard deviation
past tense	28.3	3.0	70.0	67.0	15.9
perfect aspect verbs	8.8	0.0	20.0	20.0	5.2
present tense	142.6	110.0	182.0	72.0	19.5
place adverbials	1.7	0.0	7.0	7.0	2.1
time adverbials	7.4	1.0	15.0	14.0	3.9
first person pronouns	70.7	28.0	104.0	76.0	18.7
second person pronouns	34.3	19.0	72.0	53.0	11.2
third person pronouns	21.7	0.0	62.0	62.0	14.4
pronoun IT	22.2	6.0	47.0	41.0	10.8
demonstrative pronouns	11.5	3.0	30.0	27.0	6.3
indefinite pronouns	3.6	0.0	13.0	13.0	3.3
DO as pro-verb	7.4	0.0	22.0	22.0	5.0
WH questions	1.1	0.0	4.0	4.0	1.2
nominalizations	6.6	0.0	17.0	17.0	5.0
gerunds	3.3	0.0	8.0	8.0	2.1
nouns	134.8	106.0	250.0	144.0	31.1
agentless passives	3.4	0.0	13.0	13.0	3.0
BY passives	0.0	0.0	1.0	1.0	0.2
BE as main verb	43.5	30.0	72.0	42.0	9.7
existential THERE	3.2	0.0	10.0	10.0	2.8
THAT verb complements	3.0	0.0	9.0	9.0	2.8
THAT adj. complements	0.3	0.0	2.0	2.0	0.5
WH clauses	1.1	0.0	6.0	6.0	1.4
infinitives	13.3	1.0	23.0	22.0	4.8
present participial clauses	0.0	0.0	1.0	1.0	0.2
past participial clauses	0.0	0.0	0.0	0.0	0.0
past prt. WHIZ deletions	0.1	0.0	1.0	1.0	0.3
present prt. WHIZ deletions	0.1	0.0	1.0	1.0	0.4
THAT relatives: subj. position	0.4	0.0	3.0	3.0	0.7
THAT relatives: obj. position	0.4	0.0	3.0	3.0	0.7
WH relatives: subj. position	0.9	0.0	8.0	8.0	1.8
WH relatives: obj. position	0.3	0.0	5.0	5.0	1.0
WH relatives: pied pipes	0.1	0.0	3.0	3.0	0.6
sentence relatives	0.3	0.0	3.0	3.0	0.7
adv. subordinator - cause	2.6	0.0	7.0	7.0	1.6
adv. sub. - concession	0.3	0.0	2.0	2.0	0.5
adv. sub. - condition	4.6	0.0	13.0	13.0	3.7
adv. sub. - other	0.3	0.0	2.0	2.0	0.5
prepositions	71.8	50.0	102.0	52.0	12.9
attributive adjectives	38.9	21.0	70.0	49.0	11.3
predicative adjectives	6.0	0.0	16.0	16.0	3.6
adverbs	88.5	63.0	125.0	62.0	14.8
type/token ratio	45.8	40.0	55.0	15.0	3.3
word length	4.0	3.7	4.4	0.6	0.2
conjuncts	0.5	0.0	4.0	4.0	1.0
downtoners	1.6	0.0	5.0	5.0	1.5
hedges	2.7	0.0	8.0	8.0	2.2
amplifiers	5.4	0.0	11.0	11.0	3.1
emphatics	11.3	4.0	22.0	18.0	4.8
discourse particles	6.6	0.0	15.0	15.0	3.7
demonstratives	8.4	0.0	19.0	19.0	4.5
possibility modals	9.1	3.0	17.0	14.0	4.1
necessity modals	2.6	0.0	8.0	8.0	2.1
predictive modals	6.6	0.0	16.0	16.0	3.7
public verbs	6.2	1.0	13.0	12.0	3.0
private verbs	35.6	12.0	54.0	42.0	10.4
suasive verbs	2.0	0.0	7.0	7.0	2.2
SEEM/APPEAR	0.7	0.0	4.0	4.0	1.2
contractions	54.4	21.0	89.0	68.0	12.3
THAT deletion	10.0	3.0	24.0	21.0	4.7
stranded prepositions	3.7	0.0	9.0	9.0	2.1
split infinitives	0.0	0.0	0.0	0.0	0.0
split auxiliaries	4.6	0.0	9.0	9.0	2.3
phrasal coordination	1.0	0.0	3.0	3.0	0.9
non-phrasal coordination	7.5	3.0	15.0	12.0	3.2
synthetic negation	0.9	0.0	8.0	8.0	1.7
analytic negation	16.9	7.0	29.0	22.0	6.4

Mean frequencies for Interviews

Linguistic feature	Mean	Minimum value	Maximum value	Range	Standard deviation
past tense	30.1	4.0	102.0	98.0	24.9
perfect aspect verbs	9.4	3.0	18.0	15.0	4.2
present tense	104.9	39.0	140.0	101.0	28.2
place adverbials	1.6	0.0	8.0	8.0	1.9
time adverbials	5.5	0.0	14.0	14.0	3.2
first person pronouns	50.5	25.0	90.0	65.0	15.8
second person pronouns	19.5	1.0	58.0	57.0	14.6
third person pronouns	22.2	11.0	44.0	33.0	9.8
pronoun IT	11.9	1.0	20.0	19.0	4.8
demonstrative pronouns	8.7	1.0	14.0	13.0	3.4
indefinite pronouns	2.8	0.0	8.0	8.0	2.4
DO as pro-verb	4.6	1.0	8.0	7.0	2.2
WH questions	0.5	0.0	2.0	2.0	0.7
nominalizations	17.7	4.0	34.0	30.0	8.2
gerunds	6.9	2.0	23.0	21.0	4.9
nouns	160.9	109.0	204.0	95.0	23.8
agentless passives	8.0	4.0	14.0	10.0	3.0
BY passives	0.3	0.0	2.0	2.0	0.6
BE as main verb	36.3	22.0	52.0	30.0	7.1
existential THERE	3.4	0.0	8.0	8.0	1.8
THAT verb complements	7.1	2.0	15.0	13.0	3.6
THAT adj. complements	0.4	0.0	2.0	2.0	0.6
WH clauses	0.6	0.0	3.0	3.0	0.7
infinitives	16.4	8.0	28.0	20.0	5.8
present participial clauses	0.0	0.0	0.0	0.0	0.0
past participial clauses	0.0	0.0	0.0	0.0	0.0
past prt. WHIZ deletions	0.3	0.0	2.0	2.0	0.6
present prt. WHIZ deletions	1.0	0.0	3.0	3.0	1.1
THAT relatives: subj. position	1.7	0.0	7.0	7.0	2.0
THAT relatives: obj. position	2.2	0.0	7.0	7.0	1.7
WH relatives: subj. position	2.3	0.0	7.0	7.0	2.0
WH relatives: obj. position	2.0	0.0	5.0	5.0	1.6
WH relatives: pied pipes	1.0	0.0	5.0	5.0	1.3
sentence relatives	0.5	0.0	2.0	2.0	0.7
adv. subordinator - cause	2.7	0.0	8.0	8.0	2.1
adv. sub. - concession	0.4	0.0	3.0	3.0	0.8
adv. sub. - condition	3.6	0.0	7.0	7.0	1.8
adv. sub. - other	0.8	0.0	2.0	2.0	0.7
prepositions	108.0	88.0	150.0	62.0	17.7
attributive adjectives	55.3	38.0	72.0	34.0	10.1
predicative adjectives	5.3	1.0	10.0	9.0	2.5
adverbs	71.8	53.0	88.0	35.0	11.6
type/token ratio	48.4	44.0	55.0	11.0	3.0
word length	4.4	4.1	4.8	0.8	0.2
conjuncts	1.0	0.0	4.0	4.0	1.0
downtoners	1.8	0.0	5.0	5.0	1.7
hedges	0.4	0.0	3.0	3.0	0.9
amplifiers	6.8	2.0	14.0	12.0	3.0
emphatics	9.7	3.0	18.0	15.0	3.9
discourse particles	3.0	0.0	8.0	8.0	2.0
demonstratives	11.0	6.0	17.0	11.0	3.3
possibility modals	7.3	1.0	15.0	14.0	3.0
necessity modals	2.7	0.0	6.0	6.0	1.4
predictive modals	7.0	2.0	17.0	15.0	3.9
public verbs	8.5	1.0	17.0	16.0	4.1
private verbs	23.7	13.0	42.0	29.0	8.0
suasive verbs	2.2	0.0	6.0	6.0	1.8
SEEM/APPEAR	0.7	0.0	3.0	3.0	0.9
contractions	25.4	4.0	49.0	45.0	12.3
THAT deletion	4.3	0.0	8.0	8.0	2.4
stranded prepositions	5.4	0.0	15.0	15.0	4.0
split infinitives	0.0	0.0	0.0	0.0	0.0
split auxiliaries	5.0	1.0	10.0	9.0	2.2
phrasal coordination	0.9	0.0	3.0	3.0	0.9
non-phrasal coordination	9.1	1.0	19.0	18.0	3.9
synthetic negation	1.4	0.0	4.0	4.0	1.4
analytic negation	12.6	5.0	22.0	17.0	5.3

Mean frequencies for Broadcasts

Linguistic feature	Mean	Minimum value	Maximum value	Range	Standard deviation
past tense	18.5	3.0	34.0	31.0	11.0
perfect aspect verbs	6.4	2.0	12.0	10.0	2.9
present tense	74.8	40.0	125.0	85.0	21.1
place adverbials	9.9	0.0	20.0	20.0	5.7
time adverbials	13.9	3.0	24.0	21.0	5.9
first person pronouns	11.8	0.0	40.0	40.0	9.9
second person pronouns	2.7	0.0	12.0	12.0	3.5
third person pronouns	31.7	0.0	57.0	57.0	14.1
pronoun IT	9.9	2.0	23.0	21.0	7.1
demonstrative pronouns	5.7	1.0	17.0	16.0	4.4
indefinite pronouns	0.5	0.0	1.0	1.0	0.5
DO as pro-verb	1.1	0.0	4.0	4.0	1.4
WH questions	0.1	0.0	1.0	1.0	0.3
nominalizations	8.2	1.0	42.0	41.0	9.8
gerunds	3.8	0.0	9.0	9.0	1.9
nouns	229.8	138.0	298.0	160.0	44.8
agentless passives	3.6	0.0	9.0	9.0	2.5
BY passives	0.7	0.0	4.0	4.0	1.3
BE as main verb	21.9	13.0	41.0	28.0	7.3
existential THERE	2.2	0.0	6.0	6.0	1.4
THAT verb complements	1.0	0.0	5.0	5.0	1.5
THAT adj. complements	0.2	0.0	2.0	2.0	0.5
WH clauses	0.1	0.0	1.0	1.0	0.2
infinitives	9.8	2.0	20.0	18.0	4.5
present participial clauses	0.0	0.0	0.0	0.0	0.0
past participial clauses	0.0	0.0	0.0	0.0	0.0
past prt. WHIZ deletions	4.3	0.0	15.0	15.0	4.8
present prt. WHIZ deletions	1.2	0.0	6.0	6.0	1.5
THAT relatives: subj. position	0.6	0.0	5.0	5.0	1.2
THAT relatives: obj. position	0.2	0.0	1.0	1.0	0.4
WH relatives: subj. position	1.1	0.0	5.0	5.0	1.5
WH relatives: obj. position	0.4	0.0	2.0	2.0	0.6
WH relatives: pied pipes	0.0	0.0	0.0	0.0	0.0
sentence relatives	0.0	0.0	0.0	0.0	0.0
adv. subordinator - cause	0.4	0.0	2.0	2.0	0.6
adv. sub. - concession	0.3	0.0	2.0	2.0	0.6
adv. sub. - condition	1.3	0.0	5.0	5.0	1.5
adv. sub. - other	0.6	0.0	4.0	4.0	1.0
prepositions	118.0	96.0	135.0	39.0	10.6
attributive adjectives	61.1	39.0	87.0	48.0	11.7
predicative adjectives	3.0	0.0	16.0	16.0	3.8
adverbs	86.3	56.0	114.0	58.0	18.0
type/token ratio	49.7	42.0	55.0	13.0	3.5
word length	4.4	4.2	4.8	0.6	0.2
conjuncts	0.2	0.0	2.0	2.0	0.5
downtoners	1.9	0.0	9.0	9.0	2.4
hedges	0.7	0.0	3.0	3.0	0.9
amplifiers	4.7	3.0	9.0	6.0	2.0
emphatics	7.5	2.0	14.0	12.0	3.7
discourse particles	2.1	0.0	7.0	7.0	1.9
demonstratives	10.8	5.0	19.0	14.0	3.3
possibility modals	3.2	0.0	14.0	14.0	3.5
necessity modals	0.6	0.0	2.0	2.0	0.8
predictive modals	2.1	0.0	7.0	7.0	2.1
public verbs	1.9	0.0	8.0	8.0	2.2
private verbs	10.1	1.0	28.0	27.0	6.4
suasive verbs	1.9	0.0	5.0	5.0	1.6
SEEM/APPEAR	0.4	0.0	2.0	2.0	0.7
contractions	21.5	2.0	50.0	48.0	11.7
THAT deletion	1.3	0.0	8.0	8.0	2.2
stranded prepositions	4.6	0.0	12.0	12.0	3.1
split infinitives	0.0	0.0	0.0	0.0	0.0
split auxiliaries	2.7	0.0	6.0	6.0	1.9
phrasal coordination	1.3	0.0	6.0	6.0	1.6
non-phrasal coordination	8.9	2.0	17.0	15.0	4.1
synthetic negation	0.8	0.0	4.0	4.0	1.3
analytic negation	4.3	0.0	14.0	14.0	4.2

Mean frequencies for Spontaneous Speeches

Linguistic feature	Mean	Minimum value	Maximum value	Range	Standard deviation
past tense	63.9	9.0	109.0	100.0	40.3
perfect aspect verbs	7.6	2.0	12.0	10.0	3.3
present tense	80.4	48.0	109.0	61.0	16.3
place adverbials	1.8	0.0	5.0	5.0	1.6
time adverbials	5.1	0.0	11.0	11.0	2.7
first person pronouns	60.4	22.0	122.0	100.0	29.9
second person pronouns	14.6	0.0	42.0	42.0	12.5
third person pronouns	31.9	8.0	73.0	65.0	19.1
pronoun IT	13.6	6.0	22.0	16.0	6.3
demonstrative pronouns	9.1	4.0	15.0	11.0	3.4
indefinite pronouns	1.6	0.0	4.0	4.0	1.7
DO as pro-verb	4.4	0.0	14.0	14.0	3.9
WH questions	1.0	0.0	4.0	4.0	1.2
nominalizations	18.2	0.0	41.0	41.0	14.1
gerunds	4.3	0.0	8.0	8.0	3.0
nouns	157.7	135.0	188.0	53.0	16.8
agentless passives	6.2	0.0	18.0	18.0	4.2
BY passives	0.1	0.0	1.0	1.0	0.3
BE as main verb	35.2	16.0	48.0	32.0	7.9
existential THERE	3.6	0.0	9.0	9.0	3.1
THAT verb complements	7.1	0.0	20.0	20.0	5.2
THAT adj. complements	0.4	0.0	3.0	3.0	1.0
WH clauses	1.2	0.0	4.0	4.0	1.5
infinitives	15.1	4.0	28.0	24.0	7.2
present participial clauses	0.2	0.0	1.0	1.0	0.4
past participial clauses	0.0	0.0	0.0	0.0	0.0
past prt. WHIZ deletions	0.8	0.0	3.0	3.0	0.9
present prt. WHIZ deletions	0.8	0.0	6.0	6.0	1.6
THAT relatives: subj. position	0.2	0.0	1.0	1.0	0.4
THAT relatives: obj. position	1.4	0.0	4.0	4.0	1.4
WH relatives: subj. position	4.5	0.0	8.0	8.0	2.9
WH relatives: obj. position	2.1	0.0	7.0	7.0	2.1
WH relatives: pied pipes	0.6	0.0	4.0	4.0	1.1
sentence relatives	0.3	0.0	2.0	2.0	0.6
adv. subordinator - cause	3.1	0.0	7.0	7.0	2.3
adv. sub. - concession	0.1	0.0	1.0	1.0	0.2
adv. sub. - condition	3.1	0.0	8.0	8.0	2.3
adv. sub. - other	0.8	0.0	3.0	3.0	1.0
prepositions	94.6	66.0	128.0	62.0	20.6
attributive adjectives	44.2	16.0	67.0	51.0	15.4
predicative adjectives	4.4	1.0	10.0	9.0	2.1
adverbs	65.4	47.0	86.0	39.0	11.3
type/token ratio	44.9	35.0	50.0	15.0	3.9
word length	4.2	3.8	4.7	0.9	0.3
conjuncts	0.4	0.0	3.0	3.0	0.8
downtoners	1.7	0.0	7.0	7.0	1.9
hedges	0.5	0.0	4.0	4.0	1.0
amplifiers	5.1	0.0	12.0	12.0	3.2
emphatics	5.8	1.0	10.0	9.0	2.3
discourse particles	3.6	1.0	9.0	8.0	2.4
demonstratives	11.6	4.0	18.0	14.0	4.0
possibility modals	6.6	2.0	13.0	11.0	3.1
necessity modals	1.4	0.0	5.0	5.0	1.6
predictive modals	9.1	2.0	25.0	23.0	6.1
public verbs	14.0	0.0	40.0	40.0	9.8
private verbs	21.6	14.0	39.0	25.0	6.0
suasive verbs	2.7	0.0	5.0	5.0	1.9
SEEM/APPEAR	0.4	0.0	2.0	2.0	0.7
contractions	17.8	8.0	40.0	32.0	9.5
THAT deletion	5.6	1.0	16.0	15.0	3.8
stranded prepositions	4.5	1.0	13.0	12.0	3.3
split infinitives	0.0	0.0	0.0	0.0	0.0
split auxiliaries	4.1	1.0	10.0	9.0	2.7
phrasal coordination	1.7	0.0	8.0	8.0	1.9
non-phrasal coordination	14.9	3.0	44.0	41.0	11.5
synthetic negation	1.6	0.0	4.0	4.0	1.3
analytic negation	9.1	1.0	27.0	26.0	6.9

Mean frequencies for Prepared Speeches

Linguistic feature	Mean	Minimum value	Maximum value	Range	Standard deviation
past tense	48.3	14.0	87.0	73.0	22.5
perfect aspect verbs	11.3	2.0	40.0	38.0	9.1
present tense	70.5	28.0	104.0	76.0	21.1
place adverbials	1.9	0.0	8.0	8.0	2.1
time adverbials	7.1	3.0	20.0	17.0	4.4
first person pronouns	41.8	10.0	95.0	85.0	21.4
second person pronouns	5.1	0.0	14.0	14.0	4.9
third person pronouns	37.1	16.0	58.0	42.0	15.3
pronoun IT	8.9	4.0	18.0	14.0	4.4
demonstrative pronouns	6.9	2.0	9.0	7.0	2.1
indefinite pronouns	1.5	0.0	3.0	3.0	1.2
DO as pro-verb	2.4	0.0	7.0	7.0	2.3
WH questions	0.3	0.0	2.0	2.0	0.6
nominalizations	20.6	6.0	46.0	40.0	11.5
gerunds	5.1	2.0	9.0	7.0	1.9
nouns	189.1	153.0	221.0	68.0	21.6
agentless passives	9.6	4.0	20.0	16.0	3.9
BY passives	0.2	0.0	1.0	1.0	0.4
BE as main verb	30.5	19.0	38.0	19.0	5.8
existential THERE	3.1	1.0	6.0	5.0	1.4
THAT verb complements	7.0	1.0	13.0	12.0	4.5
THAT adj. complements	0.6	0.0	2.0	2.0	0.7
WH clauses	0.2	0.0	1.0	1.0	0.4
infinitives	16.2	6.0	36.0	30.0	6.6
present participial clauses	0.2	0.0	2.0	2.0	0.6
past participial clauses	0.0	0.0	0.0	0.0	0.0
past prt. WHIZ deletions	0.9	0.0	5.0	5.0	1.4
present prt. WHIZ deletions	1.4	0.0	5.0	5.0	1.2
THAT relatives: subj. position	0.3	0.0	2.0	2.0	0.7
THAT relatives: obj. position	1.6	0.0	4.0	4.0	1.4
WH relatives: subj. position	2.4	0.0	9.0	9.0	2.3
WH relatives: obj. position	2.5	1.0	8.0	7.0	1.8
WH relatives: pied pipes	1.1	0.0	6.0	6.0	1.6
sentence relatives	0.1	0.0	1.0	1.0	0.3
adv. subordinator - cause	1.6	0.0	5.0	5.0	1.7
adv. sub. - concession	0.1	0.0	1.0	1.0	0.4
adv. sub. - condition	2.4	0.0	4.0	4.0	1.1
adv. sub. - other	0.8	0.0	5.0	5.0	1.4
prepositions	112.6	92.0	137.0	45.0	12.5
attributive adjectives	48.9	28.0	72.0	44.0	13.6
predicative adjectives	3.6	1.0	6.0	5.0	1.6
adverbs	62.2	45.0	78.0	33.0	9.8
type/token ratio	49.0	43.0	56.0	13.0	3.4
word length	4.4	4.1	4.8	0.7	0.2
conjuncts	0.5	0.0	2.0	2.0	0.7
downtoners	1.5	0.0	4.0	4.0	0.9
hedges	0.2	0.0	2.0	2.0	0.6
amplifiers	3.1	1.0	8.0	7.0	2.1
emphatics	4.8	0.0	10.0	10.0	3.2
discourse particles	2.4	0.0	6.0	6.0	2.4
demonstratives	12.9	7.0	20.0	13.0	4.2
possibility modals	5.6	1.0	12.0	11.0	3.1
necessity modals	2.6	0.0	10.0	10.0	2.9
predictive modals	5.0	0.0	11.0	11.0	3.0
public verbs	7.9	1.0	15.0	14.0	4.8
private verbs	17.6	9.0	26.0	17.0	4.9
suasive verbs	3.3	0.0	14.0	14.0	3.5
SEEM/APPEAR	0.5	0.0	2.0	2.0	0.7
contractions	13.3	3.0	45.0	42.0	10.4
THAT deletion	1.9	0.0	6.0	6.0	1.6
stranded prepositions	3.7	1.0	7.0	6.0	1.9
split infinitives	0.0	0.0	0.0	0.0	0.0
split auxiliaries	5.3	2.0	11.0	9.0	2.9
phrasal coordination	1.1	0.0	4.0	4.0	1.2
non-phrasal coordination	8.6	4.0	16.0	12.0	3.4
synthetic negation	1.8	0.0	4.0	4.0	1.4
analytic negation	8.4	1.0	16.0	15.0	4.3

Pearson correlation coefficients for all linguistic features

Key to abbreviations

PASTTNSE	*past tense*	SUB CND	*adv. sub. – condition*
PERFECTS	*perfect aspect verbs*	SUB OTHR	*adv. sub. – other*
PRES	*present tense*	PREP	*prepositions*
PL ADV	*place adverbials*	ADJ ATTR	*attributive adjectives*
TM ADV	*time adverbials*	ADJ PRED	*predicative adjectives*
PRO1	*first person pronouns*	ADVS	*adverbs*
PRO2	*second person pronouns*	TYPETOKN	*type/token ratio*
PRO3	*third person pronouns*	WRDLNGTH	*word length*
IT	*pronoun IT*	CONJNCTS	*conjuncts*
PDEM	*demonstrative pronouns*	DOWNTONE	*downtoners*
PANY	*indefinite pronouns*	GEN HDG	*hedges*
PRO DO	*DO as pro-verb*	AMPLIFR	*amplifiers*
WH QUES	*WH questions*	GEN EMPH	*emphatics*
N NOM	*nominalizations*	PRTCLE	*discourse particles*
N VBG	*gerunds*	DEM	*demonstratives*
N	*nouns*	POS MOD	*possibility modals*
AGLS PSV	*agentless passives*	NEC MOD	*necessity modals*
BY PASV	*BY passives*	PRD MOD	*predictive modals*
BE STATE	*BE as main verb*	PUB VB	*public verbs*
EX THERE	*existential THERE*	PRV VB	*private verbs*
TH CL	*THAT verb complements*	SUA VB	*suasive verbs*
ADJ CL	*THAT adj complements*	SEEM	*SEEM/APPEAR*
WH CL	*WH clauses*	CONTRAC	*contractions*
INF	*infinitives*	THAT DEL	*THAT deletion*
CL VBG	*pres participial clauses*	FINLPREP	*stranded prepositions*
CL VBN	*past participial clauses*	SPL INF	*split infinitives*
WHIZ VBN	*past prt. WHIZ del.*	SPL AUX	*split auxiliaries*
WHIZ VBG	*pres prt. WHIZ del.*	P AND	*phrasal coordination*
THTREL S	*THAT relatives: subj position*	O AND	*nonphrasal coord.*
THTREL O	*THAT relatives: obj positions*	SYNTHNEG	*synthetic negation*
REL SUBJ	*WH relatives: subj position*	NOT NEG	*analytic negation*
REL OBJ	*WH relatives: obj positions*		
REL PIPE	*WH relatives: pied pipes*		
SENT REL	*sentence relatives*		
SUB COS	*adv. subordinator – cause*		
SUB CON	*adv. sub. – concession*		

	PASTTNSE	PERFECTS	PRES	PL_ADV	TM_ADV	PRO1	PRO2	PRO3
PASTTNSE	1.00000	0.38826	-0.46964	0.09066	0.15146	0.20767	0.08508	0.68004
PERFECTS	0.38826	1.00000	-0.01617	-0.03059	0.16140	0.21244	0.17447	0.43958
PRES	-0.46964	-0.01617	1.00000	-0.21840	0.06683	0.54563	0.67463	-0.15668
PL_ADV	0.09066	-0.03059	-0.21840	1.00000	0.28275	-0.17839	-0.18327	0.05336
TM_ADV	0.15146	0.16140	0.06683	0.28275	1.00000	0.12390	0.12174	0.24769
PRO1	0.20767	0.21244	0.54563	-0.17839	0.12390	1.00000	0.66061	0.08237
PRO2	0.08508	0.17447	0.67463	-0.18327	0.12174	0.66061	1.00000	0.13895
PRO3	0.68004	0.43958	-0.15668	0.05336	0.24769	0.08237	0.13895	1.00000
IT	0.08175	0.11223	0.58245	-0.05338	0.13827	0.50378	0.58159	0.08256
PDEM	-0.13191	0.05327	0.67766	-0.14327	0.10339	0.53254	0.55424	-0.08677
PANY	0.15696	0.13283	0.43828	-0.13895	0.10865	0.50442	0.50826	0.20325
PRO_DO	0.10575	0.15091	0.61756	-0.15280	0.11347	0.58898	0.67461	0.17509
WH_QUES	0.01222	0.03829	0.39071	-0.11654	0.06070	0.35024	0.42875	0.03803
N_NOM	-0.46718	-0.24976	-0.20716	-0.17102	-0.39779	-0.45439	-0.44851	-0.50054
N_VBG	-0.25545	-0.16471	-0.17400	-0.06217	-0.25199	-0.33963	-0.32936	-0.23809
N	-0.18952	-0.22218	-0.54609	0.23642	0.00726	-0.64921	-0.64032	-0.22198
AGLS_PSV	-0.30246	-0.21462	-0.30988	-0.05442	-0.31527	-0.53324	-0.49729	-0.43401
BY_PASV	-0.25643	-0.19183	-0.27027	0.06501	-0.23745	-0.44721	-0.39437	-0.32813
BE_STATE	-0.01317	0.13137	0.67526	-0.24266	0.06773	0.52650	0.54589	0.07502
EX_THERE	0.00779	0.07520	0.24527	-0.03222	0.02522	0.14773	0.13732	-0.04950
TH_CL	-0.06171	0.09107	0.17289	-0.18172	-0.06717	0.14792	0.09175	-0.04531
ADJ_CL	-0.10634	0.11158	0.06687	-0.05342	-0.00010	-0.04023	-0.07704	-0.08351
WH_CL	0.10693	0.06669	0.30136	-0.10515	-0.04286	0.29494	0.32610	0.17048
INF	-0.00349	0.07889	0.13390	-0.15376	-0.07708	0.13200	0.08617	0.12034
CL_VBG	0.35917	0.05858	-0.31088	0.16726	-0.03561	-0.09968	-0.06359	0.34559
CL_VBN	-0.21787	-0.18393	-0.08737	-0.01068	-0.20037	-0.19572	-0.16818	-0.22565
WHIZ_VBN	-0.36383	-0.29656	-0.33674	0.11109	-0.19716	-0.52418	-0.46549	-0.42543
WHIZ_VBG	-0.15894	-0.17916	-0.35192	0.09160	-0.17633	-0.37919	-0.40021	-0.27958
THTREL_S	-0.09222	0.08081	0.11680	0.04083	0.00244	0.07057	0.06329	-0.05561
THTREL_O	-0.17682	0.06182	0.10433	-0.08907	-0.12932	0.02058	-0.05491	-0.11063
REL_SUBJ	-0.20742	-0.12933	-0.09653	-0.09257	-0.19170	-0.22820	-0.26886	-0.22284
REL_OBJ	-0.25629	-0.06956	-0.13278	-0.15400	-0.22583	-0.20847	-0.30368	-0.19753
REL_PIPE	-0.25790	-0.08099	-0.11872	-0.09351	-0.26097	-0.27557	-0.31400	-0.25780
SENT_REL	-0.05454	0.06389	0.40776	-0.08671	-0.01592	0.36091	0.31829	-0.05719
SUB_COS	-0.02387	0.07929	0.50706	-0.20644	0.05969	0.53056	0.51424	-0.00053
SUB_CON	0.07856	0.00944	-0.05924	-0.01716	-0.01555	-0.08964	-0.10116	0.14291
SUB_CND	-0.10718	0.04562	0.49314	-0.13874	-0.01222	0.30867	0.37454	0.06064
SUB_OTHR	-0.09788	-0.05035	-0.09061	-0.05159	-0.13090	-0.13466	-0.14774	-0.11600
PREP	-0.40885	-0.32014	-0.48861	0.03419	-0.27893	-0.64065	-0.65536	-0.50758
ADJ_ATTR	-0.41144	-0.29199	-0.37374	0.05141	-0.23382	-0.59229	-0.58074	-0.44570
ADJ_PRED	-0.03803	0.06175	0.26537	-0.13684	-0.09467	0.15768	0.21056	0.09366
ADVS	0.23039	0.20289	0.44484	0.20120	0.47032	0.52539	0.53574	0.32039
TYPETOKN	0.13215	0.04725	-0.45028	0.10789	0.01433	-0.35157	-0.39225	0.13939
WRDLNGTH	-0.40526	-0.26674	-0.47190	0.01614	-0.28139	-0.72163	-0.66034	-0.45480
CONJNCTS	-0.36426	-0.21571	-0.03696	-0.11496	-0.28790	-0.30885	-0.26962	-0.36039
DOWNTONE	-0.04323	-0.01081	-0.09045	-0.01456	-0.08060	-0.10304	-0.11607	-0.06267
GEN_HDG	0.00798	0.06736	0.43885	-0.04599	0.10351	0.41146	0.42659	0.04862
AMPLIFR	-0.05670	0.01666	0.47346	-0.10865	0.17105	0.48020	0.48378	-0.02743
GEN_EMPH	-0.06028	0.10107	0.63717	-0.13763	0.19199	0.49564	0.60566	0.07795
PRTCLE	-0.09094	0.09962	0.63208	-0.14472	0.31489	0.56157	0.59313	-0.03474
DEM	-0.30321	-0.03756	0.15560	-0.09785	-0.06162	-0.00996	-0.06862	-0.28221
POS_MOD	-0.16127	0.04442	0.51447	-0.21145	-0.09755	0.39220	0.39297	-0.03998
NEC_MOD	-0.21667	-0.05843	0.20159	-0.13289	-0.12389	0.02760	-0.01716	-0.11132
PRD_MOD	-0.12123	0.00715	0.27767	-0.08913	-0.03027	0.18452	0.14547	0.00764
PUB_VB	0.31804	0.17866	0.00875	-0.08672	-0.02844	0.16168	0.13743	0.25848
PRV_VB	0.16308	0.22484	0.66623	-0.21205	0.05489	0.68798	0.75392	0.24709
SUA_VB	-0.09767	-0.09035	-0.06883	-0.07080	-0.12561	-0.12319	-0.14871	-0.10397
SEEM	0.03733	0.05795	-0.00408	-0.01308	-0.04100	-0.04479	-0.04053	0.08981
CONTRAC	0.07162	0.22584	0.73228	-0.09693	0.26306	0.71809	0.78950	0.15458
THAT_DEL	0.15968	0.20932	0.64584	-0.15507	0.14620	0.66963	0.70122	0.21105
FINLPREP	0.01620	0.01360	0.38137	0.00068	0.21747	0.39486	0.35019	0.02595
SPL_INF	-0.03914	0.10029	0.08171	-0.00186	0.08781	0.07311	0.04007	0.00225
SPL_AUX	-0.07418	0.15357	-0.01256	-0.08823	-0.11512	-0.09936	-0.13630	-0.00993
P_AND	-0.12138	-0.12812	-0.35569	0.01021	-0.25447	-0.38114	-0.39155	-0.12814
O_AND	0.14402	0.09914	0.34629	-0.06129	0.21315	0.57964	0.40155	0.09991
SYNTHNEG	0.23031	0.20833	-0.16484	0.01178	-0.04100	-0.08553	-0.11496	0.23635
NOT_NEG	0.16515	0.24730	0.62933	-0.22265	0.11472	0.59457	0.67825	0.30780

	IT	PDEM	PANY	PRO_DO	WH_QUES	N_NOM	N_VBG	N
PASTTNSE	0.08175	-0.13191	0.15696	0.10575	0.01222	-0.46718	-0.25545	-0.18952
PERFECTS	0.11223	0.05327	0.13283	0.15091	0.03829	-0.24976	-0.16471	-0.22218
PRES	0.58245	0.67766	0.43828	0.61756	0.39071	-0.20716	-0.17400	-0.54609
PL_ADV	-0.05338	-0.14327	-0.13895	-0.15280	-0.11654	-0.17102	-0.06217	0.23642
TM_ADV	0.13827	0.10339	0.10865	0.11347	0.06070	-0.39779	-0.25199	0.00726
PRO1	0.50378	0.53254	0.50442	0.58898	0.35024	-0.45439	-0.33963	-0.64921
PRO2	0.58159	0.55424	0.50826	0.67461	0.42875	-0.44851	-0.32936	-0.64032
PRO3	0.08256	-0.08677	0.20325	0.17509	0.03803	-0.50054	-0.23809	-0.22198
IT	1.00000	0.56752	0.48445	0.62067	0.25244	-0.39380	-0.28411	-0.59379
PDEM	0.56752	1.00000	0.40492	0.58543	0.39301	-0.28655	-0.28251	-0.50991
PANY	0.48445	0.40492	1.00000	0.60047	0.25584	-0.39614	-0.22400	-0.52269
PRO_DO	0.62067	0.58543	0.60047	1.00000	0.40148	-0.42756	-0.26482	-0.60887
WH_QUES	0.25244	0.39301	0.25584	0.40148	1.00000	-0.19412	-0.15085	-0.28806
N_NOM	-0.39380	-0.28655	-0.39614	-0.42756	-0.19412	1.00000	0.36435	0.24086
N_VBG	-0.28411	-0.28251	-0.22400	-0.26482	-0.15085	0.36435	1.00000	0.19944
N	-0.59379	-0.50991	-0.52269	-0.60887	-0.28806	0.24086	0.19944	1.00000
AGLS_PSV	-0.46271	-0.32492	-0.41763	-0.45148	-0.23469	0.57572	0.37407	0.34418
BY_PASV	-0.37880	-0.29945	-0.35410	-0.36913	-0.19259	0.44639	0.26233	0.37035
BE_STATE	0.60417	0.63818	0.42389	0.51604	0.35928	-0.32736	-0.28196	-0.58848
EX_THERE	0.25036	0.31228	0.14422	0.18325	0.17340	-0.13277	-0.11568	-0.17155
TH_CL	0.09111	0.25278	0.05890	0.12820	0.06625	0.13699	-0.03724	-0.24515
ADJ_CL	-0.05692	0.04808	-0.08718	-0.09465	-0.03609	0.16307	0.04774	-0.06269
WH_CL	0.31056	0.25221	0.28850	0.38307	0.15112	-0.20930	-0.13329	-0.33131
INF	0.03428	-0.03732	0.13716	0.15438	-0.08213	0.06707	0.14262	-0.19750
CL_VBG	-0.13136	-0.26240	-0.01676	-0.11052	-0.14631	-0.09307	0.06272	-0.07320
CL_VBN	-0.19046	-0.15487	-0.16763	-0.18140	-0.08350	0.30114	0.16118	0.08322
WHIZ_VBN	-0.43935	-0.35327	-0.39339	-0.45580	-0.21221	0.47368	0.29987	0.45947
WHIZ_VBG	-0.38955	-0.31308	-0.31929	-0.39096	-0.20403	0.37331	0.20716	0.37838
THTREL_S	0.05872	0.11837	0.10466	0.05512	0.12853	0.01179	0.08791	-0.07083
THTREL_O	-0.04126	0.12412	0.04126	0.04731	0.05002	0.19717	0.11587	-0.02739
REL_SUBJ	-0.20842	-0.07123	-0.16871	-0.17671	-0.04964	0.29988	0.19982	0.22856
REL_OBJ	-0.23270	-0.14485	-0.26604	-0.26781	-0.11524	0.43330	0.19917	0.19372
REL_PIPE	-0.21094	-0.13470	-0.21872	-0.24581	-0.08636	0.42272	0.26822	0.21323
SENT_REL	0.35021	0.47358	0.25305	0.34428	0.26043	-0.17224	-0.13674	-0.28235
SUB_COS	0.43280	0.50330	0.39583	0.51728	0.26320	-0.24201	-0.22930	-0.43103
SUB_CON	-0.03098	-0.10413	-0.02237	-0.03630	-0.05903	-0.02294	0.07030	-0.00402
SUB_CND	0.36470	0.32808	0.37571	0.33287	0.06805	-0.12692	-0.12101	-0.44737
SUB_OTHR	-0.17064	-0.08499	-0.15069	-0.11548	-0.06327	0.21583	0.11803	0.01464
PREP	-0.56201	-0.41997	-0.54637	-0.60890	-0.33918	0.67927	0.39344	0.56834
ADJ_ATTR	-0.47257	-0.44817	-0.45845	-0.54825	-0.29692	0.57585	0.35724	0.51276
ADJ_PRED	0.08649	0.05845	0.06418	0.12369	0.08284	0.01589	0.00743	-0.32839
ADVS	0.55075	0.44553	0.45422	0.52866	0.25348	-0.60056	-0.35021	-0.56324
TYPETOKN	-0.38328	-0.48124	-0.26031	-0.39834	-0.24304	0.02640	0.14942	0.42958
WRDLNGTH	-0.59789	-0.48634	-0.54139	-0.60367	-0.28955	0.76343	0.44058	0.63217
CONJNCTS	-0.22815	-0.14260	-0.24361	-0.25352	-0.16742	0.50419	0.27541	0.04078
DOWNTONE	-0.07943	-0.06469	-0.13416	-0.11316	-0.07865	0.02928	0.07951	0.06349
GEN_HDG	0.38358	0.36472	0.47786	0.44408	0.21954	-0.30244	-0.22823	-0.39770
AMPLIFR	0.38447	0.58933	0.37816	0.44172	0.28824	-0.27921	-0.27022	-0.36763
GEN_EMPH	0.48632	0.51019	0.49368	0.56036	0.33493	-0.38657	-0.22527	-0.48304
PRTCLE	0.53498	0.69441	0.44932	0.60065	0.38904	-0.32713	-0.33620	-0.47180
DEM	0.04829	0.22779	-0.02442	-0.01469	-0.00394	0.25260	0.09815	-0.11790
POS_MOD	0.29547	0.33204	0.36169	0.37890	0.16201	-0.03543	-0.07722	-0.48899
NEC_MOD	0.04796	0.06118	-0.00241	0.02177	0.07097	0.21669	0.09114	-0.10784
PRD_MOD	0.10417	0.13758	0.13007	0.13887	0.09828	0.05516	0.00234	-0.15288
PUB_VB	0.08498	0.04029	0.15253	0.14968	0.13752	-0.07981	-0.07189	-0.19017
PRV_VB	0.62632	0.60033	0.55724	0.69143	0.40173	-0.43092	-0.29698	-0.74585
SUA_VB	-0.14103	-0.15583	-0.01137	-0.04416	-0.11445	0.26985	0.26818	0.07973
SEEM	0.04008	-0.06919	0.03240	0.03249	-0.06158	0.03998	0.00788	-0.14403
CONTRAC	0.69432	0.70670	0.55695	0.71694	0.40299	-0.51898	-0.41476	-0.62905
THAT_DEL	0.56910	0.58955	0.52159	0.65689	0.42177	-0.45604	-0.32020	-0.59845
FINLPREP	0.34546	0.57438	0.31640	0.39112	0.31576	-0.29929	-0.24537	-0.37139
SPL_INF	-0.02783	-0.00557	-0.00999	0.00057	-0.01753	-0.05368	-0.04767	0.01861
SPL_AUX	-0.10258	-0.14036	-0.07481	-0.08455	-0.16498	0.18878	0.15763	-0.04923
P_AND	-0.37876	-0.46896	-0.32003	-0.37624	-0.22611	0.30522	0.30452	0.41172
O_AND	0.34821	0.46526	0.33914	0.35708	0.30159	-0.38073	-0.34427	-0.34560
SYNTHNEG	-0.04182	-0.17931	-0.00139	-0.07831	-0.04402	-0.04479	0.04640	-0.03729
NOT_NEG	0.59400	0.56545	0.55855	0.73304	0.34282	-0.42409	-0.34022	-0.68202

	AGLS_PSV	BY_PASV	BE_STATE	EX_THERE	TH_CL	ADJ_CL	WH_CL	INF
PASTTNSE	-0.30246	-0.25643	-0.01317	0.00779	-0.06171	-0.10634	0.10693	-0.00349
PERFECTS	-0.21462	-0.19183	0.13137	0.07520	0.09107	0.11158	0.06669	0.07889
PRES	-0.30988	-0.27027	0.67526	0.24527	0.17289	0.06687	0.30136	0.13390
PL_ADV	-0.05442	0.06501	-0.24266	-0.03222	-0.18172	-0.05342	-0.10515	-0.15376
TM_ADV	-0.31527	-0.23745	0.06773	0.02522	-0.06717	-0.00010	-0.04286	-0.07708
PRO1	-0.53324	-0.44721	0.52650	0.14773	0.14792	-0.04023	0.29494	0.13200
PRO2	-0.49729	-0.39437	0.54589	0.13732	0.09175	-0.07704	0.32610	0.08617
PRO3	-0.43401	-0.32813	0.07502	-0.04950	-0.04531	-0.08351	0.17048	0.12034
IT	-0.46271	-0.37880	0.60417	0.25036	0.09111	-0.05692	0.31056	0.03428
PDEM	-0.32492	-0.29945	0.63818	0.31228	0.25278	0.04808	0.25221	-0.03732
PANY	-0.41763	-0.35410	0.42389	0.14422	0.05890	-0.08718	0.28850	0.13716
PRO_DO	-0.45148	-0.36913	0.51604	0.18325	0.12820	-0.09465	0.38307	0.15438
WH_QUES	-0.23469	-0.19259	0.35928	0.17340	0.06625	-0.03609	0.15112	-0.08213
N_NOM	0.57572	0.44639	-0.32736	-0.13277	0.13699	0.16307	-0.20930	0.06707
N_VBG	0.37407	0.26233	-0.28196	-0.11568	-0.03724	0.04774	-0.13329	0.14262
N	0.34418	0.37035	-0.58848	-0.17155	-0.24515	-0.06269	-0.33131	-0.19750
AGLS_PSV	1.00000	0.54097	-0.37758	-0.04527	0.07078	0.09538	-0.23534	-0.07089
BY_PASV	0.54097	1.00000	-0.38180	-0.16374	-0.04221	0.05751	-0.19296	-0.23197
BE_STATE	-0.37758	-0.38180	1.00000	0.43751	0.23875	0.12706	0.27170	0.09000
EX_THERE	-0.04527	-0.16374	0.43751	1.00000	0.12178	0.08144	0.14457	-0.05660
TH_CL	0.07078	-0.04221	0.23875	0.12178	1.00000	0.21122	0.02286	0.20472
ADJ_CL	0.09538	0.05751	0.12706	0.08144	0.21122	1.00000	-0.08245	0.03112
WH_CL	-0.23534	-0.19296	0.27170	0.14457	0.02286	-0.08245	1.00000	0.12417
INF	-0.07089	-0.23197	0.09000	-0.05660	0.20472	0.03112	0.12417	1.00000
CL_VBG	-0.00159	-0.01450	-0.21063	-0.12786	-0.18357	-0.05800	-0.01810	-0.01381
CL_VBN	0.33531	0.35214	-0.20412	-0.08127	-0.07683	0.00701	-0.09464	-0.08744
WHIZ_VBN	0.56125	0.56301	-0.45470	-0.16850	-0.14983	0.01544	-0.23186	-0.28238
WHIZ_VBG	0.42297	0.37657	-0.42524	-0.07526	-0.11630	-0.05604	-0.24441	-0.19599
THTREL_S	-0.01745	-0.05369	0.05708	0.08068	0.02705	0.05035	0.05633	-0.00386
THTREL_O	0.04511	-0.01663	0.10734	0.07206	0.44801	0.13178	0.00079	0.17883
REL_SUBJ	0.19836	0.17183	-0.05081	0.09760	0.07765	0.05293	0.01374	0.06235
REL_OBJ	0.24907	0.16815	-0.14566	-0.04515	0.12455	0.08730	-0.08466	0.08697
REL_PIPE	0.35460	0.25588	-0.12087	0.04589	0.09194	0.10279	-0.16019	-0.02472
SENT_REL	-0.18281	-0.15332	0.32134	0.20127	0.05037	-0.04623	0.23472	-0.07389
SUB_COS	-0.30468	-0.24305	0.47163	0.16811	0.19924	-0.03172	0.32470	0.11999
SUB_CON	0.01244	0.02862	-0.01825	-0.06953	-0.04640	-0.03269	-0.01446	0.00888
SUB_CND	-0.16992	-0.20069	0.42306	0.12062	0.21367	0.14899	0.16139	0.30321
SUB_OTHR	0.23628	0.18059	-0.07762	-0.06689	0.10402	0.17524	-0.08156	-0.01889
PREP	0.58273	0.51390	-0.55925	-0.14770	-0.04000	0.06371	-0.34626	-0.21716
ADJ_ATTR	0.44720	0.38529	-0.41951	-0.19157	-0.18188	0.06172	-0.29424	-0.08339
ADJ_PRED	-0.02421	-0.02699	0.39152	0.01593	0.08931	0.18460	0.00070	0.19998
ADVS	-0.55569	-0.48427	0.47581	0.11124	0.00569	-0.03935	0.23748	0.04522
TYPETOKN	0.02327	0.08520	-0.38867	-0.24008	-0.23486	-0.03398	-0.21584	-0.00505
WRDLNGTH	0.59398	0.50884	-0.55161	-0.20036	-0.05438	0.08220	-0.31525	-0.09416
CONJNCTS	0.42966	0.35286	-0.08362	-0.05974	0.10050	0.24313	-0.09691	-0.00341
DOWNTONE	0.08182	0.08249	-0.02695	0.03753	-0.03411	0.08582	-0.03696	-0.08725
GEN_HDG	-0.28711	-0.19900	0.29143	0.03803	-0.02957	-0.07814	0.17742	-0.04914
AMPLIFR	-0.31351	-0.24142	0.51194	0.21195	0.18894	-0.00985	0.20810	-0.04996
GEN_EMPH	-0.47067	-0.37119	0.49263	0.16055	0.00794	-0.01060	0.26296	0.09755
PRTCLE	-0.36544	-0.31556	0.54448	0.26530	0.19606	0.02649	0.18692	-0.05127
DEM	0.11165	-0.00652	0.15683	0.11435	0.26711	0.21637	0.06385	-0.01173
POS_MOD	-0.09702	-0.15700	0.35205	0.09062	0.17304	0.01727	0.23714	0.29473
NEC_MOD	0.15988	0.06424	0.10691	0.07232	0.18261	0.18087	0.01510	0.30720
PRD_MOD	-0.08748	-0.15590	0.14367	0.00553	0.16176	0.09292	0.14123	0.33962
PUB_VB	-0.12146	-0.09715	0.06830	0.10640	0.25632	-0.02620	0.23231	0.12793
PRV_VB	-0.47198	-0.37646	0.62005	0.19279	0.22514	0.00161	0.42957	0.12233
SUA_VB	0.20656	0.07315	-0.13007	-0.05069	0.09720	0.02029	-0.01055	0.31460
SEEM	-0.04468	-0.04795	0.00940	0.04293	0.07650	0.06302	-0.00524	0.12019
CONTRAC	-0.55108	-0.39708	0.63155	0.25305	0.03943	-0.03612	0.32786	-0.05114
THAT_DEL	-0.47393	-0.34769	0.55711	0.17683	0.05366	-0.06320	0.33187	0.05872
FINLPREP	-0.31985	-0.26903	0.40777	0.25784	0.13017	-0.00911	0.15948	-0.08231
SPL_INF	-0.05926	-0.03049	0.09936	-0.05530	0.01063	0.06161	0.01835	0.03383
SPL_AUX	0.24998	0.09257	-0.03576	-0.10178	0.14095	0.14227	-0.01948	0.30278
P_AND	0.27357	0.23256	-0.38136	-0.15916	-0.25930	-0.06546	-0.11810	-0.00505
O_AND	-0.37278	-0.29791	0.39080	0.20908	0.17397	-0.03598	0.23637	-0.07334
SYNTHNEG	-0.01418	-0.10676	0.04504	0.17278	0.07682	0.07913	0.13862	0.09331
NOT_NEG	-0.46781	-0.39302	0.62309	0.19554	0.21415	0.01284	0.37251	0.14087

	CL_VBG	CL_VBN	WHIZ_VBN	WHIZ_VBG	THTREL_S	THTREL_O	REL_SUBJ	REL_OBJ
PASTTNSE	0.35917	-0.21787	-0.36383	-0.15894	-0.09222	-0.17682	-0.20742	-0.25629
PERFECTS	0.05858	-0.18393	-0.29656	-0.17916	0.08081	0.06182	-0.12933	-0.06956
PRES	-0.31088	-0.08737	-0.33674	-0.35192	0.11680	0.10433	-0.09653	-0.13278
PL_ADV	0.16726	-0.01068	0.11109	0.09160	0.04083	-0.08907	-0.09257	-0.15400
TM_ADV	-0.03561	-0.20037	-0.19716	-0.17633	0.00244	-0.12932	-0.19170	-0.22583
PRO1	-0.09968	-0.19572	-0.52418	-0.37919	0.07057	0.02058	-0.22820	-0.20847
PRO2	-0.06359	-0.16818	-0.46549	-0.40021	0.06329	-0.05491	-0.26886	-0.30368
PRO3	0.34559	-0.22565	-0.42543	-0.27958	-0.05561	-0.11063	-0.22284	-0.19753
IT	-0.13136	-0.19046	-0.43935	-0.38955	0.05872	-0.04126	-0.20842	-0.23270
PDEM	-0.26240	-0.15487	-0.35327	-0.31308	0.11837	0.12412	-0.07123	-0.14485
PANY	-0.01676	-0.16763	-0.39339	-0.31929	0.10466	0.04126	-0.16871	-0.26604
PRO_DO	-0.11052	-0.18140	-0.45580	-0.39096	0.05512	0.04731	-0.17671	-0.26781
WH_QUES	-0.14631	-0.08350	-0.21221	-0.20403	0.12853	0.05002	-0.04964	-0.11524
N_NOM	-0.09307	0.30114	0.47368	0.37331	0.01179	0.19717	0.29988	0.43330
N_VBG	0.06272	0.16118	0.29987	0.20716	0.08791	0.11587	0.19892	0.19917
N	-0.07320	0.08322	0.45947	0.37838	-0.07083	-0.02739	0.22856	0.19372
AGLS_PSV	-0.00159	0.33531	0.56125	0.42297	-0.01745	0.04511	0.19836	0.24907
BY_PASV	-0.01450	0.35214	0.56301	0.37657	-0.05369	-0.01663	0.17183	0.16815
BE_STATE	-0.21063	-0.20412	-0.45470	-0.42524	0.05708	0.10734	-0.05081	-0.14566
EX_THERE	-0.12786	-0.08127	-0.16850	-0.07526	0.08068	0.07206	0.09760	-0.04515
TH_CL	-0.18357	-0.07683	-0.14983	-0.11630	0.02705	0.44801	0.07765	0.12455
ADJ_CL	-0.05800	0.00701	0.01544	-0.05604	0.05035	0.13178	0.05293	0.08730
WH_CL	-0.01810	-0.09464	-0.23186	-0.24441	0.05633	0.00079	0.01374	-0.08466
INF	-0.01381	-0.08744	-0.28238	-0.19599	-0.00386	0.17883	0.06235	0.08697
CL_VBG	1.00000	0.05891	0.02159	0.07503	-0.00508	-0.18810	-0.16192	-0.12532
CL_VBN	0.05891	1.00000	0.35105	0.20279	-0.07040	-0.04851	0.05160	0.09771
WHIZ_VBN	0.02159	0.35105	1.00000	0.41357	-0.06458	-0.02644	0.11645	0.13765
WHIZ_VBG	0.07503	0.20279	0.41357	1.00000	-0.01459	-0.07698	0.15319	0.18943
THTREL_S	-0.00508	-0.07040	-0.06458	-0.01459	1.00000	0.25104	0.00541	-0.00061
THTREL_O	-0.18810	-0.04851	-0.02644	-0.07698	0.25104	1.00000	0.15561	0.15668
REL_SUBJ	-0.16192	0.05160	0.11645	0.15319	0.00541	0.15561	1.00000	0.36910
REL_OBJ	-0.12532	0.09771	0.13765	0.18943	-0.00061	0.15668	0.36910	1.00000
REL_PIPE	-0.08815	0.14642	0.21925	0.26028	0.06279	0.18015	0.37096	0.74998
SENT_REL	-0.14632	-0.07366	-0.18745	-0.18382	0.08677	0.05296	-0.07798	-0.07251
SUB_COS	-0.23860	-0.09286	-0.34611	-0.27444	-0.03028	0.08980	-0.08761	-0.10654
SUB_CON	0.11206	-0.02482	-0.02034	-0.00597	0.06128	-0.02645	0.01522	0.00014
SUB_CND	-0.08483	-0.02777	-0.29293	-0.23329	0.08264	0.05865	-0.13929	-0.11127
SUB_OTHR	0.10640	0.19116	0.15926	0.18712	-0.05199	0.00973	0.00849	0.11228
PREP	-0.03356	0.30297	0.64904	0.48921	0.01474	0.11655	0.28696	0.39587
ADJ_ATTR	-0.04023	0.19860	0.49772	0.33613	-0.00832	0.04851	0.31553	0.26275
ADJ_PRED	0.11576	0.03240	-0.08538	-0.16130	-0.04037	0.03177	-0.13821	-0.10600
ADVS	-0.00933	-0.26795	-0.49461	-0.41098	0.04384	-0.10324	-0.31091	-0.35032
TYPETOKN	0.14928	-0.09190	0.07562	0.13777	-0.06120	-0.08946	0.00729	0.03078
WRDLNGTH	-0.07818	0.22212	0.55912	0.46403	-0.03365	0.11603	0.34836	0.37529
CONJNCTS	0.02044	0.22316	0.33687	0.20699	0.02229	0.09381	0.13466	0.24635
DOWNTONE	-0.03909	0.00268	0.08469	-0.00102	-0.02874	0.08018	0.04830	0.07255
GEN_HDG	-0.14638	-0.11696	-0.23814	-0.22048	0.00972	-0.03078	-0.16404	-0.21682
AMPLIFR	-0.25295	-0.14187	-0.29483	-0.28613	0.07977	0.13409	-0.03768	-0.12235
GEN_EMPH	-0.19033	-0.21391	-0.43386	-0.34451	0.13268	-0.02340	-0.15707	-0.24656
PRTCLE	-0.26249	-0.15178	-0.34909	-0.30183	0.05245	0.07819	-0.11638	-0.19278
DEM	-0.17412	0.03640	0.07078	-0.03889	0.15671	0.22008	0.13652	0.19602
POS_MOD	-0.08142	-0.00686	-0.24403	-0.24909	0.10787	0.04959	-0.03991	-0.06560
NEC_MOD	-0.06599	0.00874	-0.01603	-0.03930	-0.00267	0.12564	0.02186	0.11652
PRD_MOD	-0.07090	-0.01875	-0.17578	-0.08917	0.12097	0.15332	0.00979	0.03637
PUB_VB	0.01657	-0.11536	-0.21305	-0.12917	-0.06681	0.08852	-0.12329	-0.12651
PRV_VB	-0.06823	-0.15880	-0.50619	-0.43588	0.05565	0.02105	-0.20493	-0.24928
SUA_VB	0.02830	0.05978	0.16040	0.04152	0.00383	0.14251	0.07739	0.09584
SEEM	0.04054	-0.02011	-0.07407	-0.04505	-0.01812	0.02650	0.00945	0.09197
CONTRAC	-0.15134	-0.20153	-0.45852	-0.42530	0.08596	-0.04886	-0.33063	-0.34271
THAT_DEL	-0.13853	-0.16403	-0.45484	-0.37422	0.00139	-0.04618	-0.25942	-0.31410
FINLPREP	-0.06955	-0.11597	-0.28888	-0.13691	0.23360	0.14386	-0.09512	-0.08667
SPL_INF	-0.02688	-0.01358	-0.03734	-0.04148	-0.02255	0.00777	-0.04877	-0.01161
SPL_AUX	-0.04974	0.03529	0.00257	-0.04706	-0.03616	0.08935	0.07698	0.13822
P_AND	0.09670	0.15562	0.32971	0.30000	-0.05240	-0.09140	0.13646	0.25514
O_AND	-0.23061	-0.17587	-0.32174	-0.26704	0.04528	-0.01211	-0.07730	-0.13562
SYNTHNEG	0.17171	-0.09841	-0.07945	-0.02437	0.04249	0.10740	0.02142	0.00312
NOT_NEG	-0.11266	-0.18271	-0.50385	-0.41836	0.03339	0.07045	-0.27593	-0.26092

	REL_PIPE	SENT_REL	SUB_COS	SUB_CON	SUB_CND	SUB_OTHR	PREP	ADJ_ATTR
PASTTNSE	-0.25790	-0.05454	-0.02387	0.07856	-0.10718	-0.09788	-0.40885	-0.41144
PERFECTS	-0.08099	0.06389	0.07929	0.00944	0.04562	-0.05035	-0.32014	-0.29199
PRES	-0.11872	0.40776	0.50706	-0.05924	0.49314	-0.09061	-0.48861	-0.37374
PL_ADV	-0.09351	-0.08671	-0.20644	-0.01716	-0.13874	-0.05159	0.03419	0.05141
TM_ADV	-0.26097	-0.01592	0.05969	-0.01555	-0.01222	-0.13090	-0.27893	-0.23382
PRO1	-0.27557	0.36091	0.53056	-0.08964	0.30867	-0.13466	-0.64065	-0.59229
PRO2	-0.31400	0.31829	0.51424	-0.10116	0.37454	-0.14774	-0.65536	-0.58074
PRO3	-0.25780	-0.05719	-0.00053	0.14291	0.06064	-0.11600	-0.50758	-0.44570
IT	-0.21094	0.35021	0.43280	-0.03098	0.36470	-0.17064	-0.56201	-0.47257
PDEM	-0.13470	0.47358	0.50330	-0.10413	0.32808	-0.08499	-0.41997	-0.44817
PANY	-0.21872	0.25305	0.39583	-0.02237	0.37571	-0.15069	-0.54637	-0.45845
PRO_DO	-0.24581	0.34428	0.51728	-0.03630	0.33287	-0.11548	-0.60890	-0.54825
WH_QUES	-0.08636	0.26043	0.26320	-0.05903	0.06805	-0.06327	-0.33918	-0.29692
N_NOM	0.42272	-0.17224	-0.24201	-0.02294	-0.12692	0.21583	0.67927	0.57585
N_VBG	0.26822	-0.13674	-0.22930	0.07030	-0.12101	0.11803	0.39344	0.35724
N	0.21323	-0.28235	-0.43103	-0.00402	-0.44737	0.01464	0.56834	0.51276
AGLS_PSV	0.35460	-0.18281	-0.30468	0.01244	-0.16992	0.23628	0.58273	0.44720
BY_PASV	0.25588	-0.15332	-0.24305	0.02862	-0.20069	0.18059	0.51390	0.38529
BE_STATE	-0.12087	0.32134	0.47163	-0.01825	0.42306	-0.07762	-0.55925	-0.41951
EX_THERE	0.04589	0.20127	0.16811	-0.06953	0.12062	-0.06689	-0.14770	-0.19157
TH_CL	0.09194	0.05037	0.19924	-0.04640	0.21367	0.10402	-0.04000	-0.18188
ADJ_CL	0.10279	-0.04623	-0.03172	-0.03269	0.14899	0.17524	0.06371	0.06172
WH_CL	-0.16019	0.23472	0.32470	-0.01446	0.16139	-0.08156	-0.34626	-0.29424
INF	-0.02472	-0.07389	0.11999	0.00888	0.30321	-0.01889	-0.21716	-0.08339
CL_VBG	-0.08815	-0.14632	-0.23860	0.11206	-0.08483	0.10640	-0.03356	-0.04023
CL_VBN	0.14642	-0.07366	-0.09286	-0.02482	-0.02777	0.19116	0.30297	0.19860
WHIZ_VBN	0.21925	-0.18745	-0.34611	-0.02034	-0.29293	0.15926	0.64904	0.49772
WHIZ_VBG	0.26028	-0.18382	-0.27444	-0.00597	-0.23329	0.18712	0.48921	0.33613
THTREL_S	0.06279	0.08677	-0.03028	0.06128	0.08264	-0.05199	0.01474	-0.00832
THTREL_O	0.18015	0.05296	0.08980	-0.02645	0.05865	0.00973	0.11655	0.04851
REL_SUBJ	0.37096	-0.07798	-0.08761	0.01522	-0.13929	0.00849	0.28696	0.31553
REL_OBJ	0.74998	-0.07251	-0.10654	0.00014	-0.11127	0.11228	0.39587	0.26275
REL_PIPE	1.00000	-0.06292	-0.18088	0.04669	-0.07390	0.11405	0.43439	0.27582
SENT_REL	-0.06292	1.00000	0.31502	0.01530	0.21015	-0.11290	-0.24219	-0.23688
SUB_COS	-0.18088	0.31502	1.00000	-0.05823	0.23082	-0.07514	-0.39850	-0.37237
SUB_CON	0.04669	0.01530	-0.05823	1.00000	-0.04423	0.03442	-0.03274	0.07670
SUB_CND	-0.07390	0.21015	0.23082	-0.04423	1.00000	0.01123	-0.37445	-0.33738
SUB_OTHR	0.11405	-0.11290	-0.07514	0.03442	0.01123	1.00000	0.21830	0.09267
PREP	0.43439	-0.24219	-0.39850	-0.03274	-0.37445	0.21830	1.00000	0.64506
ADJ_ATTR	0.27582	-0.23688	-0.37237	0.07670	-0.33738	0.09267	0.64506	1.00000
ADJ_PRED	-0.06590	-0.02834	0.15839	0.04535	0.26768	0.15581	-0.19344	-0.12045
ADVS	-0.35121	0.24875	0.35221	0.05075	0.32582	-0.16684	-0.65997	-0.44539
TYPETOKN	0.00514	-0.18910	-0.36995	0.14254	-0.28386	-0.03124	0.14695	0.37674
WRDLNGTH	0.38770	-0.25259	-0.41817	0.05171	-0.36046	0.18729	0.77988	0.80901
CONJNCTS	0.28636	-0.11054	-0.16715	0.04465	0.06673	0.31515	0.43247	0.34708
DOWNTONE	0.04504	-0.05243	0.00891	0.12650	-0.05750	0.10887	0.11651	0.18394
GEN_HDG	-0.16591	0.19631	0.31743	0.03589	0.21168	-0.11105	-0.40781	-0.31591
AMPLIFR	-0.16531	0.28938	0.50015	-0.06013	0.20101	-0.09128	-0.34612	-0.30264
GEN_EMPH	-0.22382	0.30418	0.42918	0.05952	0.30470	-0.13370	-0.50803	-0.31658
PRTCLE	-0.18180	0.34523	0.47500	-0.11554	0.31765	-0.19531	-0.46622	-0.47044
DEM	0.17651	0.04672	0.06576	0.01176	0.05102	0.11675	0.20729	0.11614
POS_MOD	-0.07496	0.14946	0.32543	0.01015	0.45647	-0.00861	-0.34250	-0.22580
NEC_MOD	0.11899	0.08290	0.03843	-0.00644	0.32156	0.11080	-0.01624	0.05086
PRD_MOD	-0.04765	0.08758	0.10677	0.01277	0.32875	0.03109	-0.21265	-0.20704
PUB_VB	-0.12395	0.11953	0.07959	-0.01128	0.05456	-0.07128	-0.25720	-0.31672
PRV_VB	-0.24902	0.38937	0.49441	0.01378	0.38871	-0.11377	-0.67237	-0.60171
SUA_VB	0.10852	-0.11157	-0.08148	-0.04411	0.12185	0.08461	0.12092	0.04153
SEEM	0.08597	-0.00870	-0.07372	0.16331	0.02771	0.01149	-0.01100	0.07107
CONTRAC	-0.31589	0.44966	0.53200	-0.08817	0.38010	-0.21384	-0.67803	-0.62477
THAT_DEL	-0.26732	0.43533	0.50057	-0.00240	0.32138	-0.15608	-0.66118	-0.60001
FINLPREP	-0.06591	0.30842	0.33734	-0.06075	0.25376	0.00404	-0.23232	-0.40593
SPL_INF	0.01126	-0.01301	0.05135	-0.02796	0.01099	0.19895	-0.05126	-0.03090
SPL_AUX	0.10045	-0.05347	0.00219	0.09270	0.15055	0.10846	0.01359	0.13521
P_AND	0.25508	-0.21662	-0.30005	0.03133	-0.30978	0.11242	0.40050	0.47516
O_AND	-0.20455	0.32551	0.49205	-0.08851	0.19057	-0.13886	-0.44177	-0.42407
SYNTHNEG	-0.01463	-0.12890	-0.12807	-0.04264	0.01148	-0.04703	-0.07248	-0.01622
NOT_NEG	-0.25755	0.33185	0.49227	-0.02521	0.46208	-0.15676	-0.67072	-0.59850

	ADJ_PRED	ADVS	TYPETOKN	WRDLNGTH	CONJNCTS	DOWNTONE	GEN_HDG	AMPLIFR
PASTTNSE	-0.03803	0.23039	0.13215	-0.40526	-0.36426	-0.04323	0.00798	-0.05670
PERFECTS	0.06175	0.20289	0.04725	-0.26674	-0.21571	-0.01081	0.06736	0.01666
PRES	0.26537	0.44484	-0.45028	-0.47190	-0.03696	-0.09045	0.43885	0.47346
PL_ADV	-0.13684	0.20120	0.10789	0.01614	-0.11496	-0.01456	-0.04599	-0.10865
TM_ADV	-0.09467	0.47032	0.01433	-0.28139	-0.28790	-0.08060	0.10351	0.17105
PRO1	0.15768	0.52539	-0.35157	-0.72163	-0.30885	-0.10304	0.41146	0.48020
PRO2	0.21056	0.53574	-0.39225	-0.66034	-0.26962	-0.11607	0.42659	0.48378
PRO3	0.09366	0.32039	0.13939	-0.45480	-0.36039	-0.06267	0.04862	-0.02743
IT	0.08649	0.55075	-0.38328	-0.59789	-0.22815	-0.07943	0.38358	0.38447
PDEM	0.05845	0.44553	-0.48124	-0.48634	-0.14260	-0.06469	0.36472	0.58933
PANY	0.06418	0.45422	-0.26031	-0.54139	-0.24361	-0.13416	0.47786	0.37816
PRO_DO	0.12369	0.52866	-0.39834	-0.60367	-0.25352	-0.11316	0.44408	0.44172
WH_QUES	0.08284	0.25348	-0.24304	-0.28995	-0.16742	-0.07865	0.21954	0.28824
N_NOM	0.01589	-0.60056	0.02640	0.76343	0.50419	0.02928	-0.30244	-0.27921
N_VBG	0.00743	-0.35021	0.14942	0.44058	0.27541	0.07951	-0.22823	-0.27022
N	-0.32839	-0.56324	0.42958	0.63217	0.04078	0.06349	-0.39770	-0.36763
AGLS_PSV	-0.02421	-0.55569	0.02327	0.59398	0.42966	0.08182	-0.28711	-0.31351
BY_PASV	-0.02699	-0.48427	0.08520	0.50884	0.35286	0.08249	-0.19900	-0.24142
BE_STATE	0.39152	0.47581	-0.38867	-0.55161	-0.08362	-0.02695	0.29143	0.51194
EX_THERE	0.01593	0.11124	-0.24008	-0.20036	-0.05974	0.03753	0.03803	0.21195
TH_CL	0.08931	0.00569	-0.23486	-0.05438	0.10050	-0.03411	-0.02957	0.18894
ADJ_CL	0.18460	-0.03935	-0.03398	0.08220	0.24313	0.08582	-0.07814	-0.00985
WH_CL	0.00070	0.23748	-0.21584	-0.31525	-0.09691	-0.03696	0.17742	0.20810
INF	0.19998	0.04522	-0.00505	-0.09416	-0.00341	-0.08725	-0.04914	-0.04996
CL_VBG	0.11576	-0.00933	0.14928	-0.07818	0.02044	-0.03909	-0.14638	-0.25295
CL_VBN	0.03240	-0.26795	-0.09190	0.22212	0.22316	0.00268	-0.11696	-0.14187
WHIZ_VBN	-0.08538	-0.49461	0.07562	0.55912	0.33687	0.08469	-0.23814	-0.29483
WHIZ_VBG	-0.16130	-0.41098	0.13777	0.46403	0.20699	-0.00102	-0.22048	-0.28613
THTREL_S	-0.04037	0.04384	-0.06120	-0.03365	0.02229	-0.02874	0.00972	0.07977
THTREL_O	0.03177	-0.10324	-0.08946	0.11603	0.09381	0.08018	-0.03078	0.13409
REL_SUBJ	-0.13821	-0.31091	0.00729	0.34836	0.13466	0.04830	-0.16404	-0.03768
REL_OBJ	-0.10600	-0.35032	0.03078	0.37529	0.24635	0.07255	-0.21682	-0.12235
REL_PIPE	-0.06590	-0.35121	0.00514	0.38770	0.28636	0.04504	-0.16591	-0.16531
SENT_REL	-0.02834	0.24875	-0.18910	-0.25259	-0.11054	-0.05243	0.19631	0.28938
SUB_COS	0.15839	0.35221	-0.36995	-0.41817	-0.16715	0.00891	0.31743	0.50015
SUB_CON	0.04535	0.05075	0.14254	0.05171	0.04465	0.12650	0.03589	-0.06013
SUB_CND	0.26768	0.32582	-0.28386	-0.36046	0.06673	-0.05750	0.21168	0.20101
SUB_OTHR	0.15581	-0.16684	-0.03124	0.18729	0.31515	0.10887	-0.11105	-0.09128
PREP	-0.19344	-0.65997	0.14695	0.77988	0.43247	0.11651	-0.40781	-0.34612
ADJ_ATTR	-0.12045	-0.44539	0.37674	0.80901	0.34708	0.18394	-0.31591	-0.30264
ADJ_PRED	1.00000	0.11962	-0.14365	-0.19471	0.11563	0.10812	0.03542	0.04321
ADVS	0.11962	1.00000	-0.20600	-0.63647	-0.29380	0.03695	0.46047	0.46909
TYPETOKN	-0.14365	-0.20600	1.00000	0.36472	-0.02295	0.07614	-0.20726	-0.35979
WRDLNGTH	-0.19471	-0.63647	0.36472	1.00000	0.39906	0.13647	-0.39351	-0.37654
CONJNCTS	0.11563	-0.29380	-0.02295	0.39906	1.00000	0.10011	-0.15205	-0.20167
GEN_HDG	0.03542	0.46047	-0.20726	-0.39351	-0.15205	-0.00538	1.00000	0.25814
AMPLIFR	0.04321	0.46909	-0.35979	-0.37654	-0.20167	-0.00792	0.25814	1.00000
GEN_EMPH	0.12317	0.59629	-0.26820	-0.47515	-0.19812	-0.03897	0.45953	0.46886
PRTCLE	0.03263	0.48692	-0.42774	-0.48025	-0.21308	-0.09642	0.43194	0.52874
DEM	0.02584	-0.05915	-0.22333	0.12367	0.31151	0.13254	-0.06813	0.06716
POS_MOD	0.30765	0.27194	-0.27931	-0.31773	0.06220	0.04145	0.25767	0.20622
NEC_MOD	0.17465	0.02210	-0.07657	0.04219	0.22828	0.00803	-0.02768	-0.02134
PRD_MOD	0.19578	0.00549	-0.14511	-0.13655	0.04520	-0.07373	0.06081	0.02719
PUB_VB	0.01024	-0.01160	-0.09496	-0.19088	-0.16925	-0.14442	-0.01023	-0.03838
PRV_VB	0.20714	0.57979	-0.41191	-0.68072	-0.20807	-0.11483	0.46880	0.46075
SUA_VB	0.02407	-0.20627	-0.09282	0.15476	0.22174	-0.01014	-0.14535	-0.15336
SEEM	0.03776	0.09233	0.03883	0.02360	0.11387	0.05067	0.05308	-0.07247
CONTRAC	0.14549	0.65949	-0.43388	-0.70681	-0.31360	-0.12730	0.53865	0.54840
THAT_DEL	0.14098	0.51491	-0.39615	-0.65680	-0.30526	-0.15256	0.44288	0.42739
FINLPREP	-0.03818	0.37069	-0.37300	-0.42115	-0.09238	-0.12516	0.28939	0.37977
SPL_INF	0.07528	0.04261	-0.01000	-0.06409	-0.03327	-0.05573	-0.02199	0.02332
SPL_AUX	0.13455	0.05225	0.05792	0.13586	0.21466	0.16732	-0.04495	-0.10280
P_AND	-0.04946	-0.43608	0.34294	0.46940	0.10549	0.04331	-0.23766	-0.36789
O_AND	-0.02639	0.43039	-0.36203	-0.49800	-0.24764	-0.07314	0.32827	0.49339
SYNTHNEG	0.08028	0.02020	0.10228	-0.03846	-0.07156	0.06105	-0.08401	-0.12154
NOT_NEG	0.22773	0.60358	-0.37274	-0.64892	-0.22872	-0.08420	0.40539	0.41316

	GEN_EMPH	PRTCLE	DEM	POS_MOD	NEC_MOD	PRD_MOD	PUB_VB	PRV_VB
PASTTNSE	-0.06028	-0.09094	-0.30321	-0.16127	-0.21667	-0.12123	0.31804	0.16308
PERFECTS	0.10107	0.09962	-0.03756	0.04442	-0.05843	0.00715	0.17866	0.22484
PRES	0.63177	0.63208	0.15560	0.51447	0.20159	0.27767	0.00875	0.66623
PL_ADV	-0.13763	-0.14472	-0.09785	-0.21145	-0.13289	-0.08913	-0.08672	-0.21205
TM_ADV	0.19199	0.31489	-0.06162	-0.09755	-0.12389	-0.03027	-0.02844	0.05489
PRO1	0.49564	0.56157	-0.00996	0.39220	0.02760	0.18452	0.16168	0.68798
PRO2	0.60566	0.59313	-0.06862	0.39297	-0.01716	0.14547	0.13743	0.75392
PRO3	0.07795	-0.03474	-0.28221	-0.03998	-0.11132	0.00764	0.25848	0.24709
IT	0.48632	0.53498	0.04829	0.29547	0.04796	0.10417	0.08498	0.62632
PDEM	0.51019	0.69441	0.22779	0.33204	0.06118	0.13758	0.04029	0.60033
PANY	0.49368	0.44932	-0.02442	0.36169	-0.00241	0.13007	0.15253	0.55724
PRO_DO	0.56036	0.60065	-0.01469	0.37890	0.02177	0.13887	0.14968	0.69143
WH_QUES	0.33493	0.38904	-0.00394	0.16201	0.07097	0.09828	0.13752	0.40173
N_NOM	-0.38657	-0.32713	0.25260	-0.03543	0.21669	0.05516	-0.07981	-0.43092
N_VBG	-0.22527	-0.33620	0.09815	-0.07722	0.09114	0.00234	-0.07189	-0.29698
N	-0.48304	-0.47180	-0.11790	-0.48899	-0.10784	-0.15288	-0.19017	-0.74585
AGLS_PSV	-0.47067	-0.36544	0.11165	-0.09702	0.15988	-0.08748	-0.12146	-0.47198
BY_PASV	-0.37119	-0.31556	-0.00652	-0.15700	0.06424	-0.15590	-0.09715	-0.37646
BE_STATE	0.49263	0.54448	0.15683	0.35205	0.10691	0.14367	0.06830	0.62005
EX_THERE	0.16055	0.26530	0.11435	0.09062	0.07232	0.00553	0.10640	0.19279
TH_CL	0.00794	0.19606	0.26711	0.17304	0.18261	0.16176	0.25632	0.22514
ADJ_CL	-0.01060	0.02649	0.21637	0.01727	0.18087	0.09292	-0.02620	0.00161
WH_CL	0.26296	0.18692	0.06385	0.23714	0.01510	0.14123	0.23231	0.42957
INF	0.09755	-0.05127	-0.01173	0.29473	0.30720	0.33962	0.12793	0.12233
CL_VBG	-0.19033	-0.26249	-0.17412	-0.08142	-0.06599	-0.07090	0.01657	-0.06823
CL_VBN	-0.21391	-0.15178	0.03640	-0.00686	0.00874	-0.01875	-0.11536	-0.15880
WHIZ_VBN	-0.43386	-0.34909	0.07078	-0.24403	-0.01603	-0.17578	-0.21305	-0.50619
WHIZ_VBG	-0.34451	-0.30183	-0.03889	-0.24909	-0.03930	-0.08917	-0.12917	-0.43588
THTREL_S	0.13268	0.05245	0.15671	0.10787	-0.00267	0.12097	-0.06681	0.05565
THTREL_O	-0.02340	0.07819	0.22008	0.04959	0.12564	0.15332	0.08852	0.02105
REL_SUBJ	-0.15707	-0.11638	0.13652	-0.03991	0.02186	0.00979	-0.12329	-0.20493
REL_OBJ	-0.24656	-0.19278	0.19602	-0.06560	0.11652	0.03637	-0.12651	-0.24928
REL_PIPE	-0.22382	-0.18180	0.17651	-0.07496	0.11899	-0.04765	-0.12395	-0.24902
SENT_REL	0.30418	0.34523	0.04672	0.14946	0.08290	0.08758	0.11953	0.38937
SUB_COS	0.42918	0.47500	0.06576	0.32543	0.03843	0.10677	0.07959	0.49441
SUB_CON	0.05952	-0.11554	0.01176	0.01015	-0.00644	0.01277	-0.01128	0.01378
SUB_CND	0.30470	0.31765	0.05102	0.45647	0.32156	0.32875	0.05456	0.38781
SUB_OTHR	-0.13370	-0.19531	0.11675	-0.00861	0.11080	0.03109	-0.07128	-0.11377
PREP	-0.50803	-0.46622	0.20729	-0.34250	-0.01624	-0.21265	-0.25720	-0.67237
ADJ_ATTR	-0.31658	-0.47044	0.11614	-0.22580	0.05086	-0.20704	-0.31672	-0.60171
ADJ_PRED	0.12317	0.03263	0.02584	0.30765	0.17465	0.19578	0.01024	0.20714
ADVS	0.59629	0.48692	-0.05915	0.27194	0.02210	0.00549	-0.01160	0.57979
TYPETOKN	-0.26820	-0.42774	-0.22333	-0.27931	-0.07657	-0.14511	-0.09496	-0.41191
WRDLNGTH	-0.47515	-0.48025	0.12367	-0.31729	0.04219	-0.13655	-0.19088	-0.68072
CONJNCTS	-0.19812	-0.21308	0.31151	0.06220	0.22828	0.04520	-0.16925	-0.20807
DOWNTONE	-0.03897	-0.09642	0.13254	0.04145	0.00803	-0.07373	-0.14442	-0.11483
GEN_HDG	0.45953	0.43194	-0.06813	0.25767	-0.02768	0.06081	-0.01023	0.46880
AMPLIFR	0.46886	0.52874	0.06716	0.20622	-0.02134	0.02719	-0.03838	0.46075
GEN_EMPH	1.00000	0.47967	0.00381	0.32722	-0.00011	0.09513	0.03162	0.60666
PRTCLE	0.47967	1.00000	0.06227	0.30994	0.02610	0.11495	0.04200	0.54772
DEM	0.00381	0.06227	1.00000	0.09587	0.09166	0.07442	-0.02252	0.00822
POS_MOD	0.32722	0.30994	0.09587	1.00000	0.23832	0.24790	0.01170	0.43201
NEC_MOD	-0.00011	0.02610	0.09166	0.23832	1.00000	0.19705	-0.01481	0.05020
PRD_MOD	0.09513	0.11495	0.07442	0.24790	0.19705	1.00000	0.13078	0.14512
PUB_VB	0.03162	0.04200	-0.02252	0.01170	-0.01481	0.13078	1.00000	0.16664
PRV_VB	0.60666	0.54772	0.00822	0.43201	0.05020	0.14512	0.16664	1.00000
SUA_VB	-0.18655	-0.11537	0.01398	0.07187	0.22736	0.15878	0.06481	-0.17673
SEEM	0.10076	-0.04890	0.07031	0.11208	0.04199	-0.05930	-0.00489	0.07268
CONTRAC	0.65036	0.72691	-0.04073	0.34393	-0.01857	0.05174	0.08660	0.77719
THAT_DEL	0.59535	0.58640	-0.08929	0.36289	0.00086	0.13937	0.26178	0.79705
FINLPREP	0.32777	0.43395	0.11805	0.12876	-0.04857	0.00044	0.01403	0.35842
SPL_INF	0.00793	-0.02394	-0.06527	-0.02375	0.02090	0.01547	-0.03177	0.06575
SPL_AUX	-0.07705	-0.14788	0.11868	0.25280	0.32069	0.20223	-0.00166	-0.07715
P_AND	-0.26984	-0.42612	-0.10110	-0.21977	-0.01752	-0.13084	-0.12330	-0.41032
O_AND	0.39887	0.42526	0.05906	0.20338	-0.05181	0.00341	0.10676	0.42576
SYNTHNEG	-0.10635	-0.16288	0.02528	0.00973	0.08726	0.01842	0.15059	-0.06197
NOT_NEG	0.57009	0.55157	-0.04508	0.39818	0.13131	0.18040	0.22879	0.74710

	SUA_VB	SEEM	CONTRAC	THAT_DEL	FINLPREP	SPL_INF	SPL_AUX	P_AND
PASTTNSE	-0.09767	0.03733	0.07162	0.15968	0.01620	-0.03914	-0.07418	-0.12138
PERFECTS	-0.09035	0.05795	0.22584	0.20932	0.01360	0.10029	0.15357	-0.12812
PRES	-0.06883	-0.00408	0.73228	0.64584	0.38137	0.08171	-0.01256	-0.35569
PL_ADV	-0.07080	-0.01308	-0.09693	-0.15507	0.00068	-0.00186	-0.08823	0.01021
TM_ADV	-0.12561	-0.04100	0.26306	0.14620	0.21747	0.08781	-0.11512	-0.25447
PRO1	-0.12319	-0.04479	0.71809	0.66963	0.39486	0.07311	-0.09936	-0.38114
PRO2	-0.14871	-0.04053	0.78950	0.70122	0.35019	0.04007	-0.13630	-0.39155
PRO3	-0.10397	0.08981	0.15458	0.21105	0.02595	0.00225	-0.00993	-0.12814
IT	-0.14103	0.04008	0.69432	0.56910	0.34546	-0.02783	-0.10258	-0.37876
PDEM	-0.15583	-0.06919	0.70670	0.58955	0.57438	-0.00557	-0.14036	-0.46896
PANY	-0.01137	0.03240	0.55695	0.52159	0.31640	-0.00999	-0.07481	-0.32003
PRO_DO	-0.04416	0.03249	0.71694	0.65689	0.39112	0.00057	-0.08455	-0.37624
WH_QUES	-0.11445	-0.06158	0.40299	0.42177	0.31576	-0.01753	-0.16498	-0.22611
N_NOM	0.26985	0.03998	-0.51898	-0.45604	-0.29929	-0.05368	0.18878	0.30522
N_VBG	0.26818	0.00788	-0.41476	-0.32020	-0.24537	-0.04767	0.15763	0.30452
N	0.07973	-0.14403	-0.62905	-0.59845	-0.37139	0.01861	-0.04923	0.41172
AGLS_PSV	0.20656	-0.04468	-0.55108	-0.47393	-0.31985	-0.05926	0.24998	0.27357
BY_PASV	0.07315	-0.04795	-0.39708	-0.34769	-0.26903	-0.03049	0.09257	0.23256
BE_STATE	-0.13007	0.00940	0.63155	0.55711	0.40777	0.09936	-0.03576	-0.38136
EX_THERE	-0.05069	0.04293	0.25305	0.17683	0.25784	-0.05530	-0.10178	-0.15916
TH_CL	0.09720	0.07650	0.03943	0.05366	0.13017	0.01063	0.14095	-0.25930
ADJ_CL	0.02029	0.06302	-0.03612	-0.06320	-0.00911	0.06161	0.14227	-0.06546
WH_CL	-0.01055	-0.00524	0.32786	0.33187	0.15948	0.01835	-0.01948	-0.11810
INF	0.31460	0.12019	-0.05114	0.05872	-0.08231	0.03383	0.30278	-0.00505
CL_VBG	0.02830	0.04054	-0.15134	-0.13853	-0.06955	-0.02688	-0.04974	0.09670
CL_VBN	0.05978	-0.02011	-0.20153	-0.16403	-0.11597	-0.01358	0.03529	0.15562
WHIZ_VBN	0.16040	-0.07407	-0.45852	-0.45484	-0.28888	-0.03734	0.00257	0.32971
WHIZ_VBG	0.04152	-0.04505	-0.42530	-0.37422	-0.13691	-0.04148	-0.04706	0.30000
THTREL_S	0.00383	-0.01812	0.08596	0.00139	0.23360	-0.02255	-0.03616	-0.05240
THTREL_O	0.14251	0.02650	-0.04886	-0.04618	0.14386	0.00777	0.08935	-0.09140
REL_SUBJ	0.07739	0.00945	-0.33063	-0.25942	-0.09512	-0.04877	0.07698	0.13646
REL_OBJ	0.09584	0.09197	-0.34271	-0.31410	-0.08667	-0.01161	0.13822	0.25514
REL_PIPE	0.10852	0.08597	-0.31589	-0.26732	-0.06591	0.01126	0.10045	0.25508
SENT_REL	-0.11157	-0.00870	0.44966	0.43533	0.30842	-0.01301	-0.05347	-0.21662
SUB_COS	-0.08148	-0.07372	0.53200	0.50057	0.33734	0.05135	0.00219	-0.30005
SUB_CON	-0.04411	0.16331	-0.08817	-0.00240	-0.06075	-0.02796	0.09270	0.03133
SUB_CND	0.12185	0.02771	0.38010	0.32138	0.25376	0.01099	0.15055	-0.30978
SUB_OTHR	0.08461	0.01149	-0.21384	-0.15608	0.00404	0.19895	0.10846	0.11242
PREP	0.12092	-0.01100	-0.67803	-0.66118	-0.23232	-0.05126	0.01359	0.40050
ADJ_ATTR	0.04153	0.07107	-0.62477	-0.60001	-0.40593	-0.03090	0.13521	0.47516
ADJ_PRED	0.02407	0.03776	0.14549	0.14098	-0.03818	0.07528	0.13455	-0.04946
ADVS	-0.20627	0.09233	0.65949	0.51491	0.37069	0.04261	0.05225	-0.43608
TYPETOKN	-0.09282	0.03883	-0.43388	-0.39615	-0.37300	-0.01000	0.05792	0.34294
WRDLNGTH	0.15476	0.02360	-0.70681	-0.65680	-0.42115	-0.06409	0.13586	0.46940
CONJNCTS	0.22174	0.11387	-0.31360	-0.30526	-0.09238	-0.03327	0.21466	0.10549
DOWNTONE	-0.01014	0.05067	-0.12730	-0.15256	-0.12516	-0.05573	0.16732	0.04331
GEN_HDG	-0.14535	0.05308	0.53865	0.44288	0.28939	-0.02199	-0.04495	-0.23766
AMPLIFR	-0.15336	-0.07247	0.54840	0.42739	0.37977	0.02332	-0.10280	-0.36789
GEN_EMPH	-0.18655	0.10076	0.65036	0.59535	0.32777	0.00793	-0.07705	-0.26962
PRTCLE	-0.11537	-0.04890	0.72691	0.58640	0.43395	-0.02394	-0.14788	-0.42612
DEM	0.01398	0.07031	-0.04073	-0.08929	0.11805	-0.06527	0.11868	-0.10110
POS_MOD	0.07187	0.11208	0.34393	0.36289	0.12876	-0.02375	0.25280	-0.21977
NEC_MOD	0.22736	0.04199	-0.01857	0.00086	-0.04857	0.02090	0.32069	-0.01752
PRD_MOD	0.15937	-0.05930	0.05174	0.13937	0.00040	0.01547	0.20223	-0.13084
PUB_VB	0.06481	-0.00489	0.08660	0.26178	0.01403	-0.03177	-0.00166	-0.12330
PRV_VB	-0.17673	0.07268	0.77719	0.79705	0.35842	0.06575	-0.07715	-0.41032
SUA_VB	1.00000	-0.01395	-0.20596	-0.14127	-0.15252	-0.04193	0.18164	0.06597
SEEM	-0.01395	1.00000	-0.07776	0.00654	-0.08947	-0.03351	0.12310	0.00839
CONTRAC	-0.20596	-0.07776	1.00000	0.77361	0.48698	0.00379	-0.21629	-0.48526
THAT_DEL	-0.14127	0.00654	0.77361	1.00000	0.34155	0.12230	-0.15599	-0.34255
FINLPREP	-0.15252	-0.08947	0.48698	0.34155	1.00000	-0.01664	-0.22983	-0.43124
SPL_INF	-0.04193	-0.03351	0.00379	0.12230	-0.01664	1.00000	0.00997	0.13046
SPL_AUX	0.18164	0.12310	-0.21629	-0.15599	-0.22983	0.00997	1.00000	0.06516
P_AND	0.06597	0.00839	-0.48526	-0.34255	-0.43124	0.13046	0.06516	1.00000
O_AND	-0.17453	-0.09534	0.50220	0.42907	0.45475	0.06267	-0.11115	-0.36167
SYNTHNEG	0.09404	0.02395	-0.14128	-0.14513	-0.12623	-0.04757	0.15068	0.01893
NOT_NEG	-0.06461	0.03565	0.77665	0.70543	0.35257	0.00391	0.03232	-0.43728

	O_AND	SYNTHNEG	NOT_NEG
PASTTNSE	0.14402	0.23031	0.16515
PERFECTS	0.09914	0.20833	0.24730
PRES	0.34629	-0.16484	0.62933
PL_ADV	-0.06129	0.01178	-0.22265
TM_ADV	0.21315	-0.04100	0.11472
PRO1	0.57964	-0.08553	0.59457
PRO2	0.40155	-0.11496	0.67825
PRO3	0.09991	0.23635	0.30780
IT	0.34821	-0.04182	0.59400
PDEM	0.46526	-0.17931	0.56545
PANY	0.33914	-0.00139	0.55855
PRO_DO	0.35708	-0.07831	0.73304
WH_QUES	0.30159	-0.04402	0.34282
N_NOM	-0.38073	-0.04479	-0.42409
N_VBG	-0.34427	0.04640	-0.34022
N	-0.34560	-0.03729	-0.68202
AGLS_PSV	-0.37278	-0.01418	-0.46781
BY_PASV	-0.29791	-0.10676	-0.39302
BE_STATE	0.39080	0.04504	0.62309
EX_THERE	0.20908	0.17278	0.19554
TH_CL	0.17397	0.07682	0.21415
ADJ_CL	-0.03598	0.07913	0.01284
WH_CL	0.23637	0.13862	0.37251
INF	-0.07334	0.09331	0.14087
CL_VBG	-0.23061	0.17171	-0.11266
CL_VBN	-0.17587	-0.09841	-0.18271
WHIZ_VBN	-0.32174	-0.07945	-0.50385
WHIZ_VBG	-0.26704	-0.02437	-0.41836
THTREL_S	0.04528	0.04249	0.03339
THTREL_O	-0.01211	0.10740	0.07045
REL_SUBJ	-0.07730	0.02142	-0.27593
REL_OBJ	-0.13562	0.00312	-0.26092
REL_PIPE	-0.20455	-0.01463	-0.25755
SENT_REL	0.32551	-0.12890	0.33185
SUB_COS	0.49205	-0.12807	0.49227
SUB_CON	-0.08851	-0.04264	-0.02521
SUB_CND	0.19057	0.01148	0.46208
SUB_OTHR	-0.13886	-0.04703	-0.15676
PREP	-0.44177	-0.07248	-0.67072
ADJ_ATTR	-0.42407	-0.01622	-0.59850
ADJ_PRED	-0.02639	0.08028	0.22773
ADVS	0.43039	0.02020	0.60358
TYPETOKN	-0.36203	0.10228	-0.37274
WRDLNGTH	-0.49800	-0.03846	-0.64892
CONJNCTS	-0.24764	-0.07156	-0.22872
DOWNTONE	-0.07314	0.06105	-0.08420
GEN_HDG	0.32827	-0.08401	0.40539
AMPLIFR	0.49339	-0.12154	0.41316
GEN_EMPH	0.39887	-0.10635	0.57009
PRTCLE	0.42526	-0.16288	0.55157
DEM	0.05906	0.02528	-0.04508
POS_MOD	0.20338	0.00973	0.39818
NEC_MOD	-0.05181	0.08726	0.13131
PRD_MOD	0.00341	0.01842	0.18040
PUB_VB	0.10676	0.15059	0.22879
PRV_VB	0.42576	-0.06197	0.74710
SUA_VB	-0.17453	0.09404	-0.06461
SEEM	-0.09534	0.02395	0.03565
CONTRAC	0.50220	-0.14128	0.77665
THAT_DEL	0.42907	-0.14513	0.70543
FINLPREP	0.45475	-0.12623	0.35257
SPL_INF	0.06267	-0.04757	0.00391
SPL_AUX	-0.11115	0.15068	0.03232
P_AND	-0.36167	0.01893	-0.43728
O_AND	1.00000	-0.07699	0.31301
SYNTHNEG	-0.07699	1.00000	0.01277
NOT_NEG	0.31301	0.01277	1.00000

References

Aijmer, Karin. 1984. *Sort of* and *kind of* in English conversation. *Studia Linguistica* 38:118–28.

1985. *Just.* In *Papers on language and literature presented to Alvar Ellegard and Erik Frykman,* ed. by S. Backman and G. Kjellmer, pp. 1–10. Gothenburg Studies in English 60.

1986. Why is *actually* so popular in spoken English? In *English in speech and writing: a symposium,* ed. by G. Tottie and I. Bäcklund, pp. 119–30. Studia Anglistica Upsaliensia 60. Stockholm: Almqvist and Wiksell.

Akinnaso, F. Niyi. 1982. On the differences between spoken and written language. *Language and Speech* 25:97–125.

Altenberg, Bengt. 1984. Causal linking in spoken and written English. *Studia Linguistica* 38:20–69.

1986. Contrastive linking in spoken and written English. In *English in speech and writing: a symposium,* ed. by G. Tottie and I. Bäcklund, pp. 13–40. Studia Anglistica Upsaliensia 60. Stockholm: Almqvist and Wiksell.

Aronoff, Mark. 1985. Orthography and linguistic theory. *Language* 61:28–72.

Bäcklund, Ingegerd. 1984. *Conjunction-headed abbreviated clauses in English.* Studia Anglistica Upsaliensia 50. Stockholm: Almqvist and Wiksell.

1986. Beat until stiff: conjunction-headed abbreviated clauses in spoken and written English. In *English in speech and writing: a symposium,* ed. by G. Tottie and I. Bäcklund, pp. 41–56. Studia Anglistica Upsaliensia 60. Stockholm: Almqvist and Wiksell.

Basso, K.H. 1974. The ethnography of writing. In *Explorations in the ethnography of speaking,* ed. by R. Bauman and J. Sherzer, pp. 425–32. Cambridge: Cambridge University Press.

Beaman, Karen. 1984. Coordination and subordination revisited: syntactic complexity in spoken and written narrative discourse. In *Coherence in spoken and written discourse,* ed. by Deborah Tannen, pp. 45–80. Norwood, N.J.: Ablex.

Bernstein, Basil. 1970. *Class, codes, and control.* Volume 1: *Theoretical studies towards a sociology of language.* London: Routledge & Kegan Paul.

Besnier, Niko. 1986a. Spoken and written registers in a restricted-literacy setting. Unpublished Ph.D. dissertation, University of Southern California.

1986b. Register as a sociolinguistic unit: defining formality. In *Social and cognitive perspectives on language,* ed. by J. Connor-Linton, C.J. Hall and M. McGinnis, pp. 25–63. Southern California Occasional Papers in Linguistics 11. Los Angeles: University of Southern California.

Biber, Douglas. 1984. A model of textual relations within the written and spoken modes. Unpublished Ph.D. dissertation, University of Southern California.

1985. Investigating macroscopic textual variation through multi-feature/multi-dimensional analyses. *Linguistics* 23:337–60.

1986a. Spoken and written textual dimensions in English: resolving the contradictory findings. *Language* 62:384–414.

1986b. On the investigation of spoken/written differences. *Studia Linguistica* 40:1–21.

1987. A textual comparison of British and American writing. *American Speech* 62:99–119.

Forthcoming. A typology of English texts. *Linguistics.*

Biber, Douglas, and Edward Finegan. 1986. An initial typology of English text types. In *Corpus linguistics II,* ed. by Jan Aarts and Willem Meijs, pp. 19–46. Amsterdam: Rodopi.

1988a. Adverbial stance types in English. *Discourse Processes* 11:1–34.

1988b. Drift in three English genres from the 18th to the 20th centuries: a multidimensional approach. In *Corpus linguistics, hard and soft,* ed. by Merja Kyto, Ossi Ihalainen, and Matti Rissanen, pp. 83–101. Amsterdam: Rodopi.

1988c. Historical drift in three English genres. Paper presented at GURT '88, Georgetown. [Forthcoming in conference proceedings, ed. by Thomas J. Walsh. Washington, D.C.: Georgetown University Press.]

Forthcoming. Styles of stance in English: lexical and grammatical marking of evidentiality and affect. *Text* (special issue on *The pragmatics of affect,* ed. by Elinor Ochs).

Blankenship, Jane. 1962. A linguistic analysis of oral and written style. *Quarterly Journal of Speech* 48:419–22.

1974. The influence of mode, submode, and speaker predilection on style. *Speech Monographs* 41:85–118.

Blass, Thomas, and Aron W. Siegman. 1975. A psycholinguistic comparison of speech, dictation, and writing. *Language and Speech* 18:20–33.

Bloomfield, Leonard. 1933. *Language.* New York: Holt, Rinehart and Winston.

Brainerd, Barron. 1972. An exploratory study of pronouns and articles as indices of genre in English. *Language and Style* 5:239–59.

Brown, Gillian, and George Yule. 1983. *Discourse analysis.* Cambridge: Cambridge University Press.

Brown, Penelope, and Colin Fraser. 1979. Speech as a marker of situation. In *Social markers in speech,* ed. by Klaus R. Scherer and Howard Giles, pp. 33–62. Cambridge: Cambridge University Press.

Carroll, John B. 1960. Vectors of prose style. In *Style in language,* ed. by Thomas A. Sebeok, pp. 283–92. Cambridge, Mass.: MIT Press.

Cayer, Roger L., and Renee K. Sacks. 1979. Oral and written discourse of basic writers: similarities and differences. *Research in the Teaching of English* 13:121–8.

Chafe, Wallace L. 1982. Integration and involvement in speaking, writing, and oral literature. In *Spoken and written language: exploring orality and literacy*, ed. by D. Tannen, pp. 35–54. Norwood, N.J.: Ablex.

1984a. How people use adverbial clauses. In *Proceedings of the tenth annual meeting of the Berkeley Linguistics Society*, ed. by Claudia Brugman and Monica Macaulay, pp. 437–49. Berkeley: Berkeley Linguistics Society.

1984b. Speaking, writing, and prescriptivism. In *Meaning, form, and use in context: linguistic applications*, ed. by D. Schiffrin, pp. 95–103. GURT '84. Washington, D.C.: Georgetown University Press.

1985. Linguistic differences produced by differences between speaking and writing. In *Literature, language, and learning: the nature and consequences of reading and writing*, ed. by D.R. Olson, N. Torrance, and A. Hildyard, pp. 105–23. Cambridge: Cambridge University Press.

Chafe, Wallace L., and Jane Danielewicz. Forthcoming. Properties of spoken and written language. In *Comprehending oral and written language*, ed. by Rosalind Horowitz and S.J. Samuels. New York: Academic Press.

Coates, Jennifer. 1983. *The semantics of the modal auxiliaries*. London: Croom Helm.

Connor-Linton, Jeff, Christopher J. Hall, and Mary McGinnis (eds.). 1986. *Social and cognitive perspectives on language*. Southern California Occasional Papers in Linguistics 11. Los Angeles: University of Southern California.

Cook-Gumperz, Jenny, and John J. Gumperz. 1981. From oral to written culture: the transition to literacy. In *Variation in writing*, ed. by M. F. Whiteman, pp. 89–109. Hillsdale, N.J.: Erlbaum.

DeVito, Joseph A. 1966. Psychogrammatical factors in oral and written discourse by skilled communicators. *Speech Monographs* 33:73–6.

1967. Levels of abstraction in spoken and written language. *Journal of Communication* 17:354–61.

Dillon, George. 1981. *Constructing texts*. Bloomington, Ind.: Indiana University Press.

Drieman, G.H.J. 1962. Differences between written and spoken language. *Acta Psychologica* 20:36–57; 78–100.

Dubuisson, Colette, Louisette Emirkanian, and David Sankoff. 1983. *The development of syntactic complexity in narrative, informative and argumentative discourse*. CRMA–1170, Centre de Recherche de Mathématiques Appliquées, Université de Montréal.

Duranti, Alessandro. 1985. Sociocultural dimensions of discourse. In *Handbook of discourse analysis*, vol. 1, ed. by Teun van Dijk, pp. 193–230. New York: Academic Press.

Eisenstein, Elizabeth L. 1985. On the printing press as an agent of change. In

Literacy, language, and learning: the nature and consequences of reading and writing, ed. by D.R. Olson, N. Torrance, and A. Hildyard, pp. 19–33. Cambridge: Cambridge University Press.

Elsness, J. 1984. *That* or zero? A look at the choice of object clause connective in a corpus of American English. *English Studies* 65:519–33.

Erwin-Tripp, Susan. 1972. On sociolinguistic rules: alternation and co-occurrence. In *Directions in sociolinguistics*, ed. by John J. Gumperz and Dell Hymes, pp. 213–50. New York: Holt, Rinehart and Winston.

Farhady, Hossein. 1983. On the plausibility of the unitary language proficiency factor. In *Issues in language testing research*, ed. by J. W. Oller, pp. 11–28. Rowley, Mass.: Newbury House.

Farrell, Thomas. 1977. Literacy, the basics, and all that jazz. *College English* 38:443–59.

Feigenbaum, Irwin. 1978. The use of the perfect in an academic setting: a study of types and frequencies. Unpublished Ph.D. dissertation: University of Wisconsin–Milwaukee.

Ferguson, Charles A. 1959. Diglossia. *Word* 15:325–40.
1977. Baby talk as a simplified register. In *Talking to children*, ed. by C.E. Snow and C.A. Ferguson, pp. 209–33. Cambridge: Cambridge University Press.
1983. Sports announcer talk: syntactic aspects of register variation. *Language in Society* 12:153–72.

Fillmore, Charles J. 1981. Pragmatics and the description of discourse. In *Radical pragmatics*, ed. by Peter Cole, pp. 143–66. New York: Academic Press.

Finegan, Edward. 1980. *Attitudes toward English usage: the history of a war of words*. New York: Teachers College Press.
1982. Form and function in testament language. In *Linguistics and the professions*, ed. by Robert J. Di Pietro, pp. 113–20. Norwood, N.J.: Ablex.
1987. On the linguistic forms of prestige. In *The legacy of language*, ed. by Phillip C. Boardman, pp. 146–61. Reno: University of Nevada Press.

Finegan, Edward and Douglas Biber. 1986a. Toward a unified model of sociolinguistic prestige. In *Diversity and diachrony*, ed. by David Sankoff, pp. 391–8. Amsterdam: John Benjamins.
1986b. Two dimensions of linguistic complexity in English. In *Social and cognitive perspectives on language*, ed. by J. Connor-Linton, C.J. Hall, and M. McGinnis, pp. 1–24. Southern California Occasional Papers in Linguistics 11. Los Angeles: University of Southern California.

Fishman, Joshua. 1972. The sociology of language. In *Language and social context*, ed. by Pier Paolo Giglioli, pp. 45–58. New York: Penguin Books.

Ford, Cecilia E., and Sandra A. Thompson. 1986. Conditionals in discourse: a text-based study from English. In *On conditionals*, ed. by E. C. Traugott, A. T. Meulen, J. S. Reilly, and C. A. Ferguson, pp. 353–72. Cambridge: Cambridge University Press.

Francis, W. Nelson, and Henry Kucera. 1982. *Frequency analysis of English usage: lexicon and grammar.* Boston: Houghton Mifflin.

Frawley, William. 1982. Universal grammar and composition: relativization, complementation, and quantification. In *Linguistics and literacy*, ed. by William Frawley, pp. 65–90. New York: Plenum Press.

Frederiksen, Carl H., and Joseph F. Dominic (eds.). 1981. *Writing: the nature, development, and teaching of written communication.* Volume 2: *Writing: process, development and communication.* Hillsdale, N.J.: Lawrence Erlbaum Associates.

Gibson, James W., C.R. Gruner, R.J. Kibler, and F.J. Kelly. 1966. A quantitative examination of differences and similarities in written and spoken messages. *Speech Monographs* 33:444–51.

Golub, L.S. 1969. Linguistic structures in students' oral and written discourse. *Research in the Teaching of English* 3:70–85.

Goody, Jack (ed.). 1968. *Literacy in traditional societies.* Cambridge: Cambridge University Press.

1977. *The domestication of the savage mind.* Cambridge: Cambridge University Press.

Goody, Jack, and I.P. Watt. 1963. The consequences of literacy. *Comparative Studies in History and Society* 5:304–45.

Gorsuch, Richard L. 1983. *Factor analysis*, 2nd edition. Hillsdale, N.J.: Lawrence Erlbaum Associates.

Grabe, William P. 1984a. Towards defining expository prose within a theory of text construction. Unpublished Ph.D. dissertation, Department of Linguistics, University of Southern California.

1984b. Written discourse analysis. *Annual Review of Applied Linguistics* 5:101–23.

Grabe, William P., and Douglas Biber. 1987. Freshman student writing and the contrastive rhetoric hypothesis. Paper presented at SLRF 7, University of Southern California.

Green, Georgia M., and Jerry L. Morgan. 1981. Writing ability as a function of the appreciation of differences between oral and written communication. In *Writing: the nature, development, and teaching of written communication*, vol. 2, ed. by C.H. Frederiksen and J.F. Dominic, pp. 177–88. Hillsdale, N.J.: Lawrence Erlbaum Associates.

Greenfield, P.M. 1972. Oral or written language: the consequence for cognitive development in Africa, the United States and England. *Language and Speech* 15:169–78.

Gumperz, John J., Hannah Kaltman, and Mary Catherine O'Connor. 1984. Cohesion in spoken and written discourse. In *Coherence in spoken and written discourse*, ed. by Deborah Tannen, pp. 3–20. Norwood, N.J.: Ablex.

Hall, Robert A. 1964. *Introductory linguistics.* Philadelphia: Chilton Books.

Halliday, Michael A.K. 1968. The users and uses of language. In *Readings in the sociology of language*, ed. by Joshua F. Fishman, pp. 139–69. The Hague: Mouton.

1978. *Language as social semiotic: the social interpretation of language and meaning*. London: Edward Arnold.

1979. Differences between spoken and written language: some implications for literacy teaching. In *Communication through reading: Proceedings of the 4th Australian Reading Conference*, vol. 2, ed. by Glenda Page, John Elkins, and Barrie O'Connor, pp. 37–52. Adelaide, S.A.: Australian Reading Association.

Halliday, Michael A.K., and Ruqaiya Hasan. 1976. *Cohesion in English*. London: Longman.

Halpern, Jeanne W. 1984. Differences between speaking and writing and their implications for teaching. *College Composition and Communication* 35:345–57.

Harris, Mary M. 1977. Oral and written syntax attainment of second graders. *Research in the Teaching of English* 11:117–32.

Havelock, Eric A. 1963. *Preface to Plato*. Cambridge, Mass.: Harvard University Press.

Heath, Shirley Brice. 1982a. Protean shapes in literacy events: ever-shifting oral and literate traditions. In *Spoken and written language: exploring orality and literacy*, ed. by D. Tannen, pp. 91–117. Norwood, N.J.: Ablex.

1982b. What no bedtime story means: narrative skills at home and school. *Language in Society* 11:49–76.

1983. *Ways with words*. Cambridge: Cambridge University Press.

Hermeren, Lars. 1986. Modalities in spoken and written English: an inventory of forms. In *English in speech and writing: a symposium*, ed. by G. Tottie and I. Bäcklund, pp. 57–92. Studia Anglistica Upsaliensia 60. Stockholm: Almqvist and Wiksell.

Hillocks, George. 1986. *Research on written composition*. Urbana, Ill.: ERIC Clearinghouse on Reading and Communication Skills.

Hinofotis, Frances B. 1983. The structure of oral communication in an educational environment: a comparison of factor analytic rotational procedures. In *Issues in language testing research*, ed. by J.W. Oller, pp. 170–87. Rowley, Mass.: Newbury House.

Holmes, Janet. 1984. Hedging your bets and sitting on the fence: some evidence for hedges as support structures. *Te Reo* 27:47–62.

Horowitz, Milton W., and John B. Newman. 1964. Spoken and written expression: an experimental analysis. *Journal of Abnormal and Social Psychology* 68:640–7.

Householder, Fred W. 1964. *Adjectives before 'that'-clauses in English*. Bloomington, Ind.: Indiana University Linguistics Club.

1971. *Linguistic speculations*. Cambridge: Cambridge University Press.

Hu, Zhuang-Lin. 1984. Differences in mode. *Journal of Pragmatics* 8:595–606.

Hymes, Dell H. 1972. On communicative competence. In *Sociolinguistics*, ed. by J.B. Pride and Janet Holmes, pp. 269–93. Baltimore: Penguin Books.

1974. *Foundations in sociolinguistics*. Philadelphia: University of Pennsylvania Press.

Irvine, Judith. 1984/1979. Formality and informality in communicative events. In *Language in use: readings in sociolinguistics*, ed. by John Baugh and Joel Sherzer, pp. 211–28. Englewood Cliffs, N.J.: Prentice-Hall.

Janda, Richard D. 1985. Note-taking as a simplified register. *Discourse Processes* 8:437–54.

Johansson, Stig (ed.). 1982. *Computer corpora in English language research*. Bergen: Norwegian Computing Centre for the Humanities.

Johansson, Stig, Geoffrey N. Leech, and Helen Goodluck. 1978. *Manual of information to accompany the Lancaster–Oslo/Bergen Corpus of British English, for use with digital computers*. Department of English, University of Oslo.

Kay, Paul. 1977. Language evolution and speech style. In *Sociocultural dimensions of language change*, ed. by Ben G. Blount and Mary Sanches, pp. 21–33. New York: Academic Press.

Kochman, Thomas. 1981. *Black and white styles in conflict*. Chicago: University of Chicago Press.

Kroch, Anthony S. 1978. Toward a theory of social dialect variation. *Language in Society* 7:17–36.

Kroch, Anthony S., and Donald M. Hindle. 1982. A quantitative study of the syntax of speech and writing. Final Report to the National Institute of Education.

Kroch, Anthony S., and C. Small. 1978. Grammatical ideology and its effect on speech. In *Linguistic variation: models and methods*, ed. by David Sankoff, pp. 45–55. New York: Academic Press.

Kroll, Barbara. 1977. Ways communicators encode propositions in spoken and written English: a look at subordination and coordination. In *Discourse across time and space (SCOPIL no. 5)*, ed. by Elinor O. Keenan and Tina Bennett, pp. 69–108. Los Angeles: University of Southern California.

Kurzon, Dennis. 1985. Signposts for the reader: a corpus-based study of text deixis. *Text* 5:187–200.

Labov, William. 1972/1969. The logic of nonstandard English. In *Language and social context*, ed. by Paolo Giglioli, pp. 179–215. New York: Penguin Books.

1972. *Sociolinguistic patterns*. Philadelphia: University of Pennsylvania Press.

1984. Intensity. In *Meaning, form, and use in context: linguistic applications*, ed. by D. Schiffrin, pp. 43–70. GURT '84. Washington, D.C.: Georgetown University Press.

Lakoff, Robin. 1982a. Some of my favorite writers are literate: the mingling of oral and literate strategies in written communication. In *Spoken and written language: exploring orality and literacy*, ed. by D. Tannen, pp. 239–60. Norwood, N.J.: Ablex.

1982b. Persuasive discourse and ordinary conversation, with examples from advertising. In *Analyzing discourse: text and talk*, ed. by Deborah Tannen, pp. 25–42. Georgetown: Georgetown University Press.

Liggett, Sarah. 1984. The relationship between speaking and writing: an annotated bibliography. *College Composition and Communication* 35:334–44.

Marckworth, Mary L. and William J. Baker. 1974. A discriminant function analysis of co-variation of a number of syntactic devices in five prose genres. *American Journal of Computational Linguistics, Microfiche 11*.

McClure, Erica, and Esther Geva. 1983. The development of the cohesive use of adversative conjunctions in discourse. *Discourse Processes* 6:411–32.

Michaels, Sarah, and James Collins. 1984. Oral discourse styles: classroom interaction and the acquisition of literacy. In *Coherence in spoken and written discourse*, ed. by Deborah Tannen, pp. 219–44. Norwood, N.J.: Ablex.

Nystrand, Martin (ed.). 1982. *What writers know: the language, process, and structure of written discourse*. New York: Academic Press.

Ochs, Elinor. 1979. Planned and unplanned discourse. In *Discourse and syntax*, ed. by Talmy Givón, pp. 51–80. New York: Academic Press.

O'Donnell, Roy C. 1974. Syntactic differences between speech and writing. *American Speech* 49:102–10.

O'Donnell, Roy C., W.J. Griffin, and R.C. Norris. 1967. A transformational analysis of oral and written grammatical structures in the language of children in grades three, five, and seven. *Journal of Educational Research* 61:36–9.

Oller, John W. (ed.). 1983. *Issues in language testing research*. Rowley, Mass.: Newbury House.

Olson, David R. 1977. From utterance to text: the bias of language in speech and writing. *Harvard Educational Review* 47:257–81.

Olson, David R., and Nancy Torrance. 1981. Learning to meet the requirements of written text: language development in the school years. In *Writing: the nature, development, and teaching of written communication*, vol. 2, ed. by C.H. Frederiksen and J.F. Dominic, pp. 235–55. Hillsdale, N.J.: Lawrence Erlbaum Associates.

Olson, David R., Nancy Torrance, and Angela Hildyard (eds.). 1985. *Literacy, language, and learning: the nature and consequences of reading and writing*. Cambridge: Cambridge University Press.

Ong, Walter J. 1982. *Orality and literacy: the technologizing of the word*. New York: Methuen.

Osgood, Charles E. 1960. Some effects of motivation on style of encoding. In *Style in language*, ed. by Thomas A. Sebeok, pp. 293–306. Cambridge, Mass.: MIT Press.

Pellegrino, M.L. Morra, and A.A. Scopesi. 1978. Oral and written language in children: syntactical development of descriptive language. *International Journal of Psycholinguistics* 5:5–19.

Perera, Katharine. 1986. Language acquisition and writing. In *Language acquisition*, ed. by P. Fletcher and M. Garman, pp. 494–518. Cambridge: Cambridge University Press.

Philips, Susan U. 1983. *The invisible culture: communication in classroom and community on the Warm Springs Indian Reservation*. New York: Longman.

Poole, Millicent E. 1973. A comparison of the factorial structure of written coding patterns for a middle-class and a working-class group. *Language and Speech* 16:93–109.

1979. Social class, sex and linguistic coding. *Language and Speech* 22:49–67.

1983. Socioeconomic status and written language. In *The psychology of written language: developmental and educational perspectives*, ed. by Margaret Martlew, pp. 335–76. New York: John Wiley.

Poole, Millicent E., and T.W. Field. 1976. A comparison of oral and written code elaboration. *Language and Speech* 19:305–11.

Postal, Paul. 1966. Review of M.W. Dixon, *Linguistic science and logic.* *Language* 43:84–93.

Preston, Joan M., and R.C. Gardner. 1967. Dimensions of oral and written fluency. *Journal of Verbal Learning and Verbal Behavior* 6:936–45.

Price, Gayle B., and Richard L. Graves. 1980. Sex differences in syntax and usage in oral and written language. *Research in the Teaching of English* 14:147–53.

Prince, Ellen F. 1981. Toward a taxonomy of given-new information. In *Radical pragmatics*, ed. by Peter Cole, pp. 223–55. New York: Academic Press.

Quirk, Randolph, Sidney Greenbaum, Geoffrey Leech, and Jan Svartvik. 1985. *A comprehensive grammar of the English language.* London: Longman.

Rader, Margaret. 1982. Context in written language: the case of imaginative fiction. In *Spoken and written language: exploring orality and literacy*, ed. by D. Tannen, pp. 185–98. Norwood, N.J.: Ablex.

Redeker, Gisela. 1984. On differences between spoken and written language. *Discourse Processes* 7:43–55.

Rubin, Andee. 1980. A theoretical taxonomy of the differences between oral and written language. In *Theoretical issues in reading comprehension: perspectives from cognitive psychology, linguistics, artificial intelligence, and education*, ed. by Rand J. Spiro, Bertram C. Bruce, and William F. Brewer, pp. 411–38. Hillsdale, N.J.: Lawrence Erlbaum Associates.

Sahlin, Elisabeth. 1979. *'Some' and 'any' in spoken and written English.* Studia Anglistica Upsaliensia 38. Stockholm: Almqvist and Wiksell.

Sapir, Edward. 1921. *Language.* New York: Harcourt Brace and World.

de Saussure, F. 1916/1959. *Course in general linguistics* (translated by Wade Baskin). New York: Philosophical Library.

Schafer, John C. 1981. The linguistic analysis of spoken and written texts. In *Exploring speaking–writing relationships: connections and contrasts*, ed. by Barry M. Kroll and Roberta J. Vann, pp. 1–31. Urbana, Ill.: National Council of Teachers of English.

Schiffrin, Deborah. 1981. Tense variation in narrative. *Language* 57:45–62.

1982. Discourse markers: semantic resource for the construction of conversation. Unpublished Ph.D. dissertation, University of Pennsylvania.

(ed.). 1984a. *Meaning, form, and use in context: linguistic applications.* GURT '84. Washington, D.C.: Georgetown University Press.

1984b. Jewish argument as sociability. *Language in Society* 13:311–35.

1985a. Conversational coherence: the role of *well. Language* 61:640–67.

1985b. Multiple constraints on discourse options: a quantitative analysis of causal sequences. *Discourse Processes* 8:281–303.

Schourup, Lawrence C. 1985. *Common discourse particles in English conversation.* New York: Garland.

Scribner, Sylvia, and Michael Cole. 1981. *The psychology of literacy.* Cambridge, Mass.: Harvard University Press.

Shopen, Timothy. 1985. *Language typology and syntactic description.* Volume 2: *Complex constructions.* Cambridge: Cambridge University Press.

Smith, Frank. 1982. *Writing and the writer.* New York: Holt, Rinehart, and Winston.

Smith, Raoul, and William J. Frawley. 1983. Conjunctive cohesion in four English genres. *Text* 3:347–74.

Stenström, Anna-Brita. 1986. What does *really* really do? Strategies in speech and writing. In *English in speech and writing: a symposium,* ed. by G. Tottie and I. Bäcklund, pp. 149–64. Studia Anglistica Upsaliensia 60. Stockholm: Almqvist and Wiksell.

Street, Brian V. 1984. *Literacy in theory and practice.* Cambridge: Cambridge University Press.

Stubbs, Michael. 1980. *Language and literacy: the sociolinguistics of reading and writing.* London: Routledge and Kegan Paul.

    1982. Written language and society: some particular cases and general observations. In *What writers know: the language, process, and structure of written discourse,* ed. by M. Nystrand, pp. 31–55. New York: Academic Press.

Svartvik, Jan, and Randolph Quirk (eds.). *A corpus of English conversation.* Lund: CWK Gleerup.

Tannen, Deborah. 1982a. Oral and literate strategies in spoken and written narratives. *Language* 58:1–21.

    1982b. The oral/literate continuum in discourse. In *Spoken and written language: exploring orality and literacy,* ed. by D. Tannen, pp. 1–16. Norwood, N.J.: Ablex.

    1982c. The myth of orality and literacy. In *Linguistics and literacy,* ed. by William Frawley, pp. 37–50. New York: Plenum Press.

    (ed.). 1982d. *Spoken and written language: exploring orality and literacy.* Norwood, N.J.: Ablex.

    1985. Relative focus on involvement in oral and written discourse. In *Literacy, language, and learning: the nature and consequences of reading and writing,* ed. by D.R. Olson, N. Torrance, and A. Hildyard, pp. 124–47. Cambridge: Cambridge University Press.

Thompson, Sandra A. 1982. The passive in English: a discourse perspective. Unpublished ms.

    1983. Grammar and discourse: the English detached participial clause. In *Discourse perspectives on syntax,* ed. by Flora Klein-Andreu, pp. 43–65. New York: Academic Press.

    1984. 'Subordination' in formal and informal discourse. In *Meaning, form, and use in context: linguistic applications,* ed. by D. Schiffrin, pp. 85–94. GURT '84. Washington, D.C.: Georgetown University Press.

    1985. Grammar and written discourse: initial vs final purpose clauses in English. *Text* 5:55–84.

Thompson, Sandra A., and Robert E. Longacre. 1985. Adverbial clauses. In *Language typology and syntactic description*, vol. 2, ed. by T. Shopen, pp. 171–233. Cambridge: Cambridge University Press.

Tomlin, Russell S. 1985. Foreground–background information and the syntax of subordination. *Text* 5:85–122.

Tottie, Gunnel. 1981. Negation and discourse strategy in spoken and written English. In *Variation omnibus*, ed. by H. Cedergren and D. Sankoff, pp. 271–84. Edmonton, Alberta: Linguistic Research.

1982. Where do negative sentences come from? *Studia Linguistica* 36:88–105.

1983a. *Much about 'not' and 'nothing' : a study of the variation between analytic and synthetic negation in contemporary American English.* Lund: CWK Gleerup.

1983b. The missing link? Or, why is there twice as much negation in spoken English as in written English? (Proceedings from the Second Scandinavian Symposium on Syntactic Variation, ed. by S. Jacobson). *Stockholm Studies in English* 62:67–74.

1984. Is there an adverbial in this text? (And if so, what is it doing there?) In *Proceedings from the Second Nordic Conference for English Studies*, ed. by Hakan Ringbom and Matti Rissanen, pp. 299–315. Abo, Norway: Abo Akademi Foundation.

1985. The negation of epistemic necessity in present-day British and American English. *English World-Wide* 6:87–116.

1986. The importance of being adverbial: focusing and contingency adverbials in spoken and written English. In *English in speech and writing: a symposium*, ed. by G. Tottie and I. Bäcklund, pp. 93–118. Studia Anglistica Upsaliensia 60. Stockholm: Almqvist and Wiksell.

Tottie, Gunnel, Bengt Altenberg, and Lars Hermeren. 1983. *English in speech and writing* (ETOS Report 1). Lund: Engelska Institutionen.

Tottie, Gunnel, and Gerd Övergaard. 1984. The author's *would*: a feature of American English. *Studia Linguistica* 38:148–65.

Tottie, Gunnel, and Ingegerd Bäcklund (eds.). 1986. *English in speech and writing: a symposium.* Studia Anglistica Upsaliensia 60. Stockholm: Almqvist and Wiksell.

Vachek, Josef. 1973. *Written language: general problems and problems of English.* The Hague: Mouton.

1979. Some remarks on the stylistics of written language. In *Function and context in linguistic analysis*, ed. by D.J. Allerton, Edward Carney, and David Holdcroft, pp. 206–15. Cambridge: Cambridge University Press.

Vygotsky, L.S. 1962/1934. *Thought and language.* Cambridge, Mass.: MIT Press.

Weber, Elizabeth G. 1985. From feelings to knowledge: verbs of cognition. Paper presented at NWAVE XIV, Georgetown.

Weiner, E. Judith, and William Labov. 1983. Constraints on the agentless passive. *Journal of Linguistics* 19:29–58.

Wells, Gordon. 1985. Preschool literacy-related activities and success in school. In *Literacy, language, and learning: the nature and consequences of reading and writing*, ed. by D.R. Olson, N. Torrance and A. Hildyard, pp. 229–54. Cambridge: Cambridge University Press.

Wells, Rulon. 1960. Nominal and verbal style. In *Style in language*, ed. by Thomas A. Sebeok, pp. 213–20. Cambridge, Mass: MIT Press.

Widdowson, David. 1979. The process and purpose of reading. In *Explorations in applied linguistics*, ed. by David Widdowson, pp. 173–81. New York: Oxford University Press.

Williams, Joseph M. 1980. Non-linguistic linguistics and the teaching of style. *Language and Style* 13:24–40.

Winter, Eugene. 1982. *Towards a contextual grammar of English: the clause and its place in the definition of sentence*. London: George Allen and Unwin.

Young, George M. 1985. The development of logic and focus in children's writing. *Language and Speech* 28:115–27.

Zipf, G.K. 1949. *Human behavior and the principle of least effort*. Cambridge, Mass: Addison-Wesley.

Index